D1064482

The Politics of
Aristocratic Empires

The Politics of

Aristocratic

Empires

John H. Kautsky

The University of North Carolina Press   Chapel Hill

© 1982 The University of North Carolina Press

Manufactured in the United States of America

Library of Congress Cataloging in Publication Data

Kautsky, John., 1922–
    The politics of aristocratic empires.

    Bibliography: p.
    Includes index.
    1. Aristocracy. I. Title.
JC414.K38 305.5′2 81-12983
ISBN 0-8078-1502-0 AACR2

To the Memory of Karl Kautsky

Contents

Part IV: Nonaristocrats in the Politics of the Aristocracy

Part V: Conclusion

Preface

When, in the late 1960s, I worked on my book on *The Political Consequences of Modernization*, I began with a chapter on the politics of what I then called traditional societies. Its draft soon grew to such length that I decided to use only a brief summary of it and to put it aside until I had time to turn it into a book. My first chance to do serious research on the subject came in 1970–71 when, thanks to a National Science Foundation research grant, I could spend a sabbatical year at Harvard. The draft I produced there was incomplete, however—much more so than I realized at the time. I finally had the opportunity to rework it, leaving very little of it intact, during my next sabbatical leave in 1977–78, supported this time by a fellowship from the National Endowment for the Humanities. Now, four years and several more revisions later, it appears in print, an event I view with mixed feelings. I am glad that my task is finished at last, yet reluctant to give it up, for my subject is inexhaustible and much remains to be done.

I would like to think that it is not wholly accidental that my work was supported by both the National Science Foundation and the National Endowment for the Humanities. It is meant to be a social scientific study of a subject hitherto mostly reserved to historians. I ask political science questions and take my answers mostly from data made available by historians, and so I hope that the product will be of interest both to social scientists and to humanists. As virtually the first political scientist to penetrate a vast territory into which a few historical sociologists had intruded from various sides but which had been explored in thousands of little sections only by historians, I am something of a pioneer. To say this is far from being boastful, for, probably like many pioneers, I began this journey endowed not so much with heroism or foresight as with ignorance of what lay ahead, of how long or arduous a trip it would be, though I can truthfully add that I never regretted having started. Much more than was the case with my other books, I did not know where I would end up when I began and I learned far more on the way. The further I went, the more my interest and my ambition grew along with my manuscript. I was sustained by the joys of repeated discoveries, often no doubt of things others had discovered long before me but sometimes also of insights yielded by well-known data seen from a new angle.

It is precisely this view from a new angle that a newcomer trained in one discipline can usefully bring to material that has been traditionally studied by scholars in another discipline. On the comparative social science use of data provided by historians, I may quote from Theda Skocpol's preface of her recent work of historical sociology on *States and Social Revolutions*, a subject rather different from that of the present book which deals with politics without states and without social revolutions: "The comparative historian's task—and potential distinctive scholarly contribution—lies not in revealing new data about particular aspects of the large time periods and diverse places surveyed in the comparative study, but rather in establishing the interest and prima facie validity of an overall argument about causal regularities across the various historical cases. The comparativist has neither the time nor (all of) the appropriate skills to do the primary research that necessarily constitutes, in large amounts, the foundation upon which comparative studies are built. . . . The comparative analyst must be prepared to adapt the evidence presented in the works of the specialists to analytic purposes somewhat tangential to those they originally envisaged. And the comparativist must be as systematic as possible in searching out information on the same topics from case to case, even though the specialists are likely to emphasize varying topics in their research and polemics from one country to the next."[1]

My goal, then is to discover "causal regularities across the various historical cases," to develop generalizations about politics in traditional aristocratic empires—though I am well aware that, in fact, all I can produce is tentative hypotheses. I shall say more about this enterprise in the first chapter and indicate what benefits can be derived from it. What may be worth noting here is that this book is not concerned with the various historical cases as such, fascinating as they proved to me. Whenever I mentioned in the last few years that I was working on a book on aristocratic empires, I was almost invariably asked: which empires? The most accurate answer I could give was: none in particular.

If the purpose of generalization is to simplify one's view of a complex reality and thereby to make it more comprehensible, this can, of course, be done only at the cost of ignoring certain specific elements in the phenomena about which generalizations are being developed. The price I have to pay for my undertaking, then, is that I cannot say very much about any particular empire or provide any coherent picture of its politics and that I must therefore ignore even many major differences among various empires. Whether that price is too high will have to be decided by each reader in line with his or her interests. I, for one, given my interests, think the price has been worth paying, because I believe that I can account for quite a few phenomena in particular empires while—and because—I con-

1. Skocpol, *States and Social Revolutions*, p. xiv.

struct an ideal type of aristocratic politics and develop a general, if very partial and tentative, explanatory theory showing functional linkages among various elements in aristocratic empires. I think the price is all the more worth paying as there is already a vast literature on particular aristocratic empires and virtually none that does what I try to do here.

Specific historical empires are, of course, mentioned throughout this book as I try to support my generalizations with illustrations. To be sure, I have drawn my illustrations from only a small fraction of the literally innumerable traditional aristocratic empires that have existed in the past five millennia. I have had to resist the temptation to read on and on and to write on and on to provide more data on more empires. One unfortunate result of this is that some of my generalizations are supported by much more and better evidence than others that are not necessarily less important. However, to provide many more data from many more empires would have required a degree of scholarly knowledge of aristocratic empires throughout the ages and throughout the world far beyond the one I possess and could afford to acquire in a limited time. It would have expanded the scope of this book well beyond that of the essay I intended to write on the subject, and the reader whose attention was engaged by the innumerable illustrations might well have lost sight of the generalizations.

To point up the regularities and uniformities among aristocratic empires which I wish to stress throughout, I often use quotations from works on a considerable variety of specific aristocratic empires. Through the juxtaposition of similar statements by historians of, say, ninth-century France and nineteenth-century Ethiopia or of Ottoman Turkey and Inca Peru, patterns are made apparent which the historians themselves, being necessarily more specialized, may well not have seen. As it is my job here to point to the patterns formed by data from many empires rather than to point to the data themselves, I rely quite heavily on quotations in the following pages, sometimes rather lengthy ones, letting the authors I quote present specific data but—I hope—throwing new light on them and even making more sense of them by putting them in a new, comparative context and thereby moving toward explanation as well as description.

In order not to clutter the following pages unnecessarily with footnotes, I supply no documentation for historical data that are generally well known or can be found in standard historical and reference works. In my footnotes, I provide only the last names of authors and abbreviated titles with page numbers, but I give full bibliographical details in the bibliography. There I list all works cited in this book but no others.

I dedicate this book to the memory of Karl Kautsky, my grandfather, in order to acknowledge a major intellectual debt. Because doing so is important to me, yet the debt may, with reference to the present work, be by no means an obvious one, I should like to explain it. Kautsky is historically significant and best known as the most authoritative interpreter of Marxism in the generation after that of Marx and Engels, as "the man who helped to turn Marxism from an esoteric system into the doctrine of a gigantic political movement,"[2] and as the principal defender of "orthodox" or "classical" Marxism, especially against both Revisionists and Communists. Though deeply involved in politics, he was, however, and wanted to be, above all, a social scientist.[3] It is as such that Kautsky influenced the present work in various ways.

For one thing, I probably owe to Karl Kautsky the conviction that fully to understand a phenomenon it is not sufficient to know what it is and how it differs from related phenomena; one must also know how it has developed and, indeed, how it originated. It is only because I share this conception that in my studies of modernization I was driven back to the subject of traditional aristocratic empires and hence undertook the present work. In it, in turn, I trace the political nature of aristocratic empires back to the original superimposition of aristocracies on peasantries.

More generally, it was my grandfather's influence that has led me always to think of politics in its historical, evolutionary dimension and to think of history as a political scientist, that is, with a focus on conflict. Like my earlier work on modernization, this book, too, focuses on conflict, but, instead of explaining a process of change and evolution, it seeks to account for the absence of change.

In the past, when explaining political change, I followed Kautsky's Marxian scheme of accounting for change in the political "superstructure" in terms of change in the socioeconomic "base." I did so, not because I believe that there is a unidirectional causal relationship between the two or even that, as Kautsky held, the base is in some—to me undefinable—"last analysis" "ultimately" responsible for the superstructure. Rather, I merely chose economic change as a remarkably useful independent vari-

2. Lichtheim, *Marxism*, p. 267. Lichtheim says: "Karl Kautsky (1854–1938) is the key figure in the synthesis of orthodox Marxism and democratic Socialism which became current in Central Europe—and indirectly throughout Europe and North America—during the quarter century (1889–1914) of the Second International's rise and fall" (ibid., p. 264). For more complete studies of Kautsky's role in the context of the politics of German Social Democracy and the Second International, see Steenson, *Karl Kautsky*, and Salvadori, *Karl Kautsky and the Socialist Revolution*.

3. As a recent historian of Marxism, who has little sympathy for Kautsky's approach, says: "For Kautsky, Marxism was primarily the scientific, deterministic, integral apprehension of social phenomena . . . his world-view was dominated by scientific rigour devoid of sentiment and value-judgements, a belief in the unity of scientific method, the strictly causal and 'objective' interpretation of social phenomena." Kolakowski, *Main Currents of Marxism*, 2:35–36.

able in terms of which to explain my dependent variable of political change in the process of modernization.

In the present work, I use the same scheme of economic base and political superstructure serving, respectively, as my independent and dependent variable, but here it is a matter of explaining an unchanging political order in terms of an unchanging economic order. Though rarely made explicit in this book, this mode of analysis underlies its treatment of institutional and ideological elements supporting each other to form the persistent system of aristocratic politics. What for me has become a mode of analysis, I derived from Karl Kautsky's conception of history.

However, I am indebted to Kautsky for more than general conceptions and approaches. In his two-volume work on the materialist conception of history, he developed a theory—interestingly, in opposition to that of Engels—of the origins and early development of what he refers to as the state and classes and of "oriental despotism."[4] After I had completed the present book, I reread this material for the first time since I had written my doctoral dissertation on Kautsky thirty years earlier. I was amazed to find that a few of my passages, especially in the section on the conquest theory, follow Kautsky's thinking quite closely, and one or two phrases even seem to be taken almost verbatim from him. The latter may simply have stuck in my mind long after I had forgotten their source, but the broadly similar conclusions I draw from my research in sources not available half a century ago must be the result of similar thinking.

Much of the subject matter of my book was never dealt with or was barely touched on by Karl Kautsky. Furthermore, some of his interpretations of aristocratic empires, notably with respect to the role of the "state," are quite different from the results I arrive at. Nevertheless, it is only fair to acknowledge—and I do so very gladly—that this book would have been written differently or not at all were I another man's grandson and had therefore in my formative years not come under the intellectual influence of Karl Kautsky.

Time, support, and assistance are needed in addition to intellectual inspiration to complete a book like this one. I owe many debts of gratitude to institutions and individuals for providing these.

In 1970–71 and the summer of 1972, the National Science Foundation, through its Grant No. GS-2980, supported my early research and so did the Center for International Affairs of Harvard University by appointing me a Research Associate in 1970–71. The National Endowment for the Humanities awarded me a summer stipend in 1974 and a Fellowship for

---

4. Kautsky, *Die materialistische Geschichtsauffassung*, vol. 2. The points most relevant to my subject appear especially on pp. 61–143 and 204–331.

Independent Study and Research in 1977–78. Washington University granted me sabbatical leaves in 1970–71 and 1977–78 and, through its Graduate School of Arts and Sciences, provided a summer faculty research grant in 1979 and five separate faculty research grants to cover expenses in the period from 1971 to 1982. I am deeply grateful to all of these institutions for their generous support.

Gerhard E. Lenski of the University of North Carolina and my colleague at Washington University Robert H. Salisbury read the entire manuscript and offered me both encouragement and numerous valuable suggestions for improvements. Both urged me to add what are now the final two chapters, and Professor Lenski persuaded me to substitute the term "aristocratic empires" for "traditional empires." John H. Millett of Wichita State University went through my draft word for word raising extraordinarily helpful minor and major questions regarding my style and my logic. My friend Egon Schwarz at Washington University, a professional student of literature and an equally good amateur one of social science, read parts of my manuscript and proposed a number of stylistic and substantive improvements and, above all, has for years stimulated my thinking by his wide-ranging conversations. Both the reader and I should be grateful to these four scholars for helping to turn my work into a better book. Were it not for my stubborn resistance, they might have made it a better one still.

George Poteat, as my research assistant in 1970–71, diligently called my attention to useful literature, and more recently Catherine Gurganus similarly assisted me, particularly in connection with my two chapters on the peasantry, in especially helpful and insightful ways. Other graduate students in political science at Washington University helped clarify my thinking on aristocratic empires through their work in some of my seminars. For their aid, I thank all of them as well as Emma Dankoski and Valerie Karras who, with great care, understanding, and intelligence as well as patience and extraordinary cheerfulness transcribed various versions of the manuscript on the typewriter and the word processor.

Finally, I am grateful to *Studies in Comparative International Development* for permission to reprint material that was first published there in fall 1981 as my article on "The Question of Peasant Revolts in Traditional Empires." A brief summary of the material that came to form several of my chapters on the aristocracy was published as "Funktionen und Werte des Adels" in Peter Uwe Hohendahl and Paul Michael Lützeler, eds., *Legitimationskrisen des deutschen Adels 1200–1900* (Stuttgart: J. B. Metzler, 1979), pp. 1–16.

John H. Kautsky

Part I
Introduction

1

The Study of Aristocratic Empires

The Absence of Change

Traditional aristocratic empires, as analyzed in this book, are unchanging political entities. Depending on one's conception of history, this may mean that they have no history.

If by history is meant simply a record of past events, aristocratic empires obviously do have a history. To be sure, with respect to most of their inhabitants, that history is forgotten, partly because it was never recorded, but partly also because it seemed not worth recording and may still seem so, as it was endlessly repetitive. Peasants are born and die, they sow and they reap, they labor and they pay taxes. No doubt each village has its history of a changing distribution of material goods and of power and influence among the villagers, but, because village politics is only of local significance and because the possible patterns are few in number and recur in thousands of villages and through thousands of years, neither contemporary nor later historians have shown much interest in them.

The matter is different with respect to the aristocratic minority, whose doings are far more visible and have been of far greater interest to historians. Aristocrats, too, are born and die, but they do not sow or reap, they do not labor or pay taxes. They do, however, as I shall show and explain at length, engage in ceaseless conflict and competition with each other. These take the form of and are settled through wars and civil wars, coups and conspiracies, treaties and marriages. Aristocrats gain and lose, the boundaries of their territories change, empires rise and fall. This is the stuff of the history of aristocratic empires as it has come down to us and as it is still being written. No other history, that is, no other change, has been recorded, because no other change occurred. In traditional aristocratic empires there is—to be sure, by my definition—no major economic change from agrarianism to commerce or industry and hence no change in the prevailing social order or in the ideologies and institutions that express that order.

If by history is meant a record of changes in the distribution of power and wealth between major groups in the population, particularly social classes, changes in the social and economic order due to developing technology, growing production and increasing wealth, then traditional aristocratic empires have no history. It is just such a conception of history that has been prevalent in the West in the past three centuries, involving various notions of progress and, more recently, of development and modernization, these latter concepts being at least somewhat more compatible with the growing pessimism of the twentieth century than the optimistic eighteenth- and nineteenth-century concept of progress. This view of history as a unidirectional process driven by some internal dynamic has grown along with the development of science, technology, and eventually industry, both reflecting that development and, in self-fulfilling fashion, helping to advance it.[1] But while views of history, no doubt, reflect to some extent actual trends in the period when these views are prevalent, they can be irrelevant or misleading when they are applied to times and areas very different from those that gave rise to these views.

Because the conception of history as a record of progress or modernization involving major changes in the social or economic order is dominant today and is constantly being reinforced by actual developments in modern history, it is important to stress that such major changes are most exceptional in the course of the human past. In the million years of man's paleolithic existence as a hunter and gatherer, the social and economic order must have been, for all practical purposes, totally unchanging. The domestication of animals and cereals a few millennia ago and the consequent beginnings of pastoralism and agriculture brought some very gradual changes to this order but what emerged itself remained exceedingly stable.

A drastic change in the social order occurs for the first time with the rise of aristocratic empires, when aristocrats come to live off peasants, as long as five millennia ago in Mesopotamia and Egypt and as recently as five decades ago, in the case of Saudi Arabia. However, once such an empire is established, in a process that can be quite gradual or take place virtually overnight, as will be discussed in Chapter 3, below, the new social and political order, involving a new distribution of wealth and power but rest-

1. An earlier Western view, which evolved in commercialized ancient Greece and Rome and returned in the Renaissance with the revival of classical thought and commercialization, saw history as a cyclical movement, involving both progress and degeneration but therefore also changes in the social and economic order. J. B. Bury, in his classic *The Idea of Progress*, argues that the idea of progress developed only in modern times, especially in the late seventeenth century, but was absent in antiquity and in the Christian Middle Ages. More recently, Robert Nisbet has stressed that there was a belief in progress (as well as in cycles) in Greece and Rome and also in Christianity (but not in the Renaissance). Nisbet, *History of the Idea of Progress*. See also Edelstein, *The Idea of Progress in Classical Antiquity*. Neither Bury nor Nisbet deals with non-Western conceptions of history.

ing on the old agricultural economy and technology, once again persists unchanged.

To be sure, changes did eventually overtake all aristocratic empires, and not only as a result of the intervention of external forces. In fact, many aristocratic empires changed from within through a process, discussed in Chapter 2, which I call commercialization. On the other hand, it may be reasonably assumed that far more numerous small empires, many now forgotten or known only to specialists, particularly those that did not last very long, were never subject to commercialization. Often, they may eventually have been incorporated into larger commercialized empires.

Given time, most and possibly all of at least the large aristocratic empires remembered in history have tended to become, to one degree or another, commercialized. It may well be that the very existence of large empires over long periods of time tends to foster commercialization, because, with tribute flowing to it from a huge number of peasants, the ruling aristocracy can surround itself with growing numbers of servants, artisans, and traders to serve its insatiable wants for weapons and luxury articles. This new urban population may in good part depend on trade and may engage in it. At the same time, large empires favor the growth of trade, because they constitute large trading areas where exchange and transportation may be facilitated.

However, traditional aristocratic empires are defined here to exclude all the beginnings of commercialization and to ignore the dynamic that may produce more of it, that is, any dynamic resulting in cumulative change such as we associate with modern history and as underlies our view of history generally. If the result is that aristocratic empires so defined are a pure, ideal type, it is nevertheless true that real empires for long constitute or closely approximate that type.[2] The changes preparing the way for commercialization may for centuries not occur at all or be so slow as to be imperceptible and, for all practical purposes, nonexistent.[3] This becomes very evident if we compare the rate and magnitude of economic, social, and political changes of the last three hundred years of Western European history with, for example, the three thousand years of ancient Egyptian history.[4]

It is, then, the relatively overwhelming absence of major social and economic change that needs to be stressed in a discussion of aristocratic em-

2. It is for this reason that in my analysis I do not distinguish clearly between creating an ideal type and drawing generalizations from real cases.

3. For references to specific noncommercialized aristocratic empires, see the beginning of Chapter 2, below.

4. Already around the year 1600, Campanella could say "our times . . . have more history in a hundred years than the whole world in four thousand." Quoted in Bury, *The Idea of Progress*, p. 62.

pires. Such an emphasis runs counter to modern conceptions of history, but, precisely because these conceptions are a product of the last few centuries, throws more light than they can on the human past of a million years and specifically on human history in the more restricted sense of the last five thousand years for which we have written records. One of the principal purposes of this book, therefore, is to describe the unchanging elements of aristocratic empires and to explain the absence of change in them.

By generalizing across time and space, I will analyze the functions performed by individuals, groups, and classes in ideally pure traditional aristocratic empires, the institutions within which they operate, and the beliefs and attitudes they hold. An attempt will be made to explain functions and behavior, institutions and ideologies by relating them to each other and to demonstrate their place in the well-integrated body of the aristocratic empire.

Put very briefly and superficially, I shall argue that in agrarian economies where aristocrats live off peasants, the former must control the latter. Aristocrats therefore compete for control of land and peasants, principally by means of warfare, and their governments serve chiefly the functions of fighting other aristocrats and of taxing peasants. Government is not only limited, but invariably highly decentralized, because the lower aristocrat who taxes the peasant directly is more or less autonomous from the higher aristocracy. The values and ideologies of aristocrats, too, are appropriate to their dual role as exploiters and warriors.[5] The nature of the economy on the one hand and their values on the other determine what, in their own minds, aristocrats compete for, what the stakes and arenas of aristocratic politics are.

That these various elements of the aristocratic political system are functionally interrelated so as to support and reinforce each other, helps explain the stability of that system. But to account for the closed and stable character of aristocratic politics, it must also be shown that nonaristocrats can hardly or not at all intervene in it. This is done in three chapters on the peasants and townspeople.[6]

These descriptive aspects of my study of aristocratic empires will be obvious to the reader proceeding through the book. It may be well, however, to make explicit at the outset, if only by way of assertion and oversimplification, the thesis implicit in it that seeks to explain the absence of change. Why is there no dynamic, no change? Why is it that for centuries

5. The word "exploitation" has different connotations. See p. 110, below, for what I have in mind when I use it.

6. My generalizations are summarized and the thesis of this book is thus stated most explicitly in the first section of Chapter 15. The reader may find it useful to refer to it now as a statement of hypotheses and a guide to what follows.

on end the lower classes remain unable to alter their relationship with the aristocracy? Why, for that matter, does the aristocratic system itself remain so stable in spite of the instability within it, that is, why do aristocrats who continually fight and replace each other all behave and think alike? They do, because the conditions under which they live do not change, and ancient patterns of behavior remain relevant and, indeed, the only ones imaginable.

And why do the conditions and the environment in which people live in aristocratic empires not change, unlike those in modern societies? Here again, the explanation must begin with the beginnings of aristocratic empires, the imposition by what becomes an aristocracy of an exploitative relationship on agriculturists, a matter I look into in Chapter 3. Once the entire small surplus produced by peasants is appropriated for consumption by an aristocracy, nothing remains to be invested in improvements of the process of production. Neither the peasants nor the aristocrats have incentives to seek such improvements, the peasants because they could not retain any resulting gains and the aristocrats because they can augment their gains more easily by increasing the number of peasants and the amount of land subject to their exploitation.[7] Both the acceptance by peasants as well as aristocrats of the productive process as it is and the resort by aristocrats to territorial expansion as virtually the sole means of maximizing their material gains become fortified by ideology—which, in turn, remains unchanging.

The process of agricultural production, then, rather than being improved, is endlessly repeated, and there are no changes in technology except occasionally in the technology of warfare, precisely because warfare is the principal means of territorial expansion and hence of economic gain for the aristocracy. As these gains increase for individual aristocratic families or particular aristocracies until they are replaced by others, the means of consumption may grow—more palaces and temples, more gold and dia-

---

7. Gerhard Lenski explains the downward trend in the rate of technological advance beginning with the third millennium B.C., when aristocratic empires were established in the Middle East, a trend which he says was not reversed until the Industrial Revolution, by summarizing V. Gordon Childe: "Childe argues that one of the major reasons was . . . the virtual monopolization of the economic surplus by a tiny governing class. Under these conditions, the producers no longer had any incentive to improve the techniques of production, since all the gains were swallowed up by the political elite, and the elite were too far removed from the processes of production to be capable of invention. What is more, they now had almost unlimited reserves of labor at their disposal and therefore had no incentive to seek laborsaving inventions. Thus the emergence of the new distributive systems associated with agrarian societies seriously weakened the forces promoting technological advance." Lenski, *Power and Privilege*, p. 446. See Childe, *Man Makes Himself*, pp. 257–62. On the scarcity of technological innovations in ancient Greece and Rome, see Finley, "Technical Innovation and Economic Progress," and Pleket, "Technology and Society in the Graeco-Roman World."

monds, more servants and concubines. But aside from that, there are no changes in the physical environment in which people in aristocratic empires live. The natural environment remains as it had been modified by man through primitive agricultural techniques before aristocratic empires arose, and the man-made environment, consisting of tools and equipment, too, does not change. Thus, generation after generation, men keep doing the same things in the same way, they face no new problems and are not challenged to think new thoughts. Indeed, the older something is—a man, a title, a belief—the more prestige it enjoys because nothing new has rendered it out of date.[8]

All this is difficult to accept for us, because it is in sharp contrast with the world of constant and cumulative change that we are familiar with and that has shaped our conception of history. That contrast and the reasons for the absence of change in aristocratic empires can be clarified by reference to Marx's theory of social change. Karl Marx is, after all, perhaps the most outstanding representative of the view of history as unidirectional development and he formulated what is probably the most influential theory explaining this process.

According to Marx's theory, the dynamic or motor that propels history forward through a series of stages, the transitions being marked by social revolutions, is the class struggle. It is a conflict between the class that works (and thus represents the forces of production) and the class that owns the means of production. That conflict, in turn, results from the growing tension between developing forces of production and a conservative property system. "At a certain stage of their development, the material productive forces of society come in conflict with the existing relations of production, or—what is but a legal expression for the same thing—with

8. A theory explaining the absence of change somewhat different from the one stated here but not incompatible with it was suggested by Thorstein Veblen: "Any innovation calls for a greater expenditure of nervous energy in making the necessary readjustment than would otherwise be the case . . . and so presumes for its successful accomplishment, some surplus energy beyond that absorbed in the daily struggle for subsistence. Consequently it follows that progress is hindered by underfeeding and excessive physical hardship, no less effectually than by such a luxurious life as will shut out discontent by cutting off the occasion for it. The abjectly poor, and all those persons whose energies are entirely absorbed by the struggle for daily sustenance, are conservative because they cannot afford the effort of taking thought for the day after tomorrow; just as the highly prosperous are conservative because they have small occasion to be discontented with the situation as it stands today.

"From this proposition it follows that the institution of a leisure class acts to make the lower classes conservative by withdrawing from them as much as it may of the means of sustenance, and so reducing their consumption, and consequently their available energy, to such a point as to make them incapable of the effort required for the learning and adoption of new habits of thought. The accumulation of wealth at the upper end of the pecuniary scale implies privation at the lower end of the scale. It is a commonplace that, wherever it occurs, a considerable degree of privation among the body of the people is a serious obstacle to any innovation." Veblen, *The Theory of the Leisure Class*, pp. 140–41.

the property relations within which they have been at work hitherto. From forms of development of the productive forces these relations turn into their fetters. Then begins an epoch of social revolution."[9]

This theory, then, assigns the role of the ultimately dynamic element in history that is responsible for all other changes to the forces of production and assumes that these are always developing. If, for purposes of our analysis, we accept that role of the forces of production, but reject as empirically unjustified the assumption that they must be developing, we have an explanation of the absence of social and economic change in aristocratic empires. It is, incidentally, also a Marxian explanation of why Marx was wrong when he projected—or if he seemed to project—into the past as a general law of history conclusions he had derived from recent historical experience and, in good part, from his predictions of the future.[10] In aristocratic empires, the forces of production do not develop. They therefore remain quite compatible with the existing property relations or, as I would put it, with aristocratic control and exploitation. The property relations then do not turn into fetters on the productive forces that restrain the inexorable development of the latter, fetters that are eventually broken by that development—because there is no development. If the forces of production do not change, there is no need or reason for the relations of production to change. Peasants continue to carry on agriculture in an unchanging way within the unchanging system of aristocratic control and exploitation. Hence there is no growing tension, no class struggle, no social revolution. Marx's motor of history remains stalled, aristocratic empires go on for centuries or millennia.

It is only with advancing commercialization that changes are introduced into hitherto unchanging traditional aristocratic empires—to the point where I no longer define them as such. I shall deal with commercialization in the next chapter and thereby delimit our subject matter of aristocratic empires. Before that, however, a number of other introductory remarks are in order. Thus, I have to clarify just what I mean by traditional aristocratic empires and aristocracies, terms used so far without any attempt at definition, but, first of all, I must answer the question why, quite aside from the absence of major change in their history, aristocratic empires are worth studying.

9. Marx, Preface to "A Contribution to the Critique of Political Economy," pp. 4–5.

10. Marx himself seemed to recognize that the generalizations quoted above do not apply to what he called the Asiatic mode of production, a concept he never developed systematically. Thus, he said that "the Asiatic form necessarily survives longest and most stubbornly." Marx, *Pre-Capitalist Economic Formations*, p. 83. Its "characteristics make it resistant to disintegration and economic evolution, until wrecked by the external force of capitalism." Hobsbawm, "Introduction," ibid., p. 38. On Marx's thought on this subject, see also Krader, *The Asiatic Mode of Production*. See also the passage from *Capital* on "the unchangeableness of Asiatic societies," quoted in chap. 11, n. 10.

Why Study Traditional Aristocratic Empires?

This book deals with a type of political entity that no longer exists anywhere in the world, at least in its pure form that is analyzed here. What benefits can be derived from such a book? There are several possible answers to this question. One could simply be that it will contribute to a better understanding of history. And, it can be argued, any aspect of history is worth studying for the same reason that a mountain is worth climbing: because it is there. The politics of the Inca empire is no less interesting than the politics of England or Indiana—if one happens to be interested in it. To me, as a political scientist, it is not so much the politics of any one empire that fascinates me as the patterns and uniformities among different empires that I see existing across huge distances in time and space. I will turn to this matter at greater length in a moment.

One can also study premodern politics to lay the basis for an understanding of modern politics. Particularly if one is interested in the process of modernization, that is, a process of change, it is only logical to begin at the starting point of that process. We cannot recognize what is new in a situation today unless we know what the situation was yesterday. Similarly, we cannot understand how politics changes under the impact of modernization unless we have some understanding of politics before there was any modernization. A study of politics in aristocratic empires provides this understanding of politics before there was any modernization. So that they can serve as the base line from which to measure change, the aristocratic empires we consider must therefore be wholly untouched by modernization even if this precludes us from referring to any present-day polity.[11]

Another reason for studying traditional aristocratic empires to help us gain an understanding of modern societies is that the politics of virtually all societies still contains significant elements of traditionalism. Political change can be more or less rapid, but it is also necessarily more or less partial; it is

11. Gideon Sjoberg in his book on *The Preindustrial City* stresses the utility of studies of premodern "societies" for an understanding of modern ones: "Acute awareness of the social structure of preindustrial civilized societies . . . is essential for anyone who hopes to understand current processes in societies now changing over from feudal to industrial modes of organization. . . . It is these uniformities that provide a 'yardstick' for measuring and interpreting across cultural boundaries the significant social changes that are occurring" (pp. 333–34). Similarly, though in a different context, Reinhard Bendix says "if we are to understand types of 'partial development,' then we must give special attention to the 'base line' of tradition with reference to which these changes are to be gauged. To do this, a knowledge of traditional ruling groups is indispensable, and a comparative analysis can help us to define their distinguishing characteristics." Bendix, *Nation-Building and Citizenship*, p. 218. Parts of the preceding and of the following paragraph are taken more or less verbatim from my *The Political Consequences of Modernization*, p. 23.

never so complete as to wipe out all remnants of the past. Thus, an analysis of behavioral, institutional, and ideological patterns characteristic of aristocratic empires is not merely an analysis of the dead past. No one can study even the recent history of even the most industrialized countries of Europe without being struck by the pervasive persistence of many of these patterns.

That some of the most highly industrialized countries are monarchies, that the personnel of armed services is divided into officers and enlisted men, that warfare is closely associated with notions of honor and glory, that money-making and trade are viewed as degrading by some—all these things seem incongruous in modern societies for they are, indeed, inexplicable in the context of modernity. They—and numerous other institutional and ideological elements—are remnants of the traditional aristocratic order and are explicable only in its context. It is in aristocratic empires that they originated or, at any rate, in highly integrated fashion served to support and were in turn supported by the prevailing system of social relations. Some understanding of aristocratic empires, then, is needed for an understanding of many aspects of modern society.[12]

It also seems to me to be a beneficial result of a study of aristocratic empires that it may help overcome a sharp distinction often drawn between the politics of "Western" and the politics of "non-Western" societies, a distinction that has tended to interfere with the comparative study of politics. The aristocratic empires of early feudal Western Europe out of which modern Western politics developed were, with respect to all matters of concern to us here, quite like many other aristocratic empires in non-Western parts of the world. Indeed, as we shall see in the next chapter, the beginnings of modernization in the form of what I call commercialization have occurred a number of times in history in a number of aristocratic empires, non-Western as well as Western.

This is not to suggest that there are no differences between the politics of Western and non-Western countries in modern times (though the distinction does not, in fact, run along geographical or cultural lines, as the unfortunate terms "Western" and "non-Western" suggest). However, these differences are due not so much to differences in their traditional aristocratic background—a background that is similar for the two sets of societies—as they are to differences in the processes of modernization they underwent. In particular, the difference between modernization from within and modernization from without is important here. That, however,

12. Because my object is to present a picture of the characteristics of "pure" traditional aristocratic empires in this book, the persistence of traditional aristocratic elements in modern societies will not be explicitly emphasized, but I return to this matter at greater length in the final chapter.

is a subject I discussed elsewhere[13] and need not take up again in a book on aristocratic empires, except in a few pages in Chapter 15. What matters here is that these differences between the processes of modernization can by no means overcome the common effect of the traditional aristocratic background shared by Western and non-Western countries or, put more accurately, countries modernized from within and countries modernized from without. The British aristocracy and the French peasantry and their institutions and ideologies are not at all wholly different from the Indian aristocracy and the Chinese peasantry and their institutions and ideologies. A general study of aristocratic empires makes this clear, and the comparative study of politics, whether traditional or modern, benefits from this recognition.

Finally and in a sense most importantly, the study of the politics of aristocratic empires provides a broadened base for our understanding of politics. The purpose of political science is, after all, to develop generalizations about politics, not merely about modern politics. And yet, political scientists have, in fact, overwhelmingly drawn their evidence from only a tiny segment of the political experience of mankind. By confining their attention very largely to contemporary and, at any rate, twentieth-century politics, and mostly the politics of modernity and of modernization at that, they have ignored centuries and millennia of human experience. There are, of course, two excellent reasons for the myopic vision of most political scientists: most people are more interested in the present and the recent past than in the more distant past, and more numerous and more reliable data are available on the present and the recent past. But neither reason will justify any claim to the validity of generalizations about politics drawn from such limited evidence. We may have both more interest in and better access to the views of our friends than the views of strangers, but we would not base a study of the attitudes or the voting behavior of a large and varied population exclusively on interviews with our friends. The sample would be too small and unrepresentative. The same is true of the sample of political behavior on which political scientists have drawn for their generalizations.

Political scientists have not only ignored a huge reservoir of premodern data—however difficult to obtain or to understand they may be—on which to base generalizations, they have also come to look at the modern phenomena they do study from a perspective that seems quite distorted in the light of man's history of the past five millennia. For example, there is a large literature explaining the role of the military in politics as somehow "abnormal" and, to my knowledge, not a single book on the role of civilians, when it is really civilian government that is exceptional in history and, in

13. Kautsky, *The Political Consequences of Modernization*, especially pp. 17–19, 44–49.

this sense, needs explanation. A rapidly growing literature on peasant revolts often suggests that such revolts have always been common because they have been fairly frequent in modern times, but there are reasons to believe (discussed later in this book) that they were very rare and possibly nonexistent through most of peasant history.

More than that, with their perspective conditioned by the exceptional politics of recent times and of industrialized societies, political scientists operate with concepts like "public opinion," "participation," and "representation," not to mention "democracy." All of these, as commonly used, assume minimally that the people in question know—or know more than very vaguely—that they live in a country and have a government. This assumption is wrong for huge numbers of people even today and certainly for most people through most of human history. Indeed, it is questionable whether concepts like "society," "social system," and "political system," with their implications of interdependence, are applicable where great numbers of people neither know nor care about what goes on beyond the boundaries of their village or local district, do not affect it, and are not affected by it. Nor do more old-fashioned but still commonly used concepts like "state" or "country," let alone "nation," fit traditional aristocratic empires, and it is by no means clear that they have "governments" in the modern sense of that word—though I shall use the word for lack of a better one. To think of such empires in terms of such modern concepts makes their politics—that is, most of politics throughout history—difficult if not impossible to understand. On the other hand, our conception of politics and our political science are enriched if we extend them to consider aristocratic empires and learn to think of politics apart from concepts such as those just mentioned.

Given the virtually exclusive concern of political scientists with politics at the end of the second millennium A.D., no one book can hope to redress the balance at all significantly. Still, an attempt at even a tiny contribution in this direction seems worthwhile. To be sure, the present book does not deal with the million years of human existence either, but only with aristocratic empires. However, these are a major political phenomenon of the past five thousand years that are commonly referred to as our history more narrowly defined. Men lived under aristocratic empires far longer than they have under parliamentary or presidential regimes, in "democracies" or "dictatorships," and the type of politics analyzed here is, in this sense, far more typical of human politics than is present-day politics. It is politics without elections, without states, almost without government, politics without revolution or modernization.

Patterns and Generalizations

The object of this book is to develop generalizations about aristocratic empires that will help us understand their politics. I want to and I believe I can develop these generalizations because I have been struck by the far-reaching similarities and patterns recurring among aristocratic empires. These are all the more striking when one considers that many of these empires were separated from each other by thousands of years and thousands of miles and could not possibly have influenced each other. Gideon Sjoberg observes "that some writers see regularity in form across industrial systems yet implicitly deny uniformities of structure for preindustrial civilized societies. But that such regularities abound should be apparent to any observer of these societies who attains a broad space-time overview."[14]

The reason for this disparity noted by Sjoberg may well be that industrial societies have been studied by social scientists whose job it is to see regularity. For information about aristocratic empires, on the other hand, we must rely overwhelmingly on historians who typically do not attain "a broad space-time overview." On the contrary, to gain their detailed expertise, they tend to specialize in the study of particular empires or periods of history. There are innumerable books on Egypt, on Rome, and on China, most of them on some specific aspect of each empire, but how many books are there comparing two or three of these empires, let alone many others?

Being specialized, historians view matters as unique that can also be seen as fitting into regular patterns. Patterns and uniformities, after all, are in the eye of the analyst. They have no objective existence for they depend on the analyst's choice of elements to be abstracted from a total context. Even given agreement on accurate data, it is therefore objectively no more correct for one analyst to see patterns than for another one not to see them. I choose to see them and, since they exist in my eye, will try to convince the reader of their existence by stressing certain similarities rather than differences in the politics of aristocratic empires.

History as it has come down to us, from both contemporaries and historians, generally concentrates on the particular conditions surrounding particular events. The uniformity of behavioral patterns is thus obscured and, on the other hand, it is also taken for granted. This can be illustrated with reference to the recurrent phenomenon of wars of conquest of which numerous instances, scattered over four continents and five millennia, will be listed in Chapter 3. Historians recount thousands of cases of one ruler making war on another, often because one had raided the other's villages or one had insulted the other, and of the winner taking territory from the

14. Sjoberg, *The Preindustrial City*, pp. 333–34.

loser. They detail the causes, the vicissitudes and the consequences of each war, but they rarely discuss why there are rulers at all, why villages are raided or insults have to be avenged, above all why territory is worth taking and why war is the principal means to all this. They do not discuss these matters, because they take them for granted as if they were simply natural. And they take them for granted, because they have been so common in history. Precisely because of the prevalence of a pattern, the pattern as such is never analyzed.

The aristocratic assumption that warfare involving territorial expansion is natural, based as it is on centuries and often millennia of experience, has powerfully affected far into modern times both the political behavior of the successors to aristocratic governments and the perceptions of those who analyze history and society. It is only in the past few generations, under the impact of modern conditions, that this aspect of aristocratic ideology has come to be at all widely questioned and that it has become possible to see—although by no means everyone does—that wars of conquest are associated not with inborn universal human traits but with the interests of certain social groups living under certain conditions.

That human beings have, at all times and everywhere, eaten food is not surprising and requires no explanation by the historian and social scientist. As long as expansionist warfare was regarded as equally natural, it was not being explained. Once it is recognized, however, that such warfare is not as natural and inevitable as eating, the fact that there are nevertheless far-reaching uniformities of expansionist behavior across centuries, continents, and cultures becomes immensely impressive and cries out for explanation. This is all the more true as these uniformities are by no means confined to warfare and conquest, for these are closely associated with certain institutional and ideological patterns.

Is it not amazing that there should be substantial similarities between Assyrians, Almoravids, and Aztecs, between the empires of the Macedonians, the Mongols, and the Moguls, between Ostrogothic kings, Umayyad caliphs, and Ottoman sultans, between the Sassanid, Songhay, and Saudi empires, between Ptolemies, Teutonic Knights, and the Tutsi, between the Vandals, the Visigoths, and the Vikings? It is because of uniformities among aristocratic empires that Romans could deal effectively with Macedonian, Egyptian, and Parthian rulers, that Arabs could govern from the Pyrenees to the Indus, that the Mongols could dominate princes from China to Mesopotamia and Russia. Everywhere they found aristocrats exploiting peasants with similar institutional and ideological structures to facilitate this relationship. Even at the dawn of modernity in Europe, an English crusader, like Richard I, in Palestine, a Venetian traveler, like Marco Polo, in China, a Spanish conquistador, like Pizarro, in Peru probably had a better understanding of politics in these areas—because they were similar to those of aristocratic Europe—than a modern American can have in Cambodia, the Congo, or Cuba.

The search for regularities and uniformities seems particularly important with reference to aristocracies in aristocratic empires. Aristocracies have been written about overwhelmingly by historians; indeed, the histories of many empires often have been written simply as the histories of their aristocracies. Biographers and writers of fiction and drama, who have also helped shape our image of the aristocracy, stress even more than historians what is or appears to them as unique. Also, traditional aristocracies may consider themselves unique, isolated from and ignorant of all other aristocracies as they sometimes are and imbued with a belief that they are biologically different from and superior to the rest of mankind or even of divine origin. It is therefore worthwhile to show that behavioral and ideological patterns can be perceived among aristocracies across different cultures and periods of history, that, for example, the roles and attitudes of the Amhara aristocracy of Ethiopia are strikingly similar to those of the aristocracy of early feudal Europe.

On the other hand, there is much less need to emphasize regularities and uniformities among peasants. Although the peasants in any isolated village no doubt, as much as any aristocracy, considered themselves unique, their view of themselves had much less impact on the literature about them than the aristocrats' self-image had on historical writings. And the literature about peasants is mostly the work of anthropologists rather than of historians, that is, of social scientists who, at least implicitly, seek to formulate generalizations. Thus, even highly specialized village studies are typically thought of by their authors as case studies contributing to our knowledge not just of the particular village involved but of peasants in general—quite unlike most work on aristocracies.

In addition, there is a growing literature on peasant society and culture in general, which has virtually no parallel with respect to aristocracies.[15] It is true that its concern has been mostly with present-day peasants and particularly with the effects on them of modernization. However, these effects have often been so slight that the literature still throws much light on peasant society and culture in aristocratic empires. That there is such a thing as a peasant culture throughout the world is widely accepted now. Redfield wrote in 1955 that "peasant society and culture has something

15. Redfield, *Peasant Society and Culture*, must be cited first here, but subsequently there appeared such books as Wolf, *Peasants*, and Nash, *Primitive and Peasant Economic Systems*, and such readers as Potter, Diaz, and Foster, eds., *Peasant Society*; Dalton, ed., *Economic Development and Social Change*; and Shanin, ed., *Peasants and Peasant Societies*. Two more recent books, both drawing data from Southeast Asia, but generalizing about peasant societies and attitudes, are Scott, *The Moral Economy of the Peasant*, and Popkin, *The Rational Peasant*. None of the works cited here focuses specifically on peasants in aristocratic empires.

generic about it. It is a kind of arrangement of humanity with some similarities all over the world,"[16] and this is no doubt even more valid with respect to aristocratic empires than to the present when peasantries have been subjected to different forms of modernization. On the other hand, the concept of a general aristocratic culture or at least one going beyond the confines of Europe is a far less familiar one. Thus generalizations encompassing French knights and Tutsi warriors may be met with surprise and even some shock, but a demonstration of uniformities and regularities among medieval European and African villages is no longer needed.

If uniformities are, on the one hand, not to be taken for granted and, on the other hand, are quite far-reaching (and hence, to me at any rate, quite fascinating) they require explanation. It is only reasonable to assume that such uniformities have arisen out of some similar conditions and would have some similar consequences. Chapter 3 will briefly indicate the conditions that probably gave rise to aristocratic empires and the rest of the book will be devoted to their consequences.

The tentative generalizations developed in this book are supported by references to data from specific aristocratic empires only to a very limited extent. These data are meant to provide concrete illustrations of what might otherwise appear to be abstractions removed from reality and they are to show that my generalizations have some claim to validity. That they are valid universally, that is, for all empires, is not being claimed at all and could, in any case, not be proved because of the huge number of aristocratic empires in human history.

The reader must know from the outset that my goal is not to present accurate or adequate descriptions of particular historical empires or, for that matter, an accurate or adequate description of historical reality at all. This does not mean that I am writing fiction. My generalizations rest on historical evidence, but they serve to construct an ideal type of the politics of traditional aristocratic empires.[17] I seek to abstract from the infinitely complex and messy reality of history what I regard as the essential and unchanging elements of the politics of traditional aristocratic empires and to explain them in terms of their interrelationships. I will even, as noted in

16. Redfield, *Peasant Society and Culture*, p. 17. A decade later, George Foster could write: "Today scholars see peasants . . . as a major societal type only incidentally related to time and place. . . . We look upon peasants as peoples whose styles of life show certain structural, economic, social, and perhaps personality similarities (although of course not identities) . . . without reference to country or century." Foster, "Introduction: What is a Peasant?" p. 2.

17. As Raymond Aron says of Max Weber's use of ideal types: "We bring together characteristics which are more or less evident in different instances, we emphasize, eliminate, exaggerate, and finally substitute a coherent, rational whole for the confusion and incoherence of reality." Aron, "The Logic of the Social Sciences," p. 81. Weber himself said much the same in Weber, *The Methodology of the Social Sciences*, p. 90.

the next chapter, try to abstract traditional elements out of the commercialized reality of posttraditional aristocratic empires. I believe that this approach and my emphasis on uniform and recurrent patterns can contribute to an understanding of particular aristocratic empires and can also provide some basis for an understanding of processes of modernization and political change in general and in particular societies.

Not only do I generalize across numerous specific empires and across cultures, continents, and millennia, but my generalizations also cut across important distinctions, widely drawn in the literature, like that between feudal and bureaucratic empires and the one between feudalism and the "Asiatic mode of production" or "Oriental despotism" made by some writers inspired by Marx's insights in this area.[18] I am quite aware of the differences between early, still traditional West European and Japanese feudalism—I regard later feudalism as commercialized—on the one hand and other traditional aristocratic empires on the other. However, this book will stress what they all have in common, the more so as the differences have been widely noted and the notion of Western European exceptionalism is very widespread.

No doubt, this generalizing approach may seem to make me subject to the charge that I proceed ahistorically, especially because in this book, unlike in most of my other writings, the principal emphasis is not on questions of origins and development, but rather on the absence of change. Far from being ahistorical, however, my analysis is merely achronological. It is designed to show that whenever in agrarian economies a group of people can live off the surplus produced by peasants—a situation that may occur at different times and may last for different lengths of time in different areas—certain social relations prevail that give rise to a peculiar pattern of politics. It is the task of this study to demonstrate that it is reasonable to see such a pattern and to show what it is.

---

18. For thoughtful discussions of these Marxian concepts, see Lichtheim, "Oriental Despotism," and sections of Avineri, "Introduction" to Avineri, ed., *Karl Marx on Colonialism and Modernization*, pp. 2–24. For a searching analysis of their history and their applicability in the light of modern research, see Anderson, *Lineages of the Absolutist State*, pp. 462–549. Anderson argues cogently both against the indiscriminate application of the concept of feudalism to aristocratic empires other than those of medieval Western Europe and perhaps Japan and against "a ubiquitous 'Asiatism'" (ibid., p. 486). Here, neither "feudalism" nor "Oriental despotism" are used as synonyms for "traditional aristocratic empire," and my generalizations are not stretched to cover all the various types of political entities that have been designated by these terms, for, as will be pointed out shortly, I distinguish traditional aristocratic empires, on the one hand, from primitive societies and, on the other, from commercialized societies. I am also not unaware of differences among various empires, such as those between Islamic and Chinese ones (both "Oriental" or "Asiatic") which Anderson stresses (ibid., pp. 495–549), but I choose to emphasize similarities rather than differences.

A Note on the Sociological Literature
on Aristocratic Empires

Political scientists who should be concerned with the discovery and explanation of uniformities and patterns have so far given little or no attention to the study of aristocratic empires.[19] Overwhelmingly, that study has been left to historians who note uniformities only rarely and in passing. There is, however, a major sociological tradition, mostly German, stretching from Ludwig Gumplowicz and Gustav Ratzenhofer through Franz Oppenheimer and Max Weber to Richard Thurnwald and Alexander Rüstow,[20] that was interested in developing generalizations on some aspects of aristocratic empires. Also some present-day sociologists have advanced such generalizations, most notably Gideon Sjoberg, S. N. Eisenstadt, Gerhard Lenski, Reinhard Bendix, and, to some extent, Barrington Moore. The principal relevant books of these five authors[21] are in some ways similar to this work in their concerns,[22] for all are primarily

19. For the sake of completeness, I should mention one work by a political scientist, entirely devoted to aristocratic empires (though he defines them more broadly than I do): Wesson, *The Imperial Order*. Like the present book, this work generalizes about aristocratic empires, but its approach and objectives are utterly different. It describes—and judges— aristocratic empires in terms of modern concepts, which I consider quite irrelevant, denouncing them for their "totalitarianism" and "socialism" and their opposition to "democracy," "the people," the "free market," and a "laissez-faire" economy (for example, pp. 97– 101). The object of the author is to demonstrate the evil "results of power unleashed"—so far as empires "have been unrestrained one should not expect them to be good" (preface, unnumbered page)—and he paints a picture of rulers with total power imposing complete ideological and behavioral uniformity and conformity on their subjects throughout their empires, a picture far from accurate, as we shall see.

20. Gumplowicz, *Der Rassenkampf* (first published 1883), vol. 3 of *Ausgewählte Werke*; Ratzenhofer, *Die sociologische Erkenntnis* (1898); Oppenheimer, *Der Staat* (first published in 1909), translated as *The State* and later greatly expanded as vol. 2 of *System der Soziologie*; Weber, *Wirtschaft und Gesellschaft* (first published posthumously in 1921 and 1922), translated as *Economy and Society*, 3 vols., especially chap. 6 on the sociology of religion in 2:399–634, chaps. 12–13 on patrimonialism and feudalism in 3:1006–1110, and chap. 16 on the city in 3:1212–1372; Weber, *Gesammelte Aufsätze zur Religionssoziologie*, 3 vols. (1921), especially the section in vol. 1 on Confucianism and Taoism, translated as *The Religion of China*, vol. 2 on Hinduism and Buddhism, translated as *The Religion of India*, and vol. 3 on ancient Judaism, translated as *Ancient Judaism*; Thurnwald, *Werden, Wandel und Gestaltung von Staat und Kultur im Lichte der Völkerforschung*, vol. 4 of *Die menschliche Gesellschaft in ihren ethno-soziologischen Grundlagen* (1935); Rüstow, *Ursprung der Herrschaft*, vol. 1 of *Ortsbestimmung der Gegenwart* (1950).

21. Sjoberg, *The Preindustrial City*; Eisenstadt, *The Political Systems of Empires*; Lenski, *Power and Privilege*; Bendix, *Kings or People*; Moore, *Social Origins of Dictatorship and Democracy*.

22. I could read Bendix's *Kings or People* only when the manuscript of this book was virtually completed and I had not read any of the other four when I first began to think about and work on it in the early 1960s, but all of them proved very helpful.

interested in politics except Sjoberg's (which, being confined to cities, does, in any case, not need to deal with the peasantry nor with the aristocracy as distinct from the upper levels of the townspeople), and all but Moore's and Bendix's draw their illustrative evidence from societies scattered widely over the globe and through time.

However, none of these recent works focuses precisely on what is defined here as traditional aristocratic empires or uses that category. These aristocratic empires fit into Lenski's two categories of advanced horticultural societies and agrarian societies. But advanced horticultural societies include also tribal societies and societies in transition from the tribal to the traditional aristocratic order, and agrarian societies include societies where merchants have become so powerful that they are no longer purely traditional but commercialized or more or less modern, like the late Roman empire and especially late medieval and even absolutist Western Europe. Eisenstadt, whose concern is with bureaucratic empires, also draws no clear distinction between traditional ones, like Inca Peru and the Old Kingdom of ancient Egypt, and modern ones, like eighteenth-century England and France, Prussia and Austria.[23] Similarly, Bendix, even in Part I of *Kings or People* that deals with the authority of kings and their relation to the aristocracy—Part II is devoted to the rise of popular governments and to "nation-building"—covers periods in the history of Japan and Russia and especially of Germany (and Prussia) and England which, as will be explained in the next chapter, I regard as no longer traditional. Barrington Moore, being interested in "the making of the modern world," focuses on processes of change rather than on the traditional aristocratic order. And Sjoberg's work studies "past and present" preindustrial cities and thus considers such commercialized cities as ancient Rome and those in late medieval Europe and nineteenth-century China along with traditional ones. Thus, while the five books referred to all provide valuable data on politics in traditional aristocratic empires, their analyses are not confined to these empires, and it is hence by no means clear whether some of their conclu-

---

23. A more recent work by Eisenstadt, *Revolution and the Transformation of Societies*, devotes three chapters to change in "traditional societies," which evidently include "archaic and historical civilizations" from "semi-tribal or tribal federations" to China and Russia in the early twentieth century (ibid., p. 74). These chapters are concerned with politics—there are frequent references to conflict, rebellion, protest, heterodoxy, and political struggle—but Eisenstadt generally speaks of "center-periphery relations" and rarely specifies the nature and composition of the groups or elites that are in conflict. The following sentence, referring to "Imperial and Imperial-feudal systems," illustrates the level of generality on which much of his analysis moves: "Leaders in these societies sought to generate support among different groups and strata, to cooperate with different elites and functional groups, to tap various free-floating resources, and to organize and channel them to augment their own power" (ibid., p. 82).

sions, for example, on centralization, merchants and trade, and peasant revolutions, are valid with respect to traditional aristocratic empires.

The "Traditional Society," Primitive Societies, and Traditional Aristocratic Empires

The empires dealt with here are best described as traditional aristocratic empires. Either of the two adjectives not modified by the other is, as it is often used, too broad in its meaning to serve my purposes adequately. I nevertheless generally, for the sake of brevity, refer simply to aristocratic empires, but it must be remembered that they are traditional ones, that is, that they are to be distinguished from commercialized and more modern societies in which aristocrats still govern or are powerful. On the other hand, when I use the terms "traditional" and "traditionalism" alone, it must be understood that what is meant is aristocratic traditionalism, not either the more primitive or the more modern societies to which the term traditional is often applied.

Although the task of defining my concept of "aristocracy" at all fully can be postponed to a later chapter where it will be more appropriate, the preceding sentence makes clear the need to clarify what I mean by "traditional." This seems particularly necessary because doubts have been expressed as to the utility of the concepts of tradition and traditional society. These have arisen not in response to the sociological literature just mentioned but to the tendency in much of the literature on modernization to draw a simple dichotomy between tradition and modernity[24] and to lump together a wide variety of very different societies under the label traditional.

As to the first of these tendencies, I might appear to be guilty of it, because I distinguish traditional aristocratic empires from more or less "modern" commercialized, colonial, and industrial societies. These latter are, however, *more or less* modern, that is, as I have already stressed, elements of traditionalism continue to play more or less important roles in them. Thus, I certainly draw no simple dichotomy between tradition and modernity. I do try to describe and explain characteristic features of wholly nonmodern, purely traditional aristocratic empires, but know very well that there are no wholly nontraditional, pure modern societies.

24. For attacks on this tendency, see Rudolph and Rudolph, *The Modernity of Tradition*, especially Introduction, pp. 3–14; Eisenstadt, "Post-Traditional Societies and the Continuity and Reconstruction of Tradition," pp. 1–27; and especially Bendix, "Tradition and Modernity Reconsidered," pp. 323–29, republished in Bendix, *Nation-Building and Citizenship*, pp. 404–11.

As to the second tendency in the literature on modernization that has brought the concept of traditionalism into some disrepute—to group under that label all kinds of "nonmodern" societies—I am innocent of it, too. I attach the label "traditional" only to the aristocratic empires I generalize about and not to other nonmodern societies, that is, specifically, primitive societies, nor to slightly modernized societies, specifically commercialized ones. Let me illustrate this.

It has been charged, in effect, that there is no such thing as a traditional society or "tradition." As Dankwart Rustow puts it, "whereas modernity can be affirmatively defined, tradition remains largely a residual concept." To illustrate the range of traditional societies that "offer no obvious similarities," he lists "the tribes of camel herders in the Arabian desert; the villages of Tropical Africa; and the imperial civilizations once governed by the Manchus in China and the Ottomans in Turkey."[25] And Samuel Huntington, making the same point, says "Pigmy tribes, Tokugawa Japan, medieval Europe, the Hindu village are all traditional" and also labels India "the twentieth century's most complex traditional society."[26]

All of these very different societies have indeed been referred to as traditional in much of the literature, but here that adjective is not used quite so loosely. I do not deal with traditional "societies" but, for reasons that will become clear shortly, with traditional "empires" and, among the nine societies listed by the two authors, I would apply that term only to early (but not to late) medieval Europe (or at least Western Europe). I regard late medieval Western Europe, Tokugawa Japan, and the Manchu and at least the late Ottoman empires as affected to some degree by commercialization—a process dealt with in the next chapter—and hence as no longer purely traditional. Obviously, like all societies that were at one time traditional, they retain remnants of the traditional order which in these cases are so powerful that we can refer to them for an understanding of certain aspects of traditional aristocratic empires. As to twentieth-century India, it is an outstanding example of a society that has for quite some time been subjected to modernization from without, as were the Manchu and Ottoman empires in their final decades.

On the other hand, I consider Pigmy and Arabic camel-herding tribes and the villages of Tropical Africa and of India as examples of primitive societies rather than of traditional aristocratic empires. They may no longer be pure primitive societies if they have come under the impact of modernization through colonialism or through the modernized national institutions of their countries. Rather than to lump "primitive societies" and "traditional aristocratic empires" together in a category of "traditional so-

25. Rustow, *A World of Nations*, p. 12.

26. Huntington, "The Change to Change," pp. 294, 293.

cieties," I prefer to distinguish between them. Traditionalism is thus not to me, as Huntington says it is in much of the literature, the beginning point of history.[27] Not only can I not quite conceive of such a point at all, but I see aristocratic empires as arising out of primitive societies in ways discussed in Chapter 3 below.

In distinguishing my usage of the terms "traditional aristocratic empire" and "primitive society" from more common uses of the concept of "tradition," some definitions have already been suggested by implication. Some attempt at explicit definitions is now overdue. While my conception of aristocratic empires will of course emerge from this entire book, I can initially and minimally define a pure traditional aristocratic empire as a political entity that contains an aristocracy and is unaffected by commercialization or any other form of modernization. The first characteristic distinguishes it from primitive societies, but not from all societies that have come under the impact of modernization.[28] The second characteristic, of course, distinguishes the traditional aristocratic empire from societies affected by commercialization or other modernization but not from primitive ones.

A pure primitive society is defined here as consisting of a nomadic band or tribe or an individual village (even when several or many villages make up an agrarian tribe) normally numbering its members at most in the hundreds. It is not integrated into another society, but is largely or wholly self-sufficient economically and substantially or entirely autonomous politically. While there may be some division of labor, typically as between the sexes and age groups, and some specialization of functions, including that of government, and while some social stratification may appear, all members engage in productive labor, even those who may exercise some specialized governmental functions, except possibly a very few, like a chief or religious leader. In this sense, the primitive society is a classless one, and, unlike the aristocratic empire, it does not contain an aristocracy but at most a few individuals who do not engage in manual work.[29]

Obviously, this definition of primitive societies is a broad one, encompassing most societies in the human past, including hunting and gathering ones, like the Pigmies, pastoral ones, like Bedouin camel herders, and agricultural ones, like African or Indian peasant villages. It is adequate for our purposes, however, for it distinguishes primitive societies from aristocratic empires in principle. In practice, the distinction may not always

27. Ibid., pp. 296–97.

28. For my attempt to define "modernization," see my *The Political Consequences of Modernization*, pp. 19–22.

29. These and other distinctions between primitive societies and traditional empires are drawn by Sjoberg, "Folk and 'Feudal' Societies," pp. 231–39.

be quite as sharp, and transitional phenomena may appear when a tribe extending beyond a single village becomes more integrated and social stratification approaching even the appearance of a ruling class occurs. Obviously also, the term "primitive" is used here without any necessary implication of simplicity, crudeness, or backwardness, but merely because it suggests that primitive societies appear first, that is, before aristocratic empires.

Although it has not been made explicit so far, my definition of an aristocratic empire, by focusing on the aristocracy, necessarily implies that such an empire contains within itself at least a few primitive societies. An aristocracy, as I shall analyze it at great length later, is a ruling class in an agrarian economy that does not engage in productive labor but lives wholly or primarily off the labor of peasants. Hence aristocratic empires must contain not only aristocrats but also peasants who, in turn, live in agrarian primitive societies. Because, as we shall see, it takes many peasants to support one aristocrat, this also implies that aristocratic empires are necessarily a good deal larger than primitive societies.

While all aristocratic empires must contain agrarian primitive societies, not all agrarian primitive societies must be included in aristocratic empires. They can exist autonomously within such empires or independently without them. Hunting and pastoral primitive societies, too, may exist on territory included in aristocratic empires. However, unlike agrarian primitive societies, they are not essential to the existence of such empires, that is, they do not support the aristocracy and are thus about equally independent of the latter whether formally under its rule or not. Finally, it may be added that aristocratic empires may, and usually do, contain, in addition to aristocrats and peasants, people whom I shall call townspeople, but these are not an essential element in our conception of an aristocratic empire and they are hence not included in our minimal definition.

It is now clear why I prefer the term "traditional aristocratic empire" or, more briefly, "aristocratic empire" to "traditional society." For one thing, no matter how sharply I might distinguish between primitive and traditional societies, much of current usage does not do so. The term "traditional society" is bound to remain confusing therefore, and were this book entitled "The Politics of Traditional Societies," that title might arouse expectations of an analysis of politics in tribal societies.

Secondly, according to my definition of an aristocratic empire, it contains within itself or even consists of different societies. Such a conception is probably incompatible with the common concept of societies as mutually exclusive entities. Reinhard Bendix, speaking of traditional societies, refers to the "fragmentation of the social structure in economic, legal, and political terms" and he says that "in this setting the term 'society' is applied only with difficulty, since the people themselves live in fragmented subordination, while their rulers constitute 'the society' because they are the persons worthy of note in the country."[30]

I avoid these difficulties by using the term "traditional aristocratic empire" rather than "traditional society." The explicit or implicit retention of the word "traditional" should make clear that I am not dealing with commercialized, modern, or modernized societies.[31] The addition of the word "aristocratic" and the use of the word "empire" indicate that I am not concerned with individual primitive tribes or villages. Finally, the word "empire," unlike the word "society," also suggests that the entities analyzed here contain such primitive societies within themselves. Of course, I apply the term "empire" to these entities regardless of their form of government, that is, regardless of whether they are governed by emperors, other kinds of monarchs, or other aristocrats. Thus, Sparta was an empire, though it had two kings, and so was Rome, both under the Republic and the Empire.

In this book, the politics of the aristocracy are dealt with and not the politics of primitive societies, including villages within aristocratic empires, or the politics of towns, except as village and town politics affect the politics of the aristocracy. Nevertheless, given my conception of an aristocratic empire, to be elaborated later, as consisting of an aristocracy, of nearly autonomous peasant villages, and of towns which in turn consist of people attached to the aristocracy and of nearly autonomous groups of other townspeople, the book is correctly entitled "The Politics *of* Aristocratic Empires." It does not deal with all of politics *in* aristocratic empires, that is, with the politics of the vast majority of their populations that takes place within their villages and towns, but it does deal with the politics of that

---

30. Bendix, *Nation-Building and Citizenship*, p. 401.

31. To be sure, the term "traditional" has also been applied to empires existing up to the emergence of modern states, like the Chinese, Russian, and Ottoman empires into the nineteenth century, and perhaps even to the European absolutist monarchies and the Japanese Tokugawa shogunate of the seventeenth and eighteenth centuries, not to mention ancient Athens and Rome—all of which are commercialized and hence modern. The addition of the term "aristocratic" will not serve to distinguish the "traditional" empires from the more modern ones just mentioned, because in the latter, too, aristocracies remain prominent and mostly dominant. On the other hand, to refer to "early" or "ancient" empires instead of "traditional aristocratic" ones would be incorrect, because some traditional aristocratic empires have persisted into the twentieth century with little modification by modernity, like Ethiopia and the Persian Gulf and Himalayan monarchies, and one—Saudi Arabia—was even established only in the 1920s, though it came under the impact of modernization almost immediately. Given its wide and varied usage, then, "traditional" is, unfortunately, not an unambiguously clear term. However, I cannot think of a better one for my purposes and must simply urge the reader to keep in mind that I use it to exclude both primitive and commercialized or modern societies, even aristocratic ones.

small minority, the aristocracy, whose existence defines the aristocratic empire and whose politics therefore *is* the politics of the aristocratic empire.

Having mentioned three broad phases of history—the primitive, the traditional aristocratic, and the modern—I should perhaps add that they need not at all necessarily occur in that sequence, though they may do so more often than not. For one thing, the traditional aristocratic phase may be skipped altogether where primitive communities that have never been included in aristocratic empires are subjected to modernization, as happened in North America and parts of Central Africa and is now happening in New Guinea. It is also possible for the traditional aristocratic phase to be followed by the primitive one where an aristocratic empire has disintegrated or contracted to leave some primitive communities once again independent of aristocratic rule, as happened in the case of a number of major African empires or—perhaps, to the extent that they had not been subject to commercialization yet—as the three original Swiss cantons gained their independence of Habsburg rule. On the other hand, it is also possible for the traditional aristocratic phase and even a primitive phase to follow a more modern one, as was true in the cases of aristocratic empires and of once-again-independent primitive tribes and villages that emerged out of the contracting and collapsing commercialized Western Roman empire. However, in all cases, a primitive phase must precede, though not necessarily immediately, the traditional aristocratic one, for aristocratic empires rest on primitive communities. It is for this reason that it is impossible to conceive of an aristocratic empire succeeding a modern industrial society, for in the latter—as is not true under commercialization—all primitive communities are dissolved.

It is clear from the foregoing that I do not believe in any necessarily unilinear historical development. However, it is possible to postulate a certain evolutionary logic prevailing among the phases of history I have mentioned. According to it, primitive societies may be combined into aristocratic empires that, through commercialization, may become modern (and some of which may eventually become industrialized). In terms of technological development, traditional aristocratic empires are hardly a separate phase at all. Such empires, that is, aristocratic rule and exploitation, are merely superimposed on primitive peasant agriculture. It continues under these empires, though sometimes modified by irrigation and flood-control works built at the behest of the aristocracy. It is commercialization, which may be possible only in aristocratic empires, not the establishment of such empires, that brings about technological change, which may then become enormous with industrialization.

Because my interest here lies not in evolving some general scheme of historical stages but merely in distinguishing aristocratic empires from primitive societies on the one hand and from commercialized ones on the other (and because I am here not concerned with industrialized societies), I focus on the role of aristocracies as the characteristic that distinguishes those three phases from each other. I shall enlarge on this point at the beginning of the next chapter, but may note here that it is for this reason that my scheme of historical stages differs from better known, often more elaborate and, for other purposes, more useful ones.

Thus, Marx distinguished, according to their respective modes of production, among ancient slave, feudal, and capitalist class societies, preceded by primitive communism and to be followed by modern classless communism (though, as I noted, he also wrote of an Asiatic mode of production which does not fit into this evolutionary scheme and, in some ways, comes close to my aristocratic empires). Max Weber, concerned with types of domination, distinguished between the patriarchial one, the patrimonial and the feudal ones (which I will have occasion to refer to below), and the modern legal-bureaucratic one. Gerhard Lenski, in his *Power and Privilege*, focuses on the means of subsistence of various societies and classifies societies in terms of their technology into hunting and gathering, horticultural, agrarian, and industrial ones.

Even though I do not conceive of my phases of history as necessarily succeeding each other in one specific order, the following simple diagram may nevertheless be useful.[32] It illustrates the persistence of traditional aristocratic elements in modern societies and thus shows why I am able to draw on data from commercialized and hence to some degree modernized societies in this analysis of nonmodern traditional aristocratic empires, a matter to be further explained in the next chapter.

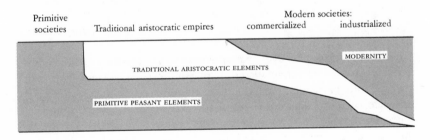

Primitive societies   Traditional aristocratic empires   Modern societies: commercialized   industrialized

MODERNITY

TRADITIONAL ARISTOCRATIC ELEMENTS

PRIMITIVE PEASANT ELEMENTS

32. I am grateful to Gerhard Lenski for suggesting that I present this kind of diagram. Obviously, the amount of space given to each historical phase in no way corresponds to its historical duration.

2

The Commercialization of
Aristocratic Empires

Traditional Aristocratic Empires
and Commercialization

As has just been suggested, I distinguish traditional aristocratic empires on the one hand from primitive societies and on the other hand from modern societies. The first distinction is, in principle, a fairly clear one, for it rests on the absence of an aristocracy in primitive societies and its presence in aristocratic empires. The distinction between aristocratic empires and modern societies also turns on the aristocracy. However, because aristocracies are obviously present in modern societies, too, we must here emphasize not the mere existence of aristocracies in aristocratic empires, but their existence as the sole ruling class. Once aristocrats come to share governmental power with nonaristocrats, that is, once nonaristocrats wield some influence in government, a crucial characteristic of aristocratic empires is no longer present, and an element of modernity has been introduced.

In practice, peasants never share power with aristocrats—agriculturalists can rule only in primitive societies, that is, in their villages—but some townspeople, particularly merchants or traders, can do so. Obviously, the influence of merchants on government is a matter of degree, and it is hence impossible to draw a sharp line between traditional aristocratic empires and commercialized and, in this sense, modern societies.[1] It can

1. That no sharp distinction can be drawn between traditional aristocratic empires and commercialized societies is no reason not to distinguish between them. As Barrington Moore says in a footnote with reference to the replacement of a subsistence economy by a market economy among peasants, itself an element of the process of commercialization: "Markets were by no means absent in premodern peasant villages. And even the modern suburban businessman may take pride in a few tomatoes grown in his backyard. It would not be necessary to mention these points were it not for anticonceptual scholarship that de-

quite reasonably be argued that where the aristocracy consumes the entire surplus produced by the peasantry there can be no trade. Consequently, the very existence of commerce introduces an element of modernity and of change into aristocratic empires. One could then define as pure traditional aristocratic empires only those containing no commercial towns-people at all.

Such empires with little or no trade do not constitute merely an ideal type abstracted from a more or less commercialized reality. Agglomerations of cultivators' villages must innumerable times in history have come under a tributary relationship to aristocracies and thus become empires, however transitory. But, contrary to the common notion that all large and long-lasting empires were commercialized, there were even some major empires which for extended periods of time had little or no trade. Let me quote sources on four such empires on three continents.

One of these virtually pure, noncommercialized aristocratic empires was the Carolingian one between the time when the Muslim conquests cut Western Europe off from Mediterranean trade and the beginnings of commercialization in the eleventh century. According to Henri Pirenne, "it is quite plain, from such evidence as we possess, that from the end of the eighth century Western Europe had sunk back into a purely agricultural state. Land was the sole source of subsistence and the sole condition of wealth. All classes of the population, from the Emperor, who had no other revenues than those derived from his landed property, down to the humblest serf, lived directly or indirectly on the products of the soil, whether they raised them by their labour, or confined themselves to collecting and consuming them. Movable wealth no longer played any part in economic life. All social existence was founded on property or on the possession of land. . . . Sale and purchase were not the normal occupation of anyone; they were expedients to which people had recourse when obliged by necessity. Commerce had so completely ceased to be one of the branches of social activity that each estate aimed at supplying all its own needs. . . . Thus we seek in vain for professional merchants. None existed, or rather none but the Jews. . . . The merchant class had disappeared."[2]

A similar description of the Vietnamese kingdom in the nine centuries between Chinese and French domination has been given: "No economic development took place in precolonial Vietnam that might have altered the basis of royal and mandarin rule. Through the entire 900 years of

---

lights in the effort to trample down historical distinctions by pointing to such trivialities. Obviously what matters is the qualitative role played by the market in the countryside: its effect on social relationships." Moore, *Social Origins of Dictatorship and Democracy*, pp. 467–68.

2. Pirenne, *Economic and Social History of Medieval Europe*, pp. 7, 10, 11, 12.

independence prior to French rule, the country's economy was static, remaining exclusively agricultural. Some villages of artisans and fishermen existed, and there were also some people employed in mining, but apart from them, the mandarins, and the Buddhist monks, the great mass of the people were peasants, engaged almost exclusively in the cultivation of rice. Both national and international trade remained insignificant, since most villages and the country as a whole were economically self-sufficient. In times when the monarchy failed to check the growth of large land holdings, feudal ambition often threatened royal authority. But no property-owning middle class of merchants, contractors, lawyers, or owners of nonagricultural enterprises ever developed to compete with the mandarins for positions of power."[3]

Through most of the Chou period (eleventh century to 221 B.C.) and in the preceding Shang period in China, "trade amounted to little more than the exchange of local materials for materials that were not produced locally. The aristocrats, provided by the peasants with food, clothing, and labor, wanted only a few items, such as jewelry and salt, that were produced in other areas. In the circumstances, there was little demand for the services of merchants." "It is accordingly impossible to imagine a prosperous and powerful merchant class."[4]

Finally, "there is no doubt that most—if not all—trade in the Inca empire was local and on a small scale. . . . There was no money and there probably were no merchants. . . . The truth is that commerce, by most ordinary definitions, did not exist on an imperial scale. . . . Marketing development in the Inca empire in general went no further than local barter by housewives. . . . Weights and measures were not used in the local markets, but simply barter of amounts measured by eye. Everything points to very small-scale trade."[5]

Still, a definition of a traditional aristocratic empire excluding all trade whatsoever would be too narrow for our purposes. I shall therefore rule out from our category of aristocratic empires only those empires where aristocrats have yielded at least some of their power to merchants or have even been more or less replaced by merchants as rulers or—which comes to the same thing—where aristocrats have become merchants themselves. Where, then, government is being conducted in good part in line with commercial considerations rather than with aristocratic values, commercialization has to that extent set in.

By these standards, quite a number of major empires, not to mention numerous minor and little known ones, qualify as traditional aristocratic

3. Buttinger, *A Dragon Defiant*, p. 54.

4. Hsu, *Ancient China in Transition*, pp. 11, 13.

5. Moore, *Power and Property in Inca Peru*, pp. 86–88.

empires. These would probably include ancient Egypt from the predynastic perhaps through the first intermediate period, that is, for very roughly two millennia until about 2000 B.C.; Ahmenid Persia from the sixth to the fourth century B.C.; the early Aryan kingdoms in India from their establishment in the second millennium to about the sixth century B.C.; China from the Shang well into the Chou period, that is, for more than a millennium to about the fifth or fourth century B.C.; Japan from the emergence of an aristocracy in the first half of the first millennium A.D. until the thirteenth century; the conquest empires in Southeastern Europe of Asiatic nomadic empire builders from the Huns in the fourth and fifth centuries through the Avars, Magyars, and Bulgars, to the Pechenegs and Cumans in the tenth to the twelfth centuries, each of which lasted at least a century or two; the early Bohemian and Polish kingdoms from the tenth to the thirteenth centuries; the various empires of the Mongols, at least in their early stages, in Central and Western Asia and Southern Russia from the thirteenth to the fifteenth centuries; the early stages of the Turkic empires of the Ottomans in the fourteenth century and the Moguls in India and the Safavids in Persia in the sixteenth century; some African empires, of which Ethiopia and that of the Tutsi lasted until quite recently; and, in Peru, the Inca empire from its legendary beginnings in the thirteenth century to its conquest by the Spaniards in the sixteenth.

In Western Europe, too, numerous traditional aristocratic empires arose as the West Roman empire disintegrated and after its fall. The Burgundians and the Visigoths established empires in Gaul in the fifth century and the Visigoths remained in Spain in the sixth and seventh centuries. In Italy the Ostrogoths ruled in the early sixth and the Lombards from the mid-sixth to the mid-eighth century. In England, beginning in the fifth century, Anglo-Saxon kingdoms were established. The Franks, beginning in the sixth century under the Merovingians, expanded across Gaul and by the end of the eighth century under Charlemagne controlled also Central Europe. Traditional aristocratic empires continued under Carolingian Frankish rule in what became France and Germany into the tenth century, and these two areas entered the period of commercialization in the eleventh century under the Capetian kings and the Saxon emperors respectively.

What was just quoted from Pirenne about the Carolingian empire seems largely true of most of Western Europe from the fifth to the tenth century. Carlo Cipolla stresses this repeatedly and is worth quoting here to show that even Western Europe, the area probably most associated in our minds with commercialization and modernization, was for a large part of its history occupied by traditional aristocratic empires. He puts it strikingly when he says that, if in the early Middle Ages there had, in Byzantium, been economists using their modern vocabulary, they would have described Western Europe as "'a backward, underdeveloped area, hampered by political struggles and by lack of security, depressed by an abnormally low level of investment.' As a matter of fact, since the beginnings of the fifth century... Western Europe had fallen into a stage of economic life near that of primitive societies."[6] "The Western societies of the Dark Ages were undoubtedly at a primitive stage of economic development and if in them a division of labor existed this was certainly on a rather low level. A good part of the goods were produced by their consumers; many other goods were exchanged on a barter basis among neighbors."[7]

Elsewhere, Cipolla describes early medieval Europe as follows: "It was a poor and primitive Europe, a Europe made up of numberless rural microcosms—the manors, largely self-sufficient, whose autarchy was in part the consequence of the decline of trade and to a large extent its cause as well.... The arts, education, trade, production, and the division of labor were reduced to a minimal level. The use of money almost completely disappeared. The population was small, production meager, and poverty extreme. The social structures were primitive. There were those who prayed, those who fought, and those who labored. The prevailing values reflected a brutal and superstitious society—fighting and praying were the only respectable activities, and those who fought did it mostly for robbing, and those who prayed did it superstitiously. Those who labored were regarded as despicable serfs."[8]

Clearly, even large and long-lasting traditional aristocratic empires are by no means exceptional in history. However, as I suggested at the beginning of Chapter 1, most and possibly all large empires may, in the long run, tend to become commercialized. In this chapter, numerous empires will be listed that did, at least to some significant degree, undergo that process —Babylonia and Phoenicia, ancient India, Greece, and Rome, all the European empires from the medieval West to Russia, the Islamic ones from the early caliphate to Mogul India and Ottoman Turkey, China, Japan, and even the Aztec empire. Obviously, there is far more widespread interest in some of these empires than in some purely traditional aristocratic ones, and far more is known of them, in good part probably

---

6. Cipolla, *Money, Prices and Civilization in the Mediterranean World*, p. 3. "There is no doubt that from the fall of the Roman Empire to the beginning of the thirteenth century Europe was an underdeveloped area in relation to the major centers of civilization at the time, whether the China of the T'ang or Sung Dynasties, the Byzantine Empire under the Macedonian dynasty, or the Arab Empire under the Ommayads or the Abbasids." Cipolla, *Before the Industrial Revolution*, p. 206. Cipolla notes that the Arabs, whose knowledge of geography improved greatly during this period, knew nothing of Europe simply because it was of no interest to them (ibid.).

7. Cipolla, *Money, Prices and Civilization*, p. 10.

8. Cipolla, *Before the Industrial Revolution*, p. 140.

precisely because they were commercialized and hence left more written records and were less isolated. Must I, then, exclude these empires, beginning with the period when they became commercialized, from consideration and as a source of data and confine my analysis to empires that I can probably regard as traditional aristocratic ones by my definition?

Fortunately, though we are here interested only in traditional aristocratic empires as such, we need not ignore commercialized ones. Commercialization, after all, may for quite a long time affect only a very few people and may not affect many of them very much. And even the minority of aristocrats who now buy and sell land or its products or of peasants who buy and sell and may even rise up in revolt in response to conditions created by commercialization are by no means wholly different in all their other behavior and attitudes from traditional aristocrats and peasants. If even advanced industrialization has not destroyed all the remnants of traditionalism, surely the beginnings of commercialization left much of the traditional aristocratic order intact.[9]

One can learn much about that traditional aristocratic order, then, by studying what is left of it after some commercialization has set in, for example, in the millennium of Chinese history from the Han to the Sung and even, to some lesser degree, in the next millennium from the Sung to the Manchus, and, of course, from feudal Europe in the late Middle Ages and even in more modern periods. Indeed, because the sources on commercialized periods are far more adequate and reliable than those on the purely traditional aristocratic ones, like Chou China or Merovingian and Carolingian Western Europe, their study is even preferable in some respects. Author and reader must merely make a deliberate attempt to distinguish between traditional elements persisting under commercialization and the effects of commercialization that have intruded into the traditional aristocratic order or have been left over in it from an earlier commercial order. Neither I nor the reader is likely to succeed in this at all times, and we may here and there ascribe to traditional aristocratic empires characteristics in fact created by commercialization, for example, if we were to deduce the attitudes of traditional aristocrats from the behavior of thirteenth-century French knights. However, on balance, this procedure seems far less risky than to ignore the rich knowledge on traditional aristocratic empires to be gained through a study of certain elements of their commercialized successors.

9. Cipolla stresses that "even the most highly developed European societies of the Middle Ages remained fundamentally agrarian. The fraction of the active population and resources engaged in trade and manufacture was small, most of the trade itself was connected with agricultural products, the . . . merchants and bankers were generally part-time landlords (as most of the artisans and sailors were part-time peasants)." Cipolla, *The Economic History of World Population*, p. 31.

It is also worth stressing that if we can learn about traditional aristocratic empires from a study of commercialized ones, that statement can also be reversed. As I just noted, commercialization affects both aristocrats and peasants only relatively slightly, and much in their institutions, ideologies, and behavior remains traditional. Consequently, while for purposes of my analysis I focus here on traditional aristocratic empires, this book should also throw a great deal of light on commercialized aristocratic empires, for example, those of late medieval Europe and imperial China. Indeed, their politics cannot be understood without an understanding of the aristocratic politics analyzed here. In the final chapter, I will then also indicate the far-reaching relevance of the latter for a well rounded comprehension even of modern politics.

Commercialization involves a number of interrelated developments. Before some of these are mentioned with reference to particular areas and periods of history, let me indicate again, very briefly, why an empire subject to it is no longer a pure traditional aristocratic one by my definition.

With growing wealth, merchants come to play a role in the politics of what were hitherto traditional aristocratic empires. They become an increasingly important source of taxes for the aristocracy and, as some of them turn into bankers, they provide loans to aristocrats. Thus, some aristocrats, who were earlier dependent for their income entirely on the peasantry, now become dependent also on some merchants. The aristocracy's dependence on the peasantry was analogous to the shepherd's dependence on his animals. The peasantry was in no position to withhold its product, and as I shall stress later, no reciprocity was therefore involved. Dependence on wealthy merchants and bankers, however, is of a very different nature, for, unlike peasants, they can withhold their services from the aristocracy or can choose which particular aristocrats to serve. They can extract concessions from the aristocracy and even play one aristocrat or aristocratic faction against another and can thus influence aristocratic decisions and gain a measure of autonomy for themselves and their towns. All this, however, means that aristocrats are no longer free to govern wholly in accordance with traditional aristocratic standards and to control completely the sphere formerly reserved entirely to them. This marks, however indistinctly, the end of the traditional empire.[10]

Typically, the growing importance of trade that makes merchants politically powerful, is accompanied by the growth of communications, urbanization, specialization, and literacy. Trade also stimulates inventions in the areas of production and transportation, and these, in turn, are related to a flowering of both applied and pure science. Nor does agriculture, the economic basis of the old traditional aristocratic empire, remain unaffected. If

10. Much of this paragraph draws on my *The Political Consequences of Modernization*, p. 50.

the landed aristocracy wants to buy the products newly made available by trade, whether by exchanging money or agricultural products for them, peasants, who may now pay their dues in cash rather than in kind, must contribute a bigger surplus out of their labor than was needed to support the aristocracy before. This can lead to more extensive and intensive agriculture, to peasant indebtedness, the alienability of land and its sale as a commodity, and the division of the peasantry into landed and landless segments. All these are symptoms that tend to accompany commercialization.

Trade can remain quite insignificant and its growth can be quite slow and gradual in an empire that then remains traditional. But once that growth passes a certain threshold, the interrelated changes just mentioned can, feeding on each other, occur relatively rapidly in the course of a century or two. Where such rather dramatic transformations took place, as in Western Europe, China, and Japan, commercialization can be defined relatively easily in terms of a particular historical period. In other cases, as in Ottoman Turkey, the corresponding changes evidently occurred more imperceptibly, and other empires, like Rome, Kievan Russia, and the caliphate, were, for different reasons, to some degree commercialized from their beginnings as empires. Let us now look more specifically at each of these cases and also mention a few others.

Commercialization in Europe

The best-known case of the commercialization of an aristocratic order is no doubt that of Western Europe, because it marked the beginning of a process of change that eventually led to the modern industrial societies of the present. These beginnings—and hence the end of the traditional aristocratic period—in Western Europe occurred at approximately the middle of the eleventh century and, in the course of the next two or three centuries, brought about some major economic, social, and political changes.[11] Land under cultivation was greatly extended by the

11. Bloch, *Feudal Society*, pp. 69–71, discusses some of these under the heading of "the economic revolution of the second feudal age," and Anderson, *Passages from Antiquity to Feudalism*, pp. 182–96, stresses their far-reaching nature in an excellent summary entitled "The Feudal Dynamic." See also Pirenne, *Economic and Social History of Medieval Europe*, and the last two chapters, entitled "The Resurgence of Town Life and of Commercial Activity" and "The Expansion and Development of Agriculture in the Eleventh Century" of Latouche, *The Birth of Western Economy*, pp. 235–99. Of course, the changes did not arrive simultaneously everywhere. Many rural areas remained largely untouched by commercialization long after the eleventh century, while on the other hand Northern Italy was ahead of the rest of Western Europe. "Even in the eighth century there existed a Po valley trade in which agricultural produce was exchanged, first for Venetian salt, then for goods of eastern

clearing of forests and wasteland and by the draining of swamps, and new lands were occupied, as in Spain and especially east of the Elbe. Important technical innovations—some known earlier and elsewhere[12]—began to spread, such as the water mill, the three-field system of crop rotation, and the use of the iron plow, the horse shoe, and the stiff harness for horse traction and hence the use of horses for plowing. All this resulted in a tremendous increase, possibly a doubling, of agricultural production and, consequently, a similar increase in the population.[13]

Related to this development and beginning about the middle of the twelfth century, there was a shift from subsistence agriculture. Formerly, producer and consumer had usually been identical, and the relatively tiny nonagricultural minority in the population received agricultural goods as payment in kind. Trade and the use of money were minimal with respect to agriculture. Now, the nonagricultural and even part of the agricultural population began to receive their agricultural goods in the market, middlemen appeared, and means of transportation, especially horse transport, improved so as to permit the shipping of produce from areas with agricultural surpluses.[14]

With the growth of communications, trade in general improved, including also trade, especially from Italy, with the Islamic and Byzantine Near East after the first Crusade (1096–99) and the conquest of Constantinople in 1204 by the crusaders of the fourth Crusade. Manufacturing, notably of cloth, grew, and cloth became a major export item from Western Europe. The increase in trade and manufacturing was linked to a growth in the size and number of towns, which were dominated by a new urban elite of successful merchants and manufacturers. Some of these towns became autonomous of aristocratic rule, as in Flanders and later in Germany and France, or even gained, with their surrounding areas, complete independence, as in Northern Italy.

Anderson, referring to Western Europe in the late Middle Ages, says that "in every country the mediaeval towns represented an absolutely

---

provenance that came through Byzantium. This commercial development was uneven, in that areas remote from trade routes and towns remained primitive." Hilton, *Bond Men Made Free*, p. 75.

12. Cipolla, *Before the Industrial Revolution*, pp. 159–60.

13. Duby, *Rural Economy and Country Life in the Medieval West*, pp. 102–3 and 119–25. Cipolla estimates that, from A.D. 1000 to 1200, the population of the British Isles grew from two to five million, of France from five to fifteen million, of Germany from three to twelve million, and of Italy from five to ten million. He adds that these figures are merely "the fruits of hazardous hypotheses." Cipolla, *Before the Industrial Revolution*, p. 4.

14. Slicher van Bath, *The Agrarian History of Western Europe*, pp. 23–25.

central economic and cultural component of the feudal order,"[15] and Bloch affirms that "from the end of the eleventh century the artisan class and the merchant class, having become much more numerous and much more indispensable to the life of the community, made themselves felt more and more vigorously in the urban setting. This applies especially to the merchant class, for the medieval economy, after the great revival of these decisive years, was always dominated, not by the producer, but by the trader."[16] It is this important role of merchants in late medieval society generally and the fact that they dominated some territories to the virtual exclusion of the aristocracy, that makes Western Europe from the eleventh century on no longer traditional.

The commercialization of Western Europe that began in the eleventh century had the most far-reaching results, for it and the industrialization that grew out of it or their profoundly upsetting consequences eventually spread to the rest of the globe. However, commercial modernization occurred independently neither for the first nor for the last time in late medieval Western Europe. There had been a number of commercialized empires in the ancient Mediterranean world[17]—Phoenicia from the tenth century B.C. on, and its colony Carthage from the ninth; Athens from the sixth century B.C. on and other commercial Greek city-states with their colonies; the Hellenistic kingdoms; and Rome in the period of the later Republic and of the Empire, including the Byzantine Eastern Roman empire which lasted through the Middle Ages.

In Rome, by about the third century B.C., a class of private merchants, financiers, and publicans (the *equites*) became important in the economy and eventually in politics. They engaged in the newly developing overseas trade, received contracts for public works, for supplying armies and fleets and for services as tax farmers in the provinces, and they acted as money lenders and bankers when tax-paying municipalities fell into arrears. Once the policies of senators and provincial governors, that is, of aristocrats, were affected by the interests of these *equites* (sometimes because aristocrats were silent partners in their companies), and wars were conducted partly in line with commercial considerations, commercialization had set in.[18] Because, as will be noted in the next chapter, Rome had no aristoc-

15. Anderson, *Passages from Antiquity to Feudalism*, p. 195. See also Pirenne, *Medieval Cities*, and Hoselitz, *Sociological Aspects of Economic Growth*, pp. 164–71.

16. Bloch, *Feudal Society*, p. 71.

17. For a brief summary, see Lévy, *The Economic Life of the Ancient World*.

18. For a careful study of the "equestrian order" and of its role in politics in Republican Rome, see Hill, *The Roman Middle Class in the Republican Period*, especially pp. 47–199. On the high development of urbanism and commerce in Imperial Rome, especially in the

racy in the early Republic into the third century and as it was commercialized from about that time on, its empire was never a purely traditional aristocratic one.

That the Roman empire was not a traditional aristocratic one is well worth noting for two reasons. First, given the interest it has held in the West as a major historical basis of Western civilization, it might well be thought of as the classical aristocratic empire; and, second, it was precisely the high level of Roman commercialization that no doubt facilitated the commercialization of Western Europe in the late Middle Ages. Indeed, Byzantium, including the areas conquered from the Byzantine empire by the Arabs in the seventh century, never reverted to traditionalism, as Western Europe did in the early Middle Ages, and it was in good part renewed contact with these areas that stimulated the commercialization of Western Europe in the eleventh century. Also, some areas in Northern Italy, in part under Byzantine influence, form a bridge between Roman imperial and late medieval commercialization. It was, incidentally, no doubt because of the relative modernity of ancient Rome as compared to the subsequent early medieval period in Western Europe that Roman law was adopted by the governments of commercialized and eventually industrialized societies as more appropriate than Germanic-feudal law, which lacked the clear conception of exclusive private property of Roman law.

To say that an empire became commercialized does not necessarily mean that trade came to dominate its economy, but merely that the aristocracy no longer governed alone and solely in line with aristocratic values. This much was certainly true in the commercialized classical world, but even in Athens the citizen remained ideally a nonworking warrior, almost continuously at war and living off the labor of slaves and metics at home and tribute-paying subject cities abroad.[19] There is some question as to just how important trade and merchants were in the Greek and Roman economy and politics. Perry Anderson emphasizes that "behind this urban culture and polity lay no urban *economy* in any way commensurate with it: on the contrary, the material wealth which sustained its intellectual and civic vitality was drawn overwhelmingly from the countryside. The classical world was massively, unalterably rural in its basic quantitative proportions. Agriculture represented throughout its history the absolutely dominant domain of production, invariably furnishing the main fortunes of

---

golden age of the Antonine emperors, mainly in the second century A.D., see Rostovtzeff, *The Social and Economic History of the Roman Empire*, especially chapter 5, and, for a summary, Bernardi, "The Economic Problems of the Roman Empire at the Time of its Decline," pp. 29–31.

19. This is stressed and the role of trade and traders in Greek political life is held to be relatively small by Hasebroek, *Trade and Politics in Ancient Greece*.

the cities themselves. The Graeco-Roman towns were never predominantly communities of manufacturers, traders or craftsmen: they were, in origin and principle, urban congeries of landowners. Every municipal order from democratic Athens to oligarchic Sparta or senatorial Rome, was essentially dominated by agrarian proprietors."[20] Their estates were worked by slaves so that urban life in classical antiquity rested on slave-operated agriculture.[21]

Yet, massive investment in slave labor to carry on agricultural production (as well as mining and much of the artisans' work in the cities) sharply distinguished the classical Greek city states and Rome from traditional aristocratic empires where agriculture is carried on by peasants who are not bought and sold and where slavery typically plays a relatively minor role in the economy. In addition, the substantial role of cities and of merchants in the economy and politics of classical Greece and of Rome in the later Republic and in the Empire makes these empires commercial rather than traditional aristocratic ones.

Commercialization in China, Russia, and Japan

Commercialization also occurred in a number of other empires. Whether it went far enough to deprive them of their traditional aristocratic character may well remain unclear in some cases, for my principal criterion distinguishing traditional aristocratic empires from commercialized ones—substantial power being wielded by merchants—is itself by no means a clear one. However, a few cases—notably those of China, Russia and Japan—are worth mentioning here as instances of far-reaching commercialization independently following on broad lines the pattern familiar to us from the Western European experience.

China under the Sung dynasty (960–1279) underwent a transformation similar to the one that occurred in Western Europe at about the same time. Mark Elvin speaks of "the medieval revolution which made the Chinese economy after about 1100 the most advanced in the world." He

20. Anderson, *Passages from Antiquity to Feudalism*, p. 19.

21. For a very different interpretation by another Marxist writer, see Wason, *Class Struggles in Ancient Greece*, who says: "In the Greek city states affected by the economic revolution there grew up a merchant class powerful enough to smash the old state structure and social hierarchy. After a period of dictatorship exercised through tyrants, they established bourgeois republics, or city states based essentially on the merchant class with the support at first of peasants and artisans; states in which trade and finance eventually dominated the whole life of the community" (p. 50). On how Greek terrain and climate discouraged the development of an aristocracy fighting on horseback and of a centralized bureaucracy or priesthood, see Gouldner, *Enter Plato*, pp. 5–9.

devotes chapters to the revolutions in, respectively, farming, water transport, money and credit, market structure and urbanization, and science and technology, which leave no doubt that "the Chinese economy had become commercialized."[22] Anderson points to a situation strikingly in contrast to that characteristic of traditional aristocratic empires where the aristocracy lives almost entirely off the peasantry: "In the Southern Sung State of the later 12th and 13th centuries, commercial revenues greatly exceeded agrarian revenues. This new fiscal balance reflected not merely the growth of domestic and foreign trade, but also the enlargement of the manufacturing base of the whole economy, the expansion of mining, and the spread of cash cropping in agriculture. . . . The Chinese Empire of the Sung epoch was unquestionably the wealthiest and most advanced economy on the globe in the 11th and 12th centuries,"[23] that is, in the same period when commercialization in Western Europe had begun.

According to one view of Chinese history, the Mongol invasion and the subsequent Yüan and Ming dynasties put an end to these "modernizing" developments of the Southern Sung, that is, to the ongoing commercialization of China. "The roads which led to Southern Sung . . . led nowhere, and the process of historical evolution was in one sense interrupted. . . . The levelling of social distinctions based on ascribed characteristics and the beginnings of capitalistic enterprise were essentially ended."[24] Hodgson speaks of "the abortive industrial revolution in Sung China" and says that a process very similar to modernization in northwest Europe "had been stopped in later Sung China under the nomad dynasties. The Occidental florescence did not taper off."[25] Scholars who contrast the development of post-Sung China to that of Western Europe also stress the small significance of foreign trade and the absence of free cities: "the Chinese city was under the domination of officials rather than of merchants."[26] Barrington Moore says that "imperial Chinese society never created an urban trading and manufacturing class comparable to that which grew out of the later stages of feudalism in Western Europe, though at times there were some starts in this direction."[27] Etienne Balazs, who also places the beginnings of Chinese capitalism in the Sung period, stresses repeatedly that a sup-

22. Elvin, *The Pattern of the Chinese Past*, pp. 7, 172. See also Haeger, ed., *Crisis and Prosperity in Sung China*, especially chaps. 1, 2, and 4, and Anderson, *Lineages of the Absolutist State*, pp. 528–30, and the sources cited there.

23. Ibid., p. 530.

24. Haeger, "Introduction," p. 12; see also ibid., p. 99.

25. Hodgson, *The Venture of Islam*, 3:197, 183.

26. Fairbank, Eckstein, and Yang, "Economic Change in Early Modern China," p. 15. See also Balazs, *Chinese Civilization and Bureaucracy*, p. 70.

27. Moore, *Social Origins of Dictatorship and Democracy*, p. 174.

posedly all-powerful scholar-official class kept a bourgeoisie from developing because it left no scope or security for individual enterprise.[28]

On the other hand, Wolfram Eberhard suggests that the changes of the Sung period did not end with it. "As a consequence of a set of changes which began in the 8th century A.D. and became very influential by the 11th century, cities began to grow greatly from the 11th century on, and many of them gradually lost their character as administrative centers. . . . They became centers of a new 'urban' or 'bourgeois' culture which was carried by a new social group, gentleman-merchants. . . . This development certainly appears similar to the contemporary development in Japan (and probably *is* similar), but also similar to the developments in Europe in the same centuries, though the similarities here are perhaps superficial."[29] Eberhard even believes that until the early eighteenth century, Chinese industry "had been hardly inferior to Western industry" and that it was only the invention of the steam engine that put Western industry far ahead. As to other differences, such as those stressed by Max Weber, "the more our knowledge of China increases, the more we see that such elements as a business spirit, organizational forms, labor supply, etc. all existed in China."[30]

Perry Anderson may bridge the apparent gap between these two interpretations. He stresses, on the one hand, that "the great, unprecedented breakthroughs of the Sung economy—above all in metallurgy—spent themselves in the subsequent epochs: the radical transformation of industry and society they promised never occurred." But while scientific and technological growth came to an end—though, according to Anderson, only in the Ming period—and hence industry failed to develop, Anderson speaks of "the presence of a vast internal market, which reached deep into

28. Balazs, *Chinese Civilization and Bureaucracy*, especially p. 53; see also Wright, "Introduction," ibid., pp. xv–xvi.

29. Eberhard, *Social Mobility in Traditional China*, p. 268; see also ibid., pp. 259–63.

30. Ibid., p. 258. As to the comparison of Chinese and Western European scientific and technological development, Joseph Needham, the author of numerous works on the history of science, including the five-volume *Science and Civilization in China*, stated that he was "not convinced that Europe was technologically and industrially ahead of China until about A.D. 1450." Needham, "Commentary on Lynn White, Jr., 'What Accelerated Technological Progress in the Western Middle Ages?'" p. 327. And he elaborates: "The fact is that in the spontaneous autochthonous development of Chinese society no drastic change parallel to the Renaissance and the 'scientific revolution' in the West occurred at all. I often like to sketch the Chinese evolution as represented by a relatively slowly rising curve, noticeably running at a higher level, sometimes a much higher level, than European parallels between, say, the second and the fifteenth centuries A.D. But then . . . the curve of science and technology in Europe begins to rise in a violent, almost exponential, manner, overtaking the level of the Asian societies." Needham, "Poverties and Triumphs of the Chinese Scientific Tradition," p. 139.

the countryside, and of very large accumulations of merchant capital" and mentions that "Yangtze merchants often accumulated huge fortunes in commerce, while Shansi bankers were to spread branches across the whole country in the Ch'ing epoch." To be sure, merchants as a group did not wield political power; "they were denied corporate political identity, but not personal social mobility. Conversely, gentry were later to appropriate opportunities for profit in mercantile activities,"[31] that is, aristocrats engaged in commerce, a sure sign of commercialization.[32]

What matters to us here is that imperial China, then, was in its last millennium no longer a traditional aristocratic empire. However, there are good reasons to argue that China ceased to be such an empire long before the Sung period and at about the time of the end of the feudal Chou period in 256 B.C. Already in the late Chou period, "craft production and both local and interregional commerce developed substantially. Those advances are evidenced particularly in the development of iron technology, the growth of cities, and the use of money. . . . Great smelters, reportedly employed more than 200 workmen, and ironmongers were prominent among the rising new class of rich merchants. . . . Cities began to grow as industrial and commercial centers. . . . Money became a significant factor in the expanding Chinese economy."[33] During the following Ch'in period (256–207 B.C), "population was growing everywhere, spurred by such innovations as the use of iron, which considerably improved the technology of agriculture: in plowing, for example. The means of transportation improved, too, facilitating the trade relations that began to form and to link new burgeoning urban districts. This process made it harder (as in late feudal Europe) to pin people to servile status on land."[34] Subsequently, "great fortunes were created during the Han age through the shrewd monopoly of certain trades and occupations and also through the clever avoidance of laws by means of bribes and influence. The use and control of money became important as early as 154 B.C., when the dynasty had to go to the moneylenders to feed and equip the troops used to put down the revolt of the feudatories. They found they could get credit only from one banker and had to pay an interest of ten times the amount of the loan, at that. The bankers made their fortunes from industry and business and from consolidating landholdings. They had been the chief beneficiaries of war and empire."[35]

31. Anderson, *Lineages of the Absolutist State*, pp. 541, 542, 544–45.

32. See also Chang, *The Income of the Chinese Gentry*, chap. 6 on "Mercantile Activities as a Source of Income," which deals, however, chiefly with the nineteenth-century gentry.

33. Hucker, *China's Imperial Past*, pp. 65–66.

34. Levenson and Schurmann, *China: An Interpretive History*, p. 68.

35. Harrison, *The Chinese Empire*, p. 142.

With merchants and bankers becoming so powerful, these changes may well be regarded as marking the beginning of commercialization. It will be important for us to keep in mind, therefore, that post-Chou China, like late medieval Western Europe, was no longer purely traditional, for this helps account for deviations in these areas from patterns prevailing in traditional aristocratic empires, for example with respect to interclass mobility and especially to peasant revolts, which, as we shall see, typically occur on any large scale only in response to commercialization.

In medieval Russia, both in the Kievan empire (or federation of princedoms) and in Novgorod, aristocrats had from their beginnings in the ninth century engaged in trade themselves. Indeed, from the eleventh century on, Novgorod was a more or less independent commercial republic. Of the early Kievan princes, Bendix says: "The protection of trade and the exaction of tribute from the subject population were probably indistinguishable from unprovoked raids and the distribution of booty as a means of organizing campaigns."[36] Even the early shifting Russian aristocratic empires were thus not traditional, but the Mongol invasion of the thirteenth century put an end to the Kievan empire whose reliance on commerce had already been undermined by the growing predominance of Italian cities in Byzantine and Eastern Mediterranean trade, and Novgorod was conquered by aristocratic Moscow under Ivan the Great in the fifteenth century.

About that time, however, after Mongol strength had waned, a second and more powerful wave of commercial modernization began in Russia. It took a form similar to that in Western Europe four centuries earlier, involving improvements in agricultural techniques and tools and a growth of domestic and foreign trade. "These signs of recovery that appeared in the fifteenth century proved the prelude to a remarkable upswing in the next century. . . . Much of the 'natural' economy that had been typical of the earlier period still persisted. But it is clear that Russia . . . entered upon a new era of economic growth in the sixteenth century."[37] This era was marked by a vast expansion of land put under cultivation, great increases in population, and the growth of trade, of the use of money, and of commercial cities—Moscow was said to be larger than London in the mid-sixteenth century.[38] In Russia, as in Western Europe, then, merchants became powerful, but unlike in the West this did not mean a reduction in the power of the aristocracy, for "noblemen there were active merchants. . . . The tsar himself, like his ancient forebears, the princes of Kiev, was

36. Bendix, *Kings or People*, p. 89.

37. Blum, *Lord and Peasant in Russia*, pp. 119–20.

38. Ibid., pp. 117–34, 123.

the single most important business man in the entire empire."[39] Thus, commercialization takes Russia out of our category of traditional aristocratic empires beginning with about the fifteenth century.

In Japan, too, in the thirteenth and especially the fourteenth century, when the so-called Ashikaga period (1336–1568) began, "there was a spread of commodity production in the countryside, . . . and the volume of monetary circulation increased. Rural productivity improved with better farm tools and increased use of animal traction, and agrarian output rose steeply in many areas. Foreign trade expanded, while artisan and merchant guilds of a type similar to those of mediaeval Europe developed in the towns."[40] "During the next two centuries the overseas commercial interests of the Japanese grew rapidly. . . . This growth of foreign trade no doubt gave impetus to economic development within Japan, and the sixteenth century witnessed rapid economic growth . . . and the rise of purely commercial towns." Reischauer even mentions the development of incipient "free cities" that maintained their "independence from control by the feudal classes"[41] until the late sixteenth century, and Anderson refers to "autonomous merchant towns reminiscent of those of mediaeval Europe. . . . The port of Sakai was to be termed an oriental 'Venice' by Jesuit travellers."[42]

On the other hand, as in Russia, not all merchants were distinct from the aristocracy. "By the late fourteenth century the Ashikaga *shogun* and the lords of western Japan were themselves financing trading expeditions to the continent. . . . The feudal lords of the coastal fringes of western Japan came to depend on the profits of foreign trade for a major part of their income . . . From the start, the Japanese overseas traders probably included among their numbers many hereditary members of the warrior class."[43] As in the case of Russia in the fifteenth century, the growth of commerce and of the power of merchants and the involvement of the aristocracy in trade removes Japan from our category of traditional aristocratic empires beginning in about the fourteenth century.

39. Ibid., p. 129.

40. Anderson, *Lineages of the Absolutist State*, p. 438. For evidence of this "dramatic economic growth," see Hall, *Japan from Prehistory to Modern Times*, pp. 121–26.

41. Reischauer, "Japanese Feudalism," pp. 43–44.

42. Anderson, *Lineages of the Absolutist State*, p. 440. "The growth of Sakai is of interest in the political as well as the economic history of Japan; it shows very clearly the development of a class of well-to-do . . . townspeople, and of merchants of great wealth enjoying an unusual degree of independence." Sansom, *A History of Japan*, 2:271. Sakai was governed by "a Council of Thirty-six . . . composed of the richest merchants" (ibid., p. 304). See also Hall, *Japan*, p. 123.

43. Reischauer, "Japanese Feudalism," pp. 43–44.

Other Instances of Commercialization

The areas mentioned—the ancient Eastern Mediterranean world and Rome, Western Europe, Russia, China, and Japan—were not the only ones where traditional aristocratic empires eventually ceased to be traditional by becoming more or less commercialized. For example, trade became important in ancient Babylonia, with investments being made in loans and in land that was worked by wage laborers, so that that empire should probably be regarded as no longer a traditional aristocratic one. "During a period of almost 2,000 years, Babylon was to be a famous commercial metropolis, whose accursed memory is to be found in the Bible and even in the Book of Revelation."[44]

In ancient India, in the Magadha kingdom beginning in the sixth century B.C. and certainly in the Maurya empire founded in the fourth century B.C., "the king became increasingly dependent on the guilds, and the financial power of these craft merchant associations qualifies them for comparison with those of medieval Europe. . . . In return for financing the imperial ambitions of the prince, these merchants often gained important rights and privileges. Wealth made possible greater social mobility, and it was not uncommon for members of the lower orders of society to attain positions of prestige."[45]

Similarly, miles and millennia away, as "a rather late development in Aztec society,"[46] trade became so important that, according to one author, "the economy . . . probably depended on trade quite as much as on tribute,"[47] and merchants became privileged and powerful politically. Jacques Soustelle, too, says that the Aztec merchant class "had become indispensable: its wealth became an instrument of greater and greater power as the ruling class progressively abandoned the frugality of the earlier generations." Soustelle even speculates that, had the Spaniards not destroyed the Aztec empire, "perhaps these 'merchant lords' . . . would have become the chiefs of a bourgeoisie that would either have become part of the ruling class or would have displaced it and taken its power."[48]

The early Arab empires, notably the Umayyad and Abbasid caliphates and the Fatimid one in Egypt, inspired by a religion born in commercial

44. Lévy, *The Economic Life of the Ancient World*, p. 9.

45. Drekmeier, *Kingship and Community in Early India*, pp. 165–66.

46. von Hagen, *The Aztec: Man and Tribe*, p. 179.

47. Davies, *The Aztecs*, p. 136.

48. Soustelle, *Daily Life of the Aztecs*, p. 65. Among the Maya, too, trade was highly developed and merchants "belonged to an honored profession." von Hagen, *World of the Maya*, p. 87.

Mecca and heirs to Byzantine commercialism in the areas they conquered, were commercialized virtually from their beginnings. "Muslim civilization was indefectibly urban, promoting commodity production, mercantile enterprise and monetary circulation in the cities which linked it together, from the first."[49] Maxime Rodinson says: "Not only did the Muslim world know a capitalistic sector, but this sector was apparently the most extensive and highly developed in history before the establishment of the world market created by the Western European bourgeoisie, and this did not outstrip it in importance until the sixteenth century."[50] And Anderson writes: "The Abbasid State presided over the maximum florescence of Islamic trade, industry and science: at its apogee in the early 9th century, it was the wealthiest and most advanced civilization in the world. Merchants, bankers, manufacturers, speculators and tax farmers accumulated huge sums in the great cities: urban crafts diversified and multiplied; a commercial sector emerged in agriculture; long-distance shipping girded the oceans; astronomy, physics and mathematics were transposed from Greek into Arabic culture."[51]

Yet if we define commercialization in terms of the political power of merchants, not so much as individuals but as a class, these empires were perhaps substantially traditional aristocratic ones—certainly more so than late medieval Western Europe or Japan though perhaps no more than China—for "towns had no corporate political identity, their merchants little collective social power. Urban charters were unknown, and town life was everywhere subject to the more or less arbitrary will of princes or emirs."[52] Rodinson summarizes this ambiguous position of Arab merchants when he writes: "this bourgeoisie, conscious as it was of itself, of its strength and value, never achieved political power as a class, even though many of its individual members succeeded in occupying the highest appointments in the state."[53]

In any case, commercialization declined once again under the Turkic successors of the Arabs who, coming out of Central Asia, founded new empires, like the Seljuk sultanate of Iraq and, later, Ottoman Turkey, Safavid Persia, and Mogul India. "In every case, it was as if the Turkifica-

49. Anderson, *Lineages of the Absolutist State*, p. 502. On commerce, banking, and craft manufacturing in the medieval Muslim world, see Labib, "Capitalism in Medieval Islam," and especially Rodinson, *Islam and Capitalism*, pp. 28–57.

50. Ibid., p. 56.

51. Anderson, *Lineages of the Absolutist State*, p. 508.

52. Ibid., p. 503.

53. Rodinson, *Islam and Capitalism*, p. 55; Anderson's and Rodinson's generalizations about early Arab empires apply also to the Mamluk one from the thirteenth through the fifteenth century. See Lapidus, *Muslim Cities in the Later Middle Ages*.

tion of the Islamic political order decisively accentuated the military cast of the original Arab systems, at the expense of their mercantile component." "The commercial vitality of the Arab epoch, which had coursed through the . . . civilization of classical Islam, now progressively ebbed away." "The business climate of Constantinople, Isfahan and Delhi in the early modern epoch was never reminiscent of that of mediaeval Baghdad or Cairo."[54] Still, the Turkic empires, too, eventually became commercialized to some degree. In the late Mogul empire, most of the agricultural surplus was put on the market. "Mughal India, then, had extensive commodity production . . . merchant capital was considerable in size and . . . an efficient system of credit not only enlarged it but also gave it great mobility."[55] What is more, aristocrats as well as merchants invested in commerce.[56] Urbanization was far advanced, with several cities reported to be as large as London and Paris in the same period, and interregional and foreign trade and banking were well developed. Many villages depended on their trade with the cities and, because they produced cash crops, also on trade with other villages for their food.[57]

Ottoman Turkey, too, became commercialized or carried on the commercialization of its Byzantine predecessors in Asia Minor and then in the Balkans, particularly in Greece. To be sure, there appears to be some disagreement on the nature of the merchants. Some say that into the nineteenth century commerce and banking in Turkey remained in the hands of foreigners, mostly Italian and French, and of ethnic minorities, especially Greeks, Armenians, and Jews, who were excluded from political power.[58] On the other hand, Halil Inalcik explicitly refers to this view as "mistaken"

54. Anderson, *Lineages of the Absolutist State*, pp. 512, 515, 516–17. Again Rodinson agrees: "From around the eleventh century A.D. domination by castes of slave-soldiers, mostly of Turkish origin, became established throughout the Middle East, with the consequence of reducing the bourgeoisie to an even more secondary role in politics, while the extent of the capitalistic sector began to shrink." Rodinson, *Islam and Capitalism*, p. 55. With reference to the same period of the decline of the Abbasid empire, Lewis speaks of "the transformation of the Islamic Near East from a commercial monetary economy to one which, despite an extensive and important foreign and transit trade, was internally a feudal economy, based on subsistence agriculture." Lewis, *The Arabs in History*, p. 158.

55. Habib, "Potentialities of Capitalistic Development in the Economy of Mughal India," pp. 70, 71; cf. also pp. 41, 77.

56. Ibid., pp. 72–73.

57. Habib, *The Agrarian System of Mughal India*, pp. 57–81.

58. See, for example, Steinhaus, *Soziologie der türkischen Revolution*, pp. 22–24, who bases this claim on agreement among "all contemporary observers." Anderson speaks of "the basically inimical relationship of the Ottoman State to cities and industry" and says that "the Sultanate nearly always intervened against the interests of the indigenous merchant communities. . . . State economic policy tended to discriminate against large-scale commercial capital." Anderson, *Lineages of the Absolutist State*, pp. 375–76.

and states that until the eighteenth century Muslims were as active as non-Muslims in commerce and banking and until the seventeenth century they were predominant.[59] Furthermore, far from seeing those engaged in commerce as excluded from political power, he says that the wealth gained by the aristocrats from the exploitation of peasants, was "invested in long-distance trade . . . or on a large scale in money lending at high interest rates. . . . From the second half of the sixteenth century onward the members of the 'military' class developed more and more into being really businessmen—merchants, landowners running large estates, and money-lending bankers." Inalcik also stresses that "the merchants could be of service to the state in various ways thanks to their accumulated fortunes of ready money; they made loans to the state, they acted as intermediaries between the state and the mass of the population in matters of taxation, they ensured a steady revenue from customs charges,"[60] all evidence of the commercialization of the Ottoman empire.

I must conclude this chapter by repeating that this book is not concerned with any form of modernization, not even with commercialization. The subject has been introduced because most of the pertinent literature does not draw the distinction between traditional aristocratic empires and commercialized ones, a distinction that, as we shall see, can be crucial in accounting for some phenomena, like peasant revolts, that are often simply ascribed to traditional aristocratic empires. For us, commercialization is important because its beginnings constitute the end of traditional aristocratic empires[61] and thus mark the boundary of my subject matter. To be sure, as I stressed, traditional aristocratic empires and commercialized ones share so many characteristics that I can draw data from the latter for my analysis of the former, and that much of my analysis of the politics of traditional aristocratic empires will, in turn, throw light on the politics of commercialized empires.

59. Inalcik, "Capital Formation in the Ottoman Empire," p. 138.

60. Ibid., pp. 136, 102–3.

61. Many more traditional aristocratic empires than came to an end through commercialization ceased to exist in their specific form when they were conquered by nomads or aristocrats who formed new empires or, more rarely, when they disintegrated into primitive communities.

3

The Origins of Aristocratic Empires

The Conquest Theory

It was the purpose of the foregoing chapter to delimit traditional aristocratic empires from the more modern societies into which commercialization can turn them. However, earlier I had also distinguished between aristocratic empires and the primitive societies which always precede them. The question now arises how aristocratic empires are formed out of primitive societies, that is, what are the origins of aristocratic empires. While a discussion of commercialization served for us mainly to define traditional aristocratic empires, an examination of their origins not merely distinguishes them from primitive societies but also lays the basis for an understanding of these empires.

An analysis of the beginnings of aristocratic empires will help us understand their peculiar character as combinations of autonomous societies among which there is little communication. Not only are racial, ethnic, cultural, linguistic, and religious cleavages within the peasantry of a single empire in fact divisions between different societies, but so is the class division between the peasantry and the aristocracy. The aristocracy, too, remains a society culturally distinct from the peasantry though it is economically dependent on it. An explanation of the origins of aristocratic empires is also an explanation of this class division, for the origin of these empires *is* the origin of aristocracies and of their superimposition on peasantries.

However, an analysis of the origins of aristocratic empires helps us understand not only the depth of the cleavages splitting their populations into autonomous societies. It also throws light on the fact, easily misunderstood in the context of modern experience, that this depth is such as generally to preclude conflict. At the end of this chapter, I shall argue that class differences, precisely because they are so great, do not produce class conflict in aristocratic empires. If one defines politics as conflict one has to look not at class divisions but elsewhere for the sources of politics in aristocratic empires. The rest of this book will try to demonstrate this, but the present chapter will help explain the deep cleavages that do not give rise to politics and thus clear the ground for a later analysis of politics, that is, of those cleavages and issues that do give rise to conflict.

Aristocratic empires have emerged time and again in history during the past several millennia (evidently first in Mesopotamia and Egypt about five thousand years ago and most recently, not far from there, in Arabia in the 1920s), and it should therefore be possible to discover some patterns in the manner in which they originated. In fact, not only were probably the great majority of aristocratic empires so small and so transitory in nature as to be totally forgotten, but we know little or nothing definite about the very beginnings of most empires—even, as we shall note particularly, of that of Rome on which, probably, more scholarly research has been carried on for a longer time than on any other.

Nevertheless, an attempt must be made to explain in very general terms how aristocratic empires could have emerged in a world of primitive societies—for even where aristocratic empires succeeded not such primitive societies but more modern commercial ones, they grew out of and were founded on primitive societies. Among such primitive societies, one can, of course, distinguish between various types, initially perhaps between gatherers and hunters (though, obviously, some people might be both). Some of the gatherers became horticulturalists, and eventually horticulturalists, particularly if they developed animal husbandry as well as agriculture, became peasants (or, more accurately, "primitive cultivators" if the term "peasants" is to be confined to agriculturalists exploited by aristocrats). On the other hand, there evolved pastoral nomads, perhaps out of the hunters who followed their herds, as some Lapps still follow their reindeer, or, as is now believed, out of horticulturalists and agriculturalists specializing in animal husbandry.[1]

In order for an aristocratic empire to evolve out of a number of primitive societies, one or more of these societies must come to be supported economically by others, that is, a division between exploiters and exploited must arise between primitive societies. Gatherers and hunters are generally neither strong enough militarily to subject other societies to exploitation nor do they produce any surplus to render them capable of being exploited. It is the pastoralists and agriculturalists, the shepherds and the cultivators, who can play a role in the establishment of aristocratic empires. Only when the cultivators are capable of producing a substantial surplus, when they live in what Gerhard Lenski calls advanced horticultural societies (defined by the use of the hoe as distinguished from the digging stick of simple horticultural societies)[2] or in agrarian societies

1. The beginning of agriculturalists and of pastoral nomads and some of their relations into modern times are discussed by Lattimore, "Inner Asian Frontiers."

2. Lenski, *Power and Privilege*, pp. 144–48. A Maya peasant family could raise enough corn

(using the plow) can aristocratic empires be built on their economies. Those who rule such societies, the aristocracies, can live off the surplus produced by them and can use some of it to build up a military and administrative apparatus with which to subject and exploit more cultivators.

Different explanations have been offered for the origins of aristocratic empires out of primitive societies, and, no doubt, different empires have originated in different ways. One hypothesis, however—that such empires originated in the conquest of some primitive societies of cultivators by primitive societies of pastoralists—is supported by sufficient evidence from many periods of history and many parts of the world and so well accounts for the character of the ethnic and class divisions that are of interest to us here that it merits our special attention.[3]

The conquest theory of the origin of the state and of social classes is an old one.[4] It has long been widely accepted by sociologists and anthropologists,[5] but it has also been criticized by a number of scholars,[6] and others

---

to survive by working forty-eight days out of the year. "With so much free time, the Maya Indian for the last two thousand years has been exploited—first by his native rulers and priests, next by his Spanish conquerors, and more recently by private owners in the hemp fields." Morley and Brainerd, *The Ancient Maya*, p. 140.

3. Historically and down to the present, "conquest theorists" have been concerned primarily with the origins of the "state," a concept not used here, rather than of aristocratic empires. However, they tend to define the state so that its origins coincide with that of social class divisions, particularly with the origins of what are defined here as aristocracies and hence of aristocratic empires.

4. Its history from Polybius through Machiavelli, Bodin, Adam Ferguson, and Herbert Spencer to its modern founder, the Polish-Austrian sociologist Gumplowicz is briefly traced by Barnes, "The Struggle of Races and Social Groups." See Gumplowicz, *Der Rassenkampf,* and also Gumplowicz, *Grundriss der Soziologie*, first published in 1885 and translated, in a new edition by Irving L. Horowitz, as *Outlines of Sociology*, especially pp. 199–205. Gumplowicz is an important, if little recognized, father of modern political science. He analyzed politics as a process of interest-group conflict and thus became a precursor of Arthur F. Bentley. See Bentley, *The Process of Government*, pp. 468–72. Gumplowicz's sociological doctrines are conveniently summarized in the article by Barnes just cited, pp. 400–419. Similar ones were expressed by his contemporary Ratzenhofer, *Die sociologische Erkenntnis*.

5. Harry Elmer Barnes said half a century ago that it had "now come to be regarded as the distinctive sociological theory of the origin of the state." "Some Contributions of Sociology to Modern Political Theory," p. 368. See also his *Sociology and Political Theory*, p. 52; Linton, *The Study of Man*, pp. 240–52; Rüstow, *Ortsbestimmung der Gegenwart*, I, especially pp. 74–92 (this entire volume seeks to relate a wide range of political, economic, social, and ideological-religious-moral phenomena in societies down to the present to their origins in conquest); Beals and Hoijer, *An Introduction to Anthropology*, p. 563; and Eberhard, *Settlement and Social Change in Asia*, pp. 5–6, 12, 279–82.

6. For example, by McLeod, *The Origin and History of Politics*, pp. 41–111, who argues, somewhat as had Friedrich Engels a half century earlier—Engels, *The Origin of the Family, Private Property and the State*, pp. 93–97—that the state arises as a result of social divisions

have modified it.[7] Briefly and simply, the theory suggests a series of stages in the relationship between, on the one hand, agrarian villages in oases and fertile river valleys and, on the other hand, nomadic tribes in steppes, deserts, and mountains near the fertile areas.[8] Each of these stages has with many variations occurred innumerable times in history.

Agriculturalists tend to be peaceable, simply because they generally have far more to lose than to gain from warfare. Being sedentary and tied to the soil by their economy, they cannot afford to leave their fields to raid other cultivators' villages nor is it likely that they could move or preserve the agricultural products they might take from them. And primitive cultivators have no interest in conquering land, because, given their primitive technology and the amount of labor available in their village, they cannot use any more land than they already have. Thus agriculturalists typically develop neither the skills nor the ideologies conducive to warfare.

Nomads, on the other hand, tend to be warlike and militarily superior to agriculturalists. Primitive hunters have experience in the use of weapons but are generally organized in such small groups as to be no threat to agrarian communities. Pastoral nomads, however, can congregate in large numbers and in disciplined organizations. Like hunters, they are highly mobile and can move with great speed where they ride horses or camels. They use weapons not only to defend their herds from wild animals but also in staging or fighting cattle-stealing raids. Cattle stealing appears to be a common phenomenon with pastoral people and can become an integral and central aspect of their culture and ideology, as with the East African

---

growing within primitive communities rather than through the conquest of one community by another. For a recent summary of different theories which holds that different states originated differently, see Krader, *Formation of the State.*

7. Lowie, *The Origin of the State*, pp. 7–42, provides much support for the theory, but agrees with McLeod that classes can also evolve internally. They arise as a result of conquest only where ideological obstacles, like religious beliefs, do not bar exploitation. Schapera, *Government and Politics in Tribal Societies*, pp. 126–34, cites several examples from South African tribal history that support the conquest theory, but finds that a class system involving subjugation and exploitation arises out of conquest only if the conquered groups differ ethnically or culturally from their conquerors. See also Mair, *Primitive Government*, especially pp. 106 and 126. On the link between the conquest theory and modern theories of imperialism, see my article, "J. A. Schumpeter and Karl Kautsky: Parallel Theories of Imperialism." Both Karl Kautsky in numerous writings cited in this article and Schumpeter in his brilliant essay, "The Sociology of Imperialism," accepted and contributed to the conquest theory.

8. The theory is fully developed and numerous illustrations are offered by Oppenheimer, *Der Staat.* His theory is summarized by Lowie, *The Origin of the State*, pp. 20–42, who accepts it with some modifications and provides examples from Africa. Linton, *The Study of Man*, pp. 240–52, perhaps following Lowie, presents substantially the same theory.

Masai. It is an early form of exploitation, but it remains irregular because its victims are mobile and not permanently inferior to the raiders.

Being accustomed and suited to warfare by training and organization and consequently by ideologies that glorify courage, revenge, and bloodshed, the nomadic shepherds are quite likely to use their military superiority for occasional or repeated raids on the cultivators' villages to take their crops from them. As Perry Anderson put it: "Nomadic societies were . . . usually hungry and poor, in their barren homelands . . . But they had one avenue of expansion to which they typically had spectacular recourse: tribute and conquest. For the horsemanship which was the basic economic skill of nomadic pastoralists also equipped them preeminently for warfare."[9] Nomadic raids on agrarian villages have characteristically occurred in areas where the fertile valleys or oases settled by cultivators border on the steppes and deserts where the nomads roam, particularly in a belt of territory stretching from the southern reaches of the Sahara across the Middle East and Central Asia to northern China. In the course of these raids, the cultivators are killed, though some may be taken as slaves for whom pastoral people, unlike hunters, have some limited use in their economy.[10]

The first stage of simple pillage and killing of the nomads' agrarian victims can—no doubt often after centuries—be replaced by a second stage if and when the cultivators' technology allows them to produce a surplus so that they can survive to produce even if deprived of some of their product. Eventually, the nomads may discover this and they may learn that it does not pay to destroy the cultivators, perhaps because they had traded with them before they robbed them. The nomads can then return time and again to the same village to take some of its product if they are willing to leave enough to the cultivators to permit most or even all of them to survive.

Provided the cultivators do not offer much resistance—and they are likely to have learned from long and bitter experience that such is usually

9. Anderson, *Passages from Antiquity to Feudalism*, p. 222.

10. A special variety of nomads—the seagoing ones—may be mentioned here, for they play the same role as the more common pastoral nomads in our analysis of the establishment of aristocratic empires. They may have developed from fishing people or from pastoral nomads who turned from land raids to piracy and raiding of seashores. Numerous such peoples appeared around the Mediterranean coast from ancient times into the nineteenth century, for example, the "Sea Peoples" threatening Egypt over a millennium before Christ, the Phoenicians, the Saracens, and the "Barbary States," but the best known ones were perhaps the Vikings or Norsemen or Normans. Polynesian aristocratic empires may, two millennia ago, have been founded by conquering seagoing nomads from southeast Asia. Thurnwald, *Die menschliche Gesellschaft*, 3:33–36.

hopeless—the nomads can then use no more violence than is necessary to frighten them into submission. In time, this relationship may become regularized, and violence may be avoided altogether if cultivators, whom we can now call peasants, will pay regular tribute to a particular nomadic tribe. In return, the peasants receive "protection," for it is now in the interest of the tribute-collecting tribe to keep other nomadic tribes away from "its" villages. Whether it is also in the interest of the peasants would depend on the intentions of those other nomads, but the peasants will in any case remain so protected whether they like it or not. This tributary relationship is, again, a common one throughout history and prevailed until quite recently, and may still prevail in some instances, between nomadic desert tribesmen and villages in oases and at the edge of the Sahara and of the desert in Arabia.[11]

As long as the nomads control only a few villages, the surplus produced by their peasants is insufficient to support them fully. They may have to remain fairly close to their villages in order to maintain the tributary relationship, but they must continue as nomadic cattle raisers using the tribute merely to supplement their livelihood. If, however, the pastoral tribe can gain control of a sufficient number of villages to live entirely off their surplus products, the nomads can settle down among the peasants. They thereby cease to be cattle raisers or, at any rate, nomads, but they do not become peasants. They remain a distinct warrior group and governing class that lives by its ability to extract from the peasants a surplus product, though in time they are no longer thought of as a distinct tribe. I shall henceforth call them the aristocracy.

The peasants, on the other hand, remain peasants; they are not turned into slaves, "for it is the essence of the conquest state that its rulers exploit societies rather than individuals."[12] They are now subjects of an aristocracy, but in their internal village affairs remain largely independent, merely, like peasants in a tributary system, handing over part of their product to their aristocracy, whether this be done now in the form of taxes or rent or of labor and services.

The assumption of the conquest theory, as we have now outlined it, that one tribe makes the conquests and then forms the aristocracy in the new

11. The Scythians, who lived in a large area in southern Russia and adjacent parts of Asia approximately from the seventh to the third century B.C., may illustrate a transitional stage between that of this tributary relationship and that of aristocratic exploitation. They have been described as having "a horse-riding, pastoral and semi-nomadic aristocracy, which dominated the settled and agricultural masses. This division is likely to reflect the initial difference in the ethnic composition of the people, the aristocracy deriving mainly from the invaders—perhaps Tatar—from the east, while the peasantry derived from the settled Tripolye people of the later Neolithic." Pounds, *An Historical Geography of Europe*, p. 50.

12. Linton, *The Study of Man*, p. 243.

empire has to be modified in many cases, but such modifications are not too important for our purposes here. On the one hand, conquests may be made not by single tribes but by alliances of tribes, as was true of the Arabs, Turks, and Mongols. On the other hand, some clans, often the original ones in the nomadic tribe, may enjoy higher status than the others and only they may become the aristocracy after the conquest. Thus, some of the German tribes, in the centuries before they invaded the Roman empire, had royal clans from which their chiefs were elected.[13] In the case of the Asiatic invaders of Eastern Europe from the Huns to the Mongols, too, it was not entire tribes that became the aristocracy in their new empires. "Military conquest and fiscal exploitation inevitably stratified the original clan communities sharply; the passage from a tribal confederation to a tributary state automatically generated a princely dynasty and ruling nobility, cleft from commoner nomads organized in regular armies commanded by them."[14]

Also, only a fraction of the nomadic tribe may engage in conquest, as when a relatively few adventurous men, grouped around a prestigious leader, set out on the warpath. In the early German tribes, which were seminomadic, war leaders formed raiding parties, recruiting their retinue sometimes from various tribes. The warriors so organized were not yet an aristocracy, that is, a separate class, but they lived off the booty they captured and the gifts and bribes they received from others in their own tribes and in other tribes, looking down on agricultural work and leaving it to others, especially women and slaves.[15] If and when such war leaders and their followers conquered territory and subjected cultivators rather than merely raiding them, they would naturally become the aristocracy.[16]

Generally, when the conquerors are from a tribe that is only seminomadic, those of its members engaged in agriculture do not participate in the campaigns of conquest. The conquerors then become the aristocrats, but they may allot some of the conquered land to the agrarian members of their own tribe. These latter become free peasants, a category that does not fit into either of our two simple categories of aristocrats and peasants, because they neither derive tribute from peasants nor pay tribute to aristocrats. Or, like the common man among the Aztecs, they do both. He had a right to the usufruct of a plot of land, he was subject to military service—regarded as both an honor and a religious rite—and to labor service and "he paid taxes: but on the other hand he must have been largely compensated for this by his share in the distribution, very like the Roman dole, of

13. Thompson, *The Early Germans*, pp. 33–35.

14. Anderson, *Passages from Antiquity to Feudalism*, p. 224.

15. Thompson, *The Early Germans*, pp. 48–60.

16. Lattimore, "Feudalism in History," p. 52.

clothes and provisions that were provided by the tribute of the provinces. His tribe was the ruling nation, and in his degree he benefited from the system."[17]

Often, however, free peasants lose their freedom eventually. Among the Aztecs, once their empire expanded and huge amounts of tribute became available, "the emperor and his chief dignitaries took the lion's share . . . and no one can tell what trifling share actually reached the common people."[18] In ancient Rome, the free peasants were expected to serve in the army and hence had to neglect their fields and to sell their lands to the aristocracy.[19] Or, being militarily weak in times of warfare, free peasants put themselves under the protection of neighboring aristocrats and thus lost their independence.

In Africa, numerous so-called despotic chieftaincies or kingdoms moved across our definitional borderline from primitive societies to aristocratic empires when they conquered neighboring tribes and subjected them to a tributary relationship. The chief or king, expected to be generous by the standards of primitive tribalism, could now distribute some of the tribute among the members of his own tribe—who might be regarded as free peasants—and he and his large family and numerous royal descendants as well as those members of his tribe he appointed as officials would form the aristocracy. A similar process may have been at work in the foundation of the Aztec and Inca empires.[20]

Indigenous Origins of Class Divisions

Racial, linguistic, and religious differences between an aristocracy and its peasantry are best (though not necessarily only) accounted for by the classical conquest hypothesis that has now been out-

17. Soustelle, *Daily Life of the Aztecs*, p. 71.

18. Ibid., pp. 83–84.

19. Roman peasants made "enormous sacrifices for the cause of Roman militarism and . . . the aristocracy responded by enforcing harsh debt laws, turning them off the land, and blocking their reinstatement onto the land." Garnsey, "Peasants in Ancient Roman Society," p. 223. On the basis of a thorough study, Brunt, with reference to the period 200–168 B.C., finds it "impossible to resist the conclusion that 10 per cent and generally more of Italian adult males were at wars year by year. This diversion of so much free labour from essential production was only possible because the profits of war enabled Italy to import supplies from abroad and above all slaves who could replace free men in agriculture, trade and industry. The military power of Rome was now based on abundant slave labour . . . But the burden of the conscription and the economic effects of Rome's conquests combined to bring about what Toynbee calls the deracination of the Italian peasantry." Brunt, *Italian Manpower*, p. 426.

20. Lenski, *Power and Privilege*, pp. 164–72.

lined. The class differences between the two, that is, differences in economic functions, in cultural characteristics associated with these functions,
and in political roles may also have originated in conquest, but they need
not have. It is also possible that the beginnings of class differences may
emerge within simple, primitive cultivator communities through indigenous processes so that some of their members may eventually come to
rule over peasants of their own community ethnically not distinct from
themselves.

Some eighty years ago, Gaetano Mosca counterposed this possibility to
that of the origins of aristocracies through conquest: "As a rule the dominance of a warrior class over a peaceful multitude is attributed to a super-
position of races, to the conquest of a relatively unwarlike group by an
aggressive one. Sometimes that is actually the case—we have examples in
India after the Aryan invasions, in the Roman Empire after the Germanic
invasions and in Mexico after the Aztec conquest. But more often, under
certain social conditions, we note the rise of a warlike ruling class in places
where there is absolutely no trace of a foreign conquest. As long as a
horde lives exclusively by the chase, all individuals can easily become
warriors. There will of course be leaders who will rule over the tribe, but
we will not find a warrior class rising to exploit, and at the same time to
protect, another class that is devoted to peaceful pursuits. As the tribe
emerges from the hunting state and enters the agricultural and pastoral
state, then, along with an enormous increase in population and a greater
stability in the means of exerting social influence, a more or less clean-cut
division into two classes will take place, one class being devoted exclusively to agriculture, the other class to war. In this event, it is inevitable
that the warrior class should little by little acquire such ascendancy over
the other as to be able to oppress it with impunity."[21]

Although such an outcome may not be as inevitable as Mosca thought,
one can imagine that where a certain division of labor between agriculturalists and cattle raisers or hunters develops within a primitive cultivator
community, the latter, both because they have more leisure and because
they become the military defenders of the village, can assume some of the
functions of the ruling stratum. I already noted the emergence of warrior
chiefs with their retinues among Germanic tribes. These became full-
fledged aristocracies only after they invaded and conquered parts of the
Roman empire. However, among the agrarian Slav tribes in Russia, Poland,
and Bohemia, similar retinues of warriors grouped around military chieftains and then around leaders of larger confederations "everywhere formed
the embryo of a landed ruling class dominating a non-servile peasantry."[22]

21. Mosca, *The Ruling Class*, p. 54.
22. Anderson, *Passages from Antiquity to Feudalism*, p. 215.

Developing indigenously, rather than by conquest, they became aristocracies when they could live off the surplus produced by slave labor on their own estates and by a still free small peasantry, and, after centuries, they became dispersed as lords of large provincial estates with an enserfed peasantry.[23] Mosca had described the process in Poland where "the warriors became nobles and masters, and the peasants, once companions and brothers, became villeins and serfs."[24]

Whereas some of the warriors of the Germanic tribes invading Western and Southern Europe became aristocrats by conquest, the emergence of an aristocracy among the Germanic people in Scandinavia, who were originally similar in their tribal constitutions to those that eventually migrated, may illustrate another way in which an upper cultivator stratum can become an aristocracy. Throughout Scandinavia, free armed agriculturalists carried on agriculture with slave labor amply supplied by the Viking raids around Western Europe and especially across the Baltic and into Russia. Richer cultivators, also described as nobles or notables, could operate larger estates with greater numbers of slaves, but they were not an aristocracy, for there was still equal representation, at least formally, of all free cultivators, rich and poor, in local assemblies and much common land-ownership. Only when, after three centuries, Viking overseas raiding came to an end in the eleventh century and the supply of slaves dried up did these local notables turn some—but never all—free cultivators into dependent tenants and thus themselves became an aristocracy.[25]

If significant differences in wealth can arise in a primitive agrarian community, it is conceivable that the poorer cultivators become dependent on the more prosperous ones. The latter can probably not exploit the former and live off their labor, because in a tightly knit tribal community wealth depends on the protection of that community, but the poor become dependent on the rich precisely because these share some of their wealth with them and provide them with protection in case of enemy attack. In

23. Ibid., pp. 230, 232–34; a similar process in Serbia is mentioned on p. 290.

24. Mosca, *The Ruling Class*, p. 55.

25. This summary follows the interpretation of Anderson, *Passages from Antiquity to Feudalism*, pp. 176–81. Other sources are vague on the origins of the Scandinavian aristocracy. See Foote and Wilson, *The Viking Achievement*, pp. 79–89 and 123–44, who say of these free cultivators: "In general, the fullest rights were only enjoyed by the free holders on inherited land . . . and when they were particularly wealthy and of proud origins, it is hard or impossible to separate them from the aristocracy. . . . A fundamental homogeneity of the yeoman class is indeed characteristic of early Scandinavian society, but there were gradations" (ibid., p. 82). "There were superior men in every locality who, for reasons that were doubtless shifting and are today inevitably obscure, held central positions in community affairs. They were of good birth" (ibid., p. 123). Jones, *A History of the Vikings*, p. 150, merely says that "above the free men was the ruling caste, the aristocracy, most of it king-allied or god-descended. Here belonged the families with wealth, land and rank."

turn, the more prosperous cultivators tend to be elected to hold the public offices and thus may come to monopolize certain governmental functions.

The differences between patricians and plebeians in ancient Rome may have originated in this manner.[26] The results of some recent research based on archaeological as well as written evidence seem to point in this direction. According to that research, economic and consequently social differentiation developed in the seventh century B.C. in the pre-urban villages that merged into the city of Rome about 575 B.C. It was then that entry into the councils of village elders (*senates*), which assisted the local "kings," that is, village chiefs, was restricted to the members of the rich families who intermarried among themselves. "The sons of the senators or *patres* were called *patricii* and were the future senators. In this way originated the *gentes patriciae*, the Roman patriciate."[27] Later, in the early Republic, the patricians have been held to have been the families of those who constituted the cavalry under the last king and took over the government of Rome after his expulsion.[28] "Cavalry and patricians are identical."[29]

It is evidently not even clear whether the early Romans of the pre-urban villages were cultivators, as much of the foregoing suggests, or shepherds. According to Gjerstad, archaeological finds demonstrate that the economy of even the pre-urban Roman villages was based on agriculture as well as cattle raising, that is, that the earliest Romans were cultivators.[30] Alföldi,

26. Tenney Frank described the process along these lines—*Roman Imperialism*, p. 6—and other historians, too, have held that the patricians were originally the richer landholders while the plebeians were the rural and urban poor. See Scullard, *A History of the Roman World from 753 to 146 B.C.*, pp. 38–42, and Boak and Sinnigen, *A History of Rome to A.D. 565*, pp. 46–47. However, there is no certainty on the origins of the division between patricians and plebeians. Frank, writing in 1914, rejected various conquest theories as the then "most widely accepted view." *Roman Imperialism*, p. 5 and the sources cited ibid., p. 12. Mommsen, who devoted more attention to the question over a century ago than many modern historians do, also explicitly rejects the original conquest hypothesis. *The History of Rome*, 1:78. According to him, the patricians were the members of the original Roman clans, while the plebeians developed out of their clients. The latter were originally freed slaves and refugees but became more numerous when the citizens of conquered towns were given client status and many immigrated into Rome as it became commercialized (ibid., pp. 66–69, 96–100). A more recent study of Roman domestic politics simply admits that "we do not know the origins of the patricians nor of their monopoly of power. They were a closed order throughout the Republic; no one was a patrician whose male ancestors had not all been patricians, and in the early times they tried to prohibit intermarriage with the other citizens, the plebeians or men of the masses (*plebs*). The distinction was one of birth, not wealth." Brunt, *Social Conflicts in the Roman Republic*, p. 47.

27. Gjerstad, "Innenpolitische und militärische Organisation in frührömischer Zeit," 1:146.

28. Alföldi, "Zur Struktur des Römerstaates im 5. Jahrhundert v. Chr."

29. Ibid., p. 243.

30. Gjerstad, "Innenpolitische und militärische Organisation," 1:139.

however, stresses that "the early Roman economy rested not on agriculture but rather on cattle raising. . . . The Romans were shepherds and their wealth consisted of cattle." In the first century of the Republic, "the land-owning breeders of cattle and horses remained militarily and politically decisive." Thus, according to Alföldi, even though these pastoral Romans were certainly not the nomads of the conquest theory, "cattle-stealing and raids for booty were with the Latin cattle-raisers . . . in the 5th century the driving force of their war-based economy. The fact that participation in war was a privilege and not a burden is connected with this. Compulsory contributions by the vanquished are also part of this form of economy: booty at the time of victory and permanent exploitation are correlated concepts."[31]

In any case, whatever the origins of the distinction between plebeians and patricians, it is important for us not to confuse it with the distinction between peasants and aristocrats. To be sure, some of the plebeians were peasants or agricultural laborers though others were urban laborers, artisans and traders, but the early patricians were as much their protectors as their exploiters and themselves engaged in manual agricultural work.

Even where some economic and political distinctions did arise within a single community, as happened in early Rome, it seems improbable that the upper stratum could become an aristocracy. Given primitive methods of production, it is hardly possible for those who work to produce enough to support not only themselves, their children, aged, widows and disabled, but also an able-bodied but nonworking aristocracy. Even members of an upper stratum, then, are engaged in the productive labor of tilling the fields and raising cattle, as were the early Roman patricians, or perhaps in the labor of hunting and therefore do not qualify as aristocrats defined as exploiters of peasants. Only in the rather exceptional cases where the necessities of life are relatively plentifully furnished by nature and can be made available with little work, can one conceive of the emergence of an aristocracy within a single village.

Of course, the greater the number of productively engaged cultivators in proportion to the village upper stratum, the more the latter can approach the character of a nonworking aristocracy. Thus, the chiefs and the priests (who may or may not be identical) of primitive tribes are sometimes fully or partially supported by their communities to have time for their specialized tasks. By this criterion alone, we could regard such chiefs and priests as aristocrats, but it is preferable to apply that concept only to a class rather than a single individual or family within a society.

Generally, it may be assumed that a village upper stratum can become an aristocracy only where it can extend its governmental control beyond its

31. Alföldi, "Zur Struktur des Römerstaates," pp. 267, 269.

own community to other agrarian villages. Only when the upper stratum has brought under its sway a number of peasants large enough to produce a surplus sufficient for it to live on is it turned into an aristocracy. But how can a village upper stratum bring additional territory and cultivators under its control? Warfare, the characteristic form of expansion chosen by aristocrats, is probably more exceptional with agrarian villages. Rome was probably one of these exceptions, perhaps because it may have begun as a Latin outpost against Etruscan expansion or because it may have been more of a cattle-raising and raiding community than an agrarian village. As I noted, primitive cultivators have little time for warfare, little mobility, and little training in the use of weapons, and they also have little to gain from war. Cultivators are unlikely, then, to engage in aggressive wars of conquest.

One means other than war by which an agriculturalist upper stratum can expand its political control beyond its own village, for which there is some historical evidence, is through alliances with other villages. Such groupings of neighboring villages may well be formed for purposes both of exchange and of military defense. They may provide an opportunity for the upper stratum of one village to come to dominate the other villages, too, and eventually to live off the labor done by the peasants in all the villages and thus to become an aristocracy.

Possibly, the Latin League of the sixth century B.C. already performed that function for the Roman patricians. More probably, it was performed by the allies and confederates Rome gained in the fourth and third centuries B.C. as a result of her expansion throughout the Italian peninsula. Evidently arrangements whereby not only allies but also tribes and villages and towns defeated by the Romans were granted various degrees of Roman citizenship or of independence under Roman control were profitable for the Roman upper stratum. It was not until the end of the first Punic War in 241 B.C. that a Roman conquest resulted in the formation of a province, that is, a territory owing tribute to Rome, in western Sicily, which had stood in a similar relationship to Carthage.[32]

By that time, one can clearly speak of a Roman aristocracy, which was not, however, identical with the patriciate, but included leading plebeian families as well. These, but not the lower classes, had already been admitted to the government in the fourth century B.C.[33] Rome can, then, be

32. Frank, *Roman Imperialism*, pp. 93–97.

33. Alföldi says that "we see not demolition of social barriers, nor the participation of the masses in the benefits and privileges of the aristocracy when the *plebs* achieved its goal; we see only. . . the successive incorporation of the leading social stratum of the *plebs*" in government. *Early Rome and the Latins*, pp. 91–92. On the patrician-plebeian aristocracy, the "nobilitas," see also Earl, *The Moral and Political Tradition of Rome*, pp. 12–14, and for a

cited as an example of an indigenous development of an aristocracy. It must be added, however, that about the time when the Roman upper stratum had clearly become an aristocracy, Rome was also becoming commercialized, as I noted in the preceding chapter, and thus never turned into a traditional aristocratic empire.

Not only the Roman aristocracy but the two best-known conquering aristocracies of the Western Hemisphere, where there were no pastoral nomads, originated through alliances. The Aztecs and the Incas, evidently seminomadic cultivators in search of land, arrived and settled in the valleys later occupied, respectively, by Mexico City and Cuzco. However, it was only after they allied themselves, in each case, with two other tribes inhabiting these valleys, that their leaders could launch on their remarkably successful careers of conquests and thus become aristocrats.[34]

Some aristocracies, then, have originated through processes different from that described in the classical conquest theory, for they do not begin as nomadic tribes conquering agrarian villages and they rule not only over other tribes but also over members of their own tribe who remained agriculturalists. Their beginnings can be traced back to internal divisions within their own tribe, whether, like some Germanic ones and the Romans, they become aristocracies only after they conquer others or, like the Scandinavian and Slavic ones, they become aristocrats before they conquer others. Still, once they do become aristocrats, they perpetuate themselves by conquests, just as do those who began as conquering nomadic tribes. Thus, the Roman, the Aztec, and the Inca aristocracies, like Germanic and Slav aristocracies, even though they originated from agrarian rather than nomadic tribes, founded typical conquest empires drawing tribute not only from Roman, Aztec or Quechua peasants or from Germanic or Slav ones, but from other conquered agrarian people.[35]

5,000 Years of Conquest Empires

Conquest and warfare become integral parts of the lives and societies of aristocrats whether their beginnings can be traced back to

---

more detailed analysis of the entrance of "wealthy and notable" plebeian families into "a new aristocracy," see Mommsen, *The History of Rome*, 1:281–92 and 336–37.

34. On alliances (confederations) as beginnings of empires, see Linton, *The Study of Man*, p. 241, who says that "conquest states are much more numerous than confederacies" (ibid., p. 243).

35. The origins of the Japanese aristocracy appear to be obscure, though it certainly existed by the time of the Yamato empire whose beginnings in the first few centuries A.D. are shrouded in legendary mystery. It seems not improbable that aristocrats emerged by indi-

nomadic or agrarian origins. Both former shepherds and former cultivator elites, once they are aristocrats, must control a number of villages in order to be aristocrats, that is, in order to live off the surplus produced by peasants. Once such aristocratic control of a number of villages—and hence an aristocratic empire—is established, whether by the offensive action of nomads or through alliances formed for defensive purposes, the aristocracy will, for reasons to be mentioned below, continue to engage in warfare, both offensive and defensive. Thus an aristocratic empire once founded may expand by the incorporation of more individual villages. Eventually, it may, in this process, come to collide with another aristocratic empire. One aristocracy may defeat the other and reduce it to tributary vassal status, thereby creating a hierarchy among aristocrats, or it may replace it altogether and merge the newly conquered empire, with all its villages, with its old one. Thus sizable empires can be created and, as their aristocracies fight with other aristocracies and take over their large empires, huge territorial entities under a single aristocracy may emerge. At any point in the process of expansion an aristocratic empire may also be conquered by a nomadic tribe or, more probably, an alliance of tribes that replaces the existing aristocracy or superimposes itself on it. Such a tribe or tribes, too, may succeed in conquering and uniting a number of existing empires, thus again creating a huge empire under a single aristocracy.[36]

Before we turn to our generalizations about the social and political structures and ideologies prevailing in aristocratic empires, it may be worthwhile to list some of the better-known instances of the pervasive role of conquest in the creation and expansion of such empires. Needless to say, such a listing, to be at all brief, must omit even many major and well-known empires, let alone the innumerable minor and less known and, obviously, the unknown ones. Indeed, to write a complete history of conquests by aristocracies would be to write much of known human history.[37] On the other hand, our list can include empires that eventually

---

genous processes out of the descendants of certain clans (*uji*) or of hereditary clan leaders or earlier tribal leaders, but they, too, formed a warrior aristocracy carrying on warfare against each other and conquering each others' territories. Hall, *Japan from Prehistory to Modern Times*, pp. 28–32; Sansom, *A History of Japan*, 1:35–38.

36. At the height of their power, the Umayyad caliphate controlled over three million square miles (about the same area as that of the present-day United States or China), the Roman and the Chinese Han empires two million square miles, and the Ahmenid Persian empire, that of Alexander the Great, and the Ottoman empire more than a million and a half square miles. Lenski, *Power and Privilege*, pp. 194–95. And the Mongol empire, the biggest of them all, must have embraced, very roughly, ten million square miles, more than any present-day country and about equal to the total size of the (British) Commonwealth.

37. A look at Langer's authoritative one-volume *Encyclopedia of World History* will confirm that much of recorded history is the history of such conquests. The sections on premodern

became commercialized if they were traditional aristocratic ones in the period of their foundation or expansion and even those few, like the Roman and Arabic ones, whose commercialization coincided with their expansion and which never or only quite briefly went through a traditional aristocratic phase, if their expansion was nevertheless principally traditional aristocratic in motivation and execution.

In ancient Egypt, there is evidence of nomads moving into the Nile valley to become aristocrats ruling peasants and then of their small states expanding by conquest in predynastic days. About five thousand years ago, a ruling family from Upper Egypt united that area with Lower Egypt by conquest. During the next three millennia of dynastic history, Egypt was occasionally threatened or conquered by various nomadic people, such as the Hyksos and other Asiatics from the east, the Nubians from the south, the Libyans from the west, and also the "Sea Peoples," who were maritime as well as terrestrial nomads, from the north. And in its last few centuries, dynastic Egypt was invaded by Ethiopians or Kushites, Assyrians, Babylonians, Persians, and finally Macedonians.

Like Egypt in the Nile Valley, the other ancient empires of the Middle East, those in the valley of the Tigris and Euphrates—notably Sumer, Babylonia, Mittani, and Assyria—as well as the Hittite empire and the later Lydian and Median kingdoms in Asia Minor and Iran were all conquest states. All were subject to conquest by nomads from the surrounding barren areas, even more than was relatively isolated Egypt. And all were adding each others' territories as well as the intervening lands, such as Syria and Palestine (as Egypt did, too, during the last millennium of dynastic history) to their own from time to time.

The ancient Israelites may be said to have been in a transitional state from tribalism to an aristocratic empire. A loose confederacy of highland peasant tribes exploited by urban merchants and absentee landowners in the city-states of the plains turned only relatively briefly into the United Monarchy under Saul and David (1020–961 B.C.), and became a full-fledged aristocratic empire only under King Solomon (961–922 B.C.). After his death, that empire was divided as a result of tribal rebellion, and eventually both its major parts, Israel and Judah, came under the rule of other conquerors.

The Greek city-states, too, were originally founded by invading nomads from the north who conquered a sedentary population in many river valleys separated by mountains. The Homeric epics still tell of aristocratic warriors and peasants owing them tribute and service, but given poor

---

history, occupying nearly one-third of its 1,300 pages of text, read overwhelmingly like an endless listing of rulers and dynasties and of their wars and the consequent boundary changes of their empires. Langer, ed., *An Encyclopedia of World History*.

conditions for agriculture (except around Sparta and in Thessaly), the Greeks turned to the sea for fishery, piracy, and eventually trade. Though the landowning warrior aristocracy remained more inclined to appropriate the profits of trade than to engage in it, this did launch Greek city-states, most notably Athens, on a course of commercialization, as noted in the preceding chapter. Only Sparta comes close to remaining an aristocratic empire. The Spartans conquered the agrarian Peloponnesian hinterland of their city and turned its inhabitants into "helots" who were collectively owned by the city and could not be bought and sold. They were thus not really slaves but rather serfs or unfree peasants, while the citizens of Sparta in effect constituted an aristocracy that could devote itself fully to governmental and especially military affairs rather than to productive labor or trade.

The entire area from the Aegean and Egypt to the Indus was within a few decades united by Ahmenid Persian conquerors, especially Cyrus the Great (550–530 B.C.) and his son Cambyses (530–521). This vast empire began to decline after a century, with emperors and their satraps fighting and murdering each other, and after another century was, in turn, conquered, and thus united with Greece, by Alexander the Great of Macedon (336–323). His empire fell apart as quickly as it had been created, succeeded by the Hellenistic kingdoms, like those of Pontus and Pergamum in Asia Minor, of the Seleucids in Mesopotamia, Syria and, for some time, Persia, and of the Ptolemies in Egypt. Although these were governed by aristocracies and were involved in perennial warfare typical of aristocratic empires, cities and trade grew in them to an extent hitherto unknown in Greek civilization. Thus, as noted earlier, these Hellenistic kingdoms, like the earlier Greek city-states and the later Roman empire, cannot be included among traditional aristocratic empires.

The Persian empire, succeeding the Seleucids and conquering its neighbors and being conquered by them, persisted under various invaders and dynasties, notably the Parthians (171 B.C.–A.D. 226), the Sassanids (226–642), the caliphate till the late ninth century, the Seljuk Turks in the eleventh, the Mongol Ilkhans from the mid-thirteenth to the mid-fourteenth century, Timur and his dynasty in the fifteenth, and the Safavids (1502–1736) and Kajars (1794–1925).

By the time Alexander conquered Persia, Rome had begun its expansion which, starting in central Italy, was to continue for half a millennium (from roughly 400 B.C. to A.D. 100). In its prearistocratic phase, Rome added tribe after tribe in Italy and then, in its posttraditional phase, empire after empire, like Carthage, Macedon, and Ptolemaic Egypt, until the Roman empire had extended its control around the entire Mediterranean and from northern Mesopotamia to southern Scotland. This period of expansion was followed by centuries of defensive warfare against nomadic invaders, like the Picts and Scots and many Germanic tribes and eventually the Huns. The latter started the Germanic tribes on a wave of migrations and conquests into the empire,[38] resulting in the fifth and sixth centuries in a series of new aristocratic empires being established, as by the Visigoths in Gaul and Spain, the Ostrogoths and the Lombards in Italy, the Vandals and Suevi in Spain and North Africa, and the Anglo-Saxons in England.

The Huns turned out to be only the first of several Turkic-Tartaric people from Asia who invaded Southeast Europe and established empires there. Both their empire and that of the Avars (from the mid-sixth to the late eighth century) in present-day Hungary were defeated by revolting tributary tribes, but the Magyars became permanent rulers in that area from the end of the ninth century. The Bulgars established a kingdom in the Balkans in the seventh century that eventually became Slavicized,[39] while Pechenegs (Patzinaks) in the tenth and eleventh and Cumans in the eleventh and twelfth centuries came to rule in Rumania and the southern Ukraine. The last of the nomadic invaders from Asia, the Mongols, will be mentioned in a moment.

Beginning in the sixth century, the Franks expanded their territory around the lower Rhine and by a series of conquests culminating under Charlemagne around 800, came to control all of present-day France (except Britanny), the Low Countries, Western Germany, Austria, Switzerland, and Northern Italy. The history of the subsequent millennium in Europe which sees the end of traditional aristocratic empires on that continent through the process of commercialization, need not even be alluded to here except to note the obvious fact that conquest of aristocrats by aristocrats remained the principal factor determining who was to govern and exploit what lands and what people.

While, in Europe, territories were time and again divided and combined and transferred from one aristocratic family and its followers to another, new agrarian areas in the East were conquered by German aristocrats, like the Teutonic Knights (especially in the thirteenth century) who put Slavic and Baltic peasants under their rule and also imported German peasants to these lands. In the ninth century, the Slavic tribes in much of Russia were conquered by bands of nomadic Vikings (Varangians or Rus) from Scandinavia, some of them mercenaries hired to defend local cities.[40] The em-

38. McGovern, *The Early Empires of Central Asia*, pp. 356–98.

39. "They do not appear to have been particularly numerous, and constituted little more than a Turkic aristocracy which lorded it over the larger Slavic and Thracian masses." Pounds, *An Historical Geography of Europe*, p. 179.

40. For a summary of scholarly controversies as to whether the Rus were, indeed, Scandinavian Vikings or perhaps Slavs and whether they were identified with the early Kievan empire or with Novgorod, see Riasanovsky, *A History of Russia*, pp. 25–30.

pires they established, especially the Kievan one, a loose federation of ceaselessly warring principalities, were not pure traditional aristocratic empires, because they rested economically on trade, including the slave trade, as much as on the exploitation of peasants. Vikings (or Norsemen) also raided all the coasts of Europe and established themselves as aristocratic rulers in a number of places, notably in Normandy in the early tenth century and in England and Sicily in the late eleventh. From the end of the eleventh into the thirteenth century, crusading European aristocrats set up more or less ephemeral feudal kingdoms, principalities, and counties through their conquests in parts of Palestine, Lebanon, Syria, Turkey, and Greece, all areas previously commercialized under Hellenistic, Roman-Byzantine, and Arab rule.

Conquest states are not confined to European history and what are commonly regarded as its antecedents in the Middle East. India, particularly the fertile Indus valley, was subject to many invasions by people from the dry and mountainous areas to its north, beginning with the Aryan conquests during the second millennium B.C.[41] During the first millennium B.C., such conquests resulted in the formation of a few kingdoms out of many smaller ones and the eventual emergence in the fourth and third centuries B.C. of the great Mauryan empire. There followed further invasions from the northwest, as by the Scythians and Kushans who founded their own empires. Much as in Europe after the fall of Rome, invading nomads and already established aristocracies fought among themselves for centuries over control of the land, and empires and dynasties rose and fell. Among the best known is the Gupta empire in the fourth and fifth centuries A.D., which united much of northern India, and the Gurjara dynasty, originally a horde of central Asiatic nomads that ruled in western India from the sixth to the eleventh century. Roughly during the same period, the Rajputs established kingdoms in northern India and maintained some autonomous princely states until 1948. Beginning in the eleventh century, there came a series of invasions by central Asian Muslim tribes into north India—Turks, Afghans, Persians, Pathans, and Mongols. The Afghan-founded Sultanate of Delhi, comprising most of northern India, lasted from the early thirteenth into the sixteenth century when it was succeeded by the Mogul empire established by a Turk descendant of Genghis Khan and Timur. His successors conquered virtually all of India, but their empire disintegrated in the eighteenth century. By then there were further invasions by Persians and Afghans, the Hindu Marathas raided, plundered, and formed kingdoms all over India, and the British, the last foreign conquerors of India, began to build their modern empire there.

The history of China, like that of India, was for millennia marked by

41. *Arya* meant "noble, well-born, free." Edwardes, *A History of India*, p. 24.

periodic invasions of the rich Huang valley by "barbarians" from the less fertile areas, generally to the north and west, who set themselves up as ruling dynasties. Some of these may have appeared in the second millennium B.C., when there were clearly people performing functions we shall associate with aristocracies. The Shang dynasty "could produce a government group which could command many lesser chiefs who in turn dominated the peasants, could make war with wheeled vehicles and sizable bodies of troops, could initiate and carry on the construction of public works, and could perform religious rites apparently on behalf of the people as a whole."[42] Beginning about 1000 B.C., the Chou people conquered much of central China. The Ch'in, another invading group, and their successors, the Han dynasty, ruled all of China and some adjacent territories, for four centuries (221 B.C.–A.D. 220). During the following centuries, when China was already to some degree commercialized, the Wei and other northern barbarian dynasties as well as Chinese dynasties, above all the T'ang (618–906), were establishing, expanding, and uniting their empires in the typical fashion of conquering aristocrats and warlords. During nearly three-fourths of the last millennium of the Chinese empire, much or all of it was ruled by conquest dynasties—the Liao dynasty of the Khitan Mongols (907–1126), the Chin dynasty of the Jurchen Tungus tribes (1115–1234), the Yüan dynasty of the Mongols (1260–1368), and the Ch'ing dynasty of the Manchus (1644–1912).

Among these dynasties, the most noteworthy as conquerors were the Mongols, for within less than a century (the thirteenth), these nomadic horsemen, led by Genghis Khan and his immediate successors, conquered not only China, but all of central Asia, Persia, the caliphate of Baghdad (Mesopotamia), the kingdoms of Georgia and Azerbaijan, and the remnants of the Kievan empire in southern Russia. Through the characteristic process of nomadic conquest of other nomadic tribes, of settled tribes, and, above all, of empires created by earlier conquerors, they thus founded the largest empire in all history. Like most conquest empires, the Mongol one soon fell apart, though Mongols ruled huge areas like China for quite some time, and one of their successors, Timur, again overran much of central Asia, Persia, Mesopotamia, Azerbaijan, and northwestern India in the late fourteenth century. The Mongol Khanate of the Golden Horde occupied southern Russia and levied tribute from the princes of all Russia for about two and a half centuries (1238 to about 1480).

42. Goodrich, *A Short History of the Chinese People*, p. 8. On nomadic conquests of China, see Eberhard, *Conquerors and Rulers*, especially pp. 112–37, who describes numerous instances of the relations between Tibetan, Mongol, and Turkish nomads on the one hand and Chinese agriculturalists on the other, some of which illustrate and combine the various stages in nomad-peasant relations mentioned above in our discussion of the conquest theory of the beginnings of aristocratic empires.

One of these Russian princes, the one in Moscow, conquered some other Russian principalities and by 1480 threw off Mongol domination. There then began the expansion of Muscovy and a no longer traditional Russian empire that in the course of the subsequent four centuries was extended west to the Baltic and into Poland, south across the Ukraine to the Black Sea and across the Caucasus, southeast deep into central Asia, and east all the way to the Pacific and indeed across it to Alaska and into California.[43]

Six centuries before the Mongol conquests and also in the course of a single century (from the death of Mohammed in 632 to the battle of Tours in 732), the Arabs, another group of nomads, burst out of their traditional barren territory and, strengthened by their conquests as they went along, created a huge empire, the Umayyad caliphate, stretching west across North Africa and Spain and east across Mesopotamia into Persia and down to the Indus. This empire, too, soon split and came to be ruled by various dynasties.

Among the converts to Islam in central Asia were the Turks. In the eleventh century, one of their branches, the Seljuks, launched on a career of conquests, expanding in the course of two centuries into Persia, Mesopotamia, and Anatolia. Starting from Anatolia, the Ottoman dynasty of Turks, itself a warrior tribe originally driven from central Asia by the Mongols in the thirteenth century, in the fourteenth and fifteenth centuries occupied almost the entire Balkan peninsula, thus putting an end to the Byzantine remnant of the Roman empire, and, in the sixteenth century, conquered most of the former Arab empire from the Caucasus and Mesopotamia in the east to Algeria in the west.

In Spain, Arabic dynasties, some of them conquering territories from each other, were in control of much of the country for four centuries from A.D. 711. Their control was gradually reduced during this period (but completely ended only in 1492) by a long succession of regional Spanish rulers, some of them descendants of the conquering Visigoths, who fought each other and the Arabs as they expanded their territories.

Having conquered Spain, Spanish aristocrats (and similarly the Portuguese) expanded their rule over the natives of much of the newly discovered Americas. Here we have yet another instance of an empire, though a commercialized rather than a traditional one, incorporating innumerable

---

43. "At the beginning of the fourteenth century, Muscovy extended over only 47,000 square kilometers. By the mid-fifteenth century, the state's territories had increased to 430,000 square kilometers, and by 1600 they had reached 5,400,000 square kilometers." "By 1688 Russia included Siberia and comprised 15,280,000 square kilometers." Bendix, *Kings or People*, pp. 108, 615. It must be noted that the expansion across Siberia was motivated not by the search for peasants and arable land, but chiefly by the fur trade, with Russian peasants being imported to this area only after the conquest.

tribes under its control, but once again, other existing empires, too, were encountered and conquered. The Aztec empire in Mexico and the Inca empire in Peru (and parts of present-day Ecuador, Bolivia, Argentina, and Chile) had themselves been formed by conquests and had levied tribute on many tribes and on earlier empires. They were but the last and hence best-known of a long series of native empires in Mexico and Peru.

Finally, in sub-Saharan Africa, too, numerous conquest states were formed, though little is known of those in the more distant past. The oldest African empire, aside from Egypt, was evidently Kush, located south of Egypt and at times occupied by the Egyptians. After 700 B.C., the Kushites in turn conquered Egypt and formed one of its dynasties and an empire stretching from Ethiopia to the Mediterranean. During the following millennium, the power of the Kushites and their kingdom of Meroe declined, and they were succeeded by the Axumites whose Axum empire is a predecessor of Ethiopia, an empire that, expanding and contracting, conquering and being conquered, lasted through the centuries into the present one. As recently as the turn of this century, the Amharic expansionism of Emperor Menelich II was designed to obtain tribute and to secure his frontiers (though now no longer against rival aristocratic empires but against European colonial powers). The dynasty claiming descent from King Solomon and the Queen of Sheba came to an end only with the overthrow in 1974 and the death in 1975 of Emperor Haile Selassie.

Further south, the warring Zimbabwe kingdoms may have been established about A.D. 500 or 600 in present-day Zimbabwe and Mozambique, probably by conquerors from the north. They were subject to many invasions for about a millennium, "each ruling group and its armies invading and conquering and settling."[44] In West Africa, the empire of Ghana, founded perhaps as early as A.D. 300 (and located a thousand miles northwest of present-day Ghana) conquered its neighbors to stretch from Timbuktu to Senegal. It fell in the eleventh century to the Almoravids, a nomad Muslim Berber dynasty that had earlier conquered Morocco and invaded Spain about the same time. There followed a period of many conquests and reconquests, and numerous kingdoms were established in West Africa. In the fourteenth and fifteenth centuries, the Mali empire became the most powerful and richest of these only to be replaced in the fifteenth and sixteenth centuries by the Songhay empire that expanded in all directions to rule all the western Sudan, an area perhaps the size of the continental United States. Further invasions from Morocco followed, and by the nineteenth century the Berber Tuareg nomads ruled in Niger, while further south the Fulani conquered the Hausa states. The Hausa-Fulani

44. Davidson, *The Lost Cities of Africa*, p. 263.

emirates of northern Nigeria continue to this day as examples of conquest states.

At the beginning of the nineteenth century, Dingiswayo, chief of a Bantu-speaking tribe, subjected hundreds of semiagrarian, seminomadic tribes in South Africa to a tributary relationship and to indirect rule and thus founded the Zulu kingdom.[45] Dingiswayo's successor Shaka destroyed the communities he conquered, incorporating their men into his army and their cattle into his herds with which to maintain his army. "Plunder was the major source of wealth."[46] Instead of continuing as an aristocratic conquest empire, the Zulu kingdom thus reverted to the status of a raiding nomadic people, albeit an extraordinarily successful one due to certain innovations in its military technology and organization. Shaka's successor, having reached the limits of his army's striking range, even raided and destroyed communities already tributary to him.[47]

Here we may mention the liquidation in recent years of the remnants of what very probably was a conquest empire in Ruanda-Burundi.[48] In Ruanda, the agricultural Hutu, who are related to the Bantus, rose in 1959 in bloody revolt and drove out the pastoral Tutsi (Watutsi), a group of Ethiopian-Amharic or Nilotic origin who had become their rulers, probably as a result of conquest, about four hundred years ago. In neighboring Burundi, the Tutsi have continued to rule (in the form of a monarchy until 1966), but here, too, the aristocracy was challenged by Hutu uprisings in 1965, 1969, and 1972, all repressed, the latter with the loss of perhaps 100,000 lives.

In our own century, the Arab Ibn Saud founded what may well be the last major aristocratic conquest empire. As happens occasionally in the course of the endless tribal feuds characteristic of nomadic pastoral people, one tribe manages to conquer and unite a few others and then, with this superior force, to go on to conquer more nomadic tribes and also peasant villages and even existing empires. Generally, these tribal alliances and their conquests are short-lived and hardly enter the annals of history. In a few instances, however—the cases of Genghis Khan and Mohammed (no nomad himself) and their successors are the most outstanding ones—this kind of warlike organization gathers strength as it goes along and remains

45. The literature on the origins of the Zulu state is well summarized by Walter, *Terror and Resistance*, chap. 6.

46. Ibid., p. 252.

47. Ibid., p. 203.

48. For a brief description of Ruanda as a conquest empire illustrating many of the points I make about aristocratic empires, see Carlston, *Social Theory and African Tribal Organization*, pp. 163–66.

united enough to conquer great territories before it is stopped by natural obstacles like oceans or mountains, by superior enemy forces, internal disunity, or overextended communications. Ibn Saud's conquests are in this pattern. By 1913 he had subjected most of the nomads of eastern Arabia (Nejd) and in the early 1920s he turned on the settled tribes of northern and western Arabia, finally conquering the Kingdom of Hejaz with Mecca, Jidda, and Medina in 1924–25. He thus founded the kingdom of Hejaz and Nejd that has been known as Saudi Arabia since 1932. That, however, was the limit of Ibn Saud's expansionism, for, unlike the Arabs thirteen centuries earlier and the Mongols seven centuries earlier, who confronted only other primitive tribes and traditional aristocratic or some-what commercialized empires, often warring among themselves, he now found himself hemmed in on all sides by areas controlled by or under the influence of a modern power, Britain.

The Absence of Class Conflict

Politics is conflict, and conflict rests on differences and cleavages within a population, that is, in the minds of the people concerned. Any analysis of politics must therefore begin with an analysis of cleavages that give rise to conflict, but it must not be assumed that all cleavages, whether perceived as such or not, do give rise to conflict.

That aristocratic empires are deeply divided is obvious from my discussion of their origins, but, as will become more evident as we proceed in this book, the principal cleavage dividing them, that between aristocrats and peasants, is so deep that it can hardly be bridged even by conflict. In the light of our experience in modern societies, such a statement makes little sense. However, aristocratic empires are not like modern societies, not only because they are not modern, but because they are not societies.

If "analytical definitions usually treat a society as a relatively independent or self-sufficient population characterized by internal organization, territoriality, cultural distinctiveness, and sexual recruitment,"[49] then the population inhabiting an aristocratic empire constitutes not one but many societies. As is clear from their beginnings, such empires are collections of agrarian societies which, remaining independent of each other, are linked to another society, the aristocracy, by being exploited by it. In addition, in the towns, there are people who, as I will note in a later chapter, do not constitute distinct societies. Aristocratic empires, then, consist "mainly of territorial and genealogical communities, rooted in thousands of more or

49. Mayhew, "Society," p. 577.

less isolated centers, mostly villages which are autonomous units, almost self-sufficient in their religious, social, political, and economic life."[50]

Wolfram Eberhard, who argues that the concept of "social system" is not relevant to the analysis of premodern societies, is worth quoting here, particularly because he has China in mind, a commercialized empire often thought to have been highly integrated both politically and culturally. He writes that "it did not matter of which race, religion, culture the rulers were. They lived their own life in their palaces and cities. They did not interfere with the life of other groups, communities, classes, layers, except that they forced them to make contributions to their support—for which they promised 'protection.' And the members of the lower layers, too, did not care who ruled them nor did they care what people in the other layers did, how they looked, which language they spoke. Each layer had its own social life, lived its own way, avoided getting into trouble with other layers and paid 'taxes' as a necessity to live in peace, as long as they were able to pay."[51]

If a system is a set of interdependent elements where a change in one affects all others, then aristocratic empires are, indeed, not social or political systems. A change in one village or one province or even its separation from an empire might affect the aristocracy but it does not affect the peasants in all the other villages and provinces. Conversely, a change in the aristocracy might have little or no effect on the peasantry.

That there is no conflict and hence no politics between aristocrats and peasants is not completely true—I shall look into this matter in more detail in my discussion of peasant revolts below—but there is no doubt that at least openly expressed conflict is very exceptional or nonexistent. This does not mean, of course, that there is little or no conflict and politics in aristocratic empires, but politics in these empires takes place principally not between classes but within classes. The aristocracy (and those attached to it in the towns, like servants and low-level bureaucrats) and each village and to some extent also town organizations like guilds are separate communities or societies and hence constitute separate political arenas. It is the object of this book to analyze politics within the aristocracy and then to investigate whether and to what extent peasants and townspeople impinge on aristocratic politics.

Only after I have shown that nonaristocrats can intervene in the politics of the aristocracy or affect its fate only exceptionally or slightly will it be clear that politics in aristocratic empires is not the politics of class conflict.

---

50. A. D. A. de Kat Angelino, *Colonial Policy* (The Hague, 1931), 1:67–68, as quoted in Gibb and Bowen, *Islamic Society and the West*, 1:211.

51. Eberhard, *Conquerors and Rulers*, p. 6.

In the meantime, it must be acknowledged that it is tempting to perceive the relation between aristocrats and peasants as one of conflict. To do so, however, is to project our modern experience backward into history.

Marx and Engels did exactly that when—before they had studied early history or had as yet much interest in Russian and Indian society—they asserted in the opening passage of the Communist Manifesto that "the history of all hitherto existing societies is the history of class struggles" and when they specifically refer to conflict between "lord and serf" as an example of such struggles. They further assert that "oppressors and oppressed stood in constant opposition to one another, carried on an uninterrupted, now hidden, now open fight, a fight that each time ended, either in a revolutionary re-constitution of society at large, or in the common ruin of the contending classes."[52] This statement, couched in the form of a historical generalization, is probably more a prediction of the fate of bourgeois society as Marx and Engels foresaw it. In any case, it is wrong as a description of the fate of aristocratic empires, which came to an end neither through peasant revolution and the reconstitution of society to serve peasant interests nor through the common ruin of the aristocracy and the peasantry. Neither outcome could occur because there was in fact no class struggle between oppressor and oppressed, between lord and serf in aristocratic empires.

That Marx and Engels—and many others in industrial society down to the present who have commented on aristocratic empires—should assume, often as a matter of course, that the relation between aristocrats and peasants is one of class conflict is not at all surprising. This assumption is not a far-fetched one because the aristocratic-peasant relationship is such a blatantly exploitative one—and it will certainly be analyzed as such here. One class that does no productive labor lives off the labor of the other class. Also, it is not inappropriate to describe the aristocracy and the peasantry as classes (and I do so here), whether classes are defined in terms of differences in wealth or status or power or of different roles in the economy. They are also, by and large, classes in the Marxian sense of the distinction between those who own and those who work the means of production, although, as I shall stress, what matters is not ownership of the land, but the fact that aristocrats always control both the land and the peasants whether, under the prevailing property system, they are landowners or not.

However, the differences between the aristocracy and the peasantry in aristocratic empires go far beyond those between classes in modern industrial societies, and the gulf between them is therefore far wider than that between modern classes. For one thing, the economic, social, and political

52. Marx and Engels, "Manifesto of the Communist Party," pp. 473, 474.

distinctions, which will be stressed in the course of my analysis, are far greater, and mobility between the classes is hence far smaller, nor is the wide gulf between the two bridged and interclass mobility eased by the existence of intermediate classes. The townspeople do not stand between the aristocracy and the peasantry; they are not a middle class like white-collar workers who occupy the gap between the blue-collar workers and managerial personnel in modern industrial societies.

In addition, aristocrats and peasants are generally separated from each other by far-reaching cultural distinctions involving differences of language and religion and sometimes of race. They are, far more than the nineteenth-century British upper and lower classes to whom Disraeli applied the term, "two nations," though the word "nation" with its modern connotations is not really applicable to them. These cultural distinctions are often accounted for by the origins of the aristocracy in an ethnically and culturally distinct community coming to rule other communities. Though the ethnic distinctions between conquerors and conquered are in time worn down, cultural ones can persist through centuries—some cultural characteristics being more resistant to change than others—and strongly reinforce the other class distinctions.[53]

Cultural and ethnic distinctions on the one hand and, on the other, class distinctions, whether defined in terms of economic functions or of wealth, of political power, or of social status, thus rest on each other to such an extent that they become virtually inseparable. The division between peasantry and aristocracy in aristocratic empires, then, is not only deeper than but also quite different in character from class divisions in modern industrial societies. The use of the same concept of "class" may therefore be somewhat misleading (although the class divisions of aristocratic empires have, of course, affected the character of the class divisions of those modern societies growing out of them). To repeat, the aristocracy and the peasantry constitute not mere classes but—or not so much classes as—different societies and different political arenas. If a class is conceived of as a grouping in conflict with another class, then, indeed, aristocracies and peasantries are not classes at all.

53. Linguistic and religious distinctions between aristocracies and peasantries, even where they formally share a single language or religion, are discussed in Chapter 11, below. On the extent to which the four conquest dynasties of China of the past millennium (Liao, Chin, Yüan, and Ch'ing) maintained their distinct tribal characteristics with respect to language and religion, military and political organization, and habits of food and dress, see Wittfogel and Feng, *History of Chinese Society: Liao*, pp. 4–16. See also Wittfogel, "Chinese Society," pp. 352–53. On the preponderant majority of foreigners or sons of foreigners from central Asia in the aristocracy of the Mogul empire (1526–1857), see Spear, "The Mughal 'Mansabdari' System," pp. 8–10.

Part II
The Aristocracy as a Ruling Class

4

The Aristocracy Defined

A Preliminary Definition of the Aristocracy

Aristocracies in certain aristocratic empires can easily be defined as those of a particular race, language, or religion. However, because racial and ethnic differences between aristocrats and peasants vary in character from empire to empire and some such differences may not exist at all in some empires, aristocracies in general across aristocratic empires cannot be defined as a group set apart from the peasantry (and other nonaristocrats) by ethnic or racial characteristics. Rather, the aristocracy must be defined in terms of the economic and political role it plays in aristocratic empires for, unlike racial and ethnic characteristics, that role is in important respects the same in all aristocratic empires.

As to their governmental and political roles, I can here merely indicate briefly and imprecisely that aristocrats are those persons in aristocratic empires who occupy and compete for the higher positions in a government whose minimal functions consist of tax collection and, almost invariably, warfare. A far fuller definition will emerge only from my discussion of the role of the aristocracy in government and politics in later chapters. In the meantime, I might quote Reinhard Bendix's brief description of the aristocracy, which summarizes a number of points to be taken up in these later chapters: "Aristocrats have usually possessed prestige and wealth. Their privileges consist in a title of nobility, freedom from taxation, and special rights associated with the control of land. Aristocrats also constitute a hierarchy of honor in which different degrees or ranks are marked by special insignia, the right to bear arms, and the preemption of activities that are believed to confer prestige. . . . Aristocratic privileges and conventions help to define the circle of those considered eligible for marriage and social intercourse."[1]

In terms of its role in the economy, the aristocracy can be initially defined simply as consisting of those in an agrarian economy who, without themselves engaging in agricultural labor, live off the land by controlling

1. Bendix, *Kings or People*, p. 106.

the peasants so as to be able to take from them a part of their product. Of course, only a small percentage of the population can be aristocrats, because each peasant produces only a relatively small surplus and the average aristocrat consumes far more than a peasant.[2]

A number of clarifications have to be added to this definition. For one thing, not all aristocrats necessarily receive all or even most of their income from the peasantry. They also may tax or rob merchants and artisans and they may sell captives as slaves. However, in traditional aristocratic empires these nonagrarian sources of income should be relatively exceptional ones for aristocrats. They should be the principal ones only for exceptional aristocrats and at most should serve to supplement aristocrats' income derived from peasants, for we exclude from our category of traditional aristocratic empires by definition those empires where trade, including slave trade, is highly developed. That exclusion also serves to eliminate aristocrats from consideration who have themselves become traders and hence do not derive their income from the peasantry.

Still, participation in trade is a matter of degree. Even if aristocrats do not become merchants, they can derive some income from trade, for they may benefit from the sale of some of the surplus products of their land. Not all their peasants are necessarily engaged entirely in subsistence agriculture. Particularly where their lands are near towns, the peasants are likely to take some of their products to market, not only to exchange them for goods produced by artisans or procured by traders, but also to sell them for cash. A good part of that cash finds its way into the pockets of the aristocracy in the form of various taxes and dues. Furthermore, products other than agricultural ones to be found on the land of aristocrats may be exchanged or sold for cash. Thus forests, quarries, deposits of salt, amber, and precious stones as well as coal and metals may all be commercially exploited in aristocratic empires, though some of them also serve subsistence purposes for the peasants and the aristocracy living on the land.

Second, aristocrats also enrich themselves by the spoils of war. That, however, requires no amendment of my definition. Booty is taken either from townspeople, which has just been mentioned, or it is taken from

---

2. Lenski, citing research on a number of commercialized empires—mid-nineteenth-century China and Russia, eighteenth-century France, and first-century B.C. Rome—shows that the aristocracy comprised from 0.6 percent of the population in France (where merchants had by then entered that class) to 1.3 percent in China. Lenski, *Power and Privilege*, p. 219. It may well have been smaller in traditional aristocratic empires. On the basis of seventeenth-century English and eighteenth- and nineteenth-century Chinese data, Lenski estimates that the aristocracy, including the ruler, usually received between one-half and two-thirds of the national income in agrarian states (ibid., p. 228). In traditional aristocratic empires, where the rich merchants of commercialized England and China were absent, the aristocracy's share is likely to have been larger.

peasants, in which case plunder is merely a special way, less regular than leveling tribute or taxes, of taking a part of the peasants' product as income. Or booty or ransom is taken from other aristocrats, which amounts to a way for the aristocrats thus enriched to derive their income indirectly from the peasantry.

Third, my definition of the aristocracy includes, of course, those who receive all or part of their income not by taking it directly from the peasantry, but indirectly through other aristocrats who pass a part of what they take from the peasantry on up to them. This is typically the position of higher aristocrats and especially of rulers of aristocratic empires. They do not take from other aristocrats in the form of plunder, but in the form of tribute owed to them, although the line between the two is not a sharp one. The payment of tribute can be seen as a more regular and peaceful surrender of booty, both tribute and plunder often being the price paid for losing a war or for being too weak to fight one successfully. Speaking of the early Middle Ages in Europe, Duby says: "Annual tribute was nothing more than the collection of booty made orderly and normal, for the benefit of any tribe that was sufficiently menacing for its neighbours to sense an interest in buying peace. . . . By this method, certain peoples drew rents from their military strength. These rents were basically similar to the dues that lords of the big *villae* were imposing on neighbouring farmers, forced by their very weakness to come under the lords' protection. The greater the military superiority, the higher stood the rent."[3]

Fourth, my definition excludes another set of persons who also receive all or most of their income from aristocrats and hence indirectly and ultimately from the peasantry. Unlike higher aristocrats and rulers, however, they receive it not as tribute due to them nor do they obtain it as the spoils of war, but it constitutes payment for services rendered to the aristocracy. These persons include servants and artists, artisans and merchants working for the aristocracy as well as the lower levels of the military, the bureaucracy, and sometimes the priesthood where these three institutions are not composed entirely of aristocrats. People in all of these occupations will be dealt with later in the chapter on townspeople. None of them are aristocrats.

However, the line between the higher levels of the military, the bureaucracy, and the priesthood, which is always composed of aristocrats, and the lower levels, which may not be, is not always a clear one.[4] Where it is not,

---

3. Duby, *The Early Growth of the European Economy*, p. 49.

4. The priesthood referred to here is that administering the religion of the aristocracy. The religion of the peasantry is distinct from that of the aristocracy, even if formally similar or identical, and the village priesthood—in any case, socially identified with the peasantry—is hence not seen here as part of the aristocratic hierarchy of the priesthood, not even as its

there may exist persons who occupy a position intermediate between aristocrats and nonaristocrats or whose position is not entirely clear, or mobility into the aristocracy from the lower ranks may be possible. Far more often, however, the line between aristocrats and nonaristocrats is sharply drawn, either to include in the aristocracy the entire military—as in the case of feudal armies in the early Middle Ages in Western Europe—the entire bureaucracy, and the entire priesthood or to bisect such institutions by a rigid division, as it is still visible in the distinction between officers and common soldiers in modern armies.

Finally, some of the members of the military, the bureaucracy, and the priesthood do not live off the peasantry indirectly by being paid for their services by aristocrats, but live directly off the peasants. This is particularly obvious in the case of a system of tax collection widely prevalent in aristocratic empires. Under it, tax collectors, whether they are part of a bureaucracy or private entrepreneurs hired by rulers, like the publicans or tax farmers in the Roman Republic and the zamindars of India, are obligated to pass a certain amount on to their ruler but can retain the difference between that amount and what they can obtain from the peasants. Such tax collectors and, more generally, administrators, priests, and soldiers living off the land seem to fit my definition of aristocrats. They may nevertheless not be aristocrats, for they, too, may merely serve the aristocracy and be paid for it, though their income does not pass through the hands or the pockets of the aristocracy. However, as a result, these soldiers, priests, and especially tax collectors may be able to increase their income by squeezing more out of the peasantry, they may gain considerable independence from the aristocracy whom they ostensibly serve, and they may even exercise more and more governing functions in their territory (governing functions may, as I shall note later, involve little more than tax collection, in any case). All this will make such people more like aristocrats; whether we should regard them as such will depend on whether they meet my definition of aristocrats as those who occupy or compete for the higher positions in the government.

In an analysis such as this one, a definition is not defective because in reality certain cases are not clearly included or excluded by it. With respect to the traditional aristocracy such cases are most likely to be found—if they are found at all—in the middle level of the military, the bureaucracy, and the priesthood, where the top levels of these hierarchies are occupied by aristocrats, but the bottom ones are not. Warfare and governmental and religious administration are always functions of the aristocracy in aristocratic empires, but nonaristocrats, too, may be involved in them, which

---

bottom level, though it may formally occupy that place. See also pp. 161 and 261–64, below.

may blur definitional lines. However, in most empires the line between aristocrats and nonaristocrats was probably a fairly sharp one marked by differences in race, language, or religion or by heredity or simply by titles.

We shall turn to heredity in a moment but might note here that it is tempting to avoid some of the difficulties we have now encountered in defining the aristocracy and to obviate the need for clarifications by simply defining aristocrats as those who hold aristocratic titles. In many aristocratic empires, this is, indeed, the way in which aristocrats define themselves. However, although most aristocrats have probably held titles to distinguish themselves from nonaristocrats, the use of such distinct titles varies too much among aristocratic empires to be employed as a defining characteristic of the aristocracy in general. It is too formal a criterion, for individuals and groups not designated by aristocratic titles may also play the roles in the economy and politics of aristocratic empires by which I define aristocrats.

Thus, in the Chinese empire, bureaucrats did not hold aristocratic titles and were distinguished from the hereditary aristocracy. The same was true of high Church officials, like bishops and abbots, in medieval Europe. Nonetheless, Chinese bureaucrats and medieval European church leaders meet our criteria as aristocrats. Also, titles may, as in the posttraditional British aristocracy, be inherited only by the eldest son upon his aristocratic father's death. Obviously, that son before his father's death and all the other children and their descendants are aristocrats, if they play the roles by which I define aristocrats, even though they may not have aristocratic titles.[5] Finally, men may play aristocratic roles even in countries that officially recognize no aristocracy. At least for the first half of the nineteenth century, those former Spanish colonies in Latin America where trade was unimportant were substantially governed by big landowners of Spanish descent living off the mostly native peasantry and ruling through the three traditional aristocratic institutions of the military, the bureaucracy, and the Church. That these men held no aristocratic titles makes the Latin American oligarchy of the early years of independence, when there were few commercial and no industrial elements in it, hardly less of an aristocracy.

Heredity

If the possession of aristocratic titles or the designation of a group as an aristocracy cannot serve to define the aristocracy for us, neither can aristocratic heredity. Just as I am inclined to think that, gener-

5. The frequent assignment of courtesy titles to younger sons and also to the eldest son while his father is still alive takes care of the need of aristocrats to designate themselves as such.

ally, everyone with an aristocratic title is an aristocrat, but that individuals without such titles can also be aristocrats, I would assume that, generally, everyone who was a child of an aristocratic family is an aristocrat, but that individuals without such a family background can, at least in some empires, also be aristocrats.

To be sure, ordinarily aristocracies are hereditary, and consequently aristocrats in many empires see themselves as differing from nonaristocrats chiefly by their possession of "noble blood," a subject to which we will return later. Generally, aristocracies become hereditary probably simply because parents commonly want to assure to their offspring the same privileges that they enjoy, and aristocratic parents usually are in a position to do so.

Where an entire tribe becomes an aristocracy, generally by conquest, the aristocracy is, from the very beginning, hereditary because membership in the tribe is, of course, hereditary. However, sometimes only the chief of the conquering tribe or only he and a relatively few warriors that were instrumental in the conquest become hereditary aristocrats. In some aristocratic empires, then, only the rulers and their families are hereditary aristocrats. They may recruit those occupying high military and administrative positions from nonaristocratic families, but in time the descendants of such individuals are likely to occupy similar high positions and thus become a hereditary aristocracy. After all, if they need to compete for high office at all with men whose fathers had not been privileged, they enjoy two immense advantages: In an environment where, typically, family connections matter more than merit, they benefit from the influence of their powerful relatives. And in an environment where the great bulk of the population lives in ignorance and isolation, they are among the very few who have experience and attitudes that qualify them for high office.[6]

The tendency of aristocracies, first recruited on the basis of merit among the members of a conquering tribe, to become hereditary is well illustrated by the short history of the Aztecs. At first, their "ruling class continually renewed itself, taking recruits from the general body of the people. . . . Any warrior who managed to capture his four prisoners became . . . a member of the upper classes, whatever his origin. Furthermore, the emperor filled the higher ranks by promotion according to merit." Having acquired honor, commoners also acquired wealth. "They were not only free from the duty of farming their own shares of land as ordinary men had to do, but they were given other shares, mostly in conquered country, which were worked for them." However, by the time the Aztec empire was destroyed by the Spaniards in 1519, less than a century after it had

---

6. For some insightful remarks on "why all ruling classes tend to become hereditary, in fact if not in law," see Mosca, *The Ruling Class*, pp. 60–65.

begun to expand beyond the local level of the three confederated cities from which it began, "there was an inclination to make distinctions hereditary—distinctions that were originally attached only to an office." The son of a dignitary or lord "in theory . . . had no privileges. . . . In fact he had many advantages from the beginning, derived from the standing of his father and a higher education. . . . A nobility was therefore coming into being." Also by the beginning of the sixteenth century, "although in theory property was still communal, in fact the land that had been attributed by way of life-interest to a [dignitary] was transmitted by him to his heirs. . . . That is to say that the sons of dignitaries who already by their birth had a kind of right to be preferred in the higher appointments were also allowed the advantage of inherited revenues. . . . Whereas the old way established one general standard for all by the sharing of communal land, inequality in landed wealth had in fact become the rule."[7]

A hereditary aristocracy, other than the ruling family, will fail to develop probably only under either of two sets of circumstances. One prevails simply if the empire does not last long enough for such an aristocracy to evolve. This is probably true of the Buganda kingdom in East Africa and certainly of the Zulu kingdom in South Africa. The other set of circumstances is one where rulers deliberately prevent the rise of a hereditary aristocracy. Inheritance guarantees an aristocrat his status as such and permits the accumulation of considerable wealth through the generations. Rulers who feel threatened by the independence thus gained by their aristocratic subordinates may try to elevate to aristocratic positions men of nonaristocratic background, who would then be dependent on the ruler,[8] and men who could not have sons to inherit their status. Thus, not only in the Papal State, where the ruler himself is a nonhereditary priest, but also in other medieval European states, celibate priests were commonly employed as high officials. In China, going back to the Chou period some two and a half millennia ago, and in the Middle East beginning in the Persian empire of about the same time, eunuchs held important positions at court but also in the military and the bureaucracy.[9] At the Chinese court, eu-

7. Soustelle, *Daily Life of the Aztecs*, pp. 45–46, 45, 47, 48, 81.

8. In the early Holy Roman Empire, "neither seneschals nor marshals of the Empire were normally chosen from any but men of servile condition. . . . The *ministeriales* continued to form the normal *entourage* of the Salian and Hohenstaufen monarchs. To them were entrusted the education of the young princes, the custody of the most important castles, and sometimes, in Italy, the great administrative offices; to them also belonged the purest tradition of imperial policy." Bloch, *Feudal Society*, p. 343.

9. For specific examples of eunuchs in such positions in the Chinese and Persian empires and the Abbasid caliphate as well as in the Roman and Byzantine empires, see Wittfogel, *Oriental Despotism*, pp. 354–58. On eunuchs in these and other empires, see also Wesson, *The Imperial Order*, pp. 120–23, and on their role in Byzantium, see Runciman, *Byzantine Civilization*, pp. 162–63.

nuchs numbered in the thousands, perhaps exceeding seventy thousand at the end of the Ming period and still fifteen hundred at the beginning of the twentieth century.[10]

Probably the best example of a nonhereditary aristocracy is furnished by the Ottoman empire at the height of its power. "The Ottoman system deliberately took slaves and made them ministers of state, it took boys from the sheep-run and the plow-tail and made them courtiers and husbands of princesses." "With hardly an exception, the men who guided Suleiman's empire to a height of unexampled glory were sons of peasants and herdsmen, of downtrodden and miserable subjects, of unlettered and half-civilized men and women." Even of his nine grand viziers, all but one "were Christian renegades, who had risen as slaves to the highest honor of the empire."[11]

These aristocrats had been taken as tribute slaves from Christian areas of the empire, because Muslims could not be enslaved. They were converted to Islam, and hence their children, being Muslims, could not be slaves and could therefore not inherit the offices their fathers had obtained. The Ottoman nobility was "the reverse of hereditary, since nobility in the father was an actual hindrance to the son and to all his descendants."[12] Thus, only nonaristocrats, and also only non-Turks, could fill aristocratic positions in the Ottoman empire (except those of the sultan himself and of judges and other clergymen), and in each generation a set of boys not descended from earlier aristocrats had to be trained for these positions.

The term "slave" with its common connotations is hardly appropriate to these officials. Indeed, there is some evidence that Muslim and urban Christian parents whose children were not eligible for "enslavement" resorted to bribery and sent their children to the country to give them the advantages in life that recruitment as slaves could bring them.[13] In any case, there is no question that these individuals were aristocrats. They were the officers—including the viziers at the top—of the sultan's household, his government, and his army. As aristocrats generally do, they enjoyed immunity from taxation and were responsible only to their own courts and officials and to the ruler. They lived in some degree of luxury, paid by the sultan and from revenues of estates and they built up households, including hundreds or thousands of slaves, and military establishments themselves which followed them when they went to war with the

10. Loewe, *Imperial China*, p. 136. See also Mitamura, *Chinese Eunuchs*.

11. Lybyer, *The Government of the Ottoman Empire*, pp. 45, 196, 167.

12. Ibid., p. 118.

13. Shaw, *History of the Ottoman Empire*, 1:114.

sultan.[14] Like Chinese imperial officials, to be mentioned in a moment, these slaves of the sultan constituted an aristocracy of office and government service, but, not being drawn from a limited class like the Chinese gentry, they were even less hereditary.

The central position in the Ottoman empire, that of the sultan, however, was filled by heredity. Thus, even in that empire, the principle of heredity was not abandoned, but was evidently sacrificed for the lower aristocracy only in order to make the hereditary ruler the more powerful. Nor, it must be stressed, did the sultan's slaves ever constitute the entire lower aristocracy, that is, the aristocracy other than his own family. There was also an older Turkish aristocracy, for as the Ottomans had conquered new territory, portions of it had been awarded to military commanders. They administered these as local rulers, living off the taxes imposed on the peasantry, including the corvée, and in return had to perform military duty in the sultan's cavalry and to maintain themselves and a few retainers and horses and arms in readiness for war.

Beginning in the late fourteenth century and more generally by the mid-fifteenth century, the sultans, in order to weaken this old aristocracy and to become more independent of it, introduced the system of forming military units of slaves and to assign leading positions in the bureaucracy to specially trained slaves.[15] In time, it was these slaves who were given land as a reward for military or governmental service, and because at least a part of the land was inherited by the sons of its holder, they themselves became a part of a hereditary aristocracy.

Thus the system of a nonhereditary slave-aristocracy entirely dependent on the sultan lasted only for about a century. Exactly when it reached its height under Suleiman the Magnificent in the mid-sixteenth century, that is, when slave-aristocrats occupied the top positions in the empire, it began to decline, for, as one would expect, these slaves used their immense power to favor their personal friends and, of course, their chil-

---

14. Lybyer, *The Government of the Ottoman Empire*, pp. 114–15.

15. It appears that a somewhat similar system was introduced for quite similar purposes in the Himalayan kingdom of Bhutan in the first half of the twentieth century. At that time (and before modernization introduced by a new king beginning in 1952 put an end to the traditional phase of Bhutanese history), the kings (*Druk Gyalpo*) sought to centralize a hitherto highly decentralized traditional empire: "Young boys, some from poor, nonelite families, were brought into the palace at an early age, trained in a wide variety of tasks and, if they proved competent, were appointed to high posts either in the palace or in the provincial and district administration. This provided the Druk Gyalpo with a cadre of administrators that were both technically competent and politically dependable. It also served to weaken the position of the local elite families that had previously provided most of the recruits for the administration." Rose, *The Politics of Bhutan*, p. 38.

dren.[16] After the death of Suleiman, the Janissaries were granted "the formal privilege of entering their sons in the corps; . . . by 1592, the majority of the Janissaries were said to be sons of Turks." "In the seventeenth century they ceased to be drawn directly from the Christian population and became a variety of military aristocracy."[17] It could be argued, then, that even this major attempt to create a nonhereditary aristocracy in the end demonstrated the tendency of aristocracies to become hereditary. As Wittfogel says, "we are not so much surprised that the Turkish office holders advanced eventually to hereditary or semihereditary tenure, but that, over a considerable period, the sultan was able to successfully block these trends by maintaining a socially rootless class of 'slave-officials.'"[18]

The same tendency of aristocrats to pass their land and their privileges on to their children is illustrated by the Russian experience. Here Ivan III in the late fifteenth century began to rely heavily on *pomestye*, a form of revocable land tenure granted in return for military service. "The granting of military fiefs in conquered territories was a means of increasing the number of dependent servitors without hereditary rights. Or so it seemed. But the pomeshchiki . . . wanted to will their benefices to their heirs. This was allowed sporadically, probably in part to ensure the continued loyalty of these servitors; but to the extent that it was allowed, pomeshchiki became hereditary landowners. This also occurred with regard to Ivan the Terrible's special military guard. In the 1560's, Ivan made the landholdings of these oprichniki hereditary. . . . Thus the legal distinction between military fiefs (pomestie) and hereditary lands (votchina) became blurred."[19]

The Chinese bureaucracy might also be mentioned here, for it was recruited on the basis of examinations, not of heredity. Actually, at various times, high bureaucrats could introduce their sons into the bureaucracy without examinations or could recommend their relatives, thus bringing an element of heredity into the bureaucracy. More important, officials

16. Shaw, *History of the Ottoman Empire*, 1:26, 30, 113, 125–27, 166, 170. See also Anderson, *Lineages of the Absolutist State*, p. 369, who stresses that the estates of the older Turkish aristocracy were not inheritable and their holders were reshuffled by every new sultan. This would, of course, not mean that the aristocracy itself was not hereditary.

17. Lybyer, *The Government of the Ottoman Empire*, pp. 69, 92; see also Anderson, *Lineages of the Absolutist State*, p. 381.

18. Wittfogel, *Oriental Despotism*, p. 362. The use of slaves as a military elite that became capable of wielding power itself was a system "to be found all over the Muslim world. Turkish slave officers from Central Asia founded the Ghaznavid State in Khorasan, and dominated the Abbasid Caliphate in its decadence in Iraq; Nubian slave regiments ringed the Fatimid Caliphate, and Circassian and Turkish slaves brought from the Black Sea manned the Mamluk State in Egypt; Slav and Italian slaves commanded the last armies of the Umayyad Caliphate in Spain, and created their own *taifa* kingdoms in Andalusia when it fell." Anderson, *Lineages of the Absolutist State*, pp. 505–6.

19. Bendix, *Kings or People*, p. 114.

were overwhelmingly recruited from the gentry, whose status and whose lands were hereditary, for, as we shall note shortly, its members were favored in various ways and were far more likely than nonaristocrats to acquire the education necessary to pass the examinations. Thus Chinese bureaucrats may not have been hereditary aristocrats in their capacity as bureaucrats, but they were nevertheless hereditary aristocrats.

It is important to point out explicitly here that I regard what is commonly referred to as the gentry in China as an aristocracy. This needs to be stressed because my usage runs counter to that of some scholars. Thus, Eberhard says specifically that "the first characteristic of this 'gentry society' —which came into being in the third century B.C. and was firmly established in the first century B.C.—was the absence of aristocracy and nobility." Yet, he proceeds to define the gentry as "a social class" and in such a way as to fit clearly into my definition of an aristocracy. He says that he agrees "with M. Fried that the criteria for the gentry include leisure, nonproductive occupation, literacy and high status, but much more so with H. Bielenstein's very clear statement that the gentry is 'the ruling class in contrast to the uneducated and primarily inactive commoners. The gentry invested their wealth in land which enabled it to remain educated. The members of the gentry either served as officials or lived as junkers on their estates.' M. Levy also underlines that the gentry were expected 'to depend for income on the perquisites of political office and the absentee ownership of land.' It is the problem of the chicken and the egg whether we say that through political office a person acquires land, or that through ownership of land he enters the bureaucracy."[20]

Balazs even regards Chinese officials as such, not merely the gentry, as an aristocracy. He says: "In my opinion, it is justifiable to define the officials as a class if account is taken of their economic basis (salaries and ownership of land), their uniform style of life, and their traditionalist outlook. Their upbringing, monopoly of education, notions of honor, and above all their character of *literati*, which distinguished them so sharply

20. Eberhard, *Conquerors and Rulers*, pp. 42, 43; the references are to Fried, *Fabric of Chinese Society*, p. 180; Bielenstein, *The Restoration of the Han Dynasty*, p. 93 n. 3; Levy, "Contrasting Factors in the Modernization of China and Japan," p. 170. I might add the characterization by another scholar of the few dominant gentry families in the Sui and T'ang dynasties, which begins by stressing ideological traits that we will later find to be quite typical of aristocracies in most aristocratic empires: "This group embodies the virtues and vices of an aristocracy—disdain for their inferiors, devotion to military virtues, an intense pride in their ancestry, and a spare and austere code of honor. Closely interconnected by bonds of marriage, they set the social tone for the early T'ang as they had for the Sui and preceding northern states. Dominating the higher levels of the nobility and bureaucracy, these families secured for themselves not only immediate political power, but also privileges for their persons and the large landed estates which were the economic underpinning of their positions." McKnight, "Fiscal Privileges and the Social Order in Sung China," p. 81.

from the illiterate masses, might weight the scale toward regarding them as a caste or as a closed intellectual aristocracy." Balazs adds, however, that the factor of the examination system—"its supposedly democratic nature was a mere legend"—that allowed the "ruling class" to maintain its monopoly "position by co-opting commoners . . . militates against the idea of a closed caste."[21]

Clearly, then, even in the relatively few cases where aristocracies are not hereditary, aristocrats generally tend eventually to make them hereditary. However, there is no need for me to exclude from my definition of aristocrats those who perform aristocratic functions, most obviously in high positions in the bureaucracies and armies of aristocratic empires, even if they are celibates, eunuchs, or slaves and thus cannot have children who can inherit their positions and regardless of whether their parents were aristocrats or not. They are aristocrats because they live off agriculture without engaging in agricultural work themselves and hold high government office.[22]

Mobility

The matter of heredity is related to that of mobility. Where the aristocracy is entirely hereditary, there is of course no possibility for a nonaristocrat to become an aristocrat. If the aristocracy is not hereditary, there may be more mobility into it—and, for that matter, out of it—although here, too, aristocrats may be chosen by very restrictive criteria.

In traditional aristocratic China, during the feudal Chou period, "a common man could become a noble no more easily than a woman could change into a man."[23] In Cambodia, "while folk literature celebrated the valour of men whose peasant origins did not prevent them gaining rank and position within the kingdom, such cases of upward social mobility were rare in the extreme."[24] The chance of a peasant becoming an aristocrat must literally have been not much better than one in many millions in most aristocratic empires. Even in the Ottoman empire, during the period

21. Balazs, *Chinese Civilization and Bureaucracy*, pp. 6–7.

22. In the Zulu kingdom, a rudimentary conquest empire of short duration, where only the kings constituted a hereditary aristocracy, "the warriors as well as the administrative staff and the royal household were largely released from the necessities of ordinary work and maintained at state expense." Walter, *Power and Resistance*, p. 192.

23. Chow, *Social Mobility in China*, p. 2.

24. Osborne, *Politics and Power in Cambodia*, p. 17.

when non-Muslim peasant boys were enslaved to be trained for high military and bureaucratic positions, only a tiny fraction of the peasantry could thus rise into the aristocracy, and after about a century even that road was closed to them. What was highly exceptional here was that for some time it was only the sons of peasants who had a chance to become aristocrats (except clerical ones).

Still, there may be opportunities for the rare nonaristocrat to move up into the aristocracy. One may arise simply through closeness to an aristocrat. Concubines and servants may gain his confidence, be consulted by him, and thus participate in a process of decision making or be entrusted with administrative tasks normally reserved to aristocrats. At the court of a powerful aristocrat, a servant may even rise to the position of a court official and thus become recognized as an aristocrat himself.

Other avenues of upward mobility may be formed by the three major hierarchies that exist in most aristocratic empires, whether they are sharply distinct or not. To the exceptional nonaristocrat, they can offer an opportunity to break through the usually rigid barrier separating the aristocracy from the rest of the population.

As long as the armed forces, the governmental bureaucracy, and the priesthood are relatively small institutions, they may be manned exclusively by aristocrats. Every soldier, every government official, every priest is then an aristocrat[25]—and often every aristocrat holds one or two or even all of these professions. However, where these institutions grow larger, the ruling aristocracy may open certain positions in them not only to members of defeated aristocracies, but even to nonaristocrats. Typically, it is the lower positions in each hierarchy that are so opened up while the higher ones remain securely in the hands of the aristocracy. The ordinary priest may be a townsman but the archbishop is an aristocrat. The government clerk may be the son of a trader but the higher official will be an aristocrat. Peasants may become common soldiers or even noncommissioned officers whether voluntarily or under compulsion, but the officers, certainly the higher ones, are aristocrats.

Once nonaristocrats have joined the lower levels of aristocratic hierarchies, exceptional individuals among them may have a chance to rise into the upper levels and thereby into the aristocracy. Where military excellence is an important aristocratic quality, as it generally is in aristocratic empires, an aristocracy could strengthen itself by occasionally elevating to aristocratic rank a common soldier who distinguished himself in battle. In medieval Europe, the Church offered a rare chance to an exceptional

25. We are not concerned here with the peasants' own—and quite separate—village institutions, including village leaders and village priests.

peasant or townsman to rise to aristocratic prominence.[26] Given priestly celibacy and the absence of heirs, this constituted less of a threat to the aristocracy than the elevation of nonaristocrats into the secular aristocracy. Finally, a lower-ranking bureaucrat might rise into the upper ranks of the bureaucracy. Particularly tax collectors and tax farmers may, as mentioned, become virtually independent of their aristocratic employers and thus become aristocrats themselves.

With commercialization, there may be a tendency toward greater mobility. The aristocracy, looking down on the nouveaux riches, perceives such a tendency as a threat and may take deliberate measures to prevent mobility. If it succeeds, commercialization may, in fact, bring only relatively little mobility. Thus, China, commercialized after the Chou period, is sometimes cited as an exception to the rule of extremely limited mobility into the aristocracy. However, Wolfram Eberhard, who studied the matter systematically found "that over the course of Chinese history, the government tried more and more to stabilize society by assigning to each class its definite position in that society, and by enacting laws to make the status of each person clearly recognizable by his personal appearance as well as by the appearance of his house. In addition, each class had certain privileges and obligations to the extent that even intermarriage between different classes was prevented." "Clearly, the ideal was a stable, static society."[27]

Nor was this merely an ideal. Eberhard says that in fact "we should not expect much social mobility in medieval China and little more in modern China."[28] For the medieval period, that is, the twelve centuries from the end of the feudal Chou period about 250 B.C. into the tenth century A.D., he shows by means of detailed studies, that there was remarkable social stability, with some gentry families remaining dominant for a thousand years, in spite of changes in dynasties and in boundaries. As to new families entering the gentry, "all of these families became important by pure violence either as soldiers in the regular or irregular army, or as members of a successful gang. They came to prominence by 'conquest,' very much in the same way as the new gentry families of foreign origin. Military action was *the* way to achieve upward mobility, not action within the bureaucracy. It cannot be maintained that in medieval China the system of official examinations created an open society on the basis of achievement, with ascribed status being of secondary importance. Rise to power by brutal force was typical for medieval China. Thus in periods of peace, in which the gentry had effective control over the country, rise to power was rare, and only

26. Gregory VII (Hildebrand), one of the most powerful Popes (1073–1085), was probably the son of an Italian artisan or peasant.

27. Eberhard, *Social Mobility in Traditional China*, pp. 197, 16.

28. Ibid., p. 22.

times of war and disturbance were periods of social change. Not until modern times has the rise to elite status been achieved normally by bureaucratic means rather than by military power."[29]

However, even in modern China, that is, in the last millennium of the empire, the examination system did not create "an open society on the basis of achievement." Especially during the earlier part of this period, "its influence on the social composition of the imperial bureaucracy was seriously restricted by institutionalized social discrimination, by hereditary claims to office . . . and, under the conquest dynasties, by the politically prominent nobles of the 'barbarian' master nationality."[30] Large groups—all women and craftsmen, shopkeepers, and merchants—were legally excluded from the examinations and hence from entry into the gentry. Merchants (who were admitted under a tiny quota in the nineteenth century) were, as a result of commercialization, precisely the one group of commoners who could, at least exceptionally, acquire the wealth and education that might have enabled them to compete in examinations. Peasants were legally free to compete, but only an exceptional peasant's son could attain the education necessary to pass the examinations. The state schools accepted virtually only sons of the gentry, private tutors were expensive and good ones rare, and only schools established by rich clans for their own boys might admit a boy from a poorer branch of the clan.[31] Obviously, the bureaucracy as a road into the aristocracy was not open to the overwhelming majority of the peasantry and "it usually took several generations for a farmer-peasant to climb."[32]

Until the seventh century A.D., only those recommended by the local governor (a member of the gentry, of course) could take the examinations, and he could be punished if his candidate turned out to be a failure. Hence he was most unlikely to recommend a peasant's son he did not know or to reject someone recommended to him by a powerful gentry family. Also, as I noted, officials could legally secure appointments for a certain number of their relatives without examination. Finally, more or less widespread corruption permitting candidates to bypass examinations always favored the gentry.[33] At least in certain periods, it was possible to purchase academic titles and one of the lower bureaucratic ranks.[34] Because only a limited number of positions needed to be filled and only a limited number of

29. Eberhard, *Conquerors and Rulers*, pp. 170–71, italics in the original.

30. Wittfogel, *Oriental Despotism*, p. 349.

31. Eberhard, *Social Mobility in Traditional China*, pp. 25–26.

32. Chow, *Social Mobility in China*, p. 9.

33. Eberhard, *Social Mobility in Traditional China*, pp. 23–25.

34. Chang, *The Chinese Gentry*, pp. 3–6.

candidates were permitted to compete in the examinations, all this further reduced the chances of a peasant ever becoming an official and thus entering the gentry. Eberhard concludes "that the examination system cannot be expected to have contributed much to upward social mobility."[35]

Furthermore, the Chinese bureaucracy was evidently not a good avenue of upward mobility even for those very few of lower-class background who had succeeded in entering it. "It seems safe to conclude that a correlation between social origin and success not only in the examinations but also in the careers after the examinations might exist. If we take the successful gentry . . . and study the social origins of these persons, we find out that in those periods which have already been analyzed almost nobody rose from low social origins."[36]

Drawing on a number of detailed studies of the social background of officials under various Chinese dynasties, Wittfogel suggests that in the Han period (206 B.C.–A.D. 220), several centuries before the examination system was introduced, "no more than 8 per cent of all officials of known social background were commoners"; in the T'ang period (618–907), when the examination system was fully developed, "less than 10 per cent were commoners"; under the Sung dynasty (960–1279) the corresponding figure was about 15 percent according to one study and perhaps only 9 according to another; under the Mongol Yüan dynasty (1234–1368) "about 15 per cent were descended from commoners"; and in the Ming period (1368–1644) it may have been as many as 23 percent. Much like Eberhard, Wittfogel concludes from these data that the examinations "added a varying amount of 'fresh blood' to the ranking officialdom. But they did not destroy the trend toward sociopolitical self-perpetuation which dominated the thoughts and actions of this group."[37] Still, these figures, referring to most of the two millennia of Chinese commercialization, small as they may be by modern standards, seem much higher than corresponding figures one would expect to find for traditional aristocratic empires.

Much of the literature—and what Wittfogel calls "popular legend"[38]—emphasizes the civil service examinations as the route for upward mobility in China. However, there were, in fact, other, informal, routes, such as migration, in addition to the use of violence just mentioned as the principal route in the medieval period. Thus, Eberhard concludes his study of the subject by noting that there was indeed social mobility in China in the past millennium, but that not every individual had an equal opportunity of moving up. "A long-term social rise can be seen," but it was a movement of

35. Eberhard, *Social Mobility in Traditional China*, p. 26.

36. Ibid., p. 27.

37. Wittfogel, *Oriental Despotism*, pp. 348, 351–52, 354.

38. Ibid., p. 348.

families rather than of individuals. While he disclaims definite conclusions, it seems to Eberhard that at least in South China, and perhaps also in Central China, social mobility "was strong—and perhaps as strong as in Western countries in the same centuries," particularly in periods of dynastic change.[39]

While I have here been chiefly concerned with upward mobility into the aristocracy, it might be noted that there was perhaps more downward mobility out of the aristocracy in China than is usual among aristocracies. Chinese aristocratic families differed from those in most aristocratic empires in that they could belong to clans composed also of nonaristocratic families. They thus regarded themselves as related by blood to nonaristocrats. Indeed, the peasant families surrounding the home of a gentry family were typically members of the same clan as the gentry family, and hence its distant relatives, quite unlike the peasants surrounding the aristocrat's castle or manor house in feudal Europe. This, no doubt, facilitated downward mobility for the Chinese aristocracy as compared to other aristocracies. Eberhard argues that, because upper-class families had more children than lower-class families in China, "some sons had to move socially downward because the generation of high-status sons was much larger than the generation of high-status fathers, while the number of jobs increased more slowly, at best in proportion to the growth of the general population. . . . We find, therefore, among the Chinese elite, the 'gentry families' a downward social mobility of individuals. Family policy attempts and usually succeeds in retaining the social level of the main house over a long period, but many branch families move down into the next level, that of farmers."[40]

If social mobility was very limited in commercialized China it seems fair to repeat our generalization that, certainly as compared to modern societies, interclass mobility in traditional aristocratic empires was extremely limited and that more often than not the aristocracy was virtually—though rarely completely—closed to newcomers and especially to peasants.

One major exception to this generalization was, once again, the Ottoman empire, at least at the height of its power in the sixteenth century. Here enslaved peasant sons, selected and promoted on the basis of their ability, were given careful intellectual and physical training to qualify them for leading positions in the army and the bureaucracy.[41] As noted earlier, these institutions did for some time into the sixteenth century constitute effective avenues of upward mobility all the way to the top position of

39. Eberhard, *Social Mobility in Traditional China*, pp. 264, 265.

40. Ibid., pp. 264–65. On downward mobility in agrarian societies in general, see also Lenski, *Power and Privilege*, pp. 289–91.

41. Shaw, *History of the Ottoman Empire*, 1:114. For a detailed description of the palace school and its curriculum, see Miller, *The Palace School of Muhammad the Conqueror*.

vizier. If contemporary witnesses are to be believed, this Ottoman system operated entirely on the basis of merit. Lybyer quotes three sixteenth-century Western European observers who were most impressed with it. One stresses that in Turkey "they judge of nobility by the worth which they see appearing in a man and they give honors according to the evidence of his past." Another one says of Suleiman, "he sows hope of certain reward in all conditions of men, who by means of virtue, may succeed in mounting to better fortune." And the third one, quoted at length, tells us that the Turks "do not measure even their own people by any other rule than that of personal merit. The only exception is the house of Ottoman; in this case, and in this case only, does birth confer distinction. . . . Each man in Turkey carries in his own hand his ancestry and his position in life, which he may make or mar as he will."[42]

Lybyer insists that "the entire system from start to finish was designed to reward merit and fully to satisfy every ambition that was backed by ability, effort, and sufficient preparation." He says that the Ottoman government —the court, the army, the bureaucracy—"was a school in which the pupils were enrolled for life. Constantly under careful drill and discipline, they advanced from stage to stage through all their days, rewarded systematically in accordance with their deserts by promotions, honors, and gifts, and punished rigorously for infraction of rules, while both rewards and punishments increased from stage to stage until the former included all that life under the Moslem scheme could offer, and the latter threatened to take away the life itself." "At the same time, reward was considered more potent than the rod. Unequalled prizes were offered in this school, so skillfully disposed and graded as to call out the utmost strivings and the best work of every pupil." "Merit was recognized everywhere, and regularly led to promotion."[43]

While Shaw hints at some favoritism on behalf of the descendants of those who constituted the government, he, too, stresses mobility on the basis of merit for he speaks of "a system of social mobility based on the possession of certain definable and attainable attributes. While children of existing members of the Ruling Class found it relatively convenient to acquire the characteristics required to retain their fathers' social status this was not automatic. It was accomplished by a long course of study in the various schools maintained by the Ruling Class to train new members and by apprenticeship in the departments of government. Ambition, ability, and good fortune determined who rose in the Ottoman Empire." And

---

42. Quoted in Lybyer, *The Government of the Ottoman Empire*, p. 85, respectively from books by Guillaume Postel, published in 1570, V. D. Tanco, published in 1558, and Ogier Ghiselin de Busbecq, published in 1581.

43. Ibid., pp. 82, 71, 72, 73.

Shaw also refers to "a fluid social structure in which talented people could rise to important positions in the service of the sultan."[44]

Nor was there lack of opportunity for mobility. "The losses occasioned by fierce and frequent wars, and by not infrequent depositions and executions, gave abundant opportunity for men to rise from below. Conquest was continually adding new offices and commands. The whole Ruling Institution was, so to speak, in a constant state of boiling, in which the human particles were rapidly rising to the top, and, alas, disappearing, while others rose as rapidly behind them. . . . The upward movement was not in the least accidental or automatic; it was conducted with keen intelligence at every stage. Now and then . . . favor disturbed the scheme; but this happened very seldom before the end of Suleiman's reign." Lybyer goes so far as to assert that "as regards sheer efficiency, unobstructed opportunity, and certainty of reward" the Ottoman system compared favorably with opportunities for upward mobility in "the free democracies of the present age," that is, of the early twentieth century.[45]

Exaggerated as this judgment may be, the Ottoman system has to be recognized as an exceptional one among aristocratic empires. However, it must be added that—if it ever operated as Lybyer described it—it did not last long and began to break down when slave-aristocrats reached the heights of power. Being aristocrats, they used their power to destroy the merit system. Shaw says that when slave-aristocrats "rose to power in the mid-sixteenth century, most appointments to positions were determined by . . . personal attachments and loyalties rather than by considerations of ability and efficiency."[46] There was an increasing tendency for those in high positions to pass on their offices, privileges, and wealth to their descendants —and thus for the aristocracy of the Ottoman empire to become more similar to those of other aristocratic empires.

In aristocratic empires, restrictions on interclass mobility probably do not have to be laid down in laws or made explicit. As we shall see, the positions occupied and the functions served by aristocrats and nonaristocrats and, consequently, their behavior and their values are so very different and are confirmed by so much symbolism, that interclass mobility appears unnatural for all except possibly a few people on the margins of the aristocracy. Everyone knows what class he belongs to, and it does not occur to him that he could move into another one.

Also, it must be kept in mind that even if there were no formal or legal barriers to the ascent of nonaristocrats into the aristocracy and even if the aristocrats' deep conviction of their own superiority did not constitute

44. Shaw, *History of the Ottoman Empire*, 1:113, 115.

45. Lybyer, *The Government of the Ottoman Empire*, pp. 83, 84.

46. Shaw, *History of the Ottoman Empire*, 1:166.

another major barrier, conditions of nonaristocratic life in aristocratic empires were generally such as to disqualify virtually all but those born and raised in the aristocracy from holding aristocratic positions. The military, the priesthood, and the bureaucracy are thus generally not effective avenues of upward mobility, because if nonaristocrats can enter them at all, they tend of necessity to be confined to lowly positions. Nonaristocrats, except the very few closely associated with aristocrats in some empires, simply did not acquire the experience, the intellectual horizon, or the training and skills required for higher positions. This is particularly clear with respect to literacy; "in a nation with a low literacy rate, where reading and writing are technical accomplishments of the civil or religious government, the resource of qualified functionaries is relatively small and normally will remain within certain families of the accepted aristocracy. Even when the state is expanding rapidly and there is a positive demand for more officials, experience at the top level is a rare faculty, so that there will be a tendency to retain the highest positions within a relatively small group. This was so in the Egyptian Empire"[47]—and in aristocratic empires generally.

47. Wilson, *The Burden of Egypt*, p. 171.

5

The Aristocracy in the Economy

Ownership and Control of Land

In aristocratic empires, aristocrats may or may not be big landowners. What matters to us here is not the particular system of property in land that prevails, but the control by the aristocracy of the land, that is, of the peasants. While the legal property relationships vary from one aristocratic empire to another, the power relationship between peasants and aristocrats is remarkably uniform. Indeed, property is often, by modern standards, not very clearly defined. "The pure concept of private property as an absolute right to use and abuse, as it was defined in Roman law, is rarely if ever encountered"[1] in aristocratic empires. Roman law was the product of the commercialized Roman empire and was readopted in commercialized Western Europe. Thus, it was only in posttraditional Europe that landownership became clearly defined, as it had been in Rome, and it was under European influence that large landownership in the modern sense was brought to other parts of the world, like Latin America, India, and the Near East, and became characteristic of the aristocracy there as it had earlier in Europe.

In China, private property in land developed with commercialization independently of European influence. "Ever since the time of the Sung (1114–1234) private ownership in land has been the dominant form of tenure in China. The state, at one time or another, reserved for its own use royal lands to sustain the court, banner lands to support the military aristocracy, lands for the purpose of military colonization, lands for the support of temples serving the state cult, and lands in the hands of provincial or district government."[2] Much of the privately owned land as well as these

---

1. Rodinson, *Islam and Capitalism*, p. 64. Hsu concludes from his study of society in Chou China that it is "misleading to think that the ancient Chinese concept of ownership was the same as the modern judicial idea of ownership. What seems to have mattered in ancient China was the actual control of a given piece of land, not the legality of its ownership. The term 'possession' is probably more apt here than 'ownership.'" Hsu, *Ancient China in Transition*, p. 110.
2. Wolf, *Peasant Wars of the Twentieth Century*, p. 106.

state lands were, by our standards, held by the aristocracy.

The widely held modern image of the aristocrat as a big landowner is derived from the experience of commercialized societies, but in aristocratic empires widely different property systems in land prevailed. However, regardless of the legal conceptions involved, the peasant was always entitled to retain enough of his product to survive (except in periods of shortage, when he might starve), and the aristocrat was entitled to the surplus produced by the peasant. One can imagine, as an extreme case, a situation where the peasant owns no land and works on the aristocrat's land and either contributes the aristocrat's share of the product in the form of rent, perhaps on a sharecropping basis, or receives his own share in the form of wages, whether by retaining part of his product or in cash. The opposite extreme would be the situation where peasants own all the land and aristocrats none and where the latter receive their share in the form of taxes.

Clearly, even in these extreme cases, the size of the respective shares of the product of the land received by the peasant and the aristocrat, that is, the degree of exploitation of the former by the latter, does not stand in any necessary relationship to the property system. In one way or another, peasants always work for the aristocrat, whether they work on his land as agricultural laborers or rent it from him or own their own land and pay taxes to him. Both renters and owners are, in addition to paying their dues as such, often compelled by law—that is, by the aristocracy—to work without compensation a certain amount of time on the aristocrat's land (where his land is distinct from theirs). Such a system, known as the corvée, coming down from ancient Rome, was passed on by the Franks to feudal Europe, and similar ones existed in ancient Egypt, in China and Japan, and, in a sense, as will be noted in a moment, in Inca Peru.

In practice, the property system in aristocratic empires is likely to lie somewhere between the two extremes just mentioned. Aristocrats may own some land outright or as grants from the ruler in return for military service, and the ruler may own land for the upkeep of his establishment, and the peasants, too, may own land on which they pay tribute.[3] But in the absence of the modern concept of ownership it is also possible for both the aristocrat and the peasant to hold some legal rights to the same piece of land—which really means that each is entitled to a part of the product— with the aristocrat typically holding rights to many more pieces of land than the individual peasant. Thus, in the feudal manor of the early Middle Ages in Western Europe, the estate was typically divided between the demesne, including the manor house, held by the lord and managed by

3. On such a system among the Aztecs, see Davies, *The Aztecs*, pp. 78–79, and Soustelle, *Daily Life of the Aztecs*, pp. 79–81.

him or his steward, and the land held by the villeins, that is, the peasants. The lord, as Bloch says, claimed "superior real property right" over the land of the villein "above all, by the right to impose taxes and demand services."[4] The peasants had to provide the lord with a portion of the product of their land and, in addition, had to supply the labor to work his demesne.[5] Still, the peasant, too, had rights to the land, even if he was a serf. "Serfdom is a rather vague notion which contains an infinite range of gradations and variations around the exploitation of a peasant enjoying variable legal rights, in particular over the land that he cultivates, by a landowner who also enjoys variable rights, which are never absolute, over his peasant and his land."[6]

Perry Anderson, even more than Bloch, stresses private landownership by the aristocrat under European feudalism: "The peasants, who occupied and tilled the land were not its owners. Agrarian property was privately controlled by a class of feudal lords, who extracted a surplus from the peasants by politico-legal relations of compulsion. This extra-economic coercion, taking the form of labour services, rents in kind or customary dues owed to the individual lord by the peasant, was exercised both on the manorial demesne attached directly to the person of the lord and on the strip tenancies or virgates cultivated by the peasant. Its necessary result was a juridical amalgamation of economic exploitation with political authority. The peasant was subject to the jurisdiction of his lord."[7]

Speaking of feudalism more broadly defined as "a system of economic and social relationships based on the legalised and institutionalised claim of a ruling group to a substantial part of the surplus of peasant production,"

4. Bloch, *Feudal Society*, p. 241. However, Bloch also explains that "it is very rare, during the whole of the feudal era, for anyone to speak of ownership. . . . For nearly all land and a great many human beings were burdened at this time with a multiplicity of obligations differing in their nature, but all apparently of equal importance. None implied that fixed proprietary exclusiveness which belonged to the conception of ownership in Roman law. The tenant who—from father to son, as a rule—ploughs the land and gathers in the crop; his immediate lord, to whom he pays dues and who, in certain circumstances, can resume possession of the land; the lord of the lord, and so on, right up the feudal scale—how many persons are there who can say, each with as much justification as the other, 'That is my field!' Even this is an understatement. For the ramifications extended horizontally as well as vertically and account should be taken of the village community, which normally recovered the use of the whole of its agricultural land as soon as it was cleared of crops; of the tenant's family, without whose consent the property could not be alienated; and of the families of the successive lords" (ibid., pp. 115, 116).

5. Slicher van Bath, *The Agrarian History of Western Europe*, pp. 40–49, and Pirenne, *Economic and Social History of Medieval Europe*, pp. 57–66.

6. Rodinson, *Islam and Capitalism*, p. 64.

7. Anderson, *Passages from Antiquity to Feudalism*, p. 147.

Rodney Hilton puts less emphasis on private landownership but quite as much on the element of coercion as Anderson: "The members of the ruling group usually appear as landowners, though the concept of land-ownership is by no means precise, for it often appears as the ownership of rights over the working occupiers of the land, rather than of ownership of the land itself. Since . . . the ruling group was not economically necessary to peasants, who already effectively possessed their own means of subsistence (contrasted, for instance, with propertyless wage workers), the element of coercion in the transfer of the peasant surplus to the lord was quite open. It was guaranteed by the possession by the lords of military force. . . . But, since the exercise of force is best legitimised by legal sanction, lords from high to low developed rights of private jurisdiction for the regulation of their relations with the peasant communities."[8]

It is the relationship of exploitation that results from the coercive political and military authority of the aristocrat, that is, from his control of the peasants, that matters to us here. Unlike any particular property system, it is the universal aspect of the relationship between peasantry and aristocracy and the very basis of the existence of the aristocracy. A look at non-European property systems where peasants were in effective possession of their land will illustrate this. In Peru, while in a sense the Inca owned all the land in his empire, land actually belonged to the peasant communities.[9] Peasants paid taxes in the form of service on fields set aside in each village for the Inca, that is, for the imperial aristocracy and, in fact, also the local one, and for "the Sun," that is, the priests. They also served on various government projects, like road building.

Similarly, Islamic empires, like the Umayyad and Abbasid caliphates, Ottoman Turkey, Safavid Persia, and Mogul India, followed a doctrine formally established under the Caliph Omar II (717–720) "that all land was by right of conquest the property of the sovereign, on which subjects paid rents to the Caliph,"[10] from which the ruler in turn supported his military and bureaucratic aristocracy. In practice, "after the initial Arab conquests in the Middle East, the local peasantry in the subject lands were typically left in undisturbed possession of their plots," and in Mogul India, as in Turkey, "the indigenous peasantry was guaranteed permanent and hereditary occupation of its plots."[11] However, under the Abbasids, the Otto-

---

8. Hilton, "Peasant Society," p. 71.

9. Sally Falk Moore stresses that the controversy over whether the Inca or the peasant communities held title to the land resulted from Spanish conceptions of property rights. In fact, "it does not make any practical difference who held the title." Rights to land were "concurrent." Moore, *Power and Property in Inca Peru*, p. 46.

10. Anderson, *Lineages of the Absolutist State*, p. 497; see also ibid., pp. 515, 518.

11. Ibid., pp. 498–99, 518.

mans, and the Moguls, military and bureaucratic aristocrats received land grants to exploit the peasantry as tax farmers and absentee landlords, there being no territorial aristocracy in Islamic aristocratic empires.

Whatever the property system, then, and however clearly defined or vague it may be, in all aristocratic empires peasants are controlled and hence exploited by aristocrats.[12] That exploitation rests on political relationships rather than on any specific property system is well stated by Rodinson when he points out "that the division of the social product was effected . . . in accordance with the 'natural' human tendency of each group to maximize the advantages that its situation could bring. Whatever moral and ideological precepts may exist, in every state the rights and interests of any social category are fully respected in the share-out of the social product only if this category is represented in the state and possesses sufficient strength to compel such respect. Neither of these conditions was fulfilled in the traditional Muslim state"[13] with respect to the peasantry, nor, I may add, in any other aristocratic empire. In all such empires, the peasants are not represented in the "state" of the aristocracy because they are not part of it and, being defenseless against the aristocracy, they can be and are exploited. Exploitation is, indeed, the principal and only necessary link between the peasants' societies in their villages and the society of the aristocracy, regardless of who "owns" the land. In all cases, while the peasant produces and consumes, the aristocrat does not produce and yet consumes —and generally consumes far more than the peasant. What the aristocrat consumes must be part of the peasant's product whether it is delivered in the form of labor and services, rent, dues, or taxes.[14]

12. It is not only property relations as between aristocrats and peasants that vary from empire to empire, but also the property systems prevailing among peasants. These, too, are independent of the overriding fact of exploitation. "Private ownership of land, more or less well defined, appears in primitive communities and there is no correlation between this type of appropriation and the exploitation of the community by a higher community. The first states whose structure we can get to know through history or archaeology, and the simplest of the types of state existing in our own time which are known to us through ethnological observation, are based on exploitation of the surplus of communities in which private appropriation is combined in infinitely varied ways with the rights of the community. . . . Everywhere there is a hierarchy, a variety of multiple rights of the various communities, families, lineages, religious and political authorities, etc., over the land and its fruits." Rodinson, *Islam and Capitalism*, pp. 63–64.

13. Ibid., p. 73. Being principally interested in the relationship of Islam to the economy of Muslim societies, Rodinson refers to "the calls to justice and charity found in the sacred writings of Islam" and says, "as ever, God's good counsel proved powerless unless backed by institutions that gave power to those human beings whose interest it was to cause this counsel to become reality" (ibid., p. 74).

14. Referring to an Indian manuscript, Habib, *The Agrarian System of Mughal India*, p. 90, writes: "To what, asks Bhimsen, did Southern India owe its innumerable temples, some of

Exploitation of Peasants

Until now, I have simply assumed that the aristocracy lives off the surplus produced by the peasants. It is now time to ask where that surplus comes from, a matter not quite as simple as may at first appear. After all, it is probably generally true that, given low levels of productivity and in the absence of birth control, sufficient numbers of cultivators will be born and will survive to insure that the village as a whole will always tend to exist on the verge of starvation if it lives free of any aristocratic exploitation. How, then, is aristocratic exploitation of the peasantry possible, that is, how can peasants be deprived of a surplus if they produce no surplus?

First of all, it must be stressed that exploitation is, indeed, impossible if the available technology is such that even with maximum exertion individual cultivators can produce no surplus. In a village society with that type of technology, no nonproducers, like the old and the sick, survive, except some of the children who are essential as future producers.[15] Any reduction in the food supply by exploitation would thus kill producers and would reduce production. Under such circumstances, a village can be raided and robbed and thereby destroyed, but it cannot be subjected to continuing exploitation. In practice, even if a tiny surplus could be extracted, this would not be sufficient to pay for the expenses involved in extracting it, especially the maintenance of the necessary military and administrative machinery.

Consequently, there have not been aristocratic empires ever since there have been cultivators on the one hand and pastoralists on the other. Such empires can arise only at a time in history when agricultural technology has developed to a point where a fairly substantial surplus can be produced.

---

them without peer in the world? To the fact, says he, that the soil is immensely productive while the subsistence needs of the inhabitants are so few. The *rajas* devoted the huge surplus which thus resulted to the construction of temples, for want of anything better as much as from their own religious bent. . . . He thus assumes as a matter of course that the possession of everything produced in excess of the barest amount necessary for survival should have vested in the hands of the rulers." A traveler who in 1675–76 visited a local Indian king who fought the Mogul emperor with a peasant army, quotes him as referring to his peasants as "Naked, Starved Rascals" and saying of them: "money is inconvenient for them: give them Victuals and an Arse-Clout, it is enough." Quoted ibid., pp. 350, 90, from John Fryer, *A New Account of East India and Persia being Nine Years' Travels, 1672–81* (London: Hakluyt Society, 1912), 2:67, 66.

15. Cipolla estimates that in agrarian societies, "in general, more than one-third of the population is below 15 years of age; . . . this means that the non-active young population represents a heavy burden for the active population and this is one of the reasons why agricultural societies put children to work at an early age." Cipolla, *The Economic History of World Population*, p. 83.

Now, due to population growth, no such surplus may, in fact, be produced, but the village is capable of surviving and of continuing the process of production when deprived of part of its food supply by exploitation.

Of course, no matter how advanced the technology, exploitation is not possible beyond a certain limit. That limit is reached when the goose that lays the golden egg is killed. Given the aristocrats' irresistible power over the peasants, it is always tempting for them to increase their demands. However, if too little food—or too little time to produce food for themselves—is left to the peasants, they are weakened, they die, or, where that is possible, they run away, and the productivity and the tax yield of the village decline.[16] Thus, if aristocrats subject a village already on the verge of starvation to a tax amounting to, say, a third of its product and thus permit only two-thirds of its population to survive, these survivors may be unable to produce as much as did the entire village before. Once a third of the peasants have died, the income of the aristocracy will therefore have decreased. If the aristocracy persists in appropriating the same proportion of the village product, that is, one-third, or if it even persists in squeezing the same absolute amount out of the village as before, more peasants will die, and in a very few generations all peasants—and therefore eventually all aristocrats (if they treat all their villages in this manner)—will be dead.

New aristocracies may well exceed the tolerable limits of exploitation and so may the exceptional local aristocrats who, like some in Mogul India, were insecure in their assignments of land and were thus "tempted to get as much out of the peasants as possible in the time available."[17] Generally, however, aristocrats learn what the limits of exploitation are and may fix them by custom or law. Habib puts it succinctly with reference to the Mogul empire: "Imperial revenue policy was obviously shaped by two basic considerations. First, . . . the tendency was to set the revenue demand at the highest rate possible so as to secure the greatest military strength for the Empire. But, secondly, it must also have been clear that if the revenue rate was raised so high as to leave the peasant not enough for his survival, the revenue collections would soon fall in absolute terms. These considerations explain why the revenue demand as set by the imperial authorities usually approximated to the surplus produce, leaving the peasant only the barest minimum needed for subsistence."[18]

Exploitation is possible, even though cultivators free of aristocratic rule produce no surplus. If the tax levied by the aristocracy consists of only 10

---

16. Maquet, *The Premise of Inequality in Ruanda*, pp. 105, 153, makes this point well with respect to the Tutsi-Hutu relationship.

17. Moore, *Social Origins of Dictatorship and Democracy*, p. 327; see also Habib, *The Agrarian System of Mughal India*, pp. 320–22.

18. Ibid., p. 319.

percent of the product of the village and only 10 percent of its population are thus doomed to starvation, the remaining 90 percent of the villagers may well be able to produce as much as did all the villagers before, that is, to produce a surplus. Or, indeed, more than 90 percent or even all the peasants can survive if they will produce the necessary surplus to pay the tax imposed by the aristocracy. In short, 90 percent of the original population must produce 100 percent of the original product or 100 percent of the original population must produce 110 percent of the original product to pay the 10 percent tax to the aristocracy, but in either case (and in any intermediate case), a surplus is being produced.

Thus, it is quite possible for aristocrats to tax peasants (or to raise taxes on peasants) who are barely surviving. This is done by forcing some to die and the rest to produce more or by forcing all of them to produce more. It would seem, then, that even if it is assumed that cultivators are always on the verge of starvation, because their population always grows to that point, and that they therefore never produce a surplus for themselves, a surplus can nevertheless be extracted from a village by compelling the peasants to remain on the verge of starvation but to produce more per capita, a process which some of them may not survive.

How can peasant per capita production be increased? The available technology is, as a practical matter, not subject to improvement. If the amount of arable land available to the village cannot be expanded, additional labor, that is, more hours of work, on the part of the entire village population may well not increase the total product much or at all. Under these circumstances imposing a tax on the village or increasing it may result in starvation for some peasants, say, 10 percent of them. Then the remaining 90 percent, using all the land and the same technology that was available to begin with, can produce the necessary surplus.

It might seem that for the remaining 90 percent of the peasants to produce that surplus, that is, to produce as much as 100 percent of the peasants did before, will require them to work harder. If—and this may or may not be true—the peasants were already working up to the limit of their capacity, perhaps to keep as many of their children alive as possible, an increase in production by the individual peasant may be impossible. How then can 90 percent of the peasants produce what 100 percent produced before? They can, if the 10 percent who are eliminated by death produced little or nothing to begin with. This may well be the case because, when the aristocracy takes 10 percent of the food supply from the village, it will probably be the least productive peasants—the old and the sick— who will die first. This will certainly happen if the peasants decide that they should be the ones to be deprived of food, but the result will be similar even if all the peasants take a 10 percent cut in their diet. The old and sick should keep dying until 90 percent of the peasants are left—the very ones who did all or most of the work even when the other ten percent were alive—and these 90 percent, retaining 90 percent of the original food supply—can then live as well as before, that is, on the verge of starvation.

On the other hand, where the original amount of land under cultivation can be expanded or where agriculture is of such a nature that additional hours or improved efficiency of work would increase the product, the original village population can be made to produce the surplus needed to pay the new or additional tax and no peasants need die.

In either case, contrary to what may be widely believed, it is only aristocratic coercion that will make the peasants produce a surplus.[19] It is the certain knowledge that the tax collector will inevitably appear and take a part of their product that makes the peasants continue to produce a surplus though they themselves cannot enjoy it but must live on the verge of starvation. In the absence of aristocratic coercion or when such coercion is removed, the agriculturalists will cultivate less land or work less hard or do both, so that the existing population will live on the verge of starvation, or, more probably, their population will grow to the point where all are once again on the verge of starvation. This would seem to be borne out by—and in turn explain—the fact that villages of primitive cultivators, that is, those not subject to aristocratic exploitation, appear to exist on as low a material level as those in aristocratic empires. In terms of what they consume, then, primitive cultivators not being taxed by aristocrats are no better off than peasants who are. They may, however, be able to maintain a population equal to one of a village subject to aristocratic exploitation with less work per capita or a larger population with the same amount of work and in this sense they are better off.

It need hardly be stressed that the tendencies sketched here do not necessarily assert themselves undisturbed in reality. Thus, aristocrats in practice do not or cannot always, as has been assumed, deprive the peasants of all of their surplus product. Aristocrats are too inefficient to do so, and peasants are too hungry and hence too eager to hold on to as much of their product as possible to permit it.[20] However, in the long run, this may

---

19. Gerhard Lenski says: "Without the elite, there would have been no economic surplus, since population growth would have kept pace with gains in productivity—at least prior to the development of modern methods of birth control. Strange as it may seem, until modern times there was an economic surplus in societies chiefly because the ambitions of the elite kept the growth of populations in check. Taking a long-run view of this problem, it is clear that the exploitative character of elites and their expropriation of the economic surplus were necessary prerequisites to social progress. Had there been no exploitative elites, there would have been no economic surplus to support the technicians, inventors, artists, philosophers, prophets, and other cultural innovators who brought modern civilization into being." Lenski, *Power and Privilege*, pp. 64–65, n. 19.

20. Speaking of early medieval Western Europe, Marc Bloch says: "Almost the only forces

merely result in an increase in the peasant population up to the point of starvation.

Aside from the aristocrats' inability to take and the peasants' reluctance to surrender the entire surplus—factors that operate almost universally to prevent all of it from being collected—special circumstances can make reality depart, at least temporarily, from the picture drawn here. Especially favorable crop conditions or some other factors causing peasants to produce more than they usually do may permit them legitimately to retain a surplus. On the other hand, crop failure or epidemics, like the Black Death, can reduce the peasant population below that permitted by the usual starvation level. War could have a similar effect if some of the peasants are withdrawn from the village population by being drafted into the army. After the initial period of suffering caused by famine or disease, a higher standard of living could result for the surviving peasants until the population once again reaches the starvation level.[21] A shortage of peasant labor might also force the landlord to reduce his demands on peasants or

---

that were . . . capable of counterbalancing (often very effectively, it is true) the abuses of power by the masters were the peasantry's remarkable capacity for passive resistance and, on the negative side, the inefficient management of the manors." Bloch, *Feudal Society*, p. 249.

21. However, war, unlike disease, destroys not only peasants but also their possessions and thus, as Cipolla stresses in the following passage, endangers the survivors as well. To be sure, aristocrats make war only on each other, never on peasants (except possibly when villages are first brought under aristocratic control or to put down rare peasant revolts). But however harmless and neutral peasants, like cattle, may be, they and their possessions are destroyed because they constitute the basis of the enemy aristocrat's wealth. "Passing armies killed or confiscated livestock, burned or confiscated food reserves, and destroyed houses, mills, barns, and other agricultural buildings. . . . From a purely economic point of view, war was a much greater evil than the plague, and all the more evil as the societies in question suffered from a relative scarcity of capital in relation to existing population. The plague destroyed men, but not capital, and those who survived the onslaught of the disease usually found themselves in more favorable economic conditions. War, instead, hit capital above all, and those who survived found themselves in conditions of the most abject misery. In the chronicles and documents of the time, descriptions abound of countrysides and towns reduced to flaming wastes and of children who, crying or begging for bread, died of hunger in the streets. Phrases such as 'the whole area was turned into a desert' or 'where men lived there are now only savage animals' recur frequently in the documents of those times. They were not rhetorical exaggerations." Cipolla, *Before the Industrial Revolution*, pp. 129–30. Cipolla also points to the link between war, famine, and epidemics: "War was disastrous largely because of its indirect consequences; that is, to the extent that it provoked greater frequency or intensity of the other two evils, namely, famines and epidemics. Famine could easily result from the destruction and the pillaging of the harvests, herds, and agricultural implements which the passing armies indulged in. Epidemics were another common by-product of wars. The sanitary and hygienic conditions of medieval and Renaissance armies were absolutely appalling. . . . Armies were more efficient in disseminating epidemics than in waging wars" (ibid., p. 151).

to pay them higher wages if he cannot compel them by force to remain on and work his land. Scantiness of population forced princes and landlords in Eastern Europe and Russia roughly from the twelfth to the sixteenth century to attract both German and native peasants to their lands that would otherwise have remained empty and unproductive. To do so, they granted them temporary immunities and exemptions from their usual obligations and offered them loans and subsidies.[22]

If the aristocrat is too inefficient to deprive the peasants of all the surplus they produce, he is certainly too inefficient or indifferent to make them produce a greater surplus. As agriculture is not, or certainly not primarily, carried on for the market and for the aristocrat's profit and as he has little if any capital invested in his land and labor, he has little interest in receiving the maximum possible production from them and no means of obtaining it. Not only is much of the aristocrat's land often not cultivated at all and few improvements are made in agricultural methods, but no attempt is made to wring from the peasants a maximum of labor. Unlike the worker in a modern enterprise carried on for profit, where labor is an investment—whether he be a slave on a plantation or a laborer in a factory —the peasant generally works under little or no supervision. His operations and their timing are determined more by custom than by the aristocrat, who is, after all, merely an element superimposed on an already existing peasant economy. The peasant enjoys a degree of protection from efficient exploitation sometimes, as in medieval Europe, by his customary rights and generally by the indifference of the aristocrat. The latter may, then, well be described as an exploiter, but he must not be thought of as an employer.[23]

Where taxes are collected in the form of labor services rather than in kind or in cash, one might expect closer supervision of the peasantry by the aristocracy or its agents and greater interference by them in village life to make sure that the required services are actually rendered. The outstanding example of an empire where the only tax laid on the peasantry was the corvée is that of the Incas.[24] But the corvée was enforced in forms parallel to that of the traditional, pre-Inca village reciprocity where families contributed their labor to community projects in return for food and beer. Thus even here, the system was largely self-enforcing and required only a minimum of organization by the central government operating through

22. Blum, *Lord and Peasant in Russia*, pp. 97–101.

23. Pirenne, *Economic and Social History of Medieval Europe*, pp. 63–64. On customary rights, see p. 115 and n. 33, below.

24. As Sally Falk Moore points out, from the point of view of the peasant, what he gave was service, but from the standpoint of the aristocrats, what they received was produce. Moore, *Power and Property in Inca Peru*, p. 49.

the local village chiefs.[25] It seems likely, then, that even in the bureaucratic Inca empire where the aristocracy lived entirely off services performed by the peasantry rather than off taxes paid in money or in kind, the peasants were not closely supervised or efficiently exploited by the aristocracy.

Exploitation and Reciprocity

Although exploitation of the peasant by the aristocrat is typically inefficient, it constitutes in any case a very one-sided relationship: the aristocrat takes and the peasant gives. I employ the term "exploitation" to describe this relation even though its distinctly negative value implications are irrelevant in our context. The verb "to exploit" is used here in the sense of "to get value or usefulness out of," as in "to exploit a mine or agricultural land" rather than in the sense of "to draw an illegitimate profit from" or "to take unfair advantage of." According to the aristocrat's laws and mores, his relationship with the peasants is obviously not an illegitimate or unfair one. As to the peasant's attitude on the matter, it will be touched on in a moment and again in the chapters on the peasantry below. Whether we choose to view the relation as unfair depends on the criteria we apply, a matter I can leave to each reader (but our views will, in any case, not help explain the behavior of aristocrats and peasants in aristocratic empires).

The peasant's role vis-à-vis the aristocrat can be well understood as akin to that of land or a mine. He is not hired or fired, but simply goes with the land; mostly he is not made to work or paid to work. Rather, he and his work are simply there, like the land itself, to be exploited by him who controls the land and everything that goes with it. That includes not only the plants and animals on it and the metals and minerals beneath it, but also the draft animals' and the peasants' labor power, which makes them all available.

In some cases, the exploitative relationship between aristocrat and peasant may be a brutally frank one, as where tax collectors appear, from the peasant's point of view, little different from the robbing and raiding no-

25. The arrangement of the peasants' marriages, which has often been ascribed to the Incas and would constitute an extreme example of central government interference in village affairs, may well have been no more than a census device whereby the central government used an existing personal and community ceremony as the point marking the assumption by the individual of liability to the corvée. Only married men were listed in the census, for, as heads of households, they were responsible through the village chief for the performance of their labor obligations. Murra, "On Inca Political Structure," p. 33. See also Métraux, *The History of the Incas*, pp. 93–94 and 98–100, and for a careful study of the Inca tax system generally, Moore, *Power and Property in Inca Peru*, pp. 48–72.

mads who may have established the exploitative relationship in the first place. However, that relationship can also be ideologically concealed by some concept of reciprocity prevailing between the peasant and the aristocrat who stands immediately above him. The aristocrat's claim to provide benefits to the peasant probably serves the function of making the peasant's exploitation more acceptable to him so that he will pay his dues and perform his labor services more willingly and cause less trouble for his lord. The claim is probably made to justify the aristocracy's rule in its own eyes, not so much in the traditional aristocratic empire, where that rule appears to be natural and god given, as in the posttraditional society, where aristocratic rule is challenged and hence for the first time in need of justification. It is then mostly in retrospect that aristocrats and historians who see the traditional world through aristocratic eyes are likely to justify aristocratic rule by aristocratic service.

Aristocrats may claim to give to their peasants two things in particular, in return for which the peasants must work for them and pay them. One of these is the right to use the aristocrat's land, where the aristocrat is the landowner. The argument assumes that the aristocrat is entitled to the land, as he certainly is according to the prevailing law, which is, of course, the aristocrat's law. But initially, it was the peasant who "owned," that is, worked the land, and the aristocrat acquired it by taking it from him or inheriting or taking it from another aristocrat. In any case, in granting the use of land to the peasant, the aristocrat does not give to the peasant anything of value; on the contrary, it is by working it that the peasant makes the land valuable for the aristocrat. By the same token, the notion that the aristocrat feeds the peasant reverses the actual relationship, because it is the peasant who produces all the food.

The second thing aristocrats claim to give to peasants is protection. If they provide physical security for the village and keep warfare away from it, they render a valuable service to the peasantry. At least, it might be said, the peasants have the assurance that they will be deprived of their surplus only once or twice a year by their own aristocrat or his tax collector rather than possibly more frequently and more irregularly by other aristocrats and robbers. Even more important, they will be allowed to survive by their own aristocrat as they might not be by others. Thus, protection may be a real benefit received by the peasants from the aristocrats. This remains true even though the motive of the latter is merely to permit the peasants to go on producing and to hold on to them and their product and even though it could be argued that peasants would need no protection, were it not for aristocrats and nomadic would-be or potential aristocrats coveting their land.[26] The protection of peasants by aristocrats, then, must be un-

---

26. One could also add that banditry, too, could be blamed on the aristocracy which pro-

derstood as an incident of conflict among aristocrats in which each protects his sources of wealth against other aristocrats.[27]

Typically, aristocrats in aristocratic empires do not interfere in the domestic affairs of the village, except to compel peasants to pay their taxes or to perform their labor services, and they leave it to the peasants to decide how these burdens are to be distributed among them. However, in some cases aristocrats may also administer justice and settle disputes in the village. The performance of this function may be seen as an aspect of the protection they provide for the peasants. Just as they protect them from external enemies to preserve the peace, they protect them from each other to maintain domestic order and assure uninterrupted production.

Even if the peasant does benefit from it, the provision of protection in return for his labor or taxes does not really involve a reciprocal relationship. Whereas the aristocrat is free to take or not to take the peasant's taxes, the peasant is not free to accept or reject the aristocrat's protection. He is compelled to pay his taxes and he is compelled to be protected, whether he likes it or not. The aristocrat is free to surrender or to grant his land, with the peasants living on it and belonging to it, to another aristocrat under whom they may be worse off. The protection of the peasants is not likely to be a major or even a serious consideration when control of land is transferred for military, diplomatic, or personal reasons from one aristocrat to another, even in the case of an individual estate, let alone in that of an entire province or empire.

On the other hand, the aristocrat will protect the peasant from other aristocrats under whose rule he might be better off. Speaking of tax collection in India, Eberhard writes: "The Moghuls among themselves justified their action, if they felt need to do so, by saying that the tax served to protect the farmer against greedy enemies who, if not restrained by their military power . . . would rob the farmers. If the farmers had known that

---

tected the peasants from it. In China, "they had no need for the Imperial apparatus except to keep marauders and bandits away from their crops. But banditry on a large enough scale to be a serious menace to the peasants was in itself very largely the consequence of exploitative officialdom." Moore, *Social Origins of Dictatorship and Democracy*, p. 205.

27. Referring to the "traditional upper class–peasant class relationships" in Iran "through the centuries," James Bill lists both claims of reciprocity mentioned here as illustrating the peasant's "checking power on the landlord": "The landlord was expected to keep the peasants alive and this meant food, clothing, shelter, and medicine. During periods of famine, earthquake, pestilence, and war, the peasant expected and received help from the landlord. . . . The peasant came to expect the protection of the landlord and his representatives against government agents and policies. The landlord often intervened to help the peasant escape crushing tax exactions and to rescue the peasant's sons from military conscription." Bill, *The Politics of Iran*, p. 19.

they were paying a price for protection they would have asked to be left alone, because no robber would have taken more than" the tax collectors.[28] A writer commenting on this passage by Eberhard says more generally: "To call the relationship between the rulers and the villagers 'functional' is to impute a degree of interdependence that does not exist. There is no economic division of labor and consequent exchange between rulers and peasantry, nor is it clarifying to say that the villagers exchange their economic produce for protection from thieves and despoilers; from the villagers' points of view, the rulers *are* the very despoilers they are supposedly protecting against."[29]

I am inclined to argue, then, that generally there is no reciprocity in the relationship between peasant and aristocrat in aristocratic empires.[30] The

28. Eberhard, *Conquerors and Rulers*, pp. 3–4. A hundred years ago, Herbert Spencer, to illustrate what he calls "the truth that the agency which maintains order may cause miseries greater than the miseries caused by disorder," reports that "a voyage up the Nile shows every observer that the people are better off where they are remote from the centre of government—that is, where administrative agencies can not so easily reach them. Nor is it only under the barbaric Turk that this happens." Spencer, *The Principles of Sociology*, 2:251, 252, para. 443.

29. Collins, "A Comparative Approach to Political Sociology," pp. 57–58. In India, "government above the village was an excrescence generally imposed by an outsider, not a necessity. . . . Because it had really nothing to do in the village where caste took care of everything, government may have seemed especially predatory. The government was not necessary to keep order." Moore, *Social Origins of Dictatorship and Democracy*, p. 339. However, referring generally to "agrarian civilizations," Barrington Moore, like many scholars, sees a reciprocal relation between peasant and aristocrat. "The general task of the secular overlord was to provide security against the external enemies. Often, but not universally, he rendered justice and settled disputes among the inhabitants of the village. . . . In return for the performance of these functions, the overlord with the priest extracted an economic surplus from the peasants" (ibid., p. 469). Moore also refers to "the ratio between services rendered and the surplus taken from the peasants," the "services" being "the contributions of those who fight, rule, and pray" (ibid., p. 471), "who perform services necessary for the agricultural cycle and the social cohesion of the village for which they receive roughly commensurate privileges and material rewards" (ibid., p. 470). Moore stresses this reciprocal relationship in order to advance "the thesis that, where the links arising out of this relationship between overlord and peasant community are strong, the tendency toward peasant rebellion (and later revolution) is feeble" (ibid., p. 469), but where these links are tenuous, as was true in China and Russia, peasant revolts occur. However, although this thesis may well hold in commercialized societies, like the China and Russia Moore has in mind, in traditional aristocratic empires the absence or rarity of peasant revolts can be explained by a number of factors to be discussed in a later chapter. There is no need to assume that exploitation inevitably leads to peasant revolts and that, if peasants do not revolt, it must be because they receive benefits from aristocrats.

30. Landsberger seems to agree when, in defining a peasant, he stresses that "a greater or lesser share of his effort is appropriated by others. . . . The person who appropriates from the peasant does so *beyond* any service he or his class has performed and . . . he is able to

entire surplus the peasant surrenders to the aristocrat is used by the latter for his own benefit; none of it is a price paid by the peasant for benefits accruing to him. Even where aristocrats organize masses of peasants to build irrigation and flood control works, as in Egypt and China, and thus increase agricultural production, the peasants remain on the verge of starvation—though there may now be more of them—and the aristocrats reap the benefits. The relationship between the aristocrat and the peasant is about as reciprocal as that between the shepherd and his animal. The shepherd will protect it from attack and let it live on and eat from his land; "in return," he takes its milk or wool and even its meat.

No doubt, some peasants do benefit from aristocratic rule—just as the sheep really does benefit when the wolf is driven off by the shepherd. Thus, peasants might be killed by nomadic raiders if it were not for aristocratic protection or in floods if it were not for flood control projects initiated by aristocrats. However, protection and flood control are provided to benefit the aristocracy, not to serve the peasantry in return for its taxes. The distinction is not merely a shadowy one referring to the motivation of the aristocracy. It is reflected in the behavior of aristocrats, who can withdraw their services at any time when it suits them, whereas peasants cannot withhold their payments as they please.

Contrary to a widely held view, it is quite possible for a system of government and exploitation to exist, even for centuries and millennia, that provides no benefits for the governed and the exploited. In aristocratic empires, at any rate, it is not true that "power must justify itself by maintaining a state of collective security and prosperity. This is the price to be paid by those who hold it—a price that is never wholly paid."[31] Any long lasting institution may have to serve a function, but it need not be functional, in the sense of beneficial, to all concerned. Exploitation is, obviously, functional to the maintenance of aristocratic empires and to the aristocracy, which simply rest on exploitation; it is not functional to the peasants who, without it, could function as primitive agriculturalists.

By arguing that peasants are exploited by definition, that is, simply by virtue of the fact that they surrender to an aristocracy any surplus they

---

exact his appropriation through control of the political system—the state, the law, and ultimately force." Landsberger, "The Role of Peasant Movements and Revolts in Development," p. 2, italics in the original.

31. Balandier, *Political Anthropology*, p. 39. See also the somewhat similar passage by Everett E. Hagen and a response by Barrington Moore quoted on pp. 314–16, below. Balandier also says that "power cannot be entirely autocratic. It seeks and receives a variable degree of support from the governed, either by routine apathy, inability to conceive of an alternative or acceptance of certain values regarded as unconditional." Balandier, *Political Anthropology*, p. 40. The first two of these conditions prevail among peasants in aristocratic empires, as will be noted below in the chapter on peasant revolts.

produce, I avoid the thorny problems of what constitutes a fair contribution by them and what, on the other hand, is unfair and hence the result of exploitation, and whether to derive concepts of exploitation by deducing them from some abstract standard of justice or from the peasants' own historically and culturally conditioned view.[32] However, this does not mean that questions of fairness and justice do not arise in the minds of aristocrats and peasants. To say that there is no reciprocity in their relationship does not mean that the peasant has no rights and the aristocrat no duties—though it would, indeed, be difficult to enforce these where they are violated. Rights and duties are simply aspects of the exploitative relationship that have become established by custom and accepted by both sides.[33] It may be the right of the peasant to retain two-thirds of his crop or to work four days a week on his own land rather than the lord's. It may be the duty of the lord to feed the peasants while they perform forced labor for him or even on certain holidays. Because he is merely returning a part of what they produced in the first place, no reciprocity is in fact involved.

However, symbolic, as distinguished from material, benefits are involved. Although the relationship between aristocrat and peasant may not seem a reciprocal one to us, it may have been seen as such in some aristocratic empires. Thus, in feudal Europe certain ceremonies reflected such an ideology, suggesting a kind of contractual relationship between aristocrat and peasant.[34] Peasants might bring food to the aristocrat on holidays, and he might offer them a feast, or they might even perceive reciprocity if the aristocrat fed them while they performed labor services for him. "This chain of gifts between a lord and his tenants must have helped to soften the sentiments of the two parties toward one another and to symbolize the reciprocity which was conceived as the foundation of their relationship."[35]

The Inca system may have served "to extend to corvée duties the feeling-tone of community reciprocal aid," and it is said that families went to work singing joyously and in their best clothes.[36] As Murra says, "the state

32. For a sophisticated treatment of these problems, see Scott, *The Moral Economy of the Peasant*, chap. 6, and also Moore, *Social Origins of Dictatorship and Democracy*, pp. 470–71.

33. On the matter of peasants being protected by custom from excessive exploitation, R. H. Hilton, writing of posttraditional thirteenth-century England, stresses "that manorial custom was not fixed. It was in fact a shifting compromise between peasant resistance based on the mutual solidarity produced by common interests and a common routine of agriculture on the one hand, and the lord's claims on the other, more or less urgent as they might be, and backed up by more or less political and military power." Hilton, "Peasant Movements in England Before 1381," p. 122.

34. Wolf, *Peasants*, p. 52.

35. Quoted in part ibid. from Homans, *English Villagers of the Thirteenth Century*, p. 269.

36. Murra, "On Inca Political Structure," p. 33.

made an ideological effort to phrase these exactions in the terminology of traditional Andean reciprocity. It is hard to say how many Inca citizens they had convinced by 1532, but their effort was at least partially successful; it convinced the European chroniclers and some modern students that the Inca crown controlled the country's whole economic and social life for what were essentially welfare purposes. In the process we underrate the continuing self-sufficiency and reciprocity of peasant endeavor, even after the Inca conquest." "The Inca state functioned like a market: it absorbed the surplus production of a self-sufficient population and 'exchanged' it by feeding those on *corvée*, the royal relatives, and the army, and by attempting to secure their allegiance."[37] The exceptional importance of the storage of food in the Inca empire points to the fact that, unlike most other aristocracies, the Incas exacted only the corvée and no other taxes from the peasantry. However, the Inca aristocracy was no different from aristocracies in all other aristocratic empires; it did not feed the peasants, they fed it.

The Landsbergers insightfully point to another way in which a one-sided relationship was made to appear reciprocal: in feudal Europe, "production for the lord . . . was the *raison d'être* of the manor as an enterprise." However, "the fact that this was not a simple, uncomplicated arrangement is attested by the variety of other duties, obligations, institutions, and even sentiments which went along with it. In the important events in the peasant's life—his marriage, his children's marriages—he was related to the lord by needing to secure his permission and to pay special dues. The overabundance of ways in which the villein's dependence upon his lord was demanded in the culture of the manor suggests that because, in point of fact, the lord was completely dependent upon the work of the peasants, a whole network of customs was devised to create the impression that the opposite was the case."[38]

In considering any benefits the peasant may derive from his relation to the aristocrat, it is important not to overlook ideological and symbolic aspects of the matter. Thus, it is possible that some peasants derive real satisfaction from serving an aristocrat who has acquired fame and glory (though it seems more likely that they would neither know nor care). They might be pleased to belong to an aristocrat who can engage in ostentatious displays of his wealth, as when they enjoy watching some ceremony.

Quite possibly peasants feel they receive some benefits in the form of spiritual welfare or some rewards after death in return for services or payments rendered to religious aristocracies, like temples in ancient Egypt or the Catholic Church in feudal Europe or in postconquest Latin America,

37. Ibid., pp. 34–35, 36.

38. Landsberger and Landsberger, "The English Peasant Revolt of 1381," pp. 111–12.

or to rulers who claimed divinity or divine descent, like those of ancient Egypt, Japan, or Inca Peru. The priest's "task has been to help give legitimacy to the prevailing social order and to provide a way of both explaining and coping with those misfortunes and disasters for which the individual peasant's traditional economic and social techniques were inadequate."[39] The peasant may receive rituals, which may be supremely important to him, in return for his contribution. These may be provided by the local aristocracy to whom he paid his taxes, as in ancient Egypt, where many aristocrats, both royal officials and local landowners, were priests, and in China, where "by ancient tradition the district magistrate was the magician of the people."[40] Because virtually all aristocrats claimed some kind of religious or at least moral sanction for their rule, peasants, who share the same kind of religious or moral assumptions, may then not only accept their role as god given and inevitable, but may even derive some satisfaction from playing their proper part in the divinely ordained order. However, as I shall note later, peasants do not generally share the religious and moral assumptions of the aristocracy; even where they formally have the same religion, the difference between the aristocracy's "great" and the peasants' "little" tradition can be far-reaching. It seems more probable, then, that peasants receive no religious benefits, which they perceive as benefits, from the aristocracy.

39. Moore, *Social Origins of Dictatorship and Democracy*, p. 469.
40. Quoted in Wolf, *Peasants*, p. 52, from Fei, *Peasant Life in China*, p. 167.

6

Limited and Decentralized Government

Limited Government

In modern societies, the term "ruling class" is frequently used but is at best a vaguely and at worst an incorrectly applied concept, more suitable as a political symbol than for descriptive purposes. The matter is different with respect to traditional aristocratic empires. Here the aristocracy can be quite accurately described as a ruling class. All positions, or at least all the high positions, in the government, whether it be that of an estate with a few villages or of a huge empire, are occupied by aristocrats, and often all aristocrats (who are adult males) occupy government positions, or at least all the major functions served by the aristocracy may be characterized as governmental.

The aristocracy in its empires is a governing class par excellence. However, as we now turn to a discussion of the aristocracy in the government of aristocratic empires, the concept of government must be deprived of the connotations it has acquired in modern societies. There it is seen as, in some measure, representing and responding to the interests of at least some of the governed and providing them with some services and benefits. Government in aristocratic empires, however, is government of the aristocracy, by the aristocracy, and for the aristocracy. It may perhaps be best understood as an extractive enterprise, created and operated by the aristocracy to maintain itself as an aristocracy, that is, as a class that lives off the labor of the peasantry and does not engage in productive labor itself. Maquet, summing up his analysis of "the function of the political organization in Ruanda," comes to much the same conclusion when he says that "this political system was a means of maintaining a certain social order in which the group of rulers and their caste appropriated to their consumption a considerable part of the country's goods without having to use their labour in the productive process."[1]

1. Maquet, *The Premise of Inequality in Ruanda*, p. 159.

An American analyst of the sixteenth-century Ottoman empire, writing before the expansion of the welfare state, clearly understood that the empire's governing institution "limited its operations almost exclusively to its own affairs"[2] and was hence in its very nature different from what we think of as government today. His remarks are so relevant to aristocratic empires generally that they are worth quoting at length. The point they make is a crucial one in our context and may yet be widely overlooked because of the application of the modern concept of government to aristocratic empires.

"The Ottoman government did not include among its functions . . . the promotion of agriculture, industry, and commerce, the organization of a system of public and universal education, the adjustment of taxation and customs duties in the interest of the welfare of its subjects, or an extension of the activities and liberties of its subjects. Benevolence toward the common people had hardly emerged into the consciousness of any sixteenth-century state. Self-maintenance in power by the most available means, which were usually military force; increase of power, authority, and territory, by similar means; and, incidentally, an assurance of the well-being of all the privileged persons who were connected with the government, in proportion to their importance: these were the chief objects aimed at by the governments of that day, whether in the West or in the East."[3]

"The duties . . . of the treasury department reveal clearly the limited purposes and activities of the Ottoman government. The support of the Ruling Institution as standing army, court, and government was provided for; the revenues . . . for the support of the Moslem institution in its religious and charitable aspects were supervised; the navy was provided for. . . . But nothing was done for the great mass of the population. They were expected to furnish the means for these activities."[4]

"As a government . . . , the Ottoman Ruling Institution maintained public order, defended the empire against its enemies, and endeavored by conquest to enlarge its possessions. . . . A large proportion of its energies was devoted to obtaining and distributing the means of its own support, to keeping its own machinery in order, and to maintaining its authority within the empire. The idea of labor for the public welfare or of effort toward progress was not present."[5]

2. Lybyer, *The Government of the Ottoman Empire*, p. 149.

3. Ibid., p. 147. And, one may add, in the Western Hemisphere, too. In the Inca empire, "the job of government was to maintain itself, to produce taxes, armies, and to keep the peace," Moore, *Power and Property in Inca Peru*, p. 116.

4. Lybyer, *The Government of the Ottoman Empire*, pp. 174–75.

5. Ibid., pp. 193–94. "As late as the mid-nineteenth century almost all of the sultan's revenues were spent on the army, the navy, the civil list, and the servicing of the public debt,

What Gibb and Bowen say of government in the Arab provinces of the Ottoman empire is generally relevant to aristocratic empires. They speak of "the paradox . . . of a government, generally apathetic, unprogressive, and careless of the welfare of its subjects, and often arbitrary and violent in its dealing with them, and a society upon whose institutions and activities such a government had little or no effect. The explanation is to be found in the very lack of a complex, all-embracing political organization. . . . We may visualize Moslem society as composed of two coexisting groups, the relations between which were for the most part formal and superficial. One group formed the governing class of soldiers and officials, the other the governed class of merchants, artisans, and cultivators. Each was organized internally on independent lines, and neither group interfered with the organization of the other in normal circumstances."[6]

Another expert on the Middle East puts it this way: "The authority of government, based almost entirely on taxation, the maintenance of an army, and an age-old tradition of dynastic rule, was felt most immediately in the towns, less directly in the villages, and hardly at all among the tribes. The provinces were ruled by military governors or landed feudatories with only occasional interference from the capital. The nomadic tribes lived in what an apt Arabic idiom calls the 'land of insolence,' respecting no outside authority. The city economies were largely regulated by the autonomous guilds of the craftsmen. In the country at large, each village was a self-contained unit economically as well as politically. The principal emissary of authority to the village, the tax-gatherer, was less of a government official than a private contractor or subcontractor who recompensed himself as liberally as he could for the advances he had paid to his employers. Often the village was responsible for tax payments collectively—a circumstance which further reduced the control of authority over the *individual* peasant."[7]

An aristocratic empire, as previously emphasized, is best conceptualized not as a society but as composed of numerous societies. The lives of the overwhelming majority of the population in aristocratic empires—the peasants and what nomads may be included in an empire—are completely bounded by the community of the tribe and the village. The autonomy of their governments is only minimally disturbed by the aristocrats' government, and their institutions persist as aristocratic conquerors and rulers come and go. For example, Indian village panchayats (councils) existed under a variety of aristocratic empires from ancient times until they broke

---

with but an insignificant fraction reserved for education, public works, and other economic and social functions of government." Rustow, "The Politics of the Near East," p. 379.

6. Gibb and Bowen, *Islamic Society and the West*, 1:209.

7. Rustow, "The Politics of the Near East," pp. 378–79, italics in the original.

up under British rule. What little legislation the government enacts is likely to affect only the aristocracy and those engaged in trade and handicrafts and to become significant only where, as in ancient Rome, such an urban commercial population becomes numerous and the empire is hence no longer a traditional aristocratic one.

Generally, customs and traditions, often reinforced by religion, rather than laws made by a government, suffice to regulate the affairs of aristocratic empires. In the Middle East, "law itself was largely beyond the scope of the ruler, whose decrees in a few points supplemented or modified a universal structure of religious law and local custom."[8] Thus, in the Ottoman empire, the sultan was bound by the *Sheri* or sacred law of Islam, which was considered permanent and not subject to change, and, in effect, by custom. Even in the area in which he could legislate—much of it concerned with the affairs of the aristocracy—"he did not so much ordain and create anew as rearrange and put in order, reorganize and regulate."[9]

Similarly, in India, "neither king nor council were conceived of as legislative bodies. Rule-application and rule-adjudication rather than rule-making were their tasks. Thus the Indian state was limited in its activities, and was conceived of as an administrative structure. The state might expand externally—military expansion was in fact part of the dharma [the higher, cosmic law] of the ruler . . . —but internally it was to do only those tasks necessary to maintain the existing order."[10] "According to classical traditions, the function of the ruler was to maintain the system, not to change it."[11]

Feudal Western European governments exercised only judicial functions; as Perry Anderson puts it: "The pure feudal hierarchy . . . excluded any 'executive' at all, in the modern sense of a permanent administrative apparatus of the State for the enforcement of the law: the parcellization of

8. Ibid., p. 379.

9. Lybyer, *The Government of the Ottoman Empire*, p. 27. See also ibid., pp. 152–63. "In theory . . . the sultan had almost absolute powers, certainly over members of the Ruling Class, and through them the government and also over his subjects. In practice, however, the situation was quite different. The nature of the Ottoman system in fact left the sultan with very limited power. First of all, the scope of his authority was limited to functions involving the exploitation of the empire's wealth, promoting the institutions and practices of Islam and the other religions of his subjects, expanding and defending the territory of the empire, and keeping order within it. Therefore, significant aspects of Ottoman life were left to be dealt with autonomously . . . by . . . groups forming the corporative substructure of Ottoman society. . . . One result of this was that decay within the political structures of empires such as that of the Ottomans had much less effect on the operation of the system than one might imagine, since the system itself was organized to accomplish almost all matters that were of interest or concern to the people." Shaw, *History of the Ottoman Empire*, 1:165.

10. Weiner, *The Politics of Scarcity*, p. 14n.

11. Weiner, "The Politics of South Asia," p. 160.

sovereignty rendered one unnecessary and impossible. At the same time, there was no room for an orthodox 'legislature' of the later type either, since the feudal order possessed no general concept of political innovation by the creation of *new* laws. Royal rulers fulfilled their station by preserving traditional laws, not by inventing novel ones. Thus political power came for a period to be virtually identified with the single 'judiciary' function of interpreting and applying the existing laws."[12] "The essential function, duty, and right of the king 'is not to make law but to promulgate it.'"[13]

By modern standards, then, the functions of government in aristocratic empires are extremely limited. It is quite misleading therefore to describe such governments by conjuring up images of modern authoritarian or "totalitarian" governments. Indeed, it may be deceptive even to describe such governments as "governments," because with respect to the scope and range of their activities and the degree to which they affect the daily lives of their subjects they are very different from the governments of industrialized societies.[14] So little does government activity in aristocratic empires matter to their subjects that most of these are undoubtedly unaware or only very dimly aware of the fact that they are subjects of aristocratic empires.

Imbued as we are with modern notions of citizenship, which imply, if not a sense of participation in government, then surely a knowledge of the existence of one's government and one's country, we easily forget that most human beings never knew of a community more comprehensive than their village or their tribe.[15] Where much of the population is unaware of the existence of "its" government, it can be assumed that that government is so limited in scope as hardly to affect the lives of most of its subjects.

The Maintenance of Domestic Peace and Order

One of the major functions of the central government of modern societies—the maintenance of domestic peace and order—need not be performed by the governments of aristocratic empires with respect to the bulk of their population. The peasants largely govern themselves

12. Anderson, *Passages from Antiquity to Feudalism*, p. 153, italics in the original.

13. McIlwain, *The Growth of Political Thought in the West*, p. 189.

14. Perhaps "domination," derived from the Latin word for lord or master, may be more appropriate than "government," which stems from the Latin word for "to steer."

15. On what they call the "parochial political culture," see Almond and Verba, *The Civic Culture*, pp. 12–19. See also the quotation from Edward Banfield on p. 302, below.

within their villages, generally in accordance with immemorial custom, and there is little conflict between villages given the lack of communication between them. Thus, the autonomy of the peasant villages is the very basis on which aristocratic empires are built.[16]

There is then no need, even in big empires, for any huge bureaucracy or police force or more than a rudimentary judicial apparatus. Even in China, a commercialized empire under a single bureaucratic government for most of two millennia, the villages were in practice autonomous. Max Weber describes this well: "A 'city' was the seat of the mandarin and was not self-governing; a 'village' was a self-governing settlement without a mandarin. . . . The village temple served as a central agency. . . . The 'temple' had jurisdiction over petty causes and very often usurped jurisdiction over causes of all sorts. The government intervened only where interests of the state were concerned. The temple court, not the court authorities of the state, enjoyed the confidence of the people. The 'temple' took care of the roads, canals, defense, safety . . . and provided schools, doctors, medicaments, and burials insofar as the sibs could not or would not do so. . . . The government again and again ignored the village as a unit, purely fiscal interest repeatedly coming to the fore."[17]

From the point of view of the aristocracy, the peasantry exists to be exploited. The problem posed by the peasantry to the aristocracy, then, is chiefly that of tax collection and this is, immediately, the problem of the local landlord or the tax collector. The peasantry requires little, if any, regulation, supervision, or intimidation beyond that necessary to extract from it a part of its product, whether in kind or in cash or in the form of labor service. Peasant revolts, as will be explained later, are rare and highly localized—if they occur at all—in aristocratic empires. Thus, the peasantry generally poses no threat to domestic peace and order.

A threat may, however, be posed by the lower aristocracy to the peace and order of the higher aristocracy. Generally, conquerors are neither capable of removing and replacing ruling aristocracies nor do they find it necessary for their objectives. Thus, "the Inca were invaders and conquerors. In each new territory they superimposed Inca government on an

16. As Marx wrote to Engels one and a quarter centuries ago: "I do not think anyone could imagine a more solid foundation for stagnant Asiatic despotism." Letter to Engels of 14 June 1853, reprinted in Avineri, ed., *Karl Marx on Colonialism and Modernization*, p. 456. Marx also wrote that "these idyllic village communities, inoffensive though they may appear, had always been the solid foundation of Oriental despotism" (Marx, "The British Rule in India," p. 94). And Engels wrote later: "Such a complete isolation of the individual communities which creates throughout the country identical, but the exact opposite of common interests, is the natural foundation for *oriental despotism* and has always found its complement in it." Engels, "Soziales aus Russland," 18:563, italics in the original.

17. Weber, *The Religion of China*, pp. 91–93.

already existing one. . . . They did not do away with the local government and replace it. They did not disturb local hereditary interests. They simply added themselves at the top and made full use of the already existing administrative machinery, incorporating the local hereditary aristocracy into" their governmental system. "The Inca did not destroy the government of the people they conquered; they sat on top of them and used them."[18]

Particularly where the conquerors are nomads as yet inexperienced in administering systems of taxation as well as other governmental functions to be mentioned below, like the maintenance of flood control and irrigation systems and the performance of religious rites, they keep nonmilitary branches of the conquered aristocracy in power. Thus, the northern conquest dynasties of China all had to rely on the existing Chinese bureaucratic aristocracy for administrative experience in running their empire, and the Seljuk Turks depended on the Persian bureaucracy of the declining Abbasid empire they conquered. Similarly, Vandal and Ostrogothic conquerors imposed themselves on top of the administration of the late Roman empire, and the Christian priesthood survived the breakup of that empire and remained largely in charge of administration, science, and art while leaving warfare to the invading Germanic tribes almost as long as traditional aristocratic empires lasted in Western Europe. Millennia earlier, conquerors of Egypt had to rely on the priesthood. It evidently had been able to keep a monopoly of administrative skills and specialized knowledge, as of astronomy, needed to predict the flooding of the Nile, the basis of Egyptian agriculture. In this fashion several layers of government, originally sometimes ethnically distinct, may develop, which can eventually harden into castes, with the latest conquerors generally retaining the military function while earlier ones now specialize as bureaucrats and priests.

However, the conquered aristocracies are not necessarily deprived of their military functions either. Though the new conquerors may be able militarily to defeat each of the aristocrats in their new territory, they cannot occupy all their land and directly rule over, that is, tax, their peasants. For this, they must rely on the defeated aristocrats, who become tributaries or vassals of their conquerors and thus part of their governmental system (though one might, with equal justification, say that the conquerors become part of an already existing governmental system).

The Chou conquerors of China exercised direct rule only over their royal domain in their original homeland and parceled their newly conquered territory out to various Chou leaders and allies. They also left much of it to the conquered indigenous clan leaders and even the descendants of the defeated Shang dynasty. Thus many small states developed

18. Moore, *Power and Property in Inca Peru*, pp. 100, 101. See also ibid., p. 122.

that became virtually independent during the later Chou period.[19] In the half-millennium between the disintegration of the Maurya empire in the late third century B.C. and the rise of the Gupta empire in A.D. 320, when India consisted of numerous warring kingdoms, "more often than not, kings followed the traditional advice to refrain from annexing conquered territory. The vanquished king, or a close relative, would be restored to the throne—the state becoming a feudatory. Or, when annexation did take place (as it did occasionally in the Gupta epoch), the former king might serve as a provincial officer."[20] When the Muslim Sultanate of Delhi (1206–1526) expanded south, local princes were often not removed but entered into tributary relations with the sultan. His successor, the Mogul emperor, left hereditary Hindu rajahs to rule territories within his empire. Similarly, the Mongol Khanate of the Golden Horde took tribute and military contingents from princes all over Russia, but left them in power.

The aristocrat in immediate control of some land and peasants usually receives his income in the form of rent or services from the peasants. Quite often, even kings and emperors have their own estates, the crown lands, on which they can rely for a direct income. However, in addition, they and the higher aristocracy generally receive income through taxation, whether they are—or are the successors to—chiefs of the original conquering tribe or the conquerors of already established aristocrats. The taxes they receive also come from the peasantry, but these cannot go directly to the higher rulers. They may be collected for the rulers by bureaucrats and tax collectors who retain part of them, but more often the lower aristocracy passes part of its income up to the higher one in the form of cash or goods, or the lower aristocracy may provide services or equipment to the higher one, particularly as required for warfare.

The conquered or lower aristocrats thus serve as agents of their conquerors or their rulers, but they always remain their potential enemies, too, ready to throw off the "yoke" of the higher aristocracy, that is, to refuse to pass on part of what they have taken from their peasants and to keep it all to themselves.[21] The higher aristocrats, of course, seek to control them by force or the threat of force or by various divide-and-rule tactics. Thus, they may assign privileges to some of the conquered over the others, they may integrate the military forces of some into their own, thus

19. Bodde, "Feudalism in China," p. 53.

20. Drekmeier, *Kingship and Community in Early India*, p. 180.

21. In Russia, "at first, the Mongols themselves collected the tribute. Then the Grand Dukes of Moscow succeeded in getting permission from the khans to do the collecting for them. . . . When the Tatar yoke began to slip, they continued to levy the tribute, but did not pay it regularly to the Mongol suzerain, and by the end of the [fifteenth] century kept it all for their own uses." Blum, *Lord and Peasant in Russia*, p. 105.

giving the conquered some interest in the conquerors' further conquests, or they may appoint some of the conquered aristocrats to collect tribute from others. Bendix, referring to the relation of the king to his vassals says: "Apparently they simultaneously needed and fought one another. Gregory of Tours commented in the seventh century that in the relations of the Merovingian ruler Clovis with his kindred, he 'needs them, and yet they are in his way.'"[22]

The resulting system of government, if it can be called that at all, amounts in some ways to what in modern British colonial practice came to be known as indirect rule and in other ways to a permanent state of actual or potential war or civil war. The medieval Holy Roman Empire illustrates both of these aspects of government in a feudal empire.[23] However, the same thing could be true of empires often described as centralized and bureaucratic. Thus a contemporary observer of the late Mogul empire in India wrote about 1700: "Usually the viceroys and governors are in a constant state of quarrel with the Hindu princes and *zamindars*—with some because they wish to seize their lands; with others to force them to pay more revenue than is customary" and "usually there is some rebellion of the rajahs and *zamindars* going on in the Moghul kingdom."[24] That, in the Inca empire, "there was great concern with rebellion and tax cheating is shown by the precautions taken. These fears probably had a foundation in fact."[25] And with reference to imperial China, Owen Lattimore speaks of "an unending rivalry between the imperial authority and the local potentates, either in their private capacity as landlords or their official capacity as delegated tax farmers for the central imperial authority, over the control and disposition of the grain surplus."[26]

In any case, it is clear that domestic peace and order are maintained and income is collected by the higher aristocracy in a very decentralized fashion. For the central government—to use a hardly applicable modern term —of this higher aristocracy, domestic peace, order, and income are all much more threatened by the lower aristocracy than by the peasantry.

22. Bendix, *Kings or People*, p. 227.

23. "To an extent, the ruler must accept the autonomy of his dependents. But since his own position requires the collection of taxes in money and kind, he must also control their jurisdictions. The extent and limits of royal authority are thus uncertain, and this uncertainty lies at the root of the protracted feuds which fill the annals of medieval history" (ibid., p. 222).

24. Quoted by Habib, *The Agrarian System of Mughal India*, p. 335, from Nicolao Manuchy, *Storia do Mogor, 1656–1712* (London: Government of India, 1907–8), 2:431–32, 462.

25. Moore, *Power and Property in Inca Peru*, p. 114.

26. Lattimore, "Inner Asian Frontiers," p. 30.

Thus, government in aristocratic empires is not only government of, by, and for the aristocrats but also government over aristocrats.

"Feudal" and "Centralized Bureaucratic" Empires

The degree of decentralization of aristocratic empires, that is, the extent of the independence of the lower from the higher aristocracy and of the ability of the former to oppose and even fight the latter, varies among aristocratic empires. Two types of empires are often distinguished, centralized bureaucratic and feudal ones.[27] The principal difference between them was pointed out by Machiavelli centuries ago: "The kingdoms known to history have been governed in two ways: either by a prince and his servants, who, as ministers by his grace and permission, assist in governing the realm; or by a prince and by barons, who hold their positions not by favour of the ruler but by the antiquity of blood."[28]

In practice, the difference between these two types of aristocratic empires is merely one of degree, and for our purposes of generalization no sharp distinction need be drawn between them. The degree of control exercised by the central government even in the bureaucratic ones must not be overestimated and is not as great as the words "centralized" and "bureaucratic" with their modern connotations suggest. By modern standards, government in all traditional aristocratic empires, whether feudal or bureaucratic, is limited and decentralized.[29]

The poor communications typical of aristocratic empires compel the local aristocracy to make decisions more or less independently of the central aristocracy. This is true whether or not, according to the prevailing aristocratic ideology, all authority is derived from the central authority, usually a monarch. "When one considers that the First Cataract was five hundred miles from the capital at Memphis and remembers that communi-

27. For an attempt to develop generalizations about the political systems of the former, see Eisenstadt, *The Political Systems of Empires*, and for a comparative historical study of the latter, see Coulborn, ed., *Feudalism in History*.

28. Machiavelli, *The Prince and the Discourses*, p. 15. For a brief summary of differences between bureaucratic and feudal empires, see Huntington, *Political Order in Changing Societies*, pp. 148–49.

29. Eisenstadt does not classify a single one of the numerous traditional bureaucratic empires he analyzes as characterized by "high centralization." All have "low" or "medium" centralization; only some not regarded here as traditional empires are classified as highly centralized, that is, Spain (1621–1701), Sweden (1770–1809), Prussia (1640–1740), France (1660–1789), and England (1509–1783). See variable VI, "Centralized Polity," in Table I in Eisenstadt, *The Political Systems of Empires*, pp. 388–93.

cations along the Nile must have been slow, it will be clear that the outlying royal officials and the outlying provincial rulers had to be accorded a generous measure of individual initiative."[30] Similarly, writing of the early feudal age in Western Europe, Bloch says: "The relative slowness of the messengers, the mishaps that at every stage threatened their progress, meant that the only effective authority was the one on the spot. Forced constantly to take the gravest steps . . . every local representative of a great potentate tended only too naturally to act for his personal advantage and thus finally to transform himself into an independent ruler."[31] To be sure, some bureaucratic empires had better systems of communication than others—the monarchs of Peru could communicate more quickly with their local subordinates than those of China—but even their position was in no way comparable to that of a modern central government.[32]

Also, given primitive means of transportation, when taxes are paid largely in kind rather than in money, they cannot be collected by a central government and disbursed by it if the empire is at all large. The empire then has to be divided into districts the extent of which is limited by the available means of transportation. In each such district, taxes are collected locally and appropriated more or less directly by the local aristocracy providing it with far-reaching autonomy and often the desire for total independence from the higher aristocracy.[33]

There are, in fact, limits to the dependence of any traditional aristocratic bureaucracy on its employer, the imperial government. Because that government cannot collect directly from the peasantry all the taxes the peasants pay and then in turn pay the bureaucrats their entire income, these are not totally dependent on the central government. It is usually first the

30. Wilson, *The Burden of Egypt*, p. 90.

31. Bloch, *Feudal Society*, p. 65.

32. In the Inca empire, "in spite of a remarkable system of communication, geographical separation and size required a rather considerable delegation of power." Moore, *Power and Property in Inca Peru*, p. 107.

33. If the taxes will not go to the ruler, the ruler may have to go to the taxes. One way in which higher aristocrats can collect local taxes is to travel about and consume the peasants' surplus at its source. While this may reduce the dependence of the higher on the lower aristocracy, it hardly reduces the autonomy of the latter. Speaking of Charlemagne, G. G. Coulton writes that he "had no means of spending a considerable part of his income but by eating and drinking it, he and his servants, straight from the farm. We see him, as we see sovereigns and great nobles all through the Middle Ages, travelling from one estate to another with his ministers and his train: eating up the year's produce in a week or a few days, and then passing on to eat up a fresh estate." Coulton, *Medieval Panorama*, p. 47. Exactly the same is reported of the Gupta empire in fourth- and fifth-century India: "Kings . . . kept on the move with army, harem, court, and secretariat, which could not be fed without eating up the surplus wherever it was produced." Kosambi, *An Introduction to the Study of Indian History*, p. 283. See also Lenski, *Power and Privilege*, p. 205.

landowners and then the bureaucrats themselves who collect the taxes for the central government and they pass only a fraction of what they collect on to the government. In Burma, public servants received no salaries at all until the mid-nineteenth century. Local officials known by a title "which means literally 'the eater of a town' . . . were given the right to enjoy whatever revenues they could extract from the towns or princely fiefs under their jurisdiction." They were expected to retain for their own remuneration about a third or a fourth of the taxes they collected for the royal treasury.[34] In China, the extralegal but generally recognized income of an official was many times his salary—Barrington Moore cites estimates ranging from four to nineteen times the regular salary.[35] Max Weber said of China that "it went without saying that the office existed for the making of a fortune, which was objectionable only if done to excess."[36]

That "the office existed for the making of a fortune" makes clear that officials in bureaucratic empires served the same function as aristocrats in all aristocratic empires: they governed, not like modern bureaucrats to represent the interests of various groups among the governed (and thereby to represent their own), but to represent only their own interests and, especially, to enrich themselves. Their income, whether it came from the share of the peasants' taxes retained by the official or from payments made to him by landowners or by lower officials, was, as is the income of all aristocrats, derived from the peasantry and it was also a source of considerable independence of the central government.

Secondly, bureaucratic officials are much like feudal aristocrats in that they can, in practice, only be recruited from a narrow stratum, usually the lower aristocracy, sometimes from merchants, for no one else, certainly not peasants, can have or acquire the necessary skills. Also, to function effectively in their local areas, officials must cooperate with the local aristocracy, and it takes an aristocrat to cooperate with an aristocrat. Both the official's own aristocratic position, that is, his control of land and peasants, even if they are not in the area where he serves, and his links to the local aristocracy provide him with a power base independent of the central government.

Then, there is the matter of heredity and mobility discussed earlier. Even if they do not formally constitute a hereditary aristocracy, the officials in bureaucratic empires, like any advantaged group (except celibate ones) in any society, tend to pass their privileges on to their children. The latter, therefore, owe their positions to their birth rather than to the central government. Often, in the absence or virtual absence of a money economy,

34. Pye, *Politics, Personality, and Nation Building*, p. 70.
35. Moore, *Social Origins of Dictatorship and Democracy*, p. 172.
36. Weber, *The Religion of China*, p. 59.

bureaucrats are paid by being assigned land, that is, the right to live off the peasants on it. That land and the bureaucratic office that goes with it, too, are inherited by the bureaucrats' children which, again, blurs the distinction between bureaucratic and feudal empires and provides far-reaching independence to local aristocrats.

The central government itself is commonly loosely organized in aristocratic empires. Offices are not clearly distinguished in terms of their functions, and different elements in the government operate more or less independently of and even in conflict with each other. Aristocratic office-holders generally claim their offices by some right rather than by merit,[37] and may enjoy a good deal of autonomy when much or all of their wealth and incomes are derived independently of the ruler and when each has his own retinue and followers and sometimes his own territorial base. In the Ottoman empire, government integration should have been relatively high, at least in the sixteenth century, for all the government officials, including the highest ones, were the sultan's slaves, subject to appointment and removal (and execution) by him. Yet even here Lybyer speaks of "a tendency of the Ruling Institution toward decentralization and division into its component parts."[38] And Shaw agrees that "even within the Ruling Class the very complexity of the system made it extremely difficult for a single man—however autocratic he might have been in theory—to grasp the details sufficiently for him to require the bureaucrats to do what he wanted and ensure that they did so."[39] Indeed, once the sultan's bureaucratic slave-aristocrats received inheritable fiefs as rewards for their service, the distinction between the bureaucratic and the feudal character of the Ottoman empire becomes shadowy.

Finally, we must recall that in bureaucratic as well as in all traditional aristocratic empires few decisions are made by the government. The supposedly highly centralized bureaucracy does not interfere in the lives of the great bulk of the population much more than the feudal aristocracy. Thus, the bureaucratic government of the Ottoman empire has been interpreted as "that of a large slave-family, which secured its own interests and managed to the best advantage its own affairs, which cared little for the welfare of the great majority of the people of the empire, and which had dealings with them and attended to their affairs only when obliged to do so by the pursuit of its own aims."[40] With the scope of government very

37. In Sassanid Persia, "one was not only born into the [Zoroastrian] cleric class but was also born into a particular rank in that class. The highest cleric . . . was not recruited from below but took office on the basis of heredity." Bill, *The Politics of Iran*, p. 3.

38. Lybyer, *The Government of the Ottoman Empire*, p. 38.

39. Shaw, *History of the Ottoman Empire*, 1:165.

40. Lybyer, *The Government of the Ottoman Empire*, pp. 149–50.

limited by modern standards, the difference between feudal and bureaucratic empires in the degree of authority exercised by the central aristocracy does not seem so significant.

The distinction between the two types of traditional aristocratic empires
is roughly the same as Max Weber's distinction between feudalism and
patrimonialism.[41] Under the latter, government is an extension of the
household of the ruler and rests on his paternal authority, whereas feudalism involves a contract fixing mutual obligations among warriors. Two
points should be made comparing Weber's stress on this distinction and
my tendency to deemphasize it.

First, "Weber emphasized this distinction despite his own analysis of
many transitional phenomena because he was interested in the contrast
between the Orient, where estates as distinct from status groups did not
develop, and the Occident, where such estates helped shape the development of the modern state."[42] Weber was in much of his work concerned
with stressing the uniqueness of Western historical development and with
finding its bases in antiquity—thus, he contrasted the religious tradition of
ancient Judaism to those of China and India. I, on the other hand, prefer
to stress that the bases in traditional aristocratic empires of Western and
non-Western societies are similar and believe that the differences between
the two types of societies can be accounted for by differences in the
processes of modernization they have undergone.

Second and more important here, patrimonialism and feudalism were,
for Weber, ideal types used for analytical purposes, but he emphasized,
just as I do here, that in historical reality the distinction between them was
blurred. In his chapter on patrimonialism he showed how patrimonial
officials can gain de facto independence on the basis of grants of benefices,
like rights to an office, or of hereditary land grants.[43] In a section significantly entitled "Decentralized Patrimonial Domination," Weber then explained that "even under purely bureaucratic patrimonialism no administrative technique could prevent that, as a rule, the individual parts of the
realm evaded the ruler's influence the more, the farther away they were
from his residence. . . . Because of the inadequate means of transportation, if for no other reason, the governors do not render all of the contributions to the ruler, but only the surplus remaining after the local demands
have been met; as a rule, they pay only fixed tributes and with increasing
distance they become more and more independent in their disposition
over the military and tax capacities of their provinces. This is also a consequence of the need, in view of the lack of modern means of communica-

41. Weber, *Economy and Society*, 3:1006–1110.
42. Bendix, *Max Weber*, p. 361.
43. Weber, *Economy and Society*, 3:1031–44.

tions, for rapid decision-making by the officials in the case of enemy attacks on these marches. . . . Finally, there are the very remote areas whose merely nominally dependent rulers could be forced to pay tributes only through continually renewed campaigns of extortion."[44]

It may also be noted that Weber devoted a section of his chapter on patrimonialism to "the continuous struggle of the central power with the various centrifugal local powers." He concluded that "as a rule, the prince found himself compelled to compromise with the local patrimonial authorities or other *honoratiores*; he was restrained by the possibility of an often dangerous resistance, by the lack of a military and bureaucratic apparatus capable of taking over the administration and, above all, by the power position of the local *honoratiores*."[45]

Max Weber, then, cannot be cited as a believer in a sharp distinction in historical reality between feudal and bureaucratic (or patrimonial) empires[46] or as a believer in the highly centralized character of the latter. Although there are differences with respect to the degree of centralization of authority between the two types of empires, what matters more from our point of view is that both types are ruled by aristocracies. For one thing, most bureaucratic empires developed out of societies with a powerful landed aristocracy that frequently retained a great deal of its power.[47] For another thing, the new central government bureaucracy, or at least its upper levels, itself constitutes an aristocracy, whether it is a titled and hereditary nobility or not. It may live side by side or more or less merge with the older type of feudal aristocracy or may virtually replace it.

Decentralization in "Centralized Bureaucratic" Empires: A Brief Survey

A closer look at some empires commonly described as centralized bureaucratic ones[48] may be useful here to demonstrate that, though supposedly centralized, they were nevertheless highly decentralized by modern standards and, though bureaucratic, they were neverthe-

44. Ibid., p. 1051.

45. Ibid., pp. 1055, 1058.

46. It is noteworthy that Reinhard Bendix, one of the foremost contemporary interpreters of Weber, concludes on the basis of his own study of royal-aristocratic relations that "household government and 'fief,' and hence the terms *patrimonialism* and *feudalism*, lose their original meaning." Bendix, *Kings or People*, p. 228; italics in the original.

47. Eisenstadt, *The Political Systems of Empires*, p. 176.

48. All of those mentioned in this section, except the Carolingian one, are listed as "centralized historical bureaucratic empires" by Eisenstadt, ibid., p. 11.

less, much like feudal empires, governed by aristocracies. Included in this consideration will be some commercialized empires, notably China, for it may be assumed that if even they were decentralized and aristocratic, the same would be true a fortiori of traditional aristocratic empires.

China offers a good illustration of the possibility just mentioned of a central government bureaucracy virtually replacing an older aristocracy. There, as the feudal nobles under the Chou dynasty got control of the peasants' land and could replace the earlier sporadic payments of tribute by regular tax payments, they came to employ merchants or lower aristocrats as tax collectors who developed into paid bureaucrats.[49] In time, these bureaucrats came to assume a far greater role, first under the next dynasty (Ch'in, 221–207 B.C.), which in effect put them in the place of the old aristocrats, although these survived as titled sinecure holders for about a millennium. Also, new titled aristocrats were created by the later Chinese dynasties, the Mongols, the Ming, and the Manchus, both of imperial clansmen and of those rewarded for service, especially for military service. However, beginning about two thousand years ago, it was the centrally recruited, appointed, and salaried officials who administered the territorial subdivisions of the Chinese empire.

"The nobility, to be sure, lived lives of great luxury, but the real administrative power by this time lay in the hands of the centrally appointed bureaucracy . . . which was paid in cash or grain, not in land (though much of its capital was invested in land). Thus was created the vitally important official-gentry class, which in most later periods has been the effective ruling group in China, and which, though it tended to be self-perpetuating as a class, was non-titled and individually non-hereditary in the government posts it held."[50]

These Chinese bureaucrats can be regarded as aristocrats, as we regard all top bureaucrats in aristocratic empires, though the literature generally distinguishes them from aristocrats. Like other aristocracies, the gentry from which they were drawn lived in an agrarian society without engaging in productive labor by drawing its wealth from the land, that is, from the peasantry (except—the Chinese empire being commercialized rather than traditional—to the extent that they also engaged in trade). Based on the land, the bureaucrats enjoyed a good deal of autonomy from the central government even though they functioned as its paid employees. Thus even in a relatively highly centralized bureaucratic and commercialized

49. Eberhard believes that it was merchants who became tribute collectors and officials. *Conquerors and Rulers*, p. 39. Cho-yun Hsu denies this—*Ancient China in Transition*, p. 13n.—and thinks these were recruited from the lower aristocracy, "stewards . . . and other retainers of the noble households" (ibid., p. 97).

50. Bodde, "Feudalism in China," p. 70.

empire like China, the government system remained, by modern standards, highly decentralized. Hsiao-tung Fei concludes that "there was a *de facto* limit to the authority of the central government. Local affairs, managed in the community by the gentry, were hardly interfered with by the central authorities."[51]

Eberhard, disagreeing with Wittfogel's description of Chinese government as a highly centralized Oriental despotism,[52] points out that in medieval China "the local administration was independent, the chief-executive excepted. The governor was appointed by the central government, but his whole staff, sometimes far more than one hundred persons, was chosen by the governor either from his own friends and relatives or from local gentry, normally both." The governors were small kings in their areas able to manage them effectively "even if communication with the central authority was interrupted." Eberhard concludes that "local administration was usually in the hands of the local gentry." The governor both checked it on behalf of the central gentry and had to rely on it to maintain his own independence from the central authority. Therefore "we can hardly declare the system of Chinese administration as typically centralized."[53]

Similarly, Max Weber, who describes imperial China as a "unified bureaucratic" and a "patrimonial" as distinguished from a "feudal" state, nevertheless said that "like all farflung patrimonial states with undeveloped techniques of communication the scope of administrative centralization characteristically remained very limited."[54] "Until modern times, the Chi-

---

51. Fei, *China's Gentry*, pp. 83–84.

52. Wittfogel only admits that families, "villages, guilds, and secondary religious organizations . . . enjoyed certain politically irrelevant freedoms. These freedoms—which in some instances were considerable—did not result in full autonomy. At best they established a kind of Beggars' Democracy." Wittfogel, *Oriental Despotism*, p. 126. Balazs, too, describes the Chinese empire as "totalitarian" and its bureaucracy as "omnipotent." "If by totalitarianism is meant total control by the state and its executives, the officials, then it can indeed be said that Chinese society was to a high degree totalitarian. . . . No private undertaking nor any aspect of private life could escape official regulation. . . . This welfare state superintended, to the minutest detail, every step its subjects took from the cradle to the grave. It was a regime of red tape and petty fuss—yards and yards of tape and never-ending fuss." Balazs, *Chinese Civilization and Bureaucracy*, pp. 10–11. He also speaks of the Chinese empire as "a hierarchical, authoritarian state, paternalistic yet tyrannical; a tentacular welfare state; a totalitarian Moloch of a state" (ibid., p. 17). However, elsewhere he admits that "the villages had always enjoyed some degree of autonomy. . . . Moreover, they were far enough away from the seat of authority to be protected from the arbitrary exactions of officials in the imperial administration" (ibid., p. 70). Balazs also refers to the passage from Max Weber quoted on p. 123, above, which shows that China was anything but "totalitarian."

53. Eberhard, *Conquerors and Rulers*, pp. 63–65.

54. Weber, *The Religion of China*, p. 47.

nese empire, too, despite the homogeneity of its officialdom, showed these features of a conglomeration of satrapies, in part merely nominally dependent, which were grouped around the directly administered central provinces. Just as did the Persian satrapies, the local authorities retained the revenues from their provinces and used them first of all to cover the costs of local administration; the central government received only its fixed tribute."[55] And Weber explained how the very fact that the governor was always appointed from another province, which was supposed to make him independent of the local authorities, made him "entirely dependent upon the instructions of an unofficial adviser, a native man of literary education who was thoroughly familiar with local customs.... Obviously this resulted in actual power being vested in the hands of unofficial, native subordinates."[56]

Indicating that the so-called centralized bureaucratic empire of China was not so different from a feudal one, Max Weber says that "the official, like a feudal lord or satrap, was responsible to the central government (the sub-official to the provincial government) for the delivery of certain amounts. In turn he financed most of his administrative expenditures from fees and tax-income and retained a surplus.... His personal and administrative expenditures were not separated.... Moreover, superior officials drew their incomes from the gross income of the lowest-rung official who was directly at the source of the taxes. He had to transfer to this superior the often rather small amount which represented his obligation in the traditional tax register. Upon assuming office, and on regularly recurrent occasions, he had to make the largest possible 'gifts' in order to secure the good will of the superior.... Acquiring office was very costly (study, purchase, gifts, and 'fees') and the official ... was compelled to make the most of his short term of office. In the absence of fixed taxes and guarantees he could do this."[57]

The Chinese officials owed their autonomy to the fact that they were drawn from landowning families. To be sure, their power depended not directly on landownership, but on their official rank and position in the bureaucracy and it, in turn, could be obtained only by those holding academic titles or degrees. As was already stressed by Max Weber, "the educational qualification, however, in view of the educational means employed, has been a cultural qualification, in the sense of a general education.... The Chinese examinations did not test any special skills, as do our modern national and bureaucratic examination regulations for jurists, medical doctors or technicians.... The examinations of China tested

55. Weber, *Economy and Society*, 3:1052.
56. Weber, *The Religion of China*, pp. 49–50.
57. Ibid., pp. 56–59.

whether or not the candidate's mind was thoroughly steeped in literature and whether or not he possessed the *ways of thought* suitable to a cultured man and resulting from cultivation in literature"[58]—ways of thought ordinarily not accessible to a peasant.

Furthermore, to obtain a degree, wealth was in practice a necessity, either, in some cases, to permit the purchase of the degree or, more regularly, to provide the years of freedom from physical labor necessary to become a scholar and thus to become capable of passing the government examinations that established educational qualifications. And the wealth that was a necessary, though not a sufficient, condition for becoming an official was drawn principally from landownership, as even income derived from trade was commonly invested in land. If wealth made the official, the official in turn made wealth. He would, of course, invest it in landownership, thus perpetuating his family's gentry status and returning the investment it had made in providing him with an education.

Not all members of the gentry were officials, then, but virtually all higher officials were members of the gentry, and the functions of the two overlapping groups were inextricably intertwined.[59] For the gentry landowners, the presence of the officials served as a guarantee of their rights to their landed property and hence to the rents they collected from the peasants. Also, it was through officials that landlords obtained the construction of irrigation systems that improved the peasants' crops and hence the rents they paid. The officials, on the other hand, operated through the gentry, having no direct contact with the peasants. The gentry, forming the local elite in the peasant community, "constituted an indispensable part of the local government and acted as a medium between the government and the common people. It collected taxes for the government and palliated some of the official abuses for the peasantry."[60]

Thus, though dependent for his position on the central government, the Chinese official owed that position in good part to the fact that he was a member of the gentry himself and hence was a landowner in his home

---

58. Ibid., pp. 120–21; italics in the original. Weber notes that in earlier, feudal times, Chinese education, like that of ancient Greece, stressed, in addition to rites and literature, "the arts of the dance and of arms" (ibid., p. 122), making its aristocratic character even clearer. In feudal Chou China, "driving a war chariot . . . and archery were listed among the six arts that were supposed to constitute the basic knowledge of a nobleman." "The other four arts are music, poetry or literature, arithmetic, and *li. Li* seems to have meant, at least in the Confucian usage, the theory and practice of right conduct." Hsu, *Ancient China in Transition*, pp. 68–69, 204.

59. See Moore, *Social Origins of Dictatorship and Democracy*, pp. 162–73, and Anderson, *Lineages of the Absolutist State*, pp. 545–46, on the links between the Chinese bureaucracy and landownership.

60. Chow, *Social Mobility in China*, p. 8.

district. And he could operate as an official of the central government only by serving the interests of the gentry in the district to which he was assigned.

Finally, not only were Chinese bureaucrats drawn from a substantially hereditary group, the gentry, but at various times the sons of higher officials could enter the bureaucracy without examinations. Also, at least under the last two dynasties, that is, in the last six centuries of the empire, the top three of the nine ranks of the bureaucracy were officially hereditary for two or three generations.[61] This, too, provided the bureaucrats with independence of the central government and tended to blur the line between the feudal and the bureaucratic nature of the empire.

When considering the centralization of bureaucratic empires, it is instructive to look at the Ottoman empire. Under Suleiman I, according to Eisenstadt the "period of maximum centralization of bureaucracy,"[62] the Ottoman empire consisted of, first, territories directly administered according to an "approximately uniform" system; second, territories "less directly administered under special regulations"; third, "numerous tributary provinces"; and fourth, "certain protected or vassal states." Beyond this lay regions continually raided, especially for slaves, but not yet fully conquered, and outside that region was the "land of war" subject to future conquests. In some vassal states, the aristocracy paid regular tribute to remain in power, in others it did not; in Egypt the government of the Mamluks was retained under a Turkish governor with much of the annual revenue going to Turkey. Even some areas nominally under direct administration were "in very slight obedience" with tribal chiefs remaining in power, providing military service and sometimes taxes, as in Albania, Kurdistan, and Arabia.[63]

Generally, a symptom and cause of decentralization common to aristocratic empires prevailed in the bureaucratic Ottoman empire: a hodgepodge system of taxation, often resulting from the retention or mere modification of systems that had developed in different areas under their earlier aristocratic rulers before they were incorporated into the empire—and before additional taxes might be imposed on them. The Ottoman system thus "contained a great variety of taxes . . . differing from *sanjak* to *sanjak* and from town to town; and it collected its income by various methods and through various agencies."[64]

Furthermore, "the tangled nature of the Ottoman land system . . . acted powerfully toward decentralization, since the regulation of countless de-

---

61. Ho, *The Ladder of Success in Imperial China*, pp. 24–25.

62. Eisenstadt, *The Political Systems of Empires*, p. 445.

63. Lybyer, *The Government of the Ottoman Empire*, pp. 29–30.

64. Ibid., p. 176. See also Shaw, *History of the Ottoman Empire*, 1:120–21.

tails could be attended to better from points near at hand." Some of the directly administered lands were at the time of conquest granted to Muslims in return for a small tax or granted or left to Christians who paid a higher tax. Others remained state lands, some administered by the sultan, a large portion given to mosques as endowment, and another large portion granted in fief to Muslims who in return rendered military service to the cavalry as "feudal spahis."[65] The latter, who could, within limits, pass their land on by inheritance, "collected the revenues and exercised seigniorial jurisdiction in their estates"[66] leading to de facto decentralization even in directly administered state lands. The local officials of the central government, too, though appointed by the sultan from among his slaves, "were supported by the assignment of lands which they administered themselves."[67] Finally, with law considered inextricably linked to religion, "many internal matters were left to be regulated by the subject nationalities, which were organized as churches, and by the foreign colonies which remained under their own laws."[68] Clearly, the sixteenth-century Ottoman empire, bureaucratized and centralized as it may have been compared to European feudal empires—Machiavelli cites it as such—was still highly decentralized by modern standards.

Another aristocratic empire often thought of as a centralized bureaucratic one is ancient Egypt. Max Weber wrote that "Egypt almost appears as a single tremendous *oikos* [a decentralized household] ruled patrimonially by the pharaoh" and he thought it provided the first example of "consistent patrimonial-bureaucratic administration known to us" as a result of "the overriding importance of systematic centralized river-regulation and of the construction projects during the long season in which the absence of agricultural work permitted drafting on an unprecedented scale. The state was based on compulsory labor."[69] It seems more probable that ancient Egypt was, in fact, governed by "an autocratic bureaucracy headed by the king" at most only during a few periods totaling a few centuries out of the dynastic history of nearly three millennia.[70] During such periods, the provincial governors or nomarchs were appointed by the king, but even then

65. Lybyer, *The Government of the Ottoman Empire*, pp. 32, 31. See also Shaw, *History of the Ottoman Empire*, 1:26.

66. Lybyer, *The Government of the Ottoman Empire*, p. 100. See also Shaw, *History of the Ottoman Empire*, 1:125–27, and Anderson, *Lineages of the Absolutist State*, pp. 368–69, who, probably defining the term differently, says that the spahis exercised no seigniorial jurisdiction because they "played virtually no role in rural production at all."

67. Lybyer, *The Government of the Ottoman Empire*, p. 149; see also ibid., p. 174.

68. Ibid., p. 146.

69. Weber, *Economy and Society*, 3:1013, 1044, 1045.

70. Edgerton, "The Question of Feudal Institutions in Ancient Egypt," p. 121.

they may have been chosen from the same families. Because they collected their own taxes, it is probably true that "there was never a strong centralization, and the local administration was always ready to carry on without a central power."[71] Under weak dynasties, the nomarchs tended to become hereditary, and in periods of disintegration of the central government they ruled as petty kings and fought each other.[72] According to Manchip White, "the Nomarchs who constituted the provincial aristocracy were the descendants of the chieftains who ruled the pre-dynastic tribes of the Nile Valley"[73] which would make them similar to feudal lords in that respect. Talcott Parsons, too, emphasizes that within the territories into which ancient Egypt was administratively subdivided, "the national and territorial governments operated independently, utilizing separate means of organizational effectiveness. Thus, Egyptian society contained many bases of solidarity independent of the main hierarchy emanating from the divine king. Not all particularistic elements were so atomized that the whole society was at the disposal of the royal leadership for any tasks that advanced national policy. By modern standards, the possibilities for such mobilization were limited."[74]

In ancient Rome, another bureaucratic empire, the provinces were administered by individuals appointed by the central government, the Senate under the Republic, and also the emperor under the Empire. They were generally drawn from the aristocracy and in practice must have enjoyed a good deal of independence—even though Rome had undergone considerable commercialization—both because of poor communications and, above all, because they were financially independent of the central government. While they were salaried and served only temporarily and could not become as entrenched as a feudal aristocracy, they could collect more taxes and tribute than they passed on to Rome.[75] Of the provincial governors in Republican Rome, Boak says: "Bribes, presents, illegal exactions, and open confiscations were the usual means of amassing wealth. The almost sovereign position of the governor, with his . . . freedom from immediate senatorial control, guaranteed him a free hand."[76]

71. Petrie, *Social Life in Ancient Egypt*, p. 44.

72. Edgerton, "The Question of Feudal Institutions in Ancient Egypt," pp. 124, 126.

73. White, *Ancient Egypt*, p. 57.

74. Parsons, *The Evolution of Societies*, p. 58. In a footnote to the next to the last sentence quoted here, Parsons refers to "this erroneous viewpoint" of Karl Wittfogel's.

75. On the imperial "civil service" and system of taxation, see Mattingly, *Roman Imperial Civilization*, pp. 119–36, 185–87.

76. Boak and Sinnigen, *A History of Rome Through A.D. 565*, p. 153. Also, the institutions of the conquered people—tribal or aristocratic—were largely preserved, though urbanization was advanced, so that Rostovtzeff could say that: "The Empire in the second century

In the bureaucratic Maurya empire of India in the fourth century B.C., "the provincial governors maintained their own courts and ministerial councils, and, owing to the difficulty of communication with the central government, autonomy tended to vary proportionately with distance from the imperial capital." The next major empire in India, that of the Guptas, who ruled from 320 into the sixth century A.D., "comprised a network of self-governing tribes and tributary kingdoms, their chiefs often serving as representatives of the imperial power. The central authority was remarkably tolerant of local variation. . . . The emperor has *de jure* power to dismiss his officials, but there is little doubt that the tenure of these district officers rested in fact on their local strength. Such offices tended to become hereditary."[77] The political system of the Mogul empire, another bureaucratic empire in India two millennia after the Maurya one, is described by Barrington Moore as "an agrarian bureaucracy imposed on top of a heterogeneous collection of native chieftains differing widely in resources and power." Though office was not supposed to be inherited, and the wealth of the officeholder was to revert to the central government, "the Hindu chiefs, local rulers whom the Moguls had conquered and left in authority in return for loyalty to the new regime, were an important exception." "Very widely, though not universally, the Mogul emperors found it necessary to rule and tax through native authorities. The general term for these intermediaries was *zamindars*."[78]

In the Aztec empire, a province was "no more than a financial frame within which the incorporated cities lived under widely varying political regimes. . . . In every case, each city kept its political and administrative autonomy, with the one condition that it paid its tax, supplied its military contingent and submitted its law suits to Mexico or Texcoco as the final court of appeals. There was, therefore, no true centralisation: what we call the Aztec empire was in fact a somewhat lax confederation of city-states with widely differing political organizations."[79]

Similarly, the Inca "empire was made up of different states, confederations, rural communities, and tribes, all keeping their own individuality,

---

presented more than ever the appearance of a vast federation of city-states." "The imperial bureaucracy very seldom interfered with local city affairs. It dealt almost exclusively with the collection of taxes (mostly through the cities), with the administration of the imperial and state domains, and with one part of jurisdiction." Rostovtzeff, *The Social and Economic History of the Roman Empire*, 1:135, 138.

77. Drekmeier, *Kingship and Community in Early India*, pp. 168, 186.

78. Moore, *Social Origins of Dictatorship and Democracy*, pp. 318, 319, 325. In the pre-French-colonial Cambodian kingdom, the great officials in the outer provinces were "almost independent petty rulers." Osborne, *Politics and Power in Cambodia*, p. 15.

79. Soustelle, *Daily Life of the Aztecs*, p. xxii.

traditions, and leaders."[80] In the face of misinterpretations of and by the Spanish chroniclers, the most reliable study of Inca government and law stresses the de facto decentralization of the Inca empire and repeatedly refers to its bureaucracy as a "myth."[81] Sally Falk Moore says that "there is strong evidence that the completely government-supported Inca bureaucracy so often admired may not have existed." "When the powers and obligations of each rank are examined and the source of income of officials is closely investigated, and when the hereditary nature and local ties of most offices are considered, the decimal system of ranking ceases to appear as a modern salaried bureaucracy and begins to look more like a landed aristocracy."[82]

The local officials of the Inca empire were the local rulers of the territories the Incas had conquered. They remained local rulers and they retained their own land after the conquest,[83] both "their land and government posts being generally hereditary."[84] Rather than being salaried, they "were not supported out of Inca tax-stores." Indeed, "the governors and [local aristocrats] enforced the Inca's rule, his taxes and laws, but they did not neglect to fill their own larders at the same time. This exploitation by officials for themselves was as much a part of the system as was their job in producing what Cuzco demanded. The conception of a selfless, salaried bureaucracy melts away on close inspection of the actual economic arrangements"[85] and that of a rather independent landed local aristocracy emerges, not very different from those of other aristocratic empires.

This conclusion runs counter to what Moore calls "a general overestimate of the magnitude of imperial government" in Peru. According to her careful study of the Inca tax system, "this system of centralized revenues produced by a submissive population, all at the command of the Inca, and principally for the imperial institutions—the Inca and the Sun—is largely a construct of chroniclers rather than a characteristic of Inca government."[86] "It is clear enough that neither agricultural tax produce, nor the performance of [corvée] service was expended principally on a national level. Quite the contrary, the largest part of both appears to have been expended within the locality or the area of the province. . . . The normal economic

80. Métraux, *The History of the Incas*, p. 110.

81. Moore, *Power and Property in Inca Peru*, pp. 13, 90, 98.

82. Ibid., pp. 13–14, 15; see also ibid., p. 133.

83. Ibid., pp. 14–15, 27–31.

84. Ibid., p. 131; see also ibid., pp. 94–98.

85. Ibid., pp. 131, 72.

86. Ibid., pp. 66, 49.

task of serving and supporting the local governing classes seems to have been a proportionately large part of the tax burden. . . . There is no reason to suppose that the principal tax burden was for imperial purposes."[87] The Inca's imperial establishment itself, on the other hand, was in part supported from Inca family estates,[88] just as other rulers of aristocratic empires were heavily dependent on their own crown lands.

Charlemagne's imposition of a centralized administrative system on his enlarged Frankish realm was at least an attempt to form a bureaucratic empire. Military and judicial powers were delegated to officials who were to govern the 250 to 350 counties into which the entire empire was divided. However, these counts were drawn from the great aristocratic families and were not salaried but received a share of the local revenues and landed endowments and hence enjoyed considerable independence. "When the king's power was weak, he found it difficult to transfer or dismiss a count; during the ninth century it became increasingly common for son to succeed father in this office. . . . The count was thus an agent of power who, unless the ruler was strong, was more likely to behave like a local potentate than an official, an agent whose subordination to the central power could not be taken for granted. In this they resemble some of the pashas found in Arab and Turkish states." "It must be stressed that even during periods of relative strength, the Frankish monarchy never had organs powerful enough to ensure that the decisions of royal authority were fully implemented throughout the length and breadth of the realm. The monarchy was not even in a position to maintain the public peace at a satisfactory level, that is, to provide normally effective protection for persons and property."[89] Within the century of Charlemagne's death, his centralized empire became the heartland of decentralized West European feudalism.

Finally, we may quote Mosca who, referring particularly to the Abbasid caliphs, says that "one of the most frequent causes for the rapid breaking up of the Mussulman states was the practice of allowing governors of the separate provinces to conscript troops, and to collect directly the taxes that paid for them. Such a concentration of power in their hands made it easy for them to create personal followings in their armies, so that they could proclaim their independence, or at least become independent in fact,

87. Ibid., pp. 63, 65. Just as much of the corvée performed on land formally set aside for the Inca in each village produced taxes for the local aristocracy, so "lands of the Sun . . . were not simply a great block of fields or terraces belonging to the 'Empire Church.' They were subdivided into small plots whose produce was allocated for many local purposes and local deities, only a part going to provincial capitals and to Cuzco, to support the official national religion of the realm" (ibid., p. 26).

88. Ibid., pp. 33–35.

89. Ganshof, *The Carolingians and the Frankish Monarchy*, pp. 91, 90. See also Eisenstadt, *The Political Systems of Empires*, pp. 28–29.

though paying a nominal deference to the caliph."[90]

Effective decentralization, then, is likely to prevail even in commercialized empires, let alone in traditional ones, and not only where, as in feudal ones, the local rulers control their land and peasants by inheritance. In formally centralized, bureaucratic empires, the ruler may grant the right to exploit peasants in a particular area to his bureaucrats, but while he may retain the right of eminent domain, they are likely to constitute the effective government in these areas. Even where the central government grants no land, but pays salaries to its officials, as in the Chinese and Roman empires, it is these bureaucrats who collect the taxes. Whether they are officially supposed to retain a portion as their remuneration, as was true, for example, in Charlemagne's empire, in Burma, and under the caliphate, or not, as in China and Rome,[91] they can and generally do keep more than they are entitled to and gain a good deal of independence.[92] Even mere tax farmers may assume various governmental functions that the central government may in time be unable to recapture. "Those who hold such definitively appropriated powers then become, at the very least, landlords, as opposed to mere landowners, and often come into the possession of extensive governing powers in political organization."[93] Though in form appointed officials, they try to make their positions hereditary and to pass both their property and their powers on to their sons. Thus, tax farming, initially a characteristic of centralized systems, can lead to decentralization and to a system classified as a form of "feudalism" by Max Weber who cites especially the Indian Zamindars and Rumanian Boyars as examples of tax farmers turned landlords.[94] Elsewhere he refers to "a stratum of landlords which developed out of tax farming and military prebendalization. The tax farmers and military prebendaries had to assume the administrative costs of their districts and to guarantee all military and financial contributions. If successful, these landlords had a free hand and little fear of intervention by central power."[95] It appears, then, that so-called centralized bureaucratic empires are, in fact, decentralized and that their bureaucracies are, with respect to the characteristics that matter to us, aristocracies not unlike feudal ones.

90. Mosca, *The Ruling Class*, p. 345.

91. Other examples from the kingdoms of Dahomey and of Ankole in Uganda of tax collectors exacting or retaining more than the king authorized are cited in Lenski, *Power and Privilege*, p. 176.

92. For a good summary analysis of "patrimonial," that is, inherited, and "prebendal," that is, granted, domains, see Wolf, *Peasants*, pp. 50–52.

93. Weber, *Economy and Society*, 1:261.

94. Ibid., pp. 259–61.

95. Weber, *The Religion of India*, pp. 69–70.

7

The Governmental Functions
of the Aristocracy

Warfare

Limited and decentralized as government in aristocratic empires is, as I stressed in the last chapter, certain minimal governmental functions must be performed by it, that is, by the aristocracy.

The military function is one of two minimum functions of the aristocracy —the other one being tax collection—and, in the case of conquest empires, it is also its original function. Thus, in India, "the Mogul conquest was achieved by an army, and the army became a government."[1] Similarly, "the Ottoman government had been an army before it was anything else. Like the Turkish nations of the steppe lands, the Ottoman nation was 'born of war and organized for conquest.' Fighting was originally the first business of the state and governing the second."[2] Long after the formation of the Ottoman empire, its Ruling Institution remained "at once the government, the army, and the nobility."[3] Thus to speak of the military function as a governmental function of the aristocracy is a modern and somewhat misleading description of the situation in many aristocratic empires, for example, those of feudal Western Europe: the aristocracy *is* the military and it *is* the government.

There is a powerful economic link tying the aristocracy to warfare: "The nobility was a landowning class whose profession was war: its social vocation was not an external accretion but an intrinsic function of its economic position. . . . The typical medium of interfeudal rivalry . . . was military and its structure was always potentially the zero-sum conflict of the battlefield, by which fixed quantities of ground were won or lost. For land is a

1. Lybyer, *The Government of the Ottoman Empire*, p. 285.

2. Ibid., p. 90. The quotation within this quotation is from Léon Cahun, *Introduction à l'Histoire de l'Asie: Turcs et Mongols des origines à 1405* (Paris: A. Colin & Cie., 1896), p. vii.

3. Lybyer, *The Government of the Ottoman Empire*, p. 195.

natural monopoly: it cannot be indefinitely extended, only redivided. The categorical object of noble rule was territory."[4]

Initially, warfare may be carried on to expand the holdings and thus the income of the aristocracy, but then it continues also to protect the area controlled by the aristocracy from warlike tribes and rival aristocracies. With each ruling aristocracy necessarily suspicious of the others, because each can maintain itself only by being ready for war and thus by threatening the others, preventive wars and wars of prestige are added to wars carried on for expansion and for defense. The Mogul emperor Akbar (1556–1605) said that a monarch should "ever be intent on conquest, otherwise his enemies rise in arms against him."[5]

Métraux deduces from "the character of Inca civilization . . . theories as to the nature of [their] devouring imperialism" that are, in fact, much more generally relevant to an explanation of the warfare and expansionism of aristocratic empires. To be sure, we can understand them only if we appreciate the importance to aristocrats both of intangible honor and glory and of tangible wealth, matters to be taken up in the next two chapters on the values of aristocracies and on the stakes of aristocratic politics. "First of all on a psychological level, the Incas, chiefs of warlike tribes, were accustomed to defend themselves against attack by their neighbors and to pillage them whenever the opportunity arose. Ambition, vanity, and personal rivalry may have played a part in first forming the aggressive policy of the Incas. War would then become a type of ideal to which they would conform in order to retain their prestige and dignity. . . . Each conquest increased the wealth of the state in lands and tribute . . . the conquest of a province meant new supplies of soldiers and workmen. As the number of officials needed to run the empire increased, the Inca would have to obtain new lands to be able to reward his dignitaries and officers, or to obtain raw materials for the maintenance of his civil service."[6]

Warfare, then, becomes virtually continuous in traditional empires. The temple of Janus, opened only in wartime, is said to have been closed for only two brief periods (in 235 and 29 B.C.) in the twelve-hundred-year history of the Roman empire.[7] Speaking of the post-Carolingian period, Marc Bloch refers to "the state of perpetual war—invasions as well as internal strife—in which Europe henceforth lived."[8] "One compilation

4. Anderson, *Lineages of the Absolutist State*, p. 31.

5. Quoted in Rawlinson, *India*, p. 304.

6. Métraux, *The History of the Incas*, p. 57.

7. This Roman example may not be as relevant as it is striking, however. The first few centuries of slow Roman expansion through Italy can probably not be ascribed to an aristocratic policy of conquest, and in its later centuries Rome was commercialized.

8. Bloch, *Feudal Society*, p. 160.

records that in the 234 years between 1228 and 1462, northern Russia witnessed a total of 133 foreign invasions and 90 feuds among rival principalities."[9] During the 250 years from 1450 to 1700, the Ottoman empire was not at war for only thirty-eight years.[10] Similarly, Chou China had thirty-eight "peaceful years" in the period from 722–464 B.C.[11] The Aztec empire was "always incomplete, always needing more work; so the Mexican, who in any case was of a warlike temper, rarely laid aside his arms. . . . Thus arose a tendency to think that it was the Aztecs' business to make war, and other peoples' business to work for them."[12]

If anything, empires even less touched by commercialization were even more warlike. The ancient "Oriental monarchies were created by war, maintained by continual war, and eventually destroyed by war."[13] The Inca empire was evidently permanently at war on its borders: "Either the Incas were conquering new peoples, or defending what they had taken. Many were preventive wars; others were undertaken to keep the professional army occupied."[14] And Donald Levine says that "the most cursory reading of Ethiopian history cannot but support the generalization made by Ludolphus, who wrote three centuries ago: 'The (Abyssinians) are a Warlike People and continually exercis'd in War . . . neither is there any respit but what is caus'd by the Winter, at what time by reason of the Inundations of the Rivers, they are forc'd to be quiet.' "[15] Similarly, the Tutsi of Ruanda "were never permanently at peace with their neighbors, and when they had an alliance with some of them it was in order only to be free to concentrate their forces on others."[16]

One major exception to the generalization stated here is ancient Egypt, an aristocratic empire that was at peace much of the time. Substantially isolated in the Nile valley with no fertile land immediately adjacent and accessible and with only occasional serious threats from neighboring nomads, the Old Kingdom engaged in no permanent expansion, though military expeditions were sent across the Sinai into Asia, south into the

9. Bendix, *Kings or People*, p. 108; for additional figures indicating the frequency of war in early Russian history, see ibid., pp. 89–90, 96, and 110–11. See also Blum, *Lord and Peasant in Russia*, pp. 59–60.

10. Computed from a table in Wright, *A Study of War*, p. 653.

11. Hsu, *Ancient China in Transition*, table on p. 56. In the 242 years between 463 and 222 B.C., there were eighty-nine years without wars (ibid., table on p. 64).

12. Soustelle, *Daily Life of the Aztecs*, p. xxiii.

13. Childe, *Man Makes Himself*, p. 265.

14. von Hagen, *Realm of the Incas*, p. 198.

15. Levine, "The Military in Ethiopian Politics," p. 6. The quotation is from Job Ludolphus, *A New History of Ethiopia*, 2nd ed. (London, 1684), p. 217.

16. Maquet, *The Premise of Inequality in Ruanda*, p. 116.

Sudan, and west into Libya. The Middle Kingdom pushed its domain into the Sudan and the western oases, but it was not until about half way through the three thousand years of dynastic history that "Thut-mose III was to introduce a formal and consistent policy of military and political imperialism."[17]

In the aristocratic conquest empire, the aristocracy is, above all, a war machine, and warfare is its normal way of life. The aristocracy's social organization, therefore, and its interests, habits, and ideologies are attuned to warfare from its very origins. "Since warfare was the predominant activity of the Zulu state, no part of social life was entirely free from the vicissitudes of military action. . . . Every part of the kingdom was geared to perpetual conquest."[18] Similarly, the traditional "Islamic States, like the Ottoman Empire itself, were essentially warrior and plunderer in cast: founded on conquest, their whole rationale and structure was military."[19] As Joseph Schumpeter put it, "created by wars that required it, the machine now created the wars it required"[20] and as General Burgoyne says in Bernard Shaw's *Devil's Disciple*: "My good sir, without a Conquest you cannot have an aristocracy."[21]

In the minds of aristocrats, warfare may not need any justification—it may appear to them as an obvious, normal aspect of life. Max Weber noted with reference to India, "that a king should ever fail to consider the subjugation of his neighbors by force or fraud remained inconceivable to secular and religious Hindu literature. When the founder of the Mahratt empire failed to conduct war for one year, the neighboring lords considered it a sure indication that he was mortally ill."[22] "The Inca state was based on the supposition that war is the natural state of man,"[23] and "from the Ruanda point of view this policy of imperialism and looting did not require any rationalization."[24] Among the Aztecs, a conquering tribe, not only the aristocracy, which was just becoming hereditary when their empire was destroyed, but "every man, whatever his origin, either was a warrior or wished to be one. . . . A boy-child was dedicated to war at birth. His umbilical cord was buried together with a shield and some little ar-

17. Wilson, *The Burden of Egypt*, p. 174; see also ibid., p. 82. For a detailed study, see Kemp, "Imperialism and Empire in New Kingdom Egypt."

18. Walter, *Terror and Resistance*, pp. 146–47.

19. Anderson, *Lineages of the Absolutist State*, p. 505.

20. Schumpeter, "The Sociology of Imperialism," p. 25.

21. Shaw, *The Devil's Disciple*, 2:140.

22. Weber, *The Religion of India*, p. 64.

23. von Hagen, *Realm of the Incas*, p. 196.

24. Maquet, *The Premise of Inequality in Ruanda*, p. 116.

rows, and in a set speech he was told that he had come into this world to fight."[25]

In eleventh-century France, "the noble was bred for war, trained for war, and passed his life fighting. He fought for amusement, for profit, and from a sense of duty."[26] The same is said of the aristocratic followers of raiding Viking princes in Kievan Russia when the *Tale of the Raid of Igor*, the great epic of that age a millennium ago, describes them as "swaddled under trumpets, cradled among helmets, nursed at the spear's point. . . . Like grey wolves in the field they roam, seeking honor for themselves, and glory for their prince." And they said to Prince Igor: "Go forth with us, O Prince, after tribute, that both you and we may profit thereby."[27] "It was the conception of the necessity of war, as a source of honor and as a means of livelihood, that set apart the little group of 'noble' folk from the rest of society." "Fighting was for them not merely an occasional duty to be performed for the sake of their lord, or king, or family. It represented much more—their whole purpose in life."[28] What Schumpeter says of "warrior nations" is true of the traditional aristocracy: "War is never regarded as an emergency interfering with private life; but, on the contrary, that life and vocation are fully realized *only* in war."[29]

Stressing the economic bases of warfare, Anderson argues that "warfare was not the 'sport' of princes, it was their fate; beyond the finite diversity of individual inclinations and characters, it beckoned them inexorably as a social necessity of their estate."[30] True as that is, warfare may still play a role somewhat akin to that of a sport for aristocrats, given their way and their view of life. It may be carried on under refined rules of chivalry— though European chivalry is mostly a posttraditional phenomenon—with land and peasants serving as the stakes to be won or lost. In Chou China, "The art of battle became so refined that even in fiercest combat chivalrous manners were required of the nobility. . . . Upon encountering an enemy of superior rank, a warrior had to take care not to offend him, especially if his foe happened to be a ruler. Polite words were exchanged even between a pursued charioteer and his pursuer. Courtesy in battle was the mark of a gentleman . . . a Ch'u general, challenging the Chin ruler in 632 B.C., said, with more than a mere turn of phrase, 'Will Your Excellency permit our knights and yours to play a game?' For these aristocrats, a war was also a

25. Soustelle, *Daily Life of the Aztecs*, p. 42.

26. Painter, *French Chivalry*, p. 7.

27. Quoted in Blum, *Lord and Peasant in Russia*, p. 38.

28. Bloch, *Feudal Society*, 2:299, 292.

29. Schumpeter, "The Sociology of Imperialism," p. 25; italics in the original.

30. Anderson, *Lineages of the Absolutist State*, p. 32.

game. Granet observed that it was much more than a clash of arms; it was a duel of moral values, a trial of honor."[31]

Apart from possible gains, war might be a diversion for the aristocrat who, as a knight-errant, might even travel in search of opportunities to fight. "Warfare was the means by which the upper classes provided themselves with exercise and occupation, and justified their existence."[32] "Accustomed to danger, the knight found in war yet another attraction: it offered a remedy for boredom."[33] Indeed, warfare provided an aesthetic pleasure to the aristocrat. As Bertrand de Born, the twelfth-century troubadour, sang, "I tell you, I find no such savour in food, or in wine, or in sleep, as in hearing the shout 'On! On!' from both sides, and the neighing of steeds that have lost their riders, and the cries of 'Help! Help!'; in seeing men great and small go down on the grass beyond the fosses; in seeing at last the dead, with the pennoned stumps of lances still in their sides."[34]

If warfare seems natural and inherently desirable to aristocrats, elaborate justifications may nevertheless be evolved to justify it. These often center on the typical aristocratic concept of honor, to be mentioned below, which under certain circumstances is seen as requiring warfare. Others involve the aristocracy's belief in the superiority of its race, civilization, law, or religion that compels it to war against those it regards as inferior. Thus, for the Ottoman empire, territory beyond its boundaries was considered "land of war, inhabited either by peoples whose religions were regarded as inferior, or by heretics, whom it was a duty to conquer, at least when practical." If, on the other hand, such territory was inhabited by orthodox Muslims, it had to be conquered to advance the unification of Islam. "The power and conquests of the Ottoman nation were felt to be the power and conquests of Islam."[35] Chinese emperors thought it necessary to bring the benefits of Chinese culture and order to inferior people on their borders. To the Aztecs, "men, by waging war, complied with what had been the will of the gods since the beginning of the world." "War was

31. Hsu, *Ancient China in Transition*, p. 69. The final reference is to Granet, *Chinese Civilization*, p. 270, who provides fascinating details and illustrations of courtesy in battle (ibid., pp. 267–81).

32. Brooke, *Europe in the Central Middle Ages*, p. 127.

33. Bloch, *Feudal Society*, p. 295. "Fighting filled the noble's need of something to do, a way to exert himself. It was his substitute for work. . . . The sword offered the workless noble an activity with a purpose, one that could bring him honor, status, and, if he was lucky, gain." Tuchman, *A Distant Mirror*, p. 65.

34. Quoted in Bloch, *Feudal Society*, p. 293.

35. Lybyer, *The Government of the Ottoman Empire*, pp. 29, 148.

not merely a political instrument: it was above all a religious rite, a war of holiness."[36]

Taxation

The military function is a major one performed by aristocracies, but warfare is not necessarily carried on continuously or at regular intervals. Periods of peace do intervene and, in exceptional aristocratic empires, notably in ancient Egypt, they could last for many years. The collection of income, on the other hand, is an absolutely essential aspect of aristocratic empires. If, obviously, aristocrats tax in order to have empires, it is equally true that they have empires in order to tax. To rule in aristocratic empires is, above all, to tax; "in Amharic, the official language of Ethiopia, the verb 'to rule' (*negesse*) originally meant 'to collect tribute.'"[37]

Fighting wars and obtaining income are for aristocrats closely related activities. For the most part, each one is necessary to make the other possible. Their income permits aristocrats to be a specialized warrior class that is freed from the necessity of productive labor to train for and fight wars. It also allows them to acquire weapons and equipment for warfare, to keep horses, and sometimes to hire mercenaries. On the other hand, their income is commonly obtained through warfare.

Bloch summarized the reasons for medieval European aristocrats engaging in warfare as follows: "Fighting, which was sometimes a legal obligation and frequently a pleasure, might also be required of the knight as a matter of honour. . . . But fighting was also, and perhaps above all, a source of profit—in fact, the nobleman's chief industry." On the other hand, "the return of peace meant for the 'poor knights' . . . an economic crisis as well as a disastrous loss of prestige."[38] Whereas these comments refer to the period when traditionalism was coming to an end in Western Europe, Duby, speaking of the early Middle Ages in Europe, says that "between warlike activity . . . and pillaging, there was no line of demarcation." He cites "stipulations in the laws of Ine, King of Wessex, which call for the following distinctions to be made between aggressors: if there are less than seven, they are simply thieves; if they are more numerous, they constitute

36. Soustelle, *Daily Life of the Aztecs*, pp. 203, 101. The Aztecs themselves, of course, fell victim to the Spaniards who conquered much of Latin America to spread their "true faith."

37. Kraft, "Letter from Addis Ababa," p. 50. Sally Falk Moore speaks of "the overwhelming preoccupation of the [Inca] empire government with taxes"—*Power and Property in Inca Peru*, p. 101—which accounts for the famous census and legal strictures on mobility often ascribed to a concern with social planning and paternalism (ibid., p. 132).

38. Bloch, *Feudal Society*, pp. 296, 298.

a band of brigands; but if there are over thirty-five, they may fairly be taken for an army."[39] Barrington Moore says bluntly that "European feudalism was mainly gangsterism that had become society itself and acquired respectability through the notions of chivalry," and he refers to it as a "form of self-help which victimizes others."[40]

The most direct way, then, in which war can provide an income for aristocrats and one difficult to distinguish from robbery is through the capture of booty or the taking of ransom for aristocratic prisoners. Both can be mere by-products of war but can also be the objects of warfare. And both mostly (except where booty is taken from peasants) amount to a redistribution of wealth among aristocrats. Aristocrats also obtain income from traders. The levying of tolls, market fees, and taxes on local trade may be quite regular.[41] Aristocrats who exact payments from traders using sea lanes, roads, or navigable streams under the aristocrats' control may well appear as pirates or "robber barons" to the victims, but are in their own eyes no less honorable than aristocrats who do not obtain or supplement their income in this manner. Bertrand de Born sang thus about war: "it will be a happy day; for we shall seize the usurers' goods, and no more shall beasts of burden pass along the highways by day in complete safety; nor shall the burgess journey without fear, nor the merchant on his way to France; but the man who is full of courage shall be rich."[42]

How tax collection grows out of warfare and becomes a substitute for or even a continuation of plundering and looting is evident from Prawdin's description of Mongol rulers who, by the end of the thirteenth century, had established themselves in Western Asia: "They and their Mongol warriors remained aliens in the land, nourished by consuming and exploiting the energies of the people. They were a warrior caste, habituated to battle and plunder. When their empire had acquired fixed boundaries, beyond which they could not seek loot from new and ever new enemies, they compelled their subjects to hand over to them without return all that contributed to an easy and comfortable life. 'They taxed the craftsmen who worked in the towns and villages, they taxed the fishermen who drew sustenance from the lakes and rivers, they taxed the mines and the dyeworks and the weaving establishments,' complains a chronicler. Poll-taxes, taxes on industry and other occupations, taxes on cattle, were a heavy burden upon the land; each new vizier discovered some fresh source of

39. Duby, *The Early Growth of the European Economy*, p. 49.

40. Moore, *Social Origins of Dictatorship and Democracy*, p. 214.

41. In commercialized China, "trade, and usury too, was often carried on with the connivance of officials, who strove not only to gain control over it but to snatch the profits as well; yet it was never mentioned except in terms of condemnation." Balazs, *Chinese Civilization and Bureaucracy*, p. 56.

42. Quoted in Bloch, *Feudal Society*, p. 296.

income to gratify the extravagant tastes of the Khan. Even worse than these legally prescribed taxes were the illegitimate exactions of the viceroys, the farmers of the revenue, and the commandants of the troops."[43] One suspects that to the taxpaying subjects the distinction between the "legally prescribed taxes" and the "illegitimate exactions" was neither very clear nor very important.

Enrichment through plunder is one important function of warfare, but the principal one—though not necessarily a cause of war in the minds of the belligerents—is to subject peasants to aristocratic rule, that is, to taxation. What Perry Anderson says of posttraditional European feudalism is also true of traditional aristocratic empires: "war was possibly the most *rational* and *rapid* single mode of expansion of surplus extraction available for any given ruling class under feudalism,"[44] principally through the conquest of land and peasants. Thus, as Shaw makes Julius Caesar say, "taxes are the chief business of a conqueror of the world."[45] Gordon Childe is no less blunt in pointing up the link between warfare and taxation in the ancient empires of the Middle East: "The victor's main concern was to exact a regular tribute from the vanquished people. In a general way the empires thus established were mere tribute-collecting machines. Normally the imperial government interfered in the internal affairs of subject peoples only in so far as was necessary to ensure obedience and the regular payment of taxes."[46]

As for merchants, so for peasants, the distinction between robbing and raiding on the one hand and legal collection of tribute, services, rent, or taxes on the other may for long remain quite hazy and be a matter of point of view. One social scientist simply refers to the aristocracy as "a predatory class" commonly existing in "traditional agrarian societies."[47] Even where the victims are peasants who remain permanently under aristocratic rule, and where income collection may be quite regular, it may involve violence. "Under the Abbasid dynasty, torture was a concomitant of tax gathering."[48] Thus, the tax collector may not seem very different from a robber to the peasant, and historically no sharp line can be drawn between them.

Taxes on the peasantry could simply consist of a fixed amount or a fixed

---

43. Prawdin, *The Mongol Empire*, p. 373.

44. Anderson, *Lineages of the Absolutist State*, p. 31; italics in the original.

45. Shaw, *Caesar and Cleopatra*, 2:200.

46. Childe, *Man Makes Himself*, p. 265. In the case of Inca conquests, "capitulation always involved a specific agreement to pay tribute." Moore, *Power and Property in Inca Peru*, p. 101.

47. Levine, *Wax and Gold*, p. 162.

48. Wittfogel, *Oriental Despotism*, p. 144. Wittfogel also cites references to "terror in fiscal procedures" in ancient Egypt, India, and China (ibid., pp. 143–44).

proportion of the crop or of a certain amount of labor time.[49] On the other hand, aristocrats may, over time, ingeniously invent a great variety of taxes to be imposed on the peasantry. A contemporary observer of the sixteenth-century Ottoman empire "relates how in his time the peasants were eaten, as it were, all the year by tithes, compulsory presents, land-tax, and extortion."[50] A mid-nineteenth-century traveler reports this concerning the Ethiopian peasantry: "They pay a certain portion in kind to the Ras, or other great chief, and sometimes a regular tax in money; besides this, they must furnish oxen to plough the king's lands. Their immediate governor then takes his share in kind of every grain (say a fifth), and feeds besides a certain number of soldiers at the expense of each householder: he has rights to oxen, sheep, goats, butter, honey, and every other requisite for subsistence; he must be received with joy and feasting by his subjects whenever he visits them, and can demand from them contributions on fifty pretexts—he is going on a campaign, or has just returned from one; he has lost a horse, or married a wife; his property has been consumed by fire, or he has lost his all in battle; or the sacred duty of a funeral banquet cannot be fulfilled without their aid."[51]

In Russia, around the fifteenth century, peasants paid their dues to their lord mostly in fixed amounts of grain and in labor services. In one monastery, where contemporary records have been preserved, they were obliged to do the agricultural work on the demesne as well as building and repair work, but also fishing, hunting, baking, brewing, and spinning, and to make payments in cash and in kind. In addition to what they owed their landlord, Russian peasants had to pay to the prince dues in cash, kind, and labor, which were levied on the commune collectively. Labor services included work on fortifications and on the prince's properties, carting and

49. Citing a number of sources on traditional and commercialized agrarian empires, Lenski reports that taxes or rents constituted the following proportions of the peasant's total crop: In Hammurabi's Babylon, one-third to one-half; in Egypt during the captivity, one-fifth; in Ahmenid Persia, 20 to 30 percent; in Ottoman Turkey, 10 to 50 percent; in China, 40 to 50 percent; in sixteenth-century Japan, two-thirds; in pre-British India, one-third to one-half. As to the corvée, in medieval Europe, one member of the peasant's family had to work on the lord's land from one to seven days a week; in feudal Thailand, adult male peasants worked up to one-third of the year in the king's service; and in China, some peasants spent most of their adult lives building the Great Wall. Lenski, *Power and Privilege*, pp. 267–69. In the Ethiopian monarchy, as recently as the 1970s, "landlords could legally take as much as 75 percent" of the annual crop from a sharecropping tenant. Markovitz, *Power and Class in Africa*, p. 166.

50. Lybyer, *The Government of the Ottoman Empire*, p. 144, n. 2, referring to Teodoro Spandugino Cantacusino, *Petit traicté de l'origine des Turcqz*, first published in Paris, 1519 (Paris: E. Leroux, 1896), p. 145.

51. W. Plowden, *Travels in Abyssinia* (London, 1868), p. 138, quoted in Levine, *Wax and Gold*, p. 162.

postal services, and service as beaters and stakers when the prince hunted as well as the obligation to feed his horses, huntsmen, and dogs.[52]

A detailed study, based on ecclesiastical records, of a small rural area in western France in the eleventh and twelfth centuries, where peasants were generally better off than in surrounding areas, mentions the following obligations the peasants owed the aristocracy: the *terrage*, a land tax eventually amounting to one-half the produce; the *cens* or land rent; the tithe or tenth part, paid generally to the secular aristocracy on all crops and livestock; charges for pasturing rights in the aristocracy's woodlands and charges for the right to take wood from them; charges for the right to fish in ponds and rivers most of which were owned by aristocrats; charges for the use of mills, ovens, and winepresses maintained by the aristocracy; various protection and assistance taxes, called customs; the corvée or obligation to work on the aristocrat's estate without compensation; required work on the aristocrat's castle; contributions made by the peasants to the dowry given by the aristocrat to his daughter and contributions to ransom money; fees paid by the peasant for the privilege of inheriting his tenure from his ancestor; a tax for the use of roads if the peasant walked on them outside his own lands; a sales tax on objects bought or sold in the market; and payments to the parish priest for the religious services he rendered to the peasant. Additional burdens imposed on the peasant in other parts of France included a head tax, a fine for marrying outside the aristocrat's territory, and an obligation to furnish hospitality to the knights and agents of the aristocrat.[53] After presenting a similarly long list of taxes imposed in the Ottoman empire, Shaw says that "the right to collect these taxes was considered by the Ottomans to be one of the most basic attributes of sovereignty." And he adds that the "Ruling Class," which he defined as "those involved in the governing of the state," "was created and maintained by the sultan largely for the very purpose of exercising this attribute."[54]

The amount of taxes may be based roughly on the wealth of the tax-

<hr />

52. Blum, *Lord and Peasant in Russia*, pp. 101–5. Engels similarly describes the situation of the peasant in commercialized early sixteenth-century Germany: "Most of his time, he had to work on his master's estate. Out of that which he earned in his few free hours, he had to pay tithes, dues, ground rents, war taxes, land taxes, imperial taxes, and other payments. He could neither marry nor die without paying the master. Aside from his regular work for the master, he had to gather litter, pick strawberries, pick bilberries, collect snailshells, drive the game for the hunting, chop wood, and so on. Fishing and hunting belonged to the master. The peasant saw his crop destroyed by wild game." Engels, "The Peasant War in Germany," p. 31.

53. Beech, *A Rural Society in Medieval France*, pp. 86–87, 103–4. It must be noted that the period covered in this study constitutes the beginnings of commercialization. Some of the taxes mentioned may not be typical of traditional feudal Europe. See also Bloch, *Feudal Society*, pp. 250–54, and Lenski, *Power and Privilege*, pp. 269–70.

54. Shaw, *History of the Ottoman Empire*, 1:121, 113. In Bulgaria, the Ottoman empire "im-

payers, but, because the point of taxation is to support the aristocracy, aristocrats, usually by far the wealthiest people, are not taxed at all (except that they may have to pass some of the taxes they levy on peasants on to higher aristocrats). Thus, it is reported of the Sassanian empire in the sixth century: "Taxes were fixed according to the area of land under cultivation and the number of fruit trees. This system lasted so well that it was later adopted by the Caliphs. A personal tax, to be paid quarterly, was imposed on all men from twenty to fifty years of age, except the nobility and the grandees of the empire, soldiers, priests and court officials and secretaries."[55]

The code of the T'ang dynasty (618–906) in China provided that "all members of the imperial clan registered with the Department of Imperial Genealogy, and all kindred of the fifth degree or closer of the empress, empress dowager, or grand empress dowagers, first degree kindred of consorts of the first degree or above, grandfathers, fathers, or brothers of concubines of the fifth degree or above, relatives of civil and military serving officials in the third rank and above, first mourning degree relatives of princes of commanderies, relatives of the *ta-kung* degree of mourning who are living in the same household with princes of commanderies, relatives living in the same household with dukes of states, and fathers and brothers of barons of districts are all exempt from taxes and labor services."[56] In Ming and Ch'ing China (1368–1911), "members of the officialdom . . . were exempt from the labor services to which all commoners except degree-holders were liable."[57]

For aristocrats to pay taxes would defeat the very purpose of government in aristocratic empires. It is, after all, to enable the aristocracy, which *is* the government, to take from and not give to the rest of the population, notably the peasantry.

Auxiliary Governmental Functions

It is possible for an aristocracy to perform no other functions than the military and tax collecting ones, but it is also possible that, in

posed approximately eighty different types of taxes and obligations." Lenski, *Power and Privilege*, p. 269.

55. Diez, *The Ancient Worlds of Asia*, p. 88. In Europe, into modern times "the nobles and the clergy normally enjoyed fiscal immunity. As late as 1659 in the territory of Ravenna (Italy), clergy, nobility, and foreigners were exempt from paying taxes, and they held 35, 42 and 15 percent of the land, respectively." Cipolla, *Before the Industrial Revolution*, p. 46.

56. Translated and quoted by McKnight, "Fiscal Privileges and the Social Order in Sung China," p. 84n.

57. Ho, *The Ladder of Success in Imperial China*, p. 18.

order to perform these two, certain auxiliary functions will have to be taken care of.

Aristocrats organize the construction of buildings for their purposes—castles and palaces, temples and churches—which may constitute huge projects that require generations to complete. Because the purposes of the aristocracy are governmental, such buildings can be called government buildings, but they should not be thought of as public buildings, for government is not a public affair in aristocratic empires.

Neither are other projects conducted by the aristocracy public works for they serve the needs of the aristocracy. Thus, the aristocracy may organize the building of fortifications and walls to protect the borders of its territory from incursions and invasions by nomadic tribes or rival aristocracies. The best known examples are the Great Wall of China, designed to keep out the nomads of Mongolia, the *limes* linking the Rhine and Danube frontiers of the Roman empire against Germanic tribes, and the Wall of Hadrian protecting the Roman province of Britain from the unconquered Caledonians.

Military operations on the borders of an empire or administrative communications may require the building and maintenance of roads and also bridges and post houses. Famous examples are the 1,666-mile-long "royal way" of Darius's Persian empire, the 53,000 miles of roads in the Roman empire, and the 10,000 miles in the mountainous Inca empire,[58] as well as roads in the Chinese and Mongol empires. Roads may serve to aid not only the military but also the income-collecting functions of the aristocracy when they are used to transport shipments of tribute from outlying provinces to the capital. The same was true of the Grand Canal from the Yangtse to the Yellow River on which rice was moved from the South of China to Peking, the new capital of the Mongol emperors.[59]

Obviously, peasants living in isolated villages are neither willing nor able to build castles or walls, roads or canals. To have such projects accomplished, it would be the function of the aristocracy to plan and design them and to mobilize peasant labor, generally through the corvée, to carry them out.

Similarly, the agricultural foundations of the aristocracy's income might have to be protected by systems of flood control or irrigation involving the construction and upkeep of dams, dikes, canals, and reservoirs, as in Egypt and Mesopotamia,[60] in Persia and China, and in Peru. Under the Incas,

58. See von Hagen's two beautiful books, *The Roads That Led to Rome* and *Highway of the Sun,* and also Forbes, *Notes on the History of Ancient Roads and Their Construction.*

59. Weber, *The Religion of China,* pp. 51–52.

60. On irrigation in the ancient Middle East, see Drower, "Water-Supply, Irrigation, and Agriculture," 1:520–57.

especially in the mountainous areas, where no surplus land or product was available, land set aside for the Inca (the "state") and for the Sun (the "church") and thus producing revenue for the aristocracy was not so much taken from the peasants as newly created by terracing and irrigation of previously uncultivated slopes.[61] Here the aristocracy did not merely protect or enlarge but even created sources of income by means of "public works."

Generally, peasants do not have the technical know-how required for the construction of flood control or irrigation works nor can any one village furnish the necessary labor power. It is thus again often the aristocracy that plans and designs the projects and mobilizes and organizes the manpower.[62] Evidently, continued aristocratic supervision of peasants is also required for the maintenance of flood control and irrigation works, for when the aristocracy in charge is replaced by newcomers the waterworks are left to decay. This happened in Iraq when the Abbasid caliphate was conquered by the Mongols, in Spain when Arab rulers yielded to Christian ones, and in India when the British took the place of the Moguls.

The construction and maintenance of waterworks may require far more planning and supervision and hence the development of more specialized institutions and personnel than the maintenance of agriculture, which peasants carry on in what they regard as natural fashion. Karl A. Wittfogel, starting from Marx's writings on "oriental despotism" and "Asiatic society," developed a theory[63] that argued that a peculiar type of political and social system, that of oriental despotism, grew out of the needs of "hydraulic agriculture." In a searching critique of that theory Wolfram Eberhard[64]— with respect to the matter most relevant here—shows that, at any rate in China, it was not the central government, as Wittfogel had claimed, that was responsible for the initiation or control of waterworks (except where the immediate needs of the imperial court or military needs were involved), but private individuals and local groups. Although this destroys the link between hydraulic agriculture and a highly centralized autocracy, which is crucial to Wittfogel's theory, it does not mean that the construction and perhaps also the control of waterworks are not commonly a function of the aristocracy, but merely indicates that people other than

61. Murra, "On Inca Political Structure," p. 31.

62. On the use of the corvée in China for such purposes, see Weber, *The Religion of China*, pp. 50–52. In Egypt, peasants were forced under the corvée to maintain dikes and dredge canals from the days of the Pharaohs until the end of the nineteenth century. See Petrie, *Social Life in Ancient Egypt*, pp. 22–23.

63. Wittfogel, *Oriental Despotism*.

64. Eberhard, *Conquerors and Rulers*, pp. 53–88. For another critical review, see Eisenstadt, "The Study of Oriental Despotism and Systems of Total Power."

aristocrats can, under certain circumstances, also perform it. Most of the local individuals and groups listed by Eberhard as responsible for water-works in China were probably, by my definition, aristocrats, and in other empires, for example that of the Incas, it was undoubtedly the aristocracy that performed this function.

The aristocracy might also supervise the storage of food for its army and bureaucracy and sometimes also for the other urban population. In the Inca empire, even the rural population was fed from the central government's storehouses while working on corvée on aristocratic lands or "public works" projects. This does not mean, as has been suggested, that the Incas were running either a welfare state or a "totalitarian" system, for, as is typical of aristocratic empires, the village community remained self-sufficient, and it, rather than the central government, was responsible for individual welfare. In effect, the peasants fed themselves while working for the aristocracy, for all they harvested while on corvée went into the government's storehouses from which they received their food and beer.

Other functions performed by the aristocracy to maintain the economy might include the control of mining and some manufacturing, especially of weapons, as well as the coinage of money and attempts to standardize weights and measures. However, especially these latter become important only as empires are commercialized.

The administration of religious affairs is often so closely related to military and civil administration that it, too, is in the hands of the aristocracy. It involves the organization by aristocrats of religious ceremonies and festivals, rituals and sacrifices as well as the construction and maintenance of temples or churches, tombs and monuments, and even such a prodigious feat of organization and technology as the building of the pyramids.

Because aristocrats have been defined here as those who exploit peasants and occupy high governmental positions in aristocratic empires, at least the upper levels of the clergy must be included in the aristocracy. This is true even if, as is by no means always the case, its members are distinct from the rest of the aristocracy and differently recruited. Even then the lay aristocracy and the clerical aristocracy tend to collaborate in the pursuit of common interests. What Levine says of aristocratic Ethiopia is largely true of most aristocratic empires and by no means only of Christian ones: "In general, it may be said that the clergy and nobility worked to further each other's interests. The nobility supported the clergy by giving endowments to churches and monasteries, setting up churches in newly conquered lands, and observing religious ceremonies as state functions. The clergy, in turn, served secular authority by providing a communications network for relaying and supporting official policies, excommunicating enemies, and providing counsel and morale in connection with military expeditions. Altogether, there was an easy commerce between the two elites. They felt common cause in their responsibilities and privileges vis-à-vis the masses. Occasionally there was even an exchange of personnel, when warlords ended their careers by becoming monks, or clerics acceded to high civil positions."[65]

The religion administered by the aristocracy is always the religion of the aristocracy, not that of the peasantry which, as we shall see in Chapter 11, below, tends to remain quite distinct. A conquering aristocracy will usually bring its own religion along with its army, but it may also administer the religion of the aristocracy it conquered in order to gain legitimacy in the eyes of the latter. Thus, the Manchu conquerors of China performed the religious ceremonies expected of Chinese emperors while also maintaining their own religious observances. In any case, its religion will provide legitimacy for its role to the aristocracy in its own eyes, and in this sense the religious function of the aristocracy may be seen as auxiliary to its military and tax-collecting functions. The legitimacy and authority of the aristocracy rests on claims of divine sanction and on tradition—and tradition itself is usually inextricably interwoven with religious elements in aristocratic empires. For example, in Chou China, "the nobles could justify their privileged status by maintaining that their ancestors were deities, a claim found in many cultures."[66] Those who maintain and propagate religion, then, play an important part in maintaining aristocrats in power.

This is not to suggest that, in aristocratic empires, religion serves as the "opium of the people" who, without it, would rise in revolt. The great bulk of "the people" are peasants, and these and also most of the townspeople, for reasons to be discussed, require no opium to be kept dormant. Of course, if peasants, too, accept the aristocracy's religion—and therefore its exploitation—the aristocracy can perform its military and tax-collecting functions that much more easily. However, as we shall see, peasant conversion to the aristocrats' religion, if it takes place at all, is likely to be quite superficial. The major and, indeed, virtually the only threat to ruling aristocrats stems from other aristocrats. That religion has by no means eliminated intraaristocratic conflicts and challenges to the rulers is obvious, but this does not mean that it does not serve as a conservative force. Aristocrats themselves accept the religious basis of aristocratic rule, and it is hence more difficult for them to defy their rulers.

It is especially monarchs who claim religious sanction for their rule. Thus, Egyptian pharaohs were regarded as gods on earth, and "the Meso-

65. Levine, *Wax and Gold*, p. 175.

66. Hsu, *Ancient China in Transition*, p. 14.

potamian king derived his authority from divine election"[67] and some Mesopotamian kings were also deified. Roman emperors, too, were deified during their lifetime; and the Aztec emperor was regarded as "a semi-divine personage surrounded with a religious halo"[68] and as a descendant of the god Quetzalcoatl. Many other rulers, like the Japanese emperor, the Inca, and the Mwami of Ruanda have claimed descent from the gods; Indian kings were regarded as earthly incarnations of one of the Hindu gods, and Burmese kings as descendants of Buddha. The Thai king was "a special order of being located somewhere in the realm between the natural and the supernatural."[69] The Cambodian king was the "deva-raja, a god-king whose position involved a mysterious blending of temporal authority and quasi-divine status."[70] In Java, "the ancient Hindu-Buddhist city states were headed by a king who was also a God, a divine monarch enthroned on the very peak of spiritual refinement upon a symbolically divine mountain set in the exact center of his squared-off capital."[71] The Chinese "emperor's personal position . . . was based exclusively on his charisma as the plenipotentiary ('Son') of Heaven where his ancestors resided."[72] "The essence of Iranian kingship was not mere enhancement of the human function on earth, but rather supernatural power aiming at 'renewing' the world after a celestial pattern."[73] Arab and Turkish monarchs from 632 to 1924 ruled as caliphs, that is, as successors to the prophet Mohammed and as divinely appointed rulers. In Persia, "the kings of Safavi times expended a great deal of energy tracing their origins directly to the Prophet,"[74] and Christian kings and emperors were anointed by bishops to be invested with a sacred character—"divinity doth hedge a king."[75] And one of these, the Ethiopian emperor, was until his overthrow in 1974 considered the "Elect of God" and the descendant of Solomon and successor to the kings of Israel.[76]

67. Frankfort, *Kingship and the Gods*, p. 243.

68. Soustelle, "Religion and the Mexican State," p. 7.

69. Wilson, *Politics in Thailand*, pp. 89–90.

70. Osborne, *Politics and Power in Cambodia*, p. 13.

71. Geertz, *The Religion of Java*, p. 231.

72. Weber, *The Religion of China*, p. 143.

73. Filippani-Ronconi, "The Tradition of Sacred Kingship in Iran," p. 60.

74. Bill, *The Politics of Iran*, p. 28.

75. Shakespeare, *Hamlet*, Act IV, Scene 3. On the religious and magical ideas of kingship in medieval Europe, see Bloch, *Feudal Society*, pp. 379–82.

76. For a brief summary and analysis of the legendary origins of the Ethiopian monarchy, see Jones and Monroe, *A History of Abyssinia*, pp. 10–21. For a well-documented summary with numerous examples of the deification of traditional rulers, see Wesson, *The Imperial Order*, pp. 80–86.

Aristocratic Occupations

It is clear from the foregoing discussion of the functions of the aristocracy, that certain occupations—and only these—are characteristic ones for aristocrats to hold. They serve as warriors, as rulers, as administrators, as judges, and as priests. Parenthetically, it must be stressed here that village priests are not aristocrats. They live among the peasantry and represent its religion rather than the aristocracy's. The two religions may be similar or superficially even identical in form, but they usually differ in content corresponding to the very different ways of life of peasants and aristocrats. Thus, even when village priests are formally members of the same clerical hierarchy as the aristocratic priesthood, as was the case with the Catholic and Russian Orthodox clergy, let alone when they represent a wholly different peasant religion, they are excluded from my conception of the aristocrats' priestly hierarchy and included among the peasants.

The distinction between the military, the governing, the administrative, the judicial, and the priestly function is a modern one. In aristocratic empires, where far less specialization prevails than in modern societies, aristocratic occupations are not likely to be distinguished along these lines. Thus, judges rarely, if ever, constitute a separate occupational group; the judicial function, as far as it is not simply left to the peasantry and the townspeople, is usually exercised by rulers, bureaucrats, and priests. Generally, there is a great deal of overlapping among aristocratic occupations that are, after all, practiced by aristocrats simply by virtue of the fact that they are aristocrats and that may even be inherited. What specialized knowledge is needed for the practice of an occupation is acquired because the aristocrat holds that occupation or is destined to hold it, for example, that of priest or military leader; ordinarily, he does not get the job because he has the required specialized knowledge.

Very commonly, rulers and military leaders are identical in aristocratic empires, men either having become rulers by virtue of their military leadership or serving as military leaders simply because they are rulers. In medieval Europe and the aristocratic Arab world, for example, there was no distinction between these two functions. In feudal Europe, not only kings and emperors, but all aristocrats (except some in the clergy) who were rulers of some territory, whether a barony, a county, a dukedom, or a principality, were also military men. In eleventh-century France, "the social and political nobleman had become completely identified with the fully armed warrior. With the exception of nobly-born members of the clergy, an adult male who was not a *miles* [soldier or knight] was not a noble."[77] In

---

77. Painter, *French Chivalry*, p. 3.

162 | Governmental Functions of the Aristocracy

"the traditional Middle Eastern Islamic social structure . . . in most cases, a single member of this [ruling] class had a number of power-laden functions. For example, a member of the ruling family was often at the same time a military leader and a large landlord."[78] In the Ottoman empire, "army and government were one. War was the external purpose, government the internal purpose, of one institution, composed of one body of men. . . . The high officials of government held high command in war. The generals of the army had extensive duties in regard to the affairs of the troops under them, the management of departments of state, or the government of provinces." The Ottoman government or ruling "institution kept itself in power, and defended and enlarged the empire, by being organized as an army. With exceptions, all its officers of government were soldiers and all its army officers had governmental duties."[79] It would seem that what Count Mirabeau said of modern Prussia—that it was not a country that possessed an army but an army that possessed a country— applies to any aristocratic empire where the aristocracy and the military are more or less identical.

In the Aztec empire, "at the summit the military hierarchy merged with that of the state. . . . The emperor's . . . primary function was that of commanding not only the Mexican armies but those of the allied cities. The most important of the great dignitaries who were about him had offices that were essentially military."[80] "In the traditional Ethiopian system, the political involvement of the military is not a phenomenon that needs to be explained; on the contrary, any distinction between the two realms is difficult to make. . . . During most of the last millennium the political capital of Ethiopia frequently took the form of an army camp."[81] "Just as the medieval baron was simultaneously owner of the land, military commander, judge and administrator of his fief, . . . so the Abyssinian ras dispensed justice, commanded the soldiery and levied taxes—or rather extorted from the farmer everything over and above the bare necessaries of subsistence. In certain periods of ancient Egypt the hiq, or local governor, saw to the upkeep of the canals, supervised agriculture, administered justice, exacted tribute, commanded his warriors."[82]

The ruler is often also the religious leader. Thus, the Inca and, until the 1950s, the Dalai Lama in Tibet ruled as a kind of god-king with both

78. Bill and Leiden, *Politics in the Middle East*, pp. 117–18.

79. Lybyer, *The Government of the Ottoman Empire*, pp. 91, 194.

80. Soustelle, *Daily Life of the Aztecs*, p. 44.

81. Levine, "The Military in Ethiopian Politics," pp. 6–7.

82. Mosca, *The Ruling Class*, p. 81.

temporal and spiritual powers.[83] The Popes were not only temporal rulers of the Papal State for over eleven centuries down to 1870, but some medieval ones "believed that imperial power resided in some primary way in the papal office." On the other hand, "the imperial dignity carried priestly quality. The emperor was in some mysterious way pope, the pope in some mysterious way emperor."[84] The Chinese and the Aztec emperors played major roles in religious rituals. King Ibn Saud, into the second half of this century, to the adherents of his Wahhabi Muslim sect, "was the Imam. . . . He like the past leaders of the Saud clan, wore both a spiritual and a temporal mantle of leadership."[85]

Indeed, all three functions of ruler, military commander, and priest can be combined in one person. Thus, the early Roman king "fulfilled the triple functions of generalissimo, high priest, and supreme judge."[86] The ancient Egyptian pharaoh, a god, was also a high priest and "the head of the army, and all conflicts and triumphs are ascribed to him personally."[87] The three professions of ruler, priest, and general were also combined on lower levels in ancient Egypt from the tenth to the eighth centuries B.C.: "The sacerdotal principalities were ruled by high priests who were also generals, while the military principalities were ruled by generals who were also high priests: I am not disposed to argue that the difference was important."[88] Similarly, in feudal Chou China, the monarch "was pope as well as emperor, and his noble subordinates were priests as well as barons; the noble and clerical estates were one."[89] In Japan, too, in the Yamato period, from about the fourth to the seventh century, not only the emperor, but local aristocrats "combined acts of governance with leadership in religious observance."[90] In Aztec Mexico, the priests were in some respects "hardly to be distinguished from the nobility, for the ruler himself was of priestly rank. They also went to war and took captives. The distinc-

---

83. The Dalai Lama is an example of a nonhereditary aristocrat and monarch. A commoner by birth, he was from his selection in early childhood surrounded and raised by the aristocracy, which thus derived strength from his claims to divinity.

84. Coulborn, "A Comparative Study of Feudalism," p. 238.

85. Bill and Leiden, *The Middle East*, p. 131.

86. Duruy, *History of Rome and of the Roman People*, 1:194.

87. Petrie, *Social Life in Ancient Egypt*, p. 34.

88. Edgerton, "The Question of Feudal Institutions in Egypt," p. 130.

89. Coulborn, "A Comparative Study of Feudalism," p. 238.

90. Hall, *Government and Local Power in Japan*, pp. 33–34. "This strong tradition of identity between secular and sacerdotal authority which typified the historic status of the Japanese sovereign applied equally to other *uji* chieftains during this period" (ibid., p. 34).

tion between priests and warriors is not an absolute one."[91] Medieval European kings, who were both rulers and military leaders, were not priests, but they "were considered sacred, and in some countries at least they were held to possess miraculous powers of healing."[92] On the other hand, some abbots, bishops, and archbishops were temporal territorial rulers and as such also engaged in warfare, which blurred somewhat the distinction between priests on the one hand and rulers and soldiers on the other.

The medieval religious military orders illustrate nicely the merger of religious, military, and governmental functions in the hands of the same aristocrats.[93] Founded during the Crusades, they were open only to those of "noble blood" who took the vows of monks and yet were soldiers and rulers. The Teutonic Order eventually conquered the entire south coast of the Baltic, subjecting Slavic and Baltic peasants, and the Hospitalers conquered and ruled Rhodes for two centuries until they lost it to the Turks and then ruled Malta (becoming the Knights of Malta) until Napoleon seized it. Similarly, Spanish military orders engaged in the Reconquest from the Muslims acquired large landholdings in the reconquered territory. However, although the merger of the ideals of monkhood and knighthood, combined with behavior much more knightly than monkish, still smacks of traditionalism, these orders developed at the end of the traditional period of Western European history. Indeed, they played a role in the process of commercialization, for the Templars, with their great wealth, became bankers and the Teutonic knights were instrumental in the founding of commercial cities that joined the Hanseatic League.

Although there tends to be much overlapping between governmental functions regarded as separate in modern times, there may also be some degree of specialization among the administrative, the military, and the priestly function, even if they are united at the top in the person of the ruler. Thus, in China, the bureaucracy remained distinct from the military, although even here "throughout the imperial period civil officials were time and again given military posts and military officials civil posts."[94]

---

91. Davies, *The Aztecs*, p. 80. But Soustelle says of the Aztec ruler: "A political and military chief, he certainly had multiple ritual obligations—as does everyone in an intensely religious society; but he was not a priest himself." Soustelle, "Religion and the Mexican State," p. 7.

92. Bloch, *The Royal Touch*, p. 3. "For many centuries, the kings of France and the kings of England used to 'touch scrofula.' . . . That is to say, they claimed to be able, simply by their touch, to cure people suffering from this disease, and their subjects shared a common belief in their medicinal powers" (ibid.).

93. For a summary history, see Seward, *The Monks of War*.

94. Wittfogel, *Oriental Despotism*, p. 354n.

Whereas the line between the military and the bureaucracy may have been reasonably clear in China, the priesthood was not held as a distinct occupation. In early Chou China, there was no "professional priesthood. There were, to be sure, certain men who specialized in religious rituals, divination, and the like, but their role was that of assistants rather than chiefs in the great religious ceremonies in which the aristocrats acted as their own priests."[95] In later China, it was the Confucian scholar-bureaucrats who were "the rightful representatives of the accepted state ritual."[96] Max Weber, too, stresses that "allowing for reservations with regard to Taoism, no powerful priesthood has ever existed so far as is known historically. . . . The cult of the great deities of heaven and earth . . . was an affair of the state. These cults were not managed by priests but by the holders of political power,"[97] with the emperor serving as high priest.

In other aristocratic empires, it is the priesthood that is held as an occupation separate from that of ruler, bureaucrat, and military leader. In Ottoman Turkey, the Muslim religious officials, who included judges as well as jurists and teachers, were recruited from the Muslim population, while government and military leaders were, especially in the sixteenth century, slaves of the sultan, recruited from among his non-Muslim subjects.[98] In India, too, priests on the one hand and rulers and warriors on the other were recruited from sharply distinct groups, the castes of the Brahmans and Kshatriyas respectively. Their distinct functions were not performed by the same persons, but members of both castes could be big landowners.

In feudal Europe, the clergy was regarded as a distinct occupation, but "a whole population of 'tonsured persons' whose status remained ill-defined, formed an indeterminate borderland on the frontiers"[99] between clergy and lay society. The Church was organized apart from the rest of the aristocracy, but the members of the higher clergy were not only, in any case, by my definition aristocrats, but were generally recruited from persons of aristocratic birth. Indeed, the Church provided the only alternative to a military career for aristocrats, and, through the Church, they were major landowners.[100] Furthermore, clerics were the principal bureaucrats.

95. Bodde, "Feudalism in China," p. 60.

96. Eisenstadt, *The Political Systems of Empires*, p. 56.

97. Weber, *The Religion of China*, pp. 142–43.

98. On what he calls "the Moslem Institution" of the Ottoman empire, see Lybyer, *The Government of the Ottoman Empire*, pp. 199–226.

99. Bloch, *Feudal Society*, p. 345.

100. In twelfth-century-B.C. Egypt, the priests owned 15 percent of the land, while in eighth-century France and in fourteenth-century England the Church owned one-third of

With reference to eighth-century Western Europe, Pirenne calls them "an indispensible auxiliary to civil society. The State could not dispense with their services. In the Carolingian period, when the last traces of lay education had disappeared, it was from the clergy that the State was obliged to borrow its staff of scribes, the heads of its chancellery, and all those agents or counsellors in whom a certain degree of intellectual culture was essential."[101]

The Aztecs, too, had "two parallel hierarchies: that of the State . . . and that of the Church." "As faithful as they were, the governors were not priests, and the priests did not govern."[102] Among the Aztecs and Mayas and under the Incas, the priests "constituted a distinct class and were apparently the equals of nobles. In some societies the priestly offices were hereditary; where they were not, the sons of nobles often filled the major offices. In most instances the king or emperor was regarded as the high priest, or head of the priesthood, as well as chief of state."[103] In some African empires there was also a priesthood distinct from the rest of the aristocracy. Thus, in Dahomey, the king, though an important priestly figure, had priestly competitors. "Apparently, these persons are of middle-class origin, but by virtue of the position they occupy can be considered a part of the privileged or leisure class."[104]

---

it, and a similar proportion was set aside as a religious endowment in Ottoman Turkey and for the Buddhist monasteries in Ceylon. Lenski, *Power and Privilege*, pp. 257–58.

101. Pirenne, *A History of Europe*, 1:38–39.

102. Soustelle, "Religion and the Mexican State," pp. 8, 15.

103. Lenski, *Power and Privilege*, pp. 178–79. In the Incas' "religious hierarchy the primacy belonged to the high priest of the Sun, . . . always a near relation of the Inca—his brother or uncle. . . . His assistant priests formed a sort of clerical college and were all nobles or scions of noble families." Métraux, *The History of the Incas*, p. 136.

104. Lenski, *Power and Privilege*, p. 178.

Part III
The Politics of
the Aristocracy

8

Values and Ideology of
the Aristocracy

Service and Duty, Honor and Glory

The values and ideology of traditional aristocrats must, of course, be understood in the context of their world and of the roles they play and of the functions they serve in it. Their values are derived from and shaped by their functions and in turn justify and reinforce their performance. The more an aristocrat conforms to the prevailing values of the aristocracy, the better he will—other things being equal—perform his aristocratic functions.

To serve and do one's duty are important precepts in the ideology and the lives of aristocrats.[1] Duty and service are always rendered to an aristocratic institution, like a unit of the army or the church or a kingdom or an empire, or to a higher aristocrat to whom the lower one owes fealty. The higher one, in turn, may hold obligations to the lower one, for example, to protect him. Ties of loyalty, then, commonly run up and down aristocratic hierarchies, but they evidently do not bind peers. Among them, be they lords of neighboring territories or the sons of a ruler waiting to succeed him, competitive and conflictual relations typically prevail.

The individual aristocrat, deeply imbued with a sense of duty and service, may well sacrifice his wealth or even lay down his life to fulfill his obligations as he sees them. As an epitome of the Japanese aristocratic code, the *bushido*, stated: "Wherever we may be, deep in mountain recesses or buried under the ground, any time or anywhere, our duty is to guard the interest of our Lord. . . . This is the backbone of our faith, unchanging and eternally true. Never in my life have I placed mine own

---

1. The motto of the Prince of Wales is: *"Ich dien"* (I serve). This does not mean that the Prince of Wales is a *Diener*, a servant, or, for that matter, a serf. Obviously, the word has very different connotations, as it still does today when servants may be lowly, but leaders of governments are public "servants," bureaucrats are civil "servants," and military men "serve" in the armed "services."

thoughts above those of my Lord and master. Nor will I do otherwise in all the days of my life. Even when I die I will return to life seven times to guard my Lord's house."[2]

Clearly, any institution, like an armed formation, or any aristocrat benefits from such loyalty. Thus, the tremendous importance that concepts like service and duty have in the minds of individual aristocrats strengthens an aristocracy or any of its subdivisions in its conflicts with the aristocracies of other empires or with other subdivisions. On the other hand, for the individual aristocrat, the sacredness of his duty provides guidance in his behavior and justification for the role he plays in his world and often for specific acts.

An aristocrat is, according to his ideology, expected to serve honorably, to carry out his duty, even at great personal sacrifice, because he is honor bound to do so. The concepts of duty and service then are closely related to that of honor, so central a component of aristocratic ideology that it has been referred to as "the animating principle in the noblemen's society."[3]

Honor is inherently possessed by the aristocrat, not as an individual but as a member of the aristocracy. At the same time, it is up to the individual aristocrat to behave in such a way as to maintain his honor. Although the specific requirements of behavior appropriate to avoid a loss of honor may vary among aristocracies, those of the Tutsi of Ruanda seem not atypical: A Tutsi "greatly desires to be regarded as having . . . the quality of being a man; it includes trustworthiness in keeping promises, generosity in treating one's friends well, liberality towards the poor, moral courage in accepting one's responsibilities. . . . Another quality that the Batutsi are extremely proud to have is . . . 'self-mastery.' To lose one's temper, to manifest violent emotion by crying is really shameful. Anger in particular should not be violently expressed. The demeanor of a Mututsi should always be dignified, polite, amiable, if a little supercilious."[4]

In Ethiopia, quite similarly "an etiquette of instinctual inhibition is taught" to the children of the aristocracy. "Dignity of comportment is expected at all times; a noble should not, for example, express great enthusiasm over anything."[5] The etiquette of the Javanese gentry, the *prijaji*, requires "the avoidance of any act suggesting disorder or lack of self-control. According to the Javanese, the difference between men and ani-

---

2. Quoted in Bellah, *Tokugawa Religion*, p. 91.

3. Vagts, *A History of Militarism*, p. 68. On "status honor" in a number of aristocratic empires, see also Weber, *Economy and Society*, 3:1104–5.

4. Maquet, "The Kingdom of Ruanda," p. 179. Maquet ends his paragraph by noting that "an aristocratic caste usually emphasizes those differences which constantly remind others how far removed they are from the noble set" (ibid., p. 180).

5. Levine, *Wax and Gold*, p. 156.

mals is that the former 'know order.' By order, the *prijaji* means formality of bearing, restraint of expression, and bodily self-discipline—a constant awareness of himself as being an object of perception for others and therefore obligated to present a pleasing, [refined, polite] picture. Spontaneity or naturalness of gesture or speech" is looked down upon.[6]

In general, the aristocrat's honor requires him to behave in accordance with a strict and often elaborate, though unwritten, code, like the *bushido* of the Japanese *samurai* and the *li* of the Chou aristocracy of China.[7] The qualities required by this code are—except possibly where the aristocrats in question constitute a specialized bureaucracy or priesthood—invariably, above all, military in nature, chiefly those of courage and fidelity.

Like aristocratic warriors everywhere, the Tutsi "like to be recognized as courageous. They came to Ruanda by conquest and, till the European occupation, their main social function as a caste was to make war, more often offensive than defensive. Consequently military courage . . . was highly praised. There are numerous and interminable poems made by official bards, telling stories of battle and commemorating military prowess."[8] "At the core of the *bushido* in the Tokugawa era was the belief that the *samurai* owed absolute devotion to their feudal overlords,"[9] as it is illustrated in the popular Japanese story of the forty-seven *ronin* who died to avenge the death of their lord.[10] To maintain his honor, an aristocrat may even feel compelled to act in a manner which to the nonaristocrat may appear quite irrational. Thus, he might be obliged to kill or commit suicide in order to avenge or atone for what is regarded as a lapse from honor.

The maintenance of honor is closely tied to the acquisition of glory,[11] and both, like other aristocratic values, serve to strengthen the aristocracy. This is particularly true in its original and most vital field of activity,

6. Geertz, *The Religion of Java*, p. 247.

7. "These *li* . . . were designed to cover all the major activities of life and required much time to learn. On the military side they remind us in some ways of the code of chivalry of European knighthood." Bodde, "Feudalism in China," p. 59.

8. Maquet, "The Kingdom of Ruanda," pp. 178–79.

9. Varley, *The Samurai*, p. 123.

10. Ibid., pp. 123–25. The *bushido* was formulated in the Tokugawa period, when Japan was no longer traditional and when the *samurai* "were in fact warriors who had no wars to fight" (ibid., p. 121), but it embodied the values of their idealized warrior past. On the *bushido* and its emphasis on loyalty, see also Bellah, *Tokugawa Religion*, pp. 90–98. He says of this code that "the military emphasis is crucial. Military service . . . typifies selfless devotion to the collectivity and its head, even to the point of death. Death indeed in a military context can come to symbolize that very devotion" (ibid., p. 97). On the *samurai*, see also the beautifully illustrated Turnbull, *The Samurai*.

11. Glory, according to Schopenhauer, "must be acquired, but honor must not be lost." Vagts, *A History of Militarism*, p. 70.

warfare, when military success is still largely a function of the courage and fidelity of the individual warrior. Thus, in ancient Greece, "the honor of the *aristos* rested on his military exploits and success."[12] Because the aristocrat who shows fear of death or injury on the battlefield is dishonored in his own eyes as well as in those of his fellows, his concern with his honor will tend to make him overcome and repress that fear, and he will be the better warrior for it. Speaking of courage, Bloch says "it was also because it gave scope for the exercise of this virtue that war created such joy in the hearts of men for whom daring and contempt for death were, in a sense, professional assets."[13]

Given the crucial role of warfare in aristocratic empires already discussed and the conflicts deeply dividing aristocrats, to be analyzed in the next two chapters, "violence . . . was built into the very texture of aristocratic life."[14] "Instant willingness to engage in personal combat required a high level of personal aggression and an absence of normative restraints in the highest strata of society. Not only was personal valor idealized, but bloodletting, mutilation, and the whole ferocity of battle were as well."[15]

If his code of honor requires the aristocrat to fight bravely, it might also require him to die. Nothing can be more honorable and glorious than death in battle, which is hence a fate peculiarly appropriate to and even reserved for aristocrats. Writing of Western European feudalism in the posttraditional era, Vagts states: "The glory of death on the battlefield was reserved for the armored man on horseback; and though common men were permitted to come to his assistance in some extreme cases, this was regarded as abnormal and monstrous. If they perished by his side, it was viewed with lusty mockery as a joke. Describing the Battle of Senlis in 1418, a French chronicler said: 'There was a captain who had a crowd of foot-men who all died, and there was great laughter because they were all men of poor estate.'"[16]

12. Gouldner, *Enter Plato*, p. 12.

13. Bloch, *Feudal Society*, p. 294.

14. Bendix, *Kings or People*, p. 228.

15. Ibid., p. 231. The prevalence of violence among aristocrats is illustrated by the fact that among the sons of English dukes born between 1330 and 1479—when, to be sure, England was no longer traditional—46 percent died violent deaths. The life expectancy of male members of ducal families born in this period was twenty-four years. Omitting violent deaths, however, it was thirty-one years. Hollingsworth, "A Demographic Study of the British Ducal Families," pp. 8–9.

16. Vagts, *A History of Militarism*, p. 42. The quotation is taken from Edgard Boutaric, *Institutions militaires de la France* (Paris: Henri Plon, 1863), p. 212. According to Shakespeare, the death in battle of common men who fought in the Hundred Years War was no joke, but it did remain an embarrassment to the aristocrats. When the French herald asks for an armistice at the battle of Agincourt (1415), it is

In Japan, "death in the service of one's lord was considered the most appropriate end for a *samurai*. Indeed such a death had almost a 'saving' quality in the religious sense."[17] Similarly, in the feudal warfare of Chou China, "it is a fine thing to expose oneself foolhardily. The supreme action is to devote oneself to death for the sake of the chief."[18] For the Tutsi of Ruanda, too, "some deaths were particularly glorious: for example, to be killed in battle or to lose one's life rather than surrender one's cattle, because this is to be deprived of the only means of living in a manner appropriate to one's rank."[19]

For an aristocrat, death on the battlefield is honorable even if the fight is a quite hopeless one—and, indeed, particularly then—and especially if death is incurred in defense of one's lord or of some symbol like a standard or flag to which one has sworn loyalty. Far better to fight and die honorably and gloriously, to fight to the last man, than to survive as the result of surrender. In Chou China, "it would be a supreme disgrace to flee with the standard unfurled, for if one goes to battle it is to do honour to one's flag. To run the risk of being the laughing-stock of an enemy who may cry your name aloud, or even to be haughtily spared by him, these are the worst misfortunes that can happen."[20]

As Bertrand de Born put it joyfully, "when battle is joined, let all men of good lineage think of naught but the breaking of heads and arms; for it is better to die than to be vanquished and live."[21] To be sure, honorable surrenders can be arranged in which the courage of the losers is properly recognized by the victors, and the former can honorably survive. Because, under the conditions of nearly continuous warfare typical of aristocratic

---

To book our dead, and then to bury them;
To sort our nobles from our common men;
for many of our princes (woe the while!)
Lie drown'd and soak'd in mercenary blood;
(So do our vulgar drench their peasant limbs
In blood of princes;)

Henry V, Act IV, Scene 7.

17. Bellah, *Tokugawa Religion*, p. 93. As a nineteenth-century *samurai* ideologist put it: "As our Imperial Throne is endless from the beginning, so we should let this thought sink deeply, that our loyalty must be endless. According to the words of Ama-no-oshihi-no-mikoto, 'He who dies for the sake of his lord does not die in vain, whether he goes to the sea and his corpse is left in a watery grave, or whether he goes to the mountain and the only shroud for his lifeless body is the mountain grass.' This is the way of loyalty." Quoted ibid. from Yoshida Shoin.

18. Granet, *Chinese Civilization*, p. 268.

19. Maquet, "The Kingdom of Ruanda," p. 180.

20. Granet, *Chinese Civilization*, p. 269.

21. Quoted in Bloch, *Feudal Society*, p. 293.

empires, today's victor can easily be tomorrow's loser, honorable peace terms might not be so difficult to obtain, and each side may want to avoid humiliating the other. There may thus be plenty of honor and glory to go around for both victor and vanquished, though undoubtedly there is more glory—if not necessarily more honor—in victory than in defeat.

If death in battle is honorable, any other death may be dishonorable. According to the military code of the Kshatriya, the ancient Indian warrior caste, "death in bed was not only considered dishonorable but a sin against caste *dharma*. When a Kshatriya felt his power weaken he was expected to seek death in battle."[22]

So important are his honor and glory to the aristocrat that he may engage in war primarily in order to pursue them. It is always possible for him to feel that his honor requires him to go to war because of some real or imagined insult he has suffered at the hands of some other aristocrat.[23] All his aristocratic followers are then honor-bound to go to war, too, in order to demonstrate their loyalty. Warfare, bloody as it may remain, can then become a kind of ritual, carried on in accordance with a strict code of chivalry for the defense of honor and the acquisition of glory.

Because glory is best gained in war, the absence of war poses a serious problem for aristocrats. The Aztecs avoided such a potential problem by deliberately not conquering Tlaxcala, an inimical "aristocratic republic" near their capital and in the midst of their empire, so that they could continue to fight wars with it.[24] As is often true among traditional aristocracies, their conceptions of honor and glory were intertwined with religious ideas. The Aztecs' principal way to gain glory was to capture prisoners of war who were needed for the constant human sacrifices their religion required. Thus, peace was in fact a threat to the individual with his dreams of glory and of the advancement and wealth that came with glory, but in their minds peace also threatened the world with destruction by angry gods.[25]

22. Weber, *The Religion of India*, p. 65.

23. "In the twelfth century, Perigord ran with blood because a certain lord thought that one of his noble neighbours looked like a blacksmith and had the bad taste to say so." Bloch, *Feudal Society*, p. 296.

24. Soustelle, *Daily Life of the Aztecs*, pp. xiv, 214.

25. Soustelle explains how the Aztecs institutionalized war in the context of his discussion of their religion: "Certainly it is not incorrect to interpret the history of Tenochtitlan between 1325 and 1519 as that of an imperialist state which steadily pursues its aim of expansion by conquest. But that is not all. As the Mexican dominion spread, so their very victories created a pacified zone all round them, a zone which grew wider and wider until it reached the edges of their known world. Where then were the victims to come from? For they were essential to provide the gods with their nourishment. . . . Where could one find the precious blood without which the sun and the whole frame of the universe was condemned to annihilation? It was essential to remain in a state of war, and from this need

Although war undoubtedly presents the best and preferred opportunities for aristocrats to display their courage, to gain glory, and to maintain their honor, they have generally invented peacetime substitutes to serve the same functions. The knightly tournaments of mock warfare,[26] jousts, and tilts are not even sharply distinguishable from real warfare carried on, in effect, as a sport. Similarly, dueling, a characteristic way for the individual aristocrat to respond to a challenge to his honor, is not clearly distinguishable from the sport of fencing, particularly if, as is often the case, each contestant in a duel considers his honor satisfied after inflicting merely some slight and often symbolic wounds on his opponent.[27]

Other sports pursued by the aristocracy are also such as to permit the display of the skills and qualities prized in warfare and hence to provide for the acquisition of glory and the maintenance of honor. This is true especially of sports involving horseback riding, such as racing and polo, for commonly there is an association of the aristocracy with horseback riding that may go back to the days of mounted nomads conquering peasants and certainly is linked to the fact that aristocrats frequently fight on horseback while others serve on foot. This association is evident in the very words for "knight" or "gentleman" in many European languages—*eques*, *Ritter*, *chevalier*, *caballero*, *cavaliere*—being related to the words for "rider" or "horse." It is also noteworthy that in medieval China, those most looked down upon, merchants and craftsmen, were not permitted to ride on horseback.[28] The Greeks, whose aristocracy did not fight on horseback, developed athletics as a form of contest in which skills could be displayed and glory gained.

Another sport characteristically engaged in by aristocrats is hunting, especially of a sort requiring courage and warlike skills, like big game hunting and hunting on horseback, as in fox hunting. "Edward the Confessor . . . spent much of his time 'in the glades and woods on the pleasure of hunting.' This was the normal relaxation of a king's leisure: Henry I of Ger-

---

arose the strange institution of the war of flowers. . . . The sovereigns of Mexico, Texcoco, and Tlacopan and the lords of Tlaxcala, Uexotzinco and Cholula mutually agreed that, there being no war, they would arrange combats, so that the captives might be sacrificed to the gods" (ibid., pp. 100–101).

26. For a well-illustrated article, see Williams, "The Sport of Knights."

27. On the beginnings of dueling and its persistence in posttraditional societies, see Baldick, *The Duel*. See also Bryson, *The Sixteenth-Century Italian Duel*.

28. When, after the tenth century, they were allowed to do so, they had to use saddles of a special color or ride in a special way. Eberhard, *Social Mobility in Traditional China*, p. 14. Even in the Mamluk empire, where merchants were "a rich, powerful, and socially honored class," "sometimes religious notables, scribes, and merchants were expressly forbidden to ride horses, which were reserved for the Mamluks." Lapidus, *Muslim Cities in the Later Middle Ages*, pp. 117, 266.

many was so keen a huntsman that he 'would take forty or more wild beasts in a day'; the Norman kings turned a substantial proportion of their kingdom into game preserves; hunting was the natural sport of a militant aristocracy, venting on animals the energy and spleen left over from fighting with their own kind."[29]

Because wild animals can constitute a menace to man, to his domestic animals, and to his crops and can be an important source of meat, hunting is often no mere sport. It may nevertheless be forbidden to nonaristocrats, or aristocrats may reserve for themselves certain hunting preserves or certain animals, as the Incas, who were horseless aristocrats, did in the case of the vicuña. The severity of the punishment typically inflicted on peasants for poaching may be explained by the fact that it was not seen so much or merely as a form of theft, but as an invasion of aristocratic privilege. If hunting is regarded as an aristocratic activity, then a peasant who hunts behaves like an aristocrat—which is intolerable.[30]

It should be added that, because service and duty, honor and glory are clearly, above all, military values, one might expect specialized nonmilitary hierarchies of the aristocracy not to hold these values. In fact, this is only partly true. Thus, the Chinese bureaucracy did not stress military virtues, but its Confucian emphasis on dignity, gentility, and good manners is related to the usual aristocratic conception of honor.

A conflict might also occur between the warlike values of the aristocracy and opposed religious values. A rare instance of the latter winning out is that of the Indian Maurya emperor Ashoka (273–232 B.C.) who "became appalled by the horrors of war and either turned Buddhist or was strongly influenced by Buddhism. He renounced war and became the earliest and most eloquent royal exponent of the philosophy of nonviolence. . . . He gave up the royal sport of hunting, . . . preached . . . kindness to all living things."[31] More commonly, it seems, it is the warlike values of the aristocracy that triumph even in the minds of aristocratic priesthoods formally representing what Max Weber calls "ethical religions of salvation." In such cases, the values of the specialized nonmilitary clergy, let alone of priests who are also rulers or warriors, are not so different from those of the rest of the aristocracy.

In developing his sociology of religion, Weber stresses that "the life pattern of a warrior has very little affinity with the notion of a beneficent providence, or with the systematic ethical demands of a transcendental

29. Brooke, *Europe in the Central Middle Ages*, p. 125.

30. For a vivid description of aristocratic hawking and hunting, of the destruction of peasants' crops wrought both by hunters and by animals the peasants are not allowed to kill, and of the death penalty for poaching, see Davis, *Life on a Mediaeval Barony*, pp. 57–67, 272.

31. Lamb, *India*, pp. 26–27.

god. Concepts like sin, salvation, and religious humility have not only seemed remote from all ruling strata, particularly the warrior nobles, but have indeed appeared reprehensible to its [sic] sense of honor. To accept a religion that works with such conceptions and to genuflect before the prophet or priest would appear plebeian and dishonorable to any martial hero or noble person, e.g., the Roman nobility of the age of Tacitus, or the Confucian mandarins. . . . Indeed, the chances and adventures of mundane existence fill his life to such an extent that he does not require of his religion (and accepts only reluctantly) anything beyond protection against evil magic or ceremonial rites congruent with his sense of status, such as priestly prayers for victory or for a blissful death leading directly into the hero's heaven."[32]

When ethical religions like Christianity and Islam are adopted by aristocrats, they lose their ethical character, and to that extent, the ideology of the aristocratic priesthood becomes similar to that of the aristocratic warriors. As Weber notes, "It will be recalled that Pope Urban lost no time in emphasizing to the crusaders the necessity for territorial expansion in order to acquire new benefices for their descendants. To an even greater degree than the Crusades, religious war for the Muslims was essentially an enterprise directed towards the acquisition of large holdings of real estate, because it was primarily oriented to securing feudal revenue." The paradise promised to the Muslim killed in holy war or to the Hindu warrior, Valhalla, and "any other hero heaven are not equivalent to salvation. Moreover, those religious elements of ancient Islam which had the character of an ethical religion of salvation largely receded into the background as long as Islam remained essentially a martial religion."[33] And Weber notes that the same was true of the Sikhs, of warlike Buddhist monks in Japan, and of the medieval Christian orders of celibate knights like the Templars.

Contempt for Work and Money-Making

The values of service and duty, honor and glory all justify and reinforce what aristocrats do in aristocratic empires, chiefly their military activities, but to some extent also their functions as rulers, administra-

32. Weber, *Economy and Society*, 2:472–73.

33. Ibid., p. 474. Not only Muslim, Hindu, and Germanic warriors went to their respective hero heavens. Among the Aztecs, too, "it was the warriors killed in battle or sacrificed after capture who went to dwell in the house of the sun. . . . Even these fortunate warriors did not enjoy their privilege indefinitely; after four years of the joys of accompanying the sun, they returned to earth in the guise of hummingbirds and lived on for ever, sipping the wild honey." Davies, *The Aztecs*, p. 172. See also Soustelle, *Daily Life of the Aztecs*, pp. 44, 106–7.

tors, and priests. Another component of the ideology of aristocrats, their contempt for productive labor, rationalizes their role as rulers in another manner, for that role is exercised mostly through the power to tax, that is, to take from the producers a part of their product and thus to live without producing. Like the other values of aristocrats, their contempt for manual work can be linked to their nomadic origins and, at any rate, to their way of life in aristocratic empires.

The nomads who spend their lives in the relatively exciting pursuits of warfare and raiding or the relatively easy tasks of hunting and cattle raising and the aristocrats who succeed them look down with contempt on the dull life of the cultivators tied to the soil and to an unending and unchanging routine of work. Perhaps the Old Testament reflects nomadic values when it sees agricultural work as a curse. God says to Adam: "Cursed is the ground for thy sake; in sorrow shalt thou eat of it all the days of thy life. Thorns also and thistles shall it bring forth to thee; and thou shalt eat the herb of the field. In the sweat of thy face shalt thou eat bread, till thou return unto the ground." And his father said of Noah that he "shall comfort us concerning our work and toil of our hands because of the ground which the Lord hath cursed."[34] Tacitus says of Germanic warriors: "Nor are they as easily persuaded to plough the earth and to wait for the year's produce as to challenge an enemy and earn the honour of wounds. Nay they actually think it tame and stupid to acquire by the sweat of toil what they might win by their blood."[35]

That peasants are compelled to work for aristocrats only increases the contempt of the latter for manual work and for those who work manually. The aristocrat is now distinguished from the peasant exactly by the fact that he can afford to live—and to live well—without working. Indeed, he cannot afford to work, for this would wipe out the distinction between him and the peasant and thus undermine his position vis-à-vis the peasant. Work, then, becomes associated with low-class status—as Mencius said some 2,300 years ago: "Those who earn their living by labor are destined to be ruled"[36]—and is beneath the dignity of the aristocrat; idleness, on the other hand, is regarded as noble. Difficult as this is to understand for one raised in the Protestant ethic—the product of a modernizing age—work to the aristocrat is dishonorable and demeaning, it is drudgery, which Webster defines as "ignoble or slavish toil."

34. Gen. 3:17–19; 5:29. But after the flood, "the Lord said in his heart, I will not again curse the ground any more for man's sake. . . . While the earth remaineth, seedtime and harvest, and cold and heat, and summer and winter, and day and night, shall not cease." Gen. 8:21–22.

35. Tacitus, *Germania*, XIV, p. 716.

36. Quoted by Hsiao-tung Fei, "Peasantry and Gentry," p. 4.

Thorstein Veblen, writing at the turn of the century, put it this way: "When the community passes from peaceable savagery to a predatory phase of life . . . aggression becomes the accredited form of action, and booty serves as *prima facie* evidence of successful aggression. . . . Therefore, by contrast, the obtaining of goods by other methods than seizure comes to be accounted unworthy of man in his best estate. The performance of productive work, or employment in personal service, falls under the same odium for the same reason. . . . Labor acquires a character of irksomeness by virtue of the indignity imputed to it. . . . During the predatory culture labor comes to be associated in men's habits of thought with weakness and subjection to a master. It is therefore a mark of inferiority, and therefore comes to be accounted unworthy of man in his best estate. . . . Prescription ends by making labor not only disreputable in the eyes of the community, but morally impossible to the noble, freeborn man, and incompatible with a worthy life."[37]

Even artists, who, like many artisans, create exclusively for aristocrats and whose product is appreciated by the latter, are nevertheless held in contempt if, like sculptors and painters, they work with their hands. Only art forms like poetry that involve no "work" are considered worthy of aristocrats.[38]

If aristocrats do not work, how do they spend their time? A good deal of it, for many of them, is spent in warfare, in war-related expeditions, and in preparation and training for war as well as in the sports more or less closely related to warfare I have just mentioned. Priests perform religious rituals and bureaucrats have their administrative tasks. How-

37. Veblen, *The Theory of the Leisure Class*, pp. 30, 41, 45. Veblen also tells of "a certain king of France, who is said to have lost his life through an excess of moral stamina in the observance of good form. In the absence of the functionary whose office it was to shift his master's seat, the king sat uncomplaining before the fire and suffered his royal person to be toasted beyond recovery. But in so doing he saved his Most Christian Majesty from menial contamination" (ibid., pp. 45–46).

38. Karl Kautsky makes this point citing a number of Greek authors. *Die materialistische Geschichtsauffassung*, 2:275–80. Aristotle, dealing with education in music in the *Politics* (Book VIII, Chap. vi, §§ 15–16), rejects "any professional system of instruction. . . . On such a system the player, instead of treating music as a means to his own improvement, makes it serve the pleasure—and that a vulgar pleasure—of the audience to which he is playing. That is why we regard his performance as something improper in a freeman, and more befitting a hireling. The players themselves may also become vulgar in the process." *The Politics of Aristotle*, p. 348. In a footnote, Barker says: "In something of an English fashion—at any rate as that fashion went in the eighteenth century—Aristotle feels that the freeman or 'gentleman' ought to preserve an amateur character. Even in the liberal arts—such as music, painting, and literature—he must be a dilettante, with a fine edge of appreciation, but with an edge of execution which is not too precious or virtuose" (ibid., pp. 334–35).

ever, commonly the tasks of government, aside from warfare, are not very demanding, and neither rulers nor their subordinates, even if, as in China, they are specialized bureaucrats, are engaged in them on a full-time basis.

Levine thus describes the typical activities of an ideal traditional Ethiopian aristocrat who "was at once governor, soldier, and courtier. In time of war he set forth at his own expense, with his own troops, to support the cause of the emperor, or perhaps simply to defend his own regional interests. In time of peace he might sojourn, if permitted, at the court of his king or overlord, eating and drinking with his peers, giving counsel to his liege when asked, engaged in intrigue and otherwise seeking to improve his station. When not active in warfare or the affairs of court, the nobleman would repair to his lands to supervise the agricultural production and the collection of rents from his tenants."[39]

Obviously, then, aristocrats generally enjoy a great deal of leisure. Leisure itself is regarded as noble, but it may nevertheless result in much boredom, from which aristocrats may seek to escape by turning to warring and raiding and warlike sports, as did many knights in feudal Western Europe. A minority of aristocrats may also devote themselves to contemplation or nonmanual arts. What Maquet says of the Tutsi in Ruanda is more generally applicable: "They do no manual work and have leisure to cultivate eloquence, poetry, refined manners, and the subtle art of being witty when talking and drinking hydromel with friends."[40] And in another work on Ruanda, Maquet says more generally: "Usually, an upper caste shows its superiority by, among other things, its leisure and pleasant life. It has to enjoy a greater share of the good things of life than the commoners and it has to get this apparently without effort, rather as a right than as a reward for specific tasks."[41]

Aristocrats also have much of their time taken up by compliance with the elaborate codes of etiquette and protocol that govern life not only at many courts of great monarchs but to some extent also in the households of lesser aristocrats who imitate their rulers. Veblen even argues that it is the function of manners to serve as "immaterial evidences of past leisure." "Refined tastes, manners, and habits of life are a useful evidence of gentility, because good breeding requires time, application, and expense, and

---

39. Levine, *Wax and Gold*, p. 160.

40. Maquet, "The Kingdom of Ruanda," p. 175. The fourteenth-century French aristocrat's "leisure time was spent chiefly in hunting, otherwise in games of chess, backgammon, and dice, in songs, dances, pageants, and other entertainments. Long winter evenings were occupied listening to the recital of interminable verse epics." Tuchman, *A Distant Mirror*, p. 65.

41. Maquet, *The Premise of Inequality in Ruanda*, p. 148.

can therefore not be compassed by those whose time and energy are taken up with work. A knowledge of good form is *prima facie* evidence that that portion of the well-bred person's life which is not spent under the observation of the spectator has been worthily spent in acquiring accomplishments that are of no lucrative effect. In the last analysis the value of manners lies in the fact that they are the voucher of a life of leisure. . . . The greater the degree of proficiency and the more patent the evidence of a high degree of habituation to observances which serve no lucrative or other directly useful purpose, the greater the consumption of time and substance impliedly involved in their acquisition, and the greater the resultant good repute. Hence, under the competitive struggle for proficiency in good manners, it comes about that much pains is taken with the cultivation of habits of decorum; and hence the details of decorum develop into a comprehensive discipline, conformity to which is required of all who would be held blameless in point of repute. And hence, on the other hand, this conspicuous leisure of which decorum is a ramification grows gradually into a laborious drill in deportment. . . . The pervading principle and abiding test of good breeding is the requirement of a substantial and patent waste of time."[42]

Just as good manners take time both to acquire and to practice, so does good taste—though by no means do all aristocracies develop either. Especially in long-established empires, the aristocrat is expected to "cultivate his tastes, for it now becomes incumbent on him to discriminate with some nicety between the noble and the ignoble in consumable goods. He becomes a connoisseur in creditable viands of various degrees of merit, in manly beverages and trinkets, in seemly apparel and architecture, in weapons, games, dancers, and the narcotics. This cultivation of the aesthetic faculty requires time and application, and the demands made upon the gentleman in this direction therefore tend to change his life of leisure into a more or less arduous application to the business of learning how to live a life of ostensible leisure in a becoming way."[43]

In traditional aristocratic empires, merchants do not play a big role, and aristocrats simply look down on them as they do on all nonaristocrats.

---

42. Veblen, *Theory of the Leisure Class*, pp. 47, 49, 50, 51. Veblen's leisure class is not identical with the aristocracy, as that term is used here. Much of his book deals with what he regards as the modern leisure class, which he does not sharply distinguish from the aristocracy, its direct forebear in his view. However, especially in his first four chapters, there are many insightful remarks applicable to the aristocracy. A few of these are quoted in this chapter (at some length, because of their delightful language). Indeed, Veblen begins his book with the statement that "the institution of a leisure class is found in its best development at the higher stages of the barbarian culture; as, for instance, in feudal Europe or feudal Japan" (ibid., p. 21).

43. Ibid., p. 64.

However, as their role increases with commercialization, aristocrats develop a special form of contempt for them. It is mixed with resentment, because merchants seek to and some actually do acquire wealth, an attribute that aristocrats traditionally associate with their own status. Probably related to this contempt for commerce is the notion, already found in ancient Rome, that the city, as distinguished from the country, is corrupt. This throws light on the difference between the aristocrat's contempt for work and his contempt for trade. Life in the country is clean and decent for, while peasants are contemptible because they work, they perform an essential function in the aristocratic scheme of things. They can hence be regarded as good, just as an ox, no matter how contemptible, can be a good ox. Peasants are no threat to the aristocracy and are therefore not resented like the merchant. He is held in contempt and is seen as corrupt and morally evil, because he does pose a threat.

The aristocrat's resentment of the merchant is well expressed by the troubadour Bertrand de Born: "I love to see the rich churl in distress if he dares to strive with nobles. I love to see him beg his bread in nakedness."[44] As Barrington Moore says of imperial China: "One may readily perceive that money-making activities represented a dangerous threat to the scholar-officials because it constituted an alternative ladder of prestige and an alternative ground of legitimacy for high social status. No amount of Confucian talk and no amount of sumptuary legislation could be expected to conceal forever the simple fact that someone who made lots of money could buy the good things of life, including even a substantial measure of deference."[45]

In commercialized societies, where land has become alienable, merchants may even use their wealth to acquire land and, with it, control of peasants and thus assume a role traditionally reserved for aristocrats. Merchants become even more threatening and hence contemptible to aristocrats when these latter become dependent on them for taxes and especially for loans. Debtors never have much love for their creditors; if, in addition to hating them, they can hold them in contempt, this may become an excuse for "honorably" not paying off their debts, as, for example, many a king and knight did to Jewish moneylenders in late medieval Europe.[46]

44. Quoted in Davis, *Life on a Mediaeval Barony*, p. 257.

45. Moore, *Social Origins of Dictatorship and Democracy*, p. 175.

46. For sources on similar practices in Mogul India, Tokugawa Japan, and medieval England, see Lenski, *Power and Privilege*, p. 253. However, in the Arabic empires, too, where merchants were not held in contempt, "princes and regents were bad debtors. They not only failed to pay their obligations but in times of need they confiscated the wealth of their creditors." Labib, "Capitalism in Medieval Islam," p. 93. In the Mamluk empire, "a loan at

Aristocrats look down on the merchant's preoccupation with money-making, because it runs counter to the dominant traditional value orientation that "censures any attempt to manipulate or to revise the natural order of things."[47] The aristocrat does not make money as the merchant does in the form of profit or interest, ways that appear unnatural to the aristocrat. This does not mean that he is not interested in wealth, that he is less materialistic than the merchant, as aristocratic ideology in commercialized society often asserts. However, he does not need to make money; he receives it naturally, that is, simply by virtue of being an aristocrat. Only money acquired as tribute, taxes, or rent conveys prestige, as is true also of the results of raiding and robbing, booty and ransom payments, and gifts given by higher aristocrats in return for services rendered to them or by lower aristocrats in hopes of receiving future favors.

Confucius felt that "the poise and harmony of the soul are shaken by the risks of acquisitiveness," but that, on the other hand, a gentleman needs wealth. Its proper source is income from taxes through office in the bureaucracy, "the one position becoming a superior man because the office alone allows for the perfection of personality. . . . Without permanent income the educated man can be of constant mind only with difficulty."[48] In fact, especially in commercialized societies, some aristocrats derive some of their wealth from the sale of products of their land and no doubt manage their estates in part with this in view. Nevertheless, the commercial economy of the aristocracy tends to be ignored in the aristocrats' self-image, perhaps because it is exceptional in traditional aristocratic empires or only accounts for a relatively small part of the aristocracy's wealth or because it deviates from the original pattern of the aristocrat living merely by the exploitation of peasants engaged in subsistence agriculture. Even the aristocrat who benefits from the activities of buying and selling will therefore avoid engaging in them himself. He will leave these to professional merchants and to managers or administrators of his lands, people of lower class whom he can regard with some disdain, while he is busy with the more typical aristocratic tasks of warfare and government, which often take him away from his lands for long periods.

Max Weber stressed that "all impersonal and commercial relationships . . . are bound to appear undignified and vulgar to the feudal ethic." "Feudalism is inherently contemptuous of bourgeois-commercial utili-

---

the behest of a supremely more powerful borrower in great need was a poor risk, and the merchant who offered it probably used it as a bribe to avoid more decisive extortions." Lapidus, *Muslim Cities in the Later Middle Ages*, p. 122.

47. Sjoberg, *The Preindustrial City*, p. 183; see also ibid., pp. 136, 183–84.

48. Weber, *The Religion of China*, p. 160.

tarianism and considers it as sordid greediness and as the life force specifically hostile to it. Feudal conduct leads to the opposite of the rational economic ethos and is the source of that nonchalance in business affairs which has been typical of all feudal strata, not only in contrast to the bourgeois, but also to the peasants' proverbial shrewdness."[49]

Weber interestingly links this aristocratic opposition to commercialism and utilitarianism to what he calls "the game," which presumably includes the aristocratic tournaments and sports I have just discussed. He argues that under feudal conditions, just as in the life of animals and early men, the game is not a pastime; "rather it is the natural form in which the psycho-physical capacities of the organism are kept alive and supple; the game is a form of 'training' which in its spontaneous and unbroken animal instinctiveness as yet transcends any split between the 'spiritual' and the 'material,' 'body' and 'soul,' no matter how conventionally it is sublimated. . . . Inevitably the game also occupies a most serious and important position in the life of these knightly strata; it constitutes a counterpole to all economically rational action."[50]

It is, then, not only in traditional aristocratic empires, but particularly in formerly traditional but now commercialized empires that aristocrats look on merchants with contempt and seek to distinguish themselves from merchants by keeping the latter in their place. "The Homeric Greeks regarded the professional merchant with distrust and contempt" but also subsequently "trade . . . was . . . looked upon by the Greeks for many centuries as an occupation unworthy of a freeman and a gentleman." "Prejudice and tradition . . . die hard, and even in the age of Pericles, while the Athenians were enjoying the pleasure and power that came to them from their extensive trade, their rich silver mines, their industries of one sort and another, they still clung tenaciously to the old feeling that agriculture was the only gainful occupation befitting a free man and a citizen."[51] In Rome, too, "the senators as great landlords looked down in

49. Weber, *Economy and Society*, 3:1105, 1106.

50. Ibid., pp. 1105–6.

51. Calhoun, *The Ancient Greeks and the Evolution of Standards in Business*, pp. 41, 52. "Although trade expanded, and built the greatness of Athens, the general feeling was traditionalist and distrustful; it contrasted the 'economy' founded on agriculture with the 'chrematistic' approach, founded on money, to which Aristotle expressed everyone's hostility." Lévy, *The Economic Life of the Ancient World*, p. 23. As he wrote in the *Politics* (Book VII, Chap. ix, § 3): "the life of mechanics or shopkeepers . . . is ignoble and inimical to goodness." *The Politics of Aristotle*, p. 301. And Plato had written in the *Laws* (Book XI, §§ 919–20) that "he who in any way shares in the illiberality of retail trades may be indicted for dishonoring his race by any one who likes," for these trades are "pursuits which have a very strong tendency to make men bad." *The Dialogues of Plato*, 2:658–59. In the classical

scorn on trade in any form, on free labor as sordid and tainted by contact with slaves."[52]

In imperial China and feudal Japan the view of trade as an unnatural and hence improper activity put merchants and artisans in an official rank even lower than peasants (whose activity was held to be very natural and proper), even when they stood far above peasants in their standard of living. In China, down to the Ming dynasty (1368–1644), merchants and shopkeepers had to wear clothing of a special color and of material inferior to that of peasants' clothing to indicate their low status, and if even one peasant in a family became a merchant, the entire family had to wear merchant's clothing.[53] "A traditional bias against the tradesman had already been formulated before the Han period, from considerations of both theory and expediency. It was felt that the main working effort of humanity should properly be directed to extracting nature's gifts from the soil; and that, whereas such an occupation was honourable and praiseworthy, a merchant's business, which depended on squeezing a profit from his fellow human beings, was questionable and even shameful."[54] "Trade was traditionally regarded as an occupation that went against the public interest, and the commercial profession was considered dishonorable, superfluous, and even positively harmful, because it was held responsible for immoral luxury, parasitism, and usury."[55]

In Japan, in the early Tokugawa period which began in 1600, "it was considered against the ethics or etiquette of the samurai to think or talk about money matters. A samurai thought it a disgrace to handle money, and if he was presented with money, he took it as a gross insult. His money account was kept by a low-grade official, and he was proud to show his friends that he did not even know how to count money."[56]

---

period of Greek history, "the moneyed classes regarded commerce and industry as degrading and . . . would not become merchants and manufacturers themselves." Cook, *The Greeks until Alexander*, p. 132.

52. Moore, *The Roman's World*, p. 81. Cicero wrote in *De Officiis* (Book I, Chap. XLII, § 150): "Unbecoming to a gentleman . . . and vulgar are the means of livelihood of all hired workmen whom we pay for mere manual labour, not for artistic skill; for in their case the very wage they receive is a pledge of their slavery. Vulgar we must consider those also who buy from wholesale merchants to retail immediately; for they would get no profits without a great deal of outright lying. . . . And all mechanics are engaged in vulgar trades." Cicero, *De Officiis*, p. 153.

53. Eberhard, *Social Mobility in Traditional China*, p. 14.

54. Loewe, *Everyday Life in Early Imperial China*, p. 152.

55. Balazs, *Chinese Civilization and Bureaucracy*, p. 56.

56. Takizawa, *The Penetration of Money Economy in Japan*, p. 35.

Sjoberg comments that for aristocrats "this was one means of removing themselves from identification with lower-status elements, including merchants."[57]

Geertz, speaking of present-day Indonesian traders, says: "A culturally homogeneous group, they formed a well-defined, sharply set-apart minority . . . whose values deviated in major respects from those embraced by both the gentry and the peasantry. . . . The status of the trader in the wider society has been ambiguous at best, pariah-like at worst. . . . The Javanese . . . have tended to see the trader as standing 'outside' the ethical order."[58] The same can be said of medieval Europe. Here, "the Church's attitude toward trade was wary and nicely summed up in St. Jerome's dictum: *Homo mercator vix aut numquam Deo placere potest*—the merchant can scarcely or never be pleasing to God."[59]

In contrast to the position of merchants in all these societies, it is notable that in the early Arab empires the merchant class "was respected and honoured by religious law and social opinion: the vocation of the trader and manufacturer was sanctioned by the Koran, which never dissociated profit from piety."[60] This is probably due to the fact already mentioned in Chapter 2 that, while these empires were founded by nomads conquering agrarian areas, they had never been purely traditional.[61] On the other hand, the nomadic Turkic conquerors of Turkey, Persia, and India "had known few cities and little commerce by comparison." "The traditional Arab esteem for the merchant was now no longer shared by their Turkic successors: contempt for trade was a general hallmark of the ruling class of the new States."[62]

57. Sjoberg, *The Preindustrial City*, p. 184.

58. Geertz, *Peddlers and Princes*, pp. 43–44.

59. Heilbroner, *The Making of Economic Society*, p. 39. See also Pirenne, *A History of Europe*, 2:229.

60. Anderson, *Lineages of the Absolutist State*, p. 503. Later, under the Mamluks (1250–1517), too, "the leading merchants were among the richest men of their times, often the equal of emirs. They received many official honors, were entitled to attend official ceremonies, and could be represented at official discussions. Rich merchants with the appropriate style of life were included among the notables of the city, for in Islamic society trade was not considered ignoble or derogating, nor were rents, pensions, and taxes regarded as the only worthy forms of income." Lapidus, *Muslim Cities in the Later Middle Ages*, p. 81. Lapidus even speaks of "the absorption of the merchant elite into the regime where they took up the duties of office in the state bureaucracy and the Sultan's service. On the other hand, from their own point of view, this was a situation rich in opportunities for profit and social prestige" (ibid., p. 130).

61. On the relationship of Islam to commercialism, see Rodinson, *Islam and Capitalism*, pp. 12–117.

62. Anderson, *Lineages of the Absolutist State*, pp. 512, 516.

In the Aztec empire, merchants were not only, as in the Arabic empires, deliberately used by the aristocracy to increase its income, but they played an important military role as spies and even as warriors. Hence, far from being treated with contempt, they were "in many respects highly privileged. They were allowed to own land, and some could even send their children to the special schools reserved for the children of the ruling classes. The second Moctezuma even treated them at times as noblemen, bidding them to sit at his side on important occasions." Unlike merchants elsewhere and much more like aristocrats, they devoted their wealth "as much to banquets and display as to private accumulation." And yet, even among the Aztecs, the merchants' growing importance "gave rise to resentment on the part of the established ruling classes—hence their feigned humility and their tendency to hide their riches."[63] "The ruling class would bear their rivalry only if they avoided all open conflict. . . . Death and deprivation hovered over the head of the trader who forgot his role and made the mistake of showing off his wealth."[64]

Conspicuous Consumption
and Display of Wealth

The limited opportunities in traditional aristocratic empires to invest in trade and moneylending—they become substantial only with commercialization—are ideologically rejected by aristocrats, because they are associated with the lower classes. Nor is great wealth invested in the agrarian economy. The peasants go with the land and are neither paid like workers nor bought like slaves, and they, in turn, produce and provide what simple tools and fertilizers are in use. The principal way available to aristocrats of increasing their income is to expand the cultivated land area under their control. This can be done by bringing uncultivated land under cultivation, which may involve draining or irrigating it or clearing forests and wasteland or terracing mountainsides. To insure uninterrupted and increased agricultural production aristocrats may also engage in the building of flood control and irrigation works. All these activities may require some investment of capital, both in tools and in the skilled labor of those who plan and supervise the construction efforts. However, even massive construction projects may not involve great investments because the labor of huge numbers of laborers is, in effect, free. It is provided by the corvée

63. Davies, *The Aztecs*, p. 139.
64. Soustelle, *Daily Life of the Aztecs*, p. 64.

exacted from peasants during those parts of the year when they are not needed to do agricultural work. They are not paid but merely fed, as they would be also if they stayed in their villages.

Investments made by aristocrats, then, are, relative to their income, small and exceptional. Overwhelmingly, they have no incentive to save and invest their wealth, unless expenditures for warfare are regarded as a form of investment because war may result in the acquisition of additional land and wealth. Clearly, aside from the exceptions mentioned, aristocrats exploit peasants and receive their income not in order to invest it but simply to consume it.

But how can aristocrats consume their entire income? Aristocracies in control of great numbers of peasants collect far more income than they can use for the necessities of their own food, clothing, and shelter, or even those of any nonaristocratic components of their armies, bureaucracies, and priesthoods supported by them. If they remain in power for long periods of time, they can accumulate huge amounts of wealth. The annual revenues of the Mogul emperor Aurangzeb (1658–1701) are said to have amounted to $450,000,000, more than ten times those of Louis XIV. According to an estimate of 1638, the Mogul court of India is supposed to have accumulated a treasure equivalent to one and one-half billion dollars.[65]

What, then, is the point of accumulating vast treasures? Certainly aristocrats do not have to save for a rainy day for, simply by virtue of being aristocrats, they can rely on a perpetually guaranteed income through the exploitation of peasants. Nor is there, in the absence of investment opportunities, any point in saving for investment purposes. In aristocratic ideology, therefore, to save is to be miserly and niggardly, it is dishonorable and ignoble. On the other hand, "unproductive consumption of goods is honorable."[66]

Wealth is accumulated by aristocrats in aristocratic empires not to be saved or invested but to be displayed. A visitor to the Mogul court of Aurangzeb describes his elaborate clothing and jewelry and goes on: "The throne was supported by six massy feet, said to be of solid gold, sprinkled over with rubies, emeralds, and diamonds. It was constructed by Shah-Jehan for the purpose of displaying the immense quantity of precious stones accumulated successively in the Treasury from the spoils of ancient *Rajahs* and *Pathans*, and the annual presents to the monarch which every Omrah is bound to make on certain festivals."[67]

65. Lybyer, *The Government of the Ottoman Empire*, p. 295. The dollars mentioned are presumably those of the pre-World War I period, when Lybyer wrote and when the purchasing power of the dollar was nearly ten times as great as in 1981.

66. Veblen, *The Theory of the Leisure Class*, p. 61.

67. François Bernier, *Travels in the Mogul Empire, A.D. 1656–1663* (Westminster, 1891), quoted in Lybyer, *The Government of the Ottoman Empire*, p. 289.

Aristocrats vie with each other in displaying their wealth and in order to do so stage elaborate ceremonies on all sorts of occasions, to celebrate holidays, victories, and weddings, to mark anniversaries, or to receive other aristocrats.[68] Two millennia before the Moguls, the Mauryan emperors of India are supposed to have "traveled over perfumed roads in golden palanquins garnished with pearls, or, for longer trips, on an elephant all sheathed in gold, with a long train of courtesans also in golden litters."[69]

The aristocrats' clothing and furniture are expensive and elaborate, and even their weapons and armor and various utensils may be lavishly decorated. Fine works of art are created, and magnificent palaces and churches, mosques and temples are erected, requiring not only unskilled corvée labor, but the efforts through decades of highly skilled craftsmen and artists. Rich use is made everywhere of precious stones and pearls, of rare metals and woods, sometimes imported at great expense from distant places. Artists are maintained by aristocrats, like architects, sculptors, and painters as well as poets, composers, and musicians.

Obviously, aristocrats also use their wealth to secure personal enjoyment and luxury for themselves. The subject of concubines and mistresses will be discussed at the end of this chapter, but food and especially drink and narcotics must be referred to here. To quote Veblen again: "In the nature of things, luxuries and the comforts of life belong to the leisure class. . . . Certain victuals, and more particularly certain beverages, are strictly reserved for the use of the superior class. . . . [If] intoxicating beverages and narcotics . . . are costly, they are felt to be noble and honorific. . . . Drunkenness and the other pathological consequences of the free use of stimulants therefore tend in their turn to become honorific, as being a mark, at the second remove, of the superior status of those who are able to afford the indulgence. Infirmities induced by over-indulgence are among some peoples freely recognized as manly attributes."[70]

It is quite possible that one reason for the decline of dynasties and empires, which is after all merely the decline of a small number of aristocrats, is the sort of infirmity that is induced by overindulgence.[71] Even if

68. For good descriptions of the display of wealth and luxury, the sumptuous life and complex ceremonials at the court of the Sassanians in Seleucia on the Tigris and at the court of the Abbasid caliphs in Baghdad, see Diez, *The Ancient Worlds of Asia*, pp. 91–118.

69. Wesson, *The Imperial Order*, p. 84. Similarly, a mid-sixteenth-century Spanish observer in Peru wrote of the Incas: "They traveled in great majesty, . . . seated in rich litters, fitted with loose poles of excellent wood, and enriched with gold and silver. Over the litter there were two high arches of gold set with precious stones." Quoted in von Hagen, *Realm of the Incas*, p. 122.

70. Veblen, *The Theory of the Leisure Class*, pp. 61–62.

71. Karl Kautsky, providing numerous examples, argues that the decline of empires for this reason is virtually inevitable, because the aristocrats' power brings them wealth that leads

aristocrats, unlike, for example, Alexander the Great, survive heavy drinking, they may concentrate on luxurious living, on wine, women, and song. No longer interested in or capable of providing military leadership, they leave this central aristocratic task to the leaders of warrior tribes hired as mercenaries or to lower-ranking aristocrats who had less opportunity for overindulgence. These soon become aware of their new strength and divide up the empire into their own smaller ones, or one of them, defeating the others, emerges to replace the old dynasty. Also, a militarily weakened aristocracy may lose its empire when it is beaten by a still vigorous aristocracy of a neighboring empire or by a conquering nomadic tribe. When the existence of an empire is tantamount merely to the existence of an aristocracy and when the maintenance of the empire depends on successful military expansion or at least successful military defense, the loss of physical and mental strength by a few aristocrats may be sufficient to bring about the loss of the empire.

Returning to the question of how aristocrats use and display their wealth, we find that a typical means is employment of numerous servants. Many are required to prepare and serve food and drink for an aristocrat's family, his retainers, and his staff and to clean his house, which is likely to be large and elaborately furnished. Others drive the aristocrat's carriage or carry him in a sedan chair; some take care of his clothing and may help him dress; others clean his weapons and his armor or carry his shield or his umbrella; still others tend his horses, his dogs, and his falcons. Also, there are pages and doorkeepers, dwarfs and jesters, guards and messengers, and lots of servants to wait not only on the aristocrat but also on his wife or wives and concubines and on other relatives and on aristocrats surrounding him.

The Hawaiian king's "glory was . . . served by a huge suite and crowd of servants, retainers and hangers-on, priests, singers, dancers, runners, fly swatters, spittoon carriers, pipe lighters, cloak holders, storytellers, and sundry other attendants."[72] In the Aztec empire, "both Nezaualpilli at Texcoco, with his immense harem and his forty favourite wives, of whom one alone, the daughter of the Mexican emperor Axayacatl, had more than two thousand people in her service, and Motecuhzoma II at Mexico, who was perpetually surrounded by three thousand attendants in the palace, without counting the eagles, snakes and jaguars which he kept in special quarters and which ate five hundred turkeys a day,

---

them to overindulge in drink and sex which eventually causes their downfall. *Die materialistische Geschichtsauffassung*, 2:314–23. "It was the fate of the ruling classes that the same factors on which their power rested undermined that power" (ibid., p. 320).

72. Wesson, *The Imperial Order*, p. 462. See ibid., pp. 116–18, on the tendency of court entourages of aristocratic rulers to grow.

lived like potentates in the midst of an abundance from which an ever-increasing train of followers grew rich."[73]

Clearly, there cannot be enough tasks to keep hundreds or thousands of servants busy. Fly swatters, spittoon carriers, pipe lighters, and cloak holders must be idle when they are not swatting flies, carrying spittoons, lighting pipes, or holding cloaks. Evidently, servants perform a useful function by their mere existence, not just by their work. They become, as Veblen put it, a derivative leisure class. As the aristocrat's leisure serves as evidence of his nobility, so, in a different way, does his servants' leisure. "Servants are useful more for show than for service actually performed. . . . Their service tends in the end to become nominal only. . . . The utility of these [servants] comes to consist, in great part, in their conspicuous exemption from productive labor and in the evidence which this exemption affords of their master's wealth and power."[74]

"In this way, then, there arises a subsidiary or derivative leisure class, whose office is the performance of a vicarious leisure for the behoof of the reputability of the primary or legitimate leisure class. This vicarious leisure class is distinguished from the leisure class proper by a characteristic feature of its habitual mode of life. The leisure of the master class is, at least ostensibly, an indulgence of a proclivity for the avoidance of labor and is presumed to enhance the master's own well-being and fullness of life; but the leisure of the servant class exempt from productive labor is in some sort a performance exacted from them, and is not normally or primarily directed at their own comfort. The leisure of the servant is not his own leisure."[75]

"Special training in personal service costs time and effort, and where it is obviously present in a high degree, it argues that the servant who possesses it neither is nor has been habitually engaged in any productive occupation. It is *prima facie* evidence of a vicarious leisure extending far back in the past. So that trained service has utility, not only as gratifying the master's instinctive liking for good and skillful workmanship and his propensity for conspicuous dominance over those whose lives are subservient to his own, but it has utility also as putting in evidence a much larger consumption of human service than would be shown by the mere present conspicuous leisure performed by an untrained person."[76]

Thus, "there arises a class of servants, the more numerous the better, whose sole office is fatuously to wait upon the person of their owner,

73. Soustelle, *Daily Life of the Aztecs*, pp. 84–85.
74. Veblen, *The Theory of the Leisure Class*, p. 54.
75. Ibid., pp. 55–56.
76. Ibid., pp. 56–57.

and so to put in evidence his ability unproductively to consume a large amount of service."[77] In addition to having masses of servants in and around his residence, the aristocrat might, for example while traveling or at receptions, surround himself with numerous retainers. These may serve to protect him, whether from potential enemies or merely from contact with common people, but they also always function to display his power and wealth. A relatively few servants and retainers are clearly identified with their master by living near him. But when they become more numerous, "more patent means are required to indicate the imputation of merit for the leisure performed, and to this end uniforms, badges, and liveries come into vogue."[78]

While the livery may be a mark of servitude, armed retainers, especially of a high aristocrat, may themselves be lower-ranking aristocrats, and their uniforms and badges, denoting association with the higher aristocrat, may be marks of honor. Indeed, as the number and specialization of servants in a household grow, they come to be arranged in hierarchies. Some of the higher ranking ones, like butlers and chamberlains, marshalls and seneschals could, when serving at the court of a powerful aristocrat, become quite powerful themselves. At such a court, the positions of such servants may then eventually, though probably not in the traditional period, develop into honorable positions for aristocrats. Thus, the present British Queen's Lord Steward of the Household is a duke, her Master of the Horse is an earl, her Mistress of the Robes is a duchess.[79]

Supported economically by peasants and, to some extent, by townspeople and surrounded and waited on by numerous servants, the aristocrat does not work and enjoys much leisure. His leisure, then, becomes an index of his power and wealth and, as such, must itself be displayed.[80] As Fei says of the Chinese gentry: "To them, leisure means prestige as well as privilege. By displaying the leisure at their disposal, they stand high in the eyes of the lower classes"[81]—and, as will be stressed in a moment, in the eyes of other aristocrats.

---

77. Ibid., p. 58.

78. Ibid., p. 66.

79. Montague-Smith, ed., *Debrett's Peerage* (1980), p. P22.

80. "In order to gain and to hold the esteem of men it is not sufficient merely to possess wealth or power. The wealth or power must be put in evidence, for esteem is awarded only on evidence. . . . A life of leisure is the readiest and most conclusive evidence of pecuniary strength, and therefore of superior force. . . . Conspicuous abstention from labor therefore becomes the conventional mark of superior pecuniary achievement and the conventional index of reputability." Veblen, *The Theory of the Leisure Class*, pp. 42, 43.

81. Fei, "Peasantry and Gentry," p. 7.

Just as saving is dishonorable for the aristocrat, the conspicuous consumption, display, and even destruction of wealth are considered honorable, and aristocratic ideology puts a high premium on generosity. Sometimes aristocrats quite literally throw their money away by scattering coins among the populace to demonstrate both how wealthy and how generous they are.

In ancient India, the Aryan knights were known as "dispensers of gifts. The knights were named by singers and wizards dependent upon their gifts, praising the donator, deriding and attempting magically to damage the stingy."[82] Very similarly, Bloch notes, the Western European medieval "minstrels, those professional parasites, extolled above all other duties that of generosity, *largesse*, 'lady and queen in whose light all virtues shine.'" He himself points out that many a noble preferred to amass his coins and jewelry rather than distribute them. But this was not the accepted norm. "That a knight should carefully calculate his booty and his ransoms and, on returning home, impose a heavy 'tallage' on his peasants provoked little or no criticism. Gain was legitimate; but on one condition—that it should be promptly and liberally expended. 'I can assure you,' said a troubadour when he was reproached for his brigandage, 'if I robbed you, it was to give, not to hoard.' . . . In squandering a fortune that was easily gained and easily lost, the noble sought to affirm his superiority over classes less confident in the future or more careful in providing for it. This praiseworthy prodigality might not always stop at generosity or even luxury. A chronicler has preserved for us the record of the remarkable competition in wasteful expenditure witnessed one day at a great 'court' held in Limousin. One knight had a plot of ground ploughed up and sown with small pieces of silver; another burned wax candles for his cooking; a third, 'through boastfulness,' ordered thirty of his horses to be burnt alive. What must a merchant have thought of this struggle for prestige through extravagance—which reminds us of the practices of certain primitive races? Here again different notions of honour marked the line of separation between the social groups."[83]

The attitudes and behavior of aristocracies described here appear, judged by the ethic of modern industrial society, to be wantonly wasteful. However, it makes little sense to apply such a judgment to aristocratic empires, simply because the expenditure of an amount of wealth is wasteful only if an alternative use for it is available. As I have stressed, aristocrats, given their social and economic position, see no point in saving or investing their income. The only other alternative, to spend the wealth on behalf of the peasantry or not to take it from the peasantry in the first

82. Weber, *The Religion of India*, p. 124.

83. Bloch, *Feudal Society*, p. 311.

place, need not be considered. It is simply not compatible with the very nature of an aristocratic empire and could hardly occur to an aristocrat, for it is only the product of a modern mind.

There is, then, no alternative to luxury consumption and display, but they, like other elements of aristocratic ideology, also serve the positive function of keeping the aristocracy in its dominant position. Anyone must be struck by the contrast between aristocrats and lower classes in aristocratic empires who sees the immense treasures accumulated and displayed in the palaces and religious edifices of the aristocracy and recalls the poverty of the peasantry and even the townspeople who lived when this wealth was being assembled—and, indeed, produced it. The open display of great wealth, by making the gap between the aristocracy and lower classes visible, serves the function of making it all the wider and more unbridgeable. If starving Indian peasants could see their Mogul emperor "clothed or rather loden with Diamonds, Rubies, Pearles, and other precious vanities, so great, so glorious"[84] or medieval European crowds could stare at the pomp of a coronation or religious ceremony, they could not in their wildest dreams imagine themselves in the position of the aristocracy, and the latter was the safer for it.

However, one should not overestimate how important it is for aristocrats to impress peasants. After all, peasants are so far beneath them as to be hardly worth impressing and, as we shall see at greater length later, they generally pose no danger to the position of the aristocracy. Ostentatious display and generous distribution of wealth by aristocrats is much more likely to serve a defensive function vis-à-vis other aristocrats than peasants, for individual aristocrats and groups of aristocrats are much more threatened in their power positions by other aristocrats or groups of them than by peasants. Various aspects of conflict, that is, of politics among aristocrats will be discussed later, but here it is relevant to note that conspicuous display and consumption play a role in intraaristocratic politics. Indeed, much of the display, like the interior and contents of palaces and temples, is visible only to aristocrats, many ceremonies, from feasts to religious services, are accessible only to them, and precious gifts are presented only to them. Clearly, an aristocrat who can bribe or overawe potential aristocratic opponents by such means has strengthened his position and has not wasted his wealth.

Veblen deals nicely with the political function of presents and feasts:

84. Quoted in Lybyer, *The Government of the Ottoman Empire*, p. 289, from a detailed contemporary account in Sir Thomas Roe's *Journal of his Embassy to the Court of the Great Mogul, 1615–1619* (London, 1899), of the staggering display of wealth in an annual ceremony in which the emperor's weight was matched on golden scales in silver, gold, precious stones, and jewels.

"Conspicuous consumption of valuable goods is a means of reputability to the gentleman of leisure. As wealth accumulates on his hands, his own unaided effort will not avail to sufficiently put his opulence in evidence by this method. The aid of friends and competitors is therefore brought in by resorting to the giving of valuable presents and expensive feasts and entertainments. . . . The competitor with whom the entertainer wishes to institute a comparison is, by this method, made to serve as a means to the end. He consumes vicariously for his host at the same time that he is a witness to the consumption of that excess of good things which his host is unable to dispose of singlehanded, and he is also made to witness his host's facility in etiquette."[85]

Of course, wealth is displayed and conspicuously consumed, ceremonies are held, and generous gifts are given not necessarily deliberately for the purposes indicated here. More commonly, these things are done simply because aristocrats have come to regard them as the proper things to do. Indeed, to do otherwise might be considered dishonorable, and hence no further justification is needed in the eyes of aristocrats. But that does not mean that their behavior does not, nevertheless, serve the functions I ascribed to it.

In his remarks on aristocratic love of pomp, Max Weber seems to make a similar point but he also links this attitude with the aristocrats' dislike for rational and commercial utilitarianism: "The need for 'ostentation,' glamour and imposing splendor, for surrounding one's life with utensils which are not justified by utility but, in Oscar Wilde's sense, useless in the meaning of 'beautiful,' is primarily a feudal status need and an important power instrument for the sake of maintaining one's own dominance through mass suggestion. 'Luxury' in the sense of rejecting purposive-rational control of consumption is for the dominant feudal strata nothing superfluous: it is a means of social self-assertion."[86]

It must be noted that these remarks by Weber on aristocratic love of pomp and luxury as well as those quoted earlier on aristocratic attitudes toward commercialism and "the game" and sports ascribe all these characteristics not to aristocrats in aristocratic empires in general, as I am inclined to do, but only to aristocrats in feudal empires. As we saw earlier, he distinguishes these from patrimonial empires, and he argues specifically that "patriarchal patrimonialism has a different effect upon the style of life." Unlike feudalism, it "must legitimate itself as guardian of the subjects' welfare in its own and in their eyes. The 'welfare state' is the legend of patrimonialism, deriving not from the free camaraderie of solemnly promised fealty, but from the authoritarian relationship of father and children.

85. Veblen, *The Theory of the Leisure Class*, pp. 64–65.
86. Weber, *Economy and Society*, 3:1106.

The 'father of the people' . . . is the ideal of the patrimonial states." "The 'good king,' not the hero, was the ideal glorified by mass legend."[87]

Weber sums up the differences between feudalism and patrimonialism that are relevant here by contrasting the administrative training of officials under patrimonialism to the education of feudal knights: "Patrimonial education always lacks the features of playfulness and elective affinity to art, of heroic asceticism and hero worship, of heroic honor and heroic hostility to the utilitarianism of business and office—features which feudalism inculcates and preserves. Indeed the administrative 'organization' (*amtliche Betrieb*) is an impersonal 'business' (*sachliches Geschäft*): The patrimonial official bases his honor not upon his 'being,' but on his 'functions,' he expects advantages and promotion from his 'services'; the idleness, the games and the commercial nonchalance of the knight must appear to him as slothfulness and lack of efficiency."[88]

In response to Weber's effort to draw a clear distinction between the aristocratic ideologies of feudalism and of patrimonialism, I would first of all stress once more that Weber himself spent much time showing that in historical fact there were no sharp distinctions between his two systems of traditional domination, that they overlapped and often appeared in amalgamated form. Thus, he refers to Western feudalism, that is, the classical form of feudalism, as itself "a marginal case of patrimonialism" and says that the "transitions" from the feudal fief to the patrimonial benefice are "fluid."[89] He sees feudal elements not only in medieval Western Europe and Japan but also in such empires commonly thought of as bureaucratic and thought of by him as patrimonial as those of ancient Egypt and Rome, of the medieval caliphate and the Ottoman Turks.[90] It seems clear that if there is in fact no sharp distinction between feudalism and patrimonialism, there can be no such distinction between the aristocratic ideologies of each system either.[91]

87. Ibid., p. 1106, 1107.

88. Ibid., p. 1108.

89. Ibid., pp. 1070, 1073.

90. Ibid., p. 1072.

91. Reinhard Bendix, discussing Weber's analysis, says that "it might be tempting to argue that no distinction between patrimonialism and feudalism need be made since both types have in common rulers who grant rights in return for military and administrative services. But the intellectual task Weber set himself was to make analytically useful distinctions between facts whose contrasting attributes were obscured by imperceptible gradations." Bendix, *Kings or People*, p. 369. To understand for what purpose these sharp distinctions are "analytically useful," one must recall that the object of Weber's work was to elaborate differences between the premodern histories of the Occident and the Orient and thereby to explain the unique modern history of the former. As indicated earlier, my own purpose here is quite different, and Weber's distinction is hence not useful for my analysis.

Secondly, I would argue that the distinction between the aristocratic ideologies of feudalism and of patrimonialism which Weber notes is, to the extent that it exists at all, not a distinction between these two types of empires but one among specialized aristocracies, if any, within either type of empire. The ideology which I have simply ascribed to "the" aristocracy of aristocratic empires but which Weber limits to feudal aristocracies is, indeed, the ideology of all traditional aristocracies—to the extent that they are warrior aristocracies, as most of them have been. The military aristocrats of patrimonial ancient Egypt and Rome, of China and Turkey, and, for that matter, of Inca Peru and Aztec Mexico were quite as concerned with rendering service and doing their duty and, above all, with their honor and their glory as were the knights of feudal Western Europe and Japan. And all were similar in liking pomp and luxury and disliking manual labor and commerce.

Deviations from this common aristocratic ideology occur only when some aristocrats no longer perform military functions, but specialize in the performance of other aristocratic functions, notably those of a priesthood or of a bureaucracy. The Chinese imperial scholar-bureaucracy is the outstanding example of such a nonmilitary branch of an aristocracy—and rather an exceptional one with respect to its size, its importance in governmental affairs, and its divorce from the military. Obviously, one would not expect such nonmilitary aristocracies to stress heroism and soldierly virtues in their ideologies, to be concerned with the acquisition of glory or to associate their honor with military performance. But even nonmilitary aristocrats, like specialized bureaucrats and priests, seem to emphasize the role of honor in their lives; they, too, look with contempt on those engaged in manual labor or commerce. Max Weber himself adds to the sharply contrasting picture, quoted above, of the training of feudal knights and patrimonial officials that the latter, too, have an "abhorrence of the acquisitive drive," and their "performance finds its dignity precisely in the fact that it is not a source of commercial enrichment."[92]

Nobility and Superiority

Aristocrats, whether military, bureaucratic, or priestly, commonly assert their own superiority over all others. The individual aristocrat, in relation to other aristocrats of equal rank, may well be no more arrogant than anyone else, but in relation to nonaristocrats he strikes us, by our modern standards, as arrogant indeed. He looks down on them as "common" and "mean" and thinks of himself as "noble."

92. Weber, *Economy and Society*, 3:1108–9.

The aristocrats' belief in their superiority may be linked to their background as conquerors. Their very ability to subject and to exploit other people may make it seem self-evident to them that they are superior. They may ascribe their superiority to that of their tribal gods or to the favor of their universal god, but typically, as will be stressed in the next section, they think of themselves as biologically distinct, as a separate race or breed of men, whether they are in fact racially distinct from their subjects or not. In any case, once in power, aristocrats feel that their membership in what they regard as a superior race naturally justifies their rule as they come to see the world divided into races destined to rule and races destined to be ruled.

The link between the aristocrats' conception of their superiority and their ability to conquer is also suggested by their choice of animals for their coats of arms and heraldic symbols, that is, of animals with which they wish to identify themselves. The overwhelming favorites seem to be lions and eagles, animals whose outstanding quality is the fact that they can kill all other animals or birds and are not subject to being killed by them. It may also be significant that the lion is commonly referred to as the king of beasts, and the eagle as king of birds, for this suggests that the claim to rule rests not on superior intelligence and wisdom or on superior beauty and grace—though all these are likely to be claimed by aristocrats—but simply on superior ability to kill. Otherwise, perhaps chimpanzees and crows or gazelles and birds of paradise would be the kings of their respective realms.

The aristocracy's claim to superiority becomes strikingly evident in the legal status it assigns to itself. Because the aristocracy constitutes a separate society within its empire, superimposed on the societies of the peasants, it typically functions under its own system of laws. The peasants administer their own justice according to the custom of their individual villages, or the local aristocrat does so for them (or to them) by his own or local standards.

However, even where a governing aristocracy seeks to introduce some, usually probably only slight, degree of legal uniformity throughout its empire, as was, for example, evidently true in the Inca empire, or where similar standards gradually came to prevail throughout an area like Western Europe, as is more likely to happen only after some commercialization, the aristocracy is subject to different laws from the peasantry. It would be unimaginable for an aristocrat accused of crime to be tried and judged by peasants; he must be judged by his peers and in accordance with the standards of his peers. Marc Bloch, dealing with Western European feudalism, defines the nobility (somewhat more narrowly than I define the aristocracy) by two characteristics. The second of these is hereditary status, but "first, it must have a legal status of its own, which confirms and makes effectual the superiority to which it lays claim. . . . It is necessary . . . that social privileges as well as hereditary succession should be recognized by law."[93] And speaking of the thirteenth-century nobility, he says: "Everywhere . . . —earlier in one place, later in another—we find evidence that the noble was specially protected in his person against the non-noble; that he was subject to an exceptional penal law, with heavier fines, as a rule, than those exacted from the common people; that recourse to private vengeance, regarded as inseparable from the bearing of arms, tended to be reserved for him; that the sumptuary laws assigned to him a place apart."[94]

In practice, the criminal law of aristocratic empires usually provides for heavier penalties if the victim of a crime is an aristocrat than if he is a peasant and for lighter penalties if the perpetrator of the crime is an aristocrat than if he is a peasant. According to the Code of Hammurabi, King of Babylon about thirty-seven centuries ago, "for a wrong done to a plebeian or a slave, the punishment is less than for that done to a patrician; but he who assaults one who is of higher class than himself is punished more severely than if an equal had committed the wrong."[95] Similarly, in the Inca empire, "any illegal act committed by a noble invariably carried a lesser penalty than the same act committed by a commoner. Incest, which carried the death penalty for commoners, involved merely a public reprimand for the nobility."[96] Even if, as Bloch found, aristocrats in thirteenth-century Western Europe were subject, "as a rule," to heavier fines, we must recall not only the usually huge disparity in wealth between aristocrat and peasant, but, above all, that the aristocrat, as Bloch also notes,[97] was by law exempt from the payment of taxes. Thus, the noncriminal peasant regularly paid probably far more in dues than the criminal aristocrat paid occasionally in fines.

From a modern point of view, calling for equal treatment of all citizens

93. Bloch, *Feudal Society*, p. 283. By this definition, the nobility of Western Europe emerged only in the twelfth century, that is, only after the beginnings of commercialization. Of course, there were aristocracies in Western Europe before then. In earlier times, there had been the Roman senatorial nobility as well as noble families among the Germanic peoples, but even when these had died out in the early feudal period from the ninth to the eleventh century, Bloch agrees that "if the concept of nobility as a legal class remained unknown, it is quite permissible from this period, by a slight simplification of terminology, to speak of a social class of nobles and especially, perhaps, of a noble way of life. For it was principally by the nature of its wealth, by its exercise of authority, and its social habits that this group was defined. . . . Its members derived their revenues from their control of the soil" (ibid., p. 288).

94. Ibid., p. 328.

95. Diamond, *Primitive Law*, p. 31.

96. Moore, *Power and Property in Inca Peru*, p. 75.

97. Bloch, *Feudal Society*, p. 329.

under the same law, such a system of unequal treatment simply reflects the use or abuse of power to secure unwarranted privileges. Sally Falk Moore says, "a clear purpose for which political power was used by the Inca was to free the ruling caste from restrictions on its sexual, social and economic life, restrictions which it enforced to the extent of the death penalty upon the commoner."[98] However, in aristocratic empires, peasants are not citizens or even members of the same society as aristocrats, there is no pretense of equality and no question that the aristocracy is privileged. In its own eyes, it deserves its privileges, including a less severe criminal law, because of its superiority. What to us may appear as mere rationalization, may nevertheless be deeply believed by aristocrats. Thus, at least according to a Spanish chronicler, the Incas claimed "that to an Inca of royal blood, public reprimand meant as much as the death penalty to a commoner."[99] Indeed, its own criminal law is not only justified by the aristocracy's claim to superiority, it in turn produces further evidence of that superiority in its own eyes: "Just as it was easier for a Greek aristocrat equipped with a chariot and horses to be more heroic at war than a foot soldier accompanying him, so was it possible for the Inca nobility to be more moral than the commoners who could not cloak their anti-social acts with legal privilege."[100]

Aristocrats can assert their own nobility, that is, superiority in character and culture, and find overwhelming evidence to support their claim, because that superiority is defined in terms of their own ideology. Nonaristocrats are low to them, because they do not share their aristocratic notions of duty and service and of honor and glory, because they engage in contemptible manual labor or commerce and are saving or miserly rather than generous. To aristocrats, living at least in relative splendor, peasants in particular appear crude (as they do to many of us who have inherited aristocratic attitudes in this respect), because they are dirty, and eat, dress, and are housed poorly. Aristocrats may be dirty, too, by modern standards, but their food and especially their clothing and housing are not merely better than but are utterly different from the peasants'. Even by aristocratic standards (let alone by our modern ones), peasants have a narrow intellectual

---

98. Moore, *Power and Property in Inca Peru*, p. 126.

99. Ibid., p. 75. Convinced of their superiority, aristocrats do not see the matter as we might and as Moore puts it: "The use of state power to shield the rulers of the state from certain criminal penalties, or to soften these penalties is an extremely significant one. It gives the lie to the conception of the noble noble, of the purer morality of the nobility. It suggests that the nobility, as enforcer of the law, was moved by a singularly convenient double standard. Rather than regard the exemption of the noble from common penalties as the emblem of the ethically high-minded, one could say that it was simply the privilege of the powerful" (ibid.; see also ibid., p. 134).

100. Ibid., p. 75.

horizon and hence a limited vocabulary and they do not appreciate the better things in life, good food and good drink and, above all, the arts—folk arts being usually quite sharply distinct from the more refined art forms sponsored and appreciated by the aristocracy. All these differences between aristocrats and nonaristocrats, particularly peasants, appear to the aristocrats as obvious indications of their own superiority.[101]

Thus, objective differences in the behavior and culture of different classes—and these are far-reaching in aristocratic empires—lead inevitably to subjective interpretations and perceptions and self-perceptions in terms of superiority and inferiority. These in turn can be self-fulfilling, leading to behavior that reinforces the initial differences and thereby serves to perpetuate the positions of the various classes in the aristocratic empire.

That their different positions may produce physical and attitudinal differences between rulers and ruled was already noted a century ago by Herbert Spencer: "Certain concomitant influences generate differences of nature, physical and mental, between those members of a community who have attained superior positions, and those who have remained inferior. Unlikenesses of status once initiated, led to unlikenesses of life, which by the constitutional changes they work, make the unlikeness of status more difficult to alter." He points first to "differences of diet and its effects" and refers to "the inevitable proclivity of the strong to feed themselves at the expense of the weak; and when there arise class-divisions, there habitually results better nutrition of the superior than of the inferior. . . . Naturally by such differences in diet, and accompanying differences in clothing, shelter, and strain on the energies, are eventually produced physical differences. . . .

101. Although in aristocratic empires, where one's position in society was simply taken for granted, there was probably less need to justify it in terms of achievement than in the present-day underdeveloped countries of which Everett Hagen writes, his remarks are nevertheless relevant. He speaks of "an intense need of the elite to feel themselves different in essence from the simple folk. An individual must have some justification of his position in life. In a society in which one feels that one can manipulate the world one attains one's position in part by individual achievement. In such a society one can feel that one's superiority relative to someone else is due to a difference in capacity to achieve and is therefore morally defensible. However, in a society in which one is almost helpless against the world, yet has prerogative and position, one must ascribe his position to some other cause. It is therefore necessary for the elite to feel that in essence—not because of what they can do, but in what they essentially are—they are different from the simple folk. For this reason it is necessary for them to feel repugnance to the distinctive features of the way of life of the simple folk. By feeling repugnance to what the simple folk do and like they persuade themselves that they are different and superior and that their superior status in life is justified. One distinctive characteristic of the simple folk is that they work with their hands, with tools, and in the process become dirty. As a result, manual-technical labor, any work which soils the hands or clothing, or indeed any 'labor' (unless, of course, it is 'play') is repugnant to the elite." Hagen, *On the Theory of Social Change*, p. 76.

"Simultaneously there arise between rulers and ruled, unlikenesses of bodily activity and skill. Occupied, as those of higher rank commonly are, in the chase when not occupied in war, they have a lifelong discipline of a kind conducive to various physical superiorities; while, contrariwise those occupied in agriculture, in carrying burdens, and in other drudgeries, partially lose what agility and address they naturally had. Class-predominance is thus further facilitated.

"And then there are the respective mental traits produced by daily exercise of power and by daily submission to power. The ideas, and sentiments, and modes of behavior, perpetually repeated, generate on the one side an inherited fitness for command, and on the other side an inherited fitness for obedience; with the result that, in course of time, there arises on both sides the belief that the established relations of classes are natural ones."[102] We know that the attitudes Spencer speaks of are not inherited, that under the impact of modernization peasants can rapidly lose their "fitness for obedience," but in aristocratic empires, where modes of behavior are, indeed, "perpetually repeated," these mental traits are passed on from generation to generation with the result, which Spencer notes, that class relations come to be regarded as natural.

How different characteristics, seen in terms of superiority and inferiority, are ascribed to the two major classes in an aristocratic empire in the early stages of development, where pastoralists rule over peasants—each set of characteristics well designed to keep the class to which it is ascribed in its place—is illustrated in the generalized conclusions drawn by an anthropologist from a study of Ruanda: "In a society where a people small in numbers had achieved dominance over a much larger subordinate people, the former pastoralists and keepers of cattle and the latter agriculturalists, the dominant group was considered to be intelligent, astute, authoritarian, refined, courageous, and cruel, while the subordinate group was held to be less intelligent, industrious, strong, obedient, and crude in manners. Superiority and inferiority infused social relations."[103]

Alexander Rüstow, in a volume dealing with the origins of domination in conquest, stresses how different character traits are not only ascribed to the conquerors and the conquered and their respective descendants, but are, in fact, developed by them in the process of adaptation to their different positions in the aristocratic empire: "The process of superstratifica-

102. Spencer, *The Principles of Sociology*, 2:300–302, par. 460.

103. Carlston, *Social Theory and African Tribal Organization*, p. 402; see also ibid., p. 165. This statement repeats almost verbatim one by Maquet—on whose study of Ruanda it is based—who adds that because the characteristics reflect the Tutsi point of view, "it appears that the superior caste has been able to make other people see themselves in important respects as Batutsi see them." Maquet, "The Kingdom of Ruanda," p. 185.

tion placed the victors and the vanquished as an upper and a lower stratum in extremely opposed social situations. Through the centuries and millennia, these had to operate, in the highest degree and in sharply opposed directions, so as to select, to breed, and to shape. The upper stratum, being an upper stratum, was brought up to be domineering, haughty, proud, arrogant, hard, cruel, sadistic—for the more it possessed and acted in line with these attributes the more firmly did it sit in the saddle of superimposition. The corresponding attributes of the lower stratum were to be subservient, docile, submissive, servile, lacking character, spineless, masochistic—for the more it possessed and acted in line with these attributes the better it was adjusted to the role fate had assigned to it. The virtues of the ruling stratum were audacity—without it one could not have come to rule—, openness—from whom was it necessary to conceal anything?—, liberality and generosity— for one had enough to give. In contrast to them stood the negative qualities of the subjects: cowardice—for woe to him who did not knuckle under!—, furtiveness and cunning—the defensive weapons of the weak—, niggardliness—for their masters had barely left them what was absolutely necessary. And these are precisely the attributes that are again and again, in the most different times and places, used to prove the 'bad nature' of those who have been subjected and their natural predestination to play the role of slaves. For this reason, those in the upper stratum in Greece referred to themselves, in noble modesty, as 'the beautiful and the good' and called those in the lower stratum simply 'the bad.'"[104] Those in a position of superiority regard their own characteristics as marks of superiority and the characteristics of those in a position of inferiority as marks of inferiority. To what extent the latter share this view is less clear—but not relevant here, where we are concerned now with the ideology of the aristocracy.

It might also be noted that even the animals associated with the two major classes in aristocratic empires are seen in terms of superiority and inferiority. The aristocrat's hunting hawk and dog and especially his horse are "noble," an adjective that could never be applied to the peasant's ox or donkey, let alone his pig. To this day, these latter animals are, at least in European cultures, widely, if vaguely, regarded as inferior to horses.[105] On the other hand, where the aristocracy is still close to its pastoral nomadic origins, cattle may be noble. Among the Tutsi of Ruanda, "a whole category of poetry was devoted to the praises of famous cows, individually identified. Very beautiful cows . . . were regarded as belonging to the king even if they had been produced in somebody else's herd. In many festivities cattle were presented to the king or to great chiefs. All this indicates

104. Rüstow, *Ortsbestimmung der Gegenwart*, 1:114.
105. Ibid., pp. 157–58.

that cattle were objects of keen interest and aroused feelings of pride similar to those associated in some Western sub-cultures with the ownership of hunters or luxury cars. Cattle were the privileged possession of the superior caste."[106] In Peru, the llamas delivered as tribute to the Inca government were designated as "noble llamas," those left to the peasants were "lowly llamas."[107]

In the preceding paragraphs, words like superiority and inferiority, high and low, upper and lower were used repeatedly. Such spatial concepts are the only ones available (at least in Indo-European languages) to describe social relations and seem particularly appropriate to point to the differences between aristocrats and nonaristocrats. Rüstow, in an intriguing footnote,[108] suggests that their use is not only appropriate to describe but is, indeed, derived from these differences, initially from the difference between nomads and peasants. The former, on horseback, are "high" and look "down" on the peasants; the latter, on foot, are "low" and look "up" to the nomad and aristocrat.[109] The close association between aristocrats and horses noted earlier, might, then, possibly explain the pervasive use of terms referring to differences in altitude to describe differences in class, status, and prestige. Rüstow also mentions that the towers of the castles of the conquerors (in German, *Eroberer*, those who placed themselves "above") were higher than the huts of those they "subjected" (*die Unterworfenen*, those thrown "below").[110]

Just as aristocrats identify their higher social status with the claim that they are somehow better, so our words high, eminent, exalted, elevated, superior, and supreme can, depending on the context, have normative implications and do not merely suggest physical height. Aristocratic forms of address, like "highness," "eminence," "excellence," and "majesty" all

106. Maquet, "The Kingdom of Ruanda," p. 178.

107. Cunow, *Geschichte und Kultur des Inkareiches*, p. 87.

108. Rüstow, *Ortsbestimmung der Gegenwart*, 1:306–7, n. 80.

109. Referring to the Western European aristocrat of early feudal times in contrast to the peasant infantry, Bloch writes: "He fought on horseback; and though he might on occasion dismount during battle, he always moved about on horseback. . . . Looking down from their chargers on the poor wretches who, 'shamefully' as one court romance puts it, drag their feet in the dust and mire, are stalwart soldiers, proud of being able to fight and manoeuvre swiftly, skilfully, effectively. . . . In a civilization where war was an everyday matter, there was no more vital contrast than this. . . . More than one text in applying to the lower orders the contemptuous designation of *pedones*, 'foot-soldiers'—or rather perhaps 'foot-sloggers'—raised it almost to the status of a legal term. Among the Franks, said the Arab emir Ousâma, 'all pre-eminence belongs to the horsemen. They are in truth the only men who count. Theirs it is to give counsel; theirs to render justice.'" Bloch, *Feudal Society*, pp. 290–91.

110. Rüstow, *Ortsbestimmung der Gegenwart*, 1:75.

indicate that aristocrats like to think of themselves as "above" nonaristo-crats. And demonstrations of respect to superiors—from prostrating one-self and kotowing to kneeling and curtsying to our bowing of the head—are all designed to make those who are socially inferior appear physically inferior as well.[111]

Pure Blood, Intermarriage, and Sex Relations

Just as behavioral, ideological, and cultural differences between aristocrats and nonaristocrats are interpreted by the aristocracy as proof of its superiority and nobility, so are racial differences. Wherever aristocrats are of different physical type from the people they subjected to their rule, their physical characteristics are defined as superior and beauti-ful, those of the subject people as inferior and ugly. The aristocrats' charac-teristics are regarded as a sign of nobility, whether it be the lighter skin of the Aryan conquerors of Dravidian people in India, the Amhara conquer-ors of Negroes, or the Spanish rulers of the Indians in the Americas or the taller build of the Tutsi ruling over the shorter and stouter Hutu in Ru-anda. The Tutsi aristocracy "avails itself of its appearance, regarded as 'beautiful,' to support its claims to an innate superiority. Consequently, it is an asset to its power. Tutsi have been able to use the . . . stereotypes of the physical characteristics of the Ruanda castes as confirmation of their su-periority: they have convinced all Ruanda that to be slender and light skinned is much better than to be stout and dark (this was even aestheti-cally translated into the patterns used in the ornamentations of baskets: they manifested a preference for elongated slim forms). They used the stereotypes also as a proof of their different nature which entitled them to rule and as a guarantee against social mobility: because a Hutu was usually

111. These points, too, are briefly suggested ibid., pp. 306–7, n. 80. Tracing all these mat-ters back to the difference between the nomad and aristocrat on horseback and the peasant on foot may not be justified. Laponce, "Spatial Archetypes and Political Perceptions," drawing on numerous works on religion, myths, and symbolism, argues more generally "that religious thought nearly universally values High over Low and that an ascending di-rection has a liberating effect while a descending move produces depression. . . . If power, and consequently the symbols and the institutions which incarnate it, is positively valued, . . . then power, and more specifically legitimate power, will be located Up rather than Down" (ibid., p. 20). In ancient Peru—where there were no horses—aristocrats also wanted to be "higher" than the common people and were carried in high litters, stood on stages, and lived in buildings on platforms. "The Javanese take the physical metaphor seri-ously, associating height with high status. In the old days . . . servants served the family's meals on their knees and the correct greeting of an inferior to a superior was to kneel and make the obeisance gesture . . . to the superior's knee or even to his foot." Geertz, *The Re-ligion of Java*, p. 244.

not endowed with the Tutsi physical characteristics he could not easily pass the line."[112]

Racial differences between aristocrats and their subjects are always interpreted by the former as evidence of their superiority. However, the aristocrats' conviction and need to feel that they are superior is so deep that they will also use that assumed superiority as evidence to insist that they are biologically distinct, even when in fact there are no racial differences between them and nonaristocrats. The ascription of blue blood to European aristocrats may be an example of this; the term originated in Spain where those with light skin, whose veins appeared blue, claimed to have no admixture of Moorish or Jewish "blood" and hence to be of older Spanish stock, possibly that of the Germanic Visigothic conquerors of Spain. Other phrases commonly used with respect to the aristocracy that suggest its biological distinctness are "noble blood," "high birth," and "breeding," the latter a term significantly ambiguous in its reference to both physical and cultural factors.[113] The very concept of the aristocracy —commonly held though not identical with my definition—as not merely a social class but a hereditary body is closely related to the aristocrats' insistence on their peculiar biological character. It assumes that all the children of aristocrats are aristocrats and that, ordinarily, no one else can be or become an aristocrat.[114]

To keep themselves separate and distinct from nonaristocrats, aristocrats generally outlaw intermarriage with them. This is one of the most obvious signs of their concern with the purity of their "noble blood" and one of the most common ones. In India, caste restrictions on intermarriage are widely thought to date back to racial distinctions between conquerors and conquered. "The original idea of caste (a Portuguese word meaning purity of race) is that of colour (*varna*) and it emerged when the conquering Aryans absorbed the conquered population into a new system of society."[115] Still,

---

112. Maquet, *The Premise of Inequality in Ruanda*, pp. 146–47.

113. Aristocrats "viewed the peasantry as, at best, a very different breed of people from themselves—people largely or wholly lacking in those qualities of personality which the elite prized and respected. . . . In legal documents in medieval England, the children of a peasant were not called *familia*, but *sequela*, meaning 'brood' or 'litter.' In both Europe and Asia there are documents in which the peasants on an estate were listed with the livestock." Lenski, *Power and Privilege*, p. 272.

114. Veblen, with modern as well as traditional upper classes in mind, defines "gentle blood [as] blood which has been ennobled by protracted contact with accumulated wealth or unbroken prerogative." Veblen, *The Theory of the Leisure Class*, p. 53.

115. Edwardes, *A History of India*, p. 27. On various theories of the origins of caste divisions (and also on the origins of the word "caste") see Klass, *Caste*, who rejects the "racial explanation" (especially in chap. 3), but says it is "surely the most widely accepted and most influential of all the explanations" (ibid., p. 42).

it is, as Max Weber points out, not racial distinctions per se that account for the ban on intermarriage. It is rather the distinction between aristocrats and their subjects, which may be defined in terms of racial distinctions, that is to be maintained by this ban: "Distinguished families the world over make it their honor to admit only their peers for courting their daughters while the sons are left to their devices in satisfying their sexual needs. Here and not in mythical 'race instinct' or unknown differences of 'racial traits' we reach the point at which color differences matter. Intermarriage with despised subjects never attained full social recognition. . . . This stable barrier was reinforced by magical dread. It led to the elevation of the importance of birthright, of clan charisma, in all areas of life."[116]

That it is not different physical characteristics which account for the ban on intermarriage is clear from the fact that aristocrats have refused to intermarry with nonaristocrats even where they are physically, that is, racially not distinguishable from them. In Ethiopia, "a self-respecting man of noble family would resist marrying his daughter to a commoner or person of dubious parentage, no matter how high a rank the latter obtained."[117] In China, the last three conquest dynasties (Chin, Yüan, and Ch'ing) all imposed a ban on intermarriage (with certain exceptions) between members of the northern conquering tribes and the Chinese which was maintained until 1902.[118] The pastoral Bahima conquerors of the agricultural Bairu in Uganda "of the fourteenth or fifteenth century imposed a strict prohibition of intermarriage."[119] In the Sassanid Persian empire, "the purity of blood of the upper class was prescribed and protected by law."[120]

The ultimate step in maintaining the purity of the rulers' blood was taken in Peru, Hawaii, and Egypt. The Inca (except the early ones) took his own sister as his principal wife to maintain the purity of his divine descent. Similarly, in the Hawaiian kingdom, "royal blood, being divine, was kept pure by brother-sister marriage."[121] For the same reason, the Egyptian king married his sister, half sister, cousin or his own daughter. "It was essential that his immediate heir should possess the strongest possible strain of royal blood. The spiritual potency of the king, on which the well-being of his subjects depended, was enhanced by the purity of his breeding. Theoretically, the actual blood of the sun god had been transmitted by Horus into the royal veins. The priesthood took this conception very

116. Weber, *The Religion of India*, pp. 125–26.
117. Levine, *Wax and Gold*, p. 163.
118. Wittfogel and Feng, *History of Chinese Society*, pp. 8, 9, 11–12.
119. Davidson, *The Lost Cities of Africa*, p. 237.
120. Bill, *The Politics of Iran*, p. 3.
121. Wesson, *The Imperial Order*, p. 462.

seriously. It frowned upon any watering down of the divine ichor in the Pharaonic blood-vessels by marriages outside the royal family. To safeguard the purity of the succession it was advisable that the king should procreate as many children as possible within what is called the forbidden degree. To this end he not infrequently married his own daughters."[122] Somewhat similarly, the kings of Ceylon, who were of Indian origin, occasionally imported relatives from India for the succession to the throne in order to maintain the purity of the royal blood, though they ruled in Ceylon for about two millennia.[123]

On the other hand, a very different pattern was followed in the Ottoman empire. Some of the early sultans married women from other royal families, and their children were thus of royal blood. However, perhaps as slaves became dominant at the court, the sultans married slave women, and their sons and daughters were married to slaves.[124] Thus, the Ottoman ruling family was infused with nonaristocratic blood in each generation, showing a lack of concern with the purity of its aristocratic descent quite exceptional among aristocrats.

While the aristocracy may manage to keep itself free from the admixture of nonaristocratic "blood," aristocrats rarely refrain from contributing some of their "blood" to nonaristocrats. The prohibition of intermarriage, in short, is not tantamount to a prohibition of sexual relations between aristocratic males and nonaristocratic females. Only "the mixture, at least from a sexual union, of upper-class daughters with sons of the lower stratum remained socially scorned."[125] The pattern appears to be as general as the ban on intermarriage and, no doubt, arises from the position of the aristocracy in the aristocratic empire and from that ban itself.

The aristocrat has the power to exploit his subjects, by force or by law, not only economically but also sexually. The acquisition on the part of aristocrats of sex partners by force can be traced back to their role as conquerors of peasant villages, initially often as nomadic conquerors. The conquerors, typically men only, do not merely plunder and then subject the peasants to their rule, but they may rape peasant women and abduct them as slaves or concubines. Their prestige and wealth always provides aristocrats with opportunities to seduce nonaristocratic women, and in medieval Europe their right to exploit their subjects sexually was probably even legally secured in the *jus primae noctis* or *droit de seigneur*. It evidently persisted in some rural sections of Europe into modern times, though aris-

122. White, *Ancient Egypt*, p. 15.
123. Singer, *The Emerging Elite*, p. 14.
124. Lybyer, *The Government of the Ottoman Empire*, pp. 57–58.
125. Weber, *The Religion of India*, p. 125.

tocrats generally received redemption dues paid to avoid enforcement.[126]

On the other hand, the aristocrat's sexual involvement with nonaristocratic women is, in part, a result of the very prohibition which keeps him from marrying such women. This limits his choice of marriage partners, but that choice—often it is made for him or with the advice of others—is further severely restricted to satisfy political considerations, for example, to consolidate an alliance with another aristocratic family or to acquire additional land. He and his wife, therefore, may have little attraction for each other, and, having the opportunity, he turns elsewhere for female companionship.

Where formal monogamy was required, the maintenance of concubines and mistresses by aristocrats was widely practiced and accepted, as in Europe into the early twentieth century. In other cultures, aristocrats could have many wives as well as numerous concubines. The Pharaohs and Incas had to marry their sisters as official or principal wives, but they also had harems. So, of course, did the Chinese emperors and the Turkish sultans and other Middle Eastern rulers. To be sure, some of these harems were so huge, containing hundreds and even thousands of women, that the same principle that Veblen noted with respect to servants must apply to their inmates, too: they were kept to display their unproductive leisure, "more for show than for service actually performed."[127]

Speaking of the medieval European aristocracy in general and British royalty in particular, a medieval historian says: "It was universally accepted that no man married merely for love, and many men and women no doubt made the best of the circumstances, and fell in love with their partners. More often, perhaps, some kind of friendship not closely akin to modern ideas of marriage subsisted between husband and wife, and many men (in particular) were unfaithful."[128] Bloch puts it more bluntly: "The noble's marriage, as we know, was often an ordinary business transaction, and the houses of the nobility swarmed with bastards."[129]

126. "The existence of this *jus primae noctis* . . . has been much disputed, but . . . the best authorities now accept that it existed." Taylor, *Sex in History*, p. 31. Relevant literature on both sides of the dispute is also reviewed in Westermarck, *The History of Human Marriage*, 1:174–80, and some documentary evidence of the existence of the right is cited by Bebel, *Woman Under Socialism*, pp. 56–58. See also Beaumarchais's comedy *The Marriage of Figaro* (on which the libretto of Mozart's opera is based) where Count Almaviva is intent on exercising the *jus primae noctis* with the maid Susanna upon her marriage to his manservant.

127. Veblen, *The Theory of the Leisure Class*, p. 54.

128. Brooke, *Europe in the Central Middle Ages*, p. 128.

129. Bloch, *Feudal Society*, p. 308. Marriage was considered "a phase of feudal business management, since it consisted basically of the joining of lands, the cementing of loyalties, and the production of heirs and future defenders. But the purifying, ennobling rapture of love for an ideal woman—what had that to do with details of crops and cattle, fleas and fire-

The aristocrat's interest in nonaristocratic women naturally provides opportunities for the latter. His power and wealth can no doubt make him attractive to such women. They can hope to gain power and wealth themselves by associating with him in a world where other avenues to such aristocratic privileges are virtually nonexistent for nonaristocrats and often especially for women. In some cases, an ambitious concubine or mistress might exercise power and influence otherwise quite unavailable to nonaristocrats and thus breach the wall of aristocratic exclusiveness. This is also the result of not uncommon attempts by such ambitious mothers or by the aristocratic fathers themselves to advance their nonaristocratic sons into the aristocracy, often even in competition with the aristocratic half-brothers of the latter, borne by their father's official wife or wives. In this fashion, new, if less noble, blood is infused into the aristocracy. More generally, however, the children of aristocrats by nonaristocratic mothers remain nonaristocrats, often quite unknown to or ignored by their fathers.

---

places, serfs and swamp drainage? Yet, though true love was impossible between husband and wife, without it a man was valueless." Hunt, *The Natural History of Love*, p. 137. The "ideal woman" mentioned here is, to be sure, not a peasant woman. By the eleventh century when traditionalism was beginning to end in Western Europe, the ideals of chivalry, especially as expressed by the Provençal school of lyrical poetry, called for aristocratic husbands and wives to have lovers—but these were themselves aristocrats. Bloch, *Feudal Society*, pp. 307–10, and Warre Cornish, *Chivalry*, pp. 295–306. "The life described in the romances is not restrained by chastity. It has no relation to marriage. . . . Love, if its irregular nature is overlooked, is lofty and pure, compatible with honor, self-restraint and modesty: it is the source of the noblest sentiments in man and woman" (ibid., p. 306).

9

The Stakes of Aristocratic Politics

Position and Rank

I suggested earlier that there is generally little, if any, class conflict in traditional aristocratic empires and that the source of politics must therefore be found elsewhere. What exceptions there may be to this statement in the form of peasant revolts and urban mob riots cannot be discussed until we turn to the peasantry and the townspeople, but, aside from such exceptions, politics in aristocratic empires consists of intraclass conflict.

Why would aristocrats become involved in conflict with each other or, to put it differently, what are the issues in the politics of the aristocracy? The foregoing chapters answer that question. For one thing, aristocrats want wealth and they therefore compete with each other for opportunities, above all, to exploit peasants, a competition that takes the form of conflict over the control of land on which the peasants live and work. The aristocrats' desire for wealth may also make them compete for opportunities to rob or tax traders by controlling markets or trade routes and particularly for opportunities to win the spoils of war, as in the form of booty or ransom payments.

Secondly, as was stressed in the last chapter, the aristocrat's ideology demands of him that he do his duty and perform services, that he gain glory, and that he maintain his honor. The more he does these things, the more self-respect he will enjoy and the more he will be looked up to with respect by others, the more prestige he will have with them. Such respect and prestige come to be valued in themselves by aristocrats, and opportunities to gain them are worth competing for and are probably indistinguishable from opportunities to serve and do one's duty, to gain glory and to preserve one's honor under stress. All these are matters of supreme importance to aristocrats, in their own eyes possibly as vital as their ability to exploit peasants. For the individual aristocrat or aristocratic families or other aristocratic groupings or institutions, it hence seems natural to compete with and fight other aristocrats for such opportunities, even at the risk of life and limb.

Finally, aristocrats obviously want power. They may want it merely as a means to the ends I have just listed; indeed, it is difficult to distinguish from these ends. On the other hand, one could argue that, as a ruling class, they may enjoy wielding power for its own sake. Whether they want it as an end or as a means is probably no clearer to them than it is to us, but it makes little difference, for it is very clear that aristocrats do want power and do compete for it with each other.

Although the stakes in intraaristocratic conflicts have now been listed separately as opportunities to gain wealth, power, and prestige, to serve and do one's duty, to maintain one's honor and gain glory, they are in practice and in the aristocrat's mind closely interrelated. Generally, these opportunities are provided by certain positions within the aristocracy and in the aristocratic hierarchies of the military, the bureaucracy, and the clergy. It can no doubt be the case that one position provides a better opportunity to increase one's wealth, whereas another is better suited for the acquisition of glory, but more often it may be true that the higher the position the more it provides of everything the aristocrat wants. Typically, the aristocrat who has more wealth also has more power, prestige, and glory, for each can be helpful in acquiring or retaining the others.[1]

The politics of the aristocracy, then, consists of conflict over positions, and, as always, the question settled by the political process is: who gets what? Which aristocrat shall occupy which position? To be sure, every aristocrat, by virtue of being an aristocrat, occupies some position within the aristocracy, but this would result in the absence of conflict and hence of politics only if all positions were regarded by all aristocrats as equal. In fact, they are—and are seen as—extremely unequal with respect to the amounts of wealth, power, and prestige they provide and the opportunities they offer their occupants to gain the things that fill the aristocrat's ideological needs. Thus, no matter what position an aristocrat occupies at a particular time, it may be worthwhile for him to compete with other aristocrats for better positions. Even those who have reached the highest positions in the various hierarchies of their empires, like kings and emperors, can gain still greater wealth, power, and prestige by competing with other kings and emperors. They may also compete with lower aristocrats, for example, to annex their lands.

The positions for which aristocrats compete include, perhaps most obviously, those associated with territorial control and hence with the ability,

---

1. Writing of mid-twentieth-century Thailand, David Wilson says that political status "is a complex of position, fame, and money which combine to mark clearly the high position of the individual. Into the calculation of status may go the number of a man's subordinates, the extent to which his name is known and respected, the amounts of goods and awards he can distribute to his followers." Wilson, *Politics in Thailand*, p. 276.

directly or indirectly, to exploit peasants. These range from the position of the knight or landlord who controls his estate through those of lords and rulers of intermediate territories to that of the king or emperor who rules and draws taxes from his kingdom or empire. However, there are many other positions that provide power and prestige, honor and glory, opportunities for service and opportunities to acquire wealth that are hence worth competing for. Each ruler has ministers and counselors who can advise him and who therefore themselves wield power and enjoy its benefits. Other positions involved in aristocratic politics are the higher posts in the armed forces, the bureaucracy, and the clergy. Finally, there are the positions of satraps, viceroys, or governors of provinces, which, given the far-reaching decentralization of aristocratic empires, are more or less akin to the positions of rulers, for, as I stressed earlier, the distinction between bureaucratic and feudal empires is only one of degree.

In the course of their competition, aristocrats assume various ranks which in time usually come to form firm hierarchies. Speaking of feudal Western Europe, Bloch says: "Despite the common characteristics of their military calling and their mode of life, the group of nobles *de facto*, and later *de jure*, was never in any sense a society of equals. Profound differences of wealth and power, and consequently of prestige, established a hierarchy among them, which was first tacitly recognized, and later confirmed by custom and statute. . . . Contrasts of rank were, in truth, extremely sharp within the nobility."[2] In posttraditional later medieval Europe, the aristocratic hierarchy typically ranged from knights and baronets through barons, viscounts, earls and counts, marquesses or marquis, dukes, and princes to kings and emperors. In China, five titles, originating in the feudal Chou period that began three thousand years ago, in time "crystallized into a fixed hierarchy of descending rank" and are usually translated into the five titles of the British peerage—duke, marquis, earl, viscount, and baron.[3]

But such ranking evidently does not satisfy rank-conscious aristocrats, and finer distinctions are drawn. Thus, under the Ch'in dynasty, which succeeded the Chou, there were eighteen orders of rank, and that series was increased to twenty in the Han period about two thousand years ago.[4] In Japan, "the Taiho Code (702) established four superior orders reserved for princes of the blood and ten court ranks with various subdivisions, resulting in some thirty grades altogether. . . . Family origin, court rank, government position, and wealth were closely related. . . . Naturally, pre-

2. Bloch, *Feudal Society*, pp. 332, 334.
3. Bodde, "Feudalism in China," p. 55.
4. Loewe, *Imperial China*, p. 134.

occupation with rank governed every move in this closed world of a tiny segment of Japanese society."[5] In the Mogul empire, the aristocracy was divided into thirty-three grades, but there were ranks within these ranks and three subgrades within each of these plus additional subdivisions. "When these refinements are realized, it can be seen how complicated the system in fact was, and what a field it contained for claim and counterclaim, for plot and counter-plot."[6]

In Europe, too, some aristocrats and their families were considered more noble than others within the same rank, the distinction usually being drawn according to the length of time that the title had been held by the family; the older the title, the better. There is a widespread assumption among aristocrats that their prestige and power are the more legitimate the farther back in the past they can trace their ancestry. In part, this no doubt results from the aristocratic concern with pure blood and breeding; the longer the aristocrat's pedigree, the greater the certainty that little or no common blood flows in his veins. In part, it rests on the prevailing world view in unchanging societies that things must be and will be what they have always been; hence one must be an aristocrat if one's ancestors were aristocrats. In any case, aristocrats commonly pay much attention to their genealogy. "The antiquity of a family is highly valued in Ruanda. Almost any Mututsi is able to give the names of his ancestors for six or eight generations,"[7] and in Java an aristocrat was "a man who could trace his ancestry back to the great semi-mythical kings of pre-colonial Java."[8]

In China there was a Department of Imperial Genealogy, and in Russia there developed a system, the *mestnichestvo*, formally abolished in 1682, which correlated an aristocrat's service rank with the genealogical rank of his family. "Infighting among noble families was an obvious consequence of this system. To uphold the family honor, much energy was expended on '*mestnichestvo* arithmetic' . . . litigation, feuds, and personal combat. According to the then prevailing view, death itself was preferable to the unspeakable disgrace of being placed 'below' a man whose ancestors' record did not entitle him to the higher position either at court or in the army."[9]

Lucian Pye, writing of the Burmese kingdom, which lasted till the late

5. Bendix, *Kings or People*, pp. 73–74.

6. Spear, "The Mughal 'Mansabdari' System," p. 6. In Sassanid Persia, "the society was divided into four basic classes: the clerics, the warriors, the bureaucrats, and the peasant masses. Each of these classes was further divided into separate and fixed groupings and the result was a complex and intricate hierarchical social structure." Bill, *The Politics of Iran*, p. 2.

7. Maquet, "The Kingdom of Ruanda," p. 178.

8. Geertz, *The Religion of Java*, p. 229.

9. Bendix, *Kings or People*, p. 115.

nineteenth century, says: "The scope and focus of the traditional political process meant that all actions tended to be governed by a fairly explicit hierarchical pattern of relationships in which the issue of superior and subordinate dominated every move. . . . The cardinal questions each official put to himself in all his dealings with others were, 'Who are my superiors?' and 'Who are my inferiors?' Every action was designed to clarify the answers to these questions. A man acted with shameless servility before his superiors and poured out uninhibited contempt and disdain on inferiors. . . . Burmese officials, like most traditional elites, naturally developed infinite skill and delicate sensitivities in dealing with matters of prestige, status, and power."[10]

To the aristocrat who needs to know exactly which other aristocrats rank above him or below him, such information is provided by the order of precedence. In the Ottoman empire, "the order of precedence on small as well as great occasions, and the observances proper to each such occasion were made a matter of law. . . . Each group and every officer in each group had his exact place in every ceremonial assembly and his exact rank in every procession."[11] In England, "the earliest formal Table of Precedence, 'The Order of all Estates of Nobles and Gentry in England' was drawn up in 1399. . . . The earliest statute, the House of Lords Precedence Act 1539, is still in force, though parts have become obsolete."[12]

Typically, an aristocrat acquires his rank by inheritance, although the system of inheritance may vary not only from aristocracy to aristocracy but even from family to family, titles passing in some cases only in the male line and in others also in the female one, in some cases only to one son, usually the oldest, in others to all sons. However, some titles, like the eighteen orders in the Ch'in empire, were "in principle . . . not held on a hereditary basis."[13] In Ethiopia, too, titles were not hereditary, and the emperor was free to ennoble anyone he chose, but nevertheless, "the Abyssinian nobility did form a self-conscious status group with a certain hereditary base."[14]

Obviously, at some time, even if in the dim past, aristocratic ranks must have been acquired for the first time. The leaders of a nomadic or semi-nomadic band of conquering warriors may have assumed titles along with control of territory and peasants and so may all the members or at least the

10. Pye, *Politics, Personality, and Nation Building*, p. 68.

11. Lybyer, *The Government of the Ottoman Empire*, pp. 134–35. The Ethiopian order of precedence of 1689, listing twenty-eight offices in the proper order, is reproduced in Alvares, *The Prester John of the Indies*, 2:560–61.

12. Montague-Smith, ed., *Debrett's Peerage* (1973–74), p. P16.

13. Loewe, *Imperial China*, p. 134.

14. Levine, *Wax and Gold*, p. 163.

leading members of the band. These members may have received their titles, along with their land, from their leader, and after the original conquest, ranks and titles are newly awarded typically for meritorious service to the ruler, usually military service. Because it is ordinarily only aristocrats who are in a position to render such service, it is usually one who is already an aristocrat, perhaps a younger son or an illegitimate one without a title, who is given a title, or a titled one who is promoted to a higher rank within the aristocracy. In Ethiopia, "although no man inherited a title, as son of a nobleman he might inherit the culture and facilities that would give him a much better chance than any commoner to obtain a title of his own."[15] Because promotion is possible, there is competition among aristocrats for higher ranks and for the greater amounts of wealth, power, and prestige, of honor and of glory that these ranks usually convey.

As noted earlier, aristocrats are not defined here by the fact that they hold aristocratic titles so that high bureaucrats, military men, and priests can be included in the aristocracy whether they hold aristocratic titles—and hence aristocratic ranks—or not. However, the aristocratic hierarchies of the military, the bureaucracy, and the clergy are generally themselves subdivided by rank, each designated by a title and associated with certain privileges and a certain amount of power and prestige and opportunities to gain wealth, honor, and glory, to serve and to do one's duty. Rigid subdivisions of military officer corps by rank are most familiar to us, because they have been inherited by modern armed forces even with their social implications, but the upper levels of bureaucracies and often of priesthoods in traditional and posttraditional aristocratic empires were similarly subdivided. Thus, the imperial Chinese bureaucracy "was organized with a full hierarchy of grades corresponding with a fixed scale of salaries. As a man's authority and seniority increased so also did his emoluments and privileges; in addition, a position in the hierarchy acted as a mark of social status, thereby assuring the holder of an appropriate degree of respect from other members of the community."[16] Nor is an individual aristocrat necessarily confined to a single hierarchy. Positions of territorial rulers and military commanders often go together, and in ancient Egypt, as I noted, one could simultaneously be a general, a governor, and a priest. Clearly, in the army, the bureaucracy, and the clergy, promotions to higher rank are, again, possible and thus there is competition and conflict among aristocrats.

Titles, then, are of supreme importance to the aristocrat, for they indicate most clearly his place on the aristocratic status ladder and the symbols

---

15. Ibid., p. 164.

16. Loewe, *Imperial China*, pp. 131–32.

and material awards to which he is entitled. "A passion for acquiring titles is the obverse of the Abyssinian's penchant for instituting offices and grades. A man's title . . . has been the major indicator of the deference which is due to him. Honorific titles and paraphernalia appropriate to them are perhaps the most sought after possessions in traditional Abyssinia, for they confer inalienable status. . . . Titles . . . not only were universally esteemed but also entitled the bearers to a style of life which included a presumptive right to gifts and obedience from all inferiors as well as the consumption of much wealth and power."[17]

Symbols

Usually each rank in the aristocracy itself as well as in the military, the bureaucracy, and the clergy is designated not only by a title but also by various visible symbols. In Europe, each aristocratic family has its coat of arms, and each rank is entitled to a particular type of crown, the more elaborate the higher the rank. Different types of dress and hats, flags and various insignia and badges may all be used to designate distinctions of rank in the aristocratic hierarchies of the military, the bureaucracy, and the priesthood. Houses, carriages, saddles, and even umbrellas of different types, sizes, and colors may be assigned to particular ranks of the aristocracy. Because all these outward symbols are associated with ranks and ranks are extremely important to aristocrats, the code regulating the use of these symbols must be rigidly adhered to and is often laid down by decree or law.

In the Ottoman empire, by the time of Suleiman the Magnificent, the "Law of Ceremonies had become a collection of considerable magnitude. . . . Regulations concerning such matters as the color and shape and materials of robes and turbans . . . were made a matter of law. . . . It was as much the duty of an officer to wear the proper costume, and to appear in the right place and at the right time at public ceremonies, as to attend to the business connected with his position. All the classes of members of the sultan's household, all the high officers of government . . . were clearly distinguished from each other by costume or head-dress or by both."[18]

17. Levine, *Wax and Gold*, pp. 158, 162. Levine lists dozens of Ethiopian titles held by military, civil government, and royal court officials, whose functions and titles were not clearly distinguished. Thus, the Chief Hand-Washer at the court of Menelik held the title of a "General of the Left Wing" (ibid., pp. 158–60). For a list of about two hundred "Titles Used by the Ottomans," which, however, includes numerous nicknames and titles conferred on individual sultans, see Alderson, *The Structure of the Ottoman Dynasty*, pp. 112–20.

18. Lybyer, *The Government of the Ottoman Empire*, pp. 134–35.

In Aztec Mexico, "stringent sumptuary laws were enforced, rivalling those of an oriental court. For Moctezuma's subjects, the use of jewels, feathers and even cotton clothing was governed by meticulous regulations depending on birth and distinction in war. Different styles of dress were to be established for the ruler's counsellors, the nobles, the different grades of warriors and for the people. Death was the penalty for any of the latter who wore cotton clothing, or whose mantle reached to his ankles. If such a one had the temerity to appear in a long mantle, his legs would be examined; if he bore no war wounds, alone considered to justify a garment of such length, he was instantly killed."[19] In Inca Peru, too, there were sumptuary laws involving "litter bearing, the wearing of certain cloth and certain ornaments and jewels, and the privilege of polygamy as belonging to the Inca ruling class and to other persons who were granted these privileges by the Inca,"[20] mostly the non-Inca, local aristocracy.

In eighth-century Japan, "patrician life was rigidly circumscribed down to the type of fan appropriate for each of the main rank-categories."[21] In imperial China, "among the ruling class, clothing was just as much an indication of rank as were insignia of various kinds or the number and style of one's retinue. The colour and ornamentation of the dress to be worn, the shape and type of headgear, the particular style of the girdle—all such details were laid down, for every occasion and for each grade of the hierarchy, by imperial decree, in fulfillment of ritual requirements. The official histories contain monographs entirely devoted to describing in the minutest detail the costumes, headgear, girdles, carriages and seals of the Emperor, of his close kin, and of high dignitaries of the court and other officials. A large number of decrees were concerned with questions of this kind."[22] Thus, the T'ang Code provided that "all those who contravene the regulations when having houses or carriages built, clothes, vases and other utensils made, or animals carved in stone for funerary purposes, are punished by a hundred strokes of the rod." Mandarins below the third degree were not permitted to have animals carved in stone near their tombs, and different colors were prescribed for the robes to be worn by bureaucrats of each grade.[23]

Herbert Spencer devotes entire chapters to such matters as obeisances, forms of address, titles, and badges and costumes (but does not distinguish between aristocratic empires and more primitive and more modern soci-

---

19. Davies, *The Aztecs*, p. 108. See also Soustelle, *Daily Life of the Aztecs*, pp. 138–39.

20. Moore, *Power and Property in Inca Peru*, p. 92.

21. Bendix, *Kings or People*, p. 74.

22. Gernet, *Daily Life in China*, pp. 127–28.

23. Ibid., pp. 108, 128.

eties). He quotes eighteenth- and nineteenth-century authors, saying, respectively, of Aztec Mexico that under Montezuma's laws, "no one was allowed to build a house with [several] stories except the great lords and gallant captains, on pain of death," and of Burma that "the character of house, and especially of roof appropriate to each rank, appears to be matter of regulation, or inviolable prescriptions." "Nothing less than death can expiate the crime, either of choosing a shape [for a house] that does not belong to the dignity of the master, or of painting the house white; which colour is permitted to the members of the royal family alone." In Japan, "the bigness and length of these [sedan] poles hath been determined by the political laws of the empire, proportionable to every one's quality." The sedan "is carried by two, four, eight or more men, according to the quality of the person in it." Similarly in China, "the highest officers are carried by eight bearers, others by four, and the lowest by two: this, and every other particular, being regulated by laws." In Turkey, "the hierarchy of rank is maintained and designated by the size of each Turkish functionary's boat." In Java, the umbrellas of six ranks were of six different colors.[24]

What Levine says of traditional Ethiopia seems true of aristocracies in all aristocratic empires: "The style of life of the nobility is colored above all by a seemingly unlimited command of deference. They are addressed as 'my lord' by all comers, and waited on in a hundred different ways wherever they go."[25] Aristocrats of different ranks and titles are generally entitled to different forms of address. An observation made in 1845 that in Fiji there are "various forms of salutation, according to the rank of the parties; and great attention is paid to insure that the salutation shall have the proper form"[26] is probably applicable to most aristocracies. Thus Geertz, writing of the "linguistic etiquette" of the Javanese nobility, says: "In Javanese it is nearly impossible to say anything without indicating the social relationship between the speaker and the listener in terms of status and familiarity." He shows that simple questions like "are you well?" or "where are you coming from?" are composed of wholly different words depending on whether they are addressed to a superior or an inferior, and he comments that "clearly a peculiar obsession is at work here."[27]

In Britain, the monarch is to be addressed as His (or Her) Most Gracious Majesty, his close relatives as Their Royal Highnesses, a duke as Most Noble or His Grace, a marquess as Most Honourable, and earls, viscounts, and barons as Right Honourable; on the Continent there are, in

24. Spencer, *The Principles of Sociology*, 2:197, par. 418, 198–200, par. 419.

25. Levine, *Wax and Gold*, p. 157.

26. Quoted by Spencer, *The Principles of Sociology*, 2:216, par. 429.

27. Geertz, *The Religion of Java*, p. 248.

addition to highnesses and royal and imperial highnesses, also serene and most serene and most illustrious highnesses—all terms which, if taken literally, provide a revealing self-image of the aristocracy.

Monarchs, of course, enjoy the most extravagant forms of address, for example, the king of Siam, "the Master of Life" and "Sovereign of the Earth"; the Turkish sultan, "the Shadow of God" and "Glory of the Universe"; the Chinese emperor, the "Son of Heaven" and "the Lord of Ten Thousand Years";[28] the Ethiopian emperor, the "Elect of God";[29] and the Persian emperor Shahpur II referred to himself as "King of Kings (Shahanshah), partner with the stars, brother of the Sun and the Moon."[30] Spencer quotes a London newspaper reporter of 1879 relating that he was introduced to the King of Burma by "a herald lying on his stomach . . . as follows: . . . Most Glorious Excellent Majesty, Lord of the Ishaddan, King of Elephants, master of many white elephants, lord of the mines of gold, silver, rubies, amber, and the noble serpentine, Sovereign of the Empires of Thuna-paranta and Tampadipa, and other great empires and countries, and of all the umbrella-wearing chiefs, the supporter of religion, the Sun-descended Monarch, arbiter of life, and great righteous King, King of Kings, and possessor of boundless dominions and supreme wisdom."[31] Similarly, "the Mogul emperor was known as 'Holder of the Universe.' . . . The court form of address came to more than two hundred words of adulation, covering everything from 'garland-twiner of spiritual and temporal blossoms' to 'second Alexander.' "[32]

Aristocrats insist on constantly being reminded of their rank not only by having themselves addressed in peculiar forms appropriate to that rank, but by obeisance to be paid to them in accordance with their rank. Forms of obeisance include the kissing of the aristocrat's hands or feet or of the hem of his dress or the ground he stands on, and especially the numerous ways of making oneself physically inferior before the aristocrat, ranging from lowering one's head through bowing and scraping, curtsying, bending

28. Spencer, *The Principles of Sociology*, 2:146, par. 395.

29. In Ethiopian "chronicles and hymns of praise which span seven centuries, the emperors are celebrated for superlative beauty and superhuman powers. In splendor of countenance they are likened to the sun; in awesomeness of power, to the lion, in religious character and divine force, to the kings of Israel and, at times, to God Himself." Levine, *Wax and Gold*, p. 151.

30. Filippani-Ronconi, "The Tradition of Sacred Kingship in Iran," p. 57. The recently deposed Mohammed Reza Shah had assumed the title of "Light of the Aryans" (ibid., pp. 83, 527).

31. Spencer, *The Principles of Sociology*, 2:159–60, par. 401. A similar set of titles of the Thai king Rama V, who reigned until 1910, is quoted by Wilson, *Politics in Thailand*, p. 91.

32. Wesson, *The Imperial Order*, p. 84.

the knee, going down on one knee or both knees, to kotowing or other forms of knocking the forehead on the ground and complete prostration.[33]

Just as monarchs enjoy the most extravagant forms of address, so they receive the most humbling forms of obeisance. In both Aztec Mexico and Inca Peru, the presence of the ruler could only be entered in poor clothing to maximize the differences between him and those below him, and one appeared before the Inca only carrying a burden on one's back as a symbol of servitude.[34] "Ethiopian subjects have had to prostrate themselves and refrain from lifting their eyes in [the emperor's] presence. An analogous show of deference was expected when they received royal messages from afar; the recipient had to hear the message outside his home, standing, and naked above the waist. The emperors rarely permitted themselves to be seen in public, and were often secluded by curtains while eating or drinking. They were not addressed directly, but through an interlocutor. Za'ra Ya'qob, whose officers were said to have kissed the earth each time they heard the sound of his voice, carried the demand for social distance so far that pages attached to his court were not permitted to have contact with anybody from outside, and were put to death if they dared to fraternize with local inhabitants."[35] Summarizing patterns prevailing in most of the kingdoms of Black Africa, Murdock says: "Behavior at court follows detailed rules of protocol, of which abject prostration in the presence of the monarch is a nearly universal ingredient. . . . Characteristic of African states is a great proliferation of titles . . . and competition for these is often keen."[36]

All these symbols of titles and crowns, styles of dress and address, and the observance of proper form, protocol, and etiquette are of the utmost importance in the life of the aristocracy. In Ethiopia, "a rank order was carefully respected, and confusion over protocol could provoke altercation."[37] Wearing clothing or a badge to which one is not entitled, addressing an aristocrat improperly, not bowing deeply enough to him or walking through a door ahead of him when he has precedence may all be crimes, punishable even by death, or attacks on the aristocrat's honor requiring bloody revenge. It is easy to write off the aristocrat's concern with such matters as absurd or petty or even ridiculous, as it does, indeed, appear

33. A richly documented section on what he calls "The Great Symbol of Total Submission: Prostration" in many aristocratic empires appears in Wittfogel, *Oriental Despotism*, pp. 152–54.

34. These and numerous examples of all the forms of obeisance mentioned here and of others are provided in Spencer, *The Principles of Sociology*, 2:113–40, pars. 383–91.

35. Levine, *Wax and Gold*, p. 151.

36. Murdock, *Africa*, p. 38.

37. Levine, *Wax and Gold*, p. 159.

from a modern perspective. However, this does not explain why serious and powerful men devoted so much of their time and energy, their thoughts, and attention to these matters of form. The reason, of course, is that because the various visible symbols and forms of address and obeisance were closely associated with particular ranks and positions in aristocratic hierarchies, they themselves came to convey prestige, honor, and glory. Prestige, honor, and glory, however, are supremely valuable to the aristocrat both in themselves and also as means to enhance both his power and his wealth. No wonder that a particular crown or hat, a title, or a decoration may be worth fighting and dying for. They stand for and they also are in themselves what matters most to aristocrats. Politics for many aristocrats, then, is in good part competition for the right to employ the kind of symbols listed here.

But how does the aristocrat acquire the right to employ these symbols? As with a title, unless he can simply appropriate them, they are awarded to him by a higher aristocrat in return for meritorious service, for outstanding performance of duty. Thus, different positions in the aristocracy, and most notably in the military, each designated by certain symbols, provide different degrees of opportunities to acquire glory, to maintain one's honor under stress, to render service, and to do one's duty. But it is for honorable behavior, glorious deeds, and faithful service that the aristocrat receives more symbolic awards. Just as he or one of his ancestors received his original rank or title and subsequent promotions, so he is now awarded additional titles, and visible symbols like badges and medals, additions to his coat of arms or his flag, or admission to special and exclusive bodies like orders of chivalry.

The result is more competition and conflict, more politics, within the aristocracy over who shall get the positions that bring the symbolic awards and who shall get the symbolic awards that, in turn, advance the holder to better positions. The process of competition among individual aristocrats strengthens the aristocratic institutions and the aristocracies as a whole of which the individuals are members, for it is on their behalf and in their service that the individuals seek to outdo each other performing deeds of valor or doing their duty.

It must be added that some of the symbols mentioned here might have served not only to stress distinctions within the aristocracy but also to distinguish aristocrats from a rising commercial class. The latter could afford to affect aristocratic life-styles and had to be prevented from doing so by an aristocracy that held it in contempt. But, however that may be, the experience of numerous aristocratic empires confirms that the division of aristocracies into ranks and the employment of various symbols to distinguish them from each other is a common phenomenon among traditional aristocracies.

Wealth

In addition to all the many intangible benefits I have now mentioned, aristocrats derive very tangible ones from the positions they occupy. The amount of wealth available to aristocrats depends on their position within the aristocracy and can vary widely. For most of them, it is roughly proportionate to the number of peasants and the quality of land that they control either directly or indirectly through other aristocrats. The local aristocrat who controls and exploits only a small estate may be quite poor and can barely make ends meet. On the other hand, obviously, the ruler of a large territory can become very rich. Though agriculture is the principal source of wealth in aristocratic empires, control of land can also involve the control of mines, whose products can be sold, and control of markets and trade routes that allows aristocrats to rob or to tax merchants.

Given this inequality and the possibility for every aristocrat to improve his material position by acquiring control over more land and more peasants, there can be intense competition among aristocrats for land. While control of land may possibly have some symbolic value, it is really the product of the land that is of material value. Aristocrats must therefore also engage in conflicts over how much of the product of their land they can retain and how much they must pass on to higher aristocrats in the form of taxes or services. As Bendix says: "Where the fortunes of men wax and wane with the fortunes of the house to which they belong, victory or defeat in jurisdictional feuds bears directly on the well-being of the individual. That well-being depends on the size and productivity of landholdings and on the degree to which political authorities can exact tribute in money or kind. Patriarchal jurisdictions are engaged, therefore, in efforts to better their holdings vis-à-vis their neighbors and to lessen the tribute paid to their ruler."[38]

Land can be acquired by conquest if the aristocrat is in such a position that he or his army does the conquering. Or land can be obtained as a grant made by a higher aristocrat usually in return for and in expectation of services rendered. Again, then, whether an aristocrat obtains such a grant depends on whether the position he held enabled him to render services to the higher aristocracy. Land can also be acquired as a gift from another aristocrat, perhaps to confirm an alliance, and by marriage into a landed family, all possibilities that are again open to an aristocrat if he occupies the right positions. Thus, the control of land and hence the wealth derived from the exploitation of peasants goes with certain positions in the aristocracy. The duke will have more land than the knight and will have a better chance of acquiring still more. Competition for wealth, then, takes the

38. Bendix, *Kings or People*, pp. 222–23.

form of conflict and competition for positions, the same positions that provide the intangible benefits of power, prestige, and glory and the symbols that go with them.

Positions that entail control of land and peasants are obvious sources of wealth, but they are not the only ones. Thus, positions of military leadership provide aristocrats opportunities not only to perform honorable service and deeds of valor and glory, but also to acquire the spoils of war. And booty not only enriches the aristocrat personally but can be distributed to his aristocratic followers. This gives him a chance both to gain power and influence and, in line with important aristocratic values, to behave honorably and generously.

Bureaucratic positions, too, can be a source of wealth in aristocratic empires. The principal function of the bureaucracy is tax collection, and tax collectors invariably, whether quite officially or not, retain a part of the taxes they collect. At the lower levels, they may not be aristocrats—though they may, through their control over the peasants, become aristocrats. But the higher positions in the bureaucracy are always occupied by aristocrats, and, generally, the higher the position the better the chance of retaining larger amounts of taxes as they are passed up from the local through the provincial and regional to the central bureaucracy.

Lucian Pye thus describes bureaucratic politics in the traditional Burmese kingdom: "The basic rationale behind the struggle of politics was the valiant quest of all to maximize their income while reducing their risks. Upon receiving quotas for revenue to be collected, officials would pass them on down, dividing and allocating the sums among their subordinates, who might in turn strive to negotiate an abatement and push the responsibilities onto neighboring districts. Once the revenues had been collected, the process reversed itself; each subordinate sought to keep as much as possible while each superior applied all the pressures he could to increase the amounts passed up."[39]

The degree of decentralization and hence the independence of the lower aristocracy from the higher one varies among aristocratic empires. Often, in order to function effectively, which means, above all, to be able to retain as much tax money as possible, it is necessary for the lower bureaucrats to give gifts to the higher bureaucrats. This was, for example, standard practice in the imperial Chinese bureaucracy, but similar practices prevail where the bureaucracy is not a well-defined and distinct institution and where it is simply lower aristocrats who are expected to give gifts to higher aristocrats. Obviously, the higher the position occupied by an aristocrat, the more and higher ranking aristocrats are below him on the ladder of rank

39. Pye, *Politics, Personality, and Nation Building*, p. 70.

and hence the more numerous and the bigger are the gifts he receives. Again, the higher his position the more wealth the aristocrat obtains.

Positions in the priesthood also give access to wealth to aristocrats. In ancient Egypt, temples, that is, the priests, eventually came to own huge tax-exempt estates; the Indian Brahmans were landowners; in Peru the peasants did forced labor not only on land set aside for the Inca but on land set aside for the Sun, that is, the priests; and in feudal Europe and in medieval Russia the church and monasteries, that is, again, the clergy, came to own tremendous landed estates, not least because aristocrats gave or left parts of their land to them in order to secure salvation for themselves. The latter process is only one way in which priests benefit materially from the fact that they control religious rituals and may control access to the gods or to a life after death. Aristocrats occupying positions in the priestly hierarchy can gain wealth, not only in the form of land and control over peasants, but in cash or in kind, in the form of gifts or sacrifices in return for the religious services they perform, and the higher ones will, directly from other aristocrats or indirectly from the lower clergy, receive more than those in lower positions.

Does the baron who exacts a tribute or tax from the passing merchant engage in robbery or extortion? Does the tax collector who retains part of what he collects steal or embezzle from the government? Does the priest who threatens someone with damnation or the wrath of the gods unless he is paid practice blackmail? From a modern perspective, it is tempting to ask such questions, to try to draw a line between legitimate and illegitimate ways of aristocratic revenue raising. In the context of traditional aristocratic empires, however, there is no such line; as I already noted, the very basis of such empires, the taxation of peasants, is not clearly distinguishable from robbery or extortion.

"Public authority in Ethiopia was frankly regarded as a private possession by all concerned. The incumbent might change, but the office remained—not so much a set of obligations to fulfill in behalf of the king, or the state, let alone in behalf of the subjects—but a set of opportunities for personal aggrandizement. The opportunities, both psychic and economic, were impressive."[40] Max Weber put the same thing in more general terms. Interested in elaborating the characteristics of modern bureaucracy, he pointed out that, in contrast to it, normally in the European Middle Ages, officeholding was "considered ownership of a source of income, to be exploited for rents or emoluments in exchange for the rendering of certain services."[41]

40. Levine, *Wax and Gold*, p. 161.

41. Weber, *Economy and Society*, 3:959. Cipolla, too, says that "in the feudal world of the

Weber had this to say of officials in patrimonial empires, which he distinguished in principle from feudal ones: "The patrimonial office lacks above all the bureaucratic separation of the 'private' and the 'official' sphere. For the political administration, too, is treated as a purely personal affair of the ruler, and political power is considered part of his personal property, which can be exploited by means of contributions and fees. . . . The office and the exercise of public authority serve the ruler and the official on which the office was bestowed, they do not serve impersonal purposes." Weber also wrote: "The patrimonial state offers the whole realm of the ruler's discretion as a hunting ground for accumulating wealth. Wherever traditional or stereotyped prescription does not impose strict limitations, patrimonialism gives free rein to the enrichment of the ruler himself, the court officials, favorites, governors, mandarins, tax collectors, influence peddlers, and the great merchants and financiers who function as tax farmers, purveyors and creditors."[42]

The distinction between aristocrats illegitimately enriching themselves and legitimately raising revenue for the government depends on a distinction between the aristocracy and the government, which is nonsensical when applied to traditional aristocratic empires. To put the same thing differently, the concept of corruption, defined as the use of public power for private profit, depends on the distinction between the private and the public sphere which, as Weber pointed out, does not exist in aristocratic empires. In a sense, there is no public sphere, for government is the private affair of the aristocracy carried on for its private profit. A modern observer can choose to regret this, but to attach a concept like corruption to the behavior or the role of the aristocracy is misleading, for it is a modern concept that is, by its definition, inapplicable to aristocratic empires.[43]

This appears to be generally, if only implicitly, recognized, for the very concept of a corrupt king or emperor makes no sense to us. It is popularly taken for granted that kings and princes live in luxury, perhaps in part as a result of our fairy tales, one of the few popular sources on life in what may have been the traditional past of present-day societies. In these tales, kings

---

eighth to eleventh centuries there was no distinction between public and private." Cipolla, *Before the Industrial Revolution*, p. 44. And Hsu says exactly the same of Chou China: "In this feudal society there was no clear distinction between the public affairs of a state and the private business of a lord." Hsu, *Ancient China in Transition*, p. 11.

42. Weber, *Economy and Society*, 3:1028–29, 1031, 1099.

43. "Corruption requires some recognition of the difference between public role and private interest. If the culture of the society does not distinguish between the king's role as a private person and the king's role as king, it is impossible to accuse the king of corruption in the use of public monies." Huntington, *Political Order in Changing Societies*, p. 60.

and princes are invariably rich simply because of the positions they hold. On the other hand, we can readily imagine a corrupt president or prime minister. These are salaried public servants who are considered corrupt if they derive material benefit beyond their salaries from their public offices.

Matters become confused, however, when as has happened under the impact of some modernization—and hence in no longer purely traditional aristocratic empires—aristocrats themselves adopt the titles of modern public officeholders.[44] If a prime minister happens to be king, a deputy prime minister the crown prince, and a minister of social affairs and labor another royal prince, the men in question are not modern public servants, no matter how modern their titles. They are, rather, aristocrats, that is, men who enrich themselves as a result of the positions they hold. It is only reasonable to expect them to behave like aristocrats and not to judge them by modern standards and to call them corrupt. What modernization has brought to them is not a change in their standards of behavior, but their modern titles and the wealth derived from the modern economy now available in addition to that drawn from the traditional sources.

Particularly in the oil-rich countries this additional wealth has been immense; yet some of them continue to lack, in Weber's words just quoted, "the bureaucratic separation of the 'private' and the 'official' sphere." With reference to the interwar period we read that King Ibn Saud "had tried to reorganize his Finance Department. At his request the Dutch Bank had found an expert who was asked to prepare a scheme for a thorough reorganization. . . . When the expert started to explain to His Majesty that the basis of all sound national finance was the rigid separation of the income of the Royal Family from the income of the state the whole scheme

44. At the time of writing, the king of Saudi Arabia and the ruling Amirs of Bahrein and Qatar serve as their own prime ministers, as was also true of the king of Nepal for some time in the 1960s, while the king of Cambodia, Norodom Sihanouk, abdicated in favor of his father in 1955 in order to become prime minister, and, on his father's death, chief of state. In Afghanistan, the prime minister and the foreign minister were both cousins of the king until, in 1963, the first person not of royal birth became prime minister. In 1973, it was again the king's cousin who became head of state and prime minister, minister of foreign affairs and of defense of the newly declared republic. The son of the queen of Tonga had been prime minister since 1949 until he succeeded her as ruler in 1965 and made his younger brother prime minister. The prime minister of Burundi was, for some time in the 1960s, the son-in-law of the Mwami (king), and the cabinet of the king of Swaziland has been composed mostly of his sons, sons-in-law, and cousins. The half-dozen or so top ministerial positions in the cabinets of Saudi Arabia, Kuwait, Bahrein, and Qatar are, in each case, occupied by close relatives of the ruler, mostly his brothers and half brothers (that is, the sons of his father's several wives), and a similar situation prevailed in Yemen before the rule of the Imams was ended by the revolution of 1962. As an article in the *Economist* put it after listing numerous members of the Saudi royal family in high modern positions: "Add a few score cousins, uncles and nephews and you have, in effect, Saudi Arabia's governing party." "The Family Way," p. 46.

was abandoned. The King would not submit himself to any control, no one should know what he was doing with his money. So after half a year of hard work a sadly disillusioned financial expert took his leave and there was great rejoicing in the Finance Department at his departure."[45]

St. John Philby, an admirer of Ibn Saud, continues this story.[46] He reports that, after World War II, the Saudi minister of finance "was content to write off as a lump sum the financial provision required by the king and the various provincial governors, mostly members of the royal family, for use at their unfettered discretion, and without any obligation to account for such funds."[47] What *The Economist* said of Saudi Arabia in 1955 must still be true: "A large proportion of the revenue furnished a cushioned existence and palatial private investment in real property abroad, to princes, ministers, rivals for power and other palace connections."[48] Furthermore, the traditional situation that makes it impossible to speak of aristocratic corruption also prevails in the other Arabian oil monarchies. "On the Persian Gulf, . . . states and sheikhdoms are still run on a feudal basis, and little distinction is drawn between national revenue and the privy purse of the ruler."[49]

45. van der Meulen, *The Wells of Ibn Saud*, pp. 188–89. Ibn Saud was not unique: "Until recent times European monarchs made no distinction between their private patrimonies and the treasuries of the states." Cipolla, *Before the Industrial Revolution*, p. 44.

46. Generous measures of British and American government aid went to the Saudi government during World War II "to which the Arabian response was a further orgy of extravagance and mismanagement, accompanied by the growth of corruption on a large scale in the highest quarters." "The only experiment made in recent years (1947) to conduct the administration on the basis of a published, and much publicised, budget was such a fiasco that no further attempt has been made to take the people into the confidence of the Government. . . . The budget, apart from the untouchable provision made for the royal exchequer and unpremeditated raids from the same direction on the resources of the State, would be administered at the sole discretion of the Finance Department." Philby, *Arabian Jubilee*, pp. 227, 228.

47. Philby also gives a graphic account of what happens when modernity in the form of oil wealth and of what it will buy becomes available to an aristocracy still operating by the standards of an aristocratic empire: "The oil made it possible for Arabia to indulge in extravagance out of its own resources. And it did this literally on a princely scale: leading off with the despatch of a dozen princes to the New World . . . to ransack America for motor-cars and other aids to the enjoyment of life. Other such expeditions followed, one led by the Crown Prince . . . each bringing back to Arabia substantial mementoes of its invasion of the richest country in the world, among whose wonders one member of one of these expeditions singled out as the most wonderful of them all a submarine night-club with walls of glass, through which the circumambient fish could watch the dancing!" (ibid., pp. 231–32).

48. "Spending from State Purses," p. 2.

49. Ibid. Some time ago in Kuwait, "one-third of the Sheik's revenues [was] reported to go into his privy purse, another third to be regularly invested in foreign securities, with the

Oil royalties—let alone the submarine nightclubs just referred to in a footnote—are not phenomena of traditional aristocratic empires, but the examples just cited—and it does not matter for our purposes for how long into the second half of the twentieth century they have remained or will remain valid—nicely illustrate what Weber said of aristocratic empires where office and political power are regarded as the personal property of aristocrats to be exploited for "the enrichment of the ruler himself, the court officials, favorites, governors." Where "the office and the exercise of public authority serve the ruler and the official," where "they do not serve impersonal purposes," any application of the concept of corruption seems inappropriate.

To apply this concept to aristocratic empires would lead us to describe all aristocrats in such empires as corrupt, for, as I remarked earlier, government is an extractive enterprise, it is instituted and functions precisely to enable the aristocracy to accumulate wealth and, given the distribution of power between the classes, cannot function in any other way. For the aristocracy not to take what it can from the peasantry or to return part of it to the peasantry, that is, not to be corrupt by the standards of advanced societies, would by its own standards simply make no sense.

The question is not whether aristocrats benefit from the offices or positions they hold; they obviously do. The question is which aristocrat shall benefit and how much, and that depends in good part on which aristocrat shall occupy which position in the aristocracy. It is around this question that aristocratic politics revolves.

---

balance devoted to public uses." The latter included the erection of a magnificent new palace. Baran, *The Political Economy of Growth*, pp. 107–8. Similarly, newspaper reports in 1961 indicated that of the oil revenues of Qatar, 25 percent went to its rulers, 50 percent to his relatives, and 25 percent into the state treasury (*New York Times*, 5 March 1961), while Sheikh Sulam of Bahrein who died in 1961 "personally received all oil revenues. Each year he gave two-thirds of the income to the public treasury and kept the remainder for himself and the 200 members of the royal family" (ibid., 3 November 1961).

10

The Arenas of
Aristocratic Politics

Conflicts between Empires

Much of what has come down to us as the history of traditional aristocratic empires—and, indeed, much even of the history of posttraditional societies ruled by aristocrats, like those of Europe in the later Middle Ages and into the period of absolutism—is the history of intraaristocratic conflicts. The description by an Amhara literatus of Ethiopian history as "always the same old thing—one lord fighting another to gain more power"[1] is equally valid for the history of other aristocratic empires.

Conflicts among aristocrats can divide major empires from each other, they can take place within empires, between or within factions and cliques or between and even within clans or families—nor are these different arenas of conflict clearly distinguishable from each other. Conflicts between aristocratic empires, such as wars, must not be thought of as international conflicts, simply because these empires, not being societies, are not nations held together by bonds of ethnic unity or administrative centralization or feelings of loyalty linking the government and its citizens. Rather, such conflicts are conflicts between the aristocracies or the ruling families of two empires. Even the Hundred Years War (1337–1453), well past the period of traditional aristocratic empires in Western Europe, cannot be adequately described, as it often is, as a war between England and France. It was rather a series of conflicts between shifting alliances of aristocrats, one of which included the king of England and one the king of France, over lands located in the present territory of France.

The modern distinction between international wars and civil wars cannot be applied to such a conflict, for, instead of clearly defined nations, territories under a single ruler were largely governed by him indirectly through aristocratic governors or vassals who attained various degrees of

1. Quoted in Levine, "Ethiopia: Identity, Authority, and Realism," p. 262.

de facto and de jure independence from him. Thus the innumerable wars that went on within the medieval Holy Roman Empire between the emperor and the various princes and dukes, who were his vassals, as well as among the latter, can be characterized equally well as international wars or civil wars. Similarly, in Japan feudal lords fought each other for centuries, particularly from the twelfth to the sixteenth. Because the dominant lords used the emperor's authority to legitimize their ascendancy, this warfare, too, partakes of the character of both civil and international wars.[2] The caliphate, the Hindu and Muslim empires in India, the Mongol one in Russia, and the Ottoman empire were also all torn by frequent warfare. Rulers fought their vassals, tributaries, or provincial governors and viceroys, and the latter fought among themselves.

Whether international or civil wars in modern eyes, such conflicts represent the interests of a few aristocrats on each side, sometimes even aristocrats within a single family. Because rulers of aristocratic empires often regarded their territories and the peasants on them as their personal possessions, that is, as subject to their exploitation, and because these territories were not held together by any unifying elements other than their ruler, it is not surprising that such rulers not infrequently divided their empires among their heirs. Nor is it uncommon for these heirs, whether they are brothers or, if their father had several wives, half brothers, to become embroiled in conflicts and warfare with each other as each one seeks to expand his empire and perhaps even hopes to reunite his father's empire under his own control. Thus, the Inca Huayna Capac divided his empire between his sons Huáscar and Atahualpa who fought a war (or civil war) with each other just before the arrival of the Spaniards in Peru. Similarly, the Carolingian empire was divided among the descendants of Charlemagne with numerous brothers, uncles, and cousins ruling over and contesting ever-shifting territories out of which there eventually emerged the loose kingdoms of France and Germany.

Aristocratic relatives may also become involved in war with one another when the related rulers of two or more territories each lay claim, on the basis of family relationships, to the succession of the rule of yet another territory. Indeed, given the intricate patterns of intermarriage among ruling families over wide areas, many conflicts between rulers are likely to be intrafamily struggles. During some periods of the central Middle Ages, "a single family group ruled over most of Europe. Their relationships and

2. Speaking of the early Yamato dynasty (ca. A.D. 300–645), Bendix says: "Formal subservience to the emperor by the heads of other clans did little to mitigate the murderous rivalries among them. . . . As in the early history of monarchies elsewhere, early Japanese history is a story of rivalries, intrigues, assassinations, and military campaigns among the great nobles." Bendix, *Kings or People*, pp. 65–66.

marriage alliances did not conduce to peace, but they commonly gave the warfare of the period the appearance of civil war."[3]

The international wars of aristocratic empires are also difficult to distinguish from their domestic or civil wars with respect to the stakes of these conflicts. What is to be gained or lost by aristocrats are positions providing power and glory as well as control of land and peasants. Ruling aristocrats might be reduced in status as a result of defeat and be made to serve as warriors, bureaucrats, or priests under new rulers, but still retain their superiority over their former subjects. Or the losers may continue as rulers of their territories but be subjected to the victors as their vassals or tributaries. They are thus forced to give up some power and prestige and that part of their income from their peasants that they are obligated to pass up to their new rulers. Not being deprived of all power, however, each vassal or tributary will seek a maximum of independence, that is, a maximum of both power and wealth at the expense of his formal sovereign and often also of his fellow vassals. If he gains total independence, that is, freedom to keep all his taxes, he may now be described as having fought a "war of liberation," a term as inappropriate as international or civil war.

Although wars of conquest and liberation are a common and the most obvious form that aristocratic "foreign" politics takes, it is not the only one. Other, more peaceful methods are also available to competing aristocrats, though not surprisingly, given the importance of war in aristocratic behavior and thought, the threat of violence is generally not too far in the background. Thus, treaties may be concluded under various forms of pressure, as when one aristocrat holds another one for ransom until concessions or cash payments are made—a not uncommon form of aristocratic conflict.

A special form of treaty is marriage. It is another way of acquiring power and land, that is, of carrying on and settling conflicts among aristocrats, characteristic of the fact that aristocratic politics is often family politics. "It is natural to consider the dynastic marriage policies . . . in the same context as warfare, since both were engaged in by the kings and great nobles for very much the same reasons."[4] Rulers of aristocratic empires regard their territories not merely as belonging to them but as identical with them in the sense that these territories have no other objective or subjective identity. In Shakespeare's work, aristocrats are still referred to simply by the name of their territory as York, Northumberland, or Worcester, and even kings are sometimes identified with their countries; in *King Henry V*, the two kings speak of each other as "our brother England" (Act II, Scene IV)

3. Brooke, *Europe in the Central Middle Ages*, p. 128.
4. Ibid.

and "our brother France" (Act V, Scene II).[5] If rulers *are* their empires, then family relations between rulers *are* relations between their empires,[6] and a family union through marriage becomes an alliance or even a territorial union between empires. Hence, a standard way to form an alliance between aristocrats or to acquire land is through marriage. That marriage is regarded as a substitute for conquest and also, again, that the ruler is identified with his empire and referred to by its name is nicely illustrated by the hexameter of Montecucculi, the seventeenth-century imperial general, referring to Habsburg expansion: *Alii bella gerunt, tu felix Austria nube* (let others wage war, you, fortunate Austria, marry).

Marriage as an instrument of politics is so closely linked to the role and ideology of aristocrats that it is very widely—though not universally—employed among aristocratic empires. Dynastic intermarriages are probably best known in Western Europe from the end of the traditional period on. To mention only a few out of numerous possible examples, in the twelfth century, the Norman Henry I married a descendant of the Anglo-Saxon King Alfred to gain greater legitimacy; their grandson Henry II added large parts of France to his inherited domains in that area by his marriage to Eleanor of Aquitaine; and he then married his daughters to the king of Castile, the king of Sicily, and to the duke of Bavaria and Saxony who became the father of Emperor Otto IV. Similarly, around 1300, the children of Rudolf I, the first Habsburg emperor, married into the ruling families of Bavaria, Brandenburg, Saxony, Tyrol, Bohemia, and Hungary. European royalty still intermarry and, as long as they wielded some power, they sought to cement relations between their countries by interdynastic marriages.

However, the same phenomenon occurred elsewhere, too, as may be illustrated by a few more examples. In Eastern Europe, the three daughters of an eleventh-century grand prince of Kiev were married, respectively, to a king of France, a king of Hungary, and a king of Norway, and the Hungarian Arpad dynasty from the eleventh to the thirteenth century became related by marriage to ruling houses in Russia, Sweden, Poland, Bohemia, Serbia, Byzantium, Austria, France, and Aragon.

---

5. Otto of Habsburg, then the pretender to the nonexistent Austrian throne, was, in the days of World War II, listed in the Washington, D.C., telephone directory as "Austria, Otto of."

6. How family conflicts are quite indistinguishable from "domestic" and "international" politics is well illustrated in James Goldman's play *The Lion in Winter* on the relations of King Henry II with his wife, Eleanor of Aquitaine, and their sons. To the accusation "I talk people and you answer back in provinces," Henry replies quite rightly: "They get mixed up" (p. 39).

Chinese imperial dynasties, off and on for two thousand years from the Han to the Manchu, married daughters of the imperial family to Mongol tribal chiefs on their northern borders in order to influence and to dominate them. In India, the Gupta dynasty, ruling in the north from the fourth to the sixth century, intermarried with other dynasties on the subcontinent; the sixteenth-century Mogul emperor Akbar married a Rajput princess; and King Jigme Dorji Wangchuk of Bhutan, who died in 1972, was married to a niece of the King of Sikkim.

The history of the rise of the Aztecs to power in Mexico was in good part due to successful marriages as well as successful warfare. An early fourteenth-century monarch is said to have had about twenty wives, probably the daughters of all his clan leaders, and thus to have founded a new aristocracy. His son married, in succession, three princesses of neighboring territories, and in the fifteenth century, the sister of another ruler of Tenochtitlán (Mexico City under the Aztecs) married the ruler of its sister city Tlaltelolco.[7] Soustelle says of the Aztecs and other tribes of their empire that "there was an established custom of ratifying the alliances between cities by the exchange of wives of the various dynasties."[8]

In the Middle East, some 3,300 years ago several kings of Mitanni married their daughters to Egyptian pharaohs, and in the same century the king of Babylonia entered into diplomatic marriages with the ruling families of Egypt and Assyria. Some 2,500 years ago, Cyaxares, the founder of the Median empire, gave his daughter in marriage to Nebuchadrezzar, the last great king of Babylonia, to conclude an alliance with him. And about two centuries later, Alexander the Great married the daughter of a local Persian chieftain. "The marriage to Roxane was doubtless contracted for political considerations, never very far from Alexander's mind."[9]

The early members of the Ottoman dynasty, in the fourteenth and early fifteenth centuries, entered "many purely diplomatic marriages, made for specific political reasons; examples may be cited among the numerous marriages with Byzantine princesses and with members of the"[10] different Turkoman dynasties of Anatolia and of the ruling family of Serbia. The first wife of Mohammed Reza, the shah of Iran deposed in 1979, was the daughter of King Fuad of Egypt.[11] King Ibn Saud, the founder of the last

7. Davies, *The Aztecs*, pp. 43, 48–50, 129.

8. Soustelle, *Daily Life of the Aztecs*, p. 179.

9. Peters, *The Harvest of Hellenism*, p. 48.

10. Alderson, *The Structure of the Ottoman Dynasty*, p. 86.

11. Neither of these two rulers was a traditional one, for both were descendants of military modernizers who made themselves monarchs, Fuad the great-grandson of Mohammed Ali of the early nineteenth century and the Shah the son of Reza Khan, who seized power in the 1920s.

conquest empire, had an estimated three hundred wives (though never more than four at one time). They came from influential families in his own tribe, in allied tribes with which he sought to strengthen his bonds, and in conquered tribes whose trust he wished to secure. "Ibn Saud always appreciated the political role of marital relations. The construction of such linkages helped him both to hold together his own supporters and to attract and absorb the opposition. He often married the widows and adopted the children of important allies and enemies killed in battle. . . . Through the years, Ibn Saud married into all the leading families in Arabia."[12]

Conflicts within Empires

Just as, in competing with other aristocrats, an aristocrat may recruit his followers or vassals from the territory he controls, be it an empire or a province of an empire, so their support may be mobilized along institutional rather than regional lines. Rival members of a single aristocratic family or rival families or cliques may control different parts of the traditional government apparatus, like the court, the army, the priesthood, or the bureaucracy, or sections thereof. On the other hand, the aristocrats within each branch of the government or at least its top leaders may develop common interests vis-à-vis those of other branches. Politics may then involve conflicts between the armed forces, the bureaucracy, and the clergy or clashes of the army with the navy.

A common conflict of interests exists between the ruler, like a king or emperor, supported by his trusted advisors and perhaps his entire court, on the one hand, and the lower aristocracy, whether feudal or bureaucratic, on the other hand. I have already stressed that these two levels of the aristocracy are in competition over who is to get what share of the taxes paid by peasants and others, the feudal barons or bureaucrats seeking to retain as much of what they collect as they can, the kings and their courts trying to have as much passed up to them as possible.[13] Such competition may, of course, involve not only taxes collected in cash or in kind but also services, especially military services, owed by the lower aristocracy to the king or emperor.

So frequent is conflict between the rulers and other aristocrats, that many analysts distinguish between the ruler and the aristocracy, treating

12. Bill and Leiden, *The Middle East*, p. 129.

13. Sally Falk Moore says of the Inca empire, "one can only guess at how much the governors bargained with the central government, and the [local aristocrats] with the governors for local, as against national, exploitation and expenditures." Moore, *Power and Property in Inca Peru*, p. 69.

the former as if he were not part of the latter. Obviously, there are differences worth emphasizing for certain purposes, and the distinction is particularly justifiable with reference to the posttraditional order of absolutism where the monarch becomes so preeminent as to play a quite distinct role. Still, even here it is difficult to draw a line between him and his court and, on the other hand, between the court and the aristocracy.[14] But, in any case, in a consideration of traditional aristocratic empires, which lacked the bureaucratic and policymaking centralization of absolutism, it seems preferable to include the monarch in the aristocracy, as I have been doing all along.

Monarchs themselves, even in posttraditional societies, regard themselves as aristocrats, sometimes as head of their aristocracies, sometimes merely as first among equals, and the members of their families or clans are always aristocrats. Monarchs often intermarry with nonroyal aristocrats, and nonroyal aristocrats may also become monarchs by conquest of new territory or by gaining de facto or de jure independence from another monarch's empire. Thus, no sharp line can be drawn in terms of social origin between the rulers of aristocratic empires and their families on the one hand and the rest of the aristocracy on the other.

To be sure, the person of the monarch often enjoys far greater respect and prestige than any other aristocrat. Indeed, he is quite commonly in aristocratic empires seen as a representative or descendant of god or of the gods or even is deified himself, and it is the monarch who may formally create the other aristocrats by giving them titles or land. But although he may be looked up to with much more awe and veneration than even the next highest aristocrat and although he may be a very powerful ruler—and these two characteristics may or may not go together—the monarch will still rarely act alone and on his own. When making decisions, he will rely, at least to some degree, on the advice of members of his family and of other counselors. These are usually men of aristocratic background, like high feudal lords, high bureaucrats or priests, but sometimes also men of common birth, like some court eunuchs in China or the *ministeriales* of the early Holy Roman Empire,[15] who then, by our standards, become aristocrats by virtue of their position. Similarly, to have his decisions carried out, the ruler must rely on other aristocrats. Thus, politically, as a decision maker and as an executive, the monarch cannot be distinguished from the aristocrats surrounding him and from his court.

No matter how outstanding and even divine the monarch may be, he is not secure from aristocratic competitors who conspire to replace him and who, if they succeed, will enjoy the same prestige and even divinity as

---

14. See Elias, *Die höfische Gesellschaft.*

15. Bloch, *Feudal Society*, p. 343.

their victim and predecessor. As Bendix says of Europe before the seventeenth century: "Kings, aristocrats, and magnates of the church made claims against one another. In these conflicts, each manipulated appeals to the transcendent powers without fear of seriously undermining the exclusive hold on authority they all enjoyed."[16]

In any case, monarchs are deeply enmeshed in the intraaristocratic politics of their empires and stand in a relation of mutual dependence to the rest of the aristocracy. The nonroyal aristocracy—feudal lords and landowners, military leaders, high bureaucrats and priests—may, at least to some extent, depend on the monarch for part of their income and for their positions and titles and other symbols that confirm and legitimize these positions in the eyes of their fellow aristocrats. However, they frequently hold their positions and the symbols that go with them more or less independently of the monarch, as by inheritance, and also enjoy economic independence of him, typically through the control of their own land and peasants.

On the other hand, no monarch is completely independent of all other aristocrats all of the time, though he can be independent of some aristocrats some or even all of the time. He needs counselors to advise him, court officials to help him run his extended household, which may comprise thousands of persons, priests to legitimize his rule and his policies, military leaders to help him fight his wars, and bureaucrats to collect his taxes. Though he may have an independent income from his own crown lands, he may be dependent for much or most of the support of his royal and military establishment and government on contributions more or less willingly rendered by other aristocrats.

Given this relationship of mutual dependence, rulers seek to control aristocrats, and aristocrats seek to control rulers, and each side tries to resist the efforts of the other. However, the relationship cannot be one of the ruler on one side and all other aristocrats on the other. To become independent of some aristocrats and to control them, the ruler must depend on other aristocrats and may well be used or controlled by them. For all these reasons, it seems appropriate to regard the ruler of an aristocratic empire with his court simply as one more institutional participant in intraaristocratic conflicts, along with other institutions, such as the military, the bureaucracy, and the clergy, to the extent that any of these institutions, including ruler and court, are distinguishable from the others.

In practice, the lines of conflict dividing the aristocracy may well not be the ones separating the court, military, bureaucracy, and clergy, even if these are clearly distinct institutions—and often they are not. They are more likely to cut across these lines or to subdivide these institutions.

16. Bendix, *Kings or People*, p. 7.

Thus, the ruler's court is frequently divided into cliques and factions, sometimes consisting of or headed by rivals competing to be close to the ruler, sometimes favoring different contestants for the throne or conspiring against and defending its occupant, sometimes representing different aristocratic factions and interests outside the court. If the monarch is strong, aristocrats will vie for his favor; if he is weak, they will try to substitute their own judgment for his. Either way, court intrigues are likely, and the court will be a major arena of intraaristocratic conflict.

Similarly, bureaucracies can become arenas of conflict as their members compete for power and influence and for greater wealth. They may be subdivided into regional groupings or family or clan groupings just as competing members of a priesthood may be organized around different temples or monasteries or in different priestly sects. Wittfogel remarks that "bureaucratic life is as competitive as it is dangerous." Citing an unpublished study of officials under the Han dynasty (206 B.C.–A.D. 220), the first long-lasting Chinese imperial dynasty, he states that "among those whose careers can be traced in some detail about 21 per cent at one time or another were imprisoned for derelictions during their official career. . . . More than 12 per cent were murdered or died after torture in prison, 14 per cent were executed, and 9 per cent committed suicide."[17]

In the armed forces, too, officers frequently form factions, and different military units, like army regiments or the palace guard, come into conflict with each other, often, not unnaturally, into armed conflict. Indeed, conflict within the military can be practically the sum total of intraaristocratic conflict if the aristocracy is virtually identical with the military, as it was in feudal Western Europe. Because military forces dominated by the aristocracy may, in turn, dominate governments well past the traditional period, conflicts for governmental control can continue to consist in good part of conflicts among cliques of officers, each in charge of certain military units and garrisons. This was a pattern of Latin American politics into the twentieth century, and a similar one prevailed in Thailand. Speaking of that country in the 1960s, David Wilson says that "politics has become a matter of competition between bureaucratic cliques for the benefits of government. In this competition the army—the best organized, most concentrated, and most powerful of the branches of the bureaucracy—has come out on top."[18]

17. Wittfogel, *Oriental Despotism*, p. 338.
18. Wilson, *Politics in Thailand*, p. 277.

Conflicts within Families

All conflicts among aristocrats, even those involving several empires, can be intrafamily conflicts, especially because intermarriage among aristocrats is so frequent. Conflict within aristocratic families is virtually inevitable. With few exceptions—Sparta had two kings, the Roman Republic two consuls—each level in each aristocratic hierarchy is occupied by only one person at any one time. There is only one regimental commander and one commander of the army, only one provincial governor and one viceroy, only one priest in charge of each temple and only one high priest. Above all, there is only one owner of an estate, one count in a county, one duke in a dukedom, one king in a kingdom. Where such positions are inherited or tend to be kept in the same family, as is particularly frequently the case with the positions of territorial rulers, competition for them will take place primarily within the family of the incumbent—though outsiders, too, may try to capture the position.

Competition for each position is likely to be intense because all the things aristocrats want—power and wealth, prestige and glory—and all the symbols and deference associated with them go with these positions, and there is generally more of each the higher the position. It is particularly the members of the incumbent's family who, living with him, are keenly aware of the benefits to be derived from his position, yet each of them knows that only one of them can hope to attain it. Of three princes in an aristocratic empire, only one can become king at any one time. The other two, although they could hold high positions, for example, as military leaders or governors or priests, are still doomed to remain on lower levels of the aristocracy than their brother, enjoy less power and wealth, less honor and glory.[19]

No wonder there are so many instances of son fighting father and brother fighting brother among aristocrats, not only in traditional aristocratic empires, but as long as aristocrats are powerful. Here we can pay special attention to conflict within families over who shall occupy the ruling position in a territory. Although this type of conflict can and does take place at all territorial levels from the knightly estate to the large empire, it is of course most visible at the higher levels, and our examples will be drawn from them.

Khosrow I (531–579), known as "the Just," the most illustrious member of the Sassanian dynasty of Persia, executed all his brothers and all but one of their male descendants when his succession to the throne was disputed.

19. As Eleanor of Acquitaine might have said to her and King Henry's three sons: "My, what a greedy little trinity you are: king, king, king. Two of you must learn to live with disappointment." Goldman, *The Lion in Winter*, p. 12.

The Abbasid Caliph Al-Amin (809–813) was fought by his brother and was murdered after his surrender, with the brother succeeding him as Mamun the Great (813–833). Otto I (936–973) of Germany suppressed a revolt of his son and his son-in-law, respectively the dukes of Swabia and Lorraine, in 955. Henry I of England (1100–1135) fought and defeated his brother Robert, the duke of Normandy, and then kept him imprisoned for the rest of his life. Russian history, down to the early nineteenth century, as it is commonly written, is largely a record of dynastic conflict, palace revolutions, and rivalries among court favorites. Often these involved several influential aristocratic families, but frequently they were also fought out within the family of the tsar with some members eliminating others by murder or exile.

In the early Inca empire, "in principle all the royal sons had equal rights to the throne, hence the succession led to all kinds of intrigues, rivalries and revolts and disturbed the beginning of each reign." Even in the later empire, when only the sons of the Inca's chief wife were eligible to succeed him, "it was not often that an emperor succeeded to the throne without having to fight one or other of his brothers, aided by his adversary's maternal family."[20]

Usurpation and bloody conflicts for the succession to the thrones of her Muslim rulers were also usual in the history of India. Lybyer writes that "the succession to the Mogul throne never became regular. . . . Accordingly the resources of the empire were apt to be wasted in civil wars between father and son, and between older and younger brothers. Even the sons of Baber engaged in civil war: Kamran, aided by Askari and Hindal, fought against Humayun. Akbar's . . . two elder sons drank themselves to death; but this did not prevent Selim, who became the emperor Jehangir, from rebelling against his father and hastening the latter's death. Jehangir's two sons rebelled against him in turn. Shah-Jehan's four sons, Dara, Shuja, Murad, and Aurangzeb, fought together until the last encompassed the death of the others, besides keeping his father a prisoner during the last seven years of his life. The mournful story need not be carried beyond the fierce civil war which followed the death of Aurangzeb, in which two of his sons were slain."[21] Lybyer concludes his "mournful story" by quoting a historian who wrote two hundred years ago of the Mogul empire that "to be born a prince" was "a misfortune of the worst and most embarrassing kind. He must die by clemency, or wade through the blood of his family to safety and empire."[22]

20. Métraux, *The History of the Incas*, pp. 84, 86.

21. Lybyer, *The Government of the Ottoman Empire*, p. 293.

22. Quoted ibid., from Alexander Dow, *The History of Hindostan* (3 vols., London, 1770–72).

Of the kings who ruled Ceylon from 543 B.C. to A.D. 1259, over a third reigned for less than five years, half of them for only one year or less. Singer, who presents these figures, explains that "the lives of the kings were involuntarily short" and he quotes such phrases to be found "on almost every page" of native chronicles as, "King Lemeni Tissa killed [the previous king]"; "his queen consort, Anula by name, slew the king by giving him poison"; "King Sengot became king in the forenoon, and died in the afternoon, having partaken of poison given him by the princess Sanga in the noon." Indeed, of the first sixty-one kings of Ceylon, over a third are said to have died a violent death, and in one twenty-eight-year period there were fifteen kings, all except possibly one of whom were killed or deposed.[23]

Similarly, of the thirty-seven sultans in the Ottoman dynasty, seventeen were forcibly deposed.[24] The history of that dynasty furnishes many examples of intrafamily conflict. Thus, Savci, a son of Sultan Murad I (about 1361–1389) rebelled against him; Alderson comments that "it is difficult to know whether the punishment meted out to Savci—blinding which led to his subsequent death—was inspired more by his father's or his brother's animosity, for Murad's authority and Bayezid's inheritance had been equally challenged."[25] After Murad had died at the battle of Kossovo (1389), his son Bayezid I (1389–1402) "sent servants to seek out his brother Yakub, who had distinguished himself during the battle, and was being acclaimed by his soldiers. Yakub was taken to Bayezid's tent, and was strangled with a bowstring."[26] Murad II (1421–1451) executed his brother Mustafa, who had rebelled against him. A few decades later, Sultan Bayezid II (1481–1512) "had to face a long series of rebellions on the part of his sons Ahmed, Korkud, and Selim I which caused him the greatest trouble and led to his final downfall; each was struggling for the succession and the continued existence of their father was of little importance to them. Even after Selim I had asserted his superiority over his brothers and had exe-

23. Singer, *The Emerging Elite*, pp. 16–17.

24. Alderson, *The Structure of the Ottoman Dynasty*, pp. 59–76, and the table listing all "depositions" on p. 76. Seven of these depositions occurred in the nineteenth and twentieth centuries.

25. Ibid., p. 49.

26. Gibbons, *The Foundation of the Ottoman Empire*, p. 180. "The new emir justified this crime by a verse conveniently found for him by his theologians in the Koran: 'So often as they return to sedition, they shall be subverted therein; and if they depart not from you, and offer you peace and restrain their hands from warring against you, take them and kill them wheresoever ye find them' [Sura IV, verse 94]. They declared that the temptation to treason and revolt was always present in the brothers of the ruler, and that murder was better than sedition" (ibid.).

cuted them, he was still troubled by two of his nephews. . . . Selim I was also forced to execute three of his own sons."[27]

Obviously, aristocrats seek to stabilize and secure the positions they hold by eliminating competition for them as much as possible, but typically the very effort to eliminate competition—that is, to eliminate potential or actual competitors—is merely another form of conflict and spawns more conflict. Still, even though it involves danger to them, most aristocrats want to have heirs to inherit their position and to continue their bloodline. Not so Shaka, ruler of the short-lived Zulu empire in the early nineteenth century. "The most serious threat to a ruler, he knew, was the potential rebellion of his own sons. Thus, he refused to marry or to beget heirs."[28] One of the first Europeans to visit him reports that Shaka's mother, who supervised his concubines, presented him with an infant and its mother: "He immediately seized the little innocent, and, throwing it up in the air, it was killed by the fall; the mother was instantly ordered to be put to death, whilst Shaka so severely beat his mother, Nandi, with a stick, for presuming to accuse him of being the father that she was lame for three months. When she recovered, she had the ten concubines put to death who had agreed with her proposal to show Shaka the infant."[29] Shaka did, indeed, avoid being killed by a son; he was instead killed by two of his brothers. One of these, Dingane, then murdered the other and became king and "also refused to marry and beget heirs." Eventually he, too, was murdered after another brother had rebelled against him.[30]

Generally aristocrats had children and particularly high aristocrats, especially rulers, were likely to have lots of them, because they had many wives or concubines. Often they were threatened by them and, in the next generation, had to contend with competition of numerous brothers and sisters. Examples of attempts to get rid of such fraternal competition are not lacking. "The last Burmese king, on coming to the throne in 1878, sought to eliminate all possible contenders by executing his eighty half-brothers and sisters. Since royal blood could not be shed, the relatives were all tied up in sacks and trampled on by white elephants."[31] Such procedures may not have been customary in Burma, but George Peter Murdock, in his ethnographic survey of all of Africa, includes the following among the patterns he found to be widely prevalent among what he calls the "despotic states in Negro Africa": "To prevent palace revolutions

---

27. Alderson, *The Structure of the Ottoman Dynasty*, pp. 51–52.

28. Walter, *Terror and Resistance*, p. 163.

29. Quoted ibid. from *The Diary of Henry Francis Fynn* (Pietermaritzburg, 1950), p. 29.

30. Walter, *Terror and Resistance*, pp. 174–75, 148, 211.

31. Pye, *Politics, Personality, and Nation Building*, p. 67.

a king's brothers, as the most likely usurpers, may be killed, blinded, incarcerated, or banished from the capital."[32]

The best known case of the institutionalization of such practices is probably that of the mid-fifteenth-century Ottoman empire. Here the famous law of fratricide of Sultan Mohammed (Mehmed) II (1451–1481) provided that "whoever among my illustrious children and grandchildren may come to the throne, should, for securing the peace of the world, order his brothers to be executed. Let them hereafter act accordingly."[33] Designed to secure the stability of the throne, it actually made conflict within the ruling family virtually inevitable: less favorite sons, in order to save their lives, let alone to gain power, had to revolt against their father to keep the son he favored from reaching the throne and from killing them.

Alderson, who studied the genealogy of the Ottoman dynasty in great detail, says that, as actually practiced, fratricide involved the execution not only of brothers but of "any male member of the family whose continued existence constituted a possible threat to the reigning sultan or, in some cases, to his heir-presumptive." Having listed all the victims, he finds that "there are at most eighty deaths which can be put to the account of the Law of Fratricide."[34] Almost all of them occurred in the course of two centuries, including those of the nineteen brothers—not to mention about fifteen slavewomen pregnant by his father—whom Sultan Mehmed III had executed on his accession to the throne in 1595.

Alderson explains that the Ottoman practice of fratricide "arose from a perhaps exaggerated instinct to protect the empire from fragmentation, a disease so prevalent among, and often fatal to, oriental dynasties." And he refers to "a policy—nonetheless effective because it was only implicit—for obliterating as quickly as possible all traces of the royal family, apart from the reigning sultan and his direct issue." He finds its "real justification" in the 650 years of unbroken rule by the Ottoman dynasty.[35]

Alderson also argues that "the sultans were not alone in finding their

32. Murdock, *Africa*, p. 38. "Among the Ankole of Uganda the problem was solved by having all of the king's sons engage in a struggle to death at the time of their father's death. The one that survived became king, free of further worries about sibling rivalry." Lenski, *Power and Privilege*, p. 171. The Zulu had a proverb that "the king should not eat with his brothers lest they poison him" (ibid.).

33. Quoted in Lybyer, *The Government of the Ottoman Empire*, p. 94, n. 2.

34. Alderson, *The Structure of the Ottoman Dynasty*, pp. 25, 26; see the table "List of Fratricides," ibid., pp. 30–31.

35. Ibid., pp. 25, 26. That a mid-twentieth-century Western scholar should justify a mid-fifteenth-century Turkish practice with the very same arguments used by the Ottoman aristocracy—the supreme desirability of keeping a dynasty and an empire intact—illustrates intriguingly the pervasiveness and persistence of aristocratic ideology.

244 | The Arenas of Aristocratic Politics

relatives inconvenient,"[36] and he quotes these examples of fourteenth-century Christian princes: "Pedro of Castile killed his brother Don Fadrique, Andronicus III Comnenos of Trebizond killed his two brothers, Michael and George; and Andronicus III Paleologos assassinated his brother when his father was dying."[37] Alderson himself adds that "fratricide was particularly common among Muslim dynasties because the practice of polygamy on a large scale led to a dangerous profusion of male heirs. One need not go farther afield than Persia, where . . . Şah Ismail I brought to death most of his younger brothers. Moreover, one may ask whether fratricide was any more cruel than the practice of the Byzantine emperors who blinded or otherwise disfigured their rivals, thus rendering them technically and practically unfit to rule, and condemning them to a living death."[38]

Brothers do not necessarily have to be killed to be eliminated as competitors. Sometimes imprisonment will do. I already mentioned Henry I keeping his brother Robert imprisoned for life after defeating him in the battle of Tinchebrai (1106). Similarly, King Alfonso VI of Castile had captured his brother García in 1073 and kept him imprisoned for the rest of his life. This practice, too, was institutionalized in the Ottoman empire. In the seventeenth century, when the law of fratricide fell into disuse, a new system was introduced that lasted until the end of the eighteenth century and in more relaxed form until the end of the dynasty in the early twentieth century. All the sultan's sons were, upon his death, placed in the "Kafes" (cage) quarters where they were imprisoned for life except for those who would eventually inherit the throne. Alderson's table listing "Sultans confined in the 'Kafes'" shows that virtually all sultans in the period in question spent, from their childhood on, many years—a number of them over forty years—in this "cage" before their accession to the throne.[39]

A remarkably similar custom demonstrating conflict within ruling families was practiced contemporaneously in Ethiopia. Also surviving into the late eighteenth century, this custom supposedly originated in antiquity, long before the Ottoman one. It involved "the seclusion of all the male line of the royal house save the reigning king and his sons and grandsons.

36. Ibid., p. 26.

37. Gibbons, *The Foundation of the Ottoman Empire*, p. 181. It may be added that the Pedro of Castile—Pedro the Cruel—mentioned here was eventually himself killed by his half brother Henry, who succeeded him as king.

38. Alderson, *The Structure of the Ottoman Dynasty*, p. 27.

39. Ibid., pp. 32–36. On the Ottoman law of fratricide and the confinement of princes in the Kafes, where "living in constant fear of execution, most of them suffered psychological disorders," see also Inalcik, *The Ottoman Empire*, pp. 59–61.

... As each king was crowned all his brothers were relegated to an impregnable amba and there they lived and died with their families, completely cut off from all communication with the kingdom. . . . The nearer kinsmen of the king were never released except when the direct royal line failed and one of them was summoned to the throne."[40]

Conflicts within ruling families still occur in the few near-traditional empires remaining in the twentieth century, though these traditional intrafamily feuds may now contain nontraditional elements of conflicts over issues of modernization. Thus Imam Ahmed of Yemen came to power in 1948 following the assassination of his father in which Ahmed's brother was involved. Subsequently, an attempt on the Imam's life was reported, followed by the public execution of two of his brothers. In 1959, a revolt against the Imam evidently led by his son, the crown prince and foreign minister el-Badr, was cruelly put down. The following year, the Imam jailed four of his nephews on charges of plotting against his regime. In 1961 he turned the government over to his son el-Badr as premier and interior minister, who succeeded Ahmed as Imam on the death of the latter in 1962 only to be ousted a week later by a modernizing military coup which put an end to the traditional monarchy in Yemen.

In Saudi Arabia, too, a struggle went on within the royal family. In 1958, King Saud granted full legislative and executive powers to one of his half brothers, the Crown Prince Faisal. In 1960, Saud resumed these powers and ousted Faisal from power. In 1962, Talal, another half brother, went to Nasser's Egypt denouncing both Saud and Faisal. In the same year, Faisal returned to the premiership, and in 1963 he assumed full control of the government, removing Saud's sons from important positions and securing the support of an uncle, the senior member of the royal family. In 1964, Saud demanded a return of his power and mobilized the Royal Guard, but Faisal gained its allegiance, assumed all royal powers as viceroy, and expelled seven of Saud's sons and then pardoned them. Finally, later in 1964, Saud was deposed and sent into exile, and Faisal became king. Faisal himself was assassinated by a nephew in 1975 who was, in turn, beheaded before a crowd of ten thousand.

In Laos, throughout the late 1950s and early 1960s a highly complex conflict involving shifting alliances and changing allegiances of commanders of army units, troop movements and occasional armed clashes and coups d'état went on between at least three groupings, each headed by a prince. The traditional, intraaristocratic and intrafamily nature of the conflict between Prince Souphanouvong, a member of the royal family, Prince

40. Jones and Monroe, *A History of Abyssinia*, pp. 71–72. "It was customary for each new king to exile all male relatives who were potential candidates for the Crown to a high mountain fortress." Levine, *Wax and Gold*, p. 155.

Souvanna Phouma, his half brother, and Prince Boun Oum, a pretender to the nonexisting throne of Southern Laos, was obscured by the persistent application to the three princes of the modern labels of, respectively, "leftist," "neutralist," and "rightist," and by the increasing involvement of the conflict in the larger war in Indo-China and of the three factions with different foreign supporters.[41]

Finally, we may recall that conflicts among aristocrats may be settled not only by violence but also by means of marriage. This is true also of conflicts within families, and there appears to be, therefore, a high frequency among aristocrats of marriages among cousins and between widowed brothers-in-law and sisters-in-law. One example, admittedly rather unusual, extreme, and intricate will do: in the second century B.C., the king of Egypt, Ptolemy V, married Cleopatra I, daughter of the Syrian king Antiochus. They had three children: Ptolemy VI who succeeded his father as king, Ptolemy VII who shared the rule with his brother and then succeeded him, and Cleopatra II. Ptolemy VI, according to Egyptian royal custom, married his sister Cleopatra II. When he died, Ptolemy VII married her—that is, he married both his sister and his widowed sister-in-law—and then he also married Cleopatra III who was the daughter of Ptolemy VI and of Cleopatra II, that is, he married his own niece and his stepdaughter, and his first wife was now both the mother and the aunt of his second wife. Peters refers to this arrangement as a "curious *ménage à trois*" and says that King Ptolemy VII, "who detested his sister as heartily as she disliked him, found that he could not rule in Alexandria without her, and since the lady preferred a throne to exile, even if the price were association with [him] and her equally objectionable daughter, Cleopatra II returned to Egypt in B.C. 124 and the troika somehow ran on for another eight years."[42] Clearly, such intrafamily marriages are no love matches but are designed to settle conflicts between aristocratic factions attached to various members of a ruling family and thus serve a political function similar to that of interdynastic and other aristocratic marriages.

---

41. "The machinations of the various personalities, parties, and political movements probably ought to be understood, at least in their earliest stages, as pure clique politics with little relationship to any social changes. What is involved has been the exercise of traditional loyalties and hostilities." Wilson, "Nation-Building and Revolutionary War," p. 91.

42. Peters, *The Harvest of Hellenism*, p. 181.

11

Stability and Instability

Instability of Personnel and the Limits of Policy Change

Much of the literature describes traditional aristocratic empires, in contrast to modern societies, as virtually unchanging and extremely stable. Others have objected to this characterization and point to the numerous changes in the history of such empires and to a high degree of instability. Our analysis of politics in aristocratic empires has shown that both views are right, but that a clear distinction must be drawn between what is and what is not changing and unstable.

We have seen that the issues in intraaristocratic politics are of life-and-death importance to aristocrats and that a ceaseless struggle for positions therefore goes on among aristocrats on all levels of the aristocracy. It is most visible at the higher levels where it is not mere villages or estates but large kingdoms and empires that change rulers, or where it is not mere bureaucrats or warriors but kings and emperors who take each others' places. Instability and change, then, prevail with respect to the individual aristocratic occupants of particular positions. Even the conquest of one empire by another can be thought of as this type of change for what it amounts to is precisely the replacement of one ruler and court by another. Of course, this new ruler will bring with him a number of new aristocrats, such as his family, his counselors, and his warriors, but these are typically superimposed on and may eventually become integrated with the old aristocracy.

The process of intraaristocratic politics, then, produces a high degree of instability of a certain type. Small and large territories change hands, military leaders, bureaucrats, and priests are transferred, promoted, demoted, and killed, and rulers ascend and are removed from thrones. The average length of the reign of Umayyad caliphs (661–750) was only six years and that of Seljuk sultans (1055–1194) was eleven,[1] and the averages for the rulers of a number of other dynasties in various traditional and near-

1. Computed from tables in Langer, ed., *An Encyclopedia of World History*, pp. 1307 and 273.

traditional aristocratic empires ranged from thirteen to twenty-one years,[2] significantly less than the averages for a number of modern European dynasties.[3]

Of course, some traditional rulers remained in power for decades: Clovis I, the founder of the Merovingian dynasty, was king of the Franks for thirty years (481–511), and Charlemagne held the same position three centuries later for forty-six years (768–814). Emperor Otto I was king of Germany for thirty-seven years (936–973), Suleiman I was sultan of the Ottoman Empire for forty-six years (1520–1566), and the Mogul emperor Aurangzeb ruled for forty-nine years (1658–1707) (but had six successors in seven years). However, such stability at the very top of an aristocratic regime may not be due to any lack of attempts to overthrow the ruler and may merely conceal a great deal of instability among the advisors to the ruler and many other aristocrats in somewhat lower positions, like high-ranking bureaucrats, generals, and governors. Indeed, the ruler may be able to remain in power for long only by turning aspirants for his position against each other and by keeping aristocrats under his rule involved in warfare with others, whether the latter are also under his rule or not. Thus stability at one level of the aristocracy is bought at the price of instability at another.

The high degree of instability of personnel that characterizes the politics of aristocratic empires also results in instability of policy, but this is relatively limited as compared to the possible policy changes in modern society. Aristocrats newly come to power will, of course, pursue their own specific interests, which may differ from those of their predecessors. One aristocrat might wage a war that his predecessor might not have begun or might have waged differently, one aristocrat might enter into a marriage or some other treaty relationship that another one might not. Above all, a

2. The following average lengths of individual reigns were computed for the following dynasties for the periods indicated: the Abbasid caliphate (750–1256), fourteen years (but only eight in the first two centuries) (ibid., pp. 1307–8); the Fatimid caliphate of Egypt (909–1171), nineteen years (ibid., p. 1308); the Arpad dynasty of Hungary (907–1301), thirteen years (ibid., p. 262); the Grand Princes of Moscow (1176–1505), fifteen years (but only ten until 1359) (ibid., p. 341); Ottoman sultans (1290–1839), eighteen years (Alderson, The Structure of the Ottoman Dynasty, p. 130); the Safavid dynasty of Persia (1502–1736), twenty-one years (Langer, ed., An Encyclopedia of World History, p. 566); the Mogul Emperors of India (1526–1857), seventeen years (ibid., p. 571); the Barakzai dynasty of Afghanistan (1747–1929), seventeen years (ibid., p. 899); the Kajar dynasty of Persia (1794–1925), nineteen years (ibid., p. 896); and the kings of Germany and Holy Roman Emperors (800–1002), thirteen years (ibid., p. 1311).

3. The French Bourbons (1589–1792), forty-one years (ibid., p. 478); the Hohenzollerns of Prussia (1701–1918), twenty-four years (ibid., p. 727); the House of Hanover-Saxe-Coburg-Windsor of Britain (1714–1952), twenty-four years (ibid. pp. 469 and 660); and the House of Habsburg-Lorraine (1740–1918), twenty-five years (ibid., p. 720).

new occupant of a high position will favor his own family, followers, or faction and thus produce a certain redistribution of power, prestige, and wealth within the aristocracy. Such a redistribution may follow lines of personal loyalty and trust or it may have broader policy implications, favoring, for example, the aristocracy of one region over that of another or one aristocratic hierarchy, perhaps the palace guard, over another, say, the priesthood.

However, changes of personnel take place only within the aristocracy, and hence changes of policy take place only within the possible range of aristocratic policy. When one aristocrat loses his position, he is always replaced by another aristocrat. To be sure, this is simply true by definition, because I defined anyone who occupies an aristocratic position as an aristocrat. The point, however, is that even if, very exceptionally, a person of nonaristocratic background occupies an aristocratic position, he will think and behave like an aristocrat and will not act as a representative of peasants, artisans, or merchants from whom he might be descended.

Although the personal, family, and factional interests of different aristocrats differ from each other, and the process of aristocratic politics or intraaristocratic conflict is thus accompanied by a process of policy change, it must be stressed that all these interests are shaped by and perceived in the light of the same aristocratic ideology, that all these interests respond to and interact in the same unchanging aristocratic society. The range of possible policies being pursued by aristocrats is hence quite limited.

Because aristocratic politics takes place within the aristocratic society alone and not within the total and overwhelmingly nonaristocratic population of the aristocratic empire, the issue is always which aristocrats shall rule and which aristocrats shall be favored, not whether aristocrats shall rule or whether aristocrats shall be favored—just as within a village different peasants may assume leading positions at different times, but the cows and the pigs never do. The peasantry and the townspeople—as distinguished from the very exceptional peasant or townsman who becomes an aristocrat—can no more enter the arena of aristocratic politics in traditional aristocratic empires than a cow or a pig can enter village politics.[4] Any significant redistribution of power or wealth, as between the aristocracy on the one hand and peasants and townspeople on the other, is therefore simply beyond the possible range of policy.

The taxes imposed by the aristocracy may be raised or lowered as a result of changes produced by intraaristocratic politics, like conquests or coups, but that the aristocracy shall live off taxes, that it shall consume and

4. This may sound like an extreme statement, but it merely follows from my definition of aristocratic empires. Empires where nonaristocrats significantly intervene in aristocratic politics are excluded from my category of traditional aristocratic empires by that definition.

not produce, is not subject to change. From this it follows that the aristoc-racy shall govern, which simply means that it shall be in a position to extract taxes, and that it shall carry on warfare to defend and, if possible, to expand its territory with peasants and townspeople from whom taxes are extracted. All this cannot be changed in aristocratic empires. Any policy putting an end to or even endangering aristocratic exploitation or govern-ment cannot be pursued, cannot be desired, and cannot even be conceived or dreamt of by aristocrats in their empires.

Thus, in the face of extreme instability of aristocratic personnel and of the policies associated with individual aristocrats and groups of aristocrats, empires persist, often through centuries. The policies of aristocratic ex-ploitation, government, and warfare on which these empires rest are so stable as to persist even from empire to empire, often through millennia. To put the same thing differently, instability reigns within the aristocracy, but the place of the aristocracy vis-à-vis the rest of the population is a stable one. The reason for the coexistence of stability and instability in aristo-cratic empires, then, lies in a sharp separation of the aristocracy from nonaristocrats, a fact I underlined by stressing that aristocratic empires are not societies, but contain many autonomous societies, one of them being that of the aristocracy.

Reinhard Bendix reaches a similar conclusion on the relationship of stability and instability, pointing out that the latter rests on the former: "Internal political instability mostly affects the ruling groups directly con-cerned with the affairs of the kingdom, and political instability probably has coexisted with a marked degree of social stability. The bulk of the population lived in isolated communities and households. People could do little to change their condition. Most of the time, life near the level of subsistence discouraged even the most courageous from actions that would jeopardize such security as they enjoyed. Kings and their notables could fight their protracted battles for dominance at home and abroad only on the basis of this politically submerged but economically active population."[5]

Writing of Egypt under Ottoman and Mamluk rule, Gibb and Bowen say: "One group formed the governing class of soldiers and officials, the other the governed class of merchants, artisans, and cultivators. Each was organized internally on independent lines, and neither group interfered with the organization of the other in normal circumstances. From time immemorial the governing class had lived on a percentage of the produce of the land, supplemented by various duties on goods, and the social structure of the other class had accomodated itself to this situation. In spite of political and dynastic revolutions, stability was ensured by the fact that under all changes of sovereignty the existing bureaucracy remained in

5. Bendix, *Kings or People*, p. 223.

being, and maintained the traditional practices with a minimum of alteration. The new masters stepped into the places vacated by their predecessors; the titles to assignments of land were redistributed, but the relations between landlord and peasant, official and artisan, remained on the whole unchanged."[6]

Substantially the same explanation of the stability-instability syndrome, here applied to Egypt all the way from its ancient beginnings, concludes David Wilson's study of politics in twentieth-century Thailand (the references to constitutions and elections being evidence of the impact of modernization on this thus no longer purely traditional aristocratic empire): "The alarums and excursions of Thai political life, the coups and counter-coups, the constitutional shuffling, and the madcap elections suggest chaos wrapped in confusion. At the same time a slightly more penetrating observation reveals the persistence of the same leaders, much of the same law, and most of the same institutions year after year. . . . The state of affairs appears to be a paradoxical stable instability, an inconstant constancy. . . . The stability of Thai society—which is the bedrock of Thai politics—is to be explained by its simple structure, consisting of an extremely large agrarian segment and a small ruling segment. . . . The society . . . is characterized by a gross two-class structure, in which the classes are physically as well as economically separated and differential status is satisfactorily justified. The effect of this is a paucity of interests in the socioeconomic sense impinging on the political process." This means that peasants cannot participate in politics (except on the village level) and that politics is left to the aristocracy or, as I quoted Wilson earlier, that "politics has become a matter of competition between bureaucratic cliques for the benefits of government."[7]

Continuity and Change through Conquest: Language

I have argued that policy changes made by aristocrats cannot bring about any major social changes because they can only take place within the relatively narrow limits set by unchanging aristocratic ideology and institutions and cannot involve changes in the relations between aristocrats and nonaristocrats. It is often suggested, however, that conquests of one empire by another and the consequent superimposition of a new ruling aristocracy on a territory and its inhabitants can bring great cultural changes, as they become most evident in the adoption of new

6. Gibb and Bowen, *Islamic Society and the West*, 1:209–10.

7. Wilson, *Politics in Thailand*, pp. 274–75, 277.

languages and religions, which may in turn produce social changes as well. Clearly, Roman, Germanic, Arabic, Turk, and other conquests of large territories brought long-lasting changes to their populations. The question for us, however, is whether these changes affected what I have outlined as the characteristic features of aristocratic empires and particularly of the relationship between aristocrats and nonaristocrats.

First of all, it must be stressed that aristocratic conquests do not typically create cultural unity among the conquered populations. The mere fact that a number, large or small, of villages have come under the rule of a single aristocracy is no reason why the peasants in these villages should adopt the same cultural characteristics, like the same religion and the same language and the many traditions and habits associated with religion and language. The villages remain isolated from each other, each maintaining its subsistence economy. All they have in common is the fact that all pay taxes to the same aristocracy, a fact that the peasants are not even aware of. In the absence of communication among villages, there is no incentive for peasants to merge their cultural identity, and tribal and ethnic groups even in fairly close geographical proximity may remain culturally distinct for centuries, whether they happen to live under a single government or come, in the course of time and many conquests, under different ones.

Nor does a ruling aristocracy ordinarily have an interest in imposing a single culture on all the villages under its control. Its relation to "its" villages is a very limited one of exploitation, and what goes on within the village is of little concern to the aristocracy. If the aristocrats see their conquests as motivated by the search for greater wealth or glory, or if they regard warfare and conquest simply as a normal aspect of life so that no question of motive arises in their minds, then the culture of the conquered remains irrelevant to them.[8]

The peasants, of course, are quite as disinterested in their rulers' culture as the latter are in theirs. Indeed, what we think of as major turning points in the history of aristocratic empires, like the conquest of Persia by Alex-

---

8. In Peru, "much of the linguistic and cultural diversity survived the Inca conquest." Moore, *Power and Property in Inca Peru*, p. 122. Indeed, when the Incas resettled villages of loyal peasants and their families in newly conquered territories, it was out of "fear of local rebellion . . . rather than any planned cultural assimilation of conquered peoples. There was in fact a studied attempt to keep the *mitimaes* from being assimilated into the local population. They were obliged by law to retain their separateness. They continued to dress in the manner of their provinces of origin. They continued to speak their language of origin. Dances, songs, and music were also kept" (ibid., p. 103). While Moore thus stresses the deliberate maintenance by the Incas of linguistic and cultural diversity, she does also mention Inca insistence on the acceptance of their Quechua language (ibid., pp. 102, 121, 130), but suggests that this, along with the imposition of the census and the Sun cult, may have been "merely the elaborated implementing of a tax system which had some of these consequences" (ibid., p. 128).

ander the Great, no doubt remained quite unknown to most of the peasants living in the areas in question at the time. These events would, in any case, have been a matter of indifference to them, because they did not affect them. The peasants continued to work and pay taxes, frequently to the same tax collectors and to the same aristocrats with merely part of their payments ending up in the hands of some new ruler.

Writing of the absence of any "nationalism" in medieval China, Eberhard says: "The Chinese farmer did not experience much, if any, difference between an orderly nomadic and an orderly Chinese administration. He paid his taxes anyhow. As soon as some regularity, not necessarily justice, in the tax system appeared, he accepted the situation. Reading fragments of private documents of this time, one often gets the clear feeling that farmers did not know who their rulers were."[9] A century and a half ago, Sir Charles Metcalfe, a student of Indian history and later governor-general of India wrote: "The village communities are little republics, having nearly everything they want within themselves, and almost independent of any foreign relations. They seem to last where nothing else lasts. Dynasty after dynasty tumbles down; revolution succeeds to revolution; Hindu, Pathan, Mughul, Mahratta, Sikh, English are masters in turn; but the village communities remain the same."[10]

Typically, only when commerce develops significantly must greater numbers of people be able to communicate with others beyond the confines of their own towns and villages and also with the representatives of the aristocratic government. It is then likely to be the language of the aristocracy that is used for that purpose and spreads to nonaristocrats, especially in the towns, while the rural population may long remain ignorant of it.

9. Eberhard, *Conquerors and Rulers*, pp. 135–36.

10. Quoted in Lamb, *India*, p. 40. Marx made the same point in *Capital* (vol. I, chap. 14, sec. 4) when he speaks of "the simplicity of the organisation for production in these self-sufficing communities that constantly reproduce themselves in the same form, and when accidentally destroyed, spring up again on the spot and with the same name—this simplicity supplies the key to the secret of the unchangeableness of Asiatic societies, an unchangeableness in such striking contrast with the constant dissolution and refounding of Asiatic States, and the never-ceasing changes of dynasty. The structure of the economic elements of society remains untouched by the storm-clouds of the political sky." And Marx cites a House of Commons report of 1812 on Indian affairs, quoted from George Campbell, *Modern India: A Sketch of the System of Civil Government* (London, 1852), pp. 84–85, which said with reference to Indian villages: "The inhabitants give themselves no trouble about the breaking up and division of kingdoms; while the village remains entire, they care not to what power it is transferred, or to what sovereign it devolves; its internal economy remains unchanged." Marx, *Capital*, 1:393–94. The same House of Commons report is quoted by Marx at somewhat greater length and in slightly different form in his "The British Rule in India" and in a letter to Engels of 14 June 1853, both reprinted in Avineri, ed., *Karl Marx on Colonialism and Modernization*, pp. 93 and 456.

Thus, significant linguistic uniformity over large areas resulted from conquests chiefly where commerce was highly developed, as in the case of the Roman conquests around the Mediterranean, the Arabic ones in the Fertile Crescent and across North Africa, medieval German expansion eastward across the Elbe, Spanish and Portuguese penetration into what consequently became Latin America, and Russian expansion across Siberia to the Pacific. Indeed, all of these conquests resulted in empires I would not regard as traditional aristocratic ones precisely because commerce played a major role in them.

On the other hand, many conquests, including some resulting in longlasting empires, left at most slight linguistic traces, like, for example, those of Germanic tribes in Spain and North Africa, of the Normans in Normandy and Sicily, of the Mongols in China, the Middle East, and Russia, and of other Asiatic people in Eastern Europe, like the Huns, the Avars, the Cumans, the Bulgars, and the Pechenegs. Their languages were evidently never widely adopted by the native people they conquered because they had no need to use them. One major exception was another group of Asian nomadic conquerors, the Magyars, who eventually settled in Hungary where the peasantry did come to speak their language.

Even in empires that had undergone some commercialization and that lasted for centuries and hence achieved greater linguistic homogeneity, the degree of that homogeneity must not be exaggerated. The conquerors of these large empires did not in fact spread their languages to all their inhabitants. Large sections of the Roman empire, particularly those where other written languages, like Greek, were in use, especially in the Middle East and in parts of the Balkans, did not adopt Latin. More important here, peasants even in Spain and Gaul continued to speak their Celtic languages for centuries under Roman rule and turned to Latin only in the fourth and fifth centuries when they were converted to Christianity.[11] To this day, Basque and Celtic Breton, both pre-Roman languages, have retained a foothold in Spain and France through two millennia of Roman and "Romance" domination, and more people probably used them before modernization began.

Quechua, the language of the Incas, was spread to millions of Indians within and even beyond the huge territory that made up the Inca empire as a result not of the efforts of the Incas but of those of the Catholic Church, which still uses it in its missionary activities. Thus, it was only after the fall of the Inca empire that the innumerable languages and dialects

11. Brown, *The World of Late Antiquity*, p. 130. On non-Latin languages that lasted through the Roman imperial period, even in Italy, see Pounds, *An Historical Geography of Europe*, pp. 104–5, 187.

spoken in it were (with the exception of Aymara and one other minor language) replaced by Quechua.[12]

In the Umayyad and Abbasid empires, "though Arabic and Islam were politically predominant, it took hundreds of years until the villages assimilated the religion, the language and the social traditions of the conquerors."[13] "In the period following the Arab conquests, Muslim cities were isolated in Christian, Zoroastrian, or pagan countrysides. In the early centuries of Islam before the massive conversion of Middle Eastern peoples, when most of the Muslims were the Arab conquerors and their clients, the towns were identified with an ethnic and religious elite and the countryside with a population belonging to another society. For example, in North Africa, the cities had long tended to be Arab and the rural areas Berber."[14] Indeed, Berber and Kurdic are two examples of languages still widely spoken, respectively in North Africa and Iraq, areas conquered by Arabs some thirteen hundred years ago.

After centuries of rule by German aristocrats, many Polish, Lithuanian, Latvian, and Estonian peasants continued to speak their languages; peasants in Bohemia and Moravia continued to speak Czech, although their lands were ruled by German-speaking aristocrats for over a millennium from Charlemagne to 1918; and the remnants of the Wends or Sorbs have retained their Slavic language into the present century, living within one hundred miles of Berlin surrounded by a German population. Rumanian and Slavic-speaking peasants preserved their languages through centuries of Turkish rule, Rumanian and Slovak ones under Hungarian aristocrats and Ukrainian ones under Polish aristocrats. The variety of languages spoken in the Russian empire, though much of it came under tsarist control between two and four centuries before the onset of industrialization, was very large both in its European and Asiatic parts.[15] In Latin America, innumerable Indian languages continue to be spoken—in Paraguay the language of 88 percent of the population is Guarani, and in Bolivia and Peru more people speak Quechua than Spanish[16]—though Spanish-speaking aristocrats ruled there for four centuries.[17] Obviously, the widespread

12. Métraux, *The History of the Incas*, pp. 187, 189.

13. Goitein, "Cairo: An Islamic City in the Light of the Geniza Documents," p. 81.

14. Lapidus, "Muslim Cities and Islamic Societies," p. 57.

15. Even after a century of industrialization, the present-day Soviet Union, which is substantially similar in territorial extent, still contains, according to the 1970 census, nearly one hundred nationalities, tribes, and linguistic groups.

16. Rustow, *A World of Nations*, p. 286.

17. That linguistic homogeneity is related to economic development is also evident from present-day data. The countries least economically developed, that is, economically closest

modern assumption, derived from a European nationalism that is less than two centuries old, that states are or ought to be identical with nations and that nations are identical with nationalities is wholly inapplicable to aristocratic empires. The people inhabiting them form a nation no more than they constitute a society.

Also, with relatively little communication over long distances, what single languages were in fact spoken in long-lasting commercialized empires often broke up into several different ones. Thus, vulgar Latin that had been adopted in parts of the Roman empire gradually evolved into Italian, French (and Provençal), Spanish, Catalan, Gallegan, Portuguese, and Rumanian, not to mention the enclaves of Rhaeto-Romanic, Ladinic, and Friulian in the Alps, and Vlach in the Balkan peninsula. Arabic, too, is more realistically characterized as a language group rather than a single language. Mutually incomprehensible forms of it are spoken in different Arab countries from Iraq to Morocco, all related to classical Arabic as French and Rumanian are related to Latin. There are German dialects that are mutually almost incomprehensible even today, and this was certainly more true in the days of aristocratic empires, when various forms of Old High German and of Low German, like Frisian and Saxon, were spoken.

Finally, even in the fairly exceptional cases where a single language is spoken by all the inhabitants of an aristocratic empire, it is used so differently by members of different classes that one can hardly think of it as the same language. Even in modern societies, and particularly those with an aristocratic background, there are, more or less related to regional dialects, distinct class dialects involving not only the use of "incorrect," that is, different rules of grammar, but distinct accents and intonations and even, to some extent, a distinct vocabulary.[18] Also, groups segregated from the rest of the population, like the Jews in Germany and Blacks in the United

---

to the agrarianism of aristocratic empires, are also the least homogeneous linguistically. See Banks and Textor, *A Cross-Polity Survey*, matrices 43–68 and 68–42. Among present-day underdeveloped countries those containing only one language group are quite exceptional. Thus, a single language is spoken by 70 percent or more of the population of only three of thirty-three African countries south of the Sahara (Lesotho, the Malagasy Republic, and Ruanda). Rustow, *A World of Nations*, pp. 285–87.

18. Clifford Geertz discusses in fascinating detail the results of the combination in Javanese of (1) words having "status meaning" in addition to their linguistic meaning, that is, different words being used depending on the status of the speaker and the listener, and (2) class dialects, ranked in terms of a spectrum from refined and civilized to rough and uncivilized, this "sort of ranking being characteristic, of course, of any stratified society." Geertz, *The Religion of Java*, pp. 248–49. Thus in the simple sentence "are you going to eat rice and cassava now?" different words are used for each English word except cassava, depending on who speaks to whom (ibid., pp. 249–60). On the important role of accents in the modern British class structure, see Shaw, *Pygmalion*, and, based on it, the libretto by Alan Jay Lerner of *My Fair Lady*.

States, tend to develop and retain distinct forms of speech. As class lines become blurred, as they have in twentieth-century Western Europe or the walls of segregation break down either for entire groups or for individuals, the distinctions between such dialects begin to disappear.

In aristocratic empires, where class lines are very sharply drawn and where the wall separating the aristocracy from the peasantry is so high as to inhibit almost all communication, it is only natural that widely different dialects should be spoken by these two classes. Their lives being so different, aristocrats and peasants will, in any case, speak about very different things. Thus each class requires a different vocabulary, that of the aristocracy being richer and more complex corresponding to the richer and more complex life of aristocrats. Clearly, even where aristocrats and peasants do formally employ the same language, that language does not become a bond uniting them. One could more correctly say of them what has been said of Englishmen and Americans, that they are separated by a common language. Thus in the relatively rare cases where aristocratic conquest and the formation of a new empire eventually result in such a common language, the relationship between aristocrats and peasants is not changed thereby.

Continuity and Change through Conquest: Religion

Ordinarily, aristocrats are as little concerned with the religion of their subjects as they are with their language. Hence conquest by an aristocracy holding a particular religion by no means results in the adoption of that religion by the conquered. Commonly aristocracies practice what is, by modern standards, called toleration, but what is more accurately described as indifference. In imperial China, "although the government regulated the order of service in the sacrifice to Heaven and Earth and Confucius and the emperor personally officiated in the sacrifice, and although the different dynasties promoted various deities in rank and title, these activities were mostly ceremonial and had no influence on the practical religious life of the people. Indeed, they were scarcely known to the people at large. . . . Generally speaking, throughout Chinese history, the government did not pass judgment on religious beliefs, interfere with religious practices, or determine religious creeds."[19]

However, aristocratic indifference comes in different degrees. Where an aristocracy and particularly a ruler are closely identified with certain gods—often because the aristocrats claim descent from them or, indeed,

19. Chan, *Religious Trends in Modern China*, p. 139.

claim to be these gods themselves—they may insist that their subjects worship them or pay obeisance to them. However, this may amount to a recognition of the aristocrats' overlordship more than a change in the subjects' religion as is, of course, also true of imposition of taxes on people of one religion to support an aristocracy, including a priesthood, of another.

Temples to deified Roman emperors were erected in various parts of the empire, regardless of the prevailing local religion, and the Incas insisted that all their subjects worship the Sun, from which they claimed descent, and required them to do corvée labor on land set aside in part for the priesthood of the Sun.[20] In neither case did this mean, however, that through conquest the old religion of the conquered was replaced by a new one. Rather, a new element, that is, a new god, was merely added to it. It must not be assumed that all gods say to their adherents as Jehovah did, "Thou shalt have no other gods before me. . . . Thou shalt not bow down thyself to them nor serve them: for I the Lord thy God am a jealous God."[21] Polytheistic systems are often far more flexible than the Judeo-Christian-Islamic monotheistic one.

Indeed, both Romans and Incas not only imposed new gods on their subjects but also managed to integrate the religions of the people they conquered into their own. The same was true of the Aztecs: "The Mexican was a receptive religion. The conquering Aztecs were only too happy to seize not only the provinces, but also the provincial gods. All foreign gods were welcome . . . and the priests of Tenochtitlan, eager for knowledge and curious of ritual, willingly adopted the myths and practices of the distant countries that the armies had traversed."[22]

Not only do polytheistic systems of religion not necessarily have a limited number of gods to which none can be added, but other belief systems are more concerned with interpretation of the order of the universe and the place of man and his societies in it and are hence not

20. "Inti, the Sun, ancestor of the dynasty, became the imperial god. His celestial power was the counterpart of the *Sapa Inca's* rule on earth; his worship merged with the homage paid to his son. Thus it was from political as much as from pious motives that the Incas raised temples to Inti in all the conquered territories. . . . They were not hostile to local religions, but demanded that in every province a privileged place should be accorded to their ancestor, the Sun." Métraux, *The History of the Incas*, pp. 121–23.

21. Exod. 20:3, 5. "The Spanish effort to eradicate and replace all indigenous religions seems to have led to the assumption that the Inca attempted the same *vis à vis* local cults. On the contrary, the Sun cult appears to have been simply superimposed on local cults. As Bram tells us, the religion of the Sun vanished with the Inca, and the principal struggle of the Catholic church was not against the Inca national religion, but against local cults." Moore, *Power and Property in Inca Peru*, p. 26; the reference is to Joseph Bram, *An Analysis of Inca Militarism* (New York, 1941), p. 44.

22. Soustelle, *Daily Life of the Aztecs*, p. 116.

necessarily incompatible with various religions. Thus, in China, certain ancient belief systems persisted as new religions—Confucianism (if it can be called a religion), Buddhism, and Taoism—arrived and merged with them. As recently as just before the Communist revolution, the majority of the Chinese followed "a syncretic religion embracing the ancient cult as its basis and Buddhist and Taoist elements as secondary features."[23] Similarly, in Japan the indigenous Shinto religion and Buddhism have fused to some extent so that, according to government statistics, in a population of slightly more than one hundred million, about seventy million believe in Shinto and almost eighty million regard themselves as Buddhists.[24] In Vietnam, elements of Confucianism, Buddhism, and Taoism have merged with local animism, and in Cambodia Buddhism and elements of Hinduism have been combined with the worship of local gods. Conquered people, then, and especially peasants are likely to maintain their great variety of local religions, with their specific beliefs, traditions, and practices, regardless of the religion of their aristocratic conquerors or in a form more or less superficially modified by it.

This remains largely true even in the relatively few cases where aristocrats develop religious rationalizations for their conquests that require them, in the service of their own gods, to destroy alien religions and to convert the conquered to their own religion. Thus, some of the Muslim conquerors of India destroyed Hindu temples, imposed discriminatory taxes on Hindus, and otherwise sought to convert them to Islam. Conversion as the object and, in any case, the result of conquest is especially typical of Christian aristocracies, from Charlemagne's conversion of the Saxons through the Spaniards' conquests in Latin America and the Philippines to the expansion of Amharic rule in Ethiopia at the turn of the present century.

Conversion by conquest is similar in its effects to conversion decreed by a ruler who himself accepted a new religion, usually for political reasons. This is how the Franks became Catholic Christians in 496 after Clovis I married a Burgundian princess, how the Tibetans became Buddhists after their king married a Chinese princess in 641, and how the Russians were converted to eastern (Byzantine) Christianity under Vladimir the Saint of Kiev about 990. Whether conversion takes place by conquest of a new ruler or by decree of an old one, a certain degree of religious and cultural uniformity may be established throughout villages in a large area, but in fact many of the preconversion beliefs and practices will survive, thus maintaining some of the old diversity under a surface uniformity. In Rus-

23. Chan, *Religious Trends in Modern China*, p. 141.
24. Ike, *Japan*, p. 5.

sia, for example, "among the masses, paganism and Christianity existed side by side for centuries. Illiterate village priests encouraged this blending of different creeds, since their income derived in good part from offerings to miracle-working icons and to the charismatic remnants of Christian saints."[25]

In the process of conversion and surface homogenization, the religion to be adopted by the peasants changes quite as much as their old religions. "Preaching the Christian doctrine in Kievan Russia was so difficult that the Christian faith itself was transformed. As elsewhere, the people had their own pagan beliefs and no background for understanding the new message."[26] In seventh- and eighth-century Japan "Buddhism, being an imported system of ideas adopted by the aristocracy and bureaucracy, did not permeate the masses of the people." In later centuries the masses did adopt it, but then "Buddhism did not really change the Japanese masses, but the Japanese masses changed Buddhism."[27]

Given the peasants' stubborn adherence to their old beliefs and traditions, the religion to which they are to be converted has to be adjusted to these beliefs and traditions and has to integrate them and to accept their symbols in order to be embraced by the peasants. "Thus, the Mediterranean Persephone became a Black Virgin Mary, the Aztec goddess Tonantzin in Mexico was transmuted into a Christian Virgin of Guadalupe. Similarly, in Islam the sacred black stone of the *ka'aba* in Mecca—center of pilgrimages in the pattern of Near Eastern stone worship—became under Muhammad the central symbol of the Islamic God."[28] Among modern Indians in the Andes, "God and Christ are sometimes identified with the Sun, . . . Pacha-mama, the 'Earth Mother,' protectress of crops and animals . . . becomes assimilated with the Virgin Mary, . . . [and they] see Santiago as the Lord of Lightning, Apu Illapu. Llamas are sacrificed to him."[29]

The cult of local saints by Muslims, which is in principle condemned by Islam but is widespread, is another example of the adaptation of the "great tradition" of a conqueror's religion to preexisting local "little traditions." That Muslims can invoke Christian saints and make pilgrimages to the tombs of Jewish patriarchs shows that even monotheistic religions can to some extent merge and that those who seek to impose the new religion often must make some concessions to the adherents of the old ones. "The

25. Bendix, *Kings or People*, p. 103.

26. Ibid.

27. Kato, *Form, Style, Tradition*, pp. 180, 182.

28. Wolf, *Peasants*, pp. 103–4.

29. Métraux, *The History of the Incas*, p. 191.

practices were sanctioned by the local clergy when their ineradicability had been evidenced over a sufficiently long period."[30]

The merger of the two traditions and the adaptation of the conquerors' new religion to the peasants' old ones is often a process that takes place gradually and not deliberately, as in the association of pagan midwinter solar and agricultural observances and Celtic and Germanic yule rites, with symbols like the tree, and of the Roman saturnalia with the celebration of the birth of Christ at Christmas. However, it can also be quite deliberate, as when the Spaniards placed the Inca symbol of the golden sun on the altars of their churches in Cuzco in order to attract their Indian subjects to them. Pope Gregory the Great specifically issued instructions in the year 601 that the pagan temples in Britain "should on no account be destroyed. . . . They are to be . . . dedicated to the service of the true God. In this way, we hope that the people, seeing that its temples are not destroyed, may abandon idolatry and resort to these places as before, and may come to know and adore the true God. . . . They are no longer to sacrifice beasts to the Devil, but they may kill them for food to the praise of God. . . . For it is certainly impossible to eradicate all errors from obstinate minds at one stroke, and whoever wishes to climb a mountaintop climbs gradually step by step, and not in one leap."[31]

In spite of a single religion being imposed across a large territory by its conquerors, peasants may well, under these circumstances, hold on to their old beliefs and practices in good measure. "Peasant groups often retain traditional forms of religion, while religious systems of wider scope are being built up and carried outward by the elite."[32] As a result, as Eisenstadt says of China in the T'ang period, "each of the great religions

---

30. von Grunebaum, "The Problem: Unity in Diversity," p. 28. Von Grunebaum deals more generally with the interaction between the "great tradition" of Islam and the local "little traditions," ibid., pp. 27–32. On that interaction in Hinduism, see Lamb, *India*, pp. 98–110, and Redfield, *Peasant Society and Culture*, pp. 89–99. The concepts of the great and little traditions are taken from Robert Redfield who wrote: "In a civilization there is a great tradition of the reflective few, and there is a little tradition of the largely unreflective many. The great tradition is cultivated in schools or temples; the little tradition works itself out and keeps itself going in the lives of the unlettered in their village communities. The tradition of the philosopher, theologian, and literary man is a tradition consciously cultivated and handed down; that of the little people is for the most part taken for granted and not submitted to much scrutiny or considered refinement or improvement" (ibid., p. 70).

31. Quoted by Wolf, *Peasants*, p. 103, from Bede, *A History of the English Church and People*, pp. 86–87. But Bede also reports that about the same time, Pope Gregory wrote to King Ethelbert (of Kent) asking him to "abolish the worship of idols and destroy their shrines" (ibid., p. 89).

32. Wolf, *Peasants*, p. 103.

had at least a dual theological and ideological system—an abstract system, with a marked philosophic flavor, and a popular system that emphasized the magical aspect. The cleavage between the nobility and the commoners, and the tradition of the literary education of the nobility, seem to have been closely associated to the development of such ideologies."[33]

Thus, in India, Hinduism is hardly a single religion, but ranges from High Hinduism with its belief in an all-pervading, formless omnipotent god through belief in one or more personal gods to village Hinduism focused on local demons and spirits.[34] Originally brought to India by Aryan invaders about 1500 B.C. and for long probably the religion only of the aristocracy, Hinduism had, by the fifth century A.D., "accepted the cults of invaders subsequent to the Aryans, as well as ancient native cults which apparently had continued to be the religion of the masses despite the Aryan invasions. . . . Village Hinduism—the Hinduism of close to 85 per cent of the Hindus—is quite different from the Hinduism stemming from the Sanskrit classics."[35]

A Chinese scholar has "urged that instead of dividing the religious life of the Chinese people into three compartments called Confucianism, Buddhism, and Taoism, it is far more accurate to divide it into two levels, the level of the masses and the level of the enlightened." In contrast to the enlightened, who honor Heaven, ancestors, and sometimes great teachers, but do not pray to them to have their lives changed for the better, "the masses worship thousands of idols and natural objects of ancient, Buddhist, Taoist, and other origins, making special offering to whatever deity is believed to have the power to influence their lives at the time. . . . They believe in the thirty-three Buddhist heavens, eighty-one Taoist heavens, and eighteen Buddhist hells, . . . in astrology, almanachs, dream interpretation, geomancy, witchcraft, phrenology, palmistry, the recalling of the soul, fortune-telling in all forms, charms, magic and all varieties of superstitions."[36]

Summarizing Clifford Geertz's *The Religion of Java*, Wolf contrasts the Javanese peasant religion "called *abangan* [and] in opposition to it . . . the religious complex of the traditional Javanese warrior-gentry, aiming at spiritual excellence and esthetic polish. . . . The *abangan* religion has incorporated animistic, Hinduistic, and Islamic elements, but has focused them on the performance of . . . ritual feasts. . . . What is first-order ritual and symbolism to the peasants seems *kasar* (crude) to the aristocrat whose

33. Eisenstadt, *The Political Systems of Empires*, p. 59. On "levels in religious traditions," see also Wolf, *Peasants*, pp. 100–106.

34. Lamb, *India*, pp. 98–101.

35. Ibid., pp. 100–101.

36. Chan, *Religious Trends in Modern China*, pp. 141–42.

rule is sanctioned by spiritual excellence, as expressed in his polished control of such art forms as the dance, the shadow play, music, textile design, etiquette, and language. Yet, although they are polar opposites, the two religious variants also complement each other as symbolic statements of a reciprocal social relationship."[37]

Lucian Pye writes that "it is customary to suggest that religions were able to integrate traditional societies by providing the members with a common framework of values and a common orientation toward the basic problems of life. Yet the closer we examine the historical evidence from such societies, the more we are impressed with the divergences in the content of the religious beliefs. In Burma among some of the peasantry the worship and propitiation of all manner of animistic objects, malevolent spirits, ogresses, and *nats* were hardly modified by the teachings of Buddha, while among the elite were to be found men profoundly knowledgeable in the sacred texts."[38]

Max Weber, too, linked the peasants to magic rather than ethical religion, because "the lot of peasants is so strongly tied to nature, so dependent on organic processes and natural events, and economically so little oriented to rational systematization. . . . The more agrarian the essential social pattern of a culture, e.g., Rome, India, or Egypt, the more likely it is that the agrarian element of the population will fall into a pattern of traditionalism and that at least the religion of the masses will lack ethical rationalization. . . . Only rarely does the peasantry serve as the carrier of any other sort of religion than their original magic. . . . As a general rule, the peasantry remained primarily involved with weather magic and animistic magic or ritualism; insofar as it developed any ethical religion, the focus was on a purely formalistic ethic of *do ut des* in relation to both god and priests."[39]

"That the peasant has become the distinctive prototype of the pious man who is pleasing to god is a thoroughly modern phenomenon. . . . None of the more important religions of Eastern Asia had any such notion about the religious merit of the peasant. Indeed, in the religions of India, and most consistently in the salvation religion of Buddhism, the peasant is

---

37. Wolf, *Peasants*, pp. 104–5.

38. Pye, *Politics, Personality, and Nation Building*, p. 74. For a detailed study of Burmese folk religion, see Spiro, *Burmese Supernaturalism*, who argues (especially in chap. 14) that this "nat religion" is different from and in important respects incompatible with Buddhism.

39. Weber, *Economy and Society*, 2:468–70. It should be noted that Weber contrasts the religion of the peasantry here with that of "the city which was regarded as the site of piety" (ibid., p. 471) rather than with that of the aristocracy, for he held that "as a rule, the warrior nobles, and indeed feudal powers generally, have not readily become the carriers of a rational religious ethic" (ibid., p. 472).

religiously suspect. . . . To the congregational piety of the *chaberim* the 'rustic' was virtually identical with the 'godless,' the rural dweller being politically and religiously a Jew of the second class. For it was virtually impossible for a peasant to live a pious life according to the Jewish ritual law, just as in Buddhism and Hinduism. . . . In early Christianity . . . the rustic was simply regarded as the heathen (*paganus*). Even the official doctrine of the medieval churches, as formulated by Thomas Aquinas, treated the peasant essentially as a Christian of lower rank, at any rate accorded him very little esteem."[40] Similarly, a student of medieval Muslim cities says: "For Muslims, cities often possess a special sanctity and are regarded as the sole places in which a full and truly Muslim life may be lived."[41]

Even if aristocrats impose a religion on their peasants in order to gain legitimacy thereby, there is much doubt that that religion will be accepted. Barrington Moore, thinking particularly of Hinduism, speaks of "an organic cosmology that conferred legitimacy on the role of the ruling classes, couched in some theory of the harmony of the universe that stressed resignation and the acceptance of individual fate." However, he adds that "such religions are the product of urban and priestly classes. The extent of their acceptance among peasants is problematic. In general the existence of an undercurrent of belief distinct from that of the educated strata, often in direct opposition to it, characterizes peasant societies."[42] Clearly, the wide gulf between the two cultures of the aristocracy and the peasantry is only superficially bridged by the imposition of the conqueror's religion on the conquered. In fact, their beliefs and practices remain very different, as seems, indeed, inevitable when their place in their world, their lives, and their values are so utterly different.

Let us now return to the question of whether aristocratic conquests can so modify the relationship between aristocrats and nonaristocrats, especially peasants, that we can no longer think of them as living in aristocratic empires. Most conquests of one aristocratic empire by another produce no cultural change at all for the peasantry. Aristocracies come and go, and life around the court and even the capital city may change somewhat as a result, but the peasants are hardly aware that those who benefit from the taxes they pay have changed. A particular territory may be included in various empires through the centuries, but among its peasants hardly a trace of the languages and religions of the various ruling aristocracies may be found.

On the other hand, the language of the ruling aristocracy may eventually

40. Ibid., pp. 470–71.

41. Lapidus, "Muslim Cities and Islamic Societies," p. 47.

42. Moore, *Social Origins of Dictatorship and Democracy*, pp. 455–56.

trickle down to the peasantry, and peasants may be converted to the aristocrats' religion either gradually and village by village or overnight and en masse by the fiat of the ruler. Even then, however, aristocrats and peasants have little in common. Not only is the adoption of a new language or new religion likely to be only partial and superficial, but even where it is far-reaching, the common language is in fact so deeply divided into class dialects, the common religion into the "great" and "little" traditions that what is spoken sounds hardly like a single language, what is believed and practiced is hardly a single religion. It is only with modernization involving growing contact of people across class lines that these differences begin to be bridged; in traditional aristocratic empires they are deep and permanent.

Even where aristocratic conquests produce substantial cultural and especially linguistic and religious changes among the conquered, the place of the aristocrat and of the peasant in the order of things remains unchanged. The peasants remain exploited, the aristocrats continue to exploit them, and the roles and behavior and thinking of both continue to be conditioned by this relationship.

Different languages can be used in a persistent economic and social order, and different religions can be compatible with it and can even be used to justify it, as when one set of aristocrats rules in the name of one god and those who replace them rule—in quite the same way—in the name of another. To be sure, some social institutions are closely tied to religion and change with it. A striking example is the Hindu caste system from which millions of Indians, particularly in East Bengal, were freed by conversion to Islam following Muslim conquests. Yet even this change did not change the relationship between aristocrat and peasant. The Muslim king or warrior was no kshatriya, the religious leader no brahman, the landlord was neither, but they were all still aristocrats; the Muslim peasant was no shudra and the agrarian laborer no untouchable, but they were still peasants, and the gulf between aristocrat and peasant was as wide as ever. No religion held by aristocrats, least of all one brought to or forced on peasants by them to perpetuate or facilitate their subjection, can be expected to bridge this gulf or to change significantly the relationship between the two classes.

Empires rise and fall, individual aristocrats and entire aristocracies succeed each other. A particular area could well have been under dozens of empires and aristocracies through the centuries, and the prevailing language and religion could have changed several times. But while empires come and go, the peculiar social order associated with aristocratic empires remains. It comes to an end not through the conquest of one empire by another, but only when nonaristocratic strata become able to compete with aristocrats, thus completely changing the nature of politics. Such a situation gradually evolved from within aristocratic empires a number of times in history through the development of commerce, and in Western Europe that development proceeded to a point where it spilled over all national and regional boundaries and eventually affected all remaining empires from without, so as to put an end to the aristocratic empire and its peculiar form of politics everywhere. An analysis of that process, the process of modernization, is, of course, beyond the scope of this book,[43] but we must still ask what role nonaristocratic strata, that is, the peasants and the townspeople, play in aristocratic politics. And we must turn to the question why peasants and also, for long periods of time, townspeople are generally not able to compete with aristocrats to the point where the old order of the aristocratic empire would be destroyed.

43. A brief summary of some of the political consequences of modernization is included in Chapter 15, below.

Part IV
Nonaristocrats in the
Politics of the Aristocracy

12

The Peasantry in the Politics
of the Aristocracy

The Peasant Defined

My discussion so far has been confined to the role of aristocrats in the politics of aristocratic empires. Such an analysis, by itself, cannot explain the unchanging character of the relationship between aristocrats and nonaristocrats and thus the stability of aristocratic predominance. To explain it, I must also show that nonaristocrats play no role in the politics of the aristocracy or are at least unable to change their relationship to the aristocracy. In this and the following two chapters, I therefore deal with the questions whether and to what extent peasants and townspeople can and do intervene in the politics of the aristocracy.

The peasantry, that is, the great bulk of the population of aristocratic empires, will be discussed first. For my purposes here, I do not need to present a full or even adequate discussion of the politics, let alone, more broadly, the societies and the culture of the peasantry corresponding to my analysis of the aristocracy. This is not necessary partly because the role of the peasantry in aristocratic empires has been touched on already and, more importantly, because, as I pointed out in the first chapter, there is a large and growing social scientific literature that, explicitly or implicitly, formulates generalizations on peasants.

Above all, peasant politics will not be dealt with here, because it is a subject wholly separate and different from that of the politics of the aristocracy. The intravillage political processes determining the distribution among the peasants of the village of benefits, like land and its products, and of burdens, like the share of taxes and of labor obligations owed to the aristocracy, as well as the distribution of power and influence among the peasants and the processes by which decisions are made—all these are obviously worth studying for many purposes. So is conflict between neighboring villages, for example, over hunting or grazing rights, over the use of forests or water. However, for my purposes I can treat the peasantry as if it were homogeneous and ignore what conflicts and what distinctions of rank may divide it.[1]

Studies of peasant politics cannot contribute much to an understanding of politics in aristocratic empires beyond the village level, that is, the politics of the aristocracy. As has been emphasized, the aristocracy forms its own society within such empires and aristocratic politics takes place within that society alone. Because it is the aristocracy and not the peasantry that constitutes the aristocratic empire, it is the politics of the aristocracy and not the politics of the peasantry that constitutes the politics of aristocratic empires.

My discussion of the peasantry here will, then, be confined to the questions of whether and how peasants affect aristocratic politics and why they generally do not. Matters like peasant values and ideology will be taken up only as they relate to these questions. Before I turn to them, however, I must indicate how I define the peasantry and thereby also suggest what its role in the economy of aristocratic empires is. The corresponding discussion of the aristocracy occupied two entire chapters, but in this context much less needs to be said about the peasantry. To be sure, there is a good deal of disagreement in the literature on how to define a peasant, just as I have had some difficulty in clearly defining an aristocrat. However, the difficulties in defining the peasant and particularly in distinguishing him from the primitive cultivator on the one hand and from the farmer on the other disappear in good part if one is concerned only, as we are here, with peasants in aristocratic empires.

I define peasants simply as those engaged in agriculture in aristocratic empires, though they also produce their necessities other than food, for example, their cloth and clothing, their tools and their dwellings. Thus, I include in the peasantry those in the village who carry on crafts, like weaving, carpentry, and pottery, on a part-time basis and even the relatively few full-time village craftsmen that develop in some peasant societies, as in feudal Europe and in India. I also regard as peasants their village leaders and village priests, even if they are not themselves engaged in agriculture and even if the latter are nominally part of the aristocrats' priestly hierarchy extending down into the village.

By including in my definition agriculturalists only in aristocratic empires, I indicate that the agriculture they are engaged in is technologically primitive and that it is subsistence agriculture. If their technology were not

---

1. Such distinctions can exist in traditional aristocratic empires, but they tend to become more prominent only with commercialization, as was true in China and in late medieval Europe. On the complex legal, economic, and social divisions of the peasantry in thirteenth-century England, see Homans, *English Villagers of the Thirteenth Century*, pp. 232–52.

primitive, they could produce a surplus for sale and if they did so on any significant scale and were hence no longer engaged in subsistence agriculture but in commercial agriculture, the empire they live in would no longer be a traditional one.

In some of the literature, a distinction is drawn between the primitive cultivator, who can retain everything he produces, and the peasant, who must pay taxes or rent to the aristocrat. "It is this production of a fund of rent which critically distinguishes the peasant from the primitive cultivator. . . . It is only when . . . the cultivator becomes subject to the demands and sanctions of power-holders outside his social stratum that we can appropriately speak of peasantry." "Peasants . . . are rural cultivators whose surpluses are transferred to a dominant group of rulers."[2] Like Wolf in these statements, Shanin defines the peasant in part in terms of his relation to the aristocracy when he says: "The peasantry consists of small agricultural producers who, with the help of simple equipment and labour of their families, produce mainly for their own consumption and for the fulfillment of obligations to the holders of political and economic power."[3] And, in a footnote, Barrington Moore says: "A previous history of subordination to a landed upper class recognized and enforced in the laws, . . . sharp cultural distinctions, and a considerable degree of *de facto* possession of the land, constitute the main distinguishing features of a peasantry."[4]

Somewhat in line with Wolf's, Shanin's, and Moore's definitions, I have sought to confine use of the term "peasants" to agriculturalists exploited by aristocrats, and to refer to others as primitive agriculturalists or cultivators. This gives a certain symmetry to my definitions: the aristocrat is one who exploits peasants; the peasant is one who is exploited by aristocrats. There can be no aristocrat without peasants and no peasants without aristocrat. It could quite reasonably be argued, however, that the symmetry is a false one. Whereas the exploiters cannot live without engaging in exploitation, the exploited could, of course, live without being exploited. One might well say, then, that peasants could exist without aristocrats and hence need not be distinguished from primitive cultivators. In practice, this issue does not arise here, for the agriculturalists we are concerned with live in aristocratic empires and are therefore subject to

---

2. Wolf, *Peasants*, pp. 10–11, 3–4.

3. Shanin, "Peasantry as a Political Factor," p. 240. Redfield, throughout his classic *Peasant Society and Culture*, refers to peasant societies as "part-societies" understandable only in relation to cities and larger societies. Earlier, he had argued that the word peasant "points to a human type. . . . It required the city to bring it into existence. There were no peasants before the first cities. And those surviving primitive people who do not live in terms of the city are not peasants." Redfield, *The Primitive World and Its Transformations*, p. 31.

4. Moore, *Social Origins of Dictatorship and Democracy*, p. 111n.

aristocratic rule and exploitation. Primitive cultivators, whether they are included in or distinguished from the peasantry, do not live in aristocratic empires, simply because any agriculturalist who has managed to escape aristocratic rule and exploitation, perhaps because his territory is inaccessible to the tax collector, is not a part of an aristocratic empire, even if his territory is surrounded by territory under aristocratic control.

Just as our exclusive concern with traditional aristocratic empires eliminates the problem of the distinction between primitive cultivators and peasants, so it eliminates, at least in principle, the problem of the distinction between peasants and farmers, because farmers, like primitive cultivators, do not live in aristocratic empires. It is nevertheless important to clarify the distinction between peasant and farmer, for there is a tendency for modern people to confuse the two, either because, as in the United States, there have been virtually no peasants and almost all agriculturalists have been farmers, or because, as in Western Europe, peasants have gradually become farmers and may, in the course of the transition, share some of the characteristics of both.

Redfield draws the distinction well between peasants and farmers when he calls those agriculturalists peasants whose "agriculture is a livelihood and a way of life, not a business for profit. We might say that those agriculturalists who carry on agriculture for reinvestment and business, looking on the land as capital and commodity, are not peasants but farmers."[5] To be sure, peasants, too, may be involved in an exchange economy. They may exchange, either directly or through the use of money, some of their specialized agricultural products and particularly some of the specialized products of their craftsmen with those of other villages, sometimes by direct contact with these villages, sometimes via markets, usually in towns, visited by peasants from several villages. Peasants may also exchange some of their products, expecially agricultural ones, for the products of towns.

However, villages may be far apart or separated by natural obstacles, and towns may be few in number so that only a small fraction of the peasantry in an empire is close to them. Given poor means of transportation, many peasants, then, may not be involved in an exchange economy at all, but, even for those who are, their exchanges are relatively incidental to their economy, and they are overwhelmingly engaged in subsistence agri-

5. Redfield, *Peasant Society and Culture*, p. 27. Heilbroner says: "A peasant is a social creature very different from a farmer. He is not technologically alert but, on the contrary, clings with stubborn persistence—and often even with great skill—to his well-known ways. He must, since a small error might mean starvation. He does not buy the majority of his supplies but, to a large extent, fashions them himself; similarly, he does not produce for a 'market,' but principally for himself. Finally, he is often not even free to consume his own crop, but typically he must hand over a portion—a tenth, a third, half or even more—to the owner of his land." Heilbroner, *The Making of Economic Society*, p. 22.

culture. Even those who do sell their products to other villages or to the town do so to obtain consumer goods in exchange or to find the cash with which to make required money payments of dues and taxes to the aristocracy, but not in order to make a profit to be reinvested in land and equipment. They are therefore peasants and not farmers, for the latter produce not for subsistence purposes but to sell on the market and they sell in order to make a profit and in order to invest in more production.

Above all, the peasant, unlike the farmer, does not regard the land as capital and commodity. He has "what anthropologists term 'inherited use-ownership' of it. . . . One had family land as one had one's name. It was held not by an individual but by the family, past, present, and future. . . . It was an incident of life."[6] Land becomes alienable and a commodity only under the impact of some commercialization, as happened in Greece, in Rome, in the Chinese empire, and in medieval Europe. In traditional aristocratic empires land is not bought and sold. Ability to exploit the peasants on some land—and, in that sense, land itself—may be passed from one aristocrat to another by conquest, treaty, or inheritance, but, subject to aristocratic exploitation, the peasant is "a man who is in effective control of a piece of land to which he has long been attached by ties of tradition and sentiment. The land and he are parts of one thing, one old-established body of relationships,"[7] regardless of whether the peasant is legally an owner or a tenant, free or a serf.

The Impossibility of Peaceable Peasant Intervention in Aristocratic Politics

In modern industrial societies, political power and influence is to some extent related to numbers. Even highly autocratic or dictatorial regimes find it necessary to organize and procure the support of great masses of people. It may therefore be difficult for us to understand why peasants who constitute the huge majority of the population—indeed, virtually the entire population—of aristocratic empires wield so little power and influence in the government of such empires and wield them only so rarely and sporadically. The explanation lies in the fact, repeatedly stressed here, that such empires are not societies with a single government, but composites of many societies. The government of an empire is the aristocrats' government, not the peasants'. The worlds of the peasants, isolated in each village, and of the aristocracy hardly intersect either in thought or in action. Aristocrats, of course, look down on peas-

6. Hagen, *On the Theory of Social Change*, pp. 63–64.

7. Redfield, *Peasant Society and Culture*, pp. 27–28.

ants as a lower order of human beings, but they need not devote much thought to them. That peasants keep working and are hence available for exploitation can simply be taken for granted and requires no regulatory activity on the part of the aristocracy.

Peasants may stand in awe of aristocrats, impressed by their military power, by their conspicuously displayed wealth, and by their ability to live without having to engage in productive labor. On the other hand, these very same things may also give rise to some passive resentment on the part of the peasants. However, all these feelings are likely to be quite vague, for in aristocratic empires aristocrats appear to peasants as distant, alien, utterly different and incomprehensible beings. They are, after all, members of a different society, who are housed, fed, and dressed differently, whose language and religion is different, who think differently and behave differently. This means that the peasant cannot be envious of the aristocrat, for to be envious would require him to be able to imagine that he himself might enjoy some of the wealth and privileges of the aristocrat. The distance between the two classes and the two cultures is too great to be bridged by the peasant's imagination.[8] Only under the impact of some modernization can he become actively envious and resentful.

All this means that aristocrats and peasants function in different political arenas. The aristocracy, of course, interferes in the lives of the peasants by exploiting them, but it does not intervene much in intravillage politics, because its interests are not at stake in conflicts among peasants. It is even more true that peasants do not commonly intervene in aristocratic politics —aside from individual peasants who may, on extremely rare occasions, rise into the ranks of the aristocracy and become politically influential within it. I am not concerned with them now for they simply become aristocrats and as such have been dealt with already. Here my subject is the participation of peasants as peasants in the politics of the aristocracy.

It is obvious from all I have said about aristocrats that they could never dream of permitting peasants as peasants to vote or participate in their councils (even if peasants wanted to do so, as they generally do not for reasons to be discussed soon). It is unimaginable that peasants as peasants could compete with aristocrats for positions, for the positions in question are aristocratic ones. A peasant could conceivably become a king by becoming an aristocrat, but a peasant as a peasant could never be king, for a

---

8. Even in the mid-twentieth century, Turkish villagers, when asked what they would do if they were the president of Turkey, mostly "responded by stolid silence—the traditional way of handling 'projective questions' which require people to imagine themselves or things to be different from what they 'really are.' Some were shocked by the impropriety of the very question. 'My God! How can you say such a thing?' gasped the shepherd. 'How can I . . . I cannot . . . a poor villager . . . master of the whole world.'" Lerner, *The Passing of Traditional Society*, p. 24.

peasant king—like a male woman—is a contradiction in terms, and so is a peasant governor, a peasant general, a peasant high priest.

Concepts like peasant voting, peasant representation, peasant participation in competition for aristocratic positions all make no sense in aristocratic empires.[9] However, aristocratic politics also involves competition for wealth—or for positions providing wealth—and that wealth is in large part created by peasants. Could peasants not intervene in aristocratic politics around the one relationship that links the separate worlds of the aristocracy and the peasantry, that of exploitation? Why do peasants not withhold their product from the aristocracy, why do they not refuse to work for the aristocracy, why do they not strike? By doing so, they could conceivably weaken one aristocrat as against another and thus play a part in aristocratic politics. And if they could strike on a large scale and for an extended time, they would, of course, destroy the aristocracy and its empire altogether, they would carry out a revolution—though in the context of historical development it could be called a reactionary one—and they would return to the status of free primitive cultivators.

It must first be noted that peasants do try to withhold their product from the aristocracy. They pay their rent or taxes only reluctantly and they pay as little as they can get away with. Often they try to hide their products from the tax collector, and the latter employs force and even torture to extract payments from the peasants. But although many peasants may not pay quite as much as aristocrats would like to obtain from them, their resistance is, on the whole, clearly ineffective, and it does not stop the process of exploitation and can hardly be thought of as participation in aristocratic politics.

Under some circumstances, the peasant may work as little or as slowly as possible when he performs corvée labor—which amounts to the same thing as not paying his taxes in full—and "when taxation becomes unusually burdensome, the peasant may reduce his cultivated acreage, and when the heavy demands continue, he may become a fiscal fugitive, abandoning his fields altogether. He may wander in despair, look for work elsewhere, or turn bandit or rebel."[10] Peasant flight to escape taxation became important in the Mogul empire of India and it occurred periodically in China, leading to widespread banditry. However, this type of resistance, too, is quite ineffective in putting an end to exploitation. Also, more often than not it will be carried on only by individual peasants or at most one or a few

9. In 1565, a half-millennium after the beginnings of commercialization in England, Sir Thomas Smith could still define those who were not "gentlemen" as having "no voice nor authoritie in our common wealth, and no account is made of them but onelie to be ruled, and not to rule other." Quoted in Bendix, *Kings or People*, p. 212.

10. Wittfogel, *Oriental Despotism*, pp. 331–32.

villages, for concerted action beyond the village level is very difficult to achieve for peasants, as I shall explain shortly when I turn to peasant rebellions. Such rebellions and even banditry do constitute peasant intervention in aristocratic politics, because they weaken some aristocrats as against others, but mere running away on the part of the peasant hardly does.[11]

The concept of a peasants' strike is as absurd as that of peasants voting in an aristocratic empire, that of a general strike bringing down the aristocracy as absurd as that of universal suffrage as a means of removing an aristocratic government. Peasants rarely refuse to work or even reduce the amount of work they do and they cannot even conceive of engaging in a strike, because if they do not work they do not eat. If the dues they pay to the aristocracy consist of a fixed amount of their product, peasants would merely reduce what is left for their own consumption if they worked less. But even if dues consist of a percentage of their product, they would reduce not only the aristocracy's share but also their own if they worked less. Because peasants are always close to or on the verge of starvation, they cannot afford to do this. Indeed, even if, in order to bring an aristocrat down, all the peasants under his control could strike simultaneously— so that he could not rely on the product of some peasants while others failed to produce—they would all starve to death long before he does.

If the peasant wants to live, he can no more stop working than a woodpecker can stop pecking, for working and eating are inseparable. This is reflected in the peasant's attitude toward work, an attitude as difficult to understand for those of us raised in a modern economy as is the aristocrat's contempt for work and money-making described earlier. To the peasant work is an inseparable aspect of his life; it is not a mere job undertaken to make a living, it is living.

The division, characteristic of industrial societies, of a person's life into his "own" time and that devoted to work would be quite incomprehensible to a peasant. Whereas the modern manual or white-collar worker works only during specified hours of the day—hours specified by some superior authority—the peasant works whenever it is required by the needs of his crops and animals, which means that he may work much more during certain seasons than others or do different types of work in different seasons or even at different times of the day. The modern worker also works only during certain periods of his life, typically between the comple-

---

11. In Russia, in the posttraditional period from the sixteenth to the nineteenth centuries, there were mass flights of peasants to newly settled regions. Blum, *Lord and Peasant in Russia*, pp. 163, 166–67, 552–54, 559. However, although it was "the most common form of their protest . . . , this was not a remedy for most of them, since it usually meant exchanging their old seignior for a new one" (ibid., p. 258). To that extent, some aristocrats did benefit at the expense of others as a result of peasant flight.

tion of his education and his retirement. The peasant, in contrast, works all his life; there is no period set aside for education and there is no retirement, nor is there ever unemployment. He begins working, by performing simple but useful tasks, almost as soon as he can walk, and he continues to work, as well as he can, until he dies.

Just as the peasant's day and his life are not sharply divided into working and nonworking segments, so his life is not split into two such segments in terms of space. Unlike the modern worker, who works in a factory or an office and spends his leisure hours at home and elsewhere, the peasant lives close to his fields and carries on his crafts at home. As a result, there is also not the typical modern division between coworkers and colleagues at work on the one hand and the family and personal friends at home on the other. The peasant's coworkers are his family and, to some extent, his friends.

Work then appears natural to the peasant, and his view of work is part of his view of nature. "There is an assurance that labor is not futile; that nature, or God, has some part in it."[12] As a result, not only the spheres of work and of leisure or play, but also a third sphere kept separate in the lives of modern men, that of religion, is highly integrated with the others in peasant life and thinking. The peasant's work is inseparable from his religion, planting and reaping have religious significance to him, he celebrates fertility rites and harvest festivals, the land and its products partake of the divine, whereas no modern worker thanks the deity for the products of assembly lines or of computers.

Redfield, generalizing from the attitudes of ancient Boeotian, nineteenth-century English and twentieth-century Maya peasants, ascribes to them "an intimate and reverent attitude toward the land; the idea that agricultural work is good and commerce is not so good; and an emphasis on productive industry as a prime virtue. . . . The Maya farmer . . . always treats his maize plant with reverence and the maize field as something of a holy place. . . . For ancient Greek as for recent Maya, nature is man's and god's both; nature is wrought upon, but decent respect attends the work; farming is practical action suffused with religious feeling. . . . In summary, I thought I found in the three peoples I reviewed a sober attitude toward work, a satisfaction in working long and hard in the fields, a disinclination to adventure or to speculate. I thought all this in striking contrast . . . to the view and ideals of such warrior-chieftains as are described in the *Iliad* or the *Mahabharata*."[13]

If work is a virtue and also a task that is simply prescribed by nature and hence by the gods, then one does not work merely because to stop work-

12. Redfield, *Peasant Society and Culture*, p. 132.
13. Ibid., pp. 112–14.

ing or to refuse to work would economically not be feasible or profitable. One goes on working all one's life and generation after generation because to do otherwise is simply not conceivable. The strike, then, both because it is impractical and because peasants cannot even think of it, is not a weapon available to the peasantry. They cannot use it to intervene in aristocratic politics by reducing exploitation, let alone to put an end to the aristocracy by putting an end to exploitation.

Have There Always Been Peasant Revolts?

If peasants cannot reduce or abolish their exploitation by peaceful means, including the strike, and thereby intervene in aristocratic politics, can they do so by the use of force and violence? If they cannot afford to stop working, because if they did they would starve, can they continue to work but refuse to hand over their surplus to the aristocracy, that is, to rebel against exploitation? As I try to answer this question in the following pages, terms such as "revolt," "rebellion," and "uprising" will be used more or less interchangeably. They will merely indicate the collective resort to violence by peasants for political ends, as distinguished from criminal ends, though the distinction is, especially with respect to banditry, often only a matter of point of view.[14] The term "revolution" will be reserved for large-scale peasant revolts aiming at the establishment of a different type of society, notably one more or less free of aristocratic exploitation, whether it be a new order or the restored prearistocratic primitive one.

When the term revolution is associated with a class, as when Marx speaks of bourgeois revolutions or proletarian revolutions, it may also suggest not only—or not so much—that that class makes the revolution as that it benefits from it.[15] A peasant revolution would then be a process by which the peasantry comes to power as a class and establishes a govern-

14. In a book developing generalizations about "social banditry" all over the world and in different periods of history, Eric Hobsbawm says "the point about social bandits is that they are peasant outlaws whom the lord and state regard as criminals, but who remain within peasant society, and are considered by their people as heroes, as champions, avengers, fighters for justice, perhaps even leaders of liberation, and in any case as men to be admired, helped, and supported." Hobsbawm, *Bandits*, p. 13. See also Hobsbawm, "Social Banditry," p. 143.

15. As Barrington Moore remarks: "Such expressions as bourgeois revolution and peasant revolution lump together indiscriminately those who make the revolution and its beneficiaries. Likewise these terms confuse the legal and political results of revolutions with social groups active in them." Moore, *Social Origins of Dictatorship and Democracy*, p. 428.

ment that rules in the interest of that class. I shall not use that definition, for according to it there has rarely if ever been a peasant revolution.

There may be some arguments about the extent to which peasants initiated or organized the war of independence of the three original cantons of Switzerland in 1291 and the extent to which they benefited from its results.[16] Similarly, there is some question whether armed resistance to aristocratic attempts to reduce the considerable independence of the "peasant republic" of Dithmarschen (in Holstein) from the thirteenth through the fifteenth century was a revolution. Even these exceptional cases of armed success leading to peasant independence in small and relatively inaccessible regions occurred in posttraditional Europe. In traditional aristocratic empires, peasants do not win their freedom by means of revolution; if they gain it at all and return to the status of primitive cultivators, it is where an empire collapses or contracts as a result of pressures from nomads or from another aristocratic empire.[17]

The literature on peasant revolts is overwhelmingly concerned with such revolts as responses to modernization, a subject quite different from our interest in peasant revolts in traditional aristocratic empires. However, it sometimes also suggests, more or less explicitly and whether intentionally or not, that the revolts it deals with occurred in traditional aristocratic empires, too.[18]

16. If it was not the petty nobility that was responsible for this victory, this exceptional peasant success may have been partially due to the fact that the mountainous land—in the days before tourism—was not worth much to the aristocracy. Also, the peasants, being as much engaged in hunting and in cattle raising as in agriculture, were, as typified by the mythical William Tell, unusually militant and skilled in the use of weapons. In any case, they maintained their independence in part only by alliances with some aristocrats against others, especially against the Habsburgs, and Switzerland became time and again involved in European aristocratic rivalries. Already by the mid-fourteenth century, the confederation of peasant cantons was joined by urban ones, especially Zürich and Bern, dominated by city patricians. Switzerland was then no longer a peasant republic, and in 1653 there was even a major peasant revolt that was suppressed.

17. With possible minor exceptions like those just mentioned, even peasant revolutions in the period of commercialization all failed—most of them to bring their leaders to power and all of them to produce governments friendly to peasant interests. Of the major modern revolutions that did succeed and in which peasants played a significant role, especially the Russian and Chinese ones, Barrington Moore says: "The peasants have provided the dynamite to bring down the old building. To the subsequent work of reconstruction they have brought nothing; instead they have been—even in France—its first victims" (ibid., p. 480). Eric Wolf also concludes from the examples of the Russian and Chinese Communist revolutions "that while such a revolution may be made with the aid of the peasantry, it is not made for the sake of the peasantry." Wolf, *Peasants*, p. 109.

18. James Scott speaks of "a rich historical record of peasant uprisings from classical antiquity, feudal Europe, and colonial Asia and Africa." Scott, "Peasant Revolution: A Dismal

There are probably two principal reasons for the belief that there have been peasant revolts ever since there have been peasants, that is, exploited agriculturalists. One is simply that it is easy to assume that peasant revolts have always occurred in the past because they have not been an uncommon phenomenon in modern times. And, secondly, it is easy for us, once we become aware of the conditions under which peasants lived in aristocratic empires, to assume that such conditions would drive them to revolt, in part because we think that they would drive us to revolt, in part because peasants do now sometimes revolt against similar conditions. Unfortunately, these arguments do not really prove anything about peasant revolts in aristocratic empires. That peasants may revolt when they come under the impact of modernization does not tell us whether they do or do not revolt when they come under no such impact. And that modern intellectuals think they would revolt if they were treated as peasants were treated in aristocratic empires does not mean that peasants necessarily felt the same way.[19]

Statements in the literature asserting or implying that peasant revolts occurred or were even common in aristocratic empires are typically the result of a failure to distinguish clearly between traditional aristocratic empires and societies subject to some commercialization. Such a distinction may not be needed in the context of a particular work, but it is

---

Science," p. 237. Eric Wolf, referring to precapitalist times, says that "the historical record is replete with peasant rebellions." Wolf, *Peasant Wars of the Twentieth Century*, p. 279. Barrington Moore contrasts "modern" and "earlier" peasant rebellions and as examples of earlier ones lists the German peasant wars and peasant upheavals in Russia and in "traditional China," to which two countries such upheavals were "endemic." Moore, *Social Origins of Dictatorship and Democracy*, pp. 457, 469, and also 208. Theda Skocpol, referring to prerevolutionary France, Russia, and China, writes that, "as in all agrarian states, the potential for peasant . . . revolts was endemic" in these countries and speaks of "this ever-present basic tension in society." Skocpol, *States and Social Revolutions*, p. 48. Gerhard Lenski, in dealing with peasant revolts in "agrarian societies," says that "though these are often forgotten or ignored, a careful reading of the histories of agrarian societies indicates that they were by no means uncommon." Lenski, *Power and Privilege*, p. 274. Eisenstadt, who analyzed some two dozen bureaucratic empires, including some I would regard as traditional, like the Old Kingdom of Egypt, the Carolingian, the Mongol, and the Inca empires, says that peasant "rebellions broke out in all the societies studied," but then modifies this on the next page—possibly significantly from our point of view—to read "uprisings and rebellions . . . were very frequent in most of the societies studied." Eisenstadt, *The Political Systems of Empires*, pp. 208, 209.

19. Reinhard Bendix says: "To us, widespread inequality may suggest unremitting coercion and continuous, latent rebellion. But for many centuries, the vast mass of people acquiesced in the established order out of religious awe, a desire for peace and security, and the inability to unite in a common political action. In those earlier times, the rule of the privileged few appeared to the many as if it were a force of nature." Bendix, *Kings or People*, p. 7.

obviously crucial for us who are here interested specifically only in peasant revolts in traditional aristocratic empires as I have defined them to exclude commercialization or any modernization. Thus, we do not have to deal with peasant revolts in modern Europe, for example, in sixteenth- and seventeenth-century Austria or fifteenth-, sixteenth-, and nineteenth-century Spain, nor do we have to pay attention to peasant revolts involved in modern revolutions in underdeveloped countries, as in Russia in 1905 and 1917–1920, in China, in Mexico, Bolivia, and Cuba, and in Algeria and Vietnam. Such revolts were clearly responses to modernization and may be seen as part of a larger category of revolutions of modernizers, directed against both foreign colonialism and native aristocracies.[20] All these revolts are often cited to demonstrate the frequency and ubiquity of peasant revolts, but they are irrelevant in our search for such revolts in aristocratic empires.

On the other hand, another set of major peasant revolts—those in classical antiquity and especially in medieval Western and Central Europe, tsarist Russia, medieval China, and Japan beginning with the fifteenth century, and also in India—must be considered here. They occurred at points close in time to the period of traditionalism and are sometimes thought to prove that peasants did rise up in major revolts in aristocratic empires and that therefore peasant revolts have occurred throughout history whenever there have been peasants. However, as we examine these major revolts more closely, we shall discover a striking pattern showing that such revolts break out only in the aftermath and presumably as a consequence of commercialization.[21]

Commercialization and the Major Peasant Revolts of Europe and Asia

The best-known agrarian uprisings in classical antiquity were probably the three "servile wars" fought by Rome, the first two involving major slave revolts on the large Sicilian estates (139 or 135–132 and 104 or 103–99 B.C.) and the third one, led by the Thracian gladiator Spartacus, a slave revolt on the Italian mainland (73–71 B.C.).[22] The slaves

20. I have dealt with the role of peasants in revolutions of modernizers in my *The Political Consequences of Modernization*, especially pp. 94–98 and 119–25, and *Patterns of Modernizing Revolutions*.

21. Of course, this does not mean that commercialization is necessarily in every instance followed by peasant revolts.

22. There were also massive revolts of agrarian slaves, sometimes referred to as peasants, in Roman Gaul and Spain between the second and the fifth centuries A.D. Of them E. A.

involved in these revolts, particularly those imported from far away and often soldiers taken prisoner, as most Roman slaves were, were not really peasants.[23] Far from tilling their own soil with their own families, they were laborers organized in large gangs to work on often huge estates.[24] The very fact that Roman warfare was, in part, carried on for the commercial objective of capturing prisoners to be sold as slaves and that Roman landowners invested in large slave contingents to operate their estates shows that Rome had been subject to commercialization and was hence not a traditional aristocratic empire, as I noted in Chapter 2.

A phenomenon similar to the Roman slave wars occurred in southern Iraq a millennium later. Generally, agricultural production in the Islamic empires was carried on by peasants, but here, "the growth of a class of large capitalists and entrepreneurs with considerable liquid capital at their disposal led to the purchase and employment of slaves in large numbers for agricultural use."[25] Herded together in gangs of many thousands in a plantation economy, these foreign, mostly East African, slaves rose in the Zanj insurrection that shook the Abbasid caliphate from 869 to 883. Clearly, this, too, was not a peasant revolt in a traditional aristocratic empire.

It is striking that (with some relatively minor exceptions to be mentioned in the next chapter) the first peasant revolts in Western Europe appear to be what Wolf calls "the revolutionary chiliastic movements of Europe after the eleventh century,"[26] the very same century in which commercialization began in that area, as I stressed in Chapter 2. Subsequently, more clearly defined peasant revolts became more frequent in Western Europe,[27] the most prominent ones being the uprising in Flanders

---

Thompson says: "The slaves certainly did not fight alone. They won allies from other sections of society including the middle classes . . . so that if we refer to these risings as 'peasant' revolts we must recognize that we are using the word 'peasant' only for want of a better term." Thompson, "Peasant Revolts in Late Roman Gaul and Spain," p. 11. Alliances of agrarian rebels with urban supporters are, as I shall note below, typically a posttraditional phenomenon.

23. "The First Sicilian Slave War . . . was sparked off by the presence on the *latifundia* of intelligent Syrians and Cilicians—often free men by birth." Green, "The First Sicilian Slave War," p. 24. "Many of them [were] men of education, some of high birth, . . . and they also had leaders who could organize and . . . plan and, when necessary, impose a measure of discipline." Finley, *A History of Sicily*, p. 138.

24. However, some native Sicilian small peasants, suffering from the plantation economy, may have joined the first Sicilian slave uprising.

25. Lewis, *The Arabs in History*, p. 104.

26. Wolf, *Peasants*, p. 106.

27. Immanuel Wallerstein writes: "That peasant revolts became widespread in western Europe from the thirteenth century to the fifteenth century seems to be in little doubt. . . .

from 1323 to 1328, the French Jacquerie of 1358, and the English peasant revolt of 1381.

The Jacquerie was chiefly a response to peasant misery brought about by the Hundred Years War, but all these revolts were reactions to new economic conditions due to the rise of towns, of trade, and of a money economy, which had changed the relationship between aristocrats and peasants. "They occurred in zones with powerful urban centres, which objectively acted as a ferment on these popular upheavals."[28] In each of them, townspeople played a significant role. Thus, in Flanders, "the stubbornness and length of the rebellion are also partially explicable by the fact that it was excited and supported by the craftsmen of Ypres and Bruges, who made common cause with it and temporarily impressed on the rural class the revolutionary spirit of the towns. The English insurrection of 1381 was also, like that of Western Flanders, the common work of the townspeople and those of the countryside."[29] Even in the Jacquerie, the one fourteenth-century uprising least directly affected by commercialization, there were some links between the peasants and the Third Estate in Paris which was making demands on the king and the aristocracy.

Clearly the major Western European peasant revolts of the fourteenth century are not examples of peasant revolts in traditional aristocratic empires, because Western Europe had been subject to the interrelated changes I call commercialization for about three centuries by the time they broke out. Similarly, the fifteenth-century peasant revolts in Prussia and Poland and especially those in Bohemia involved in the Hussite wars contained "commercial" elements,[30] and that is even more true of the great German Peasant War of 1524–1525.[31]

On the continent, there was a series of peasant rebellions: in northern Italy and then in coastal Flanders at the turn of the fourteenth century; in Denmark in 1340; in Majorca in 1351; the Jacquerie in France in 1358; scattered rebellions in Germany long before the great peasant war of 1525. Peasant republics sprang up in Frisia in the twelfth and thirteenth centuries, and in Switzerland in the thirteenth century." Wallerstein, *The Modern World-System*, p. 24.

28. Anderson, *Passages from Antiquity to Feudalism*, p. 205; see also Pirenne, *Economic and Social History of Medieval Europe*, pp. 189–98.

29. Ibid., p. 196. The Landsbergers say of the English peasant revolt: "As far as we have been able to determine, neither Tyler nor a single one of these many leaders, was himself a peasant. . . . they were artisans . . . [or] priests, chaplains, curates or other men of the church." Landsberger and Landsberger, "The English Peasant Revolt of 1381," p. 123.

30. "Prussia and Bohemia, where towns had traditionally been stronger, were—significantly enough—the only zones in the East which witnessed real peasant uprisings . . . in [the Hussite] armies poor peasants and artisans had marched side by side." Anderson, *Passages from Antiquity to Feudalism*, p. 253; see also ibid., pp. 249–50.

31. Still of interest and relevant here is Karl Kautsky's socioeconomic interpretation of

As to peasant revolts in Russia, Barrington Moore is quite right to call them endemic to that country. Blum says that the peasants "had not accepted the steady deterioration since the fifteenth century in their economic condition and in their personal freedom without resistance. . . . On occasion, they voiced their discontent by resorting to violence. Only a few instances of such activities are known about, though it is entirely possible that there were many more."[32] The earliest one cited by Blum occurred in 1483, and then there were other local ones in the sixteenth century and a major revolt led by Ivan Bolotnikov in 1606–1607. In 1670, Stenka Razin led one of the major Don Cossack and peasant uprisings, and there were hundreds of peasant outbreaks in the following century, including the major ones led by Bulavin in 1707–1708 and by Pugachev in 1773–1775. In the nineteenth century, before the Emancipation of the serfs in 1861, 1,467 peasant uprisings were recorded, many purely local but some involving mass revolts across whole districts.[33]

What is striking for us is that peasant revolts seem to begin in the late fifteenth century in response to a deterioration in the peasants' condition that occurred in the course of that century. This deterioration was linked to the commercialization that began in Russia in the very same century and that, as I noted in Chapter 2, took that empire out of our category of traditional aristocratic empires beginning at that time. The many hundreds of peasant uprisings in Russia in the four centuries before the Emancipation, including the famous ones by Razin and Pugachev, prove again, then, that peasants can respond by revolts to pressures on them unleashed by commercialization; they do not prove that peasants do or do not revolt in traditional aristocratic empires.

China is often, as by Moore and Eisenstadt, named as the principal example of a society that gave rise to peasant rebellions.[34] And these were, indeed, frequent there; Eberhard says they occurred "almost every year," though he adds that "rarely had they any real success."[35] What is

---

1895 of communistic religious movements in the Middle Ages and the Reformation, including the peasant wars in England, Bohemia, and Germany. See Kautsky, *Vorläufer des neueren Sozialismus*, especially 1:298–310, 316–25, and 2:66–74. Only parts of this work have been translated into English, including the sections on Bohemia and the German Peasant War. Kautsky, *Communism in Central Europe in the Time of the Reformation*, pp. 35–44 and 121–29.

32. Blum, *Lord and Peasant in Russia*, p. 258.

33. Ibid., pp. 167–68, 554–60.

34. Moore, *Social Origins of Dictatorship and Democracy*, pp. 208, 468; Eisenstadt, *The Political Systems of Empires*, p. 208.

35. Eberhard, *Conquerors and Rulers*, p. 89. Earlier, Eberhard had compiled a detailed listing of all rebellions (a total of about 120) under one of the Wei dynasties in Northern China,

more, peasant rebellions in China are not a recent phenomenon or even a relatively recent one compared to those I mentioned in Western and Central Europe and in Russia. Even if we exclude not only the T'ai P'ing Rebellion (1850–1864) and the Boxer Rebellion (1900–1903) but the entire past millennium of Chinese history (from the Sung on) as no longer traditional, we still find plenty of peasant rebellions for more than a millennium before the Sung dynasty. Some occurred as early as 209 B.C., and then there were the two major religious peasant revolts of the Han period, that of the Red Eyebrows (A.D. 18) and that of the Yellow Turbans (A.D. 184).[36]

However, as indicated in Chapter 2, China underwent a significant degree of commercialization about the third century B.C. Passages from two recent histories of China will show how that change affected the peasants whose revolts were a response to it: "Once the old Chou feudal patterns had been abandoned in favor of freehold farming and the unfettered sale and purchase of land on the open market, the small peasant class quickly fell into trouble." "Feudal serfdom gave way to freehold farming. The transition was completed in the Ch'in unification of China. . . . The change produced a classic land-tenure problem. . . . In a society of freehold farmers, some prosper and some do not. The prosperous become landlords, the luckless become tenants, and all sorts of inequities and exploitive situations arise, provoking discontent and rebellion."[37] "In the old Chou days a village paid a single annual tax, but when the Ch'in dynasty freed the land, two burdens were placed on it—the tax paid to the state and the rent paid to the landlord. Because of excessive irregular taxation, the freeholders, unable to pay their taxes, would get into debt and the powerful

---

beginning in 397 and ending in 547, excluding intraaristocratic conflicts but including some tribal uprisings of Huns. Eberhard, *Das Toba-Reich Nordchinas*, pp. 240–64. He says that similar listings of similar numbers of rebellions could be made for other periods of Chinese history. "The image of a united, peaceful China is a figment of the imagination. There are always struggles, most of them so-called agrarian struggles of the peasants, always for the same reasons" (ibid., p. 263).

36. Convenient brief "Sketches of Major Chinese Peasant Rebellions" from the first one in 209 B.C. to the Boxer Rebellion are presented in an appendix to Harrison, *The Communists and Chinese Peasant Rebellions*, pp. 227–304. Eberhard presents a "model" of typical Chinese peasant revolts developing—if they do not fail at any one of their stages—out of village youth gangs that turn to "banditry" in bad times and, driven into the mountains, fight and merge with other gangs to form armies that may conquer cities. Here the gentry joins them, the gang leader becomes dependent on the gentry for advice and trained personnel, and he becomes an aristocrat himself. Eberhard, *Conquerors and Rulers*, pp. 99–105. Typically, these revolts fail, though in three instances the gang leaders—not necessarily peasants themselves—became emperors for more than a short period and founded, respectively, the Han dynasty (206 B.C.–A.D. 220), the Later Liang dynasty (A.D. 907–923), and the Ming dynasty (1368–1644) (ibid., p. 89).

37. Hucker, *China's Imperial Past*, pp. 181, 64.

landlords would buy them out. They would become tenants paying a substantial rent. As the number of freeholders decreased and the mass of tenants began to live precariously, it took only slight economic shifts to cause vastly depressed conditions throughout the countryside."[38] It appears, then, that even though peasant rebellions began to occur in China long before they did in Europe, they started to break out, as they did in Europe, only after the beginnings of commercialization.

In Japan, too, this pattern prevails. Peasant revolts occurred from the fifteenth century on—the first major one broke out in 1428—that is, within a century of the beginnings of commercialization as I mentioned them in Chapter 2. These risings were in good part those of indebted peasants against moneylenders and other creditors,[39] itself an indication of the peasants' involvement in a commercial money economy. Also, in some cases revolting peasants "were in touch with townspeople . . . and on at least one occasion they were joined by city workers."[40]

38. Harrison, *The Chinese Empire*, p. 148. Three excerpts from contemporary Chinese writers (quoted in Balazs, *Chinese Civilization and Bureaucracy*, pp. 118–19 and 121) vividly illustrate the plight of the peasant under the T'ang (618–907) and the Sung (960–1279) dynasties. "When the peasant is ruined, he has to sell his field and his hut. If it happens to be a good year, he may just be able to pay his debts. But no sooner has the harvest been brought in than the grain bins are empty again, and, contract in hand and sack on back, he has to go off and start borrowing again. He has heavier and heavier interest to pay, and soon has not got enough to eat. If there is a famine, he falls into utter ruin. Families disperse, parents separate, they seek to become slaves, and no one will buy them. . . . The rich seize several times ten thousand *mou* of land, the poor have no land left, and attach themselves to the big powerful families and become their private retainers. They borrow seed and food and lease land as tenants. All the year round they work themselves to death without a day's rest, and when they have paid all their debts they live in constant anxiety whether they will be able to make both ends meet. The large landowners, however, live on the rents from their land, and are trouble-free and carefree. Wealth and poverty are clearly separated" (from Lu Chih, 754–824). "Those who till the fields do not own them, and those who own the fields do not till them. . . . The men at work are urged on with whip and cudgel, and the master treats them like slaves. He, on the other hand, sits at his ease and sees that his orders are carried out. . . . Of the produce of the fields, he takes half, although there is but one owner and ten laborers. Hence the owner, his half daily accumulating, attains wealth and power, while the laborer, his half merely providing his daily fare, falls into poverty and starvation" (from Su Hsün, 1009–1066). The peasant "is exposed to periodic catastrophes such as floods, droughts, frost, hail, locusts and other insects. If the harvest happens to be good, public and private debts [to the tax collectors and the usurers] use it up between them. Grain and silk have ceased to belong to him before they have even left the threshing floor or been removed from the loom. He eats the husk, wears coarse cloth, and remains neither nourished nor clothed" (from Ssu-ma Kuang, 1019–1086). That some Chinese writers could see the condition of the peasantry critically is itself a symptom of commercialization.

39. Sansom, *A History of Japan*, 2:207–9.

40. Ibid., p. 209.

More specifically, the early major peasant revolts in Japan took place in the two provinces of Yamashiro and Yamato. There, in the half-century beginning in 1428, "agrarian unrest had manifested itself in the form of peasant uprisings of such size, organization, and frequency that they must be regarded as part of a distinct and significant social movement." Varley says that: "In many ways the most significant factor that must be discussed in regard to agrarian distress in Yamashiro and Yamato is the high degree of commercial development that was characteristic of these provinces." Heavily taxed and suffering from price fluctuations, peasants had to turn for loans to a new class of affluent moneylenders, mortgaging and often losing their land to them. Thus, virtually every uprising in this period "had as sole, or at least partial, aim destruction of the pawnshops and demands for cancellation of debts."[41]

Finally, a word about India, where Barrington Moore mentions peasant revolts under the Mogul empire. These were generally led by local aristocrats resisting the Mogul bureaucracy[42] and were hence not antiaristocratic movements but rather manifestations of intraaristocratic conflict.[43] Habib provides some details on these revolts[44] and generalizes about them as follows: "The fact that either the peasant rebellions, at some stage of their development, passed under the leadership of *zamindars* (or their own leaders became *zamindars*), or, from the very beginning, the desperation of the peasants provided recruits for rebelling *zamindars*, seems to have been of decisive significance in merging the risings of the oppressed with the war between two oppressing classes." "The *zamindars'* leadership was not established over all the peasant risings; nor is there any reason to believe that all rebellious actions by *zamindars* were supported by the

41. Varley, *The Onin War*, pp. 191–94.

42. Moore, *Social Origins of Dictatorship and Democracy*, pp. 326, 329.

43. According to James Bill, in Iran under the Abbasid caliphate, "the Mazyar rebellion in the middle of the ninth century was a full-scale revolution of the peasant class against the Iranian large landowners and the Arab governors of the area." Bill, *The Politics of Iran*, p. 5. However, Mazyar was a local king who was engaged in complex conflicts with other aristocrats. "When he found that the Islamized land-owners of the Caspian were hostile to him, he came more and more to rely on the peasants and to voice their discontents." Roy Mottahedeh, "The Abbasid Caliphate in Iran," p. 76. He "encouraged the native peasants to revolt against their landlords." W. Madelung, "The Minor Dynasties of Northern Iran," p. 205. It was a matter, then, of "supplanting the ancient landed class with a new one, which, however, was not necessarily amenable to . . . egalitarian slogans." B. S. Amoretti, "Sects and Heresies," p. 508. As to the peasants' ideology, it is said to have "aimed at and succeeded in exerting on the central government and the big landowners such pressure as to bring about a changing of the guard within the ruling class, without any actual substitution of classes or any real social innovation . . . amounting to no more than a mere change in traditional authority" (ibid).

44. Habib, *The Agrarian System of Mughal India*, pp. 330–51.

peasants. But the fact remains that the most successful revolts, e.g., those of the Marathas and the Jats, were led by men, who were, or aspired to be, *zamindars*."[45] A recent historian of India writing of the Mogul empire also mentions that "the intolerable increases in revenue demands drove more and more *zamindars* as well as peasants to risk death from rebellion" and that "the harshness of . . . demands led peasants in many parts of the empire to flee from their Mughal villages and rally their support behind regional *zamindars*, Jat, Maratha, Sikh, and Rajput."[46]

In any case, the late Mogul empire was, as noted in Chapter 2, no longer a traditional aristocratic one. By the seventeenth century when the peasant revolts mentioned by Moore became frequent, it had become usual "to demand the revenue from the peasant before the harvest, when he would have absolutely nothing left. The practice was . . . the mark of a well developed money economy, for it would have been impossible to attempt it unless the officials expected that the peasants would pay up by pledging their crops beforehand to grain-merchants or money-lenders."[47] Thus, in the Mogul empire, too, peasant rebellion was linked to commercialization.

Peasant Revolts as a Consequence of Commercialization

Our quick review of the history of peasant rebellions indicates that such rebellions begin to occur in the early stages of commercialization. If this relationship, well known for individual peasant rebellions, has not been stressed as a generalization,[48] it is because few scholars

45. Ibid., pp. 333, 338.
46. Wolpert, *A New History of India*, p. 159.
47. Habib, *The Agrarian System of Mughal India*, p. 242.
48. Both Scott and Tilly have briefly generalized about modern peasant revolts. Scott says: "The development of capitalism, the commercialization of agrarian relations, and the growth of a centralizing state represent the historical locus of peasant revolts in the modern era. For, above all, these large historical forces cut through the integument of subsistence customs and traditional social relations to replace them with contracts, the market, and uniform laws." Scott, *The Moral Economy of the Peasant*, p. 189. And Charles Tilly, whose work on revolutions has been concerned almost exclusively with modern European history, has written: "The rural rebellion traced the rise of national states, markets, and bourgeois property." *The Vendée*, p. vii. For his treatment of the effects of "state making," urbanization and industrialization, commercialization and capitalism in post-1500 Europe, see Tilly, "Rural Collective Action in Modern Europe." Landsberger comes even closer to our generalization. Looking for explanations of peasant uprisings—but not, like me, of their beginnings in history—he says: "One is tempted to find a single, universally present ultimate cause, but unfortunately, this would seem to be mistaken. The economic integration of the society under consideration into a larger, possibly international, market; the consequent

have compared peasant revolts throughout the world and across time. And apparently none has distinguished, as I do, between traditional aristocratic empires and societies undergoing commercialization. Both are usually classed together as "early" or "traditional" or "agrarian" in contrast to much more recent modernity.

That peasant revolts seem to break out within a century or two of the transition from traditional aristocratic empire to commercialization is obviously no mere coincidence. The interrelated growth of agricultural production, of trade, of a money and a market economy, of towns, and of populations has a deeply upsetting effect on peasants.[49] Of course, various elements of commercialization may occur at different times and at different rates of change and each may affect different regions and different villages at different times—or not at all. Hence, peasant response to commercialization in the form of revolts may occur quite quickly or only after long delays or not at all. However, the following is likely to happen if and when peasants become involved in commerce to any substantial degree.

As peasants produce more and as, with growing trade, more luxury goods and services become available to the aristocrat, he will demand increased payments from his peasants in order to pay for these goods and services. Before commercialization, the amount to be paid by the peasants was well established by custom, but now even payments in kind are likely to be raised. If anything, this is even more true of cash payments, and, as peasants produce a surplus they can sell to the towns, they do more and more pay their taxes, rent, or dues to the aristocrat in cash. In addition to greater payments, the aristocrat may also demand more labor time from his peasants on his own land in order to increase production so that he can sell

---

drive to commercialise agriculture; and the subsequent encroachment on peasant lands and peasant rights and status in general: this sequence is certainly the most promising candidate for the position of 'universal ultimate cause.'" But he argues that the commercialization of agriculture—a narrower concept than my commercialization of aristocratic empires, but an important aspect of the latter—is not a sufficient cause of peasant uprisings. Leaning on Moore's thesis referred to on p. 113, n. 29, above, he would add a purely exploitative aristocracy that renders no services to the peasantry as one of several other possible causes. Nor does Landsberger consider the commercialization of agriculture as "even a truly necessary" cause of peasant revolts and he points to many such revolts that occurred long after commercialization. Landsberger, "Peasant Unrest: Themes and Variations," pp. 29–31. I, of course, argue only that the earliest peasant revolts in a society are likely to follow the beginnings of its commercialization, which does not preclude the occurrence of later peasant revolts once the society has been commercialized.

49. I am not here concerned with the somewhat similar impact of industrial-colonial modernization on peasants but have dealt with it in my writings cited above. On the effects of the colonial economy on peasants, see Scott, *The Moral Economy of the Peasant*, especially chaps. 3 and 4, and Table 4 on p. 66. For a review article on this and related works and some of the issues raised in them, see Robert H. Bates, "People in Villages."

more on the market and thus increase his income. Finally, as bureaucracies grow and the costs of war increase with commercialization, taxes, too, go up, whether they are collected directly from the peasant or indirectly through the lower aristocracy.[50]

While demands on him grow, the peasant is perhaps even more reluctant than he was before commercialization to part with his cash, his product, or his labor time, because he, too, could use them to improve his life. Referring to thirteenth-century England, R. H. Hilton writes: "The poor and the middling peasants, whose agriculture was only above subsistence level in so far as they had to sell their produce in order to pay their rent, resisted increased demands because they pressed on their already low standard of living. The richer peasants, accumulating both movable and landed property, struck against all aspects of seigneurial control because at every point they found their road to economic expansion blocked by the innumerable devices whose object it was to transfer as much as possible of the surplus from the holding to the lord in the form of rent, by hindering any movement and any progress which might take the peasant or his property out of the ken of the lord."[51] Whether they are materially better off as a result of

50. Engels, speaking of Germany at the beginning of the sixteenth century, deals at some length with this growing need for money on the part both of the princes then rising to a status of near sovereignty and of the lower nobility or knighthood declining as a result of changes in the technology of warfare and, among other things, says this: "The need of the princes for money grew with the taste for luxuries, with the increase of the courts and the standing armies, with the mounting costs of administration. The taxes were becoming more and more oppressive. . . . The dire need of the knighthood for money added considerably to their ruin. The luxurious life in the castles, the competition in magnificence at tournaments and feasts, the price of armaments and of horses all increased with the progress of civilisation, whereas the sources in income of the knights and barons, increased but little, if at all. Feuds with accompanying plunders and incendiarism, lying in ambush, and similar noble occupations, became in the course of time too dangerous. . . . In order to satisfy mounting requirements, the noble masters resorted to the same means as were practised by the princes; the peasantry was being robbed by the masters with greater dexterity every year. The serfs were being wrung dry. The bondsmen were burdened with ever new payments of various descriptions upon every possible occasion. Serf labour, dues, ground rents, land sale taxes, death taxes, protection moneys and so on, were increased at will in spite of old agreements. Justice was denied or sold for money, and wherever the knight could not obtain the peasant's money otherwise, he threw him into the tower without much ado, and compelled him to pay ransom." Engels, "The Peasant War in Germany," pp. 22–24.

51. Hilton, "Peasant Movements in England Before 1381," p. 122. The Landsbergers write with reference to the English peasant revolt of 1381: "Because of steady increases in production and commerce during the fourteenth century, 'all workers for a half-century or more had seen a betterment of their conditions and had become jealous of their well-being. Villeins, free peasants, artisans, merchants all wanted to acquire more comfort and material luxuries or at least safeguard the advances they had obtained.'" Landsberger and Landsberger, "The English Peasant Revolt of 1381," p. 127. The quotation within this quotation

their involvement in a money economy and whether they increase their production of cash crops voluntarily or under compulsion, peasants are under greater pressure than before. There is growing tension between peasants and aristocrats, and a relationship formerly well established is now changing. Peasant rebellions are one response to this change.

To all this must be added the effects of the alienability of land, as we just noted them in the case of China. In a money economy, the peasant may well fall into debt, partly because the taxes and dues he owes to the aristocracy are easily increased, partly because of the cyclical nature of agriculture that permits the peasant to sell his product only once or twice a year, while he still needs to buy things and therefore requires money all year. If land can be bought and sold, the peasant may have to sell it to obtain cash or he may mortgage it to obtain a loan and if, as is common, he cannot repay his debt, he will lose his land. Thus, landless peasants may develop, dependent on and exploited by those who acquired their land, be they a few more fortunate peasants in the village or merchants or money-lenders in the town who become absentee landlords. Obviously, this consequence of commercialization, too, is deeply upsetting to peasants formerly engaged in subsistence agriculture on their own land.

Finally, the peasants' resistance to these new and to them therefore unjustified burdens is reinforced or even stimulated by their new contacts with the towns. Here merchants and artisans, often organized in guilds, have now grown sufficiently strong to demand and to gain a certain measure of independence from the aristocracy (and thus to put an end to traditional aristocratic empires). To be sure, once they succeed, especially the wealthier merchants may become conservative, and in some cases, notably in Russia and Japan, some merchants were themselves aristocrats. Still, antiaristocratic townspeople, especially artisans, may give rebellious peasants support or even leadership, as appears to have been typically the case with peasant revolts following commercialization.

It must be emphasized that revolt is only an exceptional response by peasants to all these changes brought by commercialization. Not only are many peasants unaffected or only slightly affected by them, but the elements in traditional peasant life that keep peasants from revolting—to be discussed in the next chapter—are too powerful to be easily overcome. Peasant revolts remain relatively rare, then, even in commercialized societies. Lenski, who is inclined to stress the frequency of such revolts says: "Though the number of risings was impressive, the number of peasants

is from Charles Petit-Dutaillis, "Introduction historique," in André Reville and Charles Petit-Dutaillis, *Le soulèvement des travailleurs d'Angleterre en 1381* (Paris, 1898), p. xlviii.

involved was usually not. For the most part, these risings were local affairs involving at most a few hundred or a few thousand individuals. Thus, it would be a mistake to suppose that the peasantry was in a constant state of revolt. Nothing could be further from the truth."[52] Even if, as Eberhard says, there were peasant rebellions almost every year in China, evidently the empire with the greatest number of such rebellions, only a tiny fraction of all the many millions of Chinese peasants in the more than two millennia since the end of the feudal Chou period could have been involved in them.

52. Lenski, *Power and Privilege*, p. 274.

13

Obstacles to Peasant Revolts in Aristocratic Empires

The Rarity of Peasant Revolts

Whatever may have caused peasant revolts in the early stages of commercialization, their existence cannot prove that peasant revolts also occurred in traditional aristocratic empires. If even postcommercialization peasant rebellions were quite rare and if the factors responsible for them, like the development of a money and market economy, the alienability of land, and contact of peasants with urban rebels, did not exist in aristocratic empires, would we, then, be safe to conclude that there were no peasant rebellions in aristocratic empires?[1] I think not, for it seems unimaginable that nowhere and at no time in any aristocratic empire did the peasants of a single village forcibly resist or even kill a tax collector or burn down the residence of the local aristocrat and then try to fight off the nearly inevitable punitive reaction of the aristocracy.

For reasons still to be discussed, it seems probable, however, that peasant revolts were even less common and even more localized in traditional aristocratic empires than in societies being commercialized. On the other hand, there were undoubtedly more of them than we know of. The peasants themselves, being illiterate, left no written records, and aristocratic contemporary documents and observers very rarely referred to peasant revolts. If even modern historians can write books on aristocratic empires that barely mention peasants, they could be ignored even more easily by the historians and poets of those empires who lived in and depicted the world of the aristocracy, a world far apart from that of the peasants. The

---

1. It is striking that five authors cited on pp. 279–80, n. 18, above, who wish to show that peasant revolts were common in agrarian societies and who refer to numerous examples of such revolts (a sixth one cited does not), do not mention a single one in what I would regard as a traditional aristocratic empire—but this does not prove their absence in such empires.

doings of that contemptible, dirty rabble were of no interest to them, its occasional acts of resistance to heavy exactions or forced labor presented no serious problems even to the few aristocrats directly affected by them, nor could aristocrats gain much glory worth extolling by putting down peasant revolts. However, aristocratic chroniclers may also have failed to report peasant revolts simply because they were rare and localized and hence unknown to most aristocrats.[2]

That peasant revolts in traditional aristocratic empires were rare seems confirmed by the fact that so few are mentioned even in the literature specifically devoted to peasant revolts. That literature on Western and Eastern Europe, on China and Japan, concentrates almost exclusively on revolts in and after the period of commercialization. However, Rodney Hilton, in a specialized work on medieval peasant movements in Western Europe, takes on the task of surveying "the whole of the medieval period to see what evidence there is of conflicts inherent in peasant society." Hilton divides the Middle Ages into three phases: "The first phase is that of the feudalization of Western European society, roughly between the sixth and the tenth centuries."[3] This is precisely the period in which we are interested, when Western Europe was traditional, between the periods of Roman commercialism and the later medieval commercialization beginning in the eleventh century. Hilton describes this period as follows, stressing the absence of those factors that, in commercial periods, seem to be responsible for peasant revolts: "In this phase, the agrarian economy was producing very little surplus beyond that necessary to support the power, and rather primitive status distinction, of the landed aristocracy. Production for the market was low, rents tended to be in labour or in kind, there was little money in circulation and, since upper-class incomes were in produce rather than in cash, there was little effective demand for the luxury commodities of international trade. The urban element in western European life was, therefore, necessarily small. Lords and peasants constituted the overwhelming majority of the population."[4]

In a careful chapter on "Early Movements and Their Problems," Hilton then provides much evidence of a conflict of interest between peasants in medieval villages and aristocrats over such issues as levels of rent and labor services, access to common rights and rights to village self-administration, most of it, however, from the period after the tenth century when Western Europe was no longer traditional. In the entire chapter, there are only two

2. While the absence of evidence of peasant revolts in aristocratic empires does not necessarily prove that there were no such revolts, we must be careful not to conclude from that absence of evidence that there must have been peasant revolts.

3. Hilton, *Bond Men Made Free*, pp. 13, 14.

4. Ibid., p. 15.

references to peasant revolts before the eleventh century. One says that "as early as 643, an edict of the Lombard King, Rothari, refers to conspiracies of slaves (or serfs) under the leadership of freemen leading to attacks on landlords' property." The other one is to a relatively big uprising that occurred at the very end of the traditional period in Western Europe, "the peasants' war in Normandy in 996, at the beginning of Duke Richard II's reign. . . . The peasants' movement was highly organized, and involved the election of delegates from regional gatherings to a general assembly. These moves were then suppressed by the duke's uncle, Raoul, Count of Evreux, with the utmost ferocity."[5] In a later article, Hilton also writes that "conspiracies . . . of serfs in Flanders and elsewhere are mentioned in an imperial capitulary of 821, and the serf owners are instructed to suppress them."[6]

It is noteworthy that the three regions in which the early peasant revolts by Hilton took place were all commercialized before Western Europe generally underwent that process. Whether this occurred in Flanders by the early ninth century and in Lombardy as early as the mid-seventh century is not clear. However, it could be argued that there was both in Flanders and in northern Italy no such clearly traditional period as intervened in most of Western Europe between the commercialized periods of the Roman empire and of the late Middle Ages. In Flanders, wool manufacture had been perfected under Roman rule but did not come to an end with it. "The Franks, who invaded the region in the fifth century, continued the tradition of their predecessors. Until the coming of the Northmen in the ninth century, Frisian boatmen regularly carried cloth woven in Flanders."[7] As to Lombardy, it remained linked by trade to Byzantium when the Western Roman empire disintegrated, the Po served as an avenue of inland trade, and Pavia, the Lombard capital, was a great market place.

5. Ibid., pp. 65, 70–71.

6. Hilton, "Peasant Society, Peasant Movements and Feudalism in Medieval Europe," pp. 74–75. See also Bloch, *French Rural History*, p. 169. A French medievalist, writing more than half a century ago, refers, without giving further details, to "peasant revolts which broke out on all sides in Italy, Gaul, Frisia, Flanders, Saxony, at irregular intervals during the eighth and ninth centuries" and, evidently, to later ones in "Saxony, Frisia, and Holland, the revolts of 1095 in the Low Countries and France, and of 1008 in Brittany" and also to the rising in Normandy just mentioned. Boissonade, *Life and Work in Medieval Europe*, pp. 101, 148. Similarly, Dopsch, a contemporary of Boissonade, writes that "even in pre-Carolingian times there was no lack of . . . peasant rebellions. I need only mention the revolts of the people in the territory of Limoges in 579, when they were oppressed by heavy taxation." Dopsch, *Economic and Social Foundations of European Civilization*, p. 237. However, Hilton argues that the medieval report referring to this incident "indicates little more than general rural discontent." Hilton, "Peasant Society, Peasant Movements and Feudalism in Medieval Europe," p. 74.

7. Pirenne, *Economic and Social History of Medieval Europe*, pp. 35–36.

Hilton points out that "no more need be said about the precocity of northern Italy as far as the development of trade is concerned, than that even in the eighth century there existed a Po valley trade in which agricultural produce was exchanged, first for Venetian salt, then for goods of eastern provenance that came through Byzantium."[8]

In the case of Normandy at the turn of the eleventh century, a better case can probably be made for a link between the peasant revolt and commercialization. Referring to the pre-1066 period, one historian writes: "The financial system, with its payments in money instead of in kind, was the most characteristic feature of Norman administration. . . . This familiarity with hard cash, this knowledge of bookkeeping. . . . may go back to the commercial precocity of the Scandinavian traders. . . . It probably was assisted by the trade for the pursuit of which the towns of Normandy were so conveniently situated. As always, it fed on itself and increased as its creatures increased. It accounts very largely for the early disappearance of serfdom in Normandy, of serfdom, that is, which means arbitrary labour service and dues in kind, for in Normandy . . . there must have been some connection between trade and a free peasantry."[9]

It appears, then, that careful research can confirm the occurrence of only three peasant revolts in pre-eleventh-century Western Europe. Even if we assume that these took place in still entirely precommercial conditions, which is actually doubtful, and even if there were several more revolts of which we know nothing, this would indicate that, scattered over half a continent and half a millennium, peasant revolts in traditional aristocratic Western Europe were rare, indeed.[10]

Peaceableness, Unorganizability, and Lack of Leadership

Why are peasant revolts so rare in aristocratic empires? It is generally easier to explain why something happened—like peasant revolts under the impact of commercialization or modernization—than why

8. Hilton, *Bond Men Made Free*, p. 75.

9. Powicke, *The Loss of Normandy*, p. 48. On the Norman peasant revolt, see also the Earl of Onslow, *The Dukes of Normandy and their Origin*, pp. 95–96.

10. For a fascinating interpretation, based on Old Testament sources and especially the "Amarna Letters," of the origins of ancient Israel in a protracted peasant revolt in the Palestinian hill country against the local Canaanite kings who were satellites of the Egyptian empire, see Chaney, "Ancient Palestinian Peasant Movements and the Formation of Premonarchic Israel." See Gottwald, *The Tribes of Yahweh*, particularly pp. 210–19, 389–400, 584–87, 884–86, for what appears to be the definitive treatment of "the theory that Israel was in fact composed in considerable part of native Canaanites who revolted against their

something failed to happen—like frequent peasant revolts in aristocratic empires. To explain why something did not happen may suggest that it really ought to have happened, that it could reasonably have been expected to have happened and merely failed to for some peculiar reasons. That is not what is being suggested here; on the contrary, my point is that the rarity of peasant revolts in aristocratic empires is deeply rooted in the nature of peasant societies and in their position in such empires. Thus, a brief discussion of the causes of this rarity merely serves to highlight the relevant factors in peasant institutions and ideology.

The peasant's very way of life and work and the close interconnection between the two predispose him to be peaceable. Redfield notes that peasant upbringing stresses "hard work rather than a disposition to take risks and to perform personal exploits." He finds among peasants "a distaste for violence, a disfavor of prowess in any form of conspicuous aggressiveness."[11] To the aristocrat, risk taking and personal exploits, warlike (and also amorous) adventures are opportunities to prove his manliness and his worth, to maintain his honor and gain glory. Violence is a normal and, indeed, desirable aspect of life growing out of the aristocrat's position in his society. The peasant, on the other hand, who spends his time in adventures and exploits, proves not his worth, but his worthlessness, for worth is measured by one's proper function in society, and the peasant's function is to work. Violence, therefore, is to him a nuisance or a disaster. He has nothing to gain and everything to lose from it. "The tyranny of work weighs heavily upon a peasant: his life is geared to an annual routine and to planning for the year to come. Momentary alterations of routine threaten his ability to pick up the routine later."[12] Both because the peasant is tightly bound by traditions, often in the form of religious rules, and because, as Scott argues persuasively, living on the verge of starvation, he cannot afford to take risks and to gamble,[13] the peasant is averse to altering his routine—and rising in revolt would involve a major alteration.

Because of the peasant's intense involvement in his work, he is not only ideologically ill prepared for violent behavior, but he does not have the time, the interest, or the means to acquire military training and experience or weapons and equipment. In all these respects, he differs sharply from

---

overlords and joined forces with a nuclear group of invaders and/or infiltrators from the desert" (ibid., p. 210), and that "Israel is most appropriately conceived as an eclectic composite in which various underclass and outlaw elements of society joined their diffused antifeudal experiences, sentiments, and interests, thereby forming a single movement that, through trial and error, became an effective autonomous social system" (ibid., p. 491).

11. Redfield, *Peasant Society and Culture*, pp. 123, 127.

12. Wolf, *Peasant Wars of the Twentieth Century*, p. 289.

13. Scott, *The Moral Economy of the Peasant*.

the aristocrat who is, from childhood on, being prepared and trained for warfare, both ideologically and physically, and who can fight on horseback or in a chariot, well armored and well armed. The point here is not so much that the peasant is militarily inferior to the aristocrat, which matters only in the rare instances when they do clash violently, but that resort to organized violence is not likely even to occur to the peasant, because it is alien to his way of life. That much may be true even of the relatively exceptional peasants who, having served in the armies of aristocrats—and not having become professional soldiers—did acquire some experience and training in warfare and the use of weapons.

While the aristocracy as a warrior class has tremendous military superiority over the peasantry, its administrative and tax-collecting apparatus is often quite weak. Peasants may therefore not resort to violence not only because such action seems both hopeless and alien to them, but also because peaceable means of passive resistance—hiding part of their crops from the tax collector, lying to him about it, or even fleeing into the hills or the forest—are available and relatively more effective.

Many peasants are persistently undernourished and suffer from various diseases. What matters here is, again, not so much the fact that peasants are, therefore, man for man, likely to be physically weaker than aristocrats but that their condition tends to induce passivity in them. As Charles Tilly says: "Really miserable people devote so much of their energy to survival that they have none left for revolt."[14]

To be at all effective, a peasant revolt must encompass more than a single village or even a few villages.[15] Given the military superiority of aristocrats and their mobility, they can easily concentrate their forces and destroy one village or a few of them. Also, if they control a relatively large territory with many villages, they can well afford to destroy a few villages and their peasants and to accept the resultant economic loss. Only a peasant revolt spread over a fairly large area can pose both a military and an

---

14. Tilly, *The Vendée*, p. xiii. Scott, *The Moral Economy of the Peasant*, p. 191, refers to this view as "a naive notion" and says that "the onset of hunger in most societies . . . leads not to listlessness but rather to rage." However, the effects of such new starvation are likely to be quite different from those of chronic undernourishment persisting through generations. An expert in the fields of nutrition and pediatrics summarizes recent research to state that malnutrition early in life results in retardation and abnormalities in brain development and, when combined with environmental deprivation, produces behavioral changes. Winick, "Nutrition and Brain Development."

15. Lenski, *Power and Privilege*, p. 206, cites works on villages in fourteenth-century Western Europe and England, nineteenth-century Russia, and twentieth-century India and Thailand indicating that their average population ranged from 150 to 500 people, therefore including about 30 to 100 able-bodied adult males. It must be assumed that in aristocratic empires the typical village was even smaller.

economic threat to aristocrats. Such a revolt would require a degree of organization and communication beyond the individual village level that is typically quite unattainable in aristocratic empires. The peasants in one village hardly know of the existence of villages far beyond the neighboring ones and cannot conceive of collaborating with the peasants there. Beyond their own village, peasants in aristocratic empires are quite unorganized and unorganizable.

Thus, whereas to us a conflict between peasants and aristocrats may look like one between a huge majority and a tiny minority, that is not the way it can appear to the peasant. To him it would be a contest between the few dozen able-bodied members of his village on one side and, on the other, the aristocrats with their retinue who, although they may be somewhat fewer in number than the villagers, are much better trained, armed, and equipped for warfare. That such contests are extremely uneven accounts, of course, for the fact that what local peasant rebellions there may be are invariably crushed and cruelly avenged.[16] But, more important here, it also helps explain why there are so few peasant rebellions. The peasants cannot imagine a large-scale rebellion and they sense that a local one is utterly hopeless and hence do not normally even contemplate one.

Peasant localism and parochialism, which is responsible for this situation and for keeping peasants from functioning as a class or as a majority, may be worth further discussion, for it is utterly unfamiliar to us in modern industrial societies. However, it also differs sharply from the aristocrats'

16. Probably not only to set an example to any other potential rebels, but because they are outraged that their lowly subjects should have risen against them and thus against what they regard as the divinely and naturally ordained order, aristocrats typically, after reimposing their control, visit ferocious repression on the rebels and cruel punishment on their leaders. This was certainly true of rebellions in periods of commercialization from that of Spartacus in 71 b.c., the six thousand survivors of whose army were crucified along the Appian Way, through the great peasant revolts in Flanders, France, England, and Germany mentioned above, to those of Stenka Razin who in 1671 was tortured and quartered alive, and of Pugachev who was executed and in whose rebellious villages the gallows did not come down for months. It can be assumed that aristocrats acted quite similarly in traditional aristocratic empires, which we know to be true in the case of the sizable peasant rebellions in Normandy about a.d. 1000. Writing of peasant revolts in Western Europe at a somewhat later point, William Stearns Davis says: "Such revolts always have a single end. The ignorant peasants submit to no discipline. They cannot use the knight's weapons if they capture them. They cannot organize. If they seize a castle, the liquor in the cellars lays them out helpless through a week of orgy. The seigneurs instantly rally and with their great horses hunt down the rebels as creatures worse than wolves. The vengeance then taken on the insurgents is such that every ear that hears thereof must tingle. Perhaps along a league of roadway a corpse will be swinging from every tree. Such measures effectively discourage rebellion save under most exceptional circumstances. Even with atrocious seigneurs it is usually best to bow to the will of God and merely to pray for deliverance." Davis, *Life on a Mediaeval Barony*, p. 273.

way of life in their empires. Here the distinction between nomads and sedentary agriculturalists with respect to mobility persists to some extent. The military and administrative functions of the aristocracy require many aristocrats to travel frequently and sometimes over long distances. They can do so riding in ships, on horseback, or in carriages, or carried by their servants. Mobility in turn permits communication. The aristocrats of one empire are likely to be frequently in touch with one another as they carry out their various governmental and ceremonial functions—at least the high aristocracy is sometimes concentrated in a single capital city. And aristocracies of different empires, too, are in contact with each other both in wartime and peacetime. Thus, the customs and languages of the aristocracy are frequently fairly uniform over large areas, as they were in aristocratic Western Europe, China, and the Arab world, whether these areas were included in a single empire at one time or another or not. Languages or dialects and customs of the peasantry, on the other hand, differ more or less from locality to locality. In the Austrian and Swiss Alps, for example, the folk costumes and dialects of the peasantry differ to this day from valley to valley, each one only a few miles from the next one. Similarly, while aristocrats often intermarry across large distances, for instance all over Europe, peasants generally find their mates either within their own village or at most in neighboring villages.

Peasants are isolated in their villages because they are effectively tied to the land that they work, sometimes, when they are serfs, by the aristocrats' law, but in any case by economic necessity. They must remain on their land in order to survive, and mobility beyond a small radius, therefore, seems to them neither possible nor desirable. Typically, peasants move only—and that only rarely—to escape aristocratic exploitation, more often than not merely exchanging one aristocratic exploiter for another. Or they move at the behest of their aristocratic ruler who may transplant them to another estate, may use them to colonize hitherto uncultivated areas, or may carry out population transfers to secure territory by settling it with a reliable peasant population.

To be sure, to the small extent that peasants in aristocratic empires are engaged in an exchange economy, some of them leave their villages in order to visit market towns where markets are usually held every few days to exchange goods among villages and with townspeople. Peasants may also visit other villages for festivals and they may make pilgrimages to shrines and holy places. However, all this is usually true of relatively few peasants and may happen only exceptionally in their lives.

Eberhard describes the contacts of a peasant in fifth-century China, where, if anything, commercialization may have had some effect and where communications were better than where villages are separated by mountains, deserts or steppes: "Most of his contacts, including the most intimate and intense associations, were with members of his nuclear and extended family. Many villages consisted only of lineage members—and this has often remained so down to almost the present time. Even the fields were situated so that the farmer hardly met other people than his own lineage members when he worked on the land. His contacts with neighboring villages were less intense. Often, they may not have amounted to more than two or three visits per year. In these neighboring villages there lived the families of wives of the farmers. The next level was the market place, either in a place between villages or in a town. At this level, his contacts would already be of quite low intensity and numerically restricted. But here, he would also have some contacts with men from other social classes. He would meet craftsmen and artisans on the market place, and he might also have to have some contact with the state administration by meeting an official of low rank to whom he had to pay some fee which the man called a 'tax.' In his own village and environment, . . . his contact with the rulers, represented by officials, was normally restricted to the occasional visit of a low official . . . whom he and his co-villagers would try to satisfy when he asked for deliveries of grain and cloth. Other contacts with the ruling bureaucracy might be dangerous and best were avoided. They could mean being called to court, being led to prison or forced into the army."[17]

Similarly, referring to "the self-sufficing nature of the medieval village, and the peasant's comparative isolation even from neighboring villages" in Western Europe, G. G. Coulton writes: "The villages were small, ranging roughly from fifty to five hundred souls at most. . . . The people are few, and their ideas and words are few, the average peasant has probably never known by sight more than two or three hundred men in his whole life."[18] R. H. Tawney, speaking of sixteenth-century England, by no means a traditional aristocratic empire, even estimates that "most men have never seen more than a hundred separate individuals in the course of their whole lives."[19]

What contacts with the outside world peasants do have hardly impress them or affect them, evidently because ordinarily they live in isolation and are deeply steeped in their own local culture. Even of present-day Guatemalan Indians, who do travel to sell pots or to work on plantations, John Gillin reports: "The average man in one sample could name 14 other localities with which he was familiar. Yet these other places are not part of his universe, except in a most casual sense. The nearest analogy of which I can think is that of dream scenes for normal persons among ourselves. The Indians pass through other places, remember odds and ends about them,

17. Eberhard, *Conquerors and Rulers*, pp. 4–5.
18. Coulton, *The Medieval Village*, p. 65.
19. Tawney, *The Agrarian Problem in the Sixteenth Century*, p. 264.

but do not think of them as part of their structured life experience."[20] And Redfield reports that "in the city the peasant is an onlooker; he talks chiefly with other peasants."[21]

However, most peasants in aristocratic empires never see a city or town or even more than a very few villages other than their own, if any. Primarily engaged in subsistence agriculture, they depend on neither imports to nor exports from their small village community. Communications between the village and the outside world are extremely limited, and peasants in any one village are substantially independent of peasants in all other villages. There is a great deal of collaboration within each village, with peasants depending on each other in their work and in various ceremonies and helping each other in times of catastrophes, whether caused by nature or by the aristocracy. But that collaboration and mutual dependence extend at most to clan members in a few neighboring villages. There is no tradition of cooperation or even communication with peasants further afield, let alone of any organization encompassing great masses of peasants. It may not be insignificant that the Russian word "mir" stands for "village," "world," and "peace." Evidently these three concepts were synonymous in the peasant's mind—his village was his world and within it reigned peace.

It follows from all this that, as Eisenstadt says in introducing his brief discussion of the peasantry, "it was, as a rule, politically the most passive and inarticulate, and the least organized, stratum. Although intensive internal political activities might be conducted in each village or groups of villages, these activities were largely isolated and insulated from the central political processes of the society,"[22] that is, from the politics of the aristocracy. But because each village is also isolated from all or almost all others, Banfield can also say more generally that "most of the people of the world live and die without ever achieving membership in a community larger than the family or tribe. Except in Europe and America, the concerting of behavior in political associations and corporate organization is a rare and recent thing."[23] The peasants' parochialism is reduced only by com-

20. Gillin, "Ethos and Cultural Aspects of Personality," p. 197.

21. Redfield, *Peasant Society and Culture*, p. 47.

22. Eisenstadt, *The Political Systems of Empires*, p. 207.

23. Banfield, *The Moral Basis of a Backward Society*, p. 7. What we think of as ancient countries may well have remained unknown to most of their inhabitants until quite recently. Thus, it has been estimated that in Mexico at the outbreak of the Revolution in 1910, "some 90 percent of the population was traditionally village-oriented subsistence agriculturalists or peons who lived on large haciendas and had little or no awareness of the nation or its government." Scott, "Nation-Building in Latin America," p. 81. A decade later, a study of the Indian population close to Mexico City found that "the native is incapable of comprehending the idea of the country. . . . He does not know that Mexico is a Republic nor do his rights and obligations as a citizen interest him. . . . The only manifestation of

mercialization which integrates the hitherto isolated villages into a larger money and market economy; networks of villages grow up around common markets putting peasants in touch with others beyond their own villages and making them aware of shared interests and hence more organizable—all of which makes peasant revolts more possible and more likely to occur as responses to commercialization than in traditional aristocratic empires.

It is the absence of concerting of political behavior mentioned by Banfield that Marx had in mind when, in a famous passage, he compared individual peasants forming the peasant class to individual potatoes forming a sackful of potatoes. He is speaking of the mid-nineteenth century France of Napoleon III and hence stresses the individual small landowning peasants more than the primitive village community of aristocratic empires, but what he says about their inability to organize politically on a larger scale is, if anything, more relevant to peasants in such empires than to those Marx thought of: "Each individual peasant family is almost self-sufficient; it itself directly produces the major part of its consumption and thus acquires its means of life more through exchange with nature than in intercourse with society. The small holding, the peasant and his family; alongside them another small holding, another peasant and another family. A few score of these make up a village, and a few score of villages make up a Department. In this way, the great mass of the French nation is formed by a simple addition of homologous magnitudes, much as potatoes in a sack form a sackful of potatoes. In so far as millions of families live under economic conditions of existence that divide their mode of life, their interests and their culture from those of the other classes, and put them in hostile contrast to the latter, they form a class. In so far as there is merely a local interconnection among these small peasants, and the identity of their interests begets no unity, no national union and no political organisation, they do not form a class. They are consequently incapable of enforcing their class interests in their own name, whether through a parliament or

---

solidarity and love of country among the natives is the absolute and almost irrational affection that they feel for their village." Carlos Noriega Hope, "Apuntes etnográficos," in Manuel Gamio, ed., *La Problación del valle de Teotihuacán* (México: Dirección de Talleres Gráficos, 1922), 2:263, quoted in translation in Hansen, *The Politics of Mexican Development*, p. 136. In 1965, it could be said that "a Chinese national community has at best a history from forty to fifteen years. . . . Before that time, . . . the Chinese (excluding the ruling class) thought of themselves only as members of clans or inhabitants of limited geographical areas." Johnson, "The Role of Social Science in China Scholarship," p. 261. In a survey conducted in East Pakistan (now Bangladesh) in 1966, 90 percent of the people asked "to what country do you belong?" named their village or subdivision of origin or their county district, and only 7 percent named Pakistan. Inkeles, "Models and Issues in the Analysis of Soviet Society," p. 7.

through a convention. They cannot represent themselves, they must be represented. Their representative must at the same time appear as their master, as an authority over them."[24]

Marx's dictum that peasants "cannot represent themselves, they must be represented" and must be led by "an authority over them" points to the lack of suitable leadership among the peasants of the traditional villages as another reason for the absence of organization and hence of revolts reaching beyond at most a few neighboring villages. "The leadership of any substantial movement, no matter how limited its goals, requires attributes not usually acquired in the course of an ordinary peasant existence."[25] Townspeople, given their different environment and experience, may have developed such attributes, like skills in communicating with and organizing strangers, and they may have the requisite material resources to practice these skills. For uprisings to spread widely and to maintain themselves, such skills and resources of outside leaders are required to overcome the localism of peasants.[26]

Three authors who have more sympathy for peasants than Marx—and who have in mind peasant revolts that were responses to commercialization and even to more recent modernization—all agree on this point. Barrington Moore concludes bluntly: "By themselves the peasants have never been able to accomplish a revolution. . . . The peasants have to have leaders from other classes." Speaking of the period of the Communist revolution in China, he says: "In numerous accounts of village life, I have come upon no indication that the peasants were about to organize effectively or do anything about their problems of their own accord. . . . Just as in Manchu times, the peasants needed outside leadership before they

---

24. Marx, "The Eighteenth Brumaire of Louis Bonaparte," p. 608. Marx also referred to the French peasantry as "the class that represents barbarism within civilization." Marx, "The Class Struggles in France, 1848–1850," p. 591. And he and Engels pointed to the isolation of the village when, in the Communist Manifesto, they referred to urbanization as involving rescue of those who left the village "from the idiocy of rural life." Marx and Engels, "Manifesto of the Communist Party," p. 477.

25. AlRoy, *The Involvement of Peasants in Internal Wars*, p. 18.

26. The peasant movement led by Emiliano Zapata appears to be an exception to this generalization. Still, on the one hand, he was no ordinary peasant, he could read and write, had been to Mexico City and was in contact with politicians and intellectuals. Wolf, *Peasant Wars of the Twentieth Century*, pp. 29–30. On the other hand, his uprising, too, remained relatively localized in Morelos and might have been more so had it not become involved in the larger and nonpeasant-led Mexican Revolution. On Zapata, see Womack, *Zapata and the Mexican Revolution*. Hilton, who wants to demonstrate that peasants "were capable of producing their own leaders" lists a number of peasant leaders of medieval European peasant uprisings, some localized and some not, who "were almost certainly drawn from the ranks of the village rich." Hilton, "Peasant Society, Peasant Movements and Feudalism in Medieval Europe," pp. 90–91.

would turn actively against the existing social structure."[27] Eric Wolf says that if a peasant revolt meets resistance it "dissolves if adequate leadership is not provided from without. . . . Halted in their course and pushed back into their everyday concerns . . . peasants will quickly relapse into quiescence and passivity. . . . If the peasantry is not *allowed* to relapse into its traditional narrow concerns, peasant discontent can be mobilized to fuel a revolutionary insurrection."[28] And James Scott is only slightly less emphatic on the need for "outsiders" when he says that "they are often critical to peasant movements, . . . because . . . they may provide the power, assistance, and supralocal organization that helps peasants *act*."[29]

Spontaneous uprisings by the peasants of a single village can be imagined, and such uprisings could spread to a few neighboring villages. However, the peasants' "dependence upon non-peasants for political, military, and other leadership skills . . . increases with the scope of insurgencies."[30] Thus, none of the major peasant revolts discussed in the last chapter as consequences of commercialization was both led by peasants and conducted by them in isolation from nonpeasants. Spartacus's slave rebels— not really peasants anyway—were commanded by a former soldier and a gladiator; the great peasant revolts in Western and Central Europe in the fourteenth, fifteenth, and sixteenth centuries and also some peasant risings in Japan involved townspeople and petty nobles; none of the major peasant leaders in Russia—Bolotnikov, Razin, Bulavin, Pugachev—was him-

---

27. Moore, *Social Origins of Dictatorship and Democracy*, pp. 479, 221–22. Moore adds that "these observations do not in the least imply that the Chinese peasants were innately stupid or lacked initiative or courage. . . . The meaning is merely that, up to the last moment in many areas, the tentacles of the old order wrapped themselves around the individual with sufficient power to prevent him from acting as an isolated unit or, quite often, even thinking about such action" (ibid., p. 222). That peasants cannot even think of revolt when they are totally caught up in the old village order is the important point here, not that they are stupid. Innately peasants presumably have as much intelligence as other human beings, although malnutrition from infancy on may well stunt its development and life-long confinement to the narrow village environment may prevent its growth in some directions. Endowment with courage as with intelligence no doubt varies from individual to individual, but it is no insult to peasants as a class to note that military courage is in good part a function of combat experience and skill. Those who have had no chance to acquire these, like rookie soldiers—and peasants—are more likely to be fearful in combat than battle-hardened veterans—and aristocrats. As to initiative, Moore himself indicated that peasants exercise it only under outside leadership.

28. Wolf, *Peasants*, p. 108; italics in the original.

29. Scott, *The Moral Economy of the Peasant*, pp. 173–74; italics in the original.

30. AlRoy, *The Involvement of Peasants in Internal Wars*, p. 16. "Can the peasantry produce its own leadership? I believe the answer is fairly clear: The more extensive and national, and the more permanent the movement becomes, the less likely it is to be, or at least to remain, in the hands of peasants." Landsberger, "Peasant Unrest," p. 47.

self an ordinary peasant; Chinese peasant revolts were joined and led by members of the gentry once they moved beyond the local level; and peasant rebellions merged with those of the local aristocracy in Mogul India. It may be added that the major twentieth-century revolutions in underdeveloped countries in which peasants played a significant role were invariably led by intellectuals.[31]

It appears that all peasant revolts that spread beyond local confines in societies undergoing commercialization or modernization from without did so under nonpeasant leadership or in alliance with nonpeasant movements. The latter may account for the rare cases, to be mentioned in a moment, when victorious peasant leaders themselves became aristocrats. If peasant revolts could spread only because of nonpeasant leadership, then the absence of such leadership in traditional aristocratic empires may be a major reason for the virtual absence of peasant revolts transcending local confines in such empires. Commercialization and, more recently, modernization from without are followed by peasant revolts not only because they affect the conditions under which peasants live but also because they produce revolutionary groups in the towns, bring the peasants in contact with them, and make them available as the peasants' leaders.

It would be wholly unreasonable to assume that in traditional aristocratic empires peasants by themselves can more easily initiate, organize, and coordinate large-scale revolutions than in societies subject to commercialization. If nonpeasant leaders are needed for this purpose even in the latter type of societies, then they are, if anything, even more essential in traditional aristocratic empires. However, in aristocratic empires there are no such people. The townspeople, including artisans and merchants, are not revolutionary (as we shall see in the next chapter) and have little contact with the peasantry, and the modernizing revolutionaries who have led revolutions in twentieth-century underdeveloped countries do not exist in empires we have defined as untouched by modernization. The only nonpeasants (including former peasants) who may provide leadership for peasants are aristocrats, and, even if they lead peasants in revolts, these are intraaristocratic conflicts in which peasants are used for aristocratic ends, not antiaristocratic peasant revolutions.[32]

---

31. Wolf notes that in all the six revolutions he studied—the Mexican, Russian, Chinese, Vietnamese, Algerian, and Cuban—"dissatisfied peasants whom the market created" provided a constituency for intellectuals. *Peasant Wars of the Twentieth Century*, p. 289. See also my tabular summary of the biographies of thirty-two top leaders of revolutions of modernizers, showing that almost all of them were intellectuals and none was a peasant, in the appendix to my article, "Revolutionary and Managerial Elites in Modernizing Regimes," pp. 466–67.

32. It is interesting to note that Engels, writing more than one and a quarter centuries ago, summarized the factors inhibiting peasant revolts discussed above as effective on the eve of

The Peasant's View of Social Change

There may be yet another element inherent in peasant life in aristocratic empires that is responsible for the rarity of peasant revolts and particularly for the absence of peasant revolutions aiming at a different type of society. As it involves peasant views, any discussion of it must be somewhat speculative, because no direct evidence, such as survey data, on how peasants in aristocratic empires view their world can be available. Still, tentative conclusions can be drawn from what we know of peasants' lives in aristocratic empires and from what is known of the views of peasants in recent times who have not yet been seriously affected by modernization.

The question here is whether and to what extent peasants in aristocratic empires can conceive of change in their existing condition and of themselves as agents of such change. If they cannot conceive of any change occurring or being brought about by them, they will not revolt simply because there will be nothing for which to revolt. If they can conceive of limited change, they might engage in revolts with limited goals. If they can conceive of achieving a social order wholly different from their existing one, then they might possibly engage in revolutions with far-reaching goals.

There is no doubt that peasants are capable of conceiving of some change and of bringing it about. They must become aware of changes affecting their conditions for better or worse if they occur quickly enough to provide an opportunity for comparison with preceding conditions. Thus, crop failure, particularly when not accompanied by a reduction of taxes, or an increase in the taxes imposed on them are obviously felt by the peasants and are likely to be resented. As Barrington Moore puts it: "Economic deterioration by slow degrees can become accepted by its victims as part of the normal situation. Especially where no alternative is clearly visible, more and more privation can gradually find acceptance in the peasants' standards of what is right and proper. What infuriates peasants (and not

---

the German Peasant War in the early sixteenth century: "Incensed as were the peasants under terrific pressure, it was still difficult to arouse them to revolt. Being spread over large areas, it was highly difficult for them to come to a common understanding; the old habit of submission inherited from generation to generation, the lack of practise in the use of arms in many regions, the unequal degree of exploitation depending on the personality of the master, all combined to keep the peasant quiet. . . . Moreover, the peasants alone could never make a revolution as long as they were confronted by the organised power of the princes, nobility and the cities. Only by allying themselves with other classes could they have a chance of victory, but how could they have allied themselves with other classes when they were equally exploited by all?" Engels, "The Peasant War in Germany," pp. 31–32.

just peasants) is a new and sudden imposition or demand that strikes many people at once and that is a break with accepted rules and customs."[33]

Peasants, then, have a strong sense of "what is right and proper," they have "accepted rules and customs."[34] These are themselves a reflection of their inability, to be discussed in a moment, to conceive of bringing about a world very different from the one they have experienced. Their standards of what is right are not shaped by some desire for improvement, let alone by a utopian vision, but simply by what has been. Peasants who have for generations paid a fourth of their product in taxes or rent will consider this right and proper even though they have suffered on the verge of starvation. However, were their dues to be raised to a third of their product and especially were this to be done suddenly, they may consider this wrong and improper and they might even, if other conditions are favorable, rise up in rebellion.

Speaking of various forms of rural rebellion, Tilly says: "Their common denominator is the redress of specific violations of rural rights. . . . Where those rights are well established, when merchants or landlords or officials violate those rights, and when the village has enough organization and resources to resist, some form of rebellion occurs."[35] James Scott agrees with Tilly: "It would be my guess that the great majority of peasant movements historically, far from being affairs of rising expectations, have rather been defensive efforts to preserve customary rights or to restore them once they have been lost. . . . The righting of wrongs always involves a material gain for the poor, but we grossly misconstrue the experience of the peasantry if we treat these gains as mere advantage-seeking rather than as the restoration of rights which have been violated."[36]

The kind of local peasant revolts that are the only ones peasants are capable of making without outside leadership are defensive in character, then, aiming merely at the restoration of the status quo ante prevailing before some deterioration in the peasants' condition. Indeed, this defensive element is also a major one even in most of the peasant revolts responding to the impact of commercialization, which can lead to a noticeable deterioration in the peasants' lives. However, these revolutions, like the English, German, and major Russian peasant revolts, are typically also characterized by chiliasm and utopianism, involving far-reaching demands for equality and the end of aristocratic exploitation.

33. Moore, *Social Origins of Dictatorship and Democracy*, p. 474.

34. On peasant views of economic justice and of what constitutes tolerable and intolerable exploitation, which may well have prevailed in aristocratic empires, too, see Scott, *The Moral Economy of the Peasant*, especially chap. 6.

35. Tilly, *The Vendée*, p. viii.

36. Scott, "Peasant Revolution," pp. 237, 239.

Tilly says that rural rebellions cease to be merely defensive only "by allying with other groups of rebels, with different grievances, outside the rural area."[37] If he is right that peasant revolts are "reactive" and can become "proactive"[38] only under the influence of "other groups of rebels . . . outside the rural area," we must again remember that in aristocratic empires, unlike the more modern societies that Moore, Scott, and Tilly have in mind, there are no such groups of nonpeasant rebels. Like the outside leaders who can organize peasants on a large scale—with whom they are in fact identical—the outsiders who can formulate more far-reaching programs and demands on behalf of peasants, who can visualize achieving a world different from the existing one, who can lead a proactive movement are themselves a product of commercialization or modernization. In aristocratic empires they do not exist, which means that what peasant revolts there might be in such empires can only be defensive and reactive as well as highly localized.

To the extent that peasant revolts, in traditional aristocratic empires and even in commercialized societies, are defensive, they aim merely at a return to a previously prevailing lower level of exploitation, not at a radical transformation of the relationship between peasant and aristocrat, much less the abolition of exploitation and thereby of the aristocracy. If the term revolution stands only for revolts with such more far-reaching goals, then most peasant revolts and certainly those without outside leaders are not revolutions. Thus, what Eric Hobsbawm writes of the objectives of social banditry applies to peasant revolts as well: they are not "very ambitious. They are, essentially, the maintenance or restoration of a stable pattern of traditional social relationships; not a call for the abolition of exploitation, but a protest against its abuses."[39] "Social banditry, though a protest, is a modest and unrevolutionary protest. It protests not against the fact that peasants are poor and oppressed, but against the fact that they are sometimes excessively poor and oppressed. Bandit heroes are not expected to make a world of equality. They can only right wrongs and prove that sometimes oppression can be turned upside down."[40]

Even in the very exceptional cases—none in traditional aristocratic empires—when peasant revolts are successful, in the sense that the peasant

37. Tilly, *The Vendée*, p. viii.

38. Tilly distinguishes between reactive and proactive collective action—reactive action involving resistance to the exercise of a new claim to resources currently under the control of a group, while proactive action involves a group taking the initiative on the basis of claims it lays to resources not previously accorded to it. Tilly, "Town and Country in Revolution," p. 281.

39. Hobsbawm, "Social Banditry," p. 145.

40. Hobsbawm, *Primitive Rebels*, p. 24.

army defeats the aristocratic government, the result is merely oppression "turned upside down," the most outstanding cases being those of three Chinese peasant or bandit leaders becoming emperors and founders of new dynasties (the Han in 206 B.C., the Later Liang in A.D. 907, and the Ming in 1368). Barrington Moore says of Chinese peasant uprisings "that these were rebellions, not revolutions; that is, they did not alter the basic structure of society."[41] And Eberhard, who studied these uprisings carefully, concurs: "Peasant movements in China were not revolutionary movements; they were rebellions or revolts. This is proved by the fact that as soon as the gentry joined the movement (which was an essential step towards success), the rebels regularly began to create an organization which was identical with the organization of the regime they were trying to overthrow."[42]

Similarly, the Syrian slave who led the Sicilian uprising in the first servile war in the second century B.C. proclaimed himself king on the Hellenistic Seleucid model, and his followers "had no economic programme except to take over for their own benefit the existing institutions."[43] Exactly the same thing has been said of the Zanj slave rebellion in Iraq a thousand years later: "It had no real programme of reform, no general aim of abolishing slavery, but was rather a revolt of specific slaves to better their own position."[44] This has also been noted of the great revolt of slaves, peasants, and army deserters, led by one Maternus, in Gaul and Spain in the late second century A.D.: "Maternus and his followers were not themselves the representatives or forerunners of any future form of society: their ideas included no new mode of social existence. Their purpose was merely to replace one Emperor by another, albeit one of their own."[45]

Referring to the slave and peasant revolts of the Bacaudae in late third-century Gaul, who had sought to secede from Roman rule and to form an independent territory, E. A. Thompson's remarks are even more relevant to the small local uprisings of peasants that may take place in aristocratic empires than to the responses to some degree of commercialization by peasants and slaves in late Roman Gaul, peasants in imperial China, slaves in ninth-century Iraq, and "social bandits" in nineteenth- and twentieth-century Italy and Spain: "The various revolts of the Gallic and Spanish peasantry, even when they were successful for years on end, released no new productive forces. If Aelianus and Amandus had been able to win

41. Moore, *Social Origins of Dictatorship and Democracy*, pp. 201–2.

42. Eberhard, *Conquerors and Rulers*, p. 105.

43. Green, "The First Sicilian Slave War," p. 20. See also Finley, *A History of Sicily*, p. 141.

44. Lewis, *The Arabs in History*, p. 104.

45. Thompson, "Peasant Revolts in Late Roman Gaul and Spain," pp. 13–14.

permanent independence for Armorica, they would not have been able to introduce any fundamental change into the class structure of their society. . . . Aelianus and Amandus, then, if they had been successful, could have changed the personnel of the ruling classes in Armorica, but they could not have changed the nature of those classes themselves."[46]

That peasant revolts do not result in a wholly new mode of production is, according to the Marxian scheme, which Thompson seems to have in mind, understandable in the absence of new material productive forces. However, why do peasants not try to return to the role of primitive cultivators by putting an end to all aristocratic exploitation? It is probably because they can only envision a return to a situation they were familiar with in the past, but they cannot conceive of attaining something that to them would be wholly new.

It is reasonable to assume that the peasant in aristocratic empires may be able to imagine and even to wish for a different social order, particularly a world without taxes and dues and hence without an aristocracy. It is probably because he can imagine such a world that he runs away from his village and tries to escape to that other world—though, in fact, peasants run away only very exceptionally, possibly only in commercialized societies, and perhaps only in the hope of serving a less demanding aristocrat. In any case, what the peasant cannot imagine is that in his own world—in his village and in his aristocrat's territory—his wishes and dreams could ever be realized and that he could do anything to realize them. Thus to wish for something and not to act on it is no more inconsistent for the peasant than it would be for us to wish for good weather every day but neither to expect it nor to work to bring it about. For peasants in aristocratic empires, major social change may possibly be a wish or a dream, it cannot be a goal or a policy.

Inability to organize on a large scale and military inferiority are good reasons for the rarity of peasant revolts—as distinguished from revolutions —and certainly for their failure when they do occur. However, it is the peasant's inability to conceive of a practically attainable alternative to the existing order that is the most profound cause of the total absence of peasant revolutions in aristocratic empires, if by revolution we mean a radical transformation of the relationship between peasant and aristocrat. Obviously, the peasant cannot demand changes he cannot himself see as attainable.

46. Ibid., p. 20.

Acceptance of the World as It Is

That anyone should regard the existing social order as practically immutable is difficult for us to understand and hence requires further discussion. It runs counter to all of our experience, for we have, in our own lifetimes, seen great technological changes revolutionize the economy and change the social structure of our societies. Changing communication and transportation systems, the growth of suburbs, changes in urban neighborhoods can be observed with our own eyes, and their social and cultural consequences are not difficult to visualize. We have experienced enough political change all over the world in the past few decades not to be able to entertain the notion that political systems are static and unchangeable. We all know that our grandparents lived in a world different from our own and we therefore assume that our grandchildren will live in a world different from ours.

So much do we take change for granted that it is difficult for us to realize that, in the history of humanity, we are quite exceptional in this respect. For the great masses of mankind, certainly for primitive people but especially also for peasants until a very few centuries ago in a few countries and until a very few decades ago in most of the world—and to millions of peasants to this day—the concept of social change simply does not exist. The social, like the physical, environment is regarded by them as given by nature and hence as immutable.

There appear to be two reasons for this. One is that the peasant in an aristocratic empire totally lacks our experience of change, a point to which I will turn in a moment. However, the peasant's inability or very limited ability to affect his environment, both physical and social, is also relevant in accounting for his view of both as unchangeable. "It never occurs to him to think that he might act so as to change things. The world is as it is."[47] Sidney Verba, too, points out that the peasant's attitudes toward his physical and his political environment are related and similar: "In a culture in which men's orientation toward nature is essentially one of fatalism and resignation their orientation toward government is likely to be much the same. Political cultures in which the activities of the government are considered in the same class with such natural calamities as earthquakes and storms—to be suffered but outside the individual's control—are by no means rare, and one would assume that such an attitude would be closely related to a fatalistic attitude toward man's role in relation to nature. . . . Such a combination of fatalism toward nature and toward government may be general in peasant societies."[48] Thus, the arrival of the tax collector in

47. Hagen, *On the Theory of Social Change*, p. 71.
48. Verba, "Comparative Political Culture," p. 522.

the village must appear to the peasant much like the descent of a hailstorm: it is most unwelcome and might be a great disaster, one might even seek to escape from it or to protect one's possessions from it, but it must be expected periodically, for there has never been a time in memory without it; and it must be accepted, for it is quite beyond the power of the peasant to change it.

The following quotations from three different authors explain well why, given his way of life, it is quite reasonable for the peasant to accept the world unquestioningly as it is. Hagen's remarks about "the impotence of the peasant," like the other quotations refer to present-day underdeveloped countries, but they are even more relevant to aristocratic empires: "To the peasant, life is a mystery in a profound sense in which it is not a mystery to modern man. There is favorable weather, and his crops flourish. Or drought or excessive rain comes, and they fail. Or storms destroy them. His cattle live, bringing moderate prosperity; or they die, bringing disaster. Above all, his wife and his children live or die for causes he cannot clearly understand (though he spins webs of explanation concerning all of these things). Half of the children he begets die before the age of five years, or, if he lives in a less favorable environment, half may die before the age of one. . . . Before all of these events he is helpless unless he can induce the spirits to help him. To state that he feels impotent may give a wrong connotation, for it may imply that he feels that his position is not as it should be. He probably does not. He merely takes for granted that the phenomena of the world around him are arbitrary and not amenable to analysis, and that they control him."[49]

"Why are peasants fatalistic? One reason is that they have a relatively low degree of mastery over their natural and social environments. . . . Peasants lack the knowledge, skills, and resources necessary to cope with phenomena such as drought, floods, and famine. The causes of these conditions are looked upon as a visitation from gods or evil spirits, whom man can propitiate but not control. Under circumstances that condemn a farmer to subsistence living and a comparatively short life span, it is not surprising that villagers have few illusions about the possibility of improving their lot. A fatalistic outlook, the assumption that whatever happens is the will of God or Allah, is perhaps the best adjustment the individual can make to an apparently hopeless situation. Indeed, fatalistic attitudes may have been highly efficient and functional in the past as means of psychological adaptation to a harsh environment."[50]

"G. Destanne de Bernis has shown in a very scholarly way, using mathe-

49. Hagen, *On the Theory of Social Change*, p. 65.

50. Rogers, *Modernization Among Peasants*, p. 274.

matical methods and with a close and deep knowledge of Tunisian country life, that, if the peasants of the Muslim countries are indeed fatalistic, this is not at all an irrational attitude on their part, but represents a just estimation of the enormous, and discouraging, weight of the chancy factors that condition the success of their efforts. 'Anyone so placed would be fatalistic, at the very least,' this writer comments with justification, and he adds that 'every traditional rural civilization, if by this we mean one that has not been altered by the impact of technical progress, is sunk in fatalism.' He shows that mediaeval Christendom knew the same mentality for the same reasons."[51]

"Just as it does not occur to the peasant that he can influence any of a wide range of phenomena of the physical world that are of great emotional importance to him, so it does not occur to him that the social structure is amenable to change. One should not conclude, however, that he is apathetic, despairing, and sullen. . . . In the traditional society he seems to take both his physical environment and the social structure as data. Consciously, he neither grieves nor rejoices at them. They are simply there, and natural."[52]

That the peasant does not rejoice in the existing social order may seem obvious, but it is worth stressing, for that he accepts life as it is without question could be misunderstood to mean that he accepts it contentedly or even happily. Disease and starvation cause him pain, and it is not likely that the peasant suffers these happily. Inability to visualize an attainable alternative is not likely to make him enjoy the sickness or the death of his children. "Countless ballads as well as monks' sermons and treatises represent your typical villein as incessantly discontented."[53] It is, then, one thing to regard a condition as inevitable and immutable, but it is quite another to like it. That also means, however, that it is one thing not to like a condition and quite another to try to change it.

It is also important not to assume that peasants accept the existing order and do not attack or even question the aristocracy's control over them, because they benefit from it. Everett Hagen evidently believes this when he writes: "The relationships, practices, and beliefs of a society are not accidental. In a society which was continued without basic change for a long time they are always seen to satisfy the purposes and motivations of the members of the society, conscious and unconscious, if only we can find what those purposes and motives are. . . . Powerful elite might hold a large mass of people in hated peonage for a generation or two, but that elite

51. Rodinson, *Islam and Capitalism*, p. 113. The quotation within this quotation is from *Cahiers de l'I.S.E.A.*, No. 6 (Série V, no. 2), October 1960, pp. 114 ff.

52. Hagen, *On the Theory of Social Change*, p. 70.

53. Davis, *Life on a Mediaeval Barony*, p. 268.

classes could have held their positions by force for centuries and even millennia, as has been true in many traditional societies, is inconceivable."[54] Although the position of the peasants in aristocratic empires is, indeed, probably not actively hated by them, I fail to see why a situation unfavorable to them that can last for a generation or two cannot also persist for centuries and millennia if the peasants cannot resist it or even conceive of producing any change in it. Hagen, however, merely continues the above statement by saying that "one must conclude that the hierarchical structure of authority and power in traditional societies has been so stable because the simple folk as well as the elite accepted it. The simple folk must feel satisfaction in depending for decisions and direction on individuals above them, in submitting their wills to authority."[55] It is obviously true that the traditional aristocratic order was stable because "the simple folk," that is, the peasants, accepted it. It does not necessarily follow, however, that they accepted it because it gave them satisfaction, "because the personalities of the simple folk are authoritarian."[56] Indeed, they could hardly depend "for decisions and direction" on aristocrats "above them," because they were largely ignored and left to their own devices by them.

Others have thought of different kinds of benefits provided by the aristocracy to the peasantry, like protection and the provision of law and order, a matter discussed earlier.[57] To them, Barrington Moore gives an effective response that is as relevant to traditional aristocratic empires as it is to China, especially in the nineteenth century, which he has in mind. He raises the question "what then did the government do for the peasant?" and says: "Modern Western sociologists are perhaps too prone to dismiss as impossible the answer that it did practically nothing, which I suspect is the correct one. They reason that any institution which lasts a long time cannot be altogether harmful to those who live under it (which seems to me to fly in the face of huge masses of both historical and contemporary experience) and therefore undertake a rather desperate search for some function that the institution in question must perform. This is not the place to argue about methods or the way in which conscious and unconscious assumptions determine the questions raised in any scientific inquiry. Nevertheless, it seems more realistic to assume that large masses of people, and especially peasants, simply accept the social system under which they live without concern about any balance of benefits and pains, certainly without the least thought of whether a better one might be possible, unless and until something happens to threaten and destroy their daily routine.

54. Hagen, *On the Theory of Social Change*, p. 71.

55. Ibid.

56. Ibid., p. 74.

57. See pp. 111–14, above.

Hence it is quite possible for them to accept a society of whose working they are no more than victims."[58] Peasants "simply accept" the existing social system not because they benefit from it, but "without concern" for benefits, because they simply cannot conceive of attaining a different one.

Aside from the peasant's impotence, it is his lack of exposure to any actual major social change that makes it impossible for him to conceive of demanding, let alone achieving, any such change. Indeed, he is not likely even to dream much about change for, compared to modern men, he lives in an extremely stable world.[59] Little, if anything, in his experience predisposes him to conceive of any but the most marginal changes. In his village, life is a series of endlessly repeated routines. In the life of the individual, certain changes do take place, like entry into adult status, marriage, parenthood, and the occurrence of disease and—for a few—of old age, but behavior patterns appropriate to each of these have long ago evolved to which the individual is expected to conform. They are not new and constitute no change in peasant society. Thus, the peasant confronts few, if any, new situations that stimulate him to think of possible alternatives to life as he knows it. Even the few new elements to which a peasant may be exposed in his rare travels to the town or other villages or which are brought to the village by a rare visitor from the outside leave little impression. They are rejected because they do not fit into the very limited but highly integrated system of thought and behavior that constitutes the peasant's life in his village.

To be sure, natural disasters, like floods and storms, earthquakes and volcanic eruptions, as well as aristocratic warfare, which is like a natural disaster to the peasant, could drastically affect his life. However, they could only disrupt or end it but add no new elements to it. Where peasant life goes on at all, it goes on unchanged.[60]

58. Moore, *Social Origins of Dictatorship and Democracy*, p. 204.

59. The narrowness as well as the stability of the world experienced by the peasant may be measured by the size of his vocabulary. G. G. Coulton, writing in 1925, cites the German historian and ethnographer W. H. Riehl "who made exhaustive researches and found that the German peasant farmer of about 100 years ago had a vocabulary of only 600 words, all told." Coulton, *The Medieval Village*, p. 393.

60. Marx, speaking of Indian village communities and stressing that "English steam and English free trade . . . by blowing up their economical basis [had] produced the greatest, and, to speak the truth, the only *social* revolution ever heard of in Asia," comments with much distaste on their "barbarian egotism" and their "undignified, stagnatory, and vegetative life" and "passive sort of existence." He says "that they restrained the human mind within the smallest possible compass, making it the unresisting tool of superstition, enslaving it beneath traditional rules, depriving it of all grandeur and historical energies, . . . that they subjugated man to external circumstances instead of elevating man to be the sovereign of circumstances, that they transformed a self-developing social state into never changing natural destiny." Marx, "The British Rule in India," pp. 93–94; italics in the original.

In the absence of investment and of relevant scientific developments, technological change in agriculture is imperceptibly slow. Until very recently, peasants in southern Italy used the same kind of plow their ancestors had employed in the days of the Roman empire. Similarly, in Egypt, "the peasant of the twenty-seventh century B.C. lived much the same as did the peasant of the nineteenth century after Christ."[61] For centuries and millennia, then, the peasant's tools and utensils, his crops and his animals, his housing and his food, and hence his problems and his routine, his customs and his way of life, his thoughts, his hopes, his fears do not change. The experience of past generations, as it comes down to him through his traditions, remains relevant to his unchanging problems and provides answers to all the questions he might ask. Whereas in rapidly changing modern societies the aged are usually looked on with some condescension as unable to keep up with the times and hence out of date in their ideas, in peasant societies old age is typically treated with reverence. The experience of the old is as relevant as that of the young, but the old have more of it and are hence considered wiser.

If history must involve a record of change, one may well say that peasants in aristocratic empires have no history. The vast majority of the people living in aristocratic empires are mostly ignored by historians. In good part, this is no doubt the case because past historians were drawn from or partial to the aristocracy, or because the stone edifices of the aristocracy have outlasted the peasants' huts made of mud or straw, or because what records we have deal with the aristocracy.[62] However, it is also true simply because there is nothing worth recording about the peasantry, that is, there is no change in its condition.

It appears, then, that peasants in aristocratic empires generally live in resignation and passivity not only because of their military inferiority to the aristocracy but also because, in the absence of outside leaders, they

61. Wilson, *The Burden of Egypt*, p. 73. Wilson goes on to describe the peasant as shown on the tomb reliefs of the Old Kingdom: "His feet were ever sunk into the mud of the river bank, planting or reaping his master's crops, building in mudbrick for his master, or driving his master's cattle. He lived ever close to nature, with the peasant's mystic and superstitious sense of community with plant and animal. He was slender and not fully nourished, much of his work was heavy on his back, and his reward in payment in kind was slight. . . . Periodic famine and pestilence made him the fearful victim of unknown and sudden peril from vast forces which he took to be gods. . . . Perhaps his life was closely akin to the lives of the animals who were beside him day and night. He was a chattel, a beast of burden, a draught animal, intimately dependent upon the amount of green fodder on the valley floor" (ibid., p. 74).

62. "Essentially, the history of the Roman Republic is the history of the small, literate upper-class at Rome. . . . The majority has disappeared silently and their thoughts must remain forever obscure. The minority alone remains, vociferously articulate, for posterity." Earl, *The Moral and Political Tradition of Rome*, pp. 11–12.

cannot initiate or organize large-scale revolts. Except for a restoration of their "rights" to a level of exploitation to which they were accustomed, they have no objectives they regard as obtainable for which they might organize or revolt. They assume that life must be as it is and as, in their view, it has always been; no practical question of any substantial improvement in it ever arises.[63] Only the changes to which commercialization subjects peasants makes them capable of believing that they can bring about social change. Having suffered adverse changes, they can demand favorable ones, and these may now go far beyond the restoration of older forms of exploitation all the way to communistic utopias, as they appeared, for example, in the great English peasant revolt and the German Peasant War.

In aristocratic empires, aside from very rare, highly localized and merely defensive revolts, peasants do not intervene in the politics of the aristocracy. Just as there is no single social system in aristocratic empires, there is no single political system. The economic link of exploitation ties the aristocracy to the peasantry, but otherwise each village and the aristocracy constitutes not only an autonomous social system but also an autonomous political system.

This autonomy of the two principal classes in aristocratic empires—which are hence not mere classes but separate societies—keeps each from destroying or even from substantially affecting the other. As we saw in detail earlier, there may be great instability within the society of the aristocracy—and the same may be true within each village society—as individual members compete for different positions and advantages. However, the relationship between the aristocracy and the many peasant societies it exploits remains stable and unchanging.

It is both effect and cause of this stability and immutability that no one can imagine major social change,[64] and where no one can imagine it, no

---

63. Indian peasants in Guatemala are said to "live in a restricted time space. The universe of the Indian does not extend backward to a remembered past. . . . Nor do they project changes for the future. According to the Indian scheme of things life goes on in a timeless present, it has been this way as long as any one knows, and one will be content to see the pattern continue indefinitely. The object of life is to keep the scheme going according to expectations." Gillin, "Ethos and Cultural Aspects of Personality," p. 198.

64. Although I have not mentioned it in a chapter on peasant revolts, this is as true of the aristocracy and the townspeople in aristocratic empires as it is of peasants. To them, too, major social change is a wholly alien concept. Even in the late Middle Ages, European painters put their Biblical characters in medieval dress and armor and painted medieval castles in the background of their Biblical scenes. It simply did not occur to them that life in the Middle East centuries and millennia earlier could have been different from life as they knew it in medieval Italy or Germany. In aristocratic empires, everyone takes it for granted, then, that life in the past has always been like life in the present and that life in the future must also remain the same.

one can seek it. It does not follow, of course, that no major social change can take place, for if that were true, aristocratic empires would last forever. Social change did come to these empires, but not as a result of the programs or deliberate actions of any of their inhabitants. It came either quite gradually and imperceptibly as a result of commercialization, as it occurred at various times in Greece and Rome, in Europe, China and Japan, and elsewhere, or it came much more suddenly as a result of modernization from without emanating from societies that had earlier been commercialized and subsequently industrialized. Either way, that change marks the end of the traditional aristocratic empire.

14

The Townspeople in the Politics of the Aristocracy

Origins of the Townspeople

An aristocratic empire could consist exclusively of aristocrats and of peasants. In the early stages after its establishment, just after a number of villages have been conquered by nomads, or after an aristocracy has emerged out of an alliance of peasant villages, this may, indeed, be the case. However, if the new empire persists, that is, if the aristocrats remain in control of the peasants for some time, new strata of people are likely to emerge who are clearly not aristocrats nor are they peasants. I refer to them collectively as the townspeople. I prefer this term to the more commonly used "middle class," because the people in question do not occupy a middle position between the aristocracy and the peasantry. Some are attached to the aristocracy and some are simply separate from, but not necessarily between, the two major classes. Nor do they constitute a class, a term that suggests that they have much more in common than they do.

Unlike aristocrats and peasants, the people I lump together as townspeople are not an objectively defined category. Rather, as the term is used here, they constitute a residual category: everyone in the aristocratic empire who is neither an aristocrat nor a peasant is assigned to it. They are generally quite sharply distinct from peasants, but, as became clear from some of our discussion of the aristocracy, there may in some empires be a gray area between that class and some groupings of the townspeople. This is true especially in the middle ranges between the clearly aristocratic top level and the clearly nonaristocratic bottom level—if there is one—of the bureaucratic, military, and priestly hierarchies.

Our interest in the townspeople, as it was with the peasantry, is confined to the role they play in the politics of the aristocracy. Just as we were not concerned with the internal organization and politics of the village, so we shall be looking at the townspeople only to the extent necessary to establish whether and how they intervene in aristocratic politics.[1] However, before we can turn to their political role as it affects the politics of the aristocracy, I must deal with the origins and composition of townspeople.

One characteristic that all townspeople—except a few employed by the aristocracy in rural areas—share is that, like some aristocrats but unlike all but possibly a very few peasants, they live in towns and cities. The development of the townspeople is hence closely associated with urbanization; indeed, the two processes are virtually identical, for the great majority of the urban people in aristocratic empires are townspeople.

In some cases, groups of craftsmen and of merchants may be attached to nomadic tribes. If and when these become aristocrats, the craftsmen and merchants follow them into the conquered territory to form the nuclei of cities.[2] Probably more commonly, townspeople develop only after the aristocracy. Given the reluctance of aristocrats to engage in any manual labor, even an aristocrat controlling only little land and few peasants will employ some peasants as his personal servants and others as craftsmen, for example to build his house and his furniture and to make his clothing, utensils, and weapons. Such servants and craftsmen, being then neither peasants nor aristocrats, are the first townspeople.

An aristocrat obtaining only a small surplus from his land and peasants will be able to afford only a small retinue of servants and craftsmen, and some of these may remain part-time peasants who continue to live in the village. The larger and richer the territory and the greater the number of peasants under an aristocrat's control, the more people he can afford to employ and the more he will need to employ to serve him. A few of these can settle within the aristocrat's castle, but towns are likely to grow up around the castle and may then in turn be protected by walls. The ruler of a substantial area, receiving revenues directly from his own lands and indirectly through the aristocrats under his control, can surround himself with what may become a sizable town population.

Typically, then, it is the capital city, that is, the seat of the ruler, that becomes the largest city in the kingdom or empire, and the bigger or richer the empire the bigger that city tends to be. This is true not only because the ruler himself can and needs to maintain many townspeople. Other aristocrats, too, who are dependent on the ruler, are likely to establish permanent or temporary residences in the capital. They may do so for

1. For a general analysis of recurrent patterns, explained in terms of technology, in the society and economy of preindustrial towns throughout the world and in different periods of history, see Sjoberg, *The Preindustrial City*. Sjoberg's analysis does not particularly emphasize politics and is not confined to aristocratic empires.

2. Eberhard, *Settlement and Social Change in Asia*, pp. 280–81.

a variety of reasons, for example, to serve their ruler as military leaders, administrators, and priests, to be in communication with other aristocrats, to be safer from attack in the fortified city than on their country estates, and to enjoy the pleasures and cultural life of the city. In any case, the revenues of their lands and their peasants, too, now flow into the city, and these aristocrats, too, employ the services of townspeople.

The process of the growth of capitals of empires is repeated in the case of provincial capitals that become the administrative centers of particular areas within an empire. "In the minds of the Chinese the city . . . is, in its ideal form, a place in which gentry members who are administrators reside temporarily to exercise the necessary functions of government. . . . The active officials, who have to live in the city, surrounded themselves with the necessary personnel. There was an army in the city—ready to defend the villages if necessary, but not living in the villages. . . . There were all the craftsmen in the city, to build and fabricate whatever the office and its occupants needed. And there were peddlers and merchants ready to provide food and luxuries for the officials."[3]

Some cities also grow as commercial centers, but when this becomes their main function, as was true, for example, of some medieval Italian cities like Venice, Pisa, and Genoa, they and their empires thereby leave our category of traditional aristocratic empires. On the other hand, some cities in aristocratic empires may serve not only as governmental and military centers but also as religious and intellectual ones, like Jerusalem, Benares, Rome, and Mecca. In these ways, too, further wealth is brought into the cities, and the growth of the town population is stimulated.[4]

Still, most urban centers in aristocratic empires remain small. The townspeople can never be nearly as numerous as the peasantry on whom they ultimately depend, for it takes many peasants to produce a sufficient agricultural surplus to support a single townsman (let alone an aristocrat who consumes so very much more than a peasant), even assuming that means of transportation are available to move that surplus to the cities. Both Pirenne, speaking of the whole of Europe between the twelfth and the fifteenth centuries, and Sjoberg, speaking of "feudal societies" in general, estimate that "the urban population never comprised more than a tenth part of the total number of inhabitants."[5] Because both authors refer to commercialized societies as well as traditional aristocratic empires, it can be assumed that the proportion of the townspeople in the latter alone was

3. Eberhard, *Social Mobility in Traditional China*, pp. 267, 268.

4. On the relationship between the growth of empires and urbanization, see Sjoberg, *The Preindustrial City*, pp. 67–77.

5. Pirenne, *Economic and Social History of Medieval Europe*, p. 58; Sjoberg, *The Preindustrial City*, p. 83.

considerably smaller.[6] Only the major centers of some very large and long-lasting empires that became so commercialized that they were no longer traditional, such as ancient Rome and some Chinese cities, especially under the Sung dynasty, were evidently big even by modern standards, though estimates of their maximum size vary greatly, ranging from two hundred thousand to one million.[7]

Occupational Groupings of Townspeople

Directly or indirectly, virtually all townspeople serve the aristocracy. This is most obvious in the case of personal servants. Minor aristocrats will have relatively few of these, but the court of a large kingdom or empire swarms with servants specializing in numerous tasks and more or less busy taking care of the ruler and his family and of their possessions, including cooks, butlers, grooms, chambermaids, porters, footmen, doorkeepers, gardeners, and so on. Where servants are numerous, they are organized in various hierarchies headed by high-level servants in supervisory and managerial capacities. There is no sharp line between these latter and bureaucrats to be mentioned below. Because public affairs are the private business of aristocrats, their servants may also be involved in governmental matters, as when a servant manages an estate and thus governs its peasants or when a servant of a ruler is entrusted with an administrative position in the empire.

As the size of empires and with it the wealth and size of the aristocracy and of cities grow, the number and specialization of artisans and craftsmen increases. More and more, the different products used by the aristocracy and also by the townspeople themselves are manufactured (using this term

6. Cipolla emphasizes that: "Until the Industrial Revolution, everywhere in the world, towns with more than 100 thousand people remained extremely rare. Big figures are often quoted, but they generally represent gross exaggerations. As late as the sixteenth century, in Europe an average town numbered from 5 to 20 thousand people and any agglomeration with more than 20 thousand inhabitants was considered a big town. Throughout the ages, in any part of the world, the story of agricultural societies remained essentially the story of numerous small, more or less isolated microcosms." Cipolla, *The Economic History of World Population*, p. 100.

7. Sjoberg, *The Preindustrial City*, pp. 80–83, and the sources cited there. On cities of similar size in seventeenth-century Mogul India, see Habib, *The Agrarian System of Mughal India*, pp. 75–76. For descriptions of Sung cities, including estimates of their size and quotations from Marco Polo, see Balazs, *Chinese Civilization and Bureaucracy*, pp. 71–75. Soustelle estimates that the center of the Aztec empire, which was not long-lasting but had become commercialized, was inhabited by over a million people, but it consisted not only of the capital Tenochtitlán but also of a number of other preexisting towns that came to form "an enormous conurbation." Soustelle, *Daily Life of the Aztecs*, p. 9.

in its literal meaning of "made by hand") by different specialists. There thus develop wool and silk weavers, tailors and shoemakers, blacksmiths and coppersmiths, goldsmiths and silversmiths, carpenters and furniture makers, potters and tinkers, and many more. Some of these produce only crude articles; others, making fine jewelry, tapestries and rugs, or carved furniture, approach the character of artists. The latter work almost exclusively for the aristocracy, while some craftsmen also supply the townspeople, but little is sold to the peasantry, which is largely self-sufficient, too poor to buy the products of the city, and often beyond its reach.[8] Only itinerant peddlers may visit some villages to trade, and only a relatively few peasants from nearby villages who come to the markets in the town may buy some of the products of local craftsmen.

Both the low level of scientific development and the availability of cheap labor keep technology primitive, and the primitive technology of the artisan and poor systems of transportation as well as the poverty of the peasant and of many townspeople, keep a mass market from developing and keep the size of enterprises small. This in turn prevents the craftsmen from amassing sufficient capital to invest in improved technology or in more labor power. In commercialized empires, where land had become alienable but high prestige still rested with landownership, the few artisans who acquired some wealth would tend to invest it in land rather than in their enterprises, thus, as in Rome and China, seeking entry into the upper classes. This tendency may have contributed to the failure of early commercialization in such empires to lead to industrialization.[9]

The richer the aristocrats, the more their demands will grow for goods that cannot be produced in the immediate vicinity of their residences. There then develop merchants who bring such goods to the aristocrats, sometimes from far-distant lands, as in the silk and spice trade from the Far East to ancient and medieval Europe.[10] Such trade can be carried on only with luxury articles, such as jewelry and tapestry, and raw materials, such as precious metals and stones, ivory and ebony, spices and silk, that are both sufficiently valuable and small enough in bulk and weight to make

8. In ancient Egypt, "it is probable that the skilled handwork was long the specialty of trained artists in the nobles' establishments. There was no large middle class to create a demand; the noble and his household were supplied with fine work within the domain; the farmer, as at present, was not a purchaser of more than necessaries." Petrie, *Social Life in Ancient Egypt*, p. 20.

9. On the small scale of manufacturing in ancient Rome, see Moore, *The Roman's World*, pp. 81–84, and Boak and Sinnigen, *A History of Rome to A.D. 565*, pp. 380–82.

10. On Roman long-distance trade, see Moore, *The Roman's World*, pp. 85–93; Charlesworth, *Trade-Routes and Commerce of the Roman Empire*; and Warmington, *The Commerce Between the Roman Empire and India*.

their shipment over long distances economically feasible.[11] Other merchants may import material from the nearby countryside, buying both from aristocratic landowners and from peasants, and supply food and fuel to the urban population in general[12] and raw materials, like metals, wood, and wool, to the craftsmen in particular.

Not only do merchants, then, directly or indirectly, supply the needs of the aristocracy, but they become a source of taxes and duties for it, thus supplementing its income from the peasantry. Trade may therefore be sponsored by the aristocracy for this reason, too. Once aristocrats become substantially dependent on merchants, however, and their policies are affected thereby, we no longer regard the empire as a traditional aristocratic one.

A few townspeople, particularly merchants, may become moneylenders, but banking as a business develops only with commercialization, as in ancient Greece, China, and medieval Europe. Moneylending is restricted, because the aristocracy frowns on it, and dominant religions, like medieval Christianity and Islam, proscribe lending for interest. Above all, however, capital is scarce, and most of the townspeople and certainly the peasants cannot afford to borrow money. Most have no collateral at all, and often property is subject to destruction by natural disaster, and borrowers are subject to disease and early death. Thus, the risk being high, interest rates are exorbitant, and little capital is available to artisans and merchants to expand their enterprises.[13] On the other hand, the aristocrats who could afford to borrow money do not need to do so in traditional aristocratic empires. Their cash needs grow only with commercialization; then some of them do become dependent on moneylenders and banks, an indication that their empire is no longer a traditional one.

Given the absence of machinery and means of transportation driven by inanimate sources of energy (apart from water mills and windmills and sailboats), a group of unskilled laborers is likely to serve, in addition to animals, as beasts of burden and in related tasks. Porters, sedan carriers

11. Even of the commercialized Mediterranean world of the second half of the Middle Ages, Cipolla says: "Long-distance trade had to rely mainly, if not exclusively, on precious objects. For its basic daily needs any community had always to be as self-sufficient and self-sustaining as possible. . . . And trade had to rest heavily on aristocratic consumption of luxury goods." Cipolla, *Money, Prices, and Civilization*, p. 57.

12. It must be noted, however, that neither townspeople nor aristocrats are necessarily wholly dependent on merchants for their needs. Townspeople may themselves carry on agriculture on fields adjoining the town, that is, they may be part-time peasants, and aristocrats may find it more profitable to consume their peasants' product than to move it to the cities. See Lenski, *Power and Privilege*, pp. 200 n. 41, 205.

13. On "credit and capital formation," see Sjoberg, *The Preindustrial City*, pp. 214–16 and 270.

and litter bearers, and galley slaves are needed to move persons and goods, scavengers and sweepers make minimal attempts at cleanliness in a generally filthy environment, and ditchdiggers and building laborers are needed to dig moats and canals and erect walls, palaces, and temples. In rural areas, roads, castles, fortifications, and irrigation works are likely to be built by peasants doing forced labor for the aristocracy under some form of corvée, but in the city unskilled laborers have no other occupation and must therefore be considered as among the townspeople.

While servants, artisans, merchants, and laborers serve the economic needs of the aristocracy, another group of townspeople may assist the aristocracy in its governmental and administrative functions. These may be broken down in modern terms into such professions as bureaucrats, soldiers, priests, scholars, scientists, magicians, and astrologers, but in the practice of aristocratic empires two or more or even all of them may overlap.

The higher positions in the bureaucracy are generally held by aristocrats, but limited though their governmental functions are, they may need some assistance from nonaristocrats if the territory and the number of people they govern is large. Thus, in an age without typewriters or printing presses, there is need for clerks and scribes, and messengers take the place of the telegraph and telephone.[14] Tax collectors, too, may be nonaristocrats, employed either as members of the bureaucracy or as private contractors, though, as was mentioned, some may in effect become aristocrats.

As in the bureaucracy so in the military, the higher positions are always occupied by aristocrats, and sometimes, as in feudal Europe, the entire military is made up of aristocrats. On the other hand, in some empires, peasants are drafted into the army or nomads are hired to fill the lower ranks. If they serve only temporarily, we can simply classify them as peasants or nomads. However, if they become professional soldiers, they are no longer peasants or nomads and yet they do not become aristocrats, except in the rare cases where one is promoted into the aristocracy for special deeds of valor or can independently conquer some land and peasants to become an aristocrat. We must then classify such soldiers as townspeople, whether or not they are stationed in towns (as they typically were in China).

In the priesthood, too, the high officials are aristocrats, but if there is a

14. The Incas had the most rapid premodern system of communications. Through an elaborate system of relays, their specially trained runners could cover 250 miles per day along their roads, while the Roman mounted couriers could cover only 100 miles. Having no system of writing, the Incas employed no scribes but they did have a specialized group of accountants who interpreted their knot-string records ("quipus") of population, tax statements, etc. Von Hagen, *Realm of the Incas*, pp. 181–87.

lower layer, we must classify those composing it as townspeople. Where priests have a monopoly or near-monopoly of literacy, they may well be the ones to occupy administrative positions. Indeed, the very word "clerk" used to refer to a clergyman. But priests serve the aristocracy not only as administrators, but also in their religious capacity, for, as has been indicated, religion functions to legitimize the roles played by aristocrats in their empires.

The world of scholarship and science in aristocratic empires is not sharply distinguished from the religious one and, in its lower reaches, too, is drawn from the townspeople (a third meaning of the word "clerk" is "scholar"). Philosophers and legal scholars are engaged chiefly in the interpretation of sacred texts rather than in attempts at explanation or proposals of innovation. Where the social order is held to be as permanent and immutable as the natural one, innovation is considered impossible, and explanation seems irrelevant to the concerns of most men. Even what physical scientists there are, such as physicians and astronomers, are not sharply distinguishable from magicians and astrologers. They seek to invoke and to take advantage of supernatural forces rather than to control or explain natural ones. Thus, scholars and scientists, too, tend to support the established order of aristocratic predominance. Formal education, which is limited to the aristocracy and the upper levels of the townspeople, is largely religious in character and serves the same conservative function.

Sjoberg writes: "In the traditional world we are describing, the intellectual . . . is first and foremost a moralizer, an interpreter of the sacred literature that only he is thought to understand. But unlike the intellectual in many industrial cities, he does not criticize the status quo; it is his task merely to reinforce it. He is fully integrated into the social system and enjoys high prestige and authority, for, as a religious and/or educational leader, he is an expositor of the divine and carrier of the sacred tradition upon which the social order has been built. The intellectuals, then, reinforce and rationalize the authority of the sovereign by lending credence to the validity of the latter's position, by arguing in terms of absolutes and tradition."[15]

To be sure, in some empires, science and scholarship did develop apart from religion and magic, as in the evolution of mathematics by the ancient Greeks—the Pythagoreans still attached mystical meanings to numbers — Hindus, and Arabs, and in Aristotle's approaches to the physical and social sciences. However, such developments seem to appear only in commercialized empires, for highly developed trade with its concern for manipulation, rather than acceptance, of the existing order and its far-flung

15. Sjoberg, *The Preindustrial City*, p. 230; see also ibid., p. 119.

intercultural and interclass contacts stimulates questions about the nature of the world. Indeed, the rise of commerce and science marks the end of traditional aristocratic empires, and, developing within them, they become the small chinks in what is otherwise the impenetrable armor of the immutability of such empires.

In addition to those serving, directly or indirectly, the economic needs of the aristocracy and those who furnish military, administrative, and ideological support to that class, a third grouping of professions among the townspeople provides various forms of entertainment. It is not always clearly distinguishable from the two other groupings, as in the case of the court jester who is somewhat akin to a servant or of the poet or dramatist who may also be a philosopher. Broadly, one can distinguish between two categories of entertainers. A lower one, composed of jugglers, dancers and actors, singers and storytellers, gladiators and prostitutes, offers entertainment not only to the aristocracy but also to the townspeople and, to a limited extent, as at fairs and in market towns, even to peasants. It thus makes available an occasional small measure of change in the otherwise unchanging routine of their lives. Some intellectual stimulation, too, may be provided by actors, singers, and storytellers. This tends to reinforce the status quo and the position of the aristocracy, for plays, songs, and stories generally deal with religious themes or serve to glorify the deeds, past and present, of the aristocracy.[16] Thus, even when this lower category of entertainers does not directly amuse the aristocracy, it tends to serve its interests.

The higher category of entertainers serves only the aristocracy. It is made up of such artists as musicians, composers, and poets, painters, sculptors, and architects. These evolve only in response to the refined tastes of the aristocracy, for only aristocrats can appreciate their work, and (apart from a few exceptionally rich merchants who are likely to emerge only with commercialization) only aristocrats can afford to maintain them. Art —except for folk art—in aristocratic empires therefore developed only under the sponsorship of the aristocracy. Even in the posttraditional society, artists were dependent on aristocratic sponsorship for their livelihood, like the great Renaissance painters, sculptors, and architects and like composers and musicians, such as Bach and Handel in the early and Haydn and Mozart in the late eighteenth century and even Beethoven in the early nineteenth century.

The urban economy of the traditional aristocratic empire is generally not an expanding one, and opportunities to engage in productive or ser-

---

16. The Incas even deliberately manipulated history by having their professional "rememberers" recall and the romancers sing of only selected aspects of it. Von Hagen, *Realm of the Incas*, p. 188.

vice occupations are hence limited. As a result, considerable numbers of people make their living as beggars and as thieves, one group of townspeople that can hardly be said to serve the aristocracy either directly or indirectly. Among them are often women and children not supported by a gainfully employed husband or father, but there are also numerous cripples and disabled men who must beg or steal, for diseases and accidents are common, and medical treatment may be neither easily available nor very effective. The children of beggars and thieves, in turn, have little opportunity to move into any other occupations, so that these professions, like many others in the traditional city, tend to become hereditary.[17]

Where slaves exist in aristocratic empires, as they commonly do, most of them are townspeople,[18] but from our point of view they do not form a special category among them, for they appear as members of most of the various professions among townspeople. Many slaves, of course, are among the personal servants of the aristocracy. Slaves may also account for many of the unskilled laborers and for some of those serving the function of entertainment, particularly those in the lower reaches of this grouping, like dancers, gladiators, and prostitutes. However, artisans, too, may be slaves and so may even scholars, educators, and physicians, and in a number of empires, especially Muslim ones, slaves were used as soldiers. Because the aristocracy looks down on trade, it may leave its business transactions and accounts to be handled by slaves, who may thus act as merchants, clerks, and bureaucrats.

Outcastes, too, while socially and legally distinct from the rest of the population, need not be considered as a special category by us, for they all fit into some section or other of the townspeople we have already dealt with. Sjoberg[19] lists among outcastes the Eta of pre-Meiji Japan, a low-status group; the untouchables of India, a caste grouping; the Jews of medieval Europe and the Middle East, and the Muslims of Tibet and China, religious groups; lepers, a group distinguished from others by disease;

17. Adam Smith noted two centuries ago that in ancient Egypt, "every man was bound by a principle of religion to follow the occupation of his father, and was supposed to commit the most horrid sacrilege if he changed it for another." Smith, *The Wealth of Nations*, p. 62.

18. However, slaves can also be aristocrats, as some were in the Ottoman empire, mentioned several times above, and in other Muslim empires, especially Egypt, where Mamluks (i.e., "slaves") formed their own dynasty (independently, 1250–1517, and then under the Ottomans, 1517–1798). On the other hand, slaves can be peasants or miners, but if they are bought and sold in great numbers to work on large estates, as in Rome, or in mines, as in Greece, the empire in question is commercialized and no longer traditional. Plantation slavery is, like plantations themselves, a modern phenomenon. Peasants who are not bought and sold but are tied to the land they work are more properly considered serfs than slaves.

19. Sjoberg, *The Preindustrial City*, pp. 134–35.

and prostitutes, an occupational group. In the latter case, membership in the occupation evidently produces outcaste status, but even in the others, where outcaste status is defined in some other manner, it is in fact associated with certain occupations that are considered demeaning according to the dominant prevailing values. Outcastes may be sweepers and laborers doing particularly dirty work, they may be executioners, slaughterers, and tanners, who must take human or animal life, they may be barbers or entertainers, and they may be merchants. The latter, like the medieval Jews or Muslims, are better off economically than the pariah-type of outcaste and can, in turn, maintain some scholars and religious leaders among their numbers.

The Townspeople in Politics

Earlier, I could easily generalize about certain characteristics of the peasantry that seemed relevant in a consideration of its ability to participate in the politics of the aristocracy. Given their heterogeneity, the same cannot be done in the case of the townspeople. Thus, with respect to mobility, some of them, like artisans and laborers, may never move any further from their towns than peasants may move from their villages. Others, like servants of the aristocracy or bureaucrats, soldiers, and priests, will, being attached to aristocrats, travel quite as much as the latter. And a very few merchants may even traverse distances greater than those covered by any aristocrat and become acquainted with societies unknown to all others in the aristocratic empire.

As to communication among townspeople, even the lowliest among them, like laborers and beggars, are likely to be in communication with more people than the peasant in his isolated village. Clerks, artists, and artisans will communicate with many in the course of their work, and traveling merchants and perhaps performers may have even more far-flung contacts. Unlike the peasants', their contacts are likely to reach across the lines of their own status groups. Such lines are firm and rigid in the traditional urban society—outcastes and slaves may be sharply segregated as unclean, and the aristocracy admits only a very few personal servants, artists, and scholars to come close enough to it for familiarity to breed contempt—but even laborers and beggars, and certainly artisans and clerks, may be in daily touch with those of different profession and status, and traveling merchants and also bureaucrats and soldiers have dealings not only with people of different classes but also of different cultures, the inhabitants of different towns and villages.

Thus, the intellectual horizon of virtually all townspeople is likely to be wider than that of the peasants. Still, variations among them in this respect, too, are very great. The unskilled laborer or the servant confined to the kitchen or the stable would have far fewer intellectually stimulating experiences than merchants, bureaucrats, and artists or servants so close to aristocrats that they might become their confidants. In terms of formal education and literacy, the great majority of the townspeople are as deficient as the peasantry, but the urban population does include not only some priests and scribes with at least some rudimentary knowledge of reading and writing, but also a few scholars and educators, philosophers and scientists who acquired more knowledge than anyone else in the aristocratic empire, not barring even the aristocracy.

Clearly, townspeople, unlike either the peasantry or the aristocracy, perform a wide variety of unrelated functions, they hold very different occupations, they include some who may be even poorer than peasants and a very few who are even richer than some aristocrats, some who are nearly as ignorant as peasants and a few who are the best-educated men in the aristocratic empire. To this heterogeneity corresponds an absence of common values. One cannot speak of the ideology of the townspeople as we could of the ideology of the aristocracy or the peasantry. Different groups among them are bound to see the world quite differently.

Consequently, there is no feeling of cohesion among townspeople. All aristocrats are keenly aware of the fact that they are aristocrats and, no matter how much they fight among themselves, they regard themselves as a class apart from all others and united by strong bonds of common values and a common social position. While peasants lack class consciousness in the sense of knowing that they belong to a huge class, let alone having feelings of solidarity toward it, they do know very well that they are peasants, even if they do not give much thought to the matter or articulate it. They know they are quite different from aristocrats and townspeople and they are tied to their fellow villagers by strong bonds of cohesion. In contrast, townspeople cannot think of themselves as a group or a class. Some, like artisans or merchants, may identify themselves with their town; others, like servants or bureaucrats, are more likely to identify themselves with their aristocrat, but none can identify with all the others as townspeople.

Just as peasants have no organization beyond the confines of their individual villages, so townspeople in one town have no links with townspeople in other towns (except for some merchants to be mentioned in a moment). Indeed, while there are often at least some slight contacts between peasants in neighboring villages, towns, being generally farther apart, are even more isolated from each other.

Furthermore, peasant villages are separated from each other, but each one, being highly homogeneous internally, forms in effect a tight community or organization. The same cannot be said of towns in aristocratic empires. Peasants are unorganizable in large numbers because, though culturally and occupationally homogeneous, they are scattered over wide areas; townspeople are just as unorganizable because, though they may be concentrated in great numbers in a small area, they are culturally and occupationally so highly heterogeneous. Cooks and coppersmiths, ditch-diggers and dancers, magicians and moneylenders, merchants and messengers, painters and potters, priests and prostitutes, servants and soldiers, tax collectors and tinkers have little in common and share few interests.

Not only do the townspeople not have a single culture or their own internal organization, but, unlike each village and unlike the aristocracy, the town in the aristocratic empire does not constitute a political system. The townspeople can, for purposes of political analysis, be broken down into three categories. One category consists of people who play no active role in politics at all or only a very small one. People in the other two categories operate politically in different arenas. The stakes of conflict in each arena are different, and the members of each category compete only among themselves.

Even the poorest peasant has in his village a political arena where he can, though perhaps not on equal terms, compete and cooperate with his fellows to determine the distribution of benefits and burdens, but the urban poor may have no such arena. Laborers, low-level entertainers, beggars and thieves, particularly if they are slaves or outcastes, but even if they are not, often perform their functions individually. They may compete with each other for their livelihood, but they form no community or organization in whose affairs they may have a voice.[20]

Secondly, there is a category of townspeople who are politically attached to the aristocracy. Some of them live in close contact with the aristocracy, like servants, artists, performers, scholars, and magicians. Others represent the aristocracy, carrying out the aristocratic functions of civil, military, and religious administration by forming the lower levels of the aristocratic hierarchies of the bureaucracy, the military, and the priesthood.

All of these townspeople are directly dependent on the aristocracy. Servants tend to identify with their aristocratic masters, for they share with them some of the material and psychological gratifications obtained from the aristocrats' privileged position. If they displease their masters, they might well be flung from the relative comfort of their positions to return to the village as peasants or remain in the town as laborers. Artists and

---

20. Sometimes, to be sure, some of these occupational groups are organized in guilds, in which case they do have arenas in which to function politically. Though, being of very low status, such guilds can probably not operate effectively in interguild politics, occupational groups so organized do then belong to our third category to be mentioned in a moment.

scholars and the higher, but still nonaristocratic, bureaucrats, soldiers, and priests bask in the favor of the aristocracy. Far more than servants, they share in the aristocracy's high standard of living, and, like aristocrats, look down with contempt on the peasantry and most of the townspeople. Yet, like servants, they are dependent on the whim of their aristocratic sponsors or employers.

A category whose members range from lowly servants to sophisticated artists and scholars and to soldiers, tax collectors and priests on the borderlines of the aristocracy clearly cannot be encompassed in a single organization representing common interests. Indeed, even the various professions within this category do not have their own organizations. Servants, artists, and scholars are individually employed by aristocrats and never function as groups, and the organizations of the bureaucracy, the military, and the priesthood are dominated by the aristocrats who form their upper levels and are hence not organizations of the townspeople even if these make up the majority of their members.

Thus, the townspeople in this second category, like those in the first, do not have communities or arenas of their own in which to function politically. They do, however, function politically in the arena of the aristocracy. Soldiers and bureaucrats, priests and scholars, artists and even servants act on behalf of particular aristocrats in intraaristocratic conflicts, lining up on one side or the other in wars and civil wars and court intrigues to gain more power and influence, greater glory and greater wealth for their masters and thereby also for themselves. In this process, the higher ones, like middle-level soldiers, bureaucrats, and priests and even servants in supervisory positions on an estate or a court may come to compete directly with aristocrats and, if they are successful, may thereby effectively move up into the aristocracy.

The third category, finally, consists of those townspeople who play a role in their own political arenas as distinct from the arena of the aristocracy. These are primarily the merchants and artisans of various sorts, often organized in guilds, but may include laborers and entertainers, and even beggars and thieves if they are similarly organized. The guilds of craftsmen and of those who provide services are always confined to individual towns, but merchants' guilds may comprise members dealing in a particular product in a number of towns and thus form one notable exception to the localism of townspeople.

Generally, guilds regulate recruitment and training in their profession and try to maintain monopoly conditions, prices, and standards of workmanship and behavior. They often provide what are in effect insurance benefits for individual members, as by supporting their widows and orphans and by paying funeral expenses, and they stage festivals and religious rites, often for their patron saints or gods, thus providing a sense of community for their members.[21]

All these matters require the making of decisions, and both the substance of the decisions and the questions of how and, especially, by whom, the decisions are to be made pose political issues. Thus, each guild constitutes an arena of politics in which its members function. To be sure, they do not function with equal power or authority for typically guilds are hierarchically organized, divided, for example, into masters, some of whom serve as officers of the guild, journeymen, and apprentices, and the latter may not have any important voice in guild politics. To some extent, certain guilds may compete with each other or, on the other hand, collaborate on some matters of common interest. There is thus also an interguild political arena in which at least some of the leading guild members can be active.

Of more interest to us than intraguild and interguild politics is the guilds' relation to the aristocracy. Guilds do represent and protect their members vis-à-vis the aristocrats' bureaucracy and sometimes the priesthood on such matters as taxes and dues and what government regulation of the urban economy, especially of markets, might be in effect, for example with respect to weights and measures. However, in doing this and thus insuring the payment of dues to the aristocracy and compliance with its rules, the guilds in effect become instruments of aristocratic government serving to maintain and strengthen it.[22] Their position is parallel to that of the internally autonomous peasant community vis-à-vis the aristocracy, which, precisely because of its autonomy from the aristocracy, forms the very foundation of the aristocrats' empire.

Nevertheless, to the extent that guilds do influence aristocratic decisions, they can be the one nonaristocratic element (in addition to the extremely rare and relatively minor peasant revolts in aristocratic empires) that intervenes in the politics of the aristocracy. To be sure, they can influence decisions only in a very small area of aristocratic government and

21. On guilds and their functions, see ibid., pp. 187–95, which mentions guilds in Babylonia and Assyria, ancient Greece and Rome, China and Japan, India and Nepal, in medieval Muslim and Western European cities, and in Aztec Mexico. On guilds in some commercialized empires, see Baer, "Guilds in Middle Eastern History"; Inalcik, *The Ottoman Empire*, pp. 151–62; and also Burgess, *The Guilds of Peking*.

22. On this function of guilds in the Ottoman empire, see Anderson, *Lineages of the Absolutist State*, pp. 376 and 517, and Inalcik, *The Ottoman Empire*, p. 155, and, more generally, Lenski, *Power and Privilege*, p. 202, and his footnotes referring to works on guilds in Rome, Russia, Western Europe, and Japan. In the Mamluk empire, commercialized as it was, "professional, merchant, and artisan guilds were virtually nonexistent, and what rudimentary forms did exist were created by the state for its own purposes rather than by the solidarity and self-interest of the members." Lapidus, *Muslim Cities in the Later Middle Ages*, p. 96.

even there probably only weakly and rarely so that this role of the guilds calls for no major modification of our generalization that government in aristocratic empires is wholly in the hands of the aristocracy. Still, participation of the guilds in aristocratic politics means, in effect, that aristocratic empires can contain the seeds of their own destruction, even if these seeds have in fact not always sprouted. Given the interrelated economic changes involved in commercialization, it is precisely merchants and artisans in the towns, often organized in guilds, who gain power at the expense of the aristocracy and thereby put an end to traditional aristocratic empires.

In traditional, noncommercialized, aristocratic empires, merchants and artisans can, by definition, intrude into aristocratic politics only in very minor ways. Members of our second category of townspeople, like servants and priests, soldiers and bureaucrats, can intervene in major ways, but they do so as individuals, functioning as aristocratic auxiliaries or as potential aristocrats themselves, not as representatives of their particular professions, let alone of the townspeople in general. The townspeople in general simply do not function politically, they are not a group with common interests, and hence it makes no sense even to ask whether they can intervene in aristocratic politics.

Townspeople are no more capable than peasants and, for that matter, aristocrats of envisioning major social changes. Even the merchant who, as Sjoberg stresses,[23] manipulates his environment more than others in the preindustrial order, does so to such a small extent in aristocratic empires that he is unaware of it and sees his environment as given by nature. Geertz can say even of present-day Javanese traders: "As agriculture for the peasants, so petty commerce provides for the trader the permanent backdrop against which almost all his activities occur. It is his environment —as much, from his perspective, a natural phenomenon as a cultural one —and the whole of his life is shaped by it. . . . The trader sees trade as a peasant sees agriculture . . . as the expression of his essential self."[24]

In the case of peasants, their inability to visualize major social change has been stressed at some length as an important reason for the absence or rarity of peasant revolts. In the case of the townspeople, it does not have to be stressed, partly because similar factors, like complete lack of any experience with social change, are at work with them, too, but partly also because townspeople would not all desire or try to bring about the same changes even if they could imagine them.

It seems reasonable to assume that if peasants in aristocratic empires could imagine major social change and bring it about, they would get rid of

23. Sjoberg, *The Preindustrial City*, pp. 136, 183–84.

24. Geertz, *Peddlers and Princes*, pp. 30, 44.

aristocratic exploitation, that is, they would abolish the aristocracy. Clearly, servants, artists and scholars, soldiers, bureaucrats, and priests are too closely identified with and dependent on the aristocracy to desire any such change. Until the market expands with commercialization, most artisans and merchants are dependent on aristocrats as their customers. The goods they manufacture or transship and sell are neither useful nor cheap enough for nonaristocrats. Many entertainers perform and unskilled laborers work in the direct employ of the aristocracy. Even those townspeople who are wholly or partly dependent on other townspeople, like some merchants and artisans, entertainers and laborers, and beggars and thieves, depend on the aristocracy indirectly.[25]

Overwhelmingly, the wealth of aristocratic empires is created by peasants, and almost none of it goes directly from them to the townspeople. Virtually all of the surplus produced by the peasants is taken by the aristocracy. The aristocracy, in turn in the process of consuming this surplus, distributes much of it among the townspeople. Only with commercialization, when both technology and nonaristocratic markets develop, as they eventually did in Western Europe, can some of the townspeople create and acquire wealth independently of the aristocracy. In the traditional aristocratic empire, they remain economically dependent on the existing order of aristocratic predominance, just as towns owe their existence to it in the first place.

Thus, the townspeople associated with the aristocracy would not want to get rid of it even if they could think of doing so, and the townspeople economically dependent on the aristocracy could not afford to get rid of it even if they could imagine such a change. Clearly, townspeople can generally not be expected to attack or resist the aristocracy. Even urban riots in aristocratic empires, possibly the most overt form of opposition to the aristocracy on the part of townspeople, are bound to be as limited in their extent and in their goals as are peasant revolts in such empires. To be sure, one can imagine that in response to a sudden deterioration in their condition, perhaps as a result of higher taxes or dues imposed on them or lower wages or prices payed to them, some townspeople might in desperation engage in mob outbursts or riots. Particularly the poorer artisans, more probably the apprentices and journeymen than the masters, perhaps some petty traders, and the laborers and also economically marginal towns-

25. As Hobsbawm says of the "city mob" in posttraditional but still preindustrial cities like eighteenth-century Naples, Palermo, and Rome: "Miserable and destitute though it was, it was not directly exploited by the Bourbon or Papal court, but was on the contrary its parasite, sharing, however modestly, in the city's general exploitation of the provinces and the peasants. . . . The rulers and the parasitic poor thus lived in a sort of symbiosis." Hobsbawm, *Primitive Rebels*, p. 115.

people like beggars and thieves, might do so. Given better communications within a town than between villages, a greater number of people might even be caught up in a riot than in a peasant uprising.

However, while a peasant village, being homogeneous, may rise up in revolt virtually as a unit, if it rises up at all, towns are deeply divided. Artisans in one trade may protest increased market dues on their product by rioting, but artisans in other trades may be unaffected by these dues or even benefit from them competitively. Petty traders may attack bureaucrats who tax them, but other merchants may see these same bureaucrats as their customers who are not to be alienated. And the numerous townspeople attached to the aristocracy, the servants and entertainers, the scholars and priests, the soldiers and bureaucrats, will certainly not sympathize with any rioters, let alone join them, but may regard riots as directed against themselves—as they well might be.

Also, like peasant revolts, urban riots in traditional aristocratic empires can have no far-reaching goals. They, too, are aimed merely at a restoration of a status quo ante that prevailed before a sudden deterioration in the rioters' condition and the urban rioters are likely to blame that deterioration on the local tax collectors and bureaucrats, priests or soldiers, rather than on the higher aristocracy, let alone on the aristocratic order.[26] It is only with commercialization that artisans and merchants can gain sufficient independence of the aristocracy that some of them may want to free themselves from aristocratic control altogether, and it is only then that the character of urban revolts changes and, as we have seen, that such townspeople can influence and even lead peasant revolts.

Given the weakness and rarity of urban riots in traditional aristocratic empires, it is hardly necessary to emphasize, as in the case of peasant revolts, the military superiority of the aristocracy over any rioters. Rioters that are largely unarmed and unskilled in the use of weapons and generally peaceable in their outlook would be no match for the highly mobile, well-organized, well-armed, and warlike aristocracy.

With the minor exceptions of guild influence on aristocratic decisions and of riots, townspeople cannot intervene in aristocratic politics any more effectively than peasants. One cannot say of the town, as I did of the

26. This is also said by Hobsbawm of the eighteenth-century city mob whose "riots were not directed against the social system" (ibid., p. 116). And Lapidus concludes his chapter on "the common people" in the cities of the Mamluk empire by observing that "rebellions and crimes never sought to change the government but only to ameliorate specific wrongs. . . . A true proletariat, productive of new ideologies and communal forms, and so resentful of disinheritance as to wage war on the established order, never developed in Muslim cities. . . . The lower classes were caught between violence and impotence." Lapidus, *Muslim Cities in the Later Middle Ages*, p. 184.

village, that it is a social and political system separate from that of the aristocracy. The town as such is no such system at all, and many of its inhabitants function within the aristocratic social and political systems. But others, particularly if they are organized in guilds, can be seen as forming yet another system or set of systems that go to make up the aristocratic empire.

Only with growing commercialization can now rich and powerful merchants and artisans or manufacturers come to dominate the towns as a whole, as happened to some extent in ancient Greece, particularly in Athens, and again in late medieval Western Europe, and, for some time, also in Japan. Then the towns can become more or less independent of the aristocracy and, as towns, become autonomous political systems, but their emergence as such is one more indication that commercialization has put an end to the traditional aristocratic empire.

Part V
Conclusion

15

Aristocratic Politics and Modernization

Patterns of Politics in Aristocratic Empires: A Summary

It has been the object of this book to develop generalizations about politics in aristocratic empires. Throughout, I considered it necessary to provide numerous historical illustrations, not to prove the universal validity of these generalizations, but to show that they can be supported with a great deal of evidence, to demonstrate that it is reasonable to see the patterns which I point to as prevailing across thousands of years and miles.

This much was said in the first chapter. Now that we have come to the concluding ones, it will be useful to restate briefly my major generalizations, this time without any illustrations and evidence, to reorient the reader who may have lost sight of the forest for the trees. In this section, then, I sum up my essential points about politics in aristocratic empires and show how the various institutional and ideological characteristics of these empires are interrelated. In doing so, I also explain the remarkable durability and stability of these characteristics that stand in such striking contrast to the increasingly rapid changes that come with modernization and modernity.

Perhaps the greatest obstacle to an understanding of the politics of aristocratic empires is the overwhelmingly strong modern tendency to associate politics with countries or states each of which is constituted or inhabited by a nation or a people who, operating through interest groups and political parties or movements, seek to influence their government and its policies. A traditional aristocratic empire is not a country or a state, its inhabitants, without economic interdependence or cultural homogeneity, do not constitute a nation or a people, they have no interest groups, parties, or movements, and they do not influence their government; indeed, to the extent that there is a government at all, it is not theirs.

The distinction between a modern country or a state and an aristocratic empire is, in our context, a vital one, because the former is, in good part, an arena of politics and the latter is not. The bulk of the population of an aristocratic empire consists of peasants who lived in their isolated, autonomous, self-sufficient villages long before these were incorporated in an empire. That incorporation simply results from the superimposition of an aristocracy that comes, not to govern, but to tax the village. Importantly as that change affects the peasants in some ways, each village continues to exist as an isolated, autonomous, and self-sufficient unit. It remains, therefore, an independent arena of politics where peasants engage in conflict and make decisions regarding the distribution of scarce resources.

As towns develop, their populations, too, function in independent political arenas of their own, insofar as they function politically at all and are not directly attached to the aristocracy, like servants, soldiers, and lower-level bureaucrats. Finally, the aristocrats, that is, those who live off taxes without engaging in productive labor themselves, form their own political arena. Institutions that have in modern times become national—the monarchy and the court, assemblies of noblemen, the clergy, the bureaucracy, the army—are simply institutions of the aristocracy.

The superimposition of a society of aristocrats on separate societies of peasants is most easily understood as a result of conquest. And, indeed, it is by means of conquest that most empires expand, whether the aristocracy originally grew out of pastoral nomads who conquered agrarian villages or out of an agrarian elite. Conquest is initially motivated by the desire of would-be aristocrats and then of aristocrats to deprive cultivators of their surplus product. The resulting relationship between aristocrats and peasants, which becomes institutionalized and which I call one of exploitation, then makes further conquests both desirable and possible.

The exploitative relationship between aristocrats and peasants is, in my analysis, the key to an understanding of the political nature of aristocratic empires. It accounts not only for the origins of these empires and for the role of the aristocracy in their economy, but for the governmental functions of the aristocracy, principally taxation and warfare, for the limited and decentralized character of government, and, more or less directly, for the values and ideologies governing aristocratic behavior and thus for the stakes in the conflicts that constitute aristocratic politics.

Some traditional aristocrats themselves shared my view of the key role of exploitation in aristocratic politics. Thus, the following statement has been attributed to King Artaxerxes I (226–240), the founder of the Sassanian dynasty in Persia: "The authority of the prince must be defended by a military force; that force can only be maintained by taxes; all taxes must, at last, fall upon agriculture; and agriculture can never flourish except under the protection of justice and moderation."[1] Centuries later, "the political wisdom of the typical Islamic State was condensed in the expressive apothegm of its manuals of rule: 'The world is before all else a verdant garden whose enclosure is the State, the State is a government whose head is the prince, the prince is a shepherd who is assisted by the army, the army is a body of guards which is maintained by money, and money is the indispensable resource which is provided by subjects.'"[2]

Let me summarize what has been said in earlier chapters about aristocratic government and politics, starting from my definition of aristocrats as exploiters of peasants and regarding their role as such as our key explanatory factor. Government is instituted in order to tax, its function is to take from the peasants rather than to give anything to them, and it can hence be understood as an extractive enterprise. To describe such an institution as a government may be somewhat misleading for it does not, as that word suggests, serve to steer, to determine the direction of some common enterprise. In a sense, it is a private enterprise, for taxation is imposed for the private benefit of the aristocracy, and there is no public in aristocratic empires if that word refers to all or most of the population, not just the aristocracy.

In order to tax peasants, aristocrats must control them. They do not have to direct their labor or interfere in internal village politics, but they must be able to deprive them of their surplus and—which requires far greater effort—to keep other aristocrats from doing so. Because peasants and the land they work are the principal source of wealth in agrarian economies, aristocrats ceaselessly compete for the control of land and peasants. Warfare, both offensive and defensive, then, is required to conquer, expand, or maintain a tax base which is, in turn, required to permit

1. Quoted in Gibbon, *The Decline and Fall of the Roman Empire*, 1:183. Practically the same view is ascribed to the seventeenth-century Ottoman chronicler Mustafa Naima, except that he adds a fifth point to close his "Cycle of Equity": There can be no rule or state without the military; maintaining the military requires wealth; wealth is garnered from the subjects; the subjects can prosper only through justice; without rule and state there can be no justice. After citing this, Stanford Shaw comments on Ottoman political theory: "Accordingly, society was divided into two groups: the large mass of subjects, whose primary purpose in life was to produce wealth by engaging in industry, trade, and agriculture, and to pay taxes to the ruler; and a small group of rulers, themselves neither producing wealth nor paying taxes, but rather acting as instruments of the sovereign in collecting his revenues and using them to support him and his family as well as themselves." Shaw, *History of the Ottoman Empire*, 1:112. This is a statement of the political theory and certainly the political practice of all aristocratic empires, though industry and trade become significant sources of wealth only with commercialization.

2. Anderson, *Lineages of the Absolutist State*, p. 505; the quotation is from Dominique and Janine Sourdel, *La Civilisation de l'Islam Classique* (Paris: Arthaud, 1968), p. 327.

warfare. Closely related to taxation, it is the only other essential function of government in aristocratic empires.

Other functions that may be characterized as governmental and are performed by the aristocracy, often by the use of corvée peasant labor, are auxiliary to the taxing or military function or both. Flood control and irrigation works may be constructed to regularize and increase the yields of agriculture and hence of taxation; canals and roads may be built to move the taxes in kind from the villages to the residences of aristocrats and to move troops to expand or defend frontiers; food may be stored to feed soldiers and bureaucrats and even peasants while they perform corvée labor; fortifications and walls may be erected to keep nomads or rival aristocrats from raiding or occupying the aristocracy's tax-yielding land.

Religious administration, involving the performance of ceremonies and sacrifices and the construction and upkeep of religious buildings, such as temples and tombs, is carried on by a more or less specialized priestly aristocracy. By perpetuating the religion of the aristocracy, as distinguished from that of the peasants, it serves to legitimize the role of the aristocracy in its own eyes. To the extent—usually slight and superficial—that the religion is accepted by the peasants, it may also help make aristocratic rule, that is, taxation, acceptable to them. Temples and tombs, quite like palaces and castles, are constructed and maintained for the private benefit of aristocrats with part of the wealth they have taken from peasants. Where government is a private enterprise, there are no public policies and also no public buildings.

It follows from two facts already stressed that aristocratic government is, measured by modern standards, extremely limited. This is true, for one thing, because it provides neither regulations nor services for the nonaristocratic population. Even the military protection from which villages and towns may benefit, and which is often held to be a service furnished by the aristocracy in return for the taxes it receives, is better understood as a mere incident of intraaristocratic competition that involves no reciprocity between the peasantry and the aristocracy. Put in modern terms, the government of an aristocratic empire consists almost entirely of an internal revenue service and a war department.

Aristocratic government is limited, secondly, because the peasant villages and, to a degree, those elements in the towns not directly tied to the aristocracy, form autonomous societies. They govern themselves, and there is little, if any, need for the aristocracy to carry on local government and administration or police and judicial functions. Only the tax collector in his inevitable periodic visits and, sometimes, the military recruiter, represent the aristocracy in the villages and towns.

However, while aristocrats do not govern the villages and towns, aristocratic government is nevertheless highly decentralized. Even so-called centralized bureaucratic empires are, in fact, decentralized by modern standards and differ from feudal empires in this respect only as a matter of degree. Decentralization is, in part, simply a result of poor communications, but it is also due to the exploitative relationship between aristocrats and peasants. Although power relationships between the central and the local aristocracy vary from empire to empire and from time to time, the central aristocracy always depends on the local aristocracy for its taxes; it has no independent tax-collecting machinery. This is obviously true where the local aristocrats are feudal lords who tax their own peasants and are supposed to pass part of what they collect on to the higher aristocracy, be it in cash or kind or in the form of services. But, in fact, bureaucrats, even if appointed and paid by the central aristocracy, are not so different from feudal lords. They, too, are recruited from a narrow stratum, often the lower aristocracy; they, too, tend to become hereditary, and in order to function effectively they must cooperate with the local landed aristocracy.

In any case, it is always the local aristocrats who collect the taxes, whether they are feudal lords or bureaucrats, whether they do so in their own name or that of a higher aristocrat, and they always retain as large a part of the taxes as possible and pass on to the central aristocracy as small a part as possible. Thus, aristocratic empires are decentralized because the aristocrat who has direct control of the land and the peasants enjoys considerable, if varying degrees of, independence from the so-called central government. Provincial governors or satraps, like feudal lords, may then easily become or be tempted to become independent rulers in their own empires, that is, to retain all the taxes they collect from their peasants.

Directly or indirectly, the fact that aristocrats live off the labor of peasants also shapes their values and attitudes, so that with respect to aristocratic ideology, too, striking patterns and uniformities prevail across very different empires. Free from the necessity to do productive physical labor, aristocrats everywhere look down upon it with contempt. With growing commercialization, this contempt, now mixed with resentment, is often extended also to trade and moneylending. Only the aristocratic ways of gaining wealth from taxes and tribute, from robbing and raiding are considered honorable. What distinguishes aristocrats from nonaristocrats is both their wealth and the fact that they gain it simply by virtue of being aristocrats. To set themselves apart from others, then, and to legitimize their status in their own eyes, leisure and the display of wealth are regarded as honorable and desirable in themselves. Conspicuous consumption through the use of elaborate clothing and jewelry, magnificent buildings and works of art, expensive ceremonies and huge armies of mostly useless servants is not wasteful as it would be in modern societies with other investment opportunities. As a display of power it is a weapon in intraaristocratic conflicts used to overawe or to bribe potential opponents.

A related aspect of aristocrats' ideology is their universal insistence on their nobility and superiority. Obviously, they can hold this belief by simply ascribing positive value to whatever distinguishes them from the rest of the population, above all, of course, to their role in the economy and government, that is, as exploiters of peasants, but also to distinct racial characteristics or to their peculiar attitudes. In turn, their belief in their superiority justifies and legitimizes what sets aristocrats apart, above all, again, their ability to live off peasants. So convinced are aristocrats of their superiority that they often regard themselves as a distinct human breed. They then become concerned with maintaining the purity of their "blood" and outlaw intermarriage with nonaristocrats. This practice, too, serves both to maintain and to legitimize the wide gulf between aristocrats and nonaristocrats.

Another set of values held by aristocrats can be explained as rooted in the governmental and especially the military functions of the aristocracy and, in turn, serves to justify and facilitate their performance. These values thereby strengthen particular aristocrats or groupings or institutions of aristocrats in their conflicts with others. Service and duty to aristocratic leaders and especially the acquisition of glory and the maintenance of honor are values that may completely dominate the aristocrat's life and may even require him to sacrifice it. All are predominantly military in nature and thus tend to make the aristocrat a good warrior.

On the other hand, in order to live and die by these primary military values, the aristocrat needs wars. The quest for honor and glory, then, may be as important a motive for engaging in wars as the quest for land and peasants—though victory will bring the latter as well as the former. Frequent as wars are, they may not suffice to fill the aristocrat's need for honor and glory, and more or less peaceable substitutes may have to be developed to give him the opportunity to display his courage and warlike skills. This accounts for the universal predilection of aristocrats for sports like hunting, horseback riding, and fencing, not to mention tournaments, jousts, and tilts.

If politics consists of the conflicts people engage in to obtain what they consider valuable, the above makes clear what the stakes of aristocratic politics are. Most immediately, they are the control of land and peasants, that is, the capacity to tax the latter, which secures to aristocrats their status as aristocrats, their wealth, their leisure, their conspicuous consumption, their ability to look down on labor and to feel superior and noble. Secondly, there are other opportunities for gaining wealth open to tax collectors, military men, and priests as they carry out their governmental functions as a private extractive enterprise. And finally and equally important, the stakes of aristocratic conflict are opportunities to gain honor and glory, prestige and respect.

All of these stakes are variously provided by positions within aristocratic hierarchies, like feudal, military, bureaucratic, and priestly rank orders. Hence aristocratic politics is conflict among aristocrats for positions as well as for the titles, insignia, and privileges attached to particular positions. Such conflicts can take place within and between aristocratic families, within and between aristocratic institutions, like armies and courts, within and between aristocratic empires. Indeed, family feuds, civil wars, and wars may be difficult to distinguish as forms of aristocratic politics.

In the process of aristocratic politics and competition, aristocrats ceaselessly change positions; individual aristocrats, their families and factions rise and fall and so do entire dynasties and empires. But throughout this instability and however much aristocrats might differ in individual character and new empires may differ from their predecessors with respect to the culture of their rulers, aristocratic rule as such remains stable, unchanging and unchangeable. It persists as long as the agrarian economy continues and there is no extensive commercialization and unless aristocratic empires collapse to permit peasants to regain their independence, that is, freedom from taxation. While the aristocracy remains in power, however, aristocrats must behave as such, they must consume without producing and they must live off peasants. And this, in turn, conditions the nature of the government of their empires and the content and form of their ideology and their politics. Instability prevails within the aristocracy —as it may within peasant villages and within towns—but the relation of the aristocracy as a class with other classes and groupings remains stable and unaffected by changes within them.

This, of course, restates what has been stressed before, that aristocrats, peasants, and the townspeople not directly attached to the aristocracy are not mere classes in the modern sense of that term, they live in different societies, and each of them constitutes a separate arena of politics. There is little contact and hence little conflict between these societies or classes. Conflict takes place not between classes but within them.

Because change can come about only through conflict (unless, as is generally improbable, it is in everyone's interest), the absence of conflict between the classes explains the absence of change in their relationship to each other. The aristocracy has no interest in changing it, and the peasantry is not in a position to change it. It cannot, intellectually or physically, challenge a relationship clearly disadvantageous to it, because its intellectual and political horizon is limited to the village. The peasants are engaged in a process of production and employ a technology that are far older than the aristocratic empire.[3] That process and technology re-

3. Not only did the imposition of aristocratic control not bring any change, it may even have prevented any possible change. If one assumes, as I have not, that peasants free of

main stable through millennia and appropriate to the self-sufficient village economy, and peasants remain unable to think of affecting the world beyond their village, let alone of organizing beyond the village level, as they would have to do to rid themselves of or to modify aristocratic control. Thus, if the absence of conflict explains the absence of change, the absence of change also explains the absence of conflict. The two go together. Consequently, while particular aristocracies and empires rise and decline as a result of intraaristocratic politics, the relationship of the aristocracy to the peasants—that is, the aristocratic empire as a type—endures until it is at last affected by modernization, a process I will now touch on briefly.

Modernization from Within and Modernization from Without

This book has been concerned solely with aristocratic empires untouched by modernization, and an analysis of modernization is beyond its scope. However, it may not be inappropriate, in these two concluding chapters, to indicate how traditional aristocratic empires come to an end and what, if anything, is then left of the politics of the aristocracy. Some empires, for example, in Africa, disintegrated, their component villages returned to primitive independence, and their aristocracies evidently disappeared. Far more often, empires come to an end by being conquered by nomads or by aristocrats from other empires and by being converted or incorporated, in whole or in part, into other empires. That, however, is a subject we have already dealt with as an aspect of intraaristocratic conflict and politics.

What we need to consider here is the end of traditional aristocratic empires as a type of political entity. This means the end of unchallenged and unchallengeable aristocratic predominance—but not necessarily the end of the aristocracy—and therefore requires the rise of a nonaristocratic group capable of having its interests represented in the politics of the empire. In the unchanging agrarian economy, no such challenger to the aristocracy can develop, hence the traditional aristocratic empire comes to an end only as a result of major economic change, that is, of modernization. Modernization may develop gradually from within an empire or it may intrude quite abruptly from without. In both cases, it may involve the growth of trade and industry, but the differences with respect to its politi-

---

exploitation might produce a surplus, then it could be argued that, in draining away any such surplus, aristocrats deprive peasants of any capital that might otherwise be invested in improving technology and the process of production.

cal consequences are profound. Let us, if only very briefly and extremely sketchily, look at some of these differences as they have taken shape in very different political systems existing in the present-day world and then discuss how the aristocracy fared under the two kinds of modernization.

Modernization from within evolved from its native origins to advanced industrial society, without any interruption at some point by modernization from without, only in Western Europe, and its later phases occurred also in the overseas offshoots of Western Europe, like the United States and Canada, Australia and New Zealand. In this process of modernization from within, it takes centuries of conflict and accomodation with the aristocracy for some of the townspeople to evolve into a commercial and banking and eventually an industrial bourgeoisie that finally becomes more powerful than the aristocracy. Long before the aristocracy has disappeared, industrialization produces a new labor movement that attacks both the old and the new upper classes. There then emerges the classical trichotomy of nineteenth-century Western European politics of aristocratic conservatism, bourgeois liberalism, and laborite socialism that has shaped so much of our ideological-conceptual vocabulary. The rise of the bourgeoisie had also involved the rise of Protestantism and later of anticlericalism and of ethnic nationalism so that religious and ethnic divisions, where they do not coincide with class divisions, further complicate the political spectrum by the nineteenth century.

In the ensuing conflicts, increasing numbers of people, made organizable by the growth of industry and communications, including even some of the remaining peasants and the preindustrial petty bourgeoisie, become politically mobilized. No single political party or movement is capable of controlling the government by itself and of destroying its various opponents or even of disregarding their interests.[4] Experience teaches all or most of them to accomodate themselves to the existence and the interests of their opponents, and eventually tolerance, within narrower or wider limits, comes to be seen not merely as a necessity but as a virtue. The result is a political system where different political interests can coexist and be organized and, in widely varying degrees, be represented in the shaping of public policy and where their conflicts are institutionalized and carried on according to rules that are widely held to be legitimate.

Unlike modernization from within, modernization from without does not begin with gradual commercialization.[5] When Western European trade

---

4. Even fascist regimes were coalition governments representing elements of the aristocracy, organized in the military and the bureaucracy, of the bourgeoisie, of the petty bourgeoisie, and, in Catholic countries, of the Church. Nor could fascist regimes permanently destroy their opponents.

5. I draw the distinction between modernization from within and modernization from

and even mercantile colonialism, as in India and Malaysia, reached traditional or already commercialized empires in the rest of the world, they had
no drastic effects on their social structures.[6] But when Western European
industrialism spills over into aristocratic empires, it initiates a rapid revolutionary process, whether it is introduced by modern colonialism seeking
raw materials, investment opportunities, and markets for industry, or by a
native modernizing aristocracy, or by both.

The disintegrating effects of the relatively sudden intrusion of industrial
modernity on the economy and the culture of traditional aristocratic empires or commercialized ones arouses two kinds of opposition. A traditionalist opposition seeks a return to the old order, while a modernizing
one takes as its model the industrialized society that has now become
known to it. For some time, the two movements may not be sharply distinct, because they share the immediate objective of removing colonialism
or the modernizing aristocracy or, where these are allied, both from power.
Eventually, however, it is almost invariably—Iran is the most striking exception to date—the modernizing wing that becomes dominant within
the opposition and comes to power when the colonial-aristocratic regime
crumbles.

The new leadership is then typically drawn from the tiny minority in the
population that had received an advanced modern education and had absorbed some modern values. Even if a few modern native capitalists or
some of the small industrial working class or, more rarely, some of the
huge peasantry were mobilized to support the modernizing opposition,
they had no long history and experience of organization. And the great
bulk of the population, mostly peasants and also townspeople, remain
altogether unorganized, the impact of modernity on them having been too
slight and too brief to push them out of their age-old passivity.

Unless organized forces of the prerevolutionary regime, most probably
the clergy, retained some strength or elements of the traditionalist opposition maintained some degree of independence during the revolutionary
process—like Zapata's peasants in Mexico—regimes of revolutionary
modernizers face opposition only from factions of other revolutionary
modernizers. They neither represent nor confront movements with mass
participation organized along class, religious, or ethnic lines. Passionately

---

without and analyze the political consequences especially of the latter in my *The Political
Consequences of Modernization*.

6. In exceptional cases, notably those of the Aztecs and Incas, aristocratic empires were destroyed, but even then peasants, if they survived bloodshed, newly imported diseases, and
forced labor, lived on as before as peasants, and the old aristocracy was killed or integrated
into the new aristocracy of the conquerors, as had happened many times before when one
empire conquered another.

dedicated to their objectives of rapid modernization, of bringing industrialization and land reform, welfare and equality to their underdeveloped countries, modernizers are not willing and, more important, not compelled to tolerate or compromise with any opposition. In contrast to the politics of balance produced by modernization from within, there may then emerge the politics of the single party and of repression, of coup and countercoup.

To be sure, there are great differences among modernizing regimes, and their politics may change significantly if, in the face of tremendous difficulties, they succeed in industrializing their countries, as has happened so far most notably in the Soviet Union and also in Mexico. The revolutionary modernizers are then replaced by managerial-bureaucratic-technocratic ones, a process now under way in China, and growing numbers of the population should eventually become capable of advancing their interests politically.[7]

So much for a highly compressed summary of some major differences between the political consequences of modernization from within and those of modernization from without—which has, among other things, quite ignored countries modernized in part from within and in part from without, especially those of southern South America. Before turning more specifically to the fate of the aristocracy in the course of modernization, I still need to touch on the intriguing question of why modernization from within developed into advanced industrialization only in Western Europe and the overseas areas settled by Western Europeans. All other areas of the world were eventually modernized from without and have become industrialized by that route, if at all. Some, like Ethiopia in the late nineteenth century and Saudi Arabia in the 1930s, were still traditional aristocratic empires when industrial modernization from without intruded into them; others, like Russia and China in the nineteenth century, were commercialized empires; and Japan, uniquely, had already entered an early phase of industrial modernization from within herself when she was suddenly exposed to the impact from without of more advanced Western industrialization.[8]

Clearly, Western Europe was neither the only area nor even the first one in the world to undergo the beginnings of modernization from within in the form of commercialization. As I showed at some length in Chapter 2, above, commercialization, although not universal in aristocratic empires, has occurred quite a number of times in their history; it may, in fact, be

---

7. Some of the problems faced by successful modernizing regimes are dealt with in my monograph on *Patterns of Modernizing Revolutions*.

8. For a thoughtful discussion of both similarities and differences between Japanese and Western European development, see the "Conclusion" to Anderson, *Lineages of the Absolutist State*, pp. 413–31.

linked to the existence of large empires.[9] What makes Western Europe unique are not these commercial beginnings of modernization but the fact that commercial modernization eventually developed into advanced industrial modernization.[10]

This is not the place to discuss at any length whether industrialism *could* only have emerged in Western Europe. Here I merely want to suggest that, because all or almost all traditional aristocratic empires included some merchants, any of them could, given time, have become commercialized, as many in fact did. Of course, tendencies in that direction could be set back or interrupted as a result of conquests by nomads or by noncommercialized empires. And it could further be argued that any commercialized empire—or perhaps any that was not based on a slave economy—could conceivably eventually have developed an industrial economy,[11] as Japan in fact began to do. To be sure, many of them, like the Chinese and Muslim ones, failed to do so through several centuries. Also, in some cases any such potential development may have been nipped by foreign invasions of

---

9. See p. 5, above.

10. Max Weber devoted much of his work to a search for an explanation of the uniqueness of Western development, to an answer to his question "to what combination of circumstances the fact should be attributed that in Western civilization, and in Western civilization only, cultural phenomena have appeared which (as we like to think) lie in a line of development having universal significance and value." Weber, *The Protestant Ethic and the Spirit of Capitalism*, p. 13. More recently, Perry Anderson has sought to explain why Western European societies were the only ones to develop industrial capitalism. *Lineages of the Absolutist State*, especially pp. 420–31. "The answer surely lies in the perdurable inheritance of classical antiquity. . . . What rendered the unique passage to capitalism possible in Europe was *the concatenation of antiquity and feudalism*" (ibid., p. 420; italics in the original).

11. Perry Anderson holds that this was impossible in the case of the ancient empires due to limitations inherent in their economy, that "neither industry nor trade could ever accumulate capital or experience growth beyond the strict limits set by the economy of classical Antiquity as a whole. The regionalization of manufactures, because of transport costs, thwarted any industrial concentration and development of a more advanced division of labour in manufactures. A population overwhelmingly composed of subsistence peasants, slave labourers and urban paupers narrowed consumer markets down to a very slender scale." Anderson, *Passages from Antiquity to Feudalism*, pp. 80–81. However, the main limit on economic growth stressed by Anderson is the employment of masses of slaves in agriculture in classical Greece and especially Rome. Of the dynamic of this "slave mode of production," he says that it was a "very restricted one, since it rested essentially on the annexation of labour rather than the exploitation of land or the accumulation of capital; thus unlike either the feudal or the capitalist modes of production which were to succeed it, the slave mode of production possessed very little objective impetus for technological advance, since its labour-additive type of growth constituted a structural field ultimately resistant to technical innovations, although not initially exclusive of them" (ibid., p. 79). This may very well explain the absence of economic growth in Greece and Rome, which are Anderson's concern, but it does not account for a similar absence in other empires where commerce developed to some degree but where agriculture did not rest on slavery.

nomads and of their conquest empires before it could even begin to bud. But in modern times and especially clearly in the nineteenth century, it was the impact of Western European industrialism that prevented any possible native development of industry in societies that had been commercialized by that time, like Japan and perhaps Russia and possibly China, beyond any early state it may then have reached. Western European development, by spreading to the rest of the world, assured its own lasting uniqueness.

All we can know, then, is that the evolution of industrialism took place first in Western Europe. We do not and we cannot know that conditions which might eventually have given rise to a similar development were absent everywhere else, that such a development *could* never have taken place elsewhere.[12] To ask what might have happened if history had been different, for example, whether advanced industrial capitalism might eventually have developed independently in Japan or China if Europeans and Americans had never arrived there or if industrial capitalism had never evolved in Europe and America is, of course, pointless insofar as there can be no data to provide a conclusive answer. However, it is not pointless to raise the question if it is thereby made clear that, in the absence of data, we are no more justified in assuming one answer than another, in assuming

12. The same idea is expressed by Marshall Hodgson when, writing of the "Great Western Transmutation," he says: "Perhaps, given time (that is, some interruption of the Occidental development), we might have found similar transmutations taking place independently in other agrarianate-level societies, some sooner and some later, each with its own forms in terms of its own background. It cannot be ruled out that the Chinese might later have repeated more successfully their achievements of the Sung period, with its enormous and sudden expansion of iron and steel production, its proliferation of new technical advances, and its general cultural effervescence; for though this was cut short and China reagrarianized under the Mongol conquest, cultural patterns cannot be fixed forever by such events, as organisms may be. One can also imagine conditions that could eventually have given great impetus to an Islamicate India. But once one such transmutation had been completed in one place, there was no time to wait for the like to happen elsewhere. In its very nature, such a cultural change, once completed, soon involved the whole globe, and the fact of its occurrence in one particular place, foreclosed the possibility of its happening so anywhere else." Hodgson, *The Venture of Islam*, 3:199.

Maxime Rodinson, too, stresses that "the economic structure of the mediaeval Muslim world was broadly comparable to that of Europe in the same period, as also, no doubt, to that of China, Japan and India before the impact of Europe upon them" (*Islam and Capitalism*, p. 117), and that medieval Islamic ideology was no more "irrational" than medieval Christian ideology. The development of capitalism only in Europe could therefore not have been due, as Weber argued, to some superior degree of rationality peculiar to European culture or thinking and expressed particularly in the bureaucracy and the legal system. As Rodinson points out, Weber's evidence of this European rationalism is drawn mostly from the period when capitalism was already developing or predominant and may hence be a result rather than a cause of its development or possibly a result of some cause common to both (ibid., pp. 77 and 103–17).

that industrial capitalism could not, rather than could, have developed in Japan or China.

Whatever might have been, in historical fact among traditional aristocratic empires and commercialized ones only those in Western Europe and, to a certain point, Japan underwent industrial modernization from within. All others have by now come under the impact of modernization from without. What, then, have been the differential effects of the two processes on the aristocracy?

The Fate of the Aristocracy under Modernization

More often than not, modernization from without is supported or even introduced by elements in the native aristocracy, usually found in the central government of the aristocratic empire and especially in the military and the bureaucracy. They hope that modernization will strengthen their regime militarily, make the bureaucracy a more efficient tax-collecting machine, and enrich them by opening up new sources of income. A century ago, Russian tsars gained strength through modernization from without as aristocratic Arab rulers on the Persian gulf are gaining wealth today. But in the process, aristocrats also gain opposition from old strata, like some peasants, upset and drawn into politics by economic changes, and especially from new ones created by these changes, like industrial workers and, above all, modernizing intellectuals.

Even modernizing aristocrats, let alone the more traditional ones who resent modernization from without, are wholly unprepared for opposition. In traditional aristocratic empires, they had, after all, never faced anyone who questioned or attacked their role as sole rulers. Even in commercialized empires, where merchants could wield some influence and gain some independence and where peasants might occasionally even revolt, aristocrats had no serious trouble maintaining their supremacy. Now, modernization from without arrives so suddenly, even if under aristocratic sponsorship, as to give no time to aristocrats to develop ideological and institutional defenses against the sudden onslaught of organized opposition. The rulers of ancient empires, like China, Russia, and Ethiopia, whose predecessors had governed for centuries without any effective challenge, except by other aristocrats, are now toppled, and their aristocracies, so powerful until the eve of the revolution, are irretrievably destroyed and disappear in a matter of years. It seems probable that the fate of the few aristocracies still in power in countries modernized from without will not be dissimilar.

To be sure, not all antiaristocratic modernizing revolutions are equally thoroughgoing. Elements of the aristocracy, like local landowners and especially the priesthood may survive—even the Russian Orthodox clergy and the Catholic Church in Mexico have done so—and certain patterns of aristocratic rule, as in military and bureaucratic organizations, and perhaps even elements reminiscent of aristocratic ideology may be perpetuated by the revolutionary rulers or revived by their managerial-bureaucratic successors. Still, these similarities are likely to be superficial, and aristocratic remnants are weak. What is most striking about the effects of modernization from without on the aristocracy is how sudden and destructive they are, at least when compared to the effects of modernization from within.

The limitations imposed on aristocracies by commercialization, the beginning stage of modernization from within, particularly their new dependence on merchants and bankers, were indicated in general terms in Chapter 2. Such changes are sufficient to eliminate commercialized societies from the category of traditional aristocratic empires that is the subject of this book, but they by no means eliminated the aristocracy as the ruling class (except within some towns). Commercialization merely modifies the aristocrats' behavior and thinking, it does not put an end to them. Commercialized empires are no longer traditional aristocratic empires, but they remain under aristocratic predominance. And they may thus persist for very long periods, with aristocratic power sometimes rising and sometimes declining, but not necessarily diminishing over the long run, as was true of China for two millennia and of Russia for one millennium before the nineteenth century, of Rome for three-quarters of a millennium before the end of the West Roman empire, and of Byzantium for another millennium after that.

In Western Europe, some townspeople did gain in power in the period of commercialization, beginning in the eleventh century, but it would be far too simple to say that the aristocracy suffered a corresponding loss in power. Now, after a thousand years of modernization from within, that has, indeed, been the result, but during these thousand years, it was, by and large, the lower aristocracy that lost and the higher aristocracy that for long gained and only in the final centuries also lost power.

As in all aristocratic empires, there was in those of feudal Western Europe perennial conflict between higher and lower aristocrats over the distribution of the taxes taken from the peasantry. And as is usual in such empires, the lower aristocrats enjoyed the advantage of collecting the taxes in the first instance, thus making the higher aristocrats dependent on them. This balance of forces was upset by the emergence as a new factor in politics of what we may now call a bourgeoisie composed of a new urban upper class of successful merchants, bankers, and guild masters, some of whom began to turn into manufacturers.[13]

13. Most of the remainder of this chapter follows, in good part verbatim, my *The Political*

The bourgeoisie tended to look to the higher aristocrats, especially the rulers, for protection. Merchants sympathized with their centralizing tendencies, which would help overcome the obstacles to trade posed by feudalism with its innumerable boundaries, customs fees, and different systems of laws, weights, and measures, while the bankers found their most receptive customers among the higher aristocracy. With its support or benevolent neutrality, the bourgeoisie gained varying degrees of independence or autonomy from the lower aristocracy for its towns. Gradually the nonaristocratic urban governments became more secure from the attacks of the lower aristocracy, for with their help the rulers gained strength, and the lower aristocracy was weakened.

The higher aristocrats and ruling princes benefited from their emerging alliance with the bourgeoisie as they discovered in its taxes and loans an important new source of wealth. With it, they could hire and equip mercenary armies, thus gaining a welcome and gradually growing measure of independence from the lower aristocracy. In time, the three formerly highly decentralized aristocratic hierarchies found in all aristocratic empires, the military, the bureaucracy, and the clergy, were slowly transformed into centralized instruments of control in the hands of the rulers of larger territories. With the aid of the bourgeoisie and the income derived from it, these rulers could create professional armies and professional bureaucracies loyal only to them and could subordinate the clerical aristocracy to their rule. And gradually they could reduce the lower lay aristocracy from a feudal to a court aristocracy.

The development of royal power, coinciding with the rise of the bourgeoisie, had, like the latter, its beginning some time around the eleventh century. Although it may be clearly noted in the centralizing measures of the Norman kings of England, particularly Henry II (1154–1189), the development of new institutions to replace the age-old ones of the traditional aristocratic empire was a slow one. It reached its culmination in the absolutist regimes throughout Western Europe, most notably that of Louis XIV (1643–1715) of France.

From the sixteenth through the eighteenth centuries, regarding the bourgeoisie as a prime source of their own strength and wealth, the kings deliberately fostered its growth and that of its wealth through the adoption of mercantilist policies favoring manufacturing and exports over agriculture. Competing with other kings and their bourgeoisies for trade advantages and routes and commercial colonies overseas, they even engaged in trade wars, as had the merchant republics of Italy, especially Venice and

---

Consequences of Modernization, pp. 51–55.

Genoa, even earlier, thus adding a new type of warfare to those fought by traditional aristocratic empires.

However, one must not exaggerate the extent of the victory and the control of even the most absolutist kings over the lower aristocracy. Although they could staff important positions in the bureaucracy and the judiciary with members of the bourgeoisie, many of these and, even more, the high positions in the clergy and especially in the military remained in the hands of the aristocracy. Aristocrats now tended to congregate in the capital cities, which had, with the growth of centralization, grown up not only as governmental but also as cultural centers. Nevertheless, they maintained a significant measure of independence from the kings and central governments through the continued control of their own lands and peasants and the income derived from them.

Absolutist regimes, then, continued to be aristocratic, although no longer traditional regimes. Aristocratic values continued to be dominant in government, wars continued to be carried on, not only for trade but for honor and glory, in part because kings had to keep the lower aristocracy busy and happy, but also because kings themselves were, after all, aristocrats. Above all, the superior claim of the aristocracy to power and prestige, merely by virtue of its status and regardless of individual merit, continued to be asserted. However, what had gone unquestioned for centuries and millennia in the traditional aristocratic empire, was increasingly resented by the bourgeoisie and its intellectual spokesmen. They came to think of themselves as quite capable of participating in and even replacing aristocratic decision making and considered themselves entitled to do so by virtue of the increasingly crucial role they played in the economy and of their individual talents and skills that had enabled them to assume that role.

As the bourgeoisie grew stronger and the lower aristocracy grew weaker, and the former was hence no longer in need of protection against the latter, the bourgeoisie turned against its erstwhile allies, the ruling aristocrats. Regarding them and their aristocratic armies and churches as the principal remnants of aristocratic traditionalism, which they resented, they subjected them to ideological and, eventually in some cases, to armed attack.

In response to growing ideological attacks from the bourgeoisie, aristocrats were forced to build ideological defenses; in traditional aristocratic empires, no one had questioned the right of the aristocracy to rule, so that it required no more defense than the existence of the mountains or the clouds. Now, however, there evolved an ideology of conservatism designed to justify the aristocratic superiority that had so long been taken for granted, more often than not relying on a religious basis and on the old aristocratic values of service and duty, honor and glory, and the inherent superiority of noble blood. This was counterposed to bourgeois claims for rationalism, advancement by individual merit, civil liberties, free enterprise, in short, for liberalism.

Not only ideological but even armed attacks failed to dislodge the aristocracy permanently from its position of power. In England, where absolutism had never developed to the same extent as in France, the Revolution (1642–1649) could still be carried on under the banner of the rights of what had hitherto been a feudal representative institution in which, however, the bourgeoisie already enjoyed representation. Ideologically, the attack on absolutism in England was couched in part in religious terms rather than, as in France, involving an attack on the Church and even religion itself. However, even the much more explicitly antiaristocratic French Revolution a century and a half later proved to be only a major battle that forced the aristocracy to withdraw and weakened it, rather than a war that destroyed it. Exactly as in the English Revolution, the old monarchy was restored twenty-one years after the preceding king had been executed. More important, the institutional weapons that the ruling aristocracy had gradually created in the period of the rise of the bourgeoisie, the professional military, the professional bureaucracy, and the centralized clergy, proved to be even more powerful than the monarchy itself. The latter was finally removed in France after a century-long struggle, but these institutions and elements of aristocratic conservative ideology have survived into the present in all Western European societies and in France became visibly vital again in General de Gaulle's Fifth Republic (1958–1969).

The contrast between the outcome of these antiaristocratic revolutions in countries modernized from within and of the antiaristocratic revolutions in countries modernized from without is striking. Unlike in England and France, in China, Turkey, and, more recently, in Ethiopia, and even in Russia where some absolutism had developed, the old regimes were institutionally and ideologically unprepared for the opposition coming, not from a gradually rising bourgeoisie, but from quickly rising movements of revolutionary modernizers. In these countries, in contrast to their fate in England and France, the monarchy was destroyed beyond any reasonable hope of restoration, the aristocratic armies and bureaucracies were replaced by new ones, and even the surviving religious institutions were gravely debilitated.

Whereas in England and France major revolutions triumphed at least temporarily and weakened the aristocracy permanently, not in all countries where a native bourgeoisie had brought modernization from within did it become strong enough successfully to attack its former allies in the higher aristocracy. The bourgeois revolutions in Central Europe (1848), unlike those of Western Europe, fizzled and failed. In Japan, where something like European absolutism had developed under the Tokugawa Shogunate, one cannot speak of a bourgeois revolution at all. Under such circumstances, the ruling aristocracy itself can sponsor industrialization, particularly to strengthen its rule militarily when it feels threatened by already industrialized foreign powers. It helps by governmental means, such as taxes, to channel capital extracted from the peasantry into the hands of the bourgeoisie and toward industrialization. Thus, such an aristocracy, in cooperation with the bourgeoisie, becomes an agent of industrialization from within.

There then emerges an alliance between the ruling aristocracy on the one hand and the bourgeoisie on the other, particularly the bourgeoisie in banking and heavy industry. Bismarckian and Wilhelminian Germany furnishes the classical example of such a development, but parallels to it may be found in Japan after the Meiji Restoration. Such an alliance is characterized by policies benefiting both aristocratic government and bank-financed cartels in heavy industry, such as naval and colonial expansion, tariffs protecting both industry and big landowners, and the use of government, in both suppressive and paternalistic ways, to minimize the threat of an emerging labor movement to both employers and the aristocracy. I may note that this type of alliance can create a condition rather exceptional in world history—the coincidence at a single time and in a single society of a regime of the aristocracy and of strong advanced industry—that itself appears to be a precondition of a certain kind of fascist regime, representing a reaction to industrialization.

Unlike in Western Europe, then, in Germany and Japan—and Austria, Italy, and Spain are not wholly different in these respects—there had been no successful bourgeois revolutions, the ruling aristocracy sponsored industrialization, and the bourgeoisie remained dependent on the aristocracy and never developed a powerful antiaristocratic liberal ideology or movement. Obviously, both aristocratic institutions, above all the military and the bureaucracy, and aristocratic ideology with its peculiar link to warfare survived far more intact and powerful into the twentieth century in such countries without successful bourgeois revolutions than in Western Europe. Although fascist movements are certainly not aristocratic in character, the regimes they formed invariably incorporated and importantly rested on the surviving aristocratic institutions and even revived elements of aristocratic ideology, like its emphasis on duty and service, on glory and honor. In Germany, in Japan, and in Italy, then, the aristocracy played a key role in government until the end of World War II in 1945,[14] and in Spain much of the lay and clerical aristocracy was a pillar of the Franco regime until its end in 1975–76, and it has not disappeared yet.

14. Mussolini turned against the aristocracy in 1943 when he established his Italian Social Republic, and Hitler did likewise in 1944 after the unsuccessful plot to kill him.

16

Remnants and Legacies of Aristocratic Politics

Institutional Remnants

In the first chapter I stated that one major reason for studying the politics of aristocratic empires is that significant remnants of traditionalism are left in modern societies that can be understood only if one knows their origins. However, I did not pursue this theme throughout the book to avoid repeated digressions from the subject of the politics of traditional aristocratic empires. Still, to make explicit the relevance of this study for an understanding of modern societies, I may conclude it by some remarks on these remnants.

In the preceding section, I indicated that there is a tendency for aristocracies and their institutions and ideologies to be wiped out in revolutionary processes that respond to modernization from without, though obviously even there important remnants persist. In the underdeveloped world, it is the peasantry that remains as the major remnant from the days of aristocratic empires. In what may appear like a paradox, then, it is not in the industrially backward countries—except those relatively few, like Saudi Arabia, that have not yet undergone a revolution—that remnants of aristocratic institutions and thinking are strongest but, on the contrary, in countries modernized from within that have been subject to modernization for centuries and have even reached advanced levels of industrialization.

In spite of the historic link between peasantries and aristocracies it is in this century in countries where peasants were still the overwhelming majority of the population, like Russia, China, and India, that aristocrats lost their power. On the other hand, in countries where peasants have disappeared by being integrated into the industrial economy either as workers or as farmers, as in Britain, Germany, and France, the aristocracy has remained a significant factor in politics. In the following pages, then, I will deal only with countries modernized from within, that is, with Western Europe and, in a few remarks, also the United States.

As the preceding section suggested, aristocracies remained powerful well into the twentieth century in Britain and France and especially in Germany. Their role and influence even just in these three countries, let alone in other European ones, and even just in the present century, let alone in the millennium of European modernization from within, is obviously a huge subject and one far more complex than the subject of this book, because it involves the interaction of aristocracies with the forces of modernization. Nothing like even a brief analysis of it is contemplated here. All that can and need be done is to present some illustrations of the persistence into the present of elements discussed in this book and thus of the pervasiveness of traditionalism in modern politics.

Western Europe lived under aristocratic rule for most of the past two thousand years, modified by the commercialization of the Roman empire and that beginning in the late Middle Ages and in nearly pure traditional aristocratic empires in the intervening centuries. Drastic change away from aristocratic rule came only in the last very few centuries so that it is not surprising that elements of that rule should survive.

To be sure, most of the present-day European aristocracy is a modern creation rather than a survival of the traditional past. Thus, most French aristocrats are descendants of those ennobled between the sixteenth century and the Revolution of 1789, of the new aristocracy created by Napoleon, and of those who acquired titles in the nineteenth century. Similarly, only about four percent of all present British hereditary peerages were created before the sixteenth century and three-fourths of all peerages are less than two hundred years old.[1] The point, however, is that, until quite recently at least, most of these more or less new aristocrats eagerly imitated the behavior of the old ones and accepted the old aristocratic institutions and values. Thus, though the aristocratic families of the traditional aristocratic empires we have been concerned with have long ago become extinct, their institutions and values survive them.[2]

As noted in Chapter 7, aristocrats, performing the functions peculiar to them in aristocratic empires, can hold only the occupations of rulers and military men, bureaucrats (and judges), and priests. Down to our own generation in the industrially most advanced countries of Western Europe,

1. Of 952 British hereditary peerages listed in *Burke's Peerage* of 1967, 706 were created in the last two hundred years (plus 136 life peerages), only 41 were created before 1500, and none before about 1235, that is, about a century and a half after Britain ceased to be wholly traditional. Of 1,190 baronetcies existing in 1967, more than half were created in the past one hundred years and none before 1611. Townend, ed., *Burke's Peerage*, pp. 3015–20, 3025–28.

2. I have, of course, all along defined aristocrats not by heredity but by the position they occupy in the economy and the government of aristocratic empires. But with reference to modern times with their different economy and government, we are forced to fall back on the European aristocracy's self-definition by descent and by title.

only a very few careers have been considered proper ones to be chosen by an aristocrat—and these are precisely the careers aristocrats have pursued since the dawn of traditional aristocratic empires.[3]

Of course, aristocrats can no longer pursue the career of effective rulers in Western Europe today merely by being aristocrats. Prime ministers and presidents, members of cabinets and of parliaments are all directly or indirectly elected by the voters and do not occupy their positions by virtue of their birth or title. In the Third and Fourth French Republics and the German Weimar Republic, based on revolutionary breaks with the aristocratic past, aristocrats tended to stay out of party and parliamentary politics. In Britain, however, where modern representative institutions grew out of aristocratic ones without any drastic break, aristocrats serving in the House of Commons learned to appeal to the expanding electorate for votes. As party leaders, legitimated by the voters but partly, no doubt, because of their prestige as aristocrats, they can still—in this century in the Conservative Party—pursue the ancient aristocratic career of rulers.

The sole exception to the above statement that all Western European parliaments are directly or indirectly elected is the upper house of the British Parliament, the House of Lords, a majority of whose members still sit simply by virtue of being hereditary aristocrats. Clearly, this cannot be explained as a phenomenon of modernity. The same is, of course, true of the institution of monarchy that survives to this day with considerable prestige if little power in Britain, the three Low Countries, three Scandinavian countries, and, as recently restored, in Spain. More significant is the fact that until 1918 Switzerland and France—and San Marino—were the only republics in Europe (except Portugal whose king departed in 1910, but which, like some Latin American countries, was only partially modernized from within). Some of the ruling monarchs, notably the German emperor, were powerful political figures, yet their claim to authority rested entirely on the aristocratic basis of descent and noble blood.

Service in the hierarchy of the established state church, whether it be Catholic, Lutheran, or Anglican, has been considered another appropriate career for an aristocrat and so has government service in high bureaucratic positions. These latter positions were, at least until World War II, filled disproportionately by aristocrats, often because their occupants were drawn from the graduates of educational institutions which, in turn, favored aristocrats in their admission policies. Certain elite branches of the bureaucracy in particular attracted the aristocracy, sometimes the ministry of

---

3. Thorstein Veblen wrote of his leisure class: "The normal and characteristic occupations of the class in this mature phase of its life history are in form very much the same as in its earlier phase. These occupations are government, war, sports, and devout observances." Veblen, *The Theory of the Leisure Class*, p. 44.

finance, the colonial service, and invariably, the foreign service. Most government activities developed, after all, only in the modern, postaristocratic age, but taxation, the governing of occupied territories, and the conduct of foreign affairs have been a function of the aristocracy from the very beginnings of aristocratic empires and are hence seen by aristocrats as proper fields of activity. Foreign relations are, of course, closely tied to warfare and were, when empires were identified and defined by their ruling aristocrats, relations among aristocrats and, indeed, in Europe often intrafamily relations.

Even more than the diplomatic corps, the military has remained what it has been from the beginnings of traditional aristocratic empires, the profession par excellence of the aristocracy. Military officers, like high-ranking bureaucrats, have until quite recently been disproportionately recruited from the aristocracy,[4] and the aristocracy has, into the twentieth century considered the military its special domain. The link between aristocracy and military is emphasized by the fact that monarchs are invariably regarded as military officers and commonly appear in military uniform. Their heirs are given military training on the assumption, which can only be derived from the experience of aristocratic empires, that that is the best preparation for government.

The aristocracy's powerful role in the leadership of European armies as late as World War I and even World War II, notably in the Prussian-German general staff, is too well known to require further discussion. Given the key position of armies not only in warfare and foreign policy but also in domestic politics in a number of European countries, like

4. Throughout the nineteenth century, when Britain was the most highly industrialized country, half of all the officers in the British army were drawn from the aristocracy and the landed gentry, and the proportion was even higher among general officers and especially in elite regiments (88 percent in the 1st Life Guards in 1912). Even in the 1950s, 80 percent of all Sandhurst commissions went to public school boys. These data are drawn from Razzell, "Social Origins of Officers in the Indian and British Home Army," pp. 253, 256, 259, who concludes that "the landed upper classes maintained their position within the army throughout the nineteenth century and even into the twentieth" (ibid., p. 259). See also Otley, "Militarism and the Social Affiliations of the British Army Élite," a study rich in data on the social origins, education, and connections by marriage of British lieutenant generals, generals, and field marshalls from 1870 to 1959, which concludes that there was "a pronounced association between the army élite and the old ruling order in Britain" (ibid., p. 102). In the German military, aristocrats comprised the following percentages of the "elite officers": in 1872, 94 percent; 1898, 81 percent; 1911, 67 percent; 1925, 38 percent; 1932, 33 percent. In each case, the percentage for the entire officer corps is approximately half that for elite officers. These data are drawn from Janowitz, *The Professional Soldier*, p. 94, who provides similar though less complete data on the Swedish, British, and Italian military. Among these three countries, in the century up to World War II, the percentage of aristocrats among elite officers drops below 25 percent only in interwar Italy.

Germany and France, the power of aristocrats holding positions open to them only because they were aristocrats becomes apparent.

Modern clergies of established churches, but especially bureaucracies and military organizations can, in their centralized form, trace their origins back only to the absolutist phase of aristocratic rule that grew with commercialization and mercantilism. However, the absolutist regimes that created these modern institutions were themselves caught up in aristocratic attitudes inherited from the past and, far from creating them de novo, they gradually converted existing old aristocratic institutions into the modern bureaucracies and the modern military. This may well help account for the tremendous importance in these institutions of hierarchical arrangements with well-defined ranks, each with its particular powers and privileges and, above all, its title and insignia, all matters that had been of supreme concern to aristocrats in their traditional empires.

That aristocrats are still concerned with matters of rank and precedence is nicely illustrated by the fact that *Debrett's Peerage* provides a detailed four-column "Table of General Precedence" that shows, for example, that the eldest sons of dukes precede earls and that marquesses' eldest sons precede dukes' younger sons, not to mention the fact that eldest sons of the younger sons of peers precede the eldest sons of baronets.[5] *Burke's Peerage* lists all British peerages (1,088 as of 1967) and baronetcies (1,190 in 1967) in order of precedence so that each aristocrat can tell exactly what his place is.[6] Indeed, these publications, carefully listing all British aristocrats with their ancestors and children and picturing and describing in detail their coats of arms also demonstrate the continuing aristocratic passion for genealogy—which, in turn, has much to do with rank and precedence—and the symbols of power. *Burke's Genealogical and Heraldic History of the Peerage, Baronetage, and Knightage* has been published in over a hundred editions since 1826, and *Debrett's Peerage, Baronetage, Knightage, and Companionage* appeared annually since 1802 at least until 1974. They have their counterpart for the German aristocracy and for princely and ducal houses in other European countries in the *Almanach de Gotha*, published annually in French in that city from 1764 at least until 1941; and for France, in the twenty-volume *Nobiliaire Universel de France* and the nineteen-volume *Dictionnaire de la Noblesse.*[7]

The modern military retains another characteristic from the days of aristocratic empires when aristocrats led all armies, but the foot soldiers in

5. Montague-Smith, ed., *Debrett's Peerage* (1980), pp. 46–47.

6. Townend, ed., *Burke's Peerage*, pp. 3015–20, 3025–28.

7. Saint-Allais, ed., *Nobiliaire Universel*; Chenaye-Desbois et Badier, ed., *Dictionnaire de la Noblesse*. For Spain, there is Larios Martín, ed., *Nobiliario de Segovia*, and Atienza, *Nobiliario Español*.

some of them were peasants. The distinction between the officers and the common soldiers—*Gemeine* in German even more than "common" has the connotation of inferiority and meanness—in all modern armies is probably derived from that between the aristocracy and the rest of the population. Unlike distinctions of rank among the officers and among the men, the distinction between these two groups is above all a social one. Even the second lieutenant who is inferior to the master sergeant in terms of experience and perhaps even power, is regarded as his superior. Officers wear better uniforms, their insignia are golden or silver, they have separate and better living quarters, social clubs, and even washrooms, and common soldiers must acknowledge their superiority by saluting them, standing at attention in their presence, and using special forms of address. In aristocratic empires, this distinction was a natural reflection of the prevailing class divisions; in modern society, it can be understood as a remnant of the aristocratic past modified by the admission to officer rank of nonaristocrats, chiefly on the basis of education, as a concession both to the industrial middle classes and to the need for expertise in modern armed forces.[8]

Aristocrats have generally remained dominant in the military more than in any other institution and have powerfully shaped its structure and ideology down to the present. With its emphasis on duty and honor, to which we will turn in a moment, on rank, titles, and insignia, and on the visible superiority of an upper over a lower caste, the military comes closer to reflecting the character of the aristocracy in its traditional empires than any other modern institution. This is true even in countries without an aristocratic background, like the United States, where the military was copied from European models.[9]

Ideological Remnants

Serving in the military and the bureaucracy and also in the established church, many aristocrats have in modern times come to make a living as paid state employees. What might by traditional aristocratic standards be a humiliating situation is alleviated by the fact that they

8. It is also noteworthy that under the Geneva Convention officers who are prisoners of war may not, unlike enlisted men, be compelled to do physical labor (a major theme in the film *The Bridge over the River Kwai*), quite possibly on the assumption that officers are, or share the character of, aristocrats for whom manual labor is still considered demeaning.

9. However, in the United States, the distinction between officers and enlisted men was modified by extensive mobility from the enlisted to officer ranks and, at least until World War I, even the election of officers by enlisted men from their own ranks in certain military organizations. On Jacksonian hostility to the "aristocratic" military academy, see Ambrose, *Duty, Honor, Country*, chap. 4.

perceive the institutions in which they serve to be aristocratic ones, even if they reject, more or less rigidly, the newer representative governments of their countries as illegitimate. Still, not to be dependent on any salary and, indeed, not to pursue any career with a firm professional commitment is as much in line with the traditional role of the aristocrat and can hence still be regarded as equally honorable as being a military officer, bureaucrat, or priest. As Harold Laski wrote with some irony: "A gentleman is, rather than does. . . . He is interested in nothing in a professional way. He is allowed to cultivate hobbies, even eccentricities, but he must not practise a vocation. He must not concern himself with the sordid business of earning his living; and he must be able to show that, at least back to his grandfather, none of his near relations has ever been engaged in trade. . . . He must know how to ride and shoot and cast a fly. He should have relatives in the Army and Navy, and at least one connection in the diplomatic service."[10]

Traditionally, the aristocrat's ability to live without working resulted from his control of land and peasants. With commercialization, that control became translated into more clearly defined property rights. In Western Europe, as elsewhere, large estates owned by kings and princes, dukes, counts, and barons, and also by churches and monasteries, and worked by their peasants survived from the Middle Ages into the twentieth century. While not every one of them could own land any more, aristocrats have continued to think of themselves as linked to the land. The Prussian Junkers retained their estates until 1945, and even in France, particularly in its western region, aristocratic large landownership survived the Revolution and "a kind of de facto feudal relationship between aristocratic landlord and peasant tenant survived for generations, into our own time."[11] In England, "gentility has traditionally and almost aboriginally been connected with military office and with the lands held in return for fulfilling such office. . . . The plain fact remains that the gentlemen of England have mostly stayed put, for as long as possible, on their land. They have farmed it, hunted over it, delivered justice to those that lived on it, nor have they ever allowed themselves to forget their obligation to fight for it."[12]

As this passage indicates, landownership is connected not only with the military and administrative-judicial functions of the aristocracy and also its predilection for hunting, to be mentioned in a moment, but also with farming. In the traditional aristocratic empire, the aristocrat simply lived off the land and the peasants he controlled, but in modern society where the market for agricultural goods has expanded due to urbanization and industrialization and has become international in scope, the aristocrat may

10. Laski, *The Dangers of Being a Gentleman*, p. 13.
11. Wright, *Rural Revolution in France*, p. 4.
12. Raven, *The English Gentleman*, p. 36.

become a commercial farmer or planter. As a product of modernization, he invests his wealth by buying land, labor power (whether slaves or wage workers), and such machinery, fertilizer, and means of transportation as may be available and produces a product entirely for sale. Such a farmer or planter is quite as modern a businessman as an industrial capitalist and is in principle clearly different from an aristocrat.

In practice, however, the distinction between aristocrat and commercial farmer or planter is often not so clear and becomes one merely of degree. The latter, too, is likely to carry on subsistence agriculture along with commercial agriculture. Even those who are economically predominantly commercial farmers or planters may well be ideologically predominantly aristocrats. This may be, because they or their ancestors were aristocrats who used commercially either their aristocratic landholdings, as happened in Prussia east of the Elbe, or newly acquired land, as was true of some of the early plantations in Maryland, Virginia, and the Carolinas. But the aristocratic ideology might also be accepted through more or less conscious imitation by landowners of nonaristocratic descent, who find it congenial to their life on rural estates. This was true of many ante bellum planters in the southern United States, who, though not aristocrats by descent, held values and attitudes characteristic of the aristocracy.

Turning now to these surviving values and attitudes of the aristocracy, I might first quote General Robert E. Lee, a representative of the class just mentioned and of a profession that sought to live by aristocratic standards, who said: "Duty is the sublimest word in any language." The great importance of the concepts of duty and service in the minds of aristocrats was noted earlier. As in aristocratic empires so in modern times, the proper aristocrat serves what he perceives to be an aristocratic institution, and, in modern armies and bureaucracies as in traditional ones, performance of duty and obedience to the orders of higher authority both guide and can justify the individual member's behavior.

However, there may be a question to whom the performance of service and duty is owed. Even in traditional aristocratic empires, these concepts by no means prevented conflict among aristocrats, including defiance by inferior aristocrats of their superiors. And such conflicts may in turn have forced other aristocrats owing some allegiance to both sides to choose to which to remain loyal.

If, in the course of modernization, the institutions to which the aristocracy pledged its loyalty and service, for example governments or, more specifically, armies or bureaucracies, cease to be exclusively or even principally aristocratic ones and come to represent the interests of broader strata of the population, aristocrats may nevertheless continue to serve them. Aristocratic French army officers have in this century fought and died for a republic they detested, because they were loyal to the army or even to

"France."[13] Such aristocrats then become like those in present-day Britain, who, headed by the monarch, are public servants in the modern sense of that term. They are motivated by an outmoded ideology that has come to serve new functions in a new society but still helps preserve the aristocracy as aristocratic values did in the past.

However, where bureaucracies or specific branches thereof and especially the armed forces are dominated by aristocrats and represent aristocratic interests defined in terms of aristocratic values, these institutions may serve their country as they themselves define what constitutes the country and its interests. In the absolutist period, aristocrats came to identify with national royalist governments and they may well feel that the continuing bureaucracy and military represent the "country" or the "nation." However, a republican government that grew out of a break with a monarchy does not represent the "true" nation. Thus, aristocrats while dominating key executive organs of a government may nevertheless deny its legitimacy, feel alienated from it and be disloyal to it, all in the name of loyalty, service, and duty to the country.

Leading elements in the French army and bureaucracy were hostile to the governments they were a part of in every crisis of the Third Republic, from its shaky beginnings in the 1870s through the Dreyfus affair to its collapse in 1940. In the Vichy regime, the bureaucracy could rule free from the fetters imposed by party and parliamentary government, and it emerged powerful once again when the Fourth Republic crumbled under army pressure and General de Gaulle came to power.

In Germany, the aristocracy had its own government, which it could serve loyally, until 1918. The Weimar Republic, however, was not a truly German government in its eyes. Even more than in France, the army and the bureaucracy regarded themselves rather than the elected organs of the government as the real representatives of what they defined as the nation. From the beginnings of the Weimar Republic, when it was threatened by the Free Corps, to its early end at the hands of the Nazis, aristocratic elements in the army and the bureaucracy failed to support or actively opposed the government.

Whereas in France and Germany aristocrats chose service to their own institutions over service to the government, in Britain the aristocracy did

13. This and the continuing importance in modern aristocratic-military ideology of the values of service and duty, of fighting and dying bravely, and of honor and glory to be mentioned in a moment, is well illustrated by the final exchange of messages, on 7 May 1954, before the fall of Dien Bien Phu, the last French stronghold in North Vietnam. General Cogny, the French commanding general in North Vietnam: "You will fight to the end. There is no question about raising the white flag over Dien Bien Phu after your heroic resistance." General de Castries, the commander of the French garrison: "We shall fight to the end. Au revoir, mon Général. Vive la France!" Fall, *Hell in a Very Small Place*, pp. 406–7.

not face a new republican government to be alienated from. The aristocracy, particularly through the Conservative Party, had maintained identity with and a stake in the government as it became more representative. But even here, British army officers, in the so-called Curragh Mutiny, refused to follow orders of a Liberal government to move to northern Ireland in the face of a potential rebellion by Ulster opponents of the Home Rule bill of 1914, choosing dismissal from the army and putting loyalty to what they defined as the national interest above service to the government.

Aristocrats, then, continue to believe in service and duty, but they must necessarily decide to whom to render them. In the aristocratic empire, they often had to choose among aristocrats to serve. In modern times, they have faced choices between causes close to their hearts and causes they despised. It is not surprising that they chose the former, and by remaining faithful, as they saw it, to their own institutions of the military and the bureaucracy, they contributed in this century to the downfall of two French republics (1940 and 1958) and one German one (1933)—and similarly to that of the Austrian republic (1934) and the Spanish republic (1936–1939) and even of the Italian parliamentary monarchy (1922).

If the aristocracy played a crucial role in the domestic politics of Western European countries until quite recently, this is even more true in the fields of foreign relations and especially warfare. In domestic politics, numerous nonaristocratic interests have come to participate, but in foreign policy and war, the aristocracy had, through its control of the foreign service and the military, managed to limit the influence of such competing interests.

As a result, aristocratic ideology has continued, from the days of traditional aristocratic empires to the present, to play a powerful role in foreign and military affairs. In addition to the aristocratic conceptions of service and duty, it is those of glory and particularly of honor that matter here. We may not be surprised to read that half a millennium after the first beginnings of modernization in Western Europe, Francis I of France (1515–1547) "was still a knightly king, 'le roi chevalier.' He loved tournaments, he loved the chase; war was for him a splendid knightly game in which, as a gallant chevalier, he risked his life; for this was the accepted standard of the knightly nobility, it was a matter of his honor, and he was and felt bound as king by this law of knightly conduct as was any other knight."[14] A century or two later, Louis XIV (1643–1715) "no longer rode into battle as Henry IV had still done, like a knight at the head of his noblemen, but had his wars fought more and more by generals with mercenary troops," but even

14. Elias, *Die höfische Gesellschaft*, p. 225. At the beginning of the sixteenth century, Machiavelli could still write: "A prince should . . . have no other aim or thought, nor take up any other thing for his study, but war and its organisation and discipline, for that is the only art that is necessary to one who commands." Machiavelli, *The Prince and the Discourses*, p. 53.

"he made war, for the rank of conqueror was the 'noblest' and most eminent of all titles, for a king must fight wars, in a sense, because it is his function and his destiny."[15]

However, aristocratic ideological justifications of war continue to have a powerful influence on the behavior of governments in Europe and perhaps particularly in Germany well into the twentieth century. This is one of the dominant themes in Schumpeter's essay on imperialism: "Whoever seeks to understand Europe must not overlook that even today, its life, its ideology, its politics are greatly under the influence of the feudal 'substance'."[16] To be sure, these words are much less true today than when they were written during the First World War, but an understanding of aristocratic attitudes as shaped initially in the traditional warfare empire helps us understand the thinking and behavior not only of a Kaiser Wilhelm II or Tsar Nicholas II but also of a Churchill and a de Gaulle. Thus, Churchill's physician summarizing in the midst of World War II "what Winston had always felt about war" could write: "To him it was a romantic calling, the highest man could embrace, but it was a game for gentlemen, which had to be played according to the rules. . . . a game for people of quality."[17] Thus war was still a splendid game for Churchill as it had been for Francis I, a notion already centuries old in the days of the latter. And as for Francis I, so for de Gaulle, war was a matter of honor. He entitled the first volume of his war memoirs *The Call to Honour*,[18] and the concepts of honor and glory remained central to his thinking on foreign policy.

The same can, of course, be said of the thinking of the German aristocracy and hence also of the Nazis, whose relationship to the aristocracy was one of both admiration and resentment. The Prussian aristocratic military tradition, very much alive until 1945, glorified war as a "bath of steel" in which glory was to be won and honor maintained for the aristocracy and eventually for the "nation" with which the aristocracy had come to identify itself.

Aristocratic ideology, shaped in the traditional aristocratic empire, has remained important in the conduct of foreign policy of all modern countries. This is to some extent true even of those few, like the United States, that lack an aristocratic background but whose military and diplomatic establishments imitate, organizationally and ideologically, those shaped by an aristocratic past. Consequently, modern prime ministers and presidents

15. Elias, *Die höfische Gesellschaft*, pp. 226, 206.

16. Schumpeter, "The Sociology of Imperialism," p. 92.

17. Moran, *Winston Churchill*, p. 173.

18. de Gaulle, *War Memoirs*, I.

who would not dream of demanding lower taxes or higher farm subsidies in the name of national honor do not hestitate to justify their foreign policy or military moves by claiming that the maintenance of honor requires them. Modern governments that will gladly settle a conflict with an industrial corporation or a trade union on practical grounds and proudly announce their willingness to compromise in domestic affairs, will not accept settlements of foreign conflicts or of wars unless they are "honorable" and will refuse to compromise the national "honor." To be sure, a multitude of objectives, including very practical ones, can hide behind the concept of honor, but to deny that the concern with honor as such still influences the foreign and military policies of modern governments would be to underestimate the vitality of the original aristocratic values even today.

In passing, I may also refer to other symptoms of the persistence of aristocratic ideologies and culture tied to aristocratic involvement in warfare and hence to war-related activities. Dueling, the aristocrat's response to a challenge to his honor, has remained an aristocratic practice into the present century. Even more striking, the horse remains linked to the aristocracy, with the cavalry always the aristocrat's favorite branch of the army. As late as the 1930s, aristocratically inclined French army officers, writing in the royalist *Action Française* gave "full rein to their conviction that cavalry was the backbone of the Army and the horse essential to the proper cavalry spirit. (In any case, retired General Lavigne-Delville pointed out, if motorization was Radical-Socialist, the horse was conservative.)"[19] The aristocratic sports of horseback riding and hunting, especially fox hunting on horseback, remain associated with the aristocracy (and the newer upper classes seeking to imitate it) to this day.[20] "In the upper strata, riding *per se* is a universally recognised necessity, even if the rider does not hunt or jump."[21]

Contempt for manual labor is another aspect of aristocratic ideology that has survived into modern times. Of the English gentleman it is said

19. Weber, *Action Française*, p. 266. The successors to the cavalry, the armored cavalry and the armored corps, were still "the aristocratic stronghold" in the French army in the post-World War II period, 38 percent and 32 percent of all their field-grade officers in 1949 and 1958, respectively, having "noble-type names." Ambler, *Soldiers Against the State*, p. 151.

20. In the United States, on the other hand, both hunting and horseback riding were, under frontier conditions, associated with the lower rural classes. As in many other respects, it is only in the South that we find some attempt to imitate European aristocratic culture, as in the hunt country of Virginia.

21. Pear, *English Social Differences*, p. 253.

that "except in an emergency (or for a hobby) he still does not work with his hands."[22] But commerce, too, continues to be regarded as demeaning, and as new investment opportunities developed at the onset of industrialization, aristocrats, though then the wealthiest class, were very rarely the ones who provided capital for industry. When Britain was undergoing the industrial revolution, the aristocratic rulers of continental Europe—and even the nonaristocratic Napoleon who imitated them—referred to her contemptuously as "a nation of shopkeepers," implying, no doubt, that the country was devoid of honor, courage, and fidelity—and hence perfidious Albion. By the eighteenth century, British aristocrats, particularly the younger sons of noblemen, and by the nineteenth century also French aristocrats did avail themselves of new opportunities to make money, and they and their German counterparts now ran their estates along capitalist lines.

It has been increasingly hard to maintain the taboo against commerce in more and more commercialized and industrialized societies. Nevertheless, in aristocratic ideology a certain aura of disrepute has remained attached to participation in business. The English gentleman, "insofar as he has joined in commerce, . . . has either tended to admit loss of caste (however ironically) or else has persuaded himself that he is in fact acting for the general good rather than his own individual profit. . . . In the last resort, then, a gentleman whose money comes from 'business' does his damnedest to pretend it comes from something—almost anything—else."[23]

Even in America, with no aristocracy in its history, the word "business" has not always had wholly positive connotations. In other cultures and other languages the concept retains or retained until very recently a slightly negative connotation, as in the British "going into trade" and the German "Geschäfte machen," and the businessman, no matter how successful, could not, by aristocratic standards, reach the top of the status ladder. The antibusiness orientation of the aristocracy has been perpetuated in part by modern intellectuals, some of whose values resemble those of the aristocracy, both in Europe and in underdeveloped countries. One manifestation of this phenomenon may be the condescending attitude of many intellectuals in Europe and some in underdeveloped countries towards America —a country without an aristocracy—and her culture as materialistic, crude, and crass. Finally, the view of the city, in contrast to the country, as corrupt and corrupting, is still held in modern societies and it, too, may be related to the aristocratic contempt for commerce and grew with it in response to commercialization.

22. Raven, *The English Gentleman*, p. 53.
23. Ibid., pp. 53–54.

It goes without saying that aristocrats, as long as they have considered themselves as such, have also thought of themselves as a breed apart from[24] and somehow superior to the rest of mankind and have been concerned with the purity of their noble blood. In Europe, even today a proper marriage for an aristocrat is possible only within the aristocracy, though, along with the rest of aristocratic ideology, the taboo on inter-marriage with nonaristocrats is now crumbling under the impact of modernization. Members of European royal houses are still disqualified from succession to the throne if they marry a nonaristocrat or can enter only a so-called morganatic marriage, that is, one in which the wife and children do not acquire or inherit the title or position of the husband and father. This suggests that while good character or even mental or physical competence are generally not required of a ruler, in the aristocrat's mind, the ability to rule does depend on pure blood, that is, on the maintenance of a sharp separation from the lower classes. To a considerable extent, the royal families of Europe, though many of them have lost their thrones in the course of this century, still intermarry with each other.[25]

There is consequently hardly a royal family in Europe—except, in their own territories, the numerous German ruling houses who in time came to populate thrones all the way from Britain to Russia and from Scandinavia to the Balkans and Portugal—that could claim to be of the same nationality as the people it ruled. Nationality, however, is an irrelevant concept in this context, for the aristocracy is a remnant of the aristocratic, prenationalist order in Europe. It was only in 1917, in the midst of World War I, two centuries after its accession to the British throne, that the House of Hanover renamed itself the House of Windsor, replacing a German with an English name. What matters to the aristocracy is the protection of pure aristocratic blood from any admixture of common blood, not the maintenance of pure British, French or German blood.

24. In the French film of the 1930s, *La Grande Illusion*, the German aristocratic officer in charge of a prison camp in World War I and his French aristocratic officer-prisoner are shown to be united by bonds of common status and common attitudes and set apart from nonaristocratic officers, stressing remnants of traditional class lines that cut across the more modern lines of nationality even in the midst of war.

25. Among the grandchildren of Queen Victoria were the rulers or the wives of the rulers of Britain, Germany, Russia, Sweden, Norway, Greece, Rumania, and Spain. Their children, in turn, were kings and queens not only of their countries but also of Yugoslavia and Denmark. Thus the descendants of Victoria and Albert, her German consort, populated the great majority of the thrones of Europe in the early part of this century. Just like wars among the aristocratic empires of medieval Europe, as modern a conflict as World War I still cut across numerous family relations among rulers: William II of Germany was a first cousin of George V of Britain, a more distant cousin of Nicholas II of Russia, and an uncle of King Alexander I of Greece. Family relations also existed between the warring ruling houses of Austria-Hungary on the one hand and of Italy, Rumania, and Belgium on the other.

The Legacy of Aristocratic Empires

In a historical argument even more sweeping than the kind engaged in here, it could well be claimed that we owe to the aristocracy all of what is commonly known as civilization beyond that developed by primitive cultivators and nomads. If it is only exploitation that compels peasants to produce a surplus, then all of technology, science, and art, in the material realm as well as that of thought and ideas, beyond the level achieved by subsistence agriculturalists and pastoralists, as well as urbanization, is due to the existence of aristocracies. Of course, one might alternatively speculate that, had cultivators not been prevented from doing so by aristocratic exploitation, they might eventually have developed some more advanced civilization of their own.

In any case, aristocratic empires, by subjecting numerous village societies to a single aristocratic society, brought to humanity for the first time rigid class divisions and large settled territories under one government, however rudimentary. Rigid class divisions have only recently been breaking down, and territorial states under governments remain dominant features of human organization. Crucial in the relations of those who control modern states is the fear and threat of war. The functions and purposes, as well as the forms, of warfare have changed with modernization, but war between large territorial entities, aiming at and resulting in changes in their boundaries, is another legacy passed down to modern man from aristocratic empires.

Finally, it was aristocratic empires that made possible the process of commercialization that, in turn, put an end to aristocratic empires. In Western Europe, it led to industrialization that destroyed aristocratic empires, whether still traditional or already commercialized, relatively recently and suddenly, by impinging on them from without. And Western European commercialization and then industrialization, working through some centuries and more gradually, changed the aristocratic empires of Western Europe from within.

It is this latter process that has been stressed in this final chapter, for in it the aristocracy long continued to play a key role. However, even in Western Europe, the past century or so has witnessed the decline of the aristocracy. Its values have been diluted, its influence, even in what used to be its own institutions of the military, the bureaucracy, and the clergy, has been reduced, and it is now disappearing as a distinct social class. In France and Germany, this decline has been punctuated by powerful rearguard actions, some of which were fought successfully and decisively affected world history, as by helping to produce the Nazi regime and World War II. In

Britain, the decline has been more gradual, taking place through a merger with the bourgeoisie.[26]

However, in the very process of its decline and even its disappearance, the aristocracy has helped shape the present and the future. Both the emergence of the political Left and of the welfare state are major examples of this. Western European socialism as a mass movement was in large part a reaction to the inequality and discrimination to which the rapidly growing working class was subjected. Socialism is not a response to modern capitalism alone, as it also developed in the United States, but rather to capitalism growing up in an environment still dominated by the rigid class lines first drawn in traditional aristocratic empires. The new bourgeoisie, as a wealthy upper class, eventually found its place in that environment, more or less in alliance with the aristocracy. Industrial labor, however, simply did not fit, it was excluded and treated as an alien element and it reacted as such by creating its own friendly society—the socialist (and, more recently in France and Italy, also the communist) labor movement—within the larger hostile society. It is fair to say, then, that the Western European aristocracy had a great deal to do with shaping the character not only of the political Right but also that of the Left. The absence of an aristocracy in American history is responsible not only for the absence of conservatism (in the European sense of that word) but also for that of socialism.[27]

One of the major demands of the labor movement has been what can be summed up under the label of the welfare state, and its attainment helped integrate that movement into the larger society socially and politically. This process, now far advanced in Britain and Germany but still progressing in France, which was for long industrially behind those two countries, has helped break down the rigid class lines created by the aristocracy. But the institution of the welfare state, too, owes something to the aristocracy (aside from being a response to socialist movements that were themselves a response to an aristocratically conditioned class society). To be sure, the welfare state owes nothing to the traditional aristocratic empire whose government was decentralized and limited and provided no services to the

26. Members of the latter now probably outnumber scions of old aristocratic families in the peerage, and even some of those without titles have acquired country estates and an education in the public schools. On the other hand, aristocrats have gone into business and married the daughters of the bourgeoisie.

27. As Louis Hartz said: "It is not accidental that America which has uniquely lacked a feudal tradition has uniquely lacked also a socialist tradition." Hartz, *The Liberal Tradition in America*, p. 6.

mass of the population. The emergence of the welfare state was eased, however, by the existence and widespread acceptance of powerful bureaucracies inherited from aristocratic absolutism and influenced by an aristocracy that had always identified itself with the "state" and could hence come to think of itself as representing, even if in a somewhat patronizing manner, the "people."

The bourgeoisie and its nineteenth-century liberalism saw government, which was still in good part the government of the aristocracy, as an enemy to be weakened and limited. The aristocracy identified with it and had no objection to a strong and active government and bureaucracy not only in foreign affairs but also in social ones. There were even aristocrats who believed in "tory socialism" and contemplated an alliance against their bourgeois rivals with the new labor movements, especially as long as these were weak and posed no threat to the aristocracy. Powerful aristocratic remnants, then, helped neutralize bourgeois opposition to the welfare state and were by no means an obstacle to its growth. Here, too, if one looks for explanations of differences between American and Western European politics, one can do worse than to begin one's analysis with the absence of an aristocracy in the United States.[28]

Finally, it could even be argued—though this is clearly not the place to do so—that it was the presence of an aristocracy and the political responses to it of the past two centuries that account in good part for the emergence in Western Europe of political parties that have distinct programs and ideologies and that direct their appeals to and represent the interests of distinct segments of the population. Here surely is one of the basic differences between the politics of Western Europe and that of the United States where there are no such parties and where the nature of electoral and legislative politics is hence quite different. It may also be not entirely accidental that the relative decline of such parties in Western Europe since World War II coincides with the decline of the aristocracy.

Today the world is everywhere very different from the one described in this book. Modern politics is drastically unlike the politics of aristocratic empires. But modern politics would not be what it is if there had been no aristocratic empires in the past. If we would hope to understand the politics of our own time, we must know something of the politics of aristocratic empires.

28. Hartz argues in his *The Liberal Tradition in America*: "Any attempt to uncover the nature of an American society without feudalism can only be accomplished by studying it in conjunction with a European society where the feudal structure and the feudal ethos did in fact survive. This is not to deny our national uniqueness, . . . but actually to affirm it. How can we know the uniqueness of anything except by contrasting it with what is not unique?" (ibid., p. 4).

Bibliography

Alderson, A. D. *The Structure of the Ottoman Dynasty*. Oxford: Clarendon Press, 1956.

Alföldi, Andreas. *Early Rome and the Latins*. Ann Arbor: University of Michigan Press, 1963.

————. "Zur Struktur des Römerstaates im 5. Jahrhundert v. Chr." In *Les Origines de la République Romaine* by Einar Gjerstad et al., pp. 223–78. Genève: Fondation Hardt, 1967.

Almanach de Gotha. Annuaire Généalogique, Diplomatique et Statistique. Gotha: Justus Perthes, 1764– .

Almond, Gabriel A., and Verba, Sidney. *The Civic Culture*. Princeton, N.J.: Princeton University Press, 1963.

AlRoy, Gil Carl. *The Involvement of Peasants in Internal Wars*. Research Monograph No. 24, Center of International Studies, Princeton University, June 1966.

Alvares, Francisco. *The Prester John of the Indies*. Edited by C. F. Beckingham and G. W. B. Huntingford. 2 vols. Cambridge: Hakluyt Society; Cambridge University Press, 1961.

Ambler, John Steward. *Soldiers Against the State: The French Army in Politics*. Garden City, N.Y.: Doubleday-Anchor Books, 1968.

Ambrose, Stephen E. *Duty, Honor, Country: A History of West Point*. Baltimore: Johns Hopkins Press, 1966.

Amoretti, B. S. "Sects and Heresies." In *The Cambridge History of Iran*. Vol. 4, *The Period from the Arab Invasion to the Saljuqs*, edited by R. N. Frye, pp. 481–519. Cambridge: University Press, 1975.

Anderson, Perry. *Lineages of the Absolutist State*. London: NLB, 1974.

————. *Passages from Antiquity to Feudalism*. London: NLB, 1974.

Aristotle. *The Politics of Aristotle*. Translated by Ernest Barker. Oxford: Clarendon Press, 1946.

Aron, Raymond. "The Logic of the Social Sciences." In *Max Weber*, edited by Dennis Wrong, pp. 77–89. Englewood Cliffs, N.J.: Prentice-Hall, 1970.

Atienza, Julio de, ed. *Nobiliario Español*. 2nd rev. ed. Madrid: Aguilar, 1954.

Avineri, Shlomo, ed. *Karl Marx on Colonialism and Modernization*. Garden City, N.Y.: Doubleday & Co., 1968.

Baer, Gabriel. "Guilds in Middle Eastern History." In *Studies in the Economic History of the Middle East*, edited by M. A. Cook, pp. 11–30. London: Oxford University Press, 1970.

Balandier, Georges. *Political Anthropology*. New York: Pantheon Books, 1970.

Balazs, Etienne. *Chinese Civilization and Bureaucracy: Variations on a Theme*. New Haven, Conn.: Yale University Press, 1964.

Baldick, Robert. *The Duel: A History of Duelling*. New York: Clarkson Potter, 1965.

Banfield, Edward C. *The Moral Basis of a Backward Society*. Glencoe, Ill.: Free Press, 1958.

Banks, Arthur S., and Textor, Robert B. *A Cross-Polity Survey*. Cambridge, Mass.: The M.I.T. Press, 1963.

Baran, Paul A. *The Political Economy of Growth*. New York: Monthly Review Press, 1957.

Barnes, Harry Elmer. *Sociology and Political Theory*. New York: Alfred A. Knopf, 1924.

————. "Some Contributions of Sociology to Modern Political Theory." In *A History of Political Theories. Recent Times*, edited by Charles E. Merriam and Harry Elmer Barnes, pp. 357–402. New York: Macmillan Co., 1924.

————. "The Struggle of Races and Social Groups as a Factor in the Development of Political and Social Institutions." *The Journal of Race Development* 9 (April 1919): 394–419.

Bates, Robert H. "People in Villages: Microlevel Studies in Political Economy." *World Politics* 31 (October 1978): 129–49.

Beals, R. L., and Hoijer, H. *An Introduction to Anthropology*. 3rd ed. New York: Macmillan Co., 1965.

Bebel, August. *Woman Under Socialism*. Translated from the 33rd German ed. by Daniel de Leon. New York: New York Labor News Press, 1904.

Bede. *A History of the English Church and People*. Harmondsworth, Middlesex: Penguin Books, 1955.

Beech, George T. *A Rural Society in Medieval France: The Gâtine of Poitou in the Eleventh and Twelfth Centuries*. Baltimore: Johns Hopkins Press, 1964.

Bellah, Robert N. *Tokugawa Religion: The Values of Pre-Industrial Japan*. Glencoe, Ill.: The Free Press, 1957.

Bendix, Reinhard. *Kings or People: Power and the Mandate to Rule*. Berkeley: University of California Press, 1978.

————. *Max Weber: An Intellectual Portrait*. Garden City, N.Y.: Doubleday-Anchor Books, 1962.

————. *Nation-Building and Citizenship*. New enl. ed. Berkeley: University of California Press, 1977.

————. "Tradition and Modernity Reconsidered." *Comparative Studies in Society and History* 9 (April 1967): 292–346.

Bentley, Arthur F. *The Process of Government*. Bloomington, Ind.: The Principia Press, 1935.

Bernardi, Aurelio. "The Economic Problems of the Roman Empire at the Time of its Decline." In *The Economic Decline of Empires*, edited by Carlo M. Cipolla, pp. 16–83. London: Methuen & Co., 1970.

Bielenstein, Hans. *The Restoration of the Han Dynasty*. Göteborg: Elander, 1953.

Bill, James Alban. *The Politics of Iran: Groups, Classes, and Modernization*. Columbus, Ohio: Charles E. Merrill, 1972.

————, and Leiden, Carl. *The Middle East: Politics and Power*. Boston: Allyn and Bacon, 1974.

————, and Leiden, Carl. *Politics in the Middle East*. Boston: Little, Brown & Co., 1979.

Bloch, Marc. *Feudal Society*. Chicago: University of Chicago Press, 1961.

———. *French Rural History: An Essay on its Basic Characteristics*. Berkeley: University of California Press, 1966.

———. *The Royal Touch: Sacred Monarchy and Scrofula in England and France*. London: Routledge & Kegan Paul, 1973.

Blum, Jerome. *Lord and Peasant in Russia from the Ninth to the Nineteenth Century*. New York: Atheneum, 1965.

Boak, Arthur E. R., and Sinnigen, William G. *A History of Rome to A.D. 565*. 5th ed. New York: Macmillan, 1965.

Bodde, Derk. "Feudalism in China." In *Feudalism in History*, edited by Rushton Coulborn, pp. 49–92. Princeton, N.J.: Princeton University Press, 1956.

Boissonade, P. *Life and Work in Medieval Europe*. London: Kegan Paul, Trench, Trubner & Co., 1927.

Brooke, Christopher. *Europe in the Central Middle Ages, 962–1154*. New York: Holt, Rinehart and Winston, 1964.

Brown, Peter R. L. *The World of Late Antiquity*. New York: Harcourt Brace Jovanovich, 1971.

Brunt, P. A. *Italian Manpower, 225 B.C.–A.D. 14*. London: Oxford University Press, 1971.

———. *Social Conflicts in the Roman Republic*. New York: W. W. Norton & Co., 1971.

Bryson, Frederick R. *The Sixteenth-Century Italian Duel: A Study in Renaissance Social History*. Chicago: University of Chicago Press, 1938.

Burgess, John Steward. *The Guilds of Peking*. New York: Columbia University Press, 1928.

Burke's Genealogical and Heraldic History of the Peerage, Baronetage, and Knightage. Edited by Peter Townend, 104th ed. London: Burke's Peerage, 1967.

Bury, J. B. *The Idea of Progress: An Inquiry into its Origin and Growth*. New York: Dover Publications, 1955.

Buttinger, Joseph. *A Dragon Defiant: A Short History of Vietnam*. New York: Praeger, 1972.

Calhoun, George M. *The Ancient Greeks and the Evolution of Standards in Business*. Boston: Houghton Mifflin Co., 1926.

Carlston, Kenneth S. *Social Theory and African Tribal Organization: The Development of Socio-Legal Theory*. Urbana: University of Illinois Press, 1968.

Chan, Wing-tsit. *Religious Trends in Modern China*. New York: Columbia University Press, 1953.

Chaney, Marvin L. "Ancient Palestinian Peasant Movements and the Formation of Premonarchic Israel," unpublished paper, San Francisco Theological Seminary, San Anselmo, Calif., n.d.

Chang, Chung-li. *The Chinese Gentry: Studies on their Role in Nineteenth-Century Chinese Society*. Seattle: University of Washington Press, 1955.

———. *The Income of the Chinese Gentry*. Seattle: University of Washington Press, 1962.

Charlesworth, M. P. *Trade-Routes and Commerce of the Roman Empire*. Hildesheim: Georg Olms, 1961.

Chenaye-Desbois et Badier, François Alexandre Aubert de la, ed. *Dictionnaire de la Noblesse de la France*. 19 vols. 3rd ed. Paris, 1868–76; Nendeln, Liechtenstein: Kraus Reprint, 1969.

Childe, Gordon V. *Man Makes Himself*. London: Watts & Co., 1936.

Chow, Yung-teh. *Social Mobility in China: Status Careers Among the Gentry in a Chinese Community*. New York: Atherton Press, 1966.

Cicero, M. Tullius. *De Officiis*, with an English translation by Walter Miller. Cambridge, Mass.: Harvard University Press, 1961.

Cipolla, Carlo M. *Before the Industrial Revolution: European Society and Economy, 1000–1700*. New York: W. W. Norton & Co., 1976.

————. *The Economic History of World Population*. 5th ed. Harmondsworth, Middlesex: Penguin Books, 1970.

————. *Money, Prices, and Civilization in the Mediterranean World, Fifth to Seventeenth Century*. New York: Gordian Press, 1967.

Collins, Randall. "A Comparative Approach to Political Sociology." In *State and Society. A Reader in Comparative Political Sociology*, edited by Reinhard Bendix, pp. 42–67. Boston: Little, Brown & Co., 1968.

Cook, R. M. *The Greeks Until Alexander*. New York: Frederick A. Praeger, 1962.

Coulborn, Rushton. "A Comparative Study of Feudalism." In *Feudalism in History*, edited by Rushton Coulborn, pp. 183–395. Princeton, N.J.: Princeton University Press, 1956.

————, ed. *Feudalism in History*. Princeton, N.J.: Princeton University Press, 1956.

Coulton, G. G. *Medieval Panorama: The English Scene from Conquest to Reformation*. Cambridge: University Press, 1939.

————. *The Medieval Village*. Cambridge: University Press, 1925.

Cunow, Heinrich. *Geschichte und Kultur des Inkareiches*. Amsterdam: Elsevier, 1937.

Dalton, George, ed. *Economic Development and Social Change: The Modernization of Village Communities*. Garden City, N.Y.: The Natural History Press, 1971.

Davidson, Basil. *The Lost Cities of Africa*. Boston: Little, Brown & Co., 1959.

Davies, Nigel. *The Aztecs: A History*. New York: G. P. Putnam's Sons, 1974.

Davis, William Stearns. *Life on a Mediaeval Barony: A Picture of a Typical Feudal Community in the Thirteenth Century*. New York: Harper & Brothers, 1923.

Debrett's Peerage, Baronetage, Knightage, and Companionage. Edited by Patrick Montague-Smith. Kingston, Surrey: Kelly's Directories, 1973–74.

Debrett's Peerage and Baronetage. Edited by Patrick Montague-Smith. London: Debrett's Peerage, 1980.

de Gaulle, Charles. *War Memoirs*. 3 vols. Vol. I, *The Call to Honour, 1940–1942*. New York: Simon & Schuster, 1955.

Diamond, A. S. *Primitive Law*. London: Longmans, Green & Co., 1935.

Dictionnaire de la Noblesse de la France. Edited by François Alexandre Aubert de la Chenaye-Desbois et Badier, 19 vols. 3rd ed. Paris, 1868–76; Nendeln, Liechtenstein: Kraus Reprint, 1969.

Diez, Ernst. *The Ancient Worlds of Asia*. London: Macdonald, 1961.

Dopsch, Alfons. *The Economic and Social Foundations of European Civilization*. London: Routledge and Kegan Paul, 1937.

Drekmeier, Charles. *Kingship and Community in Early India*. Stanford, Calif.: Stanford University Press, 1962.

Drower, M. S. "Water-Supply, Irrigation, and Agriculture." In *A History of Technology*, 5 vols., edited by Charles Singer, E. J. Holmyard, and A. R. Hall, 1:520–57. Oxford: Clarendon Press, 1954.

Duby, Georges. *The Early Growth of the European Economy: Warriors and Peasants from the Seventh to the Twelfth Century*. Ithaca, N.Y.: Cornell University Press, 1974.

———. *Rural Economy and Country Life in the Medieval West*. Columbia: University of South Carolina Press, 1968.

Duruy, Victor. *History of Rome and of the Roman People*. Translated by M. M. Ripley and W. J. Clarke, edited by J. P. Mahaffy. 8 vols. Boston: C. F. Jewett Publishing Co., 1883.

Earl, Donald. *The Moral and Political Tradition of Rome*. Ithaca, N.Y.: Cornell University Press, 1967.

Eberhard, Wolfram. *Conquerors and Rulers: Social Forces in Medieval China*. 2nd rev. ed. Leiden: E. J. Brill, 1965.

———. *Settlement and Social Change in Asia*. Hong Kong: Hong Kong University Press, 1967.

———. *Social Mobility in Traditional China*. Leiden: E. J. Brill, 1962.

———. *Das Toba-Reich Nordchinas: Eine soziologische Untersuchung*. Leiden: E. J. Brill, 1949.

Edelstein, Ludwig. *The Idea of Progress in Classical Antiquity*. Baltimore: Johns Hopkins Press, 1967.

Edgerton, William F. "The Question of Feudal Institutions in Ancient Egypt." In *Feudalism in History*, edited by Rushton Coulborn, pp. 120–32. Princeton, N.J.: Princeton University Press, 1956.

Edwardes, Michael. *A History of India*. New York: Farrar, Straus & Co., 1961.

Eisenstadt, S. N. *The Political Systems of Empires*. New York: The Free Press, 1963.

———. "Post-Traditional Societies and the Continuity and Reconstruction of Tradition." In *Post-Traditional Societies*, edited by S. N. Eisenstadt, pp. 1–27. New York: W. W. Norton, 1972.

———. *Revolution and the Transformation of Societies: A Comparative Study of Civilizations*. New York: The Free Press, 1978.

———. "The Study of Oriental Despotisms as Systems of Total Power." *Journal of Asian Studies* 17 (May 1958): 435–46.

Elias, Norbert. *Die höfische Gesellschaft*. Neuwied and Berlin: Luchterhand, 1969.

Elvin, Mark. *The Pattern of the Chinese Past*. Stanford, Calif.: Stanford University Press, 1973.

Engels, Frederick. *The Origin of the Family, Private Property and the State*. New York: International Publishers, 1942.

———. "The Peasant War in Germany." In Friedrich Engels, *The German Revolutions*, edited by Leonard Krieger, pp. 1–119. Chicago: University of Chicago Press, 1967.

———. "Soziales aus Russland." *Der Volksstaat*, 21 April 1875. In Karl Marx, Friedrich Engels, *Werke*, 39 vols., 18:556–67. Berlin: Dietz Verlag, 1964.

Fairbank, John K.; Eckstein, Alexander; and Yang, L. S. "Economic Change in Early Modern China: An Analytic Framework." *Economic Development and Cultural Change* 9 (October 1960): 1–26.

Fall, Bernard B. *Hell in a Very Small Place: The Siege of Dien Bien Phu.* New York: Vintage Books, 1968.

"The Family Way." In *Out of the Fire: Oil, the Gulf and the West.* Survey, *The Economist* (London), May 1975, 44–47.

Fei, Hsiao-tung. *China's Gentry.* Chicago: University of Chicago Press, 1953.

―――. *Peasant Life in China: A Field Study of Country Life in the Yangtze Valley.* New York: Oxford University Press, 1946.

―――. "Peasantry and Gentry: An Interpretation of Chinese Social Structure and its Changes." *American Journal of Sociology* 52 (July 1946): 1–17.

Filippani-Ronconi, Pio. "The Tradition of Sacred Kingship in Iran." In *Iran under the Pahlavis,* edited by George Lenczowski, pp. 51–83. Stanford, Calif.: Hoover Institution Press, 1978.

Finley, M. I. *A History of Sicily: Ancient Sicily to the Arab Conquest.* New York: Viking Press, 1968.

―――. "Technical Innovation and Economic Progress in the Ancient World." *Economic History Review,* 2nd series, 18 (August 1965): 29–45.

Foote, Peter G., and Wilson, David M. *The Viking Achievement.* New York: Praeger, 1970.

Forbes, Robert J. *Notes on the History of Ancient Roads and Their Construction.* 2nd ed. Amsterdam: A. M. Hakkert, 1964.

Foster, George M. "Introduction: What is a Peasant?" In *Peasant Society: A Reader,* edited by Jack M. Potter, May N. Diaz, and George M. Foster, pp. 2–24. Boston: Little, Brown & Co., 1967.

Frank, Tenney. *Roman Imperialism.* New York: Macmillan Co., 1914.

Frankfort, Henri. *Kingship and the Gods.* Chicago: University of Chicago Press, 1948.

Fried, Morton H. *Fabric of Chinese Society.* New York: Praeger, 1953.

Ganshof, F. L. *The Carolingians and the Frankish Monarchy: Studies in Carolingian History.* Ithaca, N.Y.: Cornell University Press, 1971.

Garnsey, Peter. "Peasants in Ancient Roman Society." *The Journal of Peasant Studies* 3 (January 1976): 21–35.

Geertz, Clifford. *Peddlers and Princes: Social Change and Economic Modernization in Two Indonesian Towns.* Chicago: University of Chicago Press, 1963.

―――. *The Religion of Java.* New York: Free Press of Glencoe, 1960.

Gernet, Jacques. *Daily Life in China on the Eve of the Mongol Invasion 1250–1276.* New York: Macmillan, 1962.

Gibb, H. A. R., and Bowen, Harold. *Islamic Society and the West.* 2 vols. Vol. 1, *Islamic Society in the Eighteenth Century.* London: Oxford University Press, 1950.

Gibbons, Herbert Adams. *The Foundation of the Ottoman Empire.* Oxford: Clarendon Press, 1916.

Gillin, John. "Ethos and Cultural Aspects of Personality." In *Heritage of Conquest,* edited by Sol Tax, pp. 193–212. Glencoe, Ill.: Free Press, 1952.

Gjerstad, Einar. "Innenpolitische und militärische Organisation in frührömischer Zeit." In *Aufstieg und Niedergang der römischen Welt: von den Anfängen Roms bis zum Ausgang der Republik,* 4 vols., edited by Hildegard Temporini, 1:136–88. Berlin: Walter de Gruyter, 1972.

Goitein, S. D. "Cairo: An Islamic City in the Light of the Geniza Documents." In *Middle Eastern Cities*, edited by Ira M. Lapidus, pp. 80–95. Berkeley: University of California Press, 1969.

Goldman, James. *The Lion in Winter*. New York: Random House, 1966.

Goodrich, L. Carrington. *A Short History of the Chinese People*. New York: Harper & Bros., 1943.

Gottwald, Norman K. *The Tribes of Yahweh: A Sociology of the Religion of Liberated Israel, 1250–1050 B.C.E.* Maryknoll, N.Y.: Orbis Books, 1979.

Gouldner, Alvin W. *Enter Plato: Classical Greece and the Origins of Social Theory*. New York: Basic Books, 1965.

Granet, Marcel. *Chinese Civilization*. New York: Meridian, 1958.

Green, Peter. "The First Sicilian Slave War." *Past and Present* 20 (November 1961): 10–29.

Gumplowicz, Ludwig. *Outlines of Sociology*. Edited by Irving L. Horowitz. New York: Paine-Whitman, 1963.

———. *Der Rassenkampf*. In Gumplowicz, *Ausgewählte Werke*, 4 vols., edited by G. Salomon. Vol. 3. Innsbruck, Austria: Wagner, 1928.

Habib, Irfan. *The Agrarian System of Mughal India (1556–1707)*. London: Asia Publishing House, 1963.

———. "Potentialities of Capitalistic Development in the Economy of Mughal India." *Journal of Economic History* 29 (March 1969): 32–78.

Haeger, John Winthrop, ed. *Crisis and Prosperity in Sung China*. Tucson: University of Arizona Press, 1975.

Hagen, Everett E. *On the Theory of Social Change: How Economic Growth Begins*. Homewood, Ill.: Dorsey Press, 1962.

Hall, John Whitney. *Government and Local Power in Japan, 500–1700*. Princeton, N.J.: Princeton University Press, 1966.

———. *Japan from Prehistory to Modern Times*. New York: Delacorte Press, 1970.

Hansen, Roger D. *The Politics of Mexican Development*. Baltimore: Johns Hopkins University Press, 1971.

Harrison, James P. *The Communists and Chinese Peasant Rebellions*. New York: Atheneum, 1969.

Harrison, John A. *The Chinese Empire*. New York: Harcourt Brace Jovanovich, 1972.

Hartz, Louis. *The Liberal Tradition in America*. New York: Harcourt, Brace & World, 1955.

Hasebroek, Johannes. *Trade and Politics in Ancient Greece*. New York: Biblo & Tannen, 1965.

Heilbroner, Robert L. *The Making of Economic Society*. Englewood Cliffs, N.J.: Prentice-Hall, 1962.

Hill, H. *The Roman Middle Class in the Republican Period*. Oxford: Basil Blackwell, 1952.

Hilton, Rodney H. *Bond Men Made Free: Medieval Peasant Movements and the English Rising of 1381*. London: Temple Smith, 1973.

———. "Peasant Movements in England before 1381." *The Economic History Review*, 2nd series, II:2 (1949): 117–36.

————. "Peasant Society, Peasant Movements and Feudalism in Medieval Europe." In *Rural Protest: Peasant Movements and Social Change*, edited by Henry A. Landsberger, pp. 67–94. London: Macmillan, 1974.

Ho, Ping-ti. *The Ladder of Success in Imperial China: Aspects of Social Mobility, 1368–1911*. New York: Columbia University Press, 1962.

Hobsbawm, Eric J. *Bandits*. New York: Delacorte Press, 1969.

————. Introduction to *Pre-Capitalist Economic Formations*, by Karl Marx. New York: International Publishers, 1965.

————. *Primitive Rebels: Studies in Archaic Forms of Social Movements in the 19th and 20th Centuries*. New York: W. W. Norton, 1959.

————. "Social Banditry." In *Rural Protest: Peasant Movements and Social Change*, edited by Henry A. Landsberger, pp. 142–57. London: Macmillan, 1974.

Hodgson, Marshall G. S. *The Venture of Islam: Conscience and History in a World Civilization*. 3 vols. Chicago: University of Chicago Press, 1974.

Hollingsworth, T. H. "A Demographic Study of the British Ducal Families." *Population Studies* (London) 11 (July 1957): 4–26.

Homans, George C. *English Villagers of the Thirteenth Century*. Cambridge, Mass.: Harvard University Press, 1941.

Hoselitz, Bert F. *Sociological Aspects of Economic Growth*. New York: The Free Press, 1960.

Hsu, Cho-yun. *Ancient China in Transition: An Analysis of Social Mobility, 722–222 B.C.* Stanford, Calif.: Stanford University Press, 1965.

Hucker, Charles O. *China's Imperial Past: An Introduction to Chinese History and Culture*. Stanford, Calif.: Stanford University Press, 1975.

Hunt, Morton M. *The Natural History of Love*. New York: Knopf, 1959.

Huntington, Samuel P. "The Change to Change: Modernization, Development, and Politics." *Comparative Politics* 3 (April 1971): 283–322.

————. *Political Order in Changing Societies*. New Haven, Conn.: Yale University Press, 1968.

Ike, Nobutaka. *Japan: The New Superstate*. San Francisco: W. H. Freeman, 1974.

Inalcik, Halil. "Capital Formation in the Ottoman Empire." *Journal of Economic History* 29 (March 1969): 97–140.

————. *The Ottoman Empire: The Classical Age 1300–1600*. New York: Praeger, 1973.

Inkeles, Alex. "Models and Issues in the Analysis of Soviet Society." *Survey* 60 (July 1966): 3–17.

Janowitz, Morris. *The Professional Soldier: A Social and Political Portrait*. New York: Free Press of Glencoe, 1960.

Johnson, Chalmers. "The Role of Social Science in China Scholarship." *World Politics* 17 (January 1965): 256–71.

Jones, A. H. M., and Monroe, Elizabeth. *A History of Abyssinia*. Oxford: Clarendon Press, 1935.

Jones, Gwyn. *A History of the Vikings*. New York: Oxford University Press, 1968.

Kato, Shuichi. *Form, Style, Tradition: Reflections on Japanese Art and Society*. Berkeley: University of California Press, 1971.

Kautsky, John H. "J. A. Schumpeter and Karl Kautsky: Parallel Theories of Imperialism." *Midwest Journal of Political Science* 5 (May 1961): 101–28.

———. *Patterns of Modernizing Revolutions: Mexico and the Soviet Union*. Sage Professional Papers in Comparative Politics, vol. 5, series no. 01–056. Beverly Hills: Sage Publications, 1975.

———. *The Political Consequences of Modernization*. New York: John Wiley, 1972.

———. "Revolutionary and Managerial Elites in Modernizing Regimes." *Comparative Politics* 1 (July 1969): 441–67.

Kautsky, Karl. *Communism in Central Europe in the Time of the Reformation*. New York: Russell and Russell, 1959.

———. *Die materialistische Geschichtsauffassung*. 2 vols. Berlin: J. H. W. Dietz Nachf., 1927.

———. *Vorläufer des neueren Sozialismus*. 2 vols. Vol. 1, 8th ed., vol. 2, 9th ed. Berlin-Bonn: J. H. W. Dietz, 1976.

Kemp, B. J. "Imperialism and Empire in New Kingdom Egypt (c. 1575–1087 B.C.)." In *Imperialism in the Ancient World*, edited by P. D. A. Garnsey and C. R. Whittaker, pp. 7–57. Cambridge: Cambridge University Press, 1978.

Klass, Morton. *Caste: The Emergence of the South Asian Social System*. Philadelphia: Institute for the Study of Human Issues, 1980.

Kolakowski, Leszek. *Main Currents of Marxism: Its Rise, Growth, and Dissolution*. 3 vols. Vol. 2, *The Golden Age*. Oxford: Clarendon Press, 1978.

Kosambi, Damodar Dharmanand. *An Introduction to the Study of Indian History*. Bombay: Popular Book Depot, 1956.

Krader, Lawrence. *The Asiatic Mode of Production: Sources, Development and Critique in the Writings of Karl Marx*. Assen, Netherlands: Van Gorcum, 1975.

———. *Formation of the State*. Englewood Cliffs, N.J.: Prentice-Hall, 1968.

Kraft, Joseph. "Letter from Addis Ababa." *The New Yorker*, 31 July 1978, pp. 46–63.

Labib, Subhi Y. "Capitalism in Medieval Islam." *Journal of Economic History* 29 (March 1969): 79–96.

Lamb, Beatrice Pitney. *India: A World in Transition*. New York: Frederick A. Praeger, 1963.

Landsberger, Betty H., and Landsberger, Henry A. "The English Peasant Revolt of 1381." In *Rural Protest: Peasant Movements and Social Change*, edited by Henry A. Landsberger, pp. 95–141. London: Macmillan, 1974.

Landsberger, Henry A. "Peasant Unrest: Themes and Variations." In *Rural Protest: Peasant Movements and Social Change*, edited by Henry A. Landsberger, pp. 1–64. London: Macmillan, 1974.

———. "The Role of Peasant Movements and Revolts in Development." In *Latin American Peasant Movements*, edited by Henry A. Landsberger, pp. 1–61. Ithaca, N.Y.: Cornell University Press, 1969.

Langer, William L., ed. *An Encyclopedia of World History*. 4th rev. ed. Boston: Houghton Mifflin Co., 1968.

Lapidus, Ira M. "Muslim Cities and Islamic Societies." In *Middle Eastern Cities*, edited by Ira M. Lapidus, pp. 47–74. Berkeley: University of California Press, 1969.

_____. *Muslim Cities in the Later Middle Ages*. Cambridge, Mass.: Harvard University Press, 1967.

Laponce, J. A. "Spatial Archetypes and Political Perceptions." *American Political Science Review* 69 (March 1975): 11–20.

Larios Martín, Jesús, ed. *Nobiliario de Segovia*. 4 vols. Segovia: Instituto Diego de Colmenares, 1956–63.

Laski, Harold J. *The Dangers of Being a Gentleman and Other Essays*. New York: Viking Press, 1940.

Latouche, Robert. *The Birth of Western Economy: Economic Aspects of the Dark Ages*. New York: Barnes and Noble, 1961.

Lattimore, Owen. "Feudalism in History." *Past and Present* 12 (November 1957): 47–57.

_____. "Inner Asian Frontiers: Chinese and Russian Margins of Expansion." *Journal of Economic History* 7 (May 1947): 25–52.

Lenski, Gerhard E. *Power and Privilege: A Theory of Social Stratification*. New York: McGraw-Hill, 1966.

Lerner, Alan Jay. Libretto of *My Fair Lady: A Musical Play*. New York: Coward-McCann, 1956.

Lerner, Daniel. *The Passing of Traditional Society: Modernizing the Middle East*. New York: The Free Press, 1964.

Levenson, Joseph R., and Schurmann, Franz. *China: An Interpretative History: From the Beginnings to the Fall of Han*. Berkeley: University of California Press, 1969.

Levine, Donald N. "Ethiopia: Identity, Authority, and Realism." In *Political Culture and Political Development*, edited by Lucian W. Pye and Sidney Verba, pp. 245–81. Princeton, N.J.: Princeton University Press, 1965.

_____. "The Military in Ethiopian Politics: Capabilities and Constraints." In *The Military Intervenes: Case Studies in Political Development*, edited by Henry Bienen, pp. 5–34. New York: Russell Sage Foundation, 1968.

_____. *Wax and Gold: Tradition and Innovation in Ethiopian Culture*. Chicago: University of Chicago Press, 1965.

Lévy, Jean-Philippe. *The Economic Life of the Ancient World*. Chicago: University of Chicago Press, 1967.

Levy, Marion J., Jr. "Contrasting Factors in the Modernization of China and Japan." *Economic Development and Cultural Change* 2 (October 1953): 161–97.

Lewis, Bernard. *The Arabs in History*. Rev. ed. New York: Harper & Row, 1967.

Lichtheim, George. *Marxism: An Historical and Critical Study*. 2nd rev. ed. New York: Praeger, 1965.

_____. "Oriental Despotism." In *The Concept of Ideology and Other Essays*, by George Lichtheim, pp. 62–93. New York: Vintage Books, 1967.

Linton, Ralph. *The Study of Man*. New York: Appleton Century Co., 1936.

Loewe, Michael. *Everyday Life in Early Imperial China During the Han Period 202 B.C.–A.D. 220*. London: B. T. Batsford, 1968.

_____. *Imperial China: The Historical Background to the Modern Age*. New York: Frederick A. Praeger, 1966.

Lowie, Robert G. *The Origins of the State*. New York: Harcourt, Brace & Co., 1927.

Lybyer, Albert Howe. *The Government of the Ottoman Empire in the Time of Suleiman the Magnificent*. Cambridge, Mass.: Harvard University Press, 1913.

McGovern, William Montgomery. *The Early Empires of Central Asia: A Study of the Scythians and the Huns and the part they played in world history*. Chapel Hill: University of North Carolina Press, 1939.

Machiavelli, Niccolò. *The Prince and the Discourses*. New York: Modern Library, 1950.

McIlwain, Charles Howard. *The Growth of Political Thought in the West*. New York: Macmillan, 1939.

McKnight, Brian E. "Fiscal Privileges and the Social Order in Sung China." In *Crisis and Prosperity in Sung China*, edited by John Winthrop Haeger, pp. 79–99. Tuscon: University of Arizona Press, 1975.

McLeod, W. C. *The Origin and History of Politics*. New York: John Wiley & Sons, 1931.

Madelung, W. "The Minor Dynasties of Northern Iran." In *The Cambridge History of Iran*, vol. 4, *The Period from the Arab Invasion to the Saljuqs*, edited by R. N. Frye, pp. 198–249. Cambridge: University Press, 1975.

Mair, Lucy. *Primitive Government*. Baltimore: Penguin Books, 1964.

Maquet, J. J. "The Kingdom of Ruanda." In *African Worlds: Studies in the Cosmological Ideas and Social Values of African Peoples*, edited by Daryll Forde, pp. 164–89. London: Oxford University Press, 1955.

_____. *The Premise of Inequality in Ruanda: A Study of Political Relations in a Central African Kingdom*. London: Oxford University Press, 1961.

Markovitz, Irving Leonard. *Power and Class in Africa*. Englewood Cliffs, N.J.: Prentice-Hall, 1977.

Marx, Karl. "The British Rule in India," *New York Daily Tribune*, 25 June 1853. In *Karl Marx on Colonialism and Modernization*, edited by Shlomo Avineri, pp. 88–95. Garden City, N.Y.: Doubleday & Co., 1968.

_____. *Capital: A Critique of Political Economy*. Chicago: Charles H. Kerr, 1918.

_____. "The Class Struggles in France, 1848–1850." In *The Marx-Engels Reader*, edited by Robert C. Tucker, pp. 585–93. 2nd ed. New York: W. W. Norton, 1978.

_____. "A Contribution to the Critique of Political Economy." In *The Marx-Engels Reader*, edited by Robert C. Tucker, pp. 3–6. 2nd ed. New York: W. W. Norton, 1978.

_____. "The Eighteenth Brumaire of Louis Bonaparte." In *The Marx-Engels Reader*, edited by Robert C. Tucker, pp. 594–617. 2nd ed. New York: W. W. Norton, 1978.

_____. *Pre-Capitalist Economic Formations*. New York: International Publishers, 1965.

_____, and Engels, Friedrich. "Manifesto of the Communist Party." In *The Marx-Engels Reader*, edited by Robert C. Tucker, pp. 473–500. 2nd ed. New York: W. W. Norton, 1978.

Mattingly, Harold. *Roman Imperial Civilisation*. London: Edward Arnold, 1957.

Mayhew, Leon H. "Society." In *International Encyclopedia of the Social Sciences*, 14:577–85. New York: Macmillan, 1968.

Métraux, Alfred. *The History of the Incas*. New York: Schocken Books, 1970.

Miller, Barnette. *The Palace School of Muhammad the Conqueror*. Cambridge, Mass.: Harvard University Press, 1941.

Mitamura, Taisuke. *Chinese Eunuchs: The Structure of Intimate Politics*. Rutland, Vt.: Charles E. Tuttle Co., 1970.

Mommsen, Theodor. *The History of Rome*. 4 vols. Translated by William P. Dickson. London: Richard Bentley, 1868.

Montague-Smith, Patrick, ed. *Debrett's Peerage and Baronetage*. London: Debrett's Peerage, 1980.

————, ed. *Debrett's Peerage, Baronetage, Knightage, and Companionage*. Kingston, Surrey: Kelly's Directories, 1973–74.

Moore, Barrington, Jr. *Social Origins of Dictatorship and Democracy: Lord and Peasant in the Making of the Modern World*. Boston: Beacon Press, 1966.

Moore, Frank Gardner. *The Roman's World*. New York: Columbia University Press, 1936.

Moore, Sally Falk. *Power and Property in Inca Peru*. New York: Columbia University Press, 1958.

Moran, Charles McM. W. *Winston Churchill: The Struggle for Survival, 1940–65, Taken from the Diaries of Lord Moran*. London: Constable, 1966.

Morley, Sylvanus Griswold, and Brainert, George W. *The Ancient Maya*. 3rd ed. Stanford, Calif.: Stanford University Press, 1956.

Mosca, Gaetano. *The Ruling Class*. New York: McGraw-Hill, 1939.

Mottahedeh, Roy. "The Abbasid Caliphate in Iran." In *The Cambridge History of Iran*, vol. 4, *The Period from the Arab Invasion to the Saljuqs*, edited by R. N. Frye, pp. 57–89. Cambridge: University Press, 1975.

Murdock, George Peter. *Africa: Its Peoples and their Culture History*. New York: McGraw-Hill, 1959.

Murra, John V. "On Inca Political Structure." In *Systems of Political Control and Bureaucracy in Human Societies*, edited by Verne F. Ray, pp. 30–41. Seattle, Wash.: American Ethnological Society, 1958.

Nash, Manning. *Primitive and Peasant Economic Systems*. San Francisco: Chandler Publishing Co., 1966.

Needham, Joseph. "Commentary on Lynn White, Jr., 'What Accelerated Technological Progress in the Western Middle Ages?'" In *Scientific Change*, edited by A. C. Crombie, pp. 327–29. New York: Basic Books, 1963.

————. "Poverties and Triumphs of the Chinese Scientific Tradition." In *Scientific Change*, edited by A. C. Crombie, pp. 117–53. New York: Basic Books, 1963.

————. *Science and Civilization in China*. 5 vols. Cambridge: The University Press, 1954–1974.

Nisbet, Robert. *History of the Idea of Progress*. New York: Basic Books, 1980.

Nobiliaire Universel de France. Edited by Nicholas Viton de Saint-Allais, 20 vols. Paris: Bureau du Nobiliaire Universel de France, 1814–21; reprinted Paris: Librairie Bachelin-Deflorenne, 1872–77.

Nobiliario de Segovia. Edited by Jesús Larios Martín, 4 vols. Segovia: Instituto Diego de Colmenares, 1956–63.

Onslow, Earl of. *The Dukes of Normandy and Their Origin*. London: Hutchinson & Co., 1945.

Oppenheimer, Franz. *Der Staat*. Frankfurt a/M: Rutten & Loening, 1919.
———. *The State*. New York: B. W. Huebsch, 1922; Free Life Editions, 1976.
———. *System der Soziologie*. 4 vols. Jena: Gustav Fischer, 1922–35.
Osborne, Milton. *Politics and Power in Cambodia: The Sihanouk Years*. Camber-well, Victoria: Longman-Australia, 1973.
Otley, C. B. "Militarism and the Social Affiliations of the British Army Élite." In *Armed Forces and Society: Sociological Essays*, edited by Jacques van Doorn, pp. 84–108. The Hague: Mouton, 1968.
Painter, Sidney. *French Chivalry*. Ithaca, N.Y.: Cornell University Press, 1957.
Parsons, Talcott. *The Evolution of Societies*. Englewood Cliffs, N.J.: Prentice-Hall, 1977.
Pear, P. H. *English Social Differences*. London: Allen & Unwin, 1956.
Peters, F. E. *The Harvest of Hellenism: A History of the Near East from Alexander the Great to the Triumph of Christianity*. New York: Simon and Schuster, 1970.
Petrie, W. M. Flinders. *Social Life in Ancient Egypt*. London: Constable & Co., 1923.
Philby, H. St. John B. *Arabian Jubilee*. New York: John Day, 1953.
Pirenne, Henri. *Economic and Social History of Medieval Europe*. New York: Harcourt, Brace and World, 1956.
———. *A History of Europe*. 2 vols. Garden City, N.Y.: Doubleday & Co., 1958.
———. *Medieval Cities: Their Origins and the Revival of Trade*. Princeton, N.J.: Princeton University Press, 1946.
Plato. *The Dialogues of Plato*. 2 vols. Translated by B. Jowett. New York: Random House, 1937.
Pleket, H. W. "Technology and Society in the Graeco-Roman World." *Acta Historiae Neerlandica* 2 (1967): 1–25.
Popkin, Samuel L. *The Rational Peasant: The Political Economy of Rural Society in Vietnam*. Berkeley: University of California Press, 1979.
Potter, Jack M.; Diaz, May N.; and Foster, George M., eds. *Peasant Society: A Reader*. Boston: Little, Brown & Co., 1967.
Pounds, Norman G. J. *An Historical Geography of Europe, 450 B.C.–A.D. 1330*. Cambridge: University Press, 1973.
Powicke, Sir Maurice. *The Loss of Normandy, 1189–1204. Studies in the History of the Angevin Empire*. 2nd rev. ed. Manchester: University Press, 1961.
Prawdin, Michael. *The Mongol Empire: Its Rise and Legacy*. New York: The Free Press, 1967.
Pye, Lucian W. *Politics, Personality, and Nation Building: Burma's Search for Identity*. New Haven, Conn.: Yale University Press, 1962.
Ratzenhofer, Gustav. *Die sociologische Erkenntnis: Positive Philosophie des socialen Lebens*. Leipzig: F. A. Brockhaus, 1898.
Raven, Simon. *The English Gentleman*. London: Anthony Blond, 1961.
Rawlinson, H. G. *India: A Short Cultural History*. New York: Frederick A. Praeger, 1952.
Razzell, P. E. "Social Origins of Officers in the Indian and British Home Army: 1758–1962." *British Journal of Sociology* 14 (September 1963): 248–60.
Redfield, Robert. *Peasant Society and Culture: An Anthropological Approach to*

Civilization. Chicago: University of Chicago Press, 1956.

————. *The Primitive World and Its Transformations*. Ithaca, N.Y.: Cornell University Press, 1953.

Reischauer, Edwin O. "Japanese Feudalism." In *Feudalism in History*, edited by Rushton Coulborn, pp. 26–48. Princeton, N.J.: Princeton University Press, 1956.

Riasanovsky, V. *A History of Russia*. New York: Oxford University Press, 1963.

Rodinson, Maxime. *Islam and Capitalism*. New York: Pantheon Books, 1973.

Rogers, Everett M. *Modernization Among Peasants: The Impact of Communication*. New York: Holt, Rinehart and Winston, 1969.

Rose, Leo E. *The Politics of Bhutan*. Ithaca, N.Y.: Cornell University Press, 1977.

Rostovtzeff, M. *The Social and Economic History of the Roman Empire*. 2 vols. 2nd rev. ed. Oxford: Clarendon Press, 1957.

Rudolph, Lloyd I., and Rudolph, Susanne Hoeber. *The Modernity of Tradition: Political Development in India*. Chicago: University of Chicago Press, 1967.

Runciman, Steven. *Byzantine Civilization*. Cleveland: World Publishing Co., 1956.

Rüstow, Alexander. *Ortsbestimmung der Gegenwart: Eine universalgeschichtliche Kulturkritik*. 3 vols. Vol. 1, *Ursprung der Herrschaft*. Erlenbach-Zürich: Eugen Rentsch, 1950.

Rustow, Dankwart A. "The Politics of the Near East." In *The Politics of the Developing Areas*, edited by Gabriel A. Almond and James S. Coleman, pp. 369–454. Princeton, N.J.: Princeton University Press, 1960.

————. *A World of Nations: Problems of Political Modernization*. Washington, D.C.: The Brookings Institution, 1967.

Saint-Allais, Nicholas Viton de, ed. *Nobiliaire Universel de France*. 20 vols. Paris: Bureau du Nobiliaire Universel de France, 1814–21; reprinted Paris: Librairie Bachelin-Deflorenne, 1872–77.

Salvadori, Massimo. *Karl Kautsky and the Socialist Revolution, 1880–1938*. London, NLB, 1979.

Sansom, George. *A History of Japan*. 3 vols. Vol. 1, *To 1334*. Vol. 2, *1334–1615*. Stanford, Calif.: Stanford University Press, 1958, 1961.

Schapera, I. *Government and Politics in Tribal Societies*. London: Watts, 1956.

Schumpeter, Joseph A. "The Sociology of Imperialism." In *Imperialism and Social Classes: Two Essays*, by Joseph Schumpeter, pp. 3–98. New York: Meridian Books, 1955.

Scott, James C. *The Moral Economy of the Peasant: Rebellion and Subsistence in Southeast Asia*. New Haven, Conn.: Yale University Press, 1976.

————. "Peasant Revolution: A Dismal Science." *Comparative Politics* 9 (January 1977): 231–48.

Scott, Robert E. "Nation-Building in Latin America." In *Nation-Building*, edited by Karl W. Deutsch and William J. Foltz, pp. 73–83. New York: Atherton Press, 1966.

Scullard, Howard H. *A History of the Roman World 753 to 146 B.C.* 2nd rev. ed. London: Methuen & Co., 1951.

Seward, Desmond. *The Monks of War: The Military Religious Orders*. Hamden, Conn.: Archon Books, 1972.

Shanin, Teodor. "Peasantry as a Political Factor." In *Peasants and Peasant Societies*, edited by Teodor Shanin, pp. 238–63. Harmondsworth, Middlesex: Penguin Books, 1971.

_____, ed. *Peasants and Peasant Societies*. Harmondsworth, Middlesex: Penguin Books, 1971.

Shaw, George Bernard. *Caesar and Cleopatra*. In *Collected Plays with Their Prefaces*. 7 vols. 2:157–292. London: The Bodley Head, 1971.

_____. *The Devil's Disciple*. In *Collected Plays with Their Prefaces*. 7 vols. 2:49–141. London: The Bodley Head, 1971.

_____. *Pygmalion*. In *Collected Plays with Their Prefaces*. 7 vols. 4:669–782. London: The Bodley Head, 1972.

Shaw, Stanford. *History of the Ottoman Empire and Modern Turkey*. 2 vols. Vol. 1, *Empire of the Gazis: The Rise and Decline of the Ottoman Empire, 1280–1808*. Cambridge: Cambridge University Press, 1976.

Singer, Marshall R. *The Emerging Elite: A Study of Political Leadership in Ceylon*. Cambridge, Mass.: The M.I.T. Press, 1964.

Sjoberg, Gideon. "Folk and 'Feudal' Societies." *American Journal of Sociology* 58 (November 1952): 231–39.

_____. *The Preindustrial City: Past and Present*. New York: The Free Press, 1960.

Skocpol, Theda. *States and Social Revolutions: A Comparative Analysis of France, Russia, and China*. Cambridge: Cambridge University Press, 1979.

Slicher van Bath, B. H. *The Agrarian History of Western Europe, A.D. 500–1850*. London: Edward Arnold, 1963.

Smith, Adam. *An Inquiry into the Nature and Causes of the Wealth of Nations*. New York: Modern Library, 1937.

Soustelle, Jacques. *Daily Life of the Aztecs on the Eve of the Spanish Conquest*. Stanford, Calif.: Stanford University Press, 1970.

_____. "Religion and the Mexican State." *Diogenes* 34 (Summer 1961): 1–15.

Spear, Percival. "The Mughal 'Mansabdari' System." In *Elites in South Asia*, edited by Edmund Leach and S. N. Mukherjee, pp. 1–15. Cambridge: University Press, 1970.

Spencer, Herbert. *The Principles of Sociology*. 3 vols. 1876–96. Reprint. Westport, Conn.: Greenwood Press, 1975.

"Spending from State Purses." In *Oil and Social Change in the Middle East, The Economist*, 2 July 1955, pp. 2–4.

Spiro, Melford E. *Burmese Supernaturalism*. Philadelphia: Institute for the Study of Human Issues, 1978.

Steenson, Gary P. *Karl Kautsky, 1854–1938: Marxism in the Classical Years*. Pittsburgh, Pa.: University of Pittsburgh Press, 1978.

Steinhaus, Kurt. *Soziologie der türkischen Revolution*. Frankfurt: Europäische Verlagsanstalt, 1969.

Tacitus, Cornelius. *Germania*. In *The Complete Works of Tacitus*. New York: Modern Library, 1942.

Takizawa, Matsuyo. *The Penetration of Money Economy in Japan*. New York: Columbia University Press, 1927.

Tawney, R. H. *The Agrarian Problem in the Sixteenth Century*. London: Longmans,

Green & Co., 1912.

Taylor, G. Rattray. *Sex in History*. New York: Vanguard Press, 1970.

Thompson, E. A. *The Early Germans*. Oxford: Clarendon Press, 1965.

――――. "Peasant Revolts in Late Roman Gaul and Spain." *Past and Present* 2 (November 1952): 11–23.

Thurnwald, Richard. *Die menschliche Gesellschaft in ihren ethno-soziologischen Grundlagen*. 5 vols. Vol. 4, *Werden, Wandel und Gestaltung von Staat und Kultur im Lichte der Völkerforschung*. Berlin-Leipzig: Walter de Gruyter & Co., 1935.

Tilly, Charles. "Rural Collective Action in Modern Europe." In *Forging Nations: A Comparative View of Rural Ferment and Revolt*, edited by Joseph Spielberg and Scott Whiteford, pp. 9–40. East Lansing: Michigan State University Press, 1976.

――――. "Town and Country in Revolution." In *Peasant Rebellion and Communist Revolution in Asia*, edited by John W. Lewis, pp. 271–349. Stanford, Calif.: Stanford University Press, 1974.

――――. *The Vendée*. Cambridge, Mass.: Harvard University Press, 1976.

Townend, Peter, ed. *Burke's Genealogical and Heraldic History of the Peerage, Baronetage, and Knightage*. 104th ed. London: Burke's Peerage, 1967.

Tuchman, Barbara W. *A Distant Mirror: The Calamitous 14th Century*. New York: Ballantine Books, 1978.

Turnbull, S. R. *The Samurai: A Military History*. New York: Macmillan, 1977.

Vagts, Alfred. *A History of Militarism: Civilian and Military*. Rev. ed. New York: Meridian Books, 1959.

van der Meulen, D. *The Wells of Ibn Sa'ud*. New York: Praeger, 1957.

Varley, H. Paul. *The Onin War*. New York: Columbia University Press, 1967.

――――. *The Samurai*. London: Weidenfeld & Nicolson, 1970.

Veblen, Thorstein. *The Theory of the Leisure Class: An Economic Study of Institutions*. Boston: Houghton-Mifflin Co., 1973.

Verba, Sidney. "Comparative Political Culture." In *Political Culture and Political Development*, edited by Lucian W. Pye and Sidney Verba, pp. 512–60. Princeton, N.J.: Princeton University Press, 1965.

von Grunebaum, Gustave E. "The Problem: Unity in Diversity." In *Unity and Variety in Muslim Civilization*, edited by Gustave von Grunebaum, pp. 17–37. Chicago: University of Chicago Press, 1955.

von Hagen, Victor Wolfgang. *The Aztec: Man and Tribe*. Rev. ed. New York: Mentor Books, 1961.

――――. *Highway of the Sun*. New York: Duell, Sloan & Pearce, 1955.

――――. *Realm of the Incas*. New York: Mentor Books, 1957.

――――. *The Roads That Led to Rome*. Cleveland: World Publishing Co., 1967.

――――. *World of the Maya*. New York: Mentor Books, 1960.

Wallerstein, Immanuel. *The Modern World-System: Capitalist Agriculture and the Origins of the European World-Economy in the Sixteenth Century*. New York: Academic Press, 1974.

Walter, Eugene Victor. *Terror and Resistance: A Study of Political Violence*. New York: Oxford University Press, 1969.

Warmington, E. H. *The Commerce Between the Roman Empire and India*. 2nd rev. ed. London: Curzon Press, 1974.

Warre Cornish, Francis. *Chivalry*. London: George Allen & Co., 1911.

Wason, Margaret O. *Class Struggles in Ancient Greece*. London: Victor Gollancz, 1947.

Weber, Eugen. *Action Française: Royalism and Reaction in Twentieth-Century France*. Stanford, Calif.: Stanford University Press, 1962.

Weber, Max. *Ancient Judaism*. Translated and edited by Hans H. Gerth and Don Martindale. Glencoe, Ill.: The Free Press, 1952.

———. *Economy and Society*. 3 vols. Edited by Guenther Roth and Claus Wittich. New York: Bedminster Press, 1968.

———. *Gesammelte Aufsätze zur Religionssoziologie*. 3 vols. Tübingen: J. C. B. Mohr, 1921.

———. *The Methodology of the Social Sciences*. Translated and edited by Edward A. Shils and Henry A. Finch. Glencoe, Ill.: The Free Press, 1949.

———. *The Protestant Ethic and the Spirit of Capitalism*. New York: Charles Scribner's Sons, 1958.

———. *The Religion of China: Confucianism and Taoism*. Translated and edited by Hans H. Gerth. Glencoe, Ill.: The Free Press, 1951.

———. *The Religion of India: The Sociology of Hinduism and Buddhism*. Translated and edited by Hans H. Gerth and Don Martindale. Glencoe, Ill.: The Free Press, 1958.

———. *Wirtschaft und Gesellschaft*. 4th ed. Edited by Johannes Winckelmann. Tübingen: J. C. B. Mohr, 1956.

Weiner, Myron. *The Politics of Scarcity: Public Pressure and Political Response in India*. Chicago: University of Chicago Press, 1962.

———. "The Politics of South Asia." In *The Politics of the Developing Areas*, edited by Gabriel A. Almond and James S. Coleman, pp. 153–246. Princeton, N.J.: Princeton University Press, 1960.

Wesson, Robert G. *The Imperial Order*. Berkeley: University of California Press, 1967.

Westermarck, Edward. *The History of Human Marriage*. 3 vols., 5th rev. ed. London: Macmillan, 1921.

White, J. E. Manchip. *Ancient Egypt*. London: Allan Wingate, 1952.

Williams, Jay. "The Sport of Knights." *Horizon* 1 (November 1958): 92–107.

Wilson, David A. "Nation-Building and Revolutionary War." In *Nation-Building*, edited by Karl W. Deutsch and William J. Foltz, pp. 84–94. New York: Atherton Press, 1966.

———. *Politics in Thailand*. Ithaca, N.Y.: Cornell University Press, 1962.

Wilson, John A. *The Burden of Egypt: An Interpretation of Ancient Egyptian Culture*. Chicago: University of Chicago Press, 1951.

Winick, Myron. "Nutrition and Brain Development." *Natural History* 89 (December 1980): 6–13.

Wittfogel, Karl A. "Chinese Society: An Historical Survey." *The Journal of Asian Studies* 16 (May 1957): 343–64.

———. *Oriental Despotism: A Comparative Study of Total Power*. New Haven, Conn.: Yale University Press, 1957.

———, and Feng, Chia-sheng. *History of Chinese Society: Liao (907–1125)*. Philadelphia: American Philosophical Society, 1949.

Wolf, Eric R. *Peasants*. Englewood Cliffs, N.J.: Prentice-Hall, 1966.
———. *Peasant Wars of the Twentieth Century*. New York: Harper & Row, 1969.
Wolpert, Stanley. *A New History of India*. New York: Oxford University Press, 1977.
Womack, John. *Zapata and the Mexican Revolution*. New York: Knopf, 1969.
Wright, Arthur F. Introduction to *Chinese Civilization and Bureaucracy*, by Etienne Balazs. New Haven, Conn.: Yale University Press, 1964.
Wright, Gordon, *Rural Revolution in France: The Peasantry in the Twentieth Century*. Stanford, Calif.: Stanford University Press, 1964.
Wright, Quincy. *A Study of War*. 2nd ed. Chicago: University of Chicago Press, 1965.

Index